EDGAR ALLAN POE IN CONTEXT

Edgar Allan Poe mastered a variety of literary forms over the course of his brief and turbulent career. As a storyteller, Poe defied convention by creating gothic tales of mystery, horror, and suspense that remain widely popular today. This collection demonstrates how Poe's experience of early nineteenth-century American life fueled his iconoclasm and shaped his literary legacy. Rather than provide critical explications of his writings, each essay explores one aspect of Poe's immediate environment, using pertinent writings – verse, fiction, reviews, and essays – to suit. Examining his geographical, social, and literary contexts, as well as those created by the publishing industry and advances in science and technology, the essays paint an unprecedented portrait of Poe's life and times. Written for a wide audience, the collection will offer scholars and students of American literature, historians, and general readers new insight into Poe's rich and complex work.

KEVIN J. HAYES is a professor of English at the University of Central Oklahoma. Editor of *The Cambridge Companion to Edgar Allan Poe*, he has published several books on American literature, history, and culture, including *Poe and the Printed Word* (2000) and *The Road to Monticello: The Life and Mind of Thomas Jefferson* (2008).

EDGAR ALLAN POE IN CONTEXT

EDITED BY

KEVIN J. HAYES

University of Central Oklahoma

CAMBRIDGE UNIVERSITY PRESS
Cambridge, New York, Melbourne, Madrid, Cape Town,
Singapore, São Paulo, Delhi, Mexico City

Cambridge University Press
32 Avenue of the Americas, New York, NY 10013-2473, USA

www.cambridge.org
Information on this title: www.cambridge.org/9781107009974

First published 2013

Printed in the United States of America

A catalog record for this publication is available from the British Library.

Library of Congress Cataloging in Publication data
Edgar Allan Poe in context / [edited by] Kevin J. Hayes.
p.   cm.
Includes bibliographical references and index.
ISBN 978-1-107-00997-4 (hardback)
1. Poe, Edgar Allan, 1809–1849 – Criticism and interpretation.   I. Hayes, Kevin J.
PS2638.E345   2013
818'.309–dc23   2012016513

ISBN 978-1-107-00997-4 Hardback

Contents

List of Illustrations   *page* viii
Notes on Contributors   ix
Preface   xv

PART ONE: GEOGRAPHICAL CONTEXTS

1   Great Britain   3
    Christopher Gair

2   The South   13
    James M. Hutchisson

3   The American West   22
    Nathaniel Lewis

4   The Sea   32
    David Dowling

5   France   41
    Andrea Goulet

6   The Near East   53
    Travis Montgomery

7   The Polar Regions   63
    Mark Canada

PART TWO: SOCIAL CONTEXTS

8   The Urban Environment   75
    Bran Nicol

9   Curiosity   85
    Lindsey Hursh

10 Alcohol, Addiction, and Rehabilitation   96
    Paul Fisher

11 Fashion, Furnishings, and Style   107
    Patricia A. Cunningham

12 The American Stage   118
    Philip Edward Phillips

13 Lions and Bluestockings   129
    Anne Boyd Rioux

14 Slavery and Abolitionism   138
    Paul Christian Jones

15 The Cult of Mourning   148
    Therese M. Rizzo

PART THREE: THE CONTEXTS OF PUBLISHING

16 The Literary Profession   159
    John Evelev

17 Magazines   169
    Jeffrey Andrew Weinstock

18 Gift Books   179
    Kathryn K. Shinn

19 Literary Piracy   188
    Michael J. Everton

20 The Art of Reviewing   198
    Jonathan Hartmann

21 The Politics of Publishing   209
    Amy Branam

PART FOUR: LITERARY CONTEXTS

22 Ancient Classics   221
    Gregory Hays

23 Rabelais and Lesage   232
    Lois Davis Vines

24 The Gothic Movement   241
    Alan Brown

25 Byron 251
Chris Beyers

26 Folk Narrative 260
Katherine Kim

27 Transcendentalism 269
Heidi Silcox

28 Charles Dickens 279
Tara Moore

29 Nathaniel Hawthorne and the Art of the Tale 288
Meghan A. Freeman

PART FIVE: SCIENTIFIC AND PSEUDOSCIENTIFIC
CONTEXTS

30 Phrenology 301
Brett Zimmerman

31 Photography 313
Satwik Dasgupta

32 Mesmerism 322
Bruce Mills

33 Architecture 332
Alvin Holm

34 The Heritage of Fiction Science 343
Peter Swirski

35 Cosmology and Cosmogony 353
Jonathan Taylor

36 Forensic Science 363
Benjamin F. Fisher

37 Technology 372
John Tresch

Further Reading 383
Index 397

Illustrations

9.1 *Tom Thumb, Full-Length Portrait, Facing Front, Standing on Table with Tablecloth*, undated daguerreotype. Library of Congress, Prints and Photographs Division, Washington, DC (reproduction number: LC–USZ62–109908). *page* 92

12.1 A playbill from the Park Theatre, New York, September 6, 1809, the first time David and Eliza Poe performed at the Park Theatre. Courtesy of the Harvard College Library. 120

12.2 H. Fossette, *Park Theatre – Park Row* (New York: Peabody and Co., 1832). Courtesy of the Boston Athenaeum. 126

30.1 From O. S. Fowler, "Elementary Phrenology," *American Phrenological Journal* 2 (1839), 322. The letters and numbers have been digitally erased and resupplied for visual clarification. 302

30.2 From "Veneration: Its Definition, Location, Function, Adaptation, and Cultivation," *American Phrenological Journal* 9 (1847), 308. 307

33.1 Alvin Holm, *The Edgar Allan Poe House* (1982). Courtesy of the artist. 340

Notes on Contributors

CHRIS BEYERS, professor of English at Assumption College, is the author of *A History of Free Verse* (2001). In addition, he has contributed chapters on poetry and poetics to *The Oxford Handbook of Early American Literature* (2008) and *The Oxford Handbook of American Literary Naturalism* (2011).

AMY BRANAM, assistant professor of English at Frostburg State University, has contributed essays to *ANQ, Edgar Allan Poe Review, In-Between, Journal of the Fantastic in the Arts*, and *Poe Studies*.

ALAN BROWN, professor of English at the University of West Alabama, has written extensively on American ghost lore. His books include *Ghost Hunters of the South* (2006) and *Ghosts along the Mississippi* (2011).

MARK CANADA is professor of English and acting dean of the College of Arts and Sciences at the University of North Carolina at Pembroke, where he teaches American literature. His publications include *Literature and Journalism in Antebellum America: Thoreau, Stowe, and Their Contemporaries Respond to the Rise of the Commercial Press* (2011) and essays about Rebecca Harding Davis, Theodore Dreiser, Edgar Allan Poe, and Thomas Wolfe.

PATRICIA A. CUNNINGHAM, associate professor of consumer and textile sciences at The Ohio State University, is the author of *Reforming Women's Fashion, 1850–1920: Politics, Health, and Art* (2003) and co-editor (with Linda Welters) of *Twentieth-Century American Fashion* (2005).

SATWIK DASGUPTA is assistant professor of English at Victoria College in Texas.

DAVID DOWLING, lecturer in English at the University of Iowa, has published widely on nineteenth-century American literary history and culture, with a special interest in the economics of authorship and the politics of the publishing world. His books include *Capital Letters: Authorship in the Antebellum Literary Market* (2009); *Chasing the White Whale: The Moby-Dick Marathon; or, What Melville Means Today* (2010); *The Business of Literary Circles in Nineteenth-Century America* (2011); and *Literary Partnerships and the Marketplace: Writers and Mentors in Nineteenth-Century America* (2012).

JOHN EVELEV is associate professor of English at the University of Missouri. His book *Tolerable Entertainment: Herman Melville and Professionalism in Antebellum New York* was published in 2006 by the University of Massachusetts Press.

MICHAEL J. EVERTON teaches graduate courses in American literature and print culture before 1900 at Simon Fraser University. He is the author of *Authorship and the Ethics of American Publishing* (2011). In addition, he has published articles in *Early American Literature, ESQ, Legacy, Southern Literary Journal,* and *Style.*

BENJAMIN F. FISHER has published numerous books about Edgar Allan Poe, including *The Essential Tales and Poems of Edgar Allan Poe* (2004); *The Cambridge Introduction to Edgar Allan Poe* (2008); and *Poe in His Own Time: A Biographical Chronicle of His Life, Drawn from Recollections, Interviews, and Memoirs by Family, Friends, and Associates* (2010). In 1993, he received a Governor's Citation from the State of Maryland for his contributions to Poe studies.

PAUL FISHER is a biographer and cultural historian who has taught literature and history at Yale, Wesleyan, Boston University, and Harvard. He is currently assistant professor of American Studies at Wellesley College. His books include *Artful Itineraries: European Art and American Careers in High Culture, 1865–1920* (2000); *House of Wits: An Intimate Portrait of the James Family* (2008); and *The Grand Affair: John Singer Sargent, His Patrons, and Sexuality in the Art World of the Belle Époque* (forthcoming).

MEGHAN A. FREEMAN recently received her PhD in English literature from Cornell University, having completed a dissertation investigating the treatment of aesthetic theory and spectatorship in British and American novels of the nineteenth century. She has taught at Tulane University and is currently assistant professor in the School of Writing, Literature, and Film at Oregon State University.

CHRISTOPHER GAIR, senior lecturer in English and American Studies and head of English Literature at the University of Glasgow, Scotland, is the author of *Complicity and Resistance in Jack London's Novels: From Naturalism to Nature* (1997), *The American Counterculture* (2007), and *The Beat Generation* (2008) and editor of *Beyond Boundaries: C.L.R. James and Postnational Studies* (2006). In addition, he has edited Stephen Crane's *Maggie: A Girl of the Streets* (2000), Jack London's *South Sea Tales* (2002), and *Symbiosis: A Journal of Transatlantic Literary and Cultural Relations*.

ANDREA GOULET, associate professor of French and undergraduate chair of comparative literature at the University of Pennsylvania, is the author of *Optiques: The Science of the Eye and the Birth of Modern French Fiction* (2006) and has co-edited journal issues on "Visual Culture" (*Contemporary French Civilization*) and "Crime Fictions" (*Yale French Studies*). She is completing a book manuscript titled *Legacies of the Rue Morgue: Scientific and Spatial Discourses in French Crime Fiction* and is co-chair of the Nineteenth-Century French Studies Association.

JONATHAN HARTMANN teaches English at the University of New Haven. He is the author of *The Marketing of Edgar Allan Poe* (2008).

KEVIN J. HAYES, professor of English at the University of Central Oklahoma, is the author of several books including *Poe and the Printed Word* (2000); *An American Cycling Odyssey, 1887* (2002); *The Road to Monticello: The Life and Mind of Thomas Jefferson* (2008); *Edgar Allan Poe* (2009); and *A Journey Through American Literature* (2012). In addition, he edited *The Cambridge Companion to Edgar Allan Poe* (2002).

GREGORY HAYS, associate professor of classics at the University of Virginia, has published articles and reviews on Greek poetry and later Latin literature, and a translation of Marcus Aurelius's *Meditations*.

ALVIN HOLM, senior partner at Alvin Holm A.I.A. Architects, a Philadelphia firm, has written widely on the history of American architecture.

LINDSEY HURSH teaches English at the University of Central Oklahoma. Her research interests primarily concern the ways in which modernist poetry anticipates postmodern theories of imitation and authenticity.

JAMES M. HUTCHISSON, professor and director of graduate study in English at The Citadel, is the author of the biography *Poe* (2005), which earned starred reviews in major journals and a coveted spot in syndicated critic James Sallis's column, "The Reading Life." His most recent book is *Edgar Allan Poe: Beyond Gothicism* (2011). He is currently working on a new life of Ernest Hemingway.

PAUL CHRISTIAN JONES is associate professor of English at Ohio University, where he teaches courses in nineteenth-century American literature. He is the author of *Unwelcome Voices: Subversive Fiction in the Antebellum South* (2005) and *Against the Gallows: Antebellum American Writers and the Movement to Abolish Capital Punishment* (2011). His essays have appeared in numerous periodicals, including *American Periodicals*, *Journal of American Studies*, *Legacy*, *Southern Literary Journal*, and *Walt Whitman Quarterly Review*.

KATHERINE KIM is a doctoral candidate at Boston College. She was the creator and co-organizer of the two-day Poe Bicentennial Celebration at Boston College in January 2009. She was one of the collaborators of the highly successful 2009–10 Boston Public Library exhibit "The Raven in the Frog Pond," curated by Dr. Paul Lewis. She is also a member of the Edgar Allan Poe Foundation of Boston, which, in conjunction with the Boston Art Commission, is developing permanent public artwork celebrating Poe.

NATHANIEL LEWIS, chair of the English department at St. Michael's College in Vermont, is the author of *Unsettling the Literary West* (2003) and co-editor (with William Handley) of *True West: Authenticity and the American West* (2004).

BRUCE MILLS, professor of English at Kalamazoo College, is the author of *Cultural Reformations: Lydia Maria Child and the Literature of Reform* (1994) and *Poe, Fuller, and the Mesmeric Arts* (2006).

TRAVIS MONTGOMERY teaches nineteenth-century American literature at the University of Mississippi. He has published essays on Willa Cather, Helen Keller, and Edgar Allan Poe.

TARA MOORE is an instructor in the English department at Pennsylvania State University's York campus. Her book *Victorian Christmas in Print* (2009) studies nineteenth-century Christmas practices, especially when they intersect with the publishing industry. She is currently preparing for Reaktion Books a work to be titled *Christmas*, which will survey the development of the modern, global Christmas.

BRAN NICOL teaches English literature at the University of Portsmouth. His books include *The Cambridge Introduction to Postmodern Fiction* (2009) and *Postmodernism and the Contemporary Novel: A Reader* (2002).

PHILIP EDWARD PHILLIPS is professor of English and interim associate dean of the University Honors College at Middle Tennessee State University, where he teaches British and American literature. He is also W. T. Bandy Fellow at the W. T. Bandy Center for Baudelaire and Modern French Studies at Vanderbilt University and a member at large of the Poe Studies Association Executive Committee. His work on Poe has appeared in *Poe Studies*, *Edgar Allan Poe Review*, and *Approaches to Teaching Poe's Prose and Poetry* (2008).

ANNE BOYD RIOUX is professor of English and women's and gender studies at the University of New Orleans. She is author of *Writing for Immortality: Women and the Emergence of High Literary Culture in America* (2004) and editor of *Wielding the Pen: Writings on Authorship by American Women of the Nineteenth Century* (2009).

THERESE M. RIZZO, assistant professor of English at the University of North Carolina at Pembroke, has published in such journals as *MELUS* and *Studies in the Humanities* and in *America and the Black Body: Identity Politics in Print and Visual Culture* (2009). Her current work focuses on submission, manipulation, and trickery in nineteenth-century American contexts.

KATHRYN K. SHINN is a doctoral candidate at Swansea University, where she is researching the life and times of eighteenth-century teacher, editor, and Orientalist Samuel Henley.

HEIDI SILCOX is a doctoral student at the University of Oklahoma. Fascinated with the relationship between literature and philosophy, she has published essays in *Analecta Husserliana*, *Kipling Journal*, and *Philosophy and Literature*.

PETER SWIRSKI, professor at the Helsinki Collegium for Advanced Studies, is the author of several books including *Between Literature and Science: Poe, Lem, and Explorations in Aesthetics, Cognitive Science, and Literary Knowledge* (2000); *From Lowbrow to Nobrow* (2005); and

American Utopia and Social Engineering in Literature, Social Thought, and Political History (2011).

JONATHAN TAYLOR, senior lecturer in creative writing at De Montfort University, Leicester, is the author of *Mastery and Slavery in Victorian Writing* (2003) and *Science and Omniscience in Nineteenth-Century Literature* (2007).

JOHN TRESCH, associate professor of the history of science at the University of Pennsylvania, is the author of *The Romantic Machine: Utopian Science and Technology after Napoleon* (2012). His essays on Edgar Allan Poe have appeared in the *British Journal of the History of Science* (1997); *The Cambridge Companion to Edgar Allan Poe* (2002); and *Observing Nature / Representing Experience: The Osmotic Dynamics of Romanticism, 1800–1850* (2007).

LOIS DAVIS VINES, professor of French and Distinguished Teaching Professor of Humanities at Ohio University, is the author of *Valéry and Poe, A Literary Legacy* (1992) and editor of *Poe Abroad: Influence, Reputation, Affinities* (1999).

JEFFREY ANDREW WEINSTOCK is professor of English and graduate program coordinator at Central Michigan University. He is the author of several books including *Scare Tactics: Supernatural Fiction by American Women* (2008) and *Charles Brockden Brown* (2011). In addition, he is the co-editor (with Tony Magistrale) of *Approaches to Teaching Poe's Prose and Poetry* (2008).

BRETT ZIMMERMAN, associate professor of English at York University in Toronto, is the author of *Herman Melville: Stargazer* (1998) and *Edgar Allan Poe: Rhetoric and Style* (2005).

Preface

The speaker of "Dream-Land," a poem Edgar Allan Poe published in 1844, tells his readers that he comes from "a wild weird clime," a mysterious place "Out of Space – Out of Time." Since Poe's death in 1849, many commentators have used this memorable pair of prepositional phrases to characterize his imaginative writings, which have seemed to them separate from the times in which he wrote, beautiful creations with little relevance to their cultural contexts. In what may be the biggest sea change in Poe studies over the past two decades, his writings are now recognized as having very much to do with his time. But this crucial shift has not occurred all at once. In recent years, Poe's writings have been studied in relation to economy, photography, phrenology, and many other cultural, historical, and intellectual phenomena, yet no one has attempted to systematically situate Poe in the contexts of his time. Such is the purpose of *Edgar Allan Poe in Context*.

This collection consists of thirty-seven short chapters grouped into thematic parts: geography, society, publishing, literature, and science. Though Edgar Allan Poe is the subject of this book, the chapters do not provide in-depth critical explications of his writings. Instead, each chapter provides a general overview of its subject and uses whatever pertinent Poe writings – verse, fiction, reviews, essays – to suit. Though some of the contributors are Poe specialists, many are not. Instead, I have selected contributors for their expertise regarding the individual contexts, thus bringing fresh perspectives to the study of Poe. I have given the contributors considerable latitude, insisting only that they write in a jargon-free style that all readers can appreciate. *Edgar Allan Poe in Context* should enhance everyone's appreciation of Poe's richly complex work.

In the first chapter, Christopher Gair examines the importance Great Britain played in Poe's life and work. Besides providing an overview of its subject, this chapter functions as an introduction to the collection as a whole: Gair touches upon several topics other contributors develop more fully. He uses Charles Dickens as an example to show the influence of English literature on Poe. The figure of Dickens recurs frequently in this book, culminating in Tara Moore's discussion of Dickens's influence on American literary culture. Gair further develops his topic by comparing Poe's attitude toward Nathaniel Hawthorne, a theme Meghan A. Freeman develops in her chapter on Hawthorne and the art of the tale. Gair closes his essay with a brief discussion of "The Man of the Crowd," a short story Poe set on the mean streets of London that is becoming increasingly important in terms of Poe's portrayal of the modern world, as Bran Nicol explains in his treatment of Poe and the urban environment, the chapter that opens Part Two.

Other chapters in Part One discuss the importance of place in Poe's life and writings. Some treat places where he lived; others treat places he only imagined. All consider different regions of the world that figure in his writings. Though born in Boston – a fact he often regretted – Poe identified more closely with the South, the subject of Chapter 2. Born just a few years after Lewis and Clark completed their epic transcontinental journey and dying the same year as the California Gold Rush, Poe lived during a time when the settling of the West was the single most important occurrence in America culture. The West forms the subject of Chapter 3. The sea, the subject of Chapter 4, is a closely related topic. As Poe himself suggested, the journey across the prairies was akin to an ocean voyage. Poe's parallel between the two is not unique: it is no coincidence that the covered wagon, the vehicle that took countless American settlers west, became known as the prairie schooner. The last three chapters of Part One treat other regions of the world. Andrea Goulet surveys Poe's relationship to France, exploring what it was that attracted him to France and what has attracted France to him. Travis Montgomery discusses Poe's creative use of materials regarding the Near East. And Mark Canada treats Poe's depiction of the polar regions. In Poe's mind, the ends of the earth became distant places where only the imagination could go.

Poe existed in a nexus of many opposing social forces: young/old, public/private, rural/urban, sick/well, drunk/sober, clean/dirty, free/enslaved, and maybe even dead/alive. These opposites were responsible for generating much of the tension in his life and his work. Part Two is devoted to the various social contexts that contributed to Poe's writings. Besides looking at the urban environment, Part Two devotes individual chapters to the theme of curiosity, a driving social and intellectual force in Poe's day; alcoholism, a growing social problem in an era when the morning "eye opener" or a "phlegm disperser" was a widespread custom;

personal attire and home decor, both of which were important to Poe because they provided external signs he could use to interpret personality; the stage, the place where Poe's actor parents plied their trade; the literary salon, where self-appointed arbiters of taste lionized the latest authors; slavery, the so-called national evil; and the cult of mourning.

Building on many ideas I touched upon in *Poe and the Printed Word*, Part Three treats the world of publishers and publishing. It begins with Chapter 16, in which John Evelev discusses the literary profession in Poe's day and, in so doing, introduces themes his fellow contributors develop in detail. The following chapter surveys the history of magazines, looking specifically at magazines Poe helped edit and others to which he contributed. Kathryn K. Shinn examines another outlet for Poe's imaginative writing: the gift book. Ornately bound and profusely illustrated, gift books gave American authors a comparatively lucrative opportunity to publish tales and poems. Other chapters in Part Three treat literary piracy, whereby American publishers took advantage of the absence of international copyright to reprint British authors, whose works often outsold those of native authors; the practice of book reviewing, which Poe revolutionized by daring to sign his reviews, avoid favoritism, and write focused reviews in a deliberate effort to improve the quality of American literature; and the politics of publishing. In this, the final chapter of Part Three, Amy Branam does something that, to my knowledge, no one has ever done before: identify the politics of editors and publishers and then draw conclusions about how Poe negotiated through the politically charged world of magazine publishing.

In addition to its chapters on Charles Dickens and Nathaniel Hawthorne, Part Four treats several other literary contexts of Poe's writings, starting with Chapter 22, in which Gregory Hays discusses the classical context. Though Poe studied at the University of Virginia with Prof. George Long, one of the leading classical scholars of the nineteenth century, he typically borrowed his classical quotations from secondary sources. In his chapter, Hays surveys some of the complexities involved with understanding Poe's classical references. The next chapter discusses how two particular French authors, François Rabelais and Alain-René Lesage, may have influenced Poe. Other chapters in Part Four treat more obvious literary contexts, examining the impact of gothic literature, the prominence of Lord Byron, and Poe's uneasy relationship with Ralph Waldo Emerson and the Transcendentalists. In addition, Katherine Kim studies Poe's imaginative use of folklore, looking at how he used many traditional genres of oral literature to original ends.

Poe was what would be called in modern parlance a "technology geek." He was intrigued with the latest scientific developments and discoveries, which influenced his imaginative writings significantly, as the chapters in Part Five demonstrate. Some chapters discuss pseudosciences that were taken seriously in Poe's day; others treat technologies with implications in the art world; and yet others discuss scientific developments Poe's fiction foreshadows.

Chapter 37, which tackles the general subject of technology, forms the conclusion to Part Five and, in a way, the conclusion to *Edgar Allan Poe in Context*. The theme of the limits and potential of technology loosely links many of the previous contexts together. The technology of sailing made it possible to know many parts of the world but ultimately left the ends of the earth unknowable. Making gas-lit streets possible, technology changed the urban environment, but the same technology that lit the nighttime streets paradoxically enhanced the city's darkness, creating urban spaces where evil could lurk. The technology of print provided a way for American authors to widely disseminate their work, but it also gave publishers a way to disseminate the work of foreign authors and thus hinder sales of American authors. And photographic technology made it increasingly difficult for anyone to escape identification, creating a cult of personality that caused authors to be judged by their faces.

PART ONE

Geographical Contexts

CHAPTER I

Great Britain

Christopher Gair

While "The Philosophy of Composition" (1846) is Edgar Allan Poe's best-known intervention in debates about literary form, little attention has been paid to the significance of its opening words: "Charles Dickens, in a note now lying before me..."[1] The reference to Dickens offers a revealing insight into the ambitions and anxieties that marked Poe's efforts to construct the figure of the American professional author during the 1830s and 1840s. For a start, the nonchalant revelation that he was on writing terms with the preeminent English-language literary figure of the age seems designed to place Poe as Dickens's American double or, if not quite that, then at least as someone circling closely in his orbit. By extension, the reference also suggests a wider, positive interest on the part of the British author in what was occurring on the other side of the literary Atlantic at a moment when Dickens's often scathing accounts of American culture in *American Notes* (1842) still elicited a mixture of anger and insecurity in the United States. While Poe's dismissal of the importance of a national literature is often taken for granted, his ability to posit himself as a synecdochal part of a national whole serves to massage the self-confidence of his audience at a moment when the call for literary nationalism made most famously by Ralph Waldo Emerson had yet to be realized in the flowering of the "American Renaissance" in the early 1850s.

The impression created, Dickens – or at least his name – disappears from the essay after the opening sentence of the second paragraph. And yet, in what follows, the Englishman remains as a ghostly presence, and Poe appears to offer a philosophy that implicitly questions the craftsmanship underpinning Dickens's primary form, the "baggy monster" of a novel Henry James would critique later that century. In his second paragraph, Poe insists, "Nothing is more clear than that every plot, worth the name, must be elaborated to its dénouement before anything be attempted with the pen." Broadly speaking, it could be argued that Dickens adhered to this principle throughout his career: most of his novels, including *Martin*

Chuzzlewit (1843), *David Copperfield* (1849), and *Bleak House* (1852–3), end with the restoration of a comfortable middle-class order for their protagonists. The economic and moral imperatives that underpin Dickens's version of social stability and that have been disrupted through a combination of individual evil (by others), cultural transgression, and misguided, usually selfish, actions on the parts of each book's principal characters are re-created once each protagonist has learned the values necessary to earn their position in society. But while Poe's claim could be applied macrocosmically to Dickens's work, it collapses in the face of the latter's sensitivity to the demands of his readership and his habitual shaping of plot development in response to readers' impressions of the latest episode of novels first published in serial form in monthly magazines. Indeed, Poe had already identified both Dickens's genius as a writer and the formal macrocosmic problems of his chosen form and his writing habits in his review of *Barnaby Rudge* (1841). Though Poe notes how, "*the intention once known*, the *traces* of the design can be found upon every page," he tempers his praise with criticism of how, in a long novel, many "points are deprived of all effect" because they make no sense without knowledge of a dénouement that will not be revealed for hundreds of pages. In addition, he ties this diffusiveness to magazine serialization of the novel in what he sees as the unnecessary insertion of accounts of the Gordon Riots (which are "altogether an afterthought," having "the appearance of being forcibly introduced"). Poe finds the "absurd fashion of periodical novel-writing" responsible for "numerous traces of indecision – traces which a dexterous supervision of the complete work might have enabled him [Dickens] to erase."[2]

In this context, it seems that "The Philosophy of Composition" refutes the formal supremacy of Dickens's chosen genre and even his preeminence as a novelist. Although Dickens's early works, *Sketches by Boz* (1836) and *The Pickwick Papers* (1836–7), contain a section of short tales and an episodic narrative that can be read in independent segments, the major works that follow demand attention to multilayered interweaving plots that unfurl over many chapters. While Poe's comments on the "extent" of a work of art might not normally be regarded as an attack on a single author, the fact that they come so soon after he cited Dickens inevitably reflects back on Dickens in highlighting what his works don't do. Indeed, this implicit attack becomes even more evident if we read "The Philosophy of Composition" as not only an explication but also as an example of Poe's practice: his insistence on the need for a piece to be "read at one sitting" to ensure the "important effect derivable from unity of impression" implies that the reference to Dickens must relate to everything that follows. Even when Poe qualifies this assertion, he elects not to do so through his contemporary.[3] Instead, he cites Daniel Defoe's *Robinson Crusoe* (1719) as an example of an occasion when "this limit may be advantageously overpassed," referring to an early (and prenational, in the case of the United States) example of literary transnationalism rather than to a transatlantic rival.

The literature, criticism, and culture of Great Britain play particularly important roles in the shaping of Poe's literary aesthetics, and Dickens occupies a central position in Poe's thoughts about the status of the writer in the early decades of the modern industrial age. While Poe is highly skeptical about the kinds of literary nationalism propounded by Emerson in "The American Scholar" (1837), this should not be taken to imply that he had no interest in the politics of American literature or anxieties about the inherent and inescapable binary relationship between British and American culture and the ongoing influence of British literature and criticism.

On one level, the facts are straightforward: in June 1815, Poe accompanied his foster parents, John and Frances Allan, to Great Britain; after disembarking in Liverpool, the family spent the summer in Scotland, with Poe attending Kirkgate School, Irvine, and lodging with John Allan's sister, Mary. The family moved to London in October and – after a brief return to school in Irvine – Poe attended a boarding school in Chelsea, run by the misses Dubourg, before, in autumn 1817, moving to the Reverend John Bransby's Manor House School in what was then the village of Stoke Newington. Poe and the Allans returned to the United States in the summer of 1820.

The relationship between this relatively brief childhood experience and Poe's later literary output is more complex and varied. Great Britain is represented in several of Poe's works, but – while its presence is essential to some narratives – it is not always central to their structure. For example, the peripheral mention of the Hebrides in "Silence: A Fable" (1839) and "The Valley of Unrest" (1845) is insignificant, while the allusion to colonial India and Warren Hastings in "A Tale of the Ragged Mountains" (1844) and the fact that the elk in "Morning on the Wissahiccon" (1844) is owned by an English family are not developed into extended critiques of transatlantic relations or other meditations on British politics or culture.

"The Philosophy of Furniture" (1840) goes further, deploying its discussion of interior decoration to contrast not only British and American furnishings, but also American obsession with money and lack of artistic good taste more generally. For Poe, the United States, being deprived of an aristocracy able to diffuse the "proper feeling," functions along purely economic lines in its confusion of "magnificence" and "beauty": thus, "inartistical arrangement, a prevalence of straight lines, glare, glitter," the "exaggerated employment of mirrors," and a "monstrous and odious uniformity" combine to corrupt taste and ideas.[4] Though adding an affection for the aristocracy to the Anglo-American lens for his attack on American manners, Poe's views here offer an artistic antecedent to Henry David Thoreau's slightly later observations on American life in "Resistance to Civil Government" (1849): Thoreau's doctrine, "the more money, the less virtue," is matched by Poe's "a man of large purse has usually a very little soul…As we grow rich, our ideas grow rusty."[5] The key difference, of course, is that while Thoreau – like his mentor, Emerson – conceals his indebtedness to British Romanticism behind an emphasis on cultural nationalism and the need to develop democratic self-reliance, Poe celebrates British aristocratic taste as a way of highlighting American flaws.

Poe draws upon his experience of living in Great Britain in the setting for several of his tales, although the extent to which they are explicitly about the importance of national identity varies. "Why the Little Frenchman Wears His Hand in a Sling" (1837) takes place in Southampton Row, Russell Square, where Poe had lived with the Allans, but otherwise does little to claim an important British genealogy. More significantly, "William Wilson" (1839) offers a modified representation of the Manor House School and of Bransby as the setting for its early scenes before shifting to Eton and Oxford. Other tales featuring Great Britain include "King Pest" (1835), "Ligeia" (1838), and the complex transatlantic satire, "How to Write a Blackwood Article" (1842), which seem as much concerned with mocking Transcendentalism and American culture as they are with mocking Edinburgh, where they are staged.

These tales do, however, exemplify Poe's double-sided relationship to Britain and question the assumptions about British superiority that underpin, for example, "The Philosophy of Furniture." Although he does not cite it, "How to Write a Blackwood Article" provides evidence to support what Paul Giles has described as Poe's ability to position himself "on an eerie dividing line between British convention and American independence." For Giles, this transatlantic negotiation is illustrated most clearly in "William Wilson" through Wilson's inability to escape the shadow self haunting him. Thus, "Wilson frames this act of doubling through a pun on constitution, which indicates not only his physical constitution, but also the political constitution of each country which is mirrored disconcertingly across the North Atlantic divide." In Giles's persuasive analysis, "The tranquillity of the rural past [English village life]...is haunted by a threat of violence and oppression [exemplified by Dr. Bransby], as if these placid scenes of English life could never quite conceal the old country's pervasive colonial impulse toward domination and mastery."[6]

While Giles's reading of "William Wilson" may help explain the mixture of reverence and suspicion in Poe's attitude to Dickens, it also offers a useful insight into some of his other nonfiction writing. Elsewhere Poe mentions Great Britain in relation to literary criticism in ways that again indicate why he should feel (at best) ambivalent about the relationship between old and new worlds. While Poe is happy to champion individual poets such as Tennyson, he is unstinting in his condemnation of what he regards as nationalistic and vitriolic attacks by British critics on American writers. Thus, in the *Broadway Journal* (October 4, 1845), he launches a stinging critique of the condescension generally aimed at American authors from across the Atlantic and of the obsequious acceptance of this by Americans:

There is not a more disgusting spectacle under the sun than our subserviency to British criticism. It is disgusting, first because it is truckling, servile, pusillanimous – secondly, because of its gross irrationality. We know the British to bear us little but ill will – we know that, in no case, do they utter unbiased opinions of American books – we know that in the few instances in which our writers have been treated with common decency in England, these writers have openly paid homage to English institutions, or have had lurking at the bottom of their hearts a secret principle war with Democracy: – we know all this, and yet, day after day, submit our necks to the degrading yoke of the crudest opinion that emanates from the fatherland. Now if we must have nationality, let it be a nationality that will throw off this yoke.[7]

The nuances of what Poe says here have tended to be lost in a critical overemphasis on his opening paragraph. In that, Poe refutes the calls for a nationalistic form of "American Letters," asserting, "That an American should confine himself to American themes, or even prefer them, is rather a political than a literary idea....After all, the world at large is the only legitimate stage for the autorial *histrio*."[8] For scholars such as Kenneth Silverman, this introduction contains the nub of Poe's argument, articulating his opposition to Emersonian calls for new men to write about new lands.[9] Characteristically, however, Poe frames this refutation in transatlantic terms that construct a call for an American literary voice, implying that American literature must move beyond such narrow parameters and that

American critics and readers must learn to trust their own judgment and abandon their reliance on the opinions of British critics. Thus, although his plea for writers to look beyond the local for material is at odds with Emerson's demand in the opening lines of "Nature" (1836) for "our own works" in a "poetry of insight and not of tradition,"[10] the framing of Poe's appeal is strikingly similar. Poe and Emerson both recognize a postcolonial mentality shaping an American literature that remains deferential to the former colonial power, and both call for a new kind of American identity (framed in masculine terms specifically by Emerson and implicitly by Poe) that will have the courage to slay the cultural and political fatherland.

For Poe, this identity is also determined by economic and class relations within the United States and in the relationship to Britain. In "International Copyright," he says the lack of international copyright law leads not only to the flooding of the American market with cheap foreign imported books, but also the "injury to our national literature [caused] by repressing the efforts of our men of genius, for genius as a general rule is poor in worldly goods and cannot write for nothing." Again, Poe's argument resembles Emerson's: each implies that the need for American writers of original material is an essential component of the democratic state and recognizes the extent to which the marginal position of the professional writer militates against their emergence. Moreover, Poe articulates what remains unsaid in Emerson's argument: the only American writers who can afford to write are the "gentlemen of elegant leisure," whose innate conservatism "leads them into imitation of...British models" because "Colonies have always naturally aped the mother land."[11]

Poe did, of course, admire some American writers, and his 1842 review of Hawthorne's *Twice-Told Tales* indicates the reasons for such respect and the need to temper it. This review also reveals Poe's relationship to British fiction. "Nathaniel Hawthorne" anticipates "The Philosophy of Composition" in its key concerns. It develops, at greater length, Poe's belief that the tale "affords unquestionably the fairest field for the exercise of the loftiest talent which can be afforded by the wide domain of mere prose" and insists upon a "unity of effect" that "cannot be thoroughly preserved in productions whose perusal cannot be completed at one sitting." As with "The Philosophy of Composition," the tale is contrasted with the "objectionable" novel, with the ideal tale designed with a single "effect" in mind and with every word contributing to "one pre-established design." Poe states "emphatically" that Hawthorne's tales "belong to the highest region of Art" and, in lengthy analyses of several tales, praises Hawthorne's "invention, creation, imagination, [and] originality." Nevertheless, Poe does find one element of Hawthorne's work unsatisfactory: while the style is "purity itself," the subjects of the tales are "insufficiently varied" with an overarching tone of "melancholy and mysticism."[12]

Poe's review of a quintessentially New England author seems, albeit sometimes elliptically, to relate to his attitudes to the strengths and weaknesses of British and American literature – and the relation between them – more widely. Hawthorne himself, in his preface to *The House of the Seven Gables* (1851), would later articulate the reasons for calling his longer works "romances" rather than "novels" in a manner that indicates Poe's perceptive recognition of the strengths and weaknesses of Hawthorne's fiction. In drawing the distinction, Hawthorne argues that the dominant European form of storytelling – the realist novel – is unsuitable to American needs. While Dickensian realism depended on the complex and multilayered class relations, urban geography, and political and legal intrigue stemming from hundreds of years of history, the relatively new and egalitarian nation, which lacked such self-evident complexities, demanded a different form. Hawthorne explains that the writer of a romance should "claim a certain latitude, both as to its fashion and material" not available to the novelist. To discover the truths of the "new" nation, Hawthorne felt it necessary to look beneath the surface and to apply the powers of the imagination to the bare bones of historical detail. Unlike in the old world, where exteriors presented the realities of individual and social identity, Hawthorne argued that in the United States the potential of the nation – the self-reliance that he called the "truth of the human heart" – could only be presented "under circumstances... of the writer's own choosing or creation" through the use of symbolism and allegory.[13]

Hawthorne's literary self-defense depends on the same transatlantic binary deployed by Poe. The "straight lines" and "monstrous and odious uniformity" identified by Poe in "The Philosophy of Furniture" are what, for Hawthorne, preclude the possibility that realist representation of contemporary American life can provide meaningful insights into the human condition. Hawthorne not only refuses to "ape the mother land" – as Poe had put it – but also gives sound reasons for developing a genre apposite to a new political and cultural landscape. Yet Poe's criticism of the "insufficiently varied" subject matter of Hawthorne's tales suggests that (at least for Poe, writing about Hawthorne's early work) Hawthorne had been unable to find a suitably diverse alternative. While it is impossible to know what Poe would have made of Hawthorne's turn to novel-length productions and whether he would have seen them as inferior to tales read at a single sitting, there is no doubt that Hawthorne's preface mirrors Poe's call for American literature to break free from its subservience to inappropriate old world generic and critical models.

The disappointing nature of Dickens's attempts to write about American life appears to preempt Hawthorne's distinctions. In *Imagining America*, Peter Conrad argues that the "equality which is the [United States'] social and economic glory is, for Dickens, its imaginative affliction: in making men equal it makes them all alike." In the American sections of *Martin Chuzzlewit*, the result is that Martin and his companion, Mark Tapley, encounter a series of national types, "without exception," as Conrad continues, "listless, hollow-cheeked, tedious, and portentously verbose."[14] Each character is introduced as "one of the most remarkable men in our country" and each is interchangeable with the last. In contrast, the infinite possibilities afforded by the maze-like nature of Dickens's London are essential components of his authorial power in a number of ways. The manner in which the knowing narrator can act as guide to readers presumed ignorant of the geographical intricacies of the city sees him piloting them through its darkest areas and eliciting a sympathetic, reformist response to the moral labyrinth allegorized through urban poverty and decay. The way that Dickens's language mimics the landscape reinforces his power: the convoluted sentences, packed with semicolons and subordinate clauses, compel careful attention from readers and enable Dickens to bridge the gap between the two very different worlds of London's poor and its more affluent classes.[15]

"The Man of the Crowd" is, in its London setting and formal effects, the most Dickensian of Poe's works. Indeed, there is a lengthy critical history accusing Poe of plagiarizing Dickens's *Sketches by Boz* (1836) in his construction of the tale. Stephen Rachman has looked closely at the similarities and differences between "The Man of the Crowd" and, in particular, "The Drunkard's Death," noting that while Poe is "clearly indebted to Dickens," he rewrites scenes to generate very different effects. For Rachman, Poe's tale shadows Dickens, as the narrator shadows the man of the crowd, and Dickens haunts Poe's text in the way the old man occupies the psyche of Poe's narrator, with Poe "borrow[ing] details from Dickens to pretend to the same kind of intimate knowledge of the city." Importantly, however, Rachman notes that Poe "transmogrifies the socially intelligible world of Dickens into a diabolical parade of types, of urban hieroglyphics ostensibly significant to the narrator only in their potential decipherability. . . . Dickens draws his characters with sympathy. Poe erases the intimate moral relationship between people and the places they inhabit by subsuming these establishments under the guise of the crowd."[16]

Rachman's analysis provides evidence of Poe's mix of indebtedness to Dickens, anxiety about the influence of Dickens both on his own work and on American literature more generally, and his skepticism about Dickensian faith in the individual at a time when the industrial revolution and the onset of what would later be labeled "modernity" were instigating rapid changes in British cultural behavior. In "The Man of the Crowd," Poe's narrator functions as a kind of proto-anthropologist, using his observation of the "tumultuous sea of human heads" to pick out a series of classes, tribes, races, divisions, and "order[s] of men" (all familiar from Dickens's fiction) that constitute the throng of London life.[17] Unlike Dickens, whose deployment of a wandering narratorial eye identifies individuals marked by idiosyncratic quirks within these groups, Poe subdivides only into what Walter Benjamin has called the "absurd kind of uniformity" of categories marked by class or occupation or "facial expression."[18] Whereas Dickens always adopts a moral perspective, outraging his readers with scenes of destitution and cruelty and provoking them to demand reform, Poe's narrator is indifferent to the ethical dimensions of what he sees and unwilling or unable to extract deep meaning from the signs he is so adept at identifying. Whereas Dickens's plots resolve into morally satisfying conclusions, Poe refuses to provide either contextual detail for what occurs or a narrator able to interpret what he has seen. At the end of the tale, the narrator concludes, "It will be in vain to follow; for I shall learn no more of him, nor of his deeds."[19]

Benjamin is correct to argue that "Poe's manner of presentation cannot be called realism. It shows a purposely distorting imagination at work."[20] Nor, however, can it be equated with the kinds of "truth" sought by Hawthorne in the American romance. Instead, it preempts the forms of artistic modernism that would herald the collapse of literary nationalism in the early decades of the twentieth century. "The Man of the Crowd" is, of course, a short story rather than a Dickensian novel, a shift that anticipates the mania for the form from time-pressed workers in the second half of the nineteenth century. More than this, it is a representation of the standardization of people, as much as of objects, as the modern world takes shape and – as such – it brings a challenge to Dickens's habit of staging his work in a recent past where this process was less advanced. Poe seems to be suggesting that contemporary London is no more suitable as a location for Dickens's winding narratives than the straight-lined America that he would visit in 1842. While Great Britain casts a lengthy shadow over both Poe and, more widely, the American arts, "The Man of the Crowd" enacts a form of postcolonial revenge, representing a colonial power (and its most famous writer of national fictions) whose influence can be challenged and transformed, and whose own moral and geographical landscape is already becoming subsumed beneath a modernity that will make its values obsolete.

NOTES

1. Edgar Allan Poe, *Essays and Reviews*, ed. G. R. Thompson (New York: Library of America, 1984), 13.
2. Ibid., 13, 232, 236.
3. Ibid., 15.
4. Edgar Allan Poe, *The Collected Works of Edgar Allan Poe*, ed. Thomas Ollive Mabbott, 3 vols. (Cambridge, MA: Belknap Press, 1969–78), vol. ii, 500.
5. Henry David Thoreau, *Reform Papers*, ed. Wendell Glick (Princeton: Princeton University Press, 1973); Poe, *Collected Works*, vol. ii, 500.
6. Paul Giles, *Transatlantic Insurrections: British Culture and the Formation of American Literature, 1730–1860* (Philadelphia: University of Pennsylvania Press, 2001), 189–90.
7. Poe, *Essays*, 1076–7.
8. Ibid., 1076.
9. Kenneth Silverman, *New Essays on Poe's Major Tales* (New York: Cambridge University Press, 1993), 11–12.
10. Ralph Waldo Emerson, *The Collected Works of Ralph Waldo Emerson*, ed. Robert E. Spiller et al., 9 vols. to date (Cambridge, MA: Belknap Press, 1971–), vol. i, 7.
11. Poe, *Essays*, 1374–5.
12. Ibid., 571, 574, 569.
13. Nathaniel Hawthorne, *The House of the Seven Gables*, ed. Fredson Bowers (Columbus: Ohio State University Press, 1965), 1.
14. Peter Conrad, *Imagining America* (London: Routledge and Kegan Paul, 1980), 55, 57.
15. For a fuller treatment of Dickens's failure to adapt his style to representations of American life, see Christopher Gair, "The 'American Dickens': Mark Twain and Charles Dickens," in *A Companion to Mark Twain*, ed. Peter Messent and Louis J. Budd (Oxford: Blackwell, 2005), 141–56.
16. Stephen Rachman, "'Es lässt sich nicht schreiben': Plagiarism and 'The Man of the Crowd,'" in *The American Face of Edgar Allan Poe*, ed. Shawn Rosenheim and Stephen Rachman (Baltimore: Johns Hopkins University Press, 1995), 72, 75–6.
17. Poe, *Collected Works*, vol. ii, 507.
18. Walter Benjamin, *Illuminations*, trans. Harry Zohn (London: Fontana, 1973), 172.
19. Poe, *Collected Works*, vol. ii, 515.
20. Benjamin, *Illuminations*, 168.

CHAPTER 2

The South

James M. Hutchisson

In many respects, Poe is the nowhere man of American literature. Born in Boston to parents who were itinerant actors, as a young child Poe led a vagabond existence, moving up and down the East Coast with his parents until his father took flight and left his mother, Eliza, to care for three children. In 1811, she ended up in Richmond, Virginia, where she suddenly took ill and died at age twenty-four. Poe was then taken in by John and Frances Allan and raised – except for a five-year period in London – in the antebellum South. He attended the University of Virginia for one year in 1826. Then, rebelling against the middle-class values of his foster father, he fled northward and into the army, where he served an assignment at Fort Independence on Castle Island in Boston harbor before transferring some six months later to Fort Moultrie, on Sullivan's Island, South Carolina, outside Charleston – the setting of his only Southern-specific story, "The Gold-Bug." He then moved back north after gaining admission to West Point. During this time, Poe paid visits back to Richmond, occasioned by the deaths of his foster mother and father. Poe then decided the army was not for him, was dismissed from the academy after seven months, and embarked on a peripatetic existence in New York, Baltimore, and Philadelphia, returning south to Richmond twice: in 1835 to work at the *Southern Literary Messenger* and in 1849 to lecture on poetry, a time when he also reunited with his childhood sweetheart and became engaged to be married before his untimely death in Baltimore on October 7. What are we to make of this unusual geographic trajectory? It has, of course, given rise to lively debate among scholars about whether Poe should be considered a Southern writer, but it has also confused the reading public in general, since all the cities in which Poe lived, however briefly, want to claim him as a native son.

As to Poe's Southernness, we confront the inescapable fact that Poe wrote almost nothing about the South. His tales, indeed, take place mostly in an invented otherworld where the surreal and the illusory are the main features of the setting – only occasionally do his stories feature the tidal marshlands of South Carolina or the history-steeped mountains and valleys of Virginia. No concrete particularities in his stories identify them as Southern; they are actually not even identifiably American in most respects – the reason, perhaps, why as long ago as 1941 the vision of the American Renaissance F. O. Matthiessen constructed made Poe the odd man out in the period.[1] Cooper and Irving wrote of expanding democratic vistas; Hawthorne of America's Puritan past; Melville of democracy and religion. Poe's tales are rooted in the Euro-Germanic tradition of gothicism, his poetry in the Greco-Roman tradition of classicism. Yet all American literature anthologies today still classify Poe as Southern. We could perhaps, as Richmond-born Ellen Glasgow did many decades ago, identify Poe as Southern not through content but through form: "Poe is, to a large extent, a distillation of the Southerner," Glasgow wrote. "The formalism of his tone, the classical element in his poetry and in many of his stories, the drift toward rhetoric, the aloof and elusive intensity, all these qualities are Southern."[2] Other critics have had more trouble: Barrett Wendell claimed Poe was only a Southerner by courtesy; in *The Mind of the South*, W. J. Cash called him "only half a Southerner"; Allen Tate remarked cagily that Poe was "a gentleman and a Southerner," but "not quite, perhaps, a Southern gentleman."[3]

In his own time, Poe was considered a Southerner. Reviewing Poe's *Tales* in the June 28, 1845 edition of the *New York Morning News*, Evert A. Duyckinck noted that Poe's stories had been published in "newspapers and magazines of the country, chiefly of the South, and have been scarcely, if at all, known to Northern and Eastern readers."[4] After Reconstruction, the South claimed Poe as a product of its culture, easily seeing his work as part of its project of memorialization, especially so since Poe's life story was a saga of a lost cause. At the Baltimore centennial celebration of Poe's birth, Oliver Huckel characterized Poe as "never unfaithful to honor," and engaged on a "noble quest" that put him through "suffering, loss, and defeat."[5] Another speaker compared Poe to John C. Calhoun because of both men's fierce individualism and independence. And, although it was not clear if he referred to a specific text or to Poe the writer in general, George Wauchope claimed Poe was the author of "our aesthetic declaration of independence" – strangely, a phrase much like what Oliver Wendell Holmes had earlier said of Emerson's "The American Scholar" when he called it America's "intellectual Declaration of Independence": a similarity that Emerson surely would have disliked.[6]

Some have argued that, if Poe's tales are not Southern in theme and form, then perhaps they are instead coded or perhaps repressed commentaries on the South – especially in the areas of race and gender. That is, if on the surface they do not deal with the concerns of the Southern writer – the burdens of memory and history, the importance of family and place, social class, and religion – then they do so allegorically. For example, "The Fall of the House of Usher" might be read as a symbolic depiction of the dying out of the Southern aristocracy since the mansion and its landscape evoke plantation images. In the tale, so such readings go, Poe employs the gothic formula to construct a kind of jeremiad about the destruction of a culture; Madeline comes to bury the past, but she does not do so in order to make possible a future. Poe's house of Usher may symbolize opposition and fear of a world that he felt threatened the Southern pastoral ideal and, possibly, the ideal of Southern womanhood, as well. Similarly, *The Narrative of Arthur Gordon Pym* has been read as a treatment of the guilt and fear emanating from slave society.[7]

It is possible to read other Poe stories as covert allegories endorsing the ethos of the antebellum South, particularly in their infrequent but obvious stereotyped characterizations of African Americans. Black characters, when they do appear, are ignorant, stupidly happy, or darkly insidious: the murderous black cook in *Pym*, the docile servant, Jupiter, in "The Gold-Bug," and – less so but still a stereotype – Pompey in "A Predicament" come to mind. The social and racial dimensions of these texts are frequently spotlighted, perhaps because beginning in the 1830s, various arguments for Anglo racial superiority gained currency in the United States. There has also been a tendency to characterize Poe as a racist because of these types of depictions. Although since proven to be the work of another writer, a review of two proslavery books in the *Southern Literary Messenger* in 1836 was once thought to have been by Poe; it became a key piece of evidence in the case for Poe's racist thinking.[8] Most likely, Poe agreed in principle with the social attitudes he absorbed through his Southern upbringing, though this does not make him overtly, in modern parlance, a racist.

Poe's poetry, too, which was for a long time distanced by critics from the social realities of nineteenth-century America, has recently been read by feminist critics in new ways. Some see the depiction of male–female relationships in Poe's poetry as analogous to the antebellum ideology of the "intimate relation" between master and slave. Others have detected in Poe's tales covert fantasies of empowerment and revenge that can be particularized as the relation between a "suffering" – that is, alternately degraded and idealized – "servant" and an omniscient master.[9]

The strongest Southern elements in Poe seem to lie mostly in three areas: his personal behavior, his temperament and cast of mind, and the sectional bias and antimodernist tendencies he showed in his critical essays, letters and marginalia, and book reviews. Poe was a first-class fantasist when it came to crafting a public image. He had a high opinion of his intellect and his writing skills and could be something of an elitist; he therefore often adopted the carefree manner of the planter-gentleman, assuming an air of privilege and propriety, even though his life was nothing like that. He could even, when necessary, half seriously cite his Southern inheritance as the cause of his indiscretions: describing an alcoholic reverie to Joseph Snodgrass, he said that sometimes he could "give way, at long intervals, to the temptation held out on all sides by the spirit of Southern conviviality."[10] It is also clear that Poe fantasized about being part of that aristocracy, as when he characterized the subscribers of the *Southern Literary Messenger* as "almost without exception the élite, both as regards wealth and intellectual culture, of the Southern aristocracy," and said that its "corps of contributors are generally men who control the public opinion of the Southerners on all topics."[11]

In fact, when he embarked on his plan to produce his own magazine, Poe looked primarily to Southerners for financial backing and subscription. As he said in a letter to his Georgia cousin, William Poe, "It is upon the South that I chiefly rely for aid in the undertaking, and I have every hope that it will not fail me in my need."[12] Later, John Tomlin of Jackson, Tennessee encouragingly wrote Poe that his magazine would surely succeed because "the warm-hearted Southerners, by whom you are known, will not let the Work die for the want of patronage. They are your friends – for they know you well, and will sustain you."[13] As it turned out, however, the South did not support Poe all that well.

Among the most hypersensitive of writers, Poe was sometimes given to theatrical, hyperbolic statements that were a profound result of growing up in the Old South. For example, in his most famous essay, "The Philosophy of Composition," Poe proclaimed that the death of a beautiful woman was the most poetic of all subjects. If we keep in mind that Poe began to formulate his critical ideas during his tenure at the *Southern Literary Messenger* in the mid to late 1830s, we can see how much of what he wrote was influenced by the lachrymose consolation poetry that appeared therein. In the January 1836 *Messenger*, for example, Poe reviewed at length the work of a leading sentimental poet of the day, Lydia Sigourney. She would later call up Poe's sectional pride when a special posthumous edition of her work was published for the benefit of her children: "To Southerners, at least," Poe would write, "we feel that nothing farther need be said."[14] Southern magazines in the 1820s and 1830s were filled with morbid poems about heartbreak at the loss of a lover to either death or desertion. Philip Pendleton Cooke, one of Poe's Virginia friends, contributed to the *Messenger* "Rosalie Lee," a lament for the death of a beautiful girl followed into the grave by her bereaved lover. Like these writers, Poe was obsessed with grief, the dread of shame, and the world's indifference toward codes of conduct and honor. Bertram Wyatt-Brown has argued that in this way, Poe sets the stage for the South's later considerations of sectionalism, war, and defeat.[15]

Poe was also well acquainted with – indeed closely connected to – the historical situation of Virginia in the 1830s. As his aesthetic and philosophical theories developed, an increasing disbelief in a cyclical view of history folded into them. "The glory of the Ancient Dominion," Poe wrote disconsolately in 1835, "is in a fainting, is in a dying condition," a shadow of "things that have been."[16] The Virginia dynasty of Washington, Jefferson, Madison, and Monroe had ended in 1825, and the intellectual leadership of the nation had moved elsewhere. The 1830s marked the most turbulent period of slaveholder versus abolitionist antagonism and the Virginia legislative debates over emancipation (1831–2). Poe had moved north in 1837 but technically not by choice – he went where the work was – and by 1841, he could still lament that there was scarcely one "person of any literary distinction in the chief city of the Old Dominion."[17] Poe's preference for beauty over truth had its origins in the historical situation of Virginia in the 1830s, specifically in Poe's identifying with the political apologias for Virginia and the South published in the *Messenger* during his tenure there. Poe probably edited many of these articles. At any rate, in his position as assistant editor (managing editor) of the periodical, he surely read them.

Poe's critical reviews show some of the Southern origins of his literary aesthetic. His opposition to didacticism and allegory, his contention (in "The Poetic Principle") that the "obstinate oils and waters of Poetry and Truth" could not be reconciled, was stated most fully in his various attacks on Henry Wadsworth Longfellow in the 1840s. The distant opening shots in his eventual full-scale verbal war with the poet can be heard in his 1842 review of Longfellow's *Ballads and Other Poems*. In an omnibus review of Longfellow's works for the *Aristidean* in April 1845, Poe cut a swathe through much of the poet's shelf of books. Poe condemned *Poems on Slavery* as "intended for the especial use of those negrophilic old ladies of the north" who were so cozy with Longfellow and William Ellery Channing, leader of the Unitarian church, to whom the volume was dedicated. In shredding the spurious assumptions behind the poem "The Slave's Dream," Poe noted that it was "a very commendable and comfortable thing, in the Professor, to sit at ease in his library chair, and write verses instructing the southerners how to give up their all with a good grace, and abusing them if they will not; but we have a singular curiosity to know how much of his own, under a change of circumstances, the Professor himself would be willing to surrender."[18] More comments like this punctuate the review, assailing Longfellow for his sectional bias.

Poe's attacks on progress in society as a vain dream of human perfectibility and his belief that history was cyclical sprang from his identification with the South. "Southern supineness," as Poe called it, and escalating Northern antagonisms hastened this decline.[19] As Poe's various reviews of Longfellow make clear – and his public attacks on Longfellow and the whole literary culture of New England, what Poe derisively called the Frogpondians – a belief in the social progress of man and a positive view of human history were inextricably linked with didactic poetry. Thus it was logical that the South should support the separation of poetry and truth. Poetry in itself posed no threat to the region, but truth certainly did – at least the supposed truth of social progress. Poe's attack on Longfellow and on other didactic poets (most all of them Northerners) was, as Kenneth Alan Hovey has said, an attempt by Poe to "free the South from the heresy of Northern thought and an attempt to free poetry from truth."[20] Both attempts were really the same thing. Poe advocated "the poem written solely for the poem's sake"[21] – a beauty that no truth could invade – because he feared the advance of historical progress.

Poe could never let go of his animosity toward the New England literary establishment. Although he published his first volume of poems as "a Bostonian," and although he associated Boston with pleasant memories of his young mother, Poe's critical exordia were harsh toward the works of Longfellow, Emerson, William Cullen Bryant, James Fenimore Cooper, and Washington Irving, because he opposed their native Puritanism, their jingoistic chauvinism, their (to him) shallow optimism, and their abidingly democratic view of society. To Poe, these men lacked artistic vision and critical earnestness. Their writing took no notice of the psychic realities of humankind – it presented instead only pastel-colored vistas of plains and gushing waterfalls, or, when it turned philosophical, of a sentimental faith in some divine being. Poe equated these themes with the North. In turn, Poe was often disproportionately kind to Southern authors like John Pendleton Kennedy, William Gilmore Simms, and Philip Pendleton Cooke, many of whom, it must be said, were far less gifted than their Northern peers and who, more to the point, employed essentially the same themes. Writing of A. B. Longstreet's *Georgia Scenes*, for example, in the March 1836 issue of the *Messenger*, Poe spoke of the author as "endowed...with an exquisitely discriminative and penetrating understanding of character in general, and of Southern character in particular." He then continued: "Seriously – if this book were printed in England it would make the fortune of its author."[22] Regarding books by minor talents like Edward C. Pinckney of Baltimore, Poe would say: "It was profoundly admired by the critical few, but had little circulation: – this for no better reason than that the author was born too far South."[23]

Poe's antiprogressivist views and his distrust of social betterment were really early reactions against the industrialization that would eventually sweep the South and dislocate it from memory and history. Poe's views anticipate those later espoused by the Agrarian circle, whose attacks on technology and the doctrine of progress are well known. A good example of Poe's position may be found in "The Colloquy of Monos and Una" (1841). Poe uses this futuristic dialogue as a vehicle for attacking precisely the same evils that the Agrarians later saw in modern civilization. Monos equates abstract theories of social betterment (egalitarianism in the abstract sense) with industrialism. These systems are assaults on nature – a view expressed in different forms in "Sonnet – To Science" (1829), "The Man That Was Used Up" (1839), "The Thousand and Second Tale of Scheherezade" (1845), and other works. In the same way as Poe, Allen Tate questioned the validity of the rationalistic idea of human perfectibility: "Reason...and the perfectibility of man-in-the-gross," he said in 1951, "were the great liberal dogmas which underlay much of our present trouble."[24]

It is significant that Poe's social attitudes were similar to those of the Agrarians, because of the reciprocal relationship between the creation of art and the writing of literary criticism. The Agrarians, or New Critics, like Poe, denied the hortatory function of poetry; the poet was not supposed to concern himself or herself with moral or political questions, except as they fell within the sphere of vision in the poem. Poe's insistence upon a close reading of the text, excluding extra-textual knowledge that might illuminate that text, makes him the first of the New Critics. The difference was that Poe's philosophical absolutism denied to the poet the coherent reality that the Agrarians believed could be shaped by the artistic ordering of experience. But if we picture Poe primarily as the apostle of beauty – the antimaterialist – he is clearly a forefather of the group that led the Southern literary renaissance in the next century.

Where does that leave Poe? In the dream land of his imaginative creations or in the adoptive homeland of his formative years of life? It is hard to argue against the profound influence of the latter. The South was where Poe came of age, where he first made his mark as a man of letters, and where he spent the beginning of his married life. It was also where, in the painful aftermath of the death of Virginia and the fallout from his professional imbroglios, he returned to put down roots, to seek a new and better life with a woman he had loved from long ago. Throughout his mostly unhappy life and his usually unpredictable peregrinations, Poe never really thought of himself as anything other than a Southerner. In a wistful account of his life story to a second cousin who finally located him in 1839, he described his nomadic existence. Near the end, he added, as much for himself as for his correspondent, a reassuring postscript. Despite his wanderings, Poe said, "Richmond is my home, and a letter to that City will always reach me in whatever part of the world I may be."[25]

NOTES

1. F. O. Matthiessen, *American Renaissance: Art and Expression in the Age of Emerson and Whitman* (New York: Oxford University Press, 1941).
2. Ellen Glasgow, *A Certain Measure: An Interpretation of Prose Fiction* (New York: Harcourt, 1943), 132.
3. Barrett Wendell, *A Literary History of America* (New York: Scribner, 1900), 487; W. J. Cash, *The Mind of the South* (New York: Knopf, 1941), 93; Allen Tate, "To Whom Is The Poet Responsible?" *Hudson Review* 4 (1951), 325.
4. Dwight Thomas and David K. Jackson, *The Poe Log: A Documentary Life of Edgar Allan Poe, 1809–1849* (Boston: G. K. Hall, 1987), 543.
5. Charles W. Kent and John S. Patton, eds., *The Book of the Poe Centenary* (Charlottesville: University of Virginia, 1909), 52.
6. Kent and Patton, *Book of the Poe Centenary*, 205; Oliver Wendell Holmes, *The Works of Oliver Wendell Holmes*, 13 vols. (Boston: Houghton Mifflin, 1892), vol. xi, 88.
7. See, for example, Nancy Buffington, "Fictions of the South: Southern Portraits of Slavery," in *A Companion to American Fiction, 1780–1865*, ed. Shirley Samuels (New York: Wiley-Blackwell, 2004), 380–3; Peter Coviello, "Poe in Love: Pedophilia, Morbidity, and the Logic of Slavery," *ELH* 70 (2003), 875–901; Maurice S. Lee, "Absolute Poe: His System of Transcendental Racism," *American Literature* 75 (2003), 751–81.
8. "Slavery," *Southern Literary Messenger* 2 (1836), 336–9.
9. Joan Dayan, "Amorous Bondage: Poe, Ladies, and Slavery," *American Literature* 66 (1994), 239–74.
10. Poe to Joseph E. Snodgrass, April 1, 1841, *The Collected Letters of Edgar Allan Poe*, ed. John Ward Ostrom, Burton R. Pollin, and Jeffrey A. Savoye, 2 vols. (New York: Gordian, 2008), vol. i, 263.
11. Thomas and Jackson, *Poe Log*, 520.
12. Poe to William Poe, August 14, 1840, *Collected Letters*, vol. i, 236.

13. John Tomlin to Poe, November 22, 1840, *The Complete Works of Edgar Allan Poe*, ed. James A. Harrison, 17 vols. (New York: Crowell, 1902), vol. xvii, 61–2.

14. Edgar Allan Poe, *Essays and Reviews*, ed. G. R. Thompson (New York: Library of America, 1984), 176.

15. Bertram Wyatt-Brown, *Southern Honor: Ethics and Behavior in the Old South* (New York: Oxford University Press, 1983). See also Richard Gray, *Southern Aberrations: Writers of the American South and the Problems of Regionalism* (Baton Rouge: Louisiana State University Press, 2000).

16. Edgar Allan Poe, "Minor's Address," *Southern Literary Messenger* 2 (1835), 66.

17. Edgar Allan Poe, *Complete Works*, vol. xv, 241.

18. Poe, *Essays*, 762–3.

19. Ibid., 904.

20. Kenneth Alan Hovey, "Critical Provincialism: Poe's Poetic Principle in Antebellum Context," *American Quarterly* 39 (1987), 349.

21. Poe, *Essays*, 76.

22. Ibid., 778.

23. Ibid., 1440.

24. Tate, "To Whom Is The Poet Responsible?" 334.

25. Poe to George W. Poe, July 14, 1839, *Collected Letters*, vol. i, 185.

CHAPTER 3

The American West

Nathaniel Lewis

ST. LOUIS, 1849

In the spring of 1849, Edgar Allan Poe, seeking support for his proposed magazine *The Stylus*, began a correspondence with E. H. N. Patterson, editor of the *Oquawka Spectator*. Patterson, who had recently taken over control of the Illinois newspaper, had essentially proposed that he publish *The Stylus* with "duplicate publication, East and West," giving Poe editorial control of its literary content.[1] Poe, who had long depended for an audience on his "warm friends, especially in the South and West," was interested in Patterson's offer for a number of reasons, not the least of which was its western location.[2] In April, Poe wrote to Patterson that, in order to forward their plans, he hoped "to take a tour through the principal States – especially West and South – visiting the small towns more particularly than the large ones – lecturing as I went to pay expenses." He expected in this way to secure at least 1,000 pledged subscribers for the new magazine. "Under such circumstances," Poe remarked, "success would be complete."[3]

In this April letter, Poe suggested that he visit Patterson in Oquawka. Although keen to pursue the opportunity, Poe recognized as well the "serious difficulties" ahead, including the obscurity of Oquawka's location, about 200 miles north of St. Louis on the Mississippi River. In his letter of May 23, Poe remarked that "your residence in Okquawka [*sic*] is certainly one of the most serious of these difficulties," and suggested that they add to the title page "Published simultaneously at New-York and *St Louis*." Perhaps to reinforce his interest in the more prominent city, Poe then wrote that, upon receiving Patterson's approval, he would "proceed to St Louis and there meet you." For his part, Patterson, with misgivings about the St. Louis publication, remained enthusiastic in his response, but Poe, slowed by sickness and exhaustion, took two months to reply, writing in August: "I most bitterly lament the event" – presumably the illness, which he took to be cholera – "which has detained me from St Louis – for I cannot help thinking that, in a personal interview, I could have brought you over to my plans. I fear that now it is too late.... [I]f you think it *possible* that your views might be changed, I will still visit you in St L. As yet, I am too feeble to travel; but by the time your reply to this reaches me, I shall have gained sufficient strength to set out."[4] Patterson quickly agreed to meet with Poe in St. Louis in mid-October, but by then Poe was dead, leaving Patterson, who never met Poe, to write an admiring obituary in his newspaper.

Had Poe made the trip to St. Louis or to Oquawka in 1849, what would he have found? While the answer may matter little to Poe's biography – he never went West – it matters quite a bit to our understanding of Poe in his historical moment, not only helping to explain his interest in Patterson's proposal but, more broadly, his considerable engagement with the literature of the West in the 1830s and 1840s. Exploration accounts, tour narratives, stories of Indians and settlers, hunting tales, Western political treatises, sermons, newspaper and magazine articles, travelogues – Poe read them and integrated (or sometimes pasted) them into his own works, notably *The Narrative of Arthur Gordon Pym* (1838), "The Journal of Julius Rodman" (1840), and his poem "Eldorado," published in April 1849, the month of his first letter to Patterson. Poe was familiar not only with the Western writings of James Fenimore Cooper and Washington Irving, but with popular works about the West by Timothy Flint, Margaret Fuller (whose *Summer on the Lakes* he praised), James Hall, Charles Fenno Hoffman, Caroline Kirkland, and many others.[5] As Edwin Fussell pointed out nearly fifty years ago, "no important American writer was more realistically concerned with, and more accurately informed about, that literature of the West which in the mid-1830's flooded the country."[6]

This essay, a triptych of places and moments from the antebellum West, will venture down in the flood to consider the context of the literature and culture of the American West in the 1830s and 1840s – or rather contexts, plural, for during this period there was no single West and no unified canon of Western writing. The cultural and demographic shifts were breathtaking: the period is bookended by the Indian Removal Act (1830) and the Gold Rush, two significant markers of extraordinary Western relocations. But even the physical boundaries of the American West were transformed in these years, notably by the annexation of Texas and the Treaty of Guadalupe Hidalgo (1848), in which the United States acquired vast regions of the Southwest from Mexico. During Poe's life, "the West" could refer, often simultaneously, to the trans-Allegheny region, the Ohio

Valley, the northern Mississippi Valley, the Louisiana Territory and later the Missouri Territory, the Indian Territory, the Rocky Mountains, and the Far West. When Francis Parkman observed in *The Oregon Trail* (1849) that "great changes are at hand in that region," he echoed a sentiment expressed by nearly every explorer, visitor, and traveler in the antebellum West, offering less a prophecy than an established truth.[7]

Despite the imposing metanarrative of frontier, settlement, and civilization, despite the familiar mythology of the region, "the West" has always been an unstable and contested term with much at stake: it has repeatedly been used to describe a region that is both the nation's periphery (the very name suggests a region off to the side, decentered) and the nation's authentic center ("the West as America"). In many ways, the West is a contradiction in terms, impossible to resolve. To read Poe in the context of the antebellum West requires that we understand that signifier's rhetorical, cultural, geographic, and epistemological instability: to read Poe in the context of the West, in other words, is always already to read him at least partially in *our* context.

In 1849, St. Louis, at the confluence of the Mississippi and Missouri Rivers, was a bustling city, the "jumping off" point or "gateway" for the crowds of emigrants and speculators heading west, many of them part of the rush to the California gold fields. Poe could have read of this city's energetic activity in Parkman's *Oregon Trail*, which in the spring of 1849 had concluded its serialized run in the *Knickerbocker Magazine* and been published by George P. Putnam. Parkman opens the book with a vibrant description: "Last spring, 1846, was a busy season in the city of St. Louis. Not only were emigrants from every part of the country preparing for the journey to Oregon and California, but an unusual number of traders were making ready their wagons and outfits for Santa Fe."[8] This scene presents a difference in degree, not kind, from the one witnessed by Charles Dickens only four years earlier on his tour. Arriving by steamboat on the Mississippi – "an enormous ditch," "a foul stream" – Dickens commented in his *American Notes* on St. Louis's impending expansions: of the "American Improvements" that "consist of wharfs and warehouses, and new buildings in all directions; and of a great many vast plans which are still 'progressing.'"[9] Poe would have appreciated this busy-ness and the opportunities for the publication of fiction and nonfiction in growing markets.

Perhaps, to continue this speculative tour, Poe and Patterson would have taken a steamboat up the Mississippi, from St. Louis to Oquawka – and if so they might have discussed the brutal fire in May of that year that destroyed much of St. Louis; they might have stopped midway in Hannibal, Missouri and visited the offices of the *Gazette* or *Missouri Courier*, even crossing paths with an errand boy named Samuel Clemens, then thirteen years old; and whether or not they discussed ex-slave John Berry Meachum's "temperance boat" – a kind of floating library and school for St. Louis's free African Americans – it would have been difficult, in going from Missouri to Illinois, to avoid some recognition of slavery and its role along this part of the frontier. St. Louis's growth depended not only on the engines of emigration and expansion, but on the regional economy of slavery – a fact recorded by the growing African American literary culture of the West. As Eric Gardner has argued, William Wells Brown's *Narrative* (1847) presented St. Louis "as a 'gateway' to the heart of slavery, a representation clearly designed to challenge the depictions of St. Louis as the gateway to the West (and thus to America's future) that dominated white texts" at the time.[10]

We can think, then, of the West in 1849 as a series of tropes available to writers and artists, whatever their aesthetic or political vision. But we can also recognize that the West's textual and cultural instability – its ultimate refusal to convey determinate meaning – was itself becoming a subtext for many of these writers. In "Julius Rodman," his most explicit and extended meditation on the West, Poe constructed a West thoroughly mediated by a textual maze of borrowings and plagiarisms, using other works of varying reliability; and yet in many ways Poe's deconstruction of the West was an oddly authentic move, for it acknowledged rather than resisted the West's moving meanings.

CINCINNATI, 1838

Cincinnati, widely known as the Queen City of the West, turned fifty in 1838. A decade before the Gold Rush, it was less a rugged frontier town or gateway to far-off adventures than a settled home to some forty thousand residents. Possessing a thriving intellectual culture and enjoying the latest publishing technologies, the city's urban presence stood in stark contrast to naïve Eastern assumptions about the West as raw and wild and remains a powerful correction to "the bias of those historians who have followed the nineteenth-century commentators in setting the 'brawling' West against the 'effete' East, and who have overlooked the close cultural and intellectual relationships between the urban centers of the seaboard and the trans-Allegheny West."[11] In other words, the very settledness of Cincinnati in 1838 unsettles entrenched notions of the West.

To be sure, in 1838 what Poe called "the theme of life in the wilderness" remained thoroughly marketable, and Poe took full advantage with that year's publication of *Pym*.[12] Audiences in the East and in England were eager to hear thrilling tales of danger and savagery. These adventure stories, anticipating the dime novels and popular Westerns of the century's second half, relied on depictions of Native Americans that can only be called racist; it is unnerving today to read writers arguing over the authenticity of their representations. Poe (the "tomahawk critic") was no exception and, for example, criticized Charles Fenno Hoffman for creating an unrealistic Indian narrator: Poe acknowledged that the Indian may be capable of sentiment, "still he has, clearly, no capacity for their various *expression*."[13] Indeed, James Hall, one of Cincinnati's most prominent authors, had published his own collections of such "legends" just a few years earlier. Then, as now, the clash of savagery and civilization made a good story to the reading (that is, largely middle-class, white, Eastern) public.

By 1838, accounts of Cincinnati were more likely to convey the theme of life in genteel society than life in the wilderness; it was "manners" that mattered. Frances Trollope's *Domestic Manners of the Americans* (1832), depicting with a caustic tongue her years in Cincinnati, caused a sensation in the United States and Europe, but it was hardly the only book to interrogate the culture of manners in Cincinnati and the West. In her underappreciated *Retrospect of Western Travel* (1838), English writer and proto-sociologist Harriet Martineau described her "exhilarating" visit to the city. Although she saw herself as a "traveller in wild regions," Martineau recounted with pleasure visiting a museum, a bookstore, and an artist's studio – and especially enjoying a series of evening parties. "The conversation of the society" at one party "was most about books, and society and its leaders at home and abroad."[14] (She pronounced Trollope's Bazaar to be "the great deformity of the city."[15]) Martineau, like many British visitors, commented on slavery, that "offense against freedom," and on the intolerance toward Catholicism (promoted, at times, by Lyman Beecher, then living in the city with his family), but her observations of sectional divisions between "native of the east and west" are particularly instructional.[16] She quoted influential Cincinnati doctor and writer Daniel Drake from a typically enthusiastic speech: "we should foster Western genius, encourage Western writers, patronize Western publishers, augment the number of Western readers, and create a Western heart."[17]

That is, at the same moment that many Eastern writers were resisting the authority of the European tradition, Drake, Timothy Flint, James Hall, and many other writers of the period were championing the independence of Western literature. And we can see in this Western sectionalism a relatively early type of the American geographic imagination – a way of conceptualizing a national literature along regional lines that would have enormous consequences in the nineteenth and twentieth centuries and that was at least obliquely part of Poe's own complex negotiations with the regional literary identities of his moment.

NEW YORK CITY, 1845

When Caroline Kirkland returned to New York City in 1843 from the frontier town of Pinckney, Michigan, she was coming home. Kirkland was a New Yorker born and raised, and despite her seven years in the Western wilds attempting to establish the new settlement with her husband, it was in New York that she established herself – as one of the New York literati. She had, in a sense, found gold in the publication of her popular *A New Home – Who'll Follow?* (1839), telling the story of her frontier life, and she came east to mine it. When Poe, who admired Kirkland and her writings, moved his family from Philadelphia to New York a year later, he was in many ways moving in her circles.

It is perhaps not surprising that so many of the most visible works of antebellum Western literature were published by writers living in the East, with limited or no experience in the West. James Fenimore Cooper was living in New York City when he wrote *The Last of the Mohicans* (1826), as was William Cullen Bryant when he wrote "The Prairies" (1833), and Washington Irving when he composed much of his *Tour on the Prairies* (1835). Although Western writers such as Daniel Drake, protective of their region's literary prospects, were often critical of Eastern authorial flaneurs, writers in the East felt no embarrassment about their Western pronouncements. Charles Fenno Hoffman (or his editor) added "Written by a New Yorker" to the title page of his popular *Winter in the West* (1835), and the tag actually served to authenticate his observations to his Eastern readers. As Kirkland emphasizes in *Western Clearings*, the extraordinary land rushes and speculations, fueled by the opening of trade and transportation routes, often turned out to be risky investments; but the West proved to be reliable cultural capital to Eastern writers who (as Fussell put it) flooded the market.

Kirkland brought out *Western Clearings* in 1845 – the year that Poe published "The Raven," became editor of the *Broadway Journal*, circulated in New York literary society, and engaged in the "Longfellow War." Published as part of Wiley and Putnam's Library of American Books, the same series that included Poe's *Tales* and *The Raven and Other Poems*, Kirkland's book contained a series of Western sketches and stories. She opens with a defense of its very existence, answering "some cynical people [who] may ask why books must be made at all."[18] "We might urge," writes Kirkland, "that these are *Western* stories – stories illustrative of a land that was once an El Dorado – stories intended to give more minute and life-like representations of a peculiar people. To those who left Eastern and civilized homes to try the new Western world, at a period when every one was mad 'With visions prompted by intense desire' after golden harvests, no apology for an attempt to convey first impressions of so new a state of things will be needed." Kirkland here makes two implicit claims, both surprisingly representative of Western literature: the first is that the West is "original," unique, and thus a source of almost infinite re-presentations. She writes: "the wild West has had few visitors and fewer describers. Its history may be homely, but it is original. It is like nothing else in the wide world, and so various that successive travelers may continue to give their views of it for years to come, without fear of exhausting its pecu-liarities."[19] Whether or not this was true, the claim itself was anything but original, and appears in one form or another in most Western writings of the period.

Kirkland's second implicit claim is equally representative but perhaps more unexpected: in writing from New York, she is not only looking West across an enormous spatial gulf, but looking backward, across a great tem-poral divide, toward a vanished history. The real West, it seems, "once an El Dorado," is a thing of the past. Such a conception of the West seems to conflict dramatically with the popular image of the region: for many white Americans, especially those living in the East, the West represented the future. Indeed, the cultural symbolism of the West-as-future is central to the myth of American exceptionalism shaped in the 1830s and 1840s, explaining at the time the Indian removals and annexation of Texas, and later solidifying the frontier thesis. By the late 1830s, the term "manifest destiny" was already widely used.[20] Well before the Louisiana Purchase (1803), Americans favored the notion that their nation was expanding westward. When Henry David Thoreau wrote that he walked "westward as into the future," he was transforming an allegory about capitalist expan-sion into one of spiritual or intellectual development – but he was rein-scribing the notion of the West-as-future.

But the literature of the West in the 1830s and 1840s is almost always looking backward. We can associate some of this with Cooper's nostalgic tone, with what appears to be his elegy for a vanishing race and vanishing wilderness. Yet such ideological poses can obscure, even while reinforcing, a number of more subtle writerly moves in the backward glance; authors used it for their own Western clearings, making space for their work by insisting that what they saw is largely gone. J. Milton Sanders's serialized story "The Miami Valley" is a typical example of this authorial positioning, unexceptional as a narrative but of interest to Poe scholars as a literal precedent for "Julius Rodman." "The Miami Valley" began its run in *Burton's Gentleman's Magazine* in August of 1838 and continued into 1840, by which time "Julius Rodman" was concurrently appearing. Sanders opens his work with a predictable claim of factual authenticity ("veracity is some apology for egotism"), but quickly moves on to establish what might be called an objective correlative: the condition of historical decline. "Fifty years ago," he writes, "the state of Ohio contained sixty-four inhabitants; it now contains nearly one million and a half souls." Sanders, emphasizing the changes in the past half century, repeatedly reminds readers that he is now old: "I am now in the 'sear and yellow leaf,' – my eyes have lost their lustre, and my frame once so vigorous, has become palsied, and comparatively powerless." He insists on these changes – changes in the land and in his body – to convey the power and even reality of the earlier West, a West defined by its hypermasculinity: "In earlier days, in the west, effeminacy was not an accomplishment, as it appears to be now, but he who could wander the dense forest, without any compass but such as God gave him; he who could bear the winter winds and summer sun, and the many hardships which must be borne in an unhabitable [*sic*] wilderness, was then considered accomplished." Those first settlers "were men of uncommon strength and fortitude," in contrast to the present "sad havoc" into which the "descendants degenerated" due to luxury and ease.[21] This trope of the original West as the salubrious source of masculine energy is familiar enough, and was already tired by the late 1830s – but more interesting here is the way that Sanders clears authorial space in order to validate the importance of his story. For Sanders, "the actors of these scenes" were no longer on "this great stage."

More broadly, in the 1830s and 1840s there were so many Western visitors, settlers, and residents, and so many accounts of the region, that authors felt obligated to justify yet another publication about the West to those "cynical people," in Kirkland's words, saturated by the flood. By implying that the West, once an El Dorado, was a mere shadow of its former glory, writers and chroniclers introduced a spectral quality to Western literature, in which "presence" was repeatedly denied. By situating Julius Rodman's journey in the early 1790s, a decade before Lewis and

Clark's expedition, Poe was having hoaxy fun with Western claims of first contact and literary claims of authenticity, but more subtly he was delivering a ghost story that, in its backward glance, not only makes a virtue of earliness and originality but makes a palimpsest of the written West. In this sense, the West is not only a figment of the future but entombed in the past, a region constructed largely by writers who doubt its very existence. And so, in the end, we might consider reading the American West in the context of Edgar Allan Poe.

NOTES

1. Poe to E. H. N. Patterson, April 30? 1849, *The Collected Letters of Edgar Allan Poe*, ed. John Ward Ostrom, Burton R. Pollin, and Jeffrey A. Savoye, 2 vols. (New York: Gordian, 2008), vol. II, 793.
2. Poe to Thomas H. Chivers, July 6, 1842, *Collected Letters*, vol. i, 350.
3. Poe to E. H. N. Patterson, April 30? 1849, *Collected Letters*, vol. ii, 794.
4. Poe to E. H. N. Patterson, August 7, 1849, *Collected Letters*, vol. ii, 829.
5. Although this essay will emphasize works that circulated during Poe's lifetime, it will not offer a source study of Poe's writings. For Poe's Western sources, see Edwin Fussell, *Frontier: American Literature and the American West* (Princeton: Princeton University Press, 1965); and Burton R. Pollin's introduction, notes, and commentaries in his edition of Poe's *Imaginary Voyages* (Boston: Twayne, 1981). For a consideration of Poe's integration of Western themes in his writing, see James L. Berta's unpublished dissertation, "Poe and the West" (Bowling Green State University, 1986); and Kevin J. Hayes, *Poe and the Printed Word* (New York: Cambridge University Press, 2002), 70–3. Ralph Leslie Rusk's two-volume *The Literature of the Midwestern Frontier* (New York: Columbia University Press, 1925) remains a compelling study of antebellum Western writing focusing on the Ohio Valley; readers today may wish for a more contemporary cultural consciousness, but the sheer size of Rusk's project is an impressive marker of that flood of Western writing. Stephanie LeMenager, *Manifest and Other Destinies: Territorial Fictions of the Nineteenth-Century United States* (Lincoln: Nebraska University Press, 2004) is an insightful revision of nineteenth-century "territorial fictions." Nathaniel Lewis, *Unsettling the Literary West* (Lincoln: Nebraska University Press, 2003) includes a chapter on Western literature in the 1830s and a section on Poe.
6. Fussell, *Frontier*, 132.
7. Francis Parkman, *The Oregon Trail; The Conspiracy of Pontiac*, ed. William R. Taylor (New York: Library of America, 1991), 176.
8. Parkman, *Oregon Trail*, 176.
9. Charles Dickens, *American Notes and Pictures from Italy* (New York: Oxford University Press, 1997), 174.
10. Eric Gardner, *Unexpected Places: Relocating Nineteenth-Century African American Literature* (Philadelphia: University of Pennsylvania Press, 2009), 25.

11. Daniel Aaron, *Cincinnati: Queen City of the West* (Columbus: Ohio State University Press, 1992), 5.

12. In his well-known review of Cooper's *Wyandotté*, Poe remarked that "this theme – life in the Wilderness – is one of intrinsic and universal interest" (*Essays and Reviews*, ed. G. R. Thompson [New York: Library of America, 1984], 479).

13. Poe, *Essays*, 1209.

14. Harriet Martineau, *Retrospect of Western Travel*, 2 vols. (London: Saunders and Otley), vol. ii, 242.

15. Ibid., 249.

16. Ibid., 241.

17. Ibid., 230.

18. Caroline Kirkland, *Western Clearings* (New York: Wiley and Putnam, 1845), v.

19. Ibid., vi.

20. Andrews Norton, *A Discourse on the Latest Form of Infidelity; Delivered at the Request of the "Association of the Alumni of the Cambridge Theological School," on the 19th of July, 1839* (Cambridge, MA: John Owen, 1839), 33.

21. J. Milton Sanders, "The Miami Valley," *Burton's Gentleman's Magazine* 3 (1838), 406–7.

CHAPTER 4

The Sea

David Dowling

Given the considerable creative power of his sea narratives, it is rather surprising that Poe took only two transatlantic voyages in his lifetime, both as a boy. Poe sorely lacked the degree of firsthand maritime experience that established the credibility of Richard Henry Dana (*Two Years before the Mast*) and Herman Melville as the foremost authorities on the sea, from its culture and commerce to its politics and society. Poe relied instead on popular and intellectual culture as the primary source material for his sea narratives, "Manuscript Found in a Bottle" (1833), *The Narrative of Arthur Gordon Pym* (1838), and "A Descent into the Maelström" (1841). One review of *Pym*, Poe's only novel, the first two installments of which were published serially in the *Southern Literary Messenger*, derided the author for his errors in usage of nautical terminology stemming from his technical unfamiliarity with sailing ships. The reviewer, William Burton, claimed that Poe drew exclusively from fictional sources for his novel in a hollow and politically pointless derivation of Daniel Defoe's *Robinson Crusoe* (1719) and Jonathan Swift's *Gulliver's Travels* (1726).

But Poe also was deeply immersed in nonfictional, yet no less legendary, maritime discourse widely circulated in the culture at the time, such as Charles Wilkes's highly publicized and federally funded expedition to the Antarctic, Jeremiah N. Reynolds's *Address, on the Subject of a Surveying and Exploring Expedition to the Pacific Ocean and South Seas* delivered to Congress and published in 1836, and Benjamin Morrell's *Narrative of Four Voyages* (1832). Compared to such credible sources, Poe was a mere landlubber fantasy writer in the eyes of reviewers like Burton, who lamented his aggressive romanticization of established sea knowledge, however exaggerated much of it was to begin with. Burton declared *Pym* a "humbug" because it pretended "that the shrewdness and common sense of the public would give it a chance of being received as truth." However, Poe's "outrageous statements" such as those describing the "river waters of the Antarctic isles" containing "a number of distinct veins, each of a distinct hue," a metaphor for racial intolerance totally imperceptible to Burton, often conveyed incisive social and political criticism.[1] Though steeped in the celebrated nautical science and history of the time, Poe's relation to the antebellum cultural context of the sea was typically sardonic, skeptical, and wickedly humorous in a way that probed the generic limits of prose fiction sea narrative.

Poe was well aware of how central the question of veracity was to the culture of sea narratives in antebellum America. Throughout his career, he had engendered a special affinity for the printed word and its capacity to sway the masses, even to stir them into riotous pandemonium. His balloon hoax of 1844 was a ruse he concocted in part to see to what extent the genre of fantastic sea voyages (this one by air) had entranced American audiences. The public's hunger for his far-fetched story of the world's first three-day transatlantic gas balloon crossing was measurable through its interface with print culture. Demand surged for newspaper stories describing the stupendous feat that broached news of technological advancement and sea adventure for which the public had established an insatiable desire.[2]

By 1844, Poe had fully realized the importance of the sea to American culture in his day, particularly its significance as a territory of exploration and conquest. Poe's sea, like the one Melville imagines in the chapter "Brit" in *Moby-Dick*, bears the same expansive pastoral reach as Walt Whitman's prairie, and thus can be construed as one of the many antebellum creative renderings of the virgin territory inherent in the concept of Manifest Destiny. Unlike Whitman's Mississippi River valley, Poe and Melville's open ocean bears a much deeper submerged dimension with an accompanying capacity for terror in the form of enraged hull-shattering whales and bloodthirsty sharks. Indigenous peoples figure in the Antarctic expedition in *Pym*, as they did in the nation's push westward, whose signal politics were visible in the support of the Indian Removal Act by such prominent and admired figures as William Cullen Bryant. Posing a threat to such expansion, unruly natives populate Poe's imaginary South Pole, echoing the efficacious slave population bent on rebellion in the southern United States, vast portions of which were unmapped and lacking infrastructure for road and rail like the largely uncharted Antarctic, the last location on earth mastered by cartographers.[3]

Upon the publication of the first installments of *Pym*, Poe fled the South for a new position in New York City in January 1837 after losing his post at the *Messenger* in the wake of an altercation with his publisher, Thomas W. White. In an attempt to salvage his uprooted career, Poe retooled his writing to capitalize on the celebrated sea narratives of the day. He knew that Morrell's *Narrative of Four Voyages* had become an instant best seller in 1832, despite having been purportedly ghost written, plagiarized, and otherwise fabricated. These strenuous allegations led his contemporaries to brand Morrell "the biggest liar in the Pacific."[4] Such charges, however, did not damage sales of his entertainingly written work, yet it did compromise his career, as he found it increasingly difficult to gain employment based on the rash of distrust regarding his book. Sea narrative existed at the crucible of adventure fantasy for entertainment and verifiable experience for scientific discovery and commercial growth. Categories of commerce, military, and adventure blurred in the process as well, as crews of merchant and naval vessels freely intermingled. Melville, for example, sailed on the *Acushnet* in 1841 from Fairhaven, Massachusetts, only to return aboard a navy ship, the frigate USS *United States*, virtually hitchhiking his way through the South Pacific on a variety of vessels that included an Australian whaler. Morrell was ostensibly a sealing captain and veteran of several Antarctic expeditions for profit. The culture's growing economy and move toward industrialization indeed had fully extended its reach into the ocean at this time, making New Bedford, Massachusetts the richest city in the world for its whale oil. By 1846, the United States had built the largest whaling fleet, boasting 735 of the 900 whale ships at sea.[5]

Morrell's exploits are those of a capitalist at sea, told in the colorful detail and pitched bravado that Melville himself would find so captivating as a romantic quest if not an overt celebration of commerce. But Poe's imitation and wholesale larceny of *Narrative of Four Voyages* does not flatter Morrell as the nautical equivalent of a Western fur tycoon like John Jacob Astor. Instead, Poe was fully aware of the licentious exaggeration of his writings, which he exploits for their intrigue and detail in constructing a world entirely alien to most antebellum readers. New data about the sea was pouring into the culture faster than ever, especially from many who had returned with stories and tattoos from the South Sea Islands. Yet many of those tales and tattoos were faked. The context at the time was characterized by the free and open scramble to produce nautical knowledge through narrations and cultural artifacts, or the semblance thereof, as rapidly as possible to turn a profit, a pattern akin to the rise in phony land claims and counterfeit currencies that led to the Panic of 1837. The Panic transpired when Andrew Jackson called for an end to specie payment to reduce inflation and eradicate circulation of false bank notes and land claims. Hard currency, however, only exacerbated the crisis, and the economy deflated rapidly, causing a run on banks and sending the market into turmoil. Harpers, like other publishers, financially suffered through the crisis and thus chose to delay publication of *Pym*.

Radical reassessments of value and currency in the economy extended to the sea and to the literary marketplace of sea stories. The Wilkes expedition, for example, won key federal support for the circumnavigation of the globe to survey and chart the seas in order to protect the whale and seal industries. Congress donated ships and personnel for the expedition. Charles Wilkes, not coincidentally, was a lieutenant with the United States Navy and thus was selected to lead the undertaking, which launched in August 1838, just one month after Harpers had regained a sufficient economic foothold to publish *Pym*. The zeitgeist was seething with romantic dreams of sea adventure, and political and economic institutions, from the federal government to the publishing industry, were ready to cash in on this new valuable commodity.

As he had with other popular genres in the literary market, Poe approached sea stories with deep skepticism. He treated them with a wicked irony that called into question the skyrocketing value of their currency in the culture while paradoxically capitalizing on it himself. The longest passage he lifted almost verbatim from Morrell tellingly defines a mollusk as "an article of commerce."[6] *Beche de mer*, the sea slug or sea cucumber in *Pym*, provides a measure of verisimilitude to make his narrative more believable, while slyly commenting on the gluttonous and ravenous hunger for such detail in his readers, who greedily consume it raw like the cannibals in *Pym*. Indeed, Poe serves up the raw material of Morrell to popular consumers of sea fiction here as a covert stab at the publishing industry's exploitation of primal urges. He fuses sexual desire (figured in the phallic creature) with the desire for literary entertainment in transforming the creature into an article of literary commerce.

In addition to ironically employing exotic detail for cultural criticism, nautical data supplied Poe with proven popular images that resonated with his signature macabre theme of descent into death. "A Descent into the Maelström," for example, derives from Edward Wilson Landor's "The Maelstrom: A Fragment," an 1834 article signaling the culture's morbid interest in death at sea. "Manuscript Found in a Bottle" also ends with a giant "dashing of a cataract," which made creative use of John Cleve Symmes's theory that giant polar vortices pulled water into the inside of the earth's 800-mile-wide crust.

For his lurid tales of nautical murder and mayhem Poe found a ready repository of situations and images not only in popular antebellum sea narratives, but also in poetry. Samuel Taylor Coleridge's "Rime of the

Ancient Mariner" features a polar sea adventure, a ship bearing death, and a series of excruciating trials through which the narrator suffers and lives to tell the tale. "Manuscript Found in a Bottle" echoes "Ancient Mariner," depicting as it does a wayward ship full of rotting corpses. Coleridge's broad, sweeping archetypes contrast with Poe's overabundance of minute detail in both "Manuscript" and *Pym*, which attempt to make palpable the largely metaphorical mythological narrative terrain of "Ancient Mariner."[7] Such minutia propagates Poe's satire of popular sea tales and legends. Poe's interrogation into the sea genre inflates its conventions to expose the ruptured seams of history and science of polar exploration on which Symmes was the wildest and most imaginative theorist. The eighteenth-century South Seas explorations of the legendary Captain James Cook had yet to be confirmed; common knowledge about distant oceans was in radical flux, and authoritative data thus became simultaneously a desired commodity and increasingly difficult to verify. This uncertainty left room for highly questionable theorists like Symmes to take center stage in the culture, which encouraged Poe's allegory of reading and misreading in *Pym* from the narrator's struggle to decipher Augustus's messages in the dark, to the inscrutable cave hieroglyphics he puzzles over, and finally to the white ethereal fog of unknowing into which he vanishes at the novel's close.

Despite being generally skeptical of sailor writing and the Antarctic pseudoscience of Symmes, Poe was nonetheless immersed in it. His understanding of the sea was not merely that of a disbelieving and distant ironist. Reynolds, whom Poe may have known, was Symmes's main disciple and advocate, accompanying him on lecture tours beginning in 1824. After Symmes's death in 1829, Reynolds continued giving lectures in his place to sold-out auditoriums in major cities. Poe's acquaintance with Reynolds's ideas suggests some acceptance of Symmes's science at the very least and helps explain his intense attraction to the surreal aspects of a theory that inspired the phantasmagoric scenes of *Pym*. Poe's fascination – a curious combination of skepticism and the need to validate it, if not a classic Freudian cocktail of fear and desire – with Symmes's theory and the intrigue of polar exploration may have even led him to solicit Reynolds for a place on his Antarctic expedition.[8] Reynolds was also likely the source of Poe's knowledge of the gruesome *Globe* mutiny of 1824, an event replete with the violence and subjugation of indigenous peoples of the sort featured in *Pym*'s riotous dénouement.[9]

Beyond Reynolds, the culture was brimming with dark sea legends, none perhaps darker or more storied that that of the Flying Dutchman, which Poe made creative use of at least twice. This legend originated when sailors allegedly spotted a ship perpetually adrift that seemed to disappear, sending the crew into a terror. When the crew landed in port, "the story spread like wildfire, and the supposed phantom was called the Flying Dutchman."[10] The image was so captivating to antebellum audiences that it spawned a veritable industry of tales, novels, poems, paintings, and even an opera on the subject. The gothic intrigue of the image of course did not escape Poe's attention, and thus any understanding of his connection with the culture of the sea must attend to the central motif. The enchanting sea takes on nightmarish dimensions in Poe's "City in the Sea," a poem describing a community enclosed by a viscous, gelatinous atmosphere. This city of the living dead drifts in an eerily stagnant motion from which one never escapes, a kind of metropolitan, submerged version of the Flying Dutchman.

The year after *Pym* appeared, Frederick Marryat published *The Phantom Ship*, and by 1843, Richard Wagner's opera *The Flying Dutchman* debuted. In Poe, the legend becomes a nautical vision of the living dead. Sighting a vessel apparently manned by a smiling and waving captain at the tiller, Pym soon realizes the figure is a rotting corpse, teeth bared and skeletal arm waving in the breeze. Just prior to the encounter, Poe transmutes the image into an ironic and satiric comment about the rampant cultural appropriation of nautical horror through a scene in which Pym dresses up like the bloated corpse of a freshly drowned shipmate to execute a mutiny through the blinding power of fear. The plan is preposterously implausible. The scene calls attention to the facile theatrics of fear as a fabricated dramatic spectacle, rendering an artful self-parody – so hyperbolic as to be unmistakably intentional – of his manipulation of sea lore for stunning gothic narrative effect, a raucous, macabre juvenile rendition of his otherwise sophisticated and serious prose exposition of the unity of effect in "The Philosophy of Composition." Poe was indeed talking back to his culture with his renditions of the death ship, branding it with approbation, disdain, and a good measure of mockery.

Poe's depiction of cannibalism in *Pym* is drawn from another ship of horrors rendered in Owen Chase's *Narrative of the Most Extraordinary and Distressing Shipwreck of the Whale-Ship Essex*, which appeared in 1821 and inspired Melville's *Moby-Dick*. After a whale rammed into the *Essex's* hull, sinking the ship, the survivors sailed for safety in small whaleboats for three months, eventually running out of provisions and resorting to cannibalism for survival. Their selection of who would be sacrificed by randomly drawing lots is comically inverted in *Pym*, as the democratic, rational, and levelheaded Parker who first suggests the fair process is fittingly the one chosen to be eaten. Poe delights in the irony of this, and adds to it by having Pym suddenly realize, after three days of gnawing on Parker's bones, precisely how to access a cash of provisions locked in a storeroom below deck.

Among the stories told at gams in the early 1840s, friendly meetings of ships at sea for captains to exchange information on the location of whales and for crewmen to relish in the welcome diversion of fresh stories and entertainment, Melville heard for the first time the tale of an eighty-five-foot sperm whale sinking the *Essex*. On July 23, 1841, the seeds for *Moby-Dick* were planted in what Eric Dolin calls "the most consequential gam of all time."[11] Tall tales, always the order of the day for gams, were exchanged, yet one particular story struck Melville as stunning for many reasons, not the least of which was that it was entirely true. What set the story apart from the usual yarns told at gams, whaling culture's key unifying ritual, was that it was told by William Henry Chase, the teenaged son of *Essex* first mate Owen Chase, and was corroborated by his father's *Narrative*. After hearing the verbal rendition, Melville was so enthusiastic that the young Chase promptly pulled the volume from his stowage and presented it to his astonished listener. *Moby-Dick*'s author was born that day. Print culture intersected with the common sailor's oral storytelling ritual at this late July gam. As Melville's recollection of reading Chase's narrative attests, "this was the first printed account of [the *Essex* disaster] I had ever seen. The reading of this wondrous story upon the landless sea and close to the very latitude of the shipwreck had a surprising effect upon me."[12]

As with the oral legend of the Flying Dutchman that had a long history before its inscription, common sailors spun such stories from both superstition and fact. Melville's exposure to "the first printed account of [the *Essex* disaster] I had ever seen" impressed him beyond measure after hearing variations for years in conversation. The "surprising effect upon me" he recalled was precisely that which Poe himself had sought to bear on his readership.[13] Like Billy's memory at the end of Melville's *Billy Budd*, the *Pequod*'s story is kept alive through the grassroots culture of the common whalemen. The story of its voyage is ironically best told by Ishmael, a common sailor, just as Billy is best commemorated by the sea dogs' song, "Billy in the Darbies," which proves as accurate and movingly sympathetic as the newspaper report of his death is preposterously erroneous and callous.

Amid this oral culture of storytelling at sea is a curious dialectic of inversion in which the authority and heroic expectations of exploration are subverted. Poe appears to have been acutely aware of this distinctly modernist development in the genre. Melville also distrusted aspects of sea narrative at key moments in *Moby-Dick* through his ironic undercutting of lengthy expositions on the whale's divinity, only to dismember him in the most brutal fashion in the ensuing pages. After witnessing a glimpse of the divine, the cabin boy Pip has no prophecy to tell other than meaningless gibberish and maniacal laughter. Ishmael's anticipation of an adventurous and stirring initiation into whale hunting in "The First Lowering" eventuates in the mocking laughter of "The Hyena" when Ishmael and his mates are unceremoniously pitched into the sea, becoming the butt of the whale's joke much less heroic warriors.

Poe's sea is not Stephen Crane's sea of the late century as depicted in the morally rudderless and utterly hollow natural world of "The Open Boat." But it marks a decided break from older forms, such as the *Bildungsroman* and exotic picaresque genres that use the ship and ocean as backdrops for their real subjects. The *Bildungsroman* traces the development of a young greenhorn facing unfamiliar landscapes and exotic locations in a series of trials and tribulations leading to adulthood. It depends on a picaresque plotting characterized by a discursive pattern of loosely linked episodes, as showcased in Henry Fielding's *History of Tom Jones* (1749). *Pym* begins in this tradition – as seen in such coming of age works as Rudyard Kipling's *Captains Courageous* and Dana's *Two Years at the Mast*, and in the rambling and sprawling exotic picaresque yarns of Daniel Defoe's *Captain Singleton*, Tobias Smollet's *Roderick Random*, and Captain Cook's journals and travelogues – and rapidly subverts it.

In the hands of Poe and Melville, the sea becomes distinctly modern in the sense that it anticipates the aesthetic function of the voyage seen in Joseph Conrad's *The Heart of Darkness* and "The Secret Sharer," for example. As they do for Melville, ships at sea provide Poe with tension-filled settings ideal for the inversion and compression of the culture's hierarchies. The ocean and its lore compelled him to probe the limitations of textual representation, especially through images of hieroglyphics, cyphering, and inscription; and death, with myriad visions of coffins, dismemberment, and clocks, his ultimate figure for the menacing doom that awaits all mortals.

NOTES

1. William Burton, "Review of New Books," *Burton's Gentleman's Magazine* 3 (1838), 211; Kevin J. Hayes, *Poe and the Printed Word* (New York: Cambridge University Press, 2000), 68.

2. John Tresch, "Extra! Extra! Poe Invents Science Fiction!" in *The Cambridge Companion to Edgar Allan Poe*, ed. Kevin J. Hayes (New York: Cambridge University Press: 2002), 113–32.

3. For a representative postcolonial view of the issue of exploration and expansion in Poe, see Paul Lyons, *American Pacificism: Oceana in the U.S. Imagination* (New York: Routledge, 2006), 48–66. Lyons takes Poe to task for the way *Pym* "has no interest in altering the terms of the nationalistic commercial project [but rather]...perversely exacerbates aspects of the ideologies of the texts that he parodies." But Poe's profaning of the discourse forces his "nineteenth-century readers to partake in their own demons" of an expansionist ideology the text of *Pym* showcases as "hopelessly blind," in Lyons's own words, which suggests a progressive element beyond mere pointless perversity.

4. David McGonigal, *Antarctica* (London: Frances Lincoln, 2003), 135.

5. Eric Jay Dolin, *Leviathan: The History of Whaling in America* (New York: Norton, 2007), 206.

6. Edgar Allan Poe, *Poetry and Tales*, ed. Patrick F. Quinn (New York: Library of America, 1984), 1147–9.

7. Eric Wilson, *The Spiritual History of Ice: Romanticism, Science, and the Imagination* (New York: Palgrave Macmillan, 2003), 192–4.

8. Susan F. Beegel, "'Mutiny and Atrocious Butchery': The Globe Mutiny as a Source for *Pym*," in *Poe's Pym: Critical Explorations*, ed. Richard Kopley (Durham, NC: Duke University Press, 1992), 12.

9. Beegel, "Mutiny," 7–19.

10. George Barrington, *Voyage to Botany Bay* (Sydney: Sydney University Press, 2004), 30.

11. Dolin, *Leviathan*, 276.

12. Thomas Knickerson, Owen Chase et al., *The Loss of the Ship Essex, Sunk by a Whale*, ed. Nathaniel Philbrick (New York: Penguin, 2000), 77.

13. Ibid.

CHAPTER 5

France

Andrea Goulet

Poe the hoaxer would have enjoyed the fuss over a letter produced in 1929: supposedly penned nearly a century earlier by Alexandre Dumas, it describes a short visit Poe made to Paris. The letter describes Poe's odd habits of sealing himself in a chamber by day and roaming the streets at night like Dupin in "The Murders in the Rue Morgue." But the Dumas letter is itself a piece of fiction: Poe never set foot in France. He did, however, display a predilection for Gallic culture through French-sounding pseudonyms ("Henri le Rennet"), character names ("Madame Eugenie Lalande"), and italicized words and phrases (*ennui, boudoir*). Such "Piquant Expressions" from foreign tongues, Poe playfully suggests, "will show not only your knowledge of the language, but your general reading and wit."[1] This light humor belies a somewhat testy desire to establish his own cosmopolitan credentials: when Poe peppered his earliest stories with citations from Rousseau, La Bruyère, Corneille, Crébillon, and Voltaire, he hoped to distinguish himself from parochial contemporaries. Poe had studied classical French at English boarding schools and later earned highest honors in the field at the University of Virginia and West Point. Though his erudition may not have run as deep as he hoped to suggest publicly, Poe knew the language well enough to decipher French cryptograms. As Poe's reputation grew, his ostentatious Gallicisms tapered off, but he remained a Francophile and would have been gratified by the enormous success his work found in France. It was, indeed, through France – specifically through translations by poet Charles Baudelaire – that Poe's work received worldwide recognition.

BAUDELAIRE'S MISSION

In 1848, while France's Orléans monarchy crumbled, Charles Baudelaire shifted his energies from revolutionary fervor to the quiet project of translating Poe's "Mesmeric Revelation." He had discovered the American author a year earlier through popular press translations, including Isabelle Meunier's version of "The Black Cat." That Baudelaire would be drawn from the newspaper's political columns toward a tale of uncanny imagination is fitting. Poe, in whom the French poet found a kindred spirit, would enable Baudelaire to articulate an aestheticism that privileged mystic symbolism over gritty politics, revelation over revolution. Theirs was a *"gout de l'infini,"* a shared commitment to the imagination's farthest realms.

The excitement Baudelaire felt upon discovering Poe went from fraternal affinity to evangelical obsession: starting in 1848, the French poet devoted sixteen years of his life to translating Poe in order to convince his compatriots of the American's genius.[2] After "Révélation magnétique" appeared in the July 15, 1848 issue of *La Liberté de penser,* Baudelaire began work on the macabre tale "Bérénice" (1852), whose grotesque intertwining of death and beauty would influence his own poetic production. Starting in 1854, *Le Pays* serially published "Histoires extraordinaires"; the thirteen stories were collected in 1856. *Histoires extraordinaires* garnered such commercial success that a second volume of twenty-three stories – *Nouvelles histoires extraordinaires* – appeared in 1857. The date is significant, as it marks the same year as the first edition of Baudelaire's own *magnum opus,* *Les Fleurs du mal.* The monumental importance now accorded to *Les Fleurs du mal* as an inaugural text of modern poetics should not obscure the intensity of Baudelaire's concurrent immersion in the world of Poe. According to his journal, Baudelaire allotted five hours a day to translating Poe's stories and only three hours to composing his own poems![3] Even as he continued to write original poetry, art criticism, and prose poems, Baudelaire remained committed to honoring his American idol: his translation of *The Narrative of Arthur Gordon Pym* came out in 1857, followed by the philosophical treatise *Eureka* (1859–63) and a new volume of stories, *Histoires grotesques et sérieuses* (1865). Baudelaire diligently translated over fifteen hundred pages of Poe's prose, including two critical essays: "The Philosophy of Composition," which exposes the labor involved in turning intuition into poetic form, and "The Poetic Principle," which elevates "The Rythmical Creation of Beauty" above "the heresies of the Didactic."

These ideas – that poetry requires active effort and that true art is free of the bourgeois shackles of utility – resonated with Baudelaire and contributed through him to the "art for art's sake" aesthetic of later French Symbolists like Paul Valéry and Stéphane Mallarmé. But it was Baudelaire's long biographical essay, "Edgar Poe, sa vie et ses oeuvres" (1852), largely derived from an essay by John W. Daniel, that consolidated the influential image of Poe as the quintessential *poète maudit.* Tragically destined to be persecuted by a narrow-minded society, Baudelaire's Poe was a "sacred soul" of sharpened sensibility, a martyr whose "spiritual and angelic nature" transcended the political particularities of nation-states, whether democratic or monarchic.[4] Baudelaire's religious vocabulary raises the stakes of writing to metaphysical proportion: a "diabolical Providence" has marked the very bodily fibers of genius-saints like Poe with signs of worldly damnation.

Poe's transcendent poetics underpin the neo-platonic side of Baudelaire's "Spleen et Idéal" equation in *Les Fleurs du mal*. But Poe's terrifying stories also provide material for the other necessary element of this dual alchemy: in his poem entitled "Spleen," Baudelaire links the English term for ill temper and irritable gloom to a decidedly Poe-esque atmosphere of spatial enclosure and psychic torture. Without plagiarizing the American author, Baudelaire riffed on Poe's themes of synesthesia and dreams, strange beauty and death, entombment and the abyss. Poe's "The Man of the Crowd" contributed to Baudelaire's articulation in prose poems of anonymous modernity; Poe's portrayals of altered mental states informed Baudelaire's dreamy "artificial paradises" of opium and wine; Poe's description in *Pym* of seabirds devouring human flesh reappeared in "Un Voyage à Cythère." And yet to articulate these influences unidirectionally is to risk eliding the uncanny temporal relation between Baudelaire and his American double. Most of the poems in *Les Fleurs du mal* were composed before Baudelaire began translating Poe, but the echoes suggest a transatlantic fusion of fraternal minds. Upon first reading Poe's work, Baudelaire claimed to recognize "not simply certain subjects, which I had dreamed of, but sentences which I had thought out, written by him twenty years before."[5] For Baudelaire, Poe's genius escapes the bounds of human temporality – as witnessed by the final entry of his personal journal, in which Poe appears once again as a religious saint: "Every morning I will pray to God...to my father, to Mariette and to Poe, as intercessors."[6]

Hagiography was not Baudelaire's only mode of interaction with Poe's work. Michel Brix has recently identified Baudelaire's private misgivings: irritation at the puerile elements of "Hans Pfaal," impatience with "The Philosophy of Composition," and a subtle reluctance to share fully Poe's aspirational voyage through alcohol to a romanticized, infinite realm.[7] And yet there is no denying the intense identification that sustained Baudelaire's sixteen-year mission to present Poe to his compatriots. Did he succeed? Absolutely. Baudelaire's scrupulous translations became the definitive texts for Francophone readers, his personal letter campaign convinced most of his contemporaries (excepting, notably, Sainte-Beuve and Barbey d'Aurevilly) that Poe was a philosopher and a genius, and his extensive prefaces vaulted the American writer onto the worldwide literary stage.

THE SYMBOLIST ANGEL

A decade after Baudelaire said a dying goodbye to his patron saint, Symbolist poet Stéphane Mallarmé used verse to recast Poe as an ascended angel whose "strange voice" remained misunderstood by the common tribe. The year was 1876 and Mallarmé had been asked to contribute to a volume commemorating the twenty-fifth anniversary of Poe's death. The sonnet he produced, "Le Tombeau d'Edgar Poe," contains some of the most famous lines ever written by one poet in honor of another. Poe appears as The Poet, transformed by eternity into Himself, an angel who could give "a purer meaning" to the words of mere men. Mallarmé ends by evoking Poe's granite tomb, which serves as a textual cenotaph, one whose density and difficulty reflect what Poe represented to the Symbolists: a master of ordered thought, a highly cerebral artist who valorized musical rhythm over didactic effect.

Having discovered Poe through Baudelaire's translations of stories and critical essays, Mallarmé set himself to the task of translating his verse. *Le Corbeau* (1875), Mallarmé's French version of "The Raven," appeared with illustrations by Edouard Manet; in 1889, thirty-six more Poe poems came out in a volume dedicated to the memory of Baudelaire. In Poe's poetry, the French Symbolist had found a model of artistic purity. Through Mallarmé, a "French Poe" of rare and ethereal genius emerged. Near the end of his life, Mallarmé described the American author as "the purest among the Spirits... made of stars, made of lightning."[8]

Mallarmé was joined in his admiration by many poets, including Rimbaud, Moréas, Kahn, and Vielé-Griffin, but Paul Valéry most publicly carried forward the Symbolist torch for Poe. From 1889, when the teenaged Valéry wrote a letter to Mallarmé praising Poe as "perhaps the most subtle artist of this century," through the 1930s, when he lectured at the Collège de France, Valéry propounded the image of Poe as a masterful calculator of artistic effect.[9] Poe's critical essays contributed to Valéry's elaboration of a literary technique devoted to the lucid description of psychological states. Poe was, to Valéry, a "demon of lucidity."[10] This phrase may seem paradoxical in its fusion of dark metaphysics with Enlightenment intellect, but it aptly captures Valéry's respect for Poe's original mixture of fancy with logic. Valéry was particularly taken by the way Poe interweaves metaphysics with science in his genre-bending cosmological text, *Eureka*. Though the Valéry–Poe connection is best known for reinforcing an "art for art's sake" poetic symbolism, Valéry's essay on *Eureka* reminds us that turn-of-the-century French thinkers sought ways of reconciling materialism with spiritualism, rational science with mystical vision.

THE "SCIENTIFIC FANTASTIC"

In 1856, Edmond Goncourt wrote that Poe had discovered a new literary world: "le miraculeux scientifique."[11] Goncourt was right to see Poe's association of science with the supernatural as a sign of things to come: by the fin-de-siècle, France's double obsession with rational positivism and occultist spiritism had dramatically merged in the flourishing genre of the fantastic. Through tales of uncanny phenomena, Jean Lorrain, Jules Lermina, Guy de Maupassant, Henri Rivière, and Villiers de l'Isle-Adam extended Poe's explorations of the limits of the rational, conscious mind.

"The Fall of the House of Usher" (1839), which straddles supernaturalism and psychosis, and "The Facts in the Case of M. Valdemar" (1845), which describes macabre mesmerism in a tone of clinical objectivity, set precedents for the French "scientific fantastic." Guy de Maupassant applied medical discourses of psychopathology to his tales of the strange. His "Apparition" (1884) recounts an inexplicable encounter in rational terms; the two versions of "Le Horlà" (1887/1888) toggle between supernatural possession and psychotic delusion; and the title punctuation of "Fou?" (1898) exposes the enduring mystery of madness in an age of scientific progress. In Maupassant's 1882 story "Magnétisme," a character laughingly dismisses a Belgian hypnotist as a mere trickster who "gives me the impression of one of those storytellers in the vein of Edgar Poe, who end up going mad from reflecting on strange cases of madness."[12] Though mental malady fascinated (and eventually destroyed) Maupassant, it was, paradoxically, Poe's rationalist approach to the topic that inspired the French author to apply the "unity of effect" technique to the creation of his own eerie tales.[13]

Poe's lucid, controlled depiction of strange psychic states distinguished him in the minds of French writers from the German master of the fantastic, E. T. A. Hoffmann. Though Poe was first considered Hoffmann's spiritual successor, the American's "mathematical spirit" and implacable logic were soon contrasted with the German's passive visions. Barbey d'Aurevilly wrote: "Poe governed his delirium; Hoffmann was ruled by his."[14] Perhaps that explains Poe's superior role in Jules Claretie's formulation about young

French writers of the fantastic: "Edgar Poe was our god and Hoffmann his prophet."[15]

The phrase appears in Claretie's introduction to Lermina's *Histoires incroyables* (1885), published under the Anglophone pseudonym William Cobb and inspired by "the poetically scientific conceptions of Edgar Allan Poe." The first tale, "Les Fous," is chockful of Poe tropes: a hallucinating narrator who ends up interned in a "Lunatic Asylum," a series of strange actions performed in hypnagogic states, the maddening cadence of a repeated sound that recalls Poe's telltale heart, and a match of whist – the game Poe described in "The Murders in the Rue Morgue" as requiring the highest analytical faculties. As with "The System of Doctor Tarr and Professor Fether," the lunatic–sane boundary is blurred: readers of "Les Fous" gradually realize that society considers its first person narrator delusional. But the question remains whether so-called insanity may actually indicate access to a higher realm of reality.

The fine edge between reason and madness fascinated Villiers de l'Isle-Adam, whose fantastic texts run deep with admiration for Poe. "Véra," in Villiers's *Contes cruels* (1883), features a Ligeia-like apparition. *L'Eve future* (1886), in which a fictionalized Thomas Alva Edison constructs a female android through techniques that fuse electric technology and hypnotic suggestion, contains numerous allusions to Poe, including epigraphs from "The Man in the Crowd" and "Morella."[16] Villiers's Edison embodies "le scientifique miraculeux" of the fin-de-siècle, the moment when technology seems to step on the threshold of the divine. Announcing his creation of an artificial woman, Edison says he will equip her with "all the passionate mysticity of Edgar Poe's Ligeia." In "Claire Lenoir" (1887), the foolish narrator Tribulat Bonhomet dismisses "l'Américain" as a writer who, despite "some hues of rhetoric," can only appeal to a banal and vulgar bourgeois audience.[17] But an informed reader, alert to Villiers's distance from his materialist, anti-Hegelian narrator, will discern the irony, for Villiers deeply revered Poe.[18] In fact, the character of Bonhomet owes his grotesque buffoonery to Poe's eccentrics, Hop-Frog, Hans Pfaal, and Prince Prospero. Most important, "Claire Lenoir" echoes Poe in its movement through rationality to the occult, its ironic use of positivistic science to access the "keyhole of Infinity."

THE DECADENT DEMON

The dark side of Poe's literary vision – horrible phantasms, sickly obsessions, morbid psychology – cast an influential shadow on France's decadent literature of the fin-de-siècle. Fertilized by Baudelaire's perverse aestheticism, the satanic flowers of the decadent movement bloomed with the garish reds of Berenice's blood-stained teeth and the ghoulish blacks of the House of Usher. Under the pen name Rachilde, Marguerite Eymery published *Monsieur Vénus* (1884) and *La Jongleuse* (1900), in which fetishized corpses and anatomized women pay tribute to the grotesque beauty of sexual perversion. Jean Lorrain, author of *Histoire des masques* (1900) and *Monsieur de Phocas* (1901), filled his texts with neurotic dreams and criminal obsession; his stories "L'Homme au complet mauve" and "L'impossible alibi" were directly inspired by Poe's "The Man of the Crowd" and "The Tell-Tale Heart."[19] Artist Odilon Redon, who entitled his 1882 lithographic album "A Edgar Poe," produced drawings and paintings steeped in the eerie, fever-ridden shades of neurotic fantasy. Redon's illustrations of Poe include "The Teeth" and "The Tell-Tale Heart," in which technique and atmosphere combine to capture Poe's striking modernity.[20]

But the quintessential statement of Poe's decadence comes from Huysmans, whose *A Rebours* (1884) contains a lengthy, inspired paean to the American writer. The novel's protagonist, a neurasthenic nobleman named Des Esseintes, has retreated from the vulgarities of the modern world to a haven of corrupt sensuality and dream-laden artifice. Only masters of sadism and deviant geniuses are allowed to grace the bookshelves of his home library: alongside Roman decadents and French Symbolists, the "profound and strange" Edgar Poe emerges as the author best matched to Des Esseintes's pathological sensibilities.[21] Poe, writes Huysmans, was the first to identify the irresistible drives of the unconscious mind, to describe the paralyzing effects of fear on the human will, and to depict the "moral agony" of fatigue's monstrous hallucinations. Poe's female characters earn praise for their convulsive neuroses, cabalistic erudition, and sterile, angelic asexuality. And though Des Esseintes dreams of surpassing the American master's forays into the sphere of sublime sensation, he succumbs with the sick pleasure of trembling nerves to the vivisecting knife of Poe's "clinique cérébrale." Thus the American "Imp of the Perverse" was corralled by French decadents into an aestheticized realm of sacrilege and sadism.

NEW GENRES: SCIENCE FICTION
AND THE ROMAN POLICIER

Poe's diverse influence on French literature can be appreciated by juxtaposing Huysmans with Jules Verne, whose scientific positivism is considered the aesthetic opposite of decadent ennui. "The Balloon Hoax" gave Verne the idea for *Cinq semaines en ballon* (1863), while "Hans Pfaall" and "Three Sundays in a Week" informed the humorous science fantasies of *De la terre à la lune* (1865) and *Le Tour du monde en 80 jours* (1873).[22] The air and sea travel in these stories fit the expansionist, positivistic ideology of Verne's *Les Voyages extraordinaires*: "to outline all the geographical, geological, physical, and astronomical knowledge amassed by modern science and to recount…the history of the universe."[23] Yet Verne's Poe is not so different from that of the French Symbolists; Verne, too, was intrigued by Poe's exploration of the uncanny.

In 1864, Verne decreed Poe the leader of a new literary movement, "the School of the Strange."[24] Noting the delirium of Poe's "inexplicable, enigmatic, impossible" imagination, Verne summarizes many of Poe's texts for his bourgeois readers.[25] He admires the analytical intelligence of the Dupin stories and praises Poe's scientific tales for rendering physics-defying feats plausible. Surprisingly, Verne ends his tribute on a note of ambivalence about Poe's materialism: by refusing to attribute marvelous phenomena to divine or supernatural causes, Poe douses his fantastic with cold water, thus reflecting "the purely practical and industrial social influence of the United States."[26] Still, the American author did not fail to inspire Verne, whose *Le Sphinx des glaces* (1897), a novel of polar exploration, constitutes a sequel to *Pym*.[27] Poe's fingerprint is evident throughout Verne's oeuvre, which abounds in cryptograms and maelstroms, ship's logs and maritime cannibalism, hoaxes and mesmerist themes.[28]

Most scholars agree that "The Murders in the Rue Morgue" (1841) was the first modern detective story. Set on a fictional street in the real Quartier St. Roch of Paris, Poe's tale was steeped in France's true crime culture, with references to the thief turned police chief Vidocq and the *Gazette des Tribunaux*.[29] In turn, the French popular press played a key role in establishing Poe's reputation as the innovator of a detective-centered crime genre. Journalist Emile Gaboriau, who delightedly reported on Poe's "Balloon Hoax" in *Le Pays*, introduced his own fictional detective, Monsieur Lecoq, in *L'Affaire Lerouge* (1866).[30] Though younger and less self-assured than Poe's Dupin, Lecoq similarly applies superior deductive reasoning to the elucidation of a murder mystery. Through Gaboriau, Poe's detective story attained worldwide foundational status. Conan Doyle's *Study in Scarlet* (1886) took its title from Gaboriau's novel and cheekily named both Dupin and Lecoq as Sherlock Holmes's inferior investigative predecessors. And generations of detective novelists have since imitated the tropes of Poe's inaugural "Rue Morgue": the locked room mystery, the mistaken arrest, the exotic killer in the heart of a modern city.

SURREALISM, CINEMA, AND THE BD

In his second *Manifesto of Surrealism* (1929), André Breton "spit" upon Poe for having introduced the scientific method of policing into his detective fiction.[31] But four years earlier, Breton had praised him as "surrealist in adventure." Though Breton cared not a whit for consistency, those of us with mere logical minds can make sense of the apparent contradiction by distinguishing Dupin, who had become a symbol of pure rationality, from the Poe of mental derangement. The "disordered imagination" of a William Wilson or the psychic automatism of an Egaeus in "Berenice" appealed to the avant-gardists of the 1920s as they explored the thin line between lucidity and the irrational unconscious. Poe's work abounds with spectral doubles and violent spasms; and his dream fantasies and absurdist humor align with the Surrealists' love of strange juxtaposition. One may even distinguish the uncanny rhythms of "The Raven" in Breton's surrealist description of an insistent phrase "that was knocking at the window" of his nocturnal mind.[32] Breton included Poe in *Anthology of Black Humor* (1840), expressing admiration for his willingness to abandon analytic will to chance.

The irrational Poe also appealed to artists like Max Ernst, who painted a distorted Berenice in 1935. Poe's tale resurfaces even in Ernst's Surrealist methods: the French artist's obsessional staring and frottage technique recall Egaeus's disturbing automatism.[33] The lucid fantasy of René Magritte's paintings is also imprinted with Poe's imagination. Magritte named a 1928 painting *The Imp of the Perverse* and made multiple versions of *The Domain of Arnheim* (1938–62).[34] And in a sly joke on textual doppelgangers and mirror images, Magritte placed a French translation of *Pym* on the mantel in *La reproduction interdite* (1937).

Alfred Hitchcock once described Poe as a father of Surrealist art, literature, and film.[35] But Poe's influence spans the history of French cinema in all its forms. "The System of Doctor Tarr and Professor Feather" inspired a fifteen-minute silent film produced by Éclair in 1912.[36] In 1981, Claude Chabrol directed a version of the same tale for French television. Jean Epstein's 1928 film adaptation of "The Fall of the House of Usher" captured Poe's atmosphere of gloomy tension through its chiaroscuro Impressionism. Decades later, New Wave directors incorporated Poe into their self-conscious cinema. In Jean-Luc Godard's *Vivre sa vie* (1962), Nana listens as Luigi reads aloud from "The Oval Portrait"; Godard also mentions Poe in *Bande à part* (1964) and *Pierrot le fou* (1965). Eric Roehmer brought his own New Wave sensibility to *Les histoires extraordinaires d'Edgar Poe* in 1965.

Perhaps the best sign that Poe has fully entered the French visual consciousness is his inclusion in the popular *bande déssinée* form. In 2006, graphic novelist Tarek [Ben Yakhlef] collaborated with Aurélien Morinière on *Baudelaire ou le roman rêvé d'Edgar Allan Poe*, a historical comic for adults. Between 2008 and 2010, Franco-Belgian publisher Casterman featured Jean-Louis Thourd's shadowy illustrations in three volumes of *Histoires extraordinaires d'Edgar Poe*: "Le Scarabée d'Or," "Usher," and "La Mort Rouge."

CONCLUSION

Poe's legacy continues to thrive in France. Paris boasts a Lycée Edgar Poe and a rue Edgar Poe (adjoining a street named for Symbolist poet Rémy de Gourmont!) Publishers continue to churn out biographies of Poe and translations of his work. (Benjamin Lacombe's illustrations for Soleil's 2009 edition of *Les contes macabres* are creepy fun). In 2010 the Darius Milhaud theater presented a stage adaptation of "The Black Cat" and "The Tell-Tale Heart" called *Assassins*; directed by Claudia Campos, it was set in a psychiatric hospital and narrated from the perspective of the criminally insane. A theatrical version of "The Fall of the House of Usher," staged with emphasis on musical atmospherics by Sylvain Maurice, ran at the Maison de la poésie from April to May 2011.

Where Americans saw a lurid horrormonger, the French have seen a misunderstood poet of the infinite, a man whose foibles were part and parcel of a genius that combines science with sensationalism, the macabre with metaphysics, and gross matter with high aesthetics. Even Poe's alcoholic dissolution, deemed morally reprehensible by many, was revalorized by Baudelaire and his successors as a sign of uncommon intensity and access to a realm of imagination unreachable by the common soul. The "French Poe" wears the mark of genius.

NOTES

1. Edgar Allan Poe, *The Collected Works of Edgar Allan Poe*, ed. Thomas Ollive Mabbott, 3 vols. (Cambridge, MA: Belknap Press, 1969–78), vol. ii, 344.

2. Charles Baudelaire, *Correspondance*, ed. Claude Pichois, 2 vols. (Paris: Gallimard, 1973), vol. i, 676.
3. Patrick F. Quinn, *The French Face of Edgar Poe* (Carbondale: Southern Illinois University Press, 1957), 102.
4. Charles Baudelaire, "Edgar Poe, sa vie et ses ouvrages," in *Baudelaire journaliste: Articles et chroniques*, ed. Alain Vaillant (Paris: Flammarion, 2011), 121–69.
5. Quoted in Quinn, *French Face*, 15.
6. Quoted in Jeffrey Meyers, *Edgar Allan Poe: His Life and Legacy* (New York: Charles Scribner's Sons, 1992), 283.
7. Michel Brix, "Baudelaire, 'Disciple' d'Edgar Poe?" *Romantisme* 122 (2003), 55–69.
8. Quoted in Rosemary Lloyd, "Edgar Poe, 'le pur entre les Esprits,'" *Magazine littéraire* 368 (1998), 35–7.
9. Lois Davis Vines, "Stéphane Mallarmé and Paul Valéry," in *Poe Abroad: Influence, Reputation, Affinities*, ed. Lois Davis Vines (Iowa City: University of Iowa Press, 1999), 172.
10. Quoted in Vines, "Stéphane Mallarmé," 173.
11. Edmond de Goncourt, *Journal des Goncourt: Mémoires de la vie littéraire*, 3 vols. (Paris: G. Charpentier, 1887–8), vol. i, 137.
12. Guy de Maupassant, *Contes et Nouvelles*, 2 vols. (Paris: Robert Laffont, 1988), vol. ii, 369.
13. Lois D. Vines, "Introduction," *Poe Abroad: Influence, Reputation, Affinities*, ed. Lois Davis Vines (Iowa City: University of Iowa Press, 1999), 13.
14. Gwenhaël Ponnau, *La Folie dans la literature fantastique* (Paris: PUF, 1997), 51.
15. Jules Claretie, "Préface," *Histoires incroyables*, by Jules Lermina (Paris: Boulanger, 1895).
16. Villiers de l'Isle-Adam, *L'Eve future* (Paris: Gallimard, 1993), 244, 297.
17. Villiers de l'Isle-Adam, *Claire Lenoir et autres contes insolites* (Paris: Flammarion, 1984), 54.
18. A. W. Raitt, *Villiers de l'Isle-Adam et le mouvement symboliste* (Paris: José Corti, 1965), 83–100.
19. Ponnau, *La Folie*, 275–6.
20. Kevin J. Hayes, "One-Man Modernist," in *The Cambridge Companion to Edgar Allan Poe*, ed. Kevin J. Hayes (New York: Cambridge University Press, 2002), 229.
21. Joris-Karl Huysmans, *A Rebours* (Paris: Gallimard, 1977), 309–11.
22. Arthur B. Evans, "Literary Intertexts in Jules Verne's *Voyages Extraordinaires*," *Science Fiction Studies* 23 (1996), 171–87.
23. Quoted in in Evans, "Literary Intertexts," 172.
24. Jules Verne, "Edgard Poë et ses oeuvres," *Musée des familles* 31 (1864), 193–208.
25. Verne, "Edgard Poë," Chapitre I.
26. Verne, "Edgard Poë," Chapitre IV.

27. Quinn, *French Face*, 104.

28. Evans, "Literary Intertexts," 180.

29. Poe gleaned some details on Paris from a story by British novelist Catherine Gore. See Kevin J. Hayes, "Mrs Gore and 'The Murders in the Rue Morgue,'" *Notes and Queries* 58 (2011), 85–7.

30. Roger Bonniot, *Emile Gaboriau ou La Naissance du roman policier* (Paris: J. Vrin, 1985).

31. André Breton, *Manifestes du surréalisme* (Paris: Pauvert, 1972), 137.

32. Breton, *Manifestes*, 31.

33. Kevin J. Hayes, *Edgar Allan Poe* (London: Reaktion, 2009), 12; Hayes, "One-Man Modernist," 238.

34. Hayes, "One-Man Modernist," 237.

35. Ibid., 235.

36. Mark Neimeyer, "Poe and Popular Culture," in *The Cambridge Companion to Edgar Allan Poe*, ed. Kevin J. Hayes (New York: Cambridge University Press, 2002), 219.

CHAPTER 6

The Near East

Travis Montgomery

As a student at the University of Virginia, Edgar Allan Poe regularly availed himself of the library. Among the books he withdrew were three volumes of Charles Rollin's *Histoire ancienne*, which treated early Carthaginian, Egyptian, Grecian, and Persian civilizations.[1] These empires flourished within a large region that was, for Poe, "the Orient," and during the nineteenth century, Islamic potentates controlled this area. Borrowing not one but *three* volumes of Rollin's chronicle, Poe displayed an early interest in the Near East, a world of worlds that figured prominently in his creative imagination, especially during his early years as a writer. This fascination was evident in several poems featuring Orientalia, and Poe's tales offered similar material. In his two-volume collection, *Tales of the Grotesque and Arabesque* (1839), for example, twenty stories featured "significant allusions or imagery drawn from the Near East."[2]

Beyond establishing Poe's enthusiasm for this region, his borrowing of the Rollin volumes has additional significance. Poe never visited the Near East – his knowledge of it essentially came from books, including travel narratives, English translations of Arabic literature, Oriental tales, volumes of Romantic poetry, novels, and works of history like Rollin's. Thus Poe's vision of the place was filtered through Western representations of Eastern cultural realities. While the Near East embraced several different ethnic groups, each with its own traditions, the prevalence of Islamic practice in the region led many Westerners to understate its cultural diversity by labeling it "the Orient" and distinguishing it from "the Occident."[3]

Within this discursive system, which Edward W. Said labeled "Orientalism," the Orient serves as a foil for the West. Orientalist discourse was especially powerful during the eighteenth and nineteenth centuries, when European imperialism flourished, and it influenced the authors who introduced Poe to the Orient. Poe was similarly inclined to view the Near East as Other, so his imaginative encounters with the region and its history were, in a word, Orientalist. Poe's case was, however, special, for while he often invoked the reductive East–West dichotomy of Orientalism, he typically used this dyad subversively, associating the Orient with aesthetic excellence and wisdom while denigrating Occidental pretensions to cultural superiority. Nevertheless, the Orient was, for Poe, more an imagined space than a geographic place, and this universe of the mind had textual origins that merit further study.

Translations of Near Eastern literature influenced his Orientalism. The *Arabian Nights*, a collection of exotic tales unified by a frame narrative, was especially popular in the Anglophone world. While many Americans found these richly imaginative tales fascinating, the stories, filtered through Western cultural lenses, reinforced negative stereotypes of Muslims. Tyrannical sultans, adulterous women, and lecherous servants filled the pages of the *Arabian Nights*, and these characterizations mirrored American perceptions of Barbary pirates, among others, as treacherous and depraved Muslims.[4] Poe was familiar with the *Arabian Nights*. He parodied the book in "The Thousand-and-Second Tale of Scheherezade," mentioned it in an 1841 review of William Harrison Ainsworth's *Guy Fawkes*, and referred to it in other tales. Although the last of the Barbary Wars ended when Poe was a child, they set foreign policy precedents and fostered popular prejudice against Islam. As they left their mark on American politics and the national psyche, these Mediterranean conflicts may have influenced Poe's ideas about Islamic culture and his reading of the *Arabian Nights*.

Another translation of a Near Eastern classic Poe might have read was George Sale's English version of the Qur'an, published in 1734. Although the first American edition of the translation did not appear until 1833, the text of Poe's *Tamerlane, Al Aaraaf, and Other Poems* (1829) suggests he knew an English edition.[5] Sale's "Preliminary Discourse," an ethnographic essay introducing the translation, and Thomas Moore's *Lalla Rookh*, a poem that treats Islam, apparently provided some of the Islamic details that appeared in Poe's early verse.[6] Poe was no Arabic scholar, and he used works like Sale's and Moore's to interpret Muslim cultures; but the inclusion of Qur'anic material in poems such as "Israfel" and "Al Aaraaf" evinced, if nothing else, a genuine interest in Islam and the Near East.

British literature also offered Poe a smorgasbord of Orientalist writings. Most prominent of these was the Oriental tale, a widely popular mode in eighteenth-century Britain. The publishing spate resulted from the dissemination of the *Arabian Nights* in English translations not from the original Arabic, but from Antoine Galland's French version, *Mille et une Nuit*. Intrigued by the exotic creatures and settings of these tales, many British writers incorporated Orientalia into their own works, which included imaginative tales that were alternately moralistic, philosophic, or satirical.[7] As this taxonomy suggests, such stories were, with some exceptions, namely the imaginative tales showcasing adventure and fantasy, primarily didactic but leavened with exotica. A famous example was Samuel Johnson's *Rasselas* (1759), the story of a melancholy Abyssinian prince who wandered the land looking for worldly happiness. Poe knew Johnson's tale, which he discussed in "The Literati of New York." Frances Sheridan's *History of Nourjahad* (1767) may have inspired "Ligeia," a story mentioning "the gazelle eyes of the tribe of the valley of Nourjahad."[8] The Oriental mode was also popular in America, and among tales of this order was "Selim" by James Kirke Paulding, a mentor to the young Poe.[9] Celebrating singularity and novelty, these Oriental narratives necessarily conveyed a sense of restlessness, a longing for aesthetic renewal and cultural change.[10] Poe recognized the creative fecundity of such writings, and in a set of marginalia published in the *Democratic Review* in November 1844, he chastised critic James Montgomery for dismissing the devices of Oriental tales as gratuitous ornament.[11] Furthermore, the subversive potential of these fictions was not lost on Poe, whose Eastern imaginings were also countercultural. Filled with Orientalia, "Ligeia" was a case in point. Recounting the narrator's failed efforts to control his Orientalized wife, "Ligeia" can be interpreted as a warning about imperial overreach.[12]

Other works of British Orientalism molded Poe's mind. Poe knew William Beckford's *Vathek*, an eighteenth-century gothic novel.[13] A heretical caliph, Vathek was a villain whose ruthless pursuit of pleasure and power ended in the Hall of Eblis, where lost souls wander incessantly with their hearts aflame, these fires representing eternal restlessness. Although he renounced Islam, Vathek was a despot, and in this respect, he resembled the tyrannical Muslim rulers depicted in Western texts. In addition, Beckford's villain was perhaps a model for Poe's Tamerlane, an Islamic warlord whose lust for conquest outweighed his desire for Ada, the love of his younger days.[14] But *Vathek* was no piece of Orientalist propaganda, for a spirit of wonder animated this volume, which included rich descriptions of faraway places and unfamiliar customs, details that Beckford, an amateur scholar of some note, strove to render authentically.

British Romantic poets, particularly Lord Byron and Thomas Moore, who shared Beckford's fascination with the Near East, wielded a much greater influence on Poe the writer than did the author of *Vathek*. Both of these poets published a considerable amount of Orientalia. Most significant were the Oriental tales of Byron, a series of narrative poems including *The Giaour, The Bride of Abydos, The Corsair,* and *Lara,* all of which featured tortured isolatoes defined by "illicit desires, guilt, remorse, and revenge, and equipped with fictitious adventures" set in Near Eastern locales.[15] Poe's guilt-ridden Tamerlane bore a striking resemblance to Byron's Giaour, who sought absolution for his sins, and perhaps the mad narrators of "Ligeia," "The Tell-Tale Heart," and other Poe stories also descend from these Byronic figures.[16] The British poet's Oriental tales had, however, a more general importance for Poe; these romances, with "their colorful settings and their lyrical mood pictures" were "escape valves for the 'lava' of [Byron's] imagination."[17] Poe also found such material useful when, as a young poet, he spurned the influence of American followers of Wordsworth, that celebrant of rural life and all things local. This domestic turn suited nationalist writers eager to promote American culture, but Poe resisted this impulse, devoting his first collections of verse to Oriental themes. Such devices were especially prominent in "Tamerlane," "Al Aaraaf," "To Helen," "The City in the Sea," and "Israfel."[18]

Another fountain of Romantic Orientalism was Thomas Moore's *Lalla Rookh*, a long narrative poem consisting of fantastical tales arranged within a frame story tracing the progress of a bridal pageant through the Mughal Empire. Profusely annotated, Moore's text educated readers about Islamic culture and Near Eastern geography, and Poe's "Al Aaraaf," with its extensive notes, evinced the influence of *Lalla Rookh*.[19] Poe also knew Moore's *Alciphron*, which employed an Egyptian setting – he reviewed an 1840 edition for *Burton's Gentleman's Magazine*.

Nineteenth-century Egyptology provided yet another arena for the Orientalist imagination in Poe's America. Renewed interest in ancient Egypt stemmed from Napoleon's 1789 invasion, an event leading to the discovery of the Rosetta Stone, a tablet used to decipher previously inscrutable hieroglyphs. The secrets of its language revealed, the world of the pharaohs inspired a surge of scholarly activity. Plundered artifacts – mummies, sarcophagi, and other antiquities – housed in European and American museums were available to the researchers. Equipped with new knowledge of the ancient world, artists responded in kind, incorporating Egyptian figures and devices into their works. This tendency was especially strong in the United States, where American Egyptomania – to borrow Scott Trafton's term – was exemplified by the Egyptian Revival, a popular architectural style.[20] Egyptomania strongly influenced Poe, whose enthusiasm for Egyptian themes is clear in "Some Words with a Mummy," a tale about an ancient nobleman who returns from the dead and scoffs at the machines and political reforms associated with Progress, a golden calf of nineteenth-century America that Poe often ridiculed. Cryptograms, codes, and ancient writing also appeared frequently in Poe's works. John T. Irwin has attributed this recurrence to Poe's admiration for Champollion, the man who deciphered the Rosetta Stone's hieroglyphs.[21]

Ancient Egypt held, however, additional interest for Poe. As Trafton has demonstrated, Egypt became a locus of ideological conflict in nineteenth-century America, and particularly fierce were controversies about race, for white and black Americans offered complicated, conflicting pictures of ancient Egypt, variously represented by both groups as an imperial ideal and a hotbed of tyranny.[22] According to Trafton, Poe addressed the controversy in *The Narrative of Arthur Gordon Pym*, which exposed the racism sustaining archaeological inquiry, a form of imaginative imperialism complementing the territorial variety.[23] American debates about Egypt were, of course, shaped by contemporary concerns about Islam derived from the Barbary experience. During Poe's lifetime, Egypt was inhabited by Muslims, who resented Napoleon's imperial forays into their homeland; the French leader's conquest proved, however, short-lived, and the land remained under Muslim control until 1882.[24] For Poe, Egypt was associated with Islam, and the land with its grand history belonged to his imagined Orient.

In addition to British fiction and verse as well as Egypt-inspired works, travel writing also shaped Poe's perceptions of the Near East. An important source was Comte de Volney's *Les ruines* (1791). Volney's work was not, strictly speaking, a travel narrative, but the author's descriptions of ruined cities derived from his wanderings in the Near East. These accounts were probably on Poe's mind when he wrote "The Doomed City" (later "The City in the Sea"), a poem about a sublime ruin of Oriental architecture.[25] Dear to Coleridge and Shelley, whom Poe admired, was James Bruce's *Travels to Discover the Source of the Nile* (1790), a work often cited by the British poets, and if Poe lacked firsthand knowledge of Bruce's book, the Romantics introduced it to him.[26] Significant, *Travels* was more than a mere travelogue, and among other things, the book contained Bruce's speculations about the origins of Egyptian hieroglyphic writing. Poe's curiosity regarding the Orient was similarly wide-ranging, as evinced in his 1836 essay "Palaestine," in which he described the region's geography and sketched its political history. This essay consisted of passages compiled from Abraham Rees's *Cyclopaedia* and other sources.[27] Full of borrowed language, Poe's "Palaestine" was no testament to its author's imaginative powers, but the essay did record his Oriental preoccupations, which he sought in other books. Indeed, Palestine provided the scene for one of his tales: "A Tale of Jerusalem," a comic yarn about the ancient city under Roman occupation.

Along with the books mentioned earlier, Poe read other accounts of travel to the Near East. One was Chateaubriand's *Itinéraire de Paris à Jerusalem*, an English translation of which Poe may have used as a source for "The Visionary."[28] Another was John L. Stephens's *Incidents of Travel in Egypt, Arabia Petraea, and the Holy Land*, which Poe reviewed in 1837. The book, written by an American, contained a considerable amount of ethnographic material, and Poe's review was generally favorable. He did, however, take issue with some of Stephens's comments about the Red Sea, insisting that Stephens "placed himself in direct opposition to all authority on the subject."[29] To justify his critique, Poe cited German scholar Carsten Niebuhr, and the review included other references to books about travel to the Near East.[30] While "Palaestine" and the Stephens review appeared after Poe had begun writing poems and tales featuring Orientalia, both essays, which showcased the author's previous reading, suggested that the Orient had long captivated him.

While writing tales in Baltimore, Poe may also have read Washington Irving's *Tales of the Alhambra* (1832), which contained travel sketches and fiction inspired by the author's 1829 journey to Granada, home of the Alhambra, the fabled Moorish palace. Of the Alhambra, Irving exultingly wrote: "How many legends and traditions, true and fabulous; how many songs and ballads, Arabian and Spanish, of love and war and chivalry, are associated with this oriental pile!"[31] For Irving, the Alhambra was an imaginative paradise: "It is a singular good fortune to be thrown into this most romantic and historical place, which has such a sway over the imaginations of readers in all parts of the world."[32] Regardless whether Poe read Irving's book, he evidently shared the celebrated man's fascination with the Orient and its creative potential for the enterprising writer.[33]

Considering the breadth of his reading and his documented interest in the Orient, Poe was probably familiar with other American writing about Muslims, for books about Islamic cultures were readily available.[34] This publishing trend was a response to public interest in Islam. Many Americans were not, however, interested in cultural dialogue. In fact, most of the writings about Islam that they read "conveyed a consistent picture of the Muslim world, an inverted image of the world the Americans were trying to create anew."[35] Thus these books promoted an Orientalist view of Islam.

These cultural stereotypes figured prominently in American accounts of the Barbary Wars. During the early national period, diplomatic relations between America and the Barbary States – Morocco, Algiers, Tunis, and Tripoli – were poor. For years, European nations had paid tribute to these principalities to secure safe passage for merchant ships traveling to the Mediterranean. When the United States emerged as an independent nation after the Revolutionary War, the Islamic rulers of the Barbary Coast expected the Americans to pay tribute as well, but the United States government, saddled with enormous debt, had difficulty meeting these demands. When Congress failed to deliver tribute payments on schedule, corsairs seized American vessels and enslaved U.S. citizens, and the resulting political crisis led to two wars in the Mediterranean.[36] When the last of these ended in 1816, Edgar Allan Poe was seven years old.

Poe did not refer directly to the Barbary Wars in his works, but he used American representations of the Near East that emerged from these conflicts for creative purposes. Many Americans perceived these wars in Orientalist terms, as popular captivity writings demonstrated. Insisting on their absolute cultural difference from North African Muslims, former captives told stories about these conflicts that served their own interests, representing the Barbary Wars as Manichean battles pitting Western "civilization" against African "barbarity."[37] Such narratives followed the binary logic of Orientalism and fueled anti-Islamic sentiment. Despite their ideological stridency, these texts were not totally celebratory of American culture. Barbary captivity offered whites visceral proof of slavery's evils, and the experience was, in some cases, transformative and humbling.[38] Royall Tyler's *The Algerine Captive: or, The Life and Adventures of Doctor Updike Underhill* (1797), a fictional account, was notably antislavery. The narrator, Updike Underhill, a Yankee physician who once inspected slaves bound for Southern plantations before becoming a slave himself, emerged from slavery an inveterate foe of his country's own peculiar institution. Some factual records, such as James Riley's *Narrative* (1817), condemned Christians who tolerated slavery at home yet considered themselves morally superior to Muslim slave masters.

Interrogating national identity when Anglo-Americans were trying to define themselves as a distinct cultural group, the Barbary captivity narrative performed important cultural work in nineteenth-century America. Poe imitated the genre in *The Narrative of Arthur Gordon Pym*, an 1838 novel that posed similar questions about the young nation and its future. With its sensational title page, accounts of captivity experiences, and ethnographic details, the novel announced its kinship to the Barbary captivity narrative, and *Pym* did, in some respects, resemble Riley's popular book.[39] Most significant, *Pym* revealed its author's impatience with nationalist zeal, and in his errors of perception and judgment, the novel's unreliable narrator exemplified the folly of imperial endeavor, the attempt to dominate an Other who remained incomprehensible to the colonizing mind.[40]

The Barbary Wars experience is crucial to understanding Poe's Orientalism. During the early national period, many Americans considered the Muslim world in general, and the Barbary States in particular, the reverse of the United States. If such identity constructions were standard in the first half of the nineteenth century, then what are readers to make of Poe's repeated appropriations of the Orient as an ideal world? In symbolic terms, these gestures reveal his antipathy to wholly imitative writing and to literary nationalism, both of which Poe avoided in his own work.

NOTES

1. Kevin J. Hayes, *Poe and the Printed Word* (New York: Cambridge University Press, 2000), 11.
2. L. Moffitt Cecil, "Poe's 'Arabesque,'" *Comparative Literature* 18 (1966), 58.
3. Edward W. Said, *Orientalism* (1978; reprinted, New York: Vintage, 1994), 2.
4. Frank Lambert, *The Barbary Wars: American Independence in the Atlantic World* (New York: Hill and Wang, 2005), 105.
5. Cecil, "Poe's 'Arabesque,'" 59; Arthur Hobson Quinn, *Edgar Allan Poe: A Critical Biography* (New York: Appleton-Century, 1941), 156.
6. Quinn, *Edgar Allan Poe*, 179–80.
7. Martha Pike Conant, *The Oriental Tale in England* (New York: Columbia University Press, 1908), xxvi.
8. Edgar Allan Poe, *Essays and Reviews*, ed. G. R. Thompson (New York: Library of America, 1984), 1150; *The Collected Works of Edgar Allan Poe*, ed. Thomas Ollive Mabbott, 3 vols. (Cambridge, MA: Belknap Press, 1968–78), vol. ii, 313.
9. For a survey of the Oriental tale in America, see David S. Reynolds, *Faith in Fiction: The Emergence of Religious Literature in America* (Cambridge, MA: Harvard University Press, 1981), 13–37.
10. Robert L. Mack, ed., *Oriental Tales* (New York: Oxford University Press, 1992), xvii.
11. Poe, *Essays*, 1316.
12. Malini Johar Schueller, *U.S. Orientalisms: Race, Nation, and Gender in Literature, 1790–1890* (Ann Arbor: University of Michigan Press, 1998), 123.
13. Poe, *Essays*, 642–7; *Collected Works*, 3: 1335.
14. Benjamin F. Fisher, *The Cambridge Introduction to Edgar Allan Poe* (New York: Cambridge University Press, 2008), 35.
15. Paul G. Trueblood, *Lord Byron*, 2nd ed. (New York: Twayne, 1977), 61.

16. On "Tamerlane" and *The Giaour*, see Edgar Allan Poe, *The Poems of Edgar Allan Poe*, ed. Killis Campbell (Boston: Ginn, 1917), xliv and 148–50; Fisher, *Cambridge Introduction*, 35.

17. Leslie A. Marchand, *Byron's Poetry: A Critical Introduction* (Boston: Houghton Mifflin, 1965), 60.

18. For Poe's opposition to Lake School poetics, see Kent P. Ljungquist, "The Poet as Critic," *The Cambridge Companion to Edgar Allan Poe*, ed. Kevin J. Hayes (New York: Cambridge University Press, 2002), 8–9. For more on Orientalia in Poe's verse, see Brian Yothers, "Poe's Poetry of the Exotic," *Critical Insights: The Poetry of Edgar Allan Poe*, ed. Steven Frye (Pasadena: Salem Press, 2010), 19–33.

19. On "Al Aaraaf" and *Lalla Rookh*, see Poe, *Poems*, xlv–xlvii, 173–4.

20. Scott Trafton, *Egypt Land: Race and Nineteenth-Century American Egyptomania* (Durham: Duke University Press, 2004), 131.

21. John T. Irwin, *American Hieroglyphics: The Symbol of the Egyptian Hieroglyhphics in the American Renaissance* (New Haven: Yale University Press, 1980), 43.

22. Trafton, *Egypt Land*, 11.

23. Ibid., 108.

24. Karen Armstrong, *Islam: A Short History* (London: Phoenix-Orion, 2005), 126–7.

25. Wilson O. Clough, "Poe's 'The City in the Sea' Revisited," *Essays on American Literature in Honor of Jay B. Hubbell*, ed. Clarence Gohdes (Durham: Duke University Press, 1967), 80.

26. Irwin, *American Hieroglyphics*, 85.

27. J. O. Bailey, "Poe's 'Palaestine,'" *American Literature* 13 (1941), 44.

28. Alfred G. Engstrom, "Chateubriand's *Intinéraire de Paris à Jerusalem* and Poe's "The Assignation'" *Modern Language Notes* 69 (1954): 506–7; Poe, *Collected Works*, vol. ii, 168.

29. Poe, *Essays*, 939.

30. Ibid.

31. Washington Irving, *Bracebridge Hall, Tales of a Traveller, The Alhambra*, ed. Andrew B. Myers (New York: Library of America, 1991), 752.

32. Quoted in Andrew Burstein, *The Original Knickerbocker: The Life of Washington Irving* (New York: Basic Books, 2007), 221.

33. In 1835, Poe briefly reviewed volume three of Irving's *Crayon Miscellany*, which narrates legends surrounding the Arab invasion of Spain, "an event," according to Poe, "momentous in the extreme" (*Essays*, 614). Significant, nowhere did Poe demonize the conquering Saracens, whose exploits Irving recounted.

34. Robert J. Allison, *The Crescent Obscured: the United States and the Muslim World, 1776–1815* (Chicago: University of Chicago Press, 2000), xvii.

35. Allison, *Crescent Obscured*, xvii.

36. Lambert, *Barbary Wars*, 9, 7.

37. Paul Baepler, Introduction, *White Slaves, African Masters: An Anthology of Barbary Captivity Narratives*, ed. Paul Baepler (University of Chicago Press, 1999), 33.

38. Paul Baepler, "The Barbary Captivity Narrative in American Culture." *Early American Literature* 39 (2004), 230–1.

39. "Unsigned Notice in *Alexander's Weekly Messenger* [August 22, 1838]," *Edgar Allan Poe: The Critical Heritage*, ed. I. M. Walker (New York: Routledge and K. Paul, 1986), 94.

40. Schueller, *U.S. Orientalisms*, 111.

CHAPTER 7

The Polar Regions

Mark Canada

The America that Poe inhabited in the early nineteenth century was deeply engaged in geographic exploration. Three years before Poe's birth in 1809, Lewis and Clark returned from their expedition across the newly acquired Louisiana Territory. Over the next half century, while Poe was growing up, serving in the U.S. Army, editing magazines, and penning his poetry and fiction, Americans surveyed the Atlantic and Pacific coasts, blazed the Oregon and Santa Fe trails, and launched expeditions to the South Pacific, the Antarctic, and the American West. Meanwhile, fellow writers such as Richard Henry Dana and Herman Melville described factual and fictional journeys to distant places. It should come as no surprise, then, that Poe exploited this ubiquitous theme of discovery in his literature. Tales such as "Manuscript Found in a Bottle," "The Unparalleled Adventure of One Hans Pfaall," and *The Narrative of Arthur Gordon Pym* are replete with journeys, discoveries, and various exotic locales. For Poe's fictional explorers, however, the real *ultima Thule* lay not in the South Seas or the South Pole, but in their own minds.

By the early nineteenth century, the expeditions of Captain Cook, Lewis and Clark, and others had expanded the boundaries of the known world – or, at least, the world known to American readers. Huge portions of the earth, however, remained to be explored, leaving real-life explorers with alluring goals – and imaginative sorts with a delicious field for speculation.[1] One American whose vivid fancy would stir many another imagination and eventually help to inspire a full-scale expedition was a retired U.S. Army captain named John Cleves Symmes, Jr. In 1818, Symmes, then in St. Louis, made a bold, thrilling proclamation:

To all the World:

I declare the earth is hollow and habitable within; containing a number of solid concentrick spheres, one within the other, and that it is open at the poles twelve or sixteen degrees. I pledge my life in support of this truth, and am ready to explore the hollow, if the world will support and aid me in the undertaking.

Under his signature, Symmes added a few notes, including this one:

I ask one hundred brave companions, well equipped, to start from Siberia, in the fall season, with reindeer and sleighs, on the ice of the frozen sea; I engage we find a warm and rich land, stocked with thrifty vegetables and animals, if not men, on reaching one degree northward of latitude 82; we will return in the succeeding spring.[2]

If Symmes could not exactly reach "all the World" with his proclamation and invitation, he did attempt to reach a good part of it. As biographer James McBride explains, he "addressed a copy of this circular to every learned institution and to every considerable town and village, as well as to numerous distinguished individuals, throughout the United States, and sent copies to several of the learned societies of Europe."[3] Two years later appeared a novel, *Symzonia; Voyage of Discovery*, attributed to one Captain Adam Seaborn, but perhaps written by Symmes or, if one modern scholar is correct, Nathaniel Ames, a sailor who wrote *A Mariner's Sketches* (1830) and other books.[4] The narrator recounts a supposed journey to the Antarctic hole and, through it, into an internal realm populated by alabaster white people who enjoy a life of prosperity and virtue.

The notion of a hollow earth was not original to Symmes. As early as 1665, Athanasius Kircher had argued in his *Mundus Subterraneus* that the earth contained a fiery core and channels connecting its interior and exterior. Englishman Edmond Halley of comet fame expressed a similar belief in a 1692 essay published in *Philosophical Transactions*. Symmes may have encountered the idea in Cotton Mather's *Christian Philosopher*, which contains a reference to Halley's theory. Scottish mathematician and physicist John Leslie also theorized about a hollow earth.[5] In any case, it was Symmes who launched a sensation in the United States. Unlike Halley and Leslie, Symmes was no scientist, and his "New Theory," as it came to be called, did not gain unanimous support from the scientific community, although at least one mathematician saw the potential for promoting scientific inquiry, even if the motivation was warped. This mathematician, Thomas Johnston Matthews, published a critique of Symmes's theory, but pledged the profits from it to support an expedition. A number of other Americans, presumably less skeptical about Symmes's idea, got on board and pushed the government to act. Despite memorials calling for exploratory expeditions in 1822 and 1823, Congress did nothing.[6] The belief in "Symmes' Hole," however, would not go away. In 1826, an anonymous author – perhaps James McBride, an acquaintance of Symmes – came out with *Symmes's Theory of Concentric Spheres*, which carried on its title page Hamlet's famous admonition: "There are more things in Heaven and

EARTH, Horatio, / Than are dreamt of in your philosophy!" As the author explained in his preface, his purpose was "to attract the attention of the learned, who are in the habit of indulging in more abstruse researches into the operation and effect of natural causes; and should it be found to merit the attention of such, it is hoped their enquiries may be so directed as to accelerate the march of scientific improvement, enlarge the field of philosophic speculation, and open to the world new objects of ambition and enterprise." The book, both a description and a defense of Symmes's theory, touches on everything from winds, monsoons, and reports of northern animal migrations on earth to Saturn's rings and apparent circles around the poles of Mars, all phenomena possibly related to the existence of concentric spheres, here and elsewhere in the solar system. It also makes explicit reference to "the tremendous whirlpool on the coast of Norway, called the Maalstroom, which sucks in, and discharges the waters of the sea with great violence," presumably the same whirlpool that serves as a setting for Poe's story "The Descent into the Maelström."[7]

A more important apostle emerged in the form of an Ohio newspaperman named Jeremiah Reynolds. In 1825, Reynolds joined Symmes on a lecture tour and proved a gifted promoter, sometimes addressing audiences himself. Three years after they began touring together, the U.S. House of Representatives called for an expedition to explore "coasts, islands, harbors, shoals, and reefs," but the Senate derailed the plan. Reynolds, however, managed to mount a private expedition and set sail with the crews of three ships, including the *Penguin*, in 1829. After several sailors abandoned the expedition, Reynolds had to give up while in South America. Although he had not made any landmark discoveries in the Antarctic, the journal he kept on the expedition may have inspired the mysterious ending to *Pym*. Symmes died in 1829, but Reynolds, after spending two years in Chile, pushed again for a government-sponsored expedition. By now, he had long since split with Symmes and was emphasizing the need for scientific inquiry instead of the possibility of holes in the poles. Finally, in 1836, Congress came through with support for an expedition. Three years passed. Various participants, including Reynolds and Secretary of the Navy Mahlon Dickerson, prepared and planned, quibbled and squabbled. When, on August 18, 1838, more than 300 men, including seven scientists and artists, left Norfolk, Virginia, Reynolds was not among them. Dickerson, who nursed at least one grudge against him, had taken steps to keep him out of the expedition. The commander was Lieutenant Charles Wilkes, chosen after others had refused or resigned. Over the next four years, Wilkes and his fellow explorers on the United States South Seas

Exploring Expedition, or "Ex. Ex.," traveled some eighty-seven thousand miles, rounding Cape Horn, cruising through Antarctic and South Pacific waters, visiting perhaps 280 islands and America's Northwest coast, and ultimately circumnavigating the globe to arrive in New York in 1842. Along the way, the men collected more than sixty thousand specimens of plants, animal skins, shells, and more (many of which would go to the new Smithsonian Institution or the National Botanic Garden) and, significant, discovered Antarctic land where it had not been known to exist – but, alas, no unknown civilizations occupying interior spheres.[8]

As an editor, Poe was aware of geographical expeditions, including the plans for this expedition in particular. He not only reviewed books about the travels of James Clark Ross and J. L. Stephens, but also referred explicitly to the South Seas expedition numerous times, both before its launch and after its completion, in his journalism and his novel, *The Narrative of Arthur Gordon Pym*. In his reviews, Poe championed both the cause and Reynolds, its chief advocate, saying, "Our pride as a vigorous commercial empire, should stimulate us to become our own pioneers in that vast island-studded ocean, destined, it may be, to become, not only the chief theatre of our traffic, but the arena of our future naval conflicts." He added that the United States had a "*duty*... to contribute a large share to that aggregate of useful knowledge, which is the common property of all." In a review that appeared in the January 1837 issue of the *Southern Literary Messenger*, the same issue in which the first installment of *The Narrative of Arthur Gordon Pym* appeared, he praised Reynolds as a man ideally suited for the position of corresponding secretary on the expedition:

How admirably well he is qualified for this task, no person can know better than ourselves. His energy, his love of polite literature, his many and various attainments, and above all, his ardent and honorable enthusiasm, point him out as the man of all men for the execution of this task. We look forward to this finale – to the published record of the expedition – with an intensity of eager expectation, which we cannot think we have ever experienced before.

Poe may have had a personal acquaintance with Reynolds, as he seems to indicate in the first sentence here and later when he says, "Gentlemen have impugned his motives – have these gentlemen ever seen him or conversed with him half an hour?" Indeed, one report links the promoter and author to the curious circumstances surrounding Poe's mysterious death in Baltimore in 1849. Before he succumbed on October 7, Poe was said to have cried out "Reynolds!" on more than one occasion. "Perhaps to his dim and tortured brain," biographer Arthur Hobson Quinn says, "he seemed to be on the brink of a great descending circle sweeping down like the phantom ship in the 'Manuscript Found in a Bottle' into 'darkness and the distance.'"⁹

While Poe's acquaintance with Reynolds and the meaning – or even existence – of his final cries are matters of conjecture, there can be no doubt that Poe was familiar with Symmes's New Theory. Thanks to the lectures, books, and newspaper coverage that Americans encountered throughout the 1820s, the theory was in the air. Furthermore, scholars have argued for Poe's familiarity with *Symzonia*.¹⁰ Indeed, Poe described related phenomena in his own fiction. Both "Manuscript Found in a Bottle" and "A Descent into the Maelström" feature plunges into oceanic holes. In the former, Poe's narrator, alluding to a theory that the earth contained a whole network of passages, says, "It is evident that we are hurrying onwards to some exciting knowledge – some never-to-be-imparted secret, whose attainment is destruction. Perhaps this current leads us to the southern pole itself."¹¹ The latter story refers explicitly to Kircher's notion of "an abyss penetrating the globe, and issuing in some remote part."¹² The protagonist of "The Unparalleled Adventure of One Hans Pfaall," furthermore, sees signs of an opening at the North Pole from his balloon as it soars toward the moon. In *The Narrative of Arthur Gordon Pym*, Poe seems to exploit popular interest in the theory to craft a tantalizing scene as Pym and his companions float in their canoe toward the South Pole. In line with Symmes's theory, the travelers encounter warmer temperatures as they approach the pole, and the mysterious white "shrouded human figure" that appears in the novel's conclusion could be identified with the inhabitants of the "internal world" in *Symzonia*. J. O. Bailey has noted numerous parallels in the two novels – references to remnants of sea vessels and unusual animals, for example, as well as detailed descriptions of penguin colonies – and argued that *Symzonia* served as a primary source for Poe as he was writing *Pym*.¹³

What did Poe's familiarity with Reynolds, Symmes's Hole, the Antarctic expedition, and the general notion of a hollow earth mean for his literature? The question has drawn attention from numerous commentators, who have proposed various interpretations. Burton Pollin has suggested that Reynolds's *Address on the Subject of a Surveying and Exploring Expedition to the Pacific Ocean and South Seas* provided material for *Pym*. Similarly, Richard Kopley has argued that Poe drew on Reynolds's "Leaves from an Unpublished Journal," which recounts his adventures on the aborted private expedition, and has used the connection to explain *Pym*'s mystifying conclusion, arguing that the giant "shrouded human figure" Pym reports seeing in the Antarctic sea is actually the figure of a penguin on the prow of a ship about to rescue him.[14] Other scholars have examined Poe's sea fiction in the context of the genre of travel narratives or the country's scientific, commercial, and political ambitions. Lisa Gitelman, for instance, characterizes *Pym* – with its "tedious and seemingly irrelevant non-original material," non-cohesive narrative, and "frustratingly anticlimactic end" – as a parody of exploration literature and argues that it "mocks the exuberance for exploration voyages and voyage accounts that gripped America in the 1830s, an enthusiasm inflamed by the desire to compete with British naval exploration and the global reaches of British empire." Matthew Teorey, noting that Poe published and republished "Manuscript Found in a Bottle" numerous times in the years leading up to the Antarctic expedition, as well as the years of and after the expedition, argues that this tale "can be read as a dramatization of his excitement about America's embarkation into imperialism – and at the same time his apparent concerns about the possible dangers of such an endeavor."[15]

Poe certainly was engaged with the goings-on of the external world, and his writings about the Antarctic expedition show an awareness of the country's scientific and commercial concerns. Still, it is difficult to imagine that the author of so much symbolic, psychological fiction was thinking only of literal seas and expeditions when he penned his sea fiction. In his reading of *Pym*, Kenneth Silverman argues, "The climax of the work, a fantasy of being swallowed and engulfed, reveals Pym's self-destructiveness to be driven by a desire to merge with the dead."[16] For Poe, furthermore, place was often a metaphor, specifically a stand-in for some aspect of the psychological landscape. The edifices portrayed in "The Haunted Palace" and "The Fall of the House of Usher" are obvious metaphors for human heads or minds, and the school that is the setting for the first part of "William Wilson," the catacombs of "The Cask of Amontillado," and the realm described in "The Domain of Arnheim" all can be read in a similar fashion. In light of Poe's fascination with psychological space, his engagement with unknown lands holds special significance. As Darryl Jones has suggested, Poe's imaginary encounters with holes and poles is part of a larger fascination with *ultima Thule*, a Latin phrase referring to a supposed island, perhaps in the vicinity of Norway or Iceland, once considered the northernmost part of the known world. Some 300 years before the birth of Christ, the Greek explorer Pytheas supposedly visited Thule in his journey north of Britain. The phrase appears in "The Pit in the Pendulum," in which Poe writes, "My cognizance of the pit had become known to the inquisitorial agents – *the pit*, whose horrors had been destined for so bold a recusant as myself – *the pit*, typical of hell, and regarded by rumor as the Ultima Thule of all their punishments."[17] A slightly amended version of the phrase appears in "Dream-Land," where it carries more of its original geographical meaning:

> By a route obscure and lonely,
> Haunted by ill angels only,
> Where an Eidolon, named NIGHT,
> On a black throne reigns upright,
> I have reached these lands but newly
> From an ultimate dim Thule –
> From a wild weird clime that lieth, sublime,
> Out of SPACE – out of TIME.[18]

If the phrase refers to an extreme in "The Pit and the Pendulum," here it points to something beyond the extreme, a separate realm entirely. Jones notes that, for French writer Gaston Broche, who may have drawn on *Pym* in writing his adaptation of the Pytheas story, the land of ultima Thule "acts as a limit-point of human speech and understanding beyond which is only silence and whiteness and consequently as a space with the potential to open up vistas of numinous terror."[19] On a literal level, the earth's actual ultima Thule – that is, the polar regions – existed, but were not yet discovered. As such, they were both alluring and threatening. The possibility of a treacherous hole leading to the bowels of the earth only added to the sense of mystery and danger.

The motif of ultima Thule was more than a tantalizing trope for evoking terror, however. It also fit squarely into Poe's conception of the mind as a place with its own remote, unknown regions. In the mid-1830s, around the same time he was writing of Reynolds and the push for a southern oceanic expedition, Poe was gushing over the promise of phrenology, the pseudoscience that postulated that the brain consisted of physical regions dedicated to various qualities, including "Amativeness," "Cautiousness," and "Language." For one enamored of a model that presented the mind as a physical entity that could be mapped, the concept of ultima Thule was the perfect metaphor for the mind. Like the earth, the mind had its own remote, mysterious region – one both alluring and threatening. For Poe, this region was the seat of imagination, what he once called "the poetical portion" of his mind.[20] In this respect, Poe was borrowing from phrenologists, who conceived of an artistic faculty in the brain. A great deal of evidence, however, suggests that Poe was also at least dimly aware of an actual psychological entity now widely recognized by modern neurological researchers. In the current model of the human mind, the right cerebral hemisphere is dominant for the processing of images and negative emotions, as well as some aspects of music, while generally lacking key linguistic functions. It also plays a key role in dreaming and may be the source of self-destructive urges. In countless works, from his gothic poems and tales to his detective fiction to his philosophical dialogues, Poe betrayed a fascination with all of these processes and impulses, as well as a compulsion to explore and cultivate the mental region responsible for them.

If ultima Thule, in its various manifestations in *Pym* and other works, indeed represents a psychological realm, perhaps even the right brain in particular, then the actions taken toward and in it assume special significance. To set off to explore ultima Thule, the region at or beyond the extremes of understanding, is to delve into a mysterious realm in the human mind, into the realm of what Freud would eventually call the "unconscious." Indeed, some experts have likened the right cerebral hemisphere to the unconscious. Because of its remote, mysterious qualities, as well as its association with self-destructive urges, such a journey – even a mental one – was both alluring and dangerous. One might be enticed by the promise of "DISCOVERY" – the word painted on a sail in "Manuscript Found in a Bottle" – and drawn inexplicably toward the unknown, as Pym and his comrades are in the final pages of *Pym*. At the same time, just as Pym and characters in both "Manuscript Found in a Bottle" and "Descent into the Maelström" face the threat of a perilous plunge and possible destruction, one who dares the unknown realm of the mind risks succumbing to madness or self-destruction. Imagination and madness, of course, have long been associated in literature, as characterizations of art and artists by Shakespeare, Dickinson, and others make evident. For Poe, the metaphor of a plunge into the earth's interior dramatized the fall into madness as a physical event.

Even for a writer such as Poe, who frequently sought to explore the world of the mind, the external events of the world could be a rich resource to mine for literary material. In the case of the United States South Seas Exploring Expedition and Americans' fascination with Symmes's Hole, these events provided him with a metaphor he could exploit in his efforts to portray the nature and exploration of an alluring, yet threatening region of the mind. Both a geographical and a mental realm, ultima Thule amounted to an invitation to ambitious sorts to take the plunge.

NOTES

1. Darryl Jones, "Ultima Thule: *Arthur Gordon Pym*, the Polar Imaginary, and the Hollow Earth," *Edgar Allan Poe Review* 11 (2010), 51–69; Mark Canada, "Flight into Fancy: Poe's Discovery of the Right Brain," *Southern Literary Journal* 33 (2001), 62–79.
2. Quoted in James McBride, *Pioneer Biography: Sketches of the Lives of Some of the Early Settlers of Butler County, Ohio*, 2 vols. (Cincinnati: Robert Clarke, 1871), vol. ii, 243–4.
3. McBride, *Pioneer Biography*, vol. ii, 244.
4. *Symzonia; Voyage of Discovery* (New York: J. Seymour, 1820); Hans-Joachim Lang and Benjamin Lease, "The Authorship of Symzonia: The Case for Nathaniel Ames," *New England Quarterly* 48 (1975), 241–52.
5. Tara E. Nummedal, "Kircher's Subterranean World and the Dignity of the Geocosm," *The Great Art of Knowing: The Baroque Encyclopedia of Athanasius Kircher*, ed. Daniel Stolzenberg (Stanford: Stanford University Press, 2001), 37–47; David Standish, *Hollow Earth: The Long and Curious History of Imagining Strange Lands, Fantastical Creatures, Advanced Civilizations, and Marvelous Machines Below the Earth's Surface* (Cambridge, MA: Da Capo, 2006), 15, 22–4, 45–50.
6. William Stanton, *The Great United States Exploring Expedition of 1838–1842* (Berkeley: University of California Press, 1975), 9–13.
7. *Symmes's Theory of Concentric Spheres; Demonstrating That the Earth Is Hollow, Habitable Within, and Widely Open About the Poles* (Cincinnati: Morgan, Lodge and Fisher, 1826), vi, 106.
8. Stanton, *The Great United States Exploring Expedition*, 13–38, 359; Jeff Rubin, "United States Exploring Expedition," *Encyclopedia of the Antarctic*, ed. Beau Riffenburgh, 2 vols. (New York: Routledge, 2007), vol. i, 1028–30.
9. Edgar Allan Poe, *Poetry and Tales*, ed. Patrick F. Quinn (New York: Library of America, 1984), 1180, and *Essays and Reviews*, ed. G. R. Thompson (New York: Library of America, 1984), 1231, 1240–1; Arthur Hobson Quinn, *Edgar Allan Poe: A Critical Biography* (New York: Appleton-Century, 1941), 640. See also Robert F. Almy, "J. N. Reynolds: A Brief Biography with Particular Reference to Poe and Symmes," *Colophon* 2 (1937), 227–45; Aubrey Starke, "Poe's Friend Reynolds," *American Literature* 11 (1939), 152–9. For a challenge to Moran's account of Poe calling "Reynolds!" on his deathbed, see William T. Bandy, "Dr. Moran and the Poe-Reynolds Myth," *Myths and Realities*, ed. Benjamin Franklin Fisher (Baltimore: Edgar Allan Poe Society, 1987), 26–36.
10. Jones, "Ultima Thule," 61; Almy, "J. N. Reynolds"; J. O. Bailey, "Sources for Poe's Arthur Gordon Pym, 'Hans Pfaal,' and Other Pieces," *PMLA* 57 (1942), 513–35; *The Science Fiction of Edgar Allan Poe*, ed. Harold Beaver (New York: Penguin, 1976), 334–6.
11. Edgar Allan Poe, *The Collected Works of Edgar Allan Poe*, ed. Thomas Ollive Mabbott, 3 vols. (Cambridge, MA: Belknap Press, 1969–1978), vol. ii, 145.

12. Ibid., vol. ii, 583.
13. Poe, *Poetry and Tales*, 985–6, 1132, 1179; J. O. Bailey, "Sources," 514–20.
14. Edgar Allan Poe, *The Imaginary Voyages*, ed. Burton R. Pollin (New York: Twayne, 1981), 18–19; Richard Kopley, "The Secret of Arthur Gordon Pym: The Text and the Source," *Studies in American Fiction* 8 (1980), 203–18.
15. Lisa Gitelman, "Arthur Gordon Pym and the Novel Narrative of Edgar Allan Poe," *Nineteenth-Century Literature* 47 (1992), 350, 353, 358; Matthew Teorey, "Into the Imperial Whirlpool: Poe's 'MS. Found in a Bottle' and the United States South Seas Exploration Expedition," *Poe Studies* 38 (2005), 43.
16. Kenneth Silverman, *Edgar A. Poe: Mournful and Never-Ending Remembrance* (New York: HarperCollins, 1991), 136.
17. Poe, *Collected Works*, vol. ii, 690.
18. Ibid., vol. i, 343–4.
19. Jones, "Ultima Thule," 51; *Oxford English Dictionary*.
20. Poe to Philip Pendleton Cooke, August 9, 1846, *The Collected Letters of Edgar Allan Poe*, ed. John Ward Ostrom, Burton R. Pollin, and Jeffrey A. Savoye, 2 vols. (New York: Gordian, 2008), vol. i, 595.

PART TWO

Social Contexts

CHAPTER 8

The Urban Environment

Bran Nicol

In his notorious 1849 obituary of Poe, Rufus Griswold notes that the author was given to "walk[ing] the streets, in madness or melancholy, with lips moving in indistinct curses, or with eyes upturned in passionate prayers for the happiness of those who at that moment were objects of his idolatry." Like many of the details in the piece, this one is cunningly designed to instill in the minds of future readers a view of Poe as a damaged, tortured figure, so imprisoned in a hellish dream world "peopled with creations and the accidents of his brain" as to render him incapable of looking objectively at the outside world, and thus producing the great art to which his gifts were tailored. This calculated attack was hugely effective. As Kevin J. Hayes has said, Griswold's piece was largely responsible for the enduring critical habit of conflating Poe's "mentally unbalanced narrators" with the author himself.[1]

Griswold himself falls back on images from the tales to legitimate his portrait of their author. In the image of Poe deliriously wandering the city streets, he seems to be drawing – perhaps unintentionally – on one of Poe's most memorable stories, "The Man of the Crowd" (1840), in which the narrator, recently recovered from illness, becomes obsessed with a decrepit old man he observes through a London coffeehouse window and impulsively follows as he wanders through the streets, mirroring his unpredictable movements and delirious immersion in the crowd. Whether or not there is any accuracy in Griswold's claim, there is no doubt that walking through the city and reflecting on the kaleidoscopic sensations of the streets was a common literary response to the urban environment of the early nineteenth century, a new world marked not only by teeming crowds of people, but by unprecedented advances in technology such as the gas lamp and the birth of consumer culture and mass media. Poe's work, like that of Dickens, Baudelaire, Engels, or Heine, stood at the forefront of this response, and early nineteenth-century urban experience provides an important context for understanding his fiction. More precisely, to explore how Poe captured the intensities of everyday life in the city means to begin not just with "The Man of the Crowd," the subject of numerous analyses by critics, but with the influence on their readings of Walter Benjamin's insights into the story and its context in his vast *Arcades Project*.

Benjamin values Poe as one of those prominent literary "students of the physiognomy of the big city." Physiognomy is the ancient pseudoscientific practice whereby a person's inner qualities are deduced from facial and other external characteristics. Reading the city as if it were a person – and the complementary practice of reading the people of the city – were common techniques in early literary engagements with the city, from the proto-modernist poetry of Baudelaire to the "physiologies," pocket-sized paperbacks sold on Paris streets that amusingly catalogued urban types. One of these types, in fact one who doubles as the very producer of such sketches, is the *flâneur*, a term originally used in Poe's time to refer to the writers and journalists (such as Nathaniel Parker Willis) who produced sketches of urban life from a strolling or panoramic perspective. But from the outset, as Benjamin is aware, the flâneur seemed to take on more mythical proportions. He described the flâneur as a "botanist on asphalt," a man who possessed the ability of a trained scientist to decode the mysterious elements of the peculiar object that confronted him: the city and its inhabitants.[2] Baudelaire characterized the flâneur as perfectly at home in the city, its exterior spaces figuring as his interior dwelling: "The crowd is his domain, just as the air is the bird's, and water that of the fish. His passion and his profession is to merge with the crowd."[3] For Benjamin, *flânerie*, the practice of urban strolling, looking, and interpreting, functioned as a defense mechanism deployed against the potentially overwhelming confrontation with different sensations and strangers on city streets, managing to transform the vastness and complexity of the city into a series of impressions consumed by readers.

Benjamin singles out "The Man of the Crowd" as a valuable text encapsulating both the comforts and limitations of this kind of fantasy. Initially the tale depicts a relatively unproblematic flânerie in action. For the first three pages, as he is safely ensconced behind the coffeehouse window, the narrator describes the different types of people who pass by outside: "noblemen, merchants, attorneys, tradesmen, stock-jobbers," clerks both "junior" and "upper," pickpockets, gamblers, dandies, military men, Jewish peddlers, beggars, invalids, servant girls, "women of the town of all kinds and of all ages," drunkards, "pie-men, porters, coal-heavers, sweeps; organ-grinders, monkey-exhibitors and ballad mongers, those who vended with those who sang; ragged artisans and exhausted laborers of every description."[4] But Benjamin also notes – unlike Baudelaire himself, who is determined to see the tale as a paradigm of the modern artist, the "eternal convalescent" who sees things intensely, as if for the first time – that its energy comes from the fact that the story documents a failure of urban physiognomy. When confronted by the sight of the old man, the narrator loses the flâneur's characteristic detachment and runs out of the coffeehouse in pursuit. What he sees up close puzzles him even more. The man is short, thin, and feeble, his clothes "filthy and ragged" yet "of beautiful texture." The narrator thinks he catches sight through the old man's coat – although he acknowledges that perhaps "my vision deceived me" – of a diamond and a dagger.[5] He resolves "to follow the stranger whithersoever he should go." Thus begins the relentless pursuit that lasts for almost twenty-four hours, a veritable marathon of stalking in which the narrator himself becomes more and more agitated as his quarry traverses the streets, changing direction on a whim, entering shops without any pretense of browsing, leading him in and out of a gin palace. As daybreak approaches, "with a mad energy," the old man leads the narrator back to the street on which he started, now thronging even more with the crowd. At this point the narrator gives up, deciding – as the conclusion of the story has it – that "This old man ... is the type and the genius of deep crime. He refuses to be alone. He is the man of the crowd." In an enigmatic allusion, the narrator goes on to link the man to the impenetrable heart of darkness of the modern world, summed up by a quotation he applies to the widely "unreadable" German translation of the *Hortulus Animae*: "es lässt sich nicht lesen [it does not let itself be read]."[6]

The first half of the story supports Benjamin's argument that the city dwellers of Europe's capitals in the nineteenth century constituted both an emergent "reading public," in that they were required to "read" and experience their surroundings like a text, and a body of mass consumers, who took in different aspects of social experience just as they browsed and purchased the vast array of goods on display. In fact, though, Benjamin contends that the particular genius of Poe's tale is that "it includes along with the earliest description of the flâneur the figuration of his end."[7] The increased size and rapidity of the crowds emphasized in the story dehumanize the people who constitute them, causing them to act mechanically and ensuring there is no place any more for a dawdler, an ambling seeker of the quick-fix emotional purchase that comes from being in the crowd. Their mechanical, uniform behavior effectively ensures, as Robert Byer has shown in a reading that builds on Benjamin's, that Poe brings a gothic sensibility to the depiction of the crowd unapparent to the same degree in his contemporaries. "The Man of the Crowd" presents the nineteenth-century crowd as an "uncanny spectacle."[8]

It is not the only occasion in Poe when we find a fascination with how the city crowd can act as one individual. In an earlier story, "The Unparalleled Adventure of One Hans Pfaall" (1835), a "vast crowd of people" watches a balloon ascend in Rotterdam. We are told that "in an instant," "ten thousand faces were upturned toward the heavens, ten thousand pipes descended simultaneously from the corners of ten thousand mouths, and a shout, which could be compared to nothing but the roaring of Niagara, resounded long, loudly and furiously, through all the city and through all the environs of Rotterdam."[9] This story provides the reverse of the perspective in "The Man of the Crowd," as it features the crowd united in viewing a single individual, who is made to seem even smaller and ridiculous than he already is, more isolated from what passes as normal behavior. Although Poe's fiction portrays the crowd much less frequently than that of a contemporary like Dickens – and indeed favors "other-worldly" or unidentifiably "ancient" settings rather than contemporary urban reality – this kind of sketch points to his status as an important nineteenth-century documenter of the urban mass.

Byer's reading of "The Man of the Crowd" is one of a whole series of sociologically inflected analyses that take their point of departure from Benjamin's and that value how the story reveals and critiques aspects of the scopic and material conditions of the modern city.[10] So many are there that Patricia Merivale has suggested that "The Man of the Crowd" almost parallels the contribution of "The Purloined Letter" to critical theory.[11] Among these readings is Tom Gunning's elaboration of Benjamin's idea that film was the perfect medium for a society conditioned by "perception in the form of shocks."[12] He argues that people were experiencing the excitement of city life – the teeming crowds, the goods in shops framed by brightly lit windows – in ways that prefigured the absorption of the viewer of film in the spectacle on screen. "The Man of the Crowd" might therefore fruitfully be read as a kind of dream of the future medium of cinema: the narrator begins in front of a large window frame watching a lit spectacle before becoming so entranced by it that he is compelled to enter the action himself.[13]

Building on Benjamin's famous description of the story as an "X-ray picture of a detective story," in which "the drapery represented by the crime has disappeared" and all that remains is "the mere armature...the pursuer, the crowd, and an unknown man," Dana Brand argues that "The Man of the Crowd" was a necessary first step in Poe's invention of one of the most enduring and popular genres to result from the increased urbanization of society in the nineteenth century: the detective story. As an "embryo" of detective fiction (a term that better describes what he believes Benjamin really means by "x-ray") "The Man of the Crowd" testifies to what Brand calls the "epistemological anxiety" provoked in the flâneur when confronted by "unprecedented and undefined" aspects of city life – the old man – which defeat his initial practice of reducing the inhabitants of the city to manageable types. Brand goes on to argue that the two elliptical concepts referred to at the end of the story – "deep crime" and illegibility – become more powerfully and graphically combined in two stories Poe wrote shortly after "The Man of the Crowd" that feature his detective Chevalier C. Auguste Dupin, "The Murders in the Rue Morgue" (1841) and "The Mystery of Marie Rôget" (1842), and which, along with "The Purloined Letter" (1845), inaugurated the genre of detective fiction.[14]

In the first two Dupin stories, readers are immediately aware that they are in a city far removed from the safe, legible, and predictable fantasy world of the city of the flâneur. In the brutally murdered corpses around which each story revolves we are given a precise vision of the kind of "deep crime" the narrator of "The Man of the Crowd" can only dimly apprehend. They show the violence and danger inherent in city living. The mother and daughter who are the victims in "The Murders in the Rue Morgue" are savagely attacked while getting ready for bed in a place one might ordinarily assume is perfectly safe: a locked room in an upper floor of their building. The eponymous victim in "The Mystery of Marie Rôget" (which Poe based on the real unsolved murder of Mary Cecilia Rogers in July 1841 in New York) disappears despite being in the very heart of a crowd – a fate that resonates powerfully with the kind of shocking urban mystery that is a common feature of our own media age. One newspaper states, "It is impossible that a person so well known to thousands as this young woman was, should have passed three blocks without someone having seen her." Dupin is unconvinced. On the contrary, he says, it is not just possible but "far more than probable, that Marie might have proceeded, at any given period, by any one of the many routes between her own residence and that of her aunt, without meeting a single individual whom she knew, or by whom she was known."[15] "The Murders in the Rue Morgue" details a similar failure of other people to assist the investigation. The neighbors who hear what they assume are the voices of the murderers of Mme. L'Espanaye and her daughter assume – naturally perhaps, since they are all of different nationalities themselves – that the ape's voice is a human speaking in a tongue they don't recognize.

By accenting the possible consequences of the anonymity the metropolis affords – an advantage to a criminal, a danger to others – Poe's newly created genre of detective fiction, Brand contends, is founded on exploiting the "aesthetic appeal of urban anxiety."[16] Yet the appearance of a detective in each story manages to keep this exposure to urban anxiety at an acceptable level by providing reassurance that the apparently illegible city ultimately can be mastered and read. Dupin is clearly a variation on the flâneur, as evidenced by his habit of going out at night and "roaming far and wide until a late hour, seeking amid the wild lights and shadows of the populous city that infinity of mental excitement which quiet observation can afford."[17] He has the flâneur's ability to read the city but has been able to hone his skills further and direct them toward a socially beneficial end. The narrator of "The Man of the Crowd" can plausibly be regarded as a prototypical detective, one who pursues his quarry through the mean streets of London in "caoutchouc overshoes" or "gumshoes."[18] Yet, when he is confounded by the "suspect's" idiosyncrasies, Dupin, a more advanced model of sleuth, can account for precisely "those elements of urban experience that appear as gaps in the reading of the flâneur." Where the flâneur's strategy is "to reduce the crowd to a set of types," to measure it against what is already known, the detective's is to assess the ways in which a crime differs from an ordinary robbery or murder. This development of the technique of urban reading means ultimately that while the detective inhabits a much more menacing and incomprehensible city than the flâneur, he too is "a reassuring figure."[19] Each type deploys his reading strategies to impose an overall, unifying vision on the chaotic elements of the city. The practice conforms to the panoptic model of disciplining a mass of people that Michel Foucault showed is at the heart of nineteenth-century structures of power. Everything that is hidden can be brought into the light by an all-seeing, policing gaze.

In some of the key works of what we might call his "urban crime fiction" – "The Man of the Crowd," "The Murders in the Rue Morgue," and "The Mystery of Marie Rôget" – Poe depicts the exciting and menacing aspects of urban reality as well as the methods of "reading" required to master its dangerous illegibility. Elsewhere in Poe is the sense that the city's chaotic energy can lure those who live in it into impulsive behavior. Where else would the "perverse" decision to confess to a murder a man has hidden successfully for years be made than when "bound[ing] like a madman through the crowded thoroughfares."[20] In "A Predicament" (1838), the urge to achieve a masterful overview of the city itself becomes fatally seductive. The pompous and self-consciously delusional narrator

(Poe's only female narrator) is overwhelmed by a sudden urge to climb a vast Gothic cathedral in Edinburgh: "I was seized with an uncontrollable desire to ascend the giddy pinnacle, and then survey the immense extent of the city." She manages to do it by standing on her black servant's back in order to reach the hole in the clock face at the top of the steeple tower. Soon, just like the narrator of "The Man of the Crowd," where the phrase is similarly portentous, she becomes "absorbed in contemplation" at "the glorious prospect below." So immersed in the spectacle is she, however, that she is decapitated by the gigantic minute hand, which pins her to the clock. Her fate is hubristic, and not just because it visits upon her the comeuppance her cruelty toward her servant, Pompey, demands (and that balances out the obvious racism that has disturbed some readers of the story). She needs to be punished for presuming she is entitled to a God's-eye view of the city rather than accepting her place amidst the chaos and squalor of its streets, for which she expressed her disgust at the beginning: "Men were talking. Women were screaming. Children were choking. Pigs were whistling. Carts they rattled. Bulls they bellowed. Cows they lowed. Horses they neighed. Cats they caterwauled. Dogs they danced."[21]

More broadly than those stories that specifically depict the crowd or the city, the urban context of Poe's fiction explains one of its most common structural and dramatic elements: its acute sense of the effects of proximity. Over and over again his stories revolve around a fascination between two men, which descends into either uncomfortable doubling or outright rivalry. This is clear in "The Man of the Crowd," of course, but also in "The Fall of the House of Usher" and "William Wilson." In "The Purloined Letter" – a Dupin detective story that eschews the urban template of the previous two stories – the obsession between the detective and the mysterious Minister D – lies behind the investigation. In some tales the proximity is clearly though implicitly the result of the realities of urban living. In the comic story "Why the Little Frenchman Wears his Hand in a Sling" the narrator is irritated to find he has a rival for his designs on his next-door neighbor, Mistress Treacle, in the figure of "the little ould furrener Frinchman that lives jist over the way, and that's a-oggling and a-goggling the houl day."[22] His attempts to warn him off, however, simply cause the rivals to become even closer, as the Frenchman ends up gripping the narrator's hand thinking it is Mistress Treacle's. Even in "Metzengerstein" (1835), which purports to be a historical account of an age-old dispute between two families in "the interior of Hungary," there is a reference to how "the inhabitants of the Castle Berlifitzing might look, from their lofty buttresses, into the very windows of the palace

Metzengerstein."[23] While probably intended as a metaphor to indicate
how obsessed with one another the families are, the image evokes a facet
of life in the time the story was written rather than when it is set – looking
through the windows of a neighbor's house.

To return to Poe's crime fiction, the proximity between city dwellers is
central to those stories that arguably figure as the origins of another line of
crime writing to have developed alongside the detective story: "noir" killer
fiction, or those accounts of depravity narrated by psychopaths who man-
age to seduce the reader into responding sympathetically – as perfected
100 years later by Jim Thompson. "The Tell-Tale Heart" (1843) is unforth-
coming about whether or not it is set in the city, and about the nature
of the relationship between the two men, but what seems intolerable to
the narrator is the sheer fact of his proximity to the old man with whom
he shares his home – an unbearable closeness conveyed by his conviction
that the old man's eye is always upon him. This is why he harasses then
murders him without ceremony, dismembers him, and buries him under
the floorboards. The immediate catalyst for the murder is the narrator's
fear that a neighbor will hear the sound of the man's beating heart as he is
persecuted. Sure enough, as soon as he has finished concealing the body,
the police arrive, having been alerted by a neighbor who has heard the old
man shriek. The proximity of others is what leads a deranged man to murder, but is also what causes him to be caught. A similar world seems to be
behind the events in "The Black Cat" (1843). After murdering his wife, the
narrator of that story is aware that he cannot remove the corpse "either by
day or by night, without the risk of being observed by the neighbors."[24]
His response is likewise to retreat further into the intimate spaces of his
own home and conceal the body in the walls of his cellar. Yet after inqui-
ries about the disappearance, and a search for his wife, both presumably
by neighbors, the police come to search his home and the wailing of the
cat – a metaphor for the difficulty of keeping secrets in the city – gives
it away.

Poe's stories suggest that the perpetration, concealment, and detection
of "deep crime" are indissociable from the modern urban environment.
To the list of peculiarly modern literary archetypes he was among the
first to create and that continue to strike a chord with readers nearly two
centuries later – the detective, the flâneur, the psychopath – we ought
therefore to add another: the menacing urban neighbor. Freud argued in
Civilization and its Discontents (1930) that the point of the commandment
to "love thy neighbor," the maxim that underscores modern society, is not
that the others with whom we share our space in modernity are lovable,

but precisely the contrary. They are loathsome, threatening, and would have "no hesitation in letting us gain some advantage or satisfy some desire."[25] To dilute this threat is exactly why we need to be commanded to love them. Freud's misanthropy here seems the consequence of writing in a chaotic modern urban environment, of taking for granted the tensions created by a vastly populated, aggressive, competitive, technological world – one portrayed with a powerful sense of immediacy almost a century earlier in the fiction of Edgar Allan Poe.

NOTES

1. Kevin J. Hayes, *Edgar Allan Poe* (London: Reaktion, 2009), 8.
2. Walter Benjamin, *Charles Baudelaire: A Lyric Poet in the Era of High Capitalism*, trans. Harry Zohn (London: Verso, 1983), 36.
3. Charles Baudelaire, *The Painter of Modern Life and Other Essays* (London: Phaidon, 1995), 9.
4. Edgar Allan Poe, *The Collected Works of Edgar Allan Poe*, ed. Thomas Ollive Mabbott, 3 vols. (Cambridge, MA: Belknap Press, 1969–78), vol. ii, 510.
5. Ibid., vol. ii, 511–12.
6. Ibid., vol. ii, 515.
7. Benjamin, *Charles Baudelaire*, 54.
8. Robert H. Byer, "Mysteries of the City: A Reading of Poe's 'The Man of the Crowd,'" in *Ideology and Classic American Literature*, ed. Sacvan Bercovitch and Myra Jehlen (New York: Cambridge University Press, 1986), 228.
9. Edgar Allan Poe, *Poetry and Tales*, ed. Patrick F. Quinn (New York: Library of America, 1984), 951.
10. Dana Brand, *The Spectator and the City: Fantasies of Urban Legibility in Nineteenth-Century England and America* (New York: Cambridge University Press, 1991); Morris Dickstein, "The City as Text: New York and the American Writer," *TriQuarterly* 83 (1991–2), 183–204; Monika M. Elbert, "'The Man of the Crowd' and the Man Outside the Crowd: Poe's Narrator and the Democratic Reader," *Modern Language Studies* 21 (1991), 16–30; Kevin J. Hayes, "Visual Culture and the Word in Edgar Allan Poe's 'Man of the Crowd,'" *Nineteenth-Century Literature* 56 (2002), 445–65; Tom McDonough, "The Crimes of the Flâneur," *October* 102 (2002), 101–22.
11. Patricia Merivale, "Gumshoe Gothics: Poe's 'The Man of the Crowd' and his Followers," in *Detecting Texts: The Metaphysical Detective Story from Poe to Postmodernism*, ed. Patricia Merivale and Susan Elizabeth Sweeney (Philadelphia: University of Pennsylvania Press, 1999), 105.
12. Walter Benjamin, *Illuminations*, trans. Harry Zohn (New York: Schocken, 1969), 171.
13. Tom Gunning, "Urban Spectatorship, Poe, Benjamin, and *Traffic in Souls* (1913)," *Wide Angle*, 19 (1997), 32.
14. Benjamin, *Charles Baudelaire*, 48; Brand, *Spectator and the City*, 88, 98.

15. Poe, *Collected Works*, vol. iii, 750.
16. Brand, *Spectator and the City*, 92.
17. Poe, *Collected Works*, vol. ii, 533.
18. Merivale, "Gumshoe Gothics," 109.
19. Brand, *Spectator and the City*, 98, 103.
20. Poe, *Collected Works*, vol. iii, 1226.
21. Ibid., vol. ii, 347.
22. Ibid., vol. ii, 464.
23. Ibid., vol. ii, 19.
24. Ibid., vol. iii, 856.
25. Sigmund Freud, *Civilization and Its Discontents*, trans. James Strachey (New York: Norton, 1989), 42.

CHAPTER 9

Curiosity

Lindsey Hursh

In *A Diary in America*, Captain Frederick Marryat recounts a conversation with a Bostonian about a mob's destruction of the Ursuline convent in Charlestown, Massachusetts in 1834. Puzzled why Americans, seemingly tolerant of different forms of worship, would destroy a religious edifice without reason, he learned that the mob merely sought to determine what was sealed inside. Marryat provides an insight into the character of the antebellum public: "Americans are excessively curious," he writes, "they cannot bear anything like a secret – that's *unconstitutional*."[1] Anything concealed from the public directly opposed the common man philosophy in Jacksonian America, which held that information should not be guarded by clergymen or scientists but should be made public so that average citizens could use that knowledge to better themselves. To become a "self-made man" – an expression coined during this period – one must first have access to all forms of information. Marryat suggests the Massachusetts mob's actions in Charlestown, illustrate the national conviction that the public should be granted equal opportunities, if not equal rights. Information kept from the public seemed decidedly un-American.

The years between the War of 1812 and the Civil War were defined partly by the public's insatiable desire for new information. Americans became obsessed with the belief that any obstacle, no matter how impressive, could be overcome with enough knowledge and determination. The Age of Jackson witnessed unprecedented territorial expansion and, with it, the acquisition of new natural resources and animals destined to become museum exhibits. Neil Harris explains: "Not only was the predisposition to accept the mechanically probable or the organically possible a result of changing technology and the growth of natural science, it was also a peculiarly patriotic position in Jacksonian America."[2] Public schools were erected; how-to manuals and scientific articles constituted the bulk of the country's literary diet; and Americans filed into lecture halls by the hundreds to learn the latest discoveries and technological developments.

Driven by curiosity, confident of their intellectual abilities, people expected lecturers and scientific articles to use technical jargon. Dense language provided authenticity, and the public demand for minute descriptions detailing intricate mechanical operations or biological processes governed presentational style. Museums were constructed or reconfigured to showcase the staggering number of new exhibits and to accommodate the expansion of lecture rooms. Technological advances led Americans to believe that "nothing mechanical was beyond the range of Nature's imagination."[3] And it was on this optimistic and curious mood that people like P. T. Barnum, Johann Maelzel, and Edgar Allan Poe capitalized.

A year after the destruction of the Ursuline convent, Maelzel's famous chess player was shown in Boston and P. T. Barnum's first successful exhibit toured New England. Joice Heth, a slave, was purported to be 161 years old. Yet her impressive age was not her attraction; the claim that she was George Washington's nurse made her an object of widespread curiosity. Though she had been exhibited prior to Barnum's tour, Barnum understood how to make her profitable. He distributed pamphlets catering to the public's demand for sensational detail, persuaded newspapers to elaborate on the pamphlets, and, when attendance waned, wrote a newspaper editorial claiming that Heth was a cleverly constructed automaton. Barnum watched his profits double as those who had already paid to see Heth once paid again to scrutinize her in light of this controversial information. Like other hoaxers, Barnum understood that the public was "more excited by controversy than by conclusiveness."[4]

Citizens of Jacksonian America had fought hard to ensure access to information and were eager for any opportunity to test their newfound knowledge. Popular writers also provided a welcome chance to pass judgment. The taste for exposure and problem solving appeared in American fiction as well. Harris identifies Edgar Allan Poe as the "preeminent practitioner" in this regard, the man who publicly exposed Maelzel's chess player as a fraud and who eventually orchestrated hoaxes of his own.[5] Many of Poe's works, if not designed as deliberate hoaxes, debunked hoaxes while expertly exploiting the paradoxical Jacksonian climate of skepticism and gullibility, creation and destruction.

The overarching plot of Poe's "The Man That Was Used Up" is a circular account of destruction and creation detailing the development of a public hero physically debilitated by battle and reassembled by his servant. General John A. B. C. Smith may be an amalgamation of Jackson and General Winfield Scott, but Poe's tale provides readers with far more than a satiric examination of a military hero; it encapsulates the atmosphere and temperament of the public during the Age of Jackson and adeptly illustrates the "wonderfully inventive age" in which the common man thrived. Like the mob that demolished the Ursuline convent, the narrator "cannot bear anything like a secret," for "the slightest appearance of mystery…puts [him] at once into a pitiable state of agitation." Poe's writing style complies with the public's demand for meticulous descriptions; the narrator states his "melancholy satisfaction in being minute," and describes General Smith from the texture and color of his hair to his "properly proportioned calf." The narrator first encounters the general at "some public meeting" where the two have a happily one-sided discussion. The narrator is not so much engaged in conversation as he is "instructed" by the general, and his delight at their unbalanced conversation reflects the common man's partiality to lectures. Again and again the general remarks on the brilliance of mechanical invention; he mentions railroads, steamboats, electromagnetics, and even foreshadows Poe's later balloon hoax with a comment on a passenger balloon that will soon run regular trips "between London and Timbuctoo." The general's lecture inflames rather than quells the curiosity of the narrator, who resolves to discover what constitutes the "remarkable something" that led him to scrutinize the general in the first place.[6]

The general is fashioned in the mold of the Barnumesque exhibit. That the narrator first meets the general at one public meeting and then seeks to discover what makes the general such an incredible specimen by attending others – a church service, a theatrical production, a soirée – underscores the public nature of an exhibit's introduction and undoing.[7] Here we also gain insight into Barnum's success, as the objects of his showcases – first Heth and later the Feejee mermaid – engaged the public's desire for controversy by calling on audiences to determine whether his curious specimens were what they were purported to be. Barnum's exhibits appealed to the public primarily as opportunities to scrutinize and pass judgment. The general's status as a military hero becomes secondary to the search for what constitutes the transfixing quality of the man who holds the title. The overly enthusiastic refrain from the narrator's would-be informants, that "we live in a wonderfully inventive age," works on the narrator's temper as a Barnum advertisement, provoking him to embark on an increasingly agitated mission to pinpoint the general's "odd air of *je ne sais quoi*." The narrator's quest inverts the process of viewing, judging, and publicly dissecting to discern the truth of an exhibit. Instead, he observes the spectacle of the general and then witnesses the construction of his disassembled parts. Unlike "Maelzel's Chess-Player" (1836), in which Poe reveals that the automaton is more man than machine, in "The Man That Was Used Up" the narrator finds his object to be more machine than man.

The inquisitive narrator in "The Man That Was Used Up" is not the victim of a deliberate hoax, but rather a witness to the debunking of a captivating automaton. In his tale, Poe reverses the circumstances of the exposure of Maelzel's chess player. The chess player was believed to be a man-made mechanical marvel, a work of technology, while the general appears to be the ideal masculine figure, a work of nature. The opposite is true in both cases. As Poe reveals, Maelzel's automaton was a mechanical façade whose chess moves were controlled by a man concealed within the machine. Conversely, Poe's general is merely the illusion of a perfect male figure, as he is composed, from his legs to his palate, of mechanical parts. In both works, Poe illustrates the deceptive nature of appearances, a theme to which he would repeatedly return and that he explores most thoroughly in "The Spectacles."

Simpson, the narrator of "The Spectacles," is considerably nearsighted, yet his poor vision does not prevent him from experiencing love at first sight when, at the theater, he spots "the beau ideal of [his] wildest and most enthusiastic visions," whom we eventually discover when the story's hoax is debunked is his great-great-grandmother.[8] The possibility of unknowingly marrying a grandparent is ludicrous to a modern reader; however, the idea is hardly more incredible than Barnum's promotion of Joice Heth as George Washington's nurse, or Richard Locke's *New York Sun* moon hoax, or, indeed, Poe's "Balloon Hoax," published less than one month after "The Spectacles."

As every successful hoax does, "The Spectacles" offers exceptionally detailed descriptions. Simpson insists that his story requires him to be "somewhat minute." Embarking on a narcissistic report of his physical features, Simpson reveals that he suffers from weak eyesight but refuses to wear glasses because he does not wish to disfigure his countenance. Simpson's stubborn refusal is a rejection of the dominant "self-made man" emphasis of Jacksonian America, which insisted that citizens pursue every option, especially those made available by technological progress, to better themselves. Unlike General Smith, whose artificial parts constitute a seemingly natural masculine cohesiveness, the addition of eyeglasses indicates to Simpson a masculine deficiency. His vision problems are not successfully hidden from the public: he eventually discovers that his bad eyesight is "notorious." His aversion to glasses reveals his true deficiency: his vain refusal to indulge in the self-made man philosophy. Poor vision does not prevent Simpson from noticing a woman seated in an opera box well above the narrator's position, nor does it prevent him from perceiving her clothing and jewelry in incredible detail. The illogicality of Simpson's remarkably thorough observation is not a blunder by Poe, but serves instead to illustrate a number of crucial aspects about the conditions and temperament of Jacksonian America.

Poe's minute descriptions were expected by the reading public and imperative to the staging of a successful hoax. From his spot on the floor, Simpson should not have been able to detect the "admirable roundness of the wrist...well set off by a bracelet...which was ornamented and clasped by a magnificent *aigrette* of jewels," especially since we later find him so nearsighted he is incapable of identifying the woman's age when he is standing beside her.⁹ "The Spectacles" emphasizes the importance Poe's contemporaries placed on detailed description and lampoons the concept of love at first sight, which had no place in an increasingly science-based world. Indeed, in the first paragraph of the story, Simpson defends love at first sight as a valid study of the fictitious science of "magneto-aesthetics." His words both reflect "the rapid diffusion of science" into popular reading material in the middle nineteenth century and highlight how hoax victims were duped by scientific terminology. Curious individuals accustomed to examining the truth or validity of objects presented to them became "easy targets for pseudoscientific explanations."¹⁰

If Simpson is representative of the wider (male) American public, then his comments indicate the prevalent view of a woman's place in society. Madame Lalande's position in an isolated, elevated box contrasts Simpson's immersion among his fellow common men on the public floor and illustrates that women were still relegated to their pedestals. Yet Poe once more subverts this cultural doctrine by transforming the elderly woman from inert spectacle to dynamic hoaxer.

Madame Lalande, like General Smith, is a character made in the mold of the Barnumesque exhibit. Her age is approximately the same as Joice Heth's actual age when Barnum exhibited her. In the manner of one viewing an exhibit, the narrator observes Lalande from afar and believes her to be the talk of his community. As Barnum and other exhibitors employed friends and "experts" to verify an exhibit's legitimacy, so Lalande petitions Simpson's friend to assist in the deception. Deliberately perpetuating Simpson's misconception of her age and identity, she gives him a miniature of herself made when she was twenty-seven. As the aggravating fragmented refrain "he's the man – " goads the narrator of "The Man That Was Used Up" into action, the miniature functions like a Barnum advertisement by inciting Simpson's excitement over their upcoming marriage.

When the narrator finally puts on the glasses provided by Lalande, he suddenly perceives that the physical qualities he once believed to be naturally youthful and therefore attractive were merely components of the deception: the blush of her cheeks is created by rouge, her black hair is a wig, her teeth are dentures, and her figure is nothing more than "an entire universe of bustle." Unlike "The Man That Was Used Up," in which we witness a man's construction from detached parts, "The Spectacles" depicts a woman's deconstruction into separate pieces. The tale leaves her disassembled or, more accurately, revealed. Both stories suggest that appearances are deceptive, a crucial message in a period that gave rise to countless public frauds and hoaxes. Yet unlike "The Man That Was Used Up," "The Spectacles" is a story of a deliberate hoax played on a person who, because of a significant character flaw, deserves to be tricked.

The artificiality of Madame Lalande's appearance is not necessitated by physical injuries sustained in military battles, but is encouraged by a society that viewed indicators of aging tantamount to physical deformity. Instead of relegating the elderly Lalande to the fringes of society, Poe creates an active player whose age does not hinder her from orchestrating a complicated hoax. By transposing reader expectations of an aged woman, Poe questions the public's conception and treatment of aging. The elderly Lalande does not require the necessary aid of glasses that Simpson insists "impresses every feature with an air . . . of age" but the twenty-two-year-old Simpson does. Instead of conforming to the role of impotent exhibit that society expected and Joice Heth symbolized, Lalande positions Simpson as the victim of a hoax.

A similar reversal from powerless spectacle to active participant occurs in Poe's "Hop-Frog." However, in this third tale, the justification of the hoax and its result is much more sinister than the one featured in "The Spectacles." The deception Lalande orchestrates is undoubtedly a reprisal for Simpson's stubbornness, yet the punishment is comical and does not have serious repercussions for Simpson, as his marriage is merely another facet of the hoax and not legal or binding. Conversely, the motivation for the hoax in "Hop-Frog" is a desire to exact punishment for the repeated abuse and exploitation of a human exhibit and culminates in the hoax victim's death.

By the time Poe published "Hop-Frog" in 1849, disorganized displays of exhibits had been replaced by more elaborate and cohesive collections of curiosities, frequently dubbed "freak shows" by exhibitors. Such collections featured people purported to hail from strange locations and often either deformed or disfigured. The general public was as intrigued by the "what is its" as the pseudoscientists were, and debate "concerning whether a particular exhibit was a new species or a *lusus naturae* raged." Previous public opinion about curiosities, most especially those who were deformed, reflected the Baconian belief that outward deformity mirrored an inward "ill-nature."[11]

As more and more curiosities were displayed to the public and exploration uncovered new animal species and tribes of Native Americans to display, public opinion shifted to view curiosities as part of "god's great order of creatures and subject to scientific study and classification."[12] When "Hop-Frog" appeared in print, deformed dwarfs were not outside the realm of typical curiosities, as they had long been staples of exhibits and regular curiosities of Barnum's famous museum. Usually an exotic background was fabricated for dwarfs and other oddities, and "promoters told the audience that the exhibit came from a mysterious part of the world – darkest Africa, the wilds of Borneo, a Turkish harem, an ancient Aztec kingdom."[13] In Poe's story the disabled dwarf and fool of the king, christened Hop-Frog because of his deformed legs, comes from "some barbarous region...that no person ever heard of – a vast distance from the court of our king."[14] Bestowed on the king as a present by one of his generals, Hop-Frog develops a close bond with Trippetta, a midget with proportional features. In terms of appearance and function, Trippetta parallels one of Barnum's most successful curiosities, Tom Thumb.

Little people were exploited by royal courts centuries before Poe created Hop-Frog and Trippetta or Barnum exhibited Tom Thumb. Poe draws upon historical accounts of such exploitation, yet his tale also capitalizes on the resurged public interest in little people. Due in part to Barnum's promotion of Tom Thumb and the Jacksonian rejection of Baconian intolerance, dwarfs were en vogue in the mid-nineteenth century and tiny Thumb was "just the sort of oddity suited to an optimistic and benevolent society bent on showing Nature's bounty, not her nightmares."[15] Like the fictional Trippetta, Thumb was normally proportioned and entertained his spectators by singing and dancing. He became the much publicized "petted darling of the English peerage and the royal court" during Barnum's 1844 European tour, just as Trippetta is "universally admired and petted" in her king's court.

If Trippetta represents a Thumb-like oddity who encourages spectator benevolence by showcasing nature's bounty, Hop-Frog is nature's nightmare and provokes audience malevolence. The incongruous treatment of Hop-Frog and Trippetta illustrates the paradoxical emotions that freaks inspired. Though many spectators saw these "others" as nature's gifts,

Figure 9.1 *Tom Thumb, Full-Length Portrait, Facing Front, Standing on Table with Tablecloth*, undated daguerreotype. Library of Congress, Prints and Photographs Division, Washington, DC (reproduction number: LC–USZ62–109908).

human oddities were still not accepted as members of society. Articles published as late as 1847 reveal a persistent intolerance of deformed people. *The Herald of Truth* asserts, "Everything in nature is beautiful, and whatever is ugly or disagreeable is unnatural."[16] This blatantly contradictory statement and the way in which Poe presents the conflicting attitudes toward Hop-Frog and Trippetta reflect the divided state of the public mind about nature's oddities. Rather than force Hop-Frog to amuse his guests like a typical court fool or Barnum oddity, the tyrannical king retains Hop-Frog in an advisory capacity because he is "so inventive in the way of getting up pageants, suggesting novel characters, and arranging costume, for masked balls, that nothing could be done, it seems, without his assistance."[17] Nevertheless, his value to the king is still primarily "a dwarf to laugh at," and the king is merciless in his treatment of Hop-Frog, forcing him to drink despite a known intolerance of alcohol and humiliating Trippetta in an attempt to injure Hop-Frog. Such cruelty prompts Hop-Frog to devise a brutal hoax that presents the king and his ministers as chained beasts to incite terror among the king's masqueraded guests, which results in the fiery demise of the king and his men. Hop-Frog's transformation is far more dramatic than Madame Lalande's, as he moves from derided freak to potent destroyer.

Instead of employing limited first person narration to present a clear Barnumesque exhibit with which the narrator and subsequently the readers become obsessed, the omniscient first person narration in "Hop-Frog" requires readers to determine the roles and motivations of the characters for themselves. With his fondness for practical jokes and tricks, the king appears to be the likely candidate for the hoaxer, fixing Hop-Frog and Trippetta as the exhibits. Yet repeated descriptions of the king as "fat," coupled with the bizarrely technical observation that he has a large "protuberance of his stomach and a constitutional swelling of the head," indicate that he too may be cast as a Barnumesque exhibit, for along with dwarfs, fat men were regular exhibits at Barnum's museum. The king and his advisors are outfitted as orangutans, also frequently displayed at oddity collections, in tight-fitting underclothes covered with tar and flax. Robert Bogdan describes how, clad "in a style that was compatible with the story, the exhibit would behave consistently with the front" and was frequently chained "allegedly to protect the audience from the beast before them."[18]

As instructed by Hop-Frog, the pretended orangutans rush into the hall "with savage cries," rattling the chains that aid in the deception and serve Hop-Frog's ultimate purpose of hanging them from the chandelier. That Hop-Frog is the creator and coordinator of the charade and ultimately the murderer of the supposed beasts challenges the public's understanding of freaks as impotent spectacles and situates him closer to the role of hoaxer. Yet it is the king's powerful position as a monarch and his exploitation of colonized dwarfs that casts him as a ruthless exhibitor who uses freaks to reinforce his dominion. Moreover, the king's role as a sedentary despot, manifested by physical rotundity, is juxtaposed with Hop-Frog's sagacity and sharp intellect, manifested by his physical dexterity and "muscular power." Thus, Poe subtly plays with the idea that appearances reflect inner nature: though Hop-Frog is victimized by the "oily" king, he is nonetheless capable of burning his tormentor alive. The ambiguity of roles in "Hop-Frog" anticipates the burgeoning of a modern moral consciousness that opposes profiting from deformed, disabled, or other marginalized people.

Contrary to "The Man That Was Used Up" and "The Spectacles," "Hop-Frog" contains little humor. Though typically and rightly classified as a revenge tale, "Hop-Frog" nevertheless addresses the hoaxing phenomenon and responds to the popularization of "freak shows" with a seriousness that reflects the gravity of the story's subject matter. At the time of its publication, hoaxing had gradually moved away from featuring fantastical moon men and automata and toward the display of humans. The public was not called upon to determine the likelihood of a balloon trip crossing the Atlantic in three days, but prompted to decide the place and purpose of society's others. Underlying each of Poe's stories is the principle with which the Jacksonian public was well acquainted, that appearances are deceiving. Aware of this truism, the contemporary public nevertheless remained curious. Just as the desire for information played an integral part in the destruction of the Ursuline convent, so is it a catalyst for the action in all three stories. "The Man That Was Used Up" features a narrator so consumed with curiosity that he resorts to physical violence when his quest for information is impeded. In "The Spectacles," Simpson's excessive interest in Madame Lalande prompts him to willingly violate social mores by professing his love for her in a letter when he fails to find a more proper means of introduction. Seemingly benign, the word "curiosity" sometimes masked more negative impulses.

The role of curiosity in "Hop-Frog" echoes the rationale for the mob's actions in Massachusetts and explores the tendency to use curiosity to obscure malicious motivations. Though curiosity leads to the demolition of the Ursuline convent in Marryat's account, the "mob was actuated by a complex of feelings: idealism and materialism, patriotism and bigotry." First, the members of the mob believed that a mysterious woman was being held against her will in the convent and sought to free her. Also, the Protestant mob viewed Catholicism itself as mysterious and secretive, and this perception "conflicted with the prevailing ethos of practicality, openness, and materialism."[19] However, the most significant reason the Ursuline convent was targeted was because the Catholic Church seemed to patriotic common men to mirror a monarchy, which was severely antithetical to antebellum American ideology. Just as the Catholic faith resembled a monarchy to the Protestant public, so is the heinous character in "Hop-Frog" portrayed as a despotic king who delights in the subjugation of others and whose destruction is painted as an unfortunate consequence of curiosity. Hop-Frog assures the watching crowd that if "only [he can] get a good look at them, [he] can soon tell who they are" and, with the appearance of one examining a curiosity, Hop-Frog thrusts a torch at them "as though endeavoring to discover who they were."[20] Under the guise of inquisitiveness, Hop-Frog destroys eight men. Though "curiosity" was claimed to be the reason people destroyed a convent, participated in hoaxes, and waited to see the newest oddity, Poe indicates in his stories that curiosity was often the pretext for defending unhealthy obsessions, orchestrating frauds, and participating in the exploitation of disfigured people.

NOTES

1. Frederick Marryat, *A Diary in America With Remarks on Its Institutions* (New York: William H. Colyer, 1839), 28.
2. Neil Harris, *Humbug: The Art of P. T. Barnum* (Chicago: University of Chicago Press, 1973), 73.
3. Ibid.
4. Ibid., 23.
5. Ibid., 85.
6. Edgar Allan Poe, *The Collected Works of Edgar Allan Poe*, ed. Thomas Ollive Mabbott, 3 vols. (Cambridge, MA: Belknap Press, 1969–78), vol. ii, 381.
7. Jonathan Elmer, *Reading at the Social Limit: Affect, Mass Culture, and Edgar Allan Poe* (Stanford: Stanford University Press, 1995), 49.
8. Poe, *Collected Works*, vol. iii, 889.
9. Ibid., vol. iii, 890.
10. Donald Zochert, "Science and the Common Man in Ante-Bellum America," in *Science in America Since 1820*, ed. Nathan Reingold (New York: Science History Publications, 1976), 20; Harris, *Humbug*, 73.
11. Robert Bogdan, *Freak Show: Presenting Human Oddities for Amusement and Profit* (Chicago: University of Chicago Press, 1988), 27; "Deformity a Sign of Ill-Nature," *New-England Galaxy* 2 (1819), 188.
12. Bogdan, *Freak Show*, 27.
13. Ibid., 105.
14. Poe, *Collected Works*, vol. iii, 1346.
15. Harris, *Humbug*, 49.
16. "Beauty and Deformity," *Herald of Truth* 1 (1847), 22.
17. Poe, *Collected Works*, vol. iii, 1347.
18. Bogdan, *Freak Show*, 105.
19. Theodore M. Hammett, "Two Mobs of Jacksonian Boston: Ideology and Interest," *Journal of American History* 62 (1976), 847–8.
20. Poe, *Collected Works*, vol. iii, 1353.

CHAPTER 10

Alcohol, Addiction, and Rehabilitation

Paul Fisher

When Edgar Allan Poe took the Sons of Temperance pledge in Richmond, Virginia in August 1849, the local *Banner of Temperance* hoped that this "pungent and forcible" writer's pen might "sometimes be employed" on behalf of alcohol abstinence.[1] Poe's fiction, however, had already dynamically engaged questions of drink, notably in the early 1840s, during the heyday of the Sons of Temperance's immediate precursor, the Washingtonian movement. The Washingtonians, founded in Baltimore in 1840, spearheaded a secular, charismatic, largely working-class temperance crusade that swept the northeastern United States, franchising hundreds of local societies and claiming more than a million members by 1842.[2] In 1843, Poe even considered joining at a point when, as David Reynolds has observed, the movement dominated the American popular landscape and offered Poe compelling literary opportunities.[3] Modeling "The Black Cat" (1843) on a temperance tale, Poe went on to write in, through, and against recognizable – and recognizably Washingtonian – temperance modes. Yet the Washingtonians provide an illuminating context for evaluating Poe's multifaceted relation to alcohol not only because of their kinship to Poe's sensibilities but also because of their profoundly different assumptions. If Poe's relation to antebellum temperance was complicated, movements like Washingtonianism proved profoundly inconsistent and self-contradictory, providing Poe discursive space for a deep critique of contemporary American attitudes toward alcohol, addiction, and rehabilitation.

The irony of Poe's joining the Sons of Temperance just a month before his drinking-related death in 1849 pales beside the many paradoxes of his larger relation to alcohol. Poe's lifetime coincided with huge cultural shifts in American alcohol consumption as well as the rise of powerful nineteenth-century temperance movements. Poe was born in Boston in 1809, just four years before the first major American temperance organization, the Massachusetts Society for the Suppression of Intemperance, was founded there in 1813. He began his alcohol addiction during the "great whiskey glut" of the 1820s, witnessed the confusing teetotalism controversies of the 1830s, and reached the height of his literary career when competing temperance ideologies and institutions dominated American popular culture in the 1840s. What's more, all his life Poe was bombarded with the contradictions inherent in both the period's heavy alcohol use and the antialcohol movement's crusade to combat drink's social ills – with devastating consequences for Poe's personal life but with highly fruitful implications for his fiction. Poe's alcohol tales treat addiction with a degree of psychological sophistication rare among his contemporaries – his idiosyncratic, critical, and illuminating portrayals of drink springing from his lifetime of hard experience.

A distorted account of Poe's drinking perpetrated partly by Rufus Wilmot Griswold, Poe's early inimical biographer, has been largely corrected, making possible a less judgmental and more accurate evaluation of Poe's alcoholism.[4] Still, Poe's serious drinking problem, elaborately documented in the biographical materials, becomes legible only when we acknowledge the degree to which Poe's addiction coincided with his cultural context, owed to it, and is fully comprehensible only through it. Correlations between Poe's drinking and contemporary cultural practices prove both numerous and illuminating, linking Poe not only to the marginalized world of scapegoated and deviant "drunkards" but also to the alcohol-related contradictions and confusions of mainstream antebellum society.

In historical context, Poe's drinking looks less deviant than tragically normative. For example, when Harriet L'Estrange Usher, an actor friend of Poe's mother, Elizabeth Poe, fed the Poe children "liberally with bread-soaked gin," administering "gin and other spirituous liquors, with sometimes laudanum" to put them to sleep, her actions might appear to originate from the chaotic, dysfunctional, bohemian context often associated with Poe's theatrical parents.[5] Alcohol historians assert, however, that, during Poe's childhood, "virtually everyone drank virtually all the time," and that "white males were taught to drink as children, even as babies," their parents hoping that gradual exposure would keep their sons from becoming alcoholics – a set of good intentions and cultural presuppositions further illustrated by Usher's insistence that she fed the children gin "to make them strong and healthy."[6]

Traditional Anglo-American beliefs about the health-giving qualities of alcohol, though challenged by doctors as early as the 1720s, persisted well into Poe's lifetime. Philadelphia physician Benjamin Rush's influential treatise attacking distilled spirits on medical grounds, *An Inquiry into*

the Effects of Ardent Spirits upon the Human Body and Mind (1794), also
catalogued, by way of disproof, the many perceived medicinal uses of spirits (e.g., protection against cold and hot weather, cure of dyspepsia, use as
a purgative); he continued to recommend beer, wine, hard cider, and other
fermented beverages, as well as weak rum punch and opium. In spite of
rare medical proscriptions against alcohol – usually American popular culture depicted doctors as hopeless souses – Poe's early life unfolded during
a period that W. J. Rorabaugh has famously described as the "Alcoholic
Republic," an era when alcohol dominated American daily life. As historian Jack Blocker has pointed out, "alcoholic beverages were a staple
of daily diet and represented the principal form of liquid nourishment"
when water was often unsafe, and milk, tea, and coffee rare or expensive.[7]
Even Poe's preferred drink of corn whiskey (his "favorite tipple" according
to Robert DeUnger) placed him squarely in the mainstream of American
experience, not its fringe, during a time when whiskey had supplanted
rum as the cheapest and most available drink in the United States. This
"whiskey glut," according to Blocker, compounded "existing conditions
and traditional attitudes" to send the "per capita consumption soaring."[8]
Cheap and abundant liquor, cultural biases that alcohol was healthful,
ubiquitous and coercive customs of hospitality, and a lack of traditional
inhibitions against overindulgence all created devastating social circumstances for Poe, who apparently inherited a susceptibility to alcohol, as the
"too free use of the Bottle" was, according to Poe's uncle, William Poe, "a
great enemy to our family."[9]

That Poe's letters contain many minimizations and denials of his drinking, sometimes surprisingly corroborated by outside affidavits, illuminates
other crucial aspects of antebellum alcohol usage. Although such evidence
is interpretable as Poe's alcoholic denial – or the byproduct of his many
well-intentioned bouts of abstinence – these instances also document nineteenth-century America's inconsistent and shifting definitions of sobriety.
Early temperance advocates, following Benjamin Rush, forbade only the use
of distilled spirits; later movements insisted on teetotalism, abstinence that
included fermented beverages such as beer, wine, and cider. For temperance movements, this controversy largely resolved by the mid-1830s, when
most societies endorsed the "long" or "teetotal" pledge.[10] Yet in everyday
American life, such confusions persisted: Poe's protestation to Joseph Evans
Snodgrass in 1841 of his "occasional use of cider, with the hope of relieving
a nervous attack" fits into this category of hopeful, medicinal ambiguity.
Also, in the antebellum period, definitions of excess or intemperance were
conflicted or in flux – habitual use and binge drinking (what observers

often called Poe's "sprees," employing a slang term newly minted for the period's alcohol excesses) being variously defined. When Poe insisted, in the same letter, that at "no period of my life was I ever what men call intemperate. I never was in the *habit* of intoxication. I never drunk drams, etc" – he was not merely dissimulating or prevaricating but also confronting deep inconsistencies in popular standards.[11]

Such contextualizations are not meant to dismiss Poe's frequent distortions and outright lies about his drinking or to suggest that he was not what we would now describe as an alcoholic. Yet Poe repeatedly demonstrated a consciousness of his society's unstable medical, moral, and social definitions of drinking. Antebellum America remained conflicted about definitions of sobriety and showed itself capable of opportunistically and quixotically changing its norms, at the same time tarring drunkards with full moral responsibility for their addictions. Moreover, Poe's habits developed in a context in which the temperance movement, as Michael Warner has persuasively argued, virtually "*invented* addiction."[12]

During Poe's lifetime, indeed, temperance burgeoned into one of the most dramatically successful of American reform movements; antiliquor campaigns made deep inroads into the country's heavy drinking habits, prompting a reduction in the absolute alcohol consumption per capita by more than half, according to one estimate, between 1830 and 1840.[13] At the same time, temperance successfully branded drunkards as social deviants. As Steven Mintz has argued, antebellum reform channeled deep anxieties about social disorder and "moral dissolution – debauchery, drunkenness, and various forms of impulsive, vicious, and unrestrained behavior" by relentlessly cataloguing "categories of people incapable of self-discipline, such as *addicts* and *alcoholics*."[14] Poe's often conspicuous public drinking made him a special target, exemplum, and scapegoat of temperance attacks – notably Thomas Dunn English's fictional caricature of Poe, against which the writer won his famous libel case in 1846. Over his career, Poe accrued plentiful reasons to distrust and resent temperance advocates' harsh appraisals of alcoholics as "wife-beaters, thugs, murderers, and loafers."[15] Even a relatively tolerant movement such as the Washingtonians could blast and demonize Poe, such as when Edmund Burke condemned Poe's appearance at the Boston Lyceum in 1845: "he should bow down his head with shame at the thought that he, in this day of light, presented himself before a moral and intelligent audience *intoxicated!*" – on this occasion, Poe was not even drunk.[16]

This attack on Poe demonstrates that, even during their short heyday in the 1840s, Washingtonian societies were far from unitary or homogeneous;

and that they had not entirely shaken off American evangelicals' tendency to stigmatize drinkers as sinners. Moreover, characteristic Washingtonian innovations, insofar as they can be generalized, create contradictory possibilities for interpretation. Recent historians have emphasized the values of egalitarianism, tolerance, reason, and personal responsibility in a movement that foregrounded "moral suasion" and offered social support to reforming alcoholics. In this rationalist, secular, and individualist-moralist mode, Washingtonian ideology, despite the movement's mostly working-class roots, remained consistent with temperance as "quintessential middle-class reform," relying on "the theme of self-control that lay at the core of middle-class identity in the nineteenth century."[17] Other commentators, however, have emphasized the Washingtonians' penchant for dramatic, lachrymose confession and histrionic spectacle. Washingtonians conducted "experience meetings" that followed charismatic Methodist models of revivalism; their gatherings amounted to working-class "raucous affairs, with minstrel acts, comic songs, and jokes bandied about in the language of the streets," with Washingtonian lodges virtually recreating "taverns without alcohol." Washingtonian leader John Bartholomew Gough vividly embodied these sensational aspects; Gough, a charismatic orator and onetime actor, terrified his listeners with stage melodrama and penny-press tales, "spine-tingling accounts of alcohol-induced crimes and horrid visions spawned of delirium tremens."[18]

Such dualities and dialectics in the Washingtonian movement, however, represented not only competing visions of addiction and rehabilitation but also deeply contradictory, often class-based constructions of selfhood, and such contradictions emerged strongly in contemporary accounts. Temperance writer Timothy Shay Arthur's admiring sketches of Washingtonian experience meetings, collected in *Six Nights with the Washingtonians* (1842), emphasized "reasoning and persuasion" as well as sentimental sympathy in the society's rehabilitation of drunkards.[19] Likewise, the young Abraham Lincoln, in his *Address Delivered before the Springfield Washingtonian Temperance Society* (1842), saw rational-sentimental Washingtonian moral suasion as capable of transforming a suffering "victim of intemperance" into a tearful "redeemed specimen of long lost humanity": "how easily it is all done, once it is resolved to be done; how simple his language, there is a logic and an eloquence in it, that few, with human feelings can resist."[20] In praising such aspects of Washingtonianism, Arthur and Lincoln identified sentiment and logic as allied and effective modes of rehabilitation and posited a self capable of transformational improvement.

In contrast, Poe in his fiction gravitated to what David Reynolds has termed "dark temperance," narratives that highlighted drink-induced crime, murder, and mayhem and that implied a very different kind of moral actor. Thus Poe's narrator in "The Black Cat," far from embodying rational self-determination, evinces chilling *illogic*; he longs for "some intellect more calm, more logical, and far less excitable" than his own to make sense of the horrific events that unfold. In the story, an apparently gentle man, gripped by drink and dark obsessions, gouges out the eye of a beloved pet cat and strangles it, and finally buries an axe in his wife's skull. His only ostensible logic is employed in "the task of concealing her body": whether to mince the corpse, incinerate it, or wall it up in the cellar. The narrator pursues this last method painstakingly, with cold, meticulous attention to techniques of masonry. His obsessive logic becomes almost more disturbing than that in "The Cask of Amontillado" (1846), another Poe alcohol tale, in which the narrator, Montresor, immures a living victim. Poe's unnamed narrator in "The Black Cat" strikes closer to home; no historical Italian aristocrat, he is a contemporary American husband narrating a "homely narrative," a "series of mere household events."²¹

Though published in the mainstream *Saturday Evening Post* in August 1843, "The Black Cat" closely resembles the sensational tales printed in the temperance papers or the penny press of the early 1840s. Like Walt Whitman's *Franklin Evans, or The Inebriate* (1842), it traces an alcoholic's horrific descent from mild citizen to brutal murderer. Poe's tale, however, betrays the special affinities of the Washingtonian mode, then at its zenith. The narrator initially demonstrates the sentimental Washingtonian subject's "docility" and "tenderness of heart." In the usual Washingtonian narrative of degeneration, his moral temperament degrades through the explicit "instrumentality of the Fiend Intemperance": He grows "more moody, more irritable, and more regardless of the feelings of others," verbally then physically abusing his wife. Poe's confessional narrator even models crucial Washingtonian audience responses in the "tears streaming from my eyes" at his own crimes.

Yet Poe's tale, quickly veering from ruminative to murderous, may not ultimately elicit readers' compassion, and his narrator remains oddly resistant to life-changing Washingtonian sentiment. Although Poe enthusiastically supplies many dark temperance features – confession, sensation, crime, horror, madness, and atrocity – he pointedly omits obvious moralizing, anything equivalent to *Franklin Evans*'s concluding chapter, in which Whitman heavy-handedly underscores his antiliquor lesson and invokes the "holy cause" of temperance.²² Stripped of the moral commentary that often laces dark temperance texts, Poe's brilliantly stark, violent, and nightmarish tale lacks any implied counter-narrative of redemption and thus seems to present "little but Horror." His narrator fittingly begins his tale ripe for the gallows, his crimes already (literally) set in stone, with no possibility for a tearful epiphany, breakdown, confession, and pledge signing to effect a Washingtonian transformation.

Indeed, for all its Washingtonian inflections, "The Black Cat" subverts rather than endorses Washingtonian methods and presuppositions. All dark temperance narratives of the 1840s, in a sense, counteracted the more tolerant, rationalist, and transformational aspirations of Washingtonian ideology. Designed to frighten but also entertain, such morality tales actually provided a skewed and highly inconvenient morality. If human nature as well as alcoholic excess really lent itself to such horrific crimes – even if drinkers were not sinners, monsters, or victims of the rum sellers, as previous temperance advocates believed – how could sympathy, moral suasion, sober fellowship, and self-reliance "cure" them? In his temperance best seller of 1854, *Ten Nights in a Bar-Room and What I Saw There*, Timothy Shay Arthur, by then disillusioned with Washingtonian optimism, exposed this very contradiction, deploying Poe-like atrocities to advocate for complete alcohol prohibition.

In 1843, however, Poe's gruesome tale countered Washingtonian rehabilitation narratives for quite different reasons. If earlier sentimental temperance tales such as Harriet Beecher Stowe's "The Drunkard Reclaimed" (1839) had insisted that alcoholics were redeemable, Poe's dark temperance skepticism radically undercut Washingtonian assumptions of drunkards' rational persuadability. Indeed, when Poe's unstable narrator, who considers himself "above the weakness of seeking to establish a sequence of cause and effect, between the disaster and the atrocity," murders his favorite cat, he declares, "*because* I knew that it had loved me, and because I felt it had given me no reason for offence; – hung it *because* I knew that in so doing I was committing a sin." In other words, the narrator commits atrocities not only because of alcohol but also "the spirit of PERVERSENESS." This perversity he further claims to be "one of the indivisible primary faculties, or sentiments, which give direction to the character of Man."

So unreliable a narrator may not be expected to plumb his own motivations, but Poe expands on this psychological paradox in a later tale, "The Imp of the Perverse" (1845), in which he invokes the contemporary pseudoscience of phrenology to posit a "radical, primitive, and irreducible sentiment" fundamental to human beings. Rationality cannot explain this urge, Poe's narrator insists: we fall into certain irrational actions "merely because we feel that we should *not*. Beyond or behind this, there is no intelligible principle." Phrenologists, along with "all the moralists who have preceded them," have fatally "overlooked" this compelling motivation: "In the pure arrogance of the reason," the narrator concludes, "we have all overlooked it."[23]

Significant, Poe also explores the limitations of hegemonic rational selves in an earlier sketch about his own household cat, tellingly entitled "Instinct versus Reason" (1840). Here Poe editorially muses on the "self-love and arrogance of man" in rating human intellect above animal instinct. Man, he concludes, "perpetually finds himself involved in the paradox of decrying instinct as an inferior faculty, while he is forced to admit its infinite superiority, in a thousand cases, over the very reason which he claims exclusively as his own. Instinct, so far from being an inferior reason, is perhaps the most exalted of all."[24] Such a theory of the supremacy of animalistic irrationality would understand addiction and rehabilitation quite differently from Washingtonianism. Yet both this piece and "The Imp of the Perverse" demonstrate that Poe was critiquing not just a specific temperance program, a particular theory of addiction and rehabilitation, but also deeper nineteenth-century constructions of selfhood that mythologized the powers of bourgeois will.

In "The Black Cat," Poe essentially transformed a temperance tale into a deeper exploration of crime, dark psychology, and unstable selfhood. Yet Poe's tale did not so much dismiss self-reliant Washingtonian hopes for alcoholic rehabilitation as expose the sometimes convenient, smug, or arrogant suppositions behind them. Such simplistic assumptions, widespread in 1840s America, informed at least two reactions to Poe's death in 1849, when two different acquaintances independently lamented that Poe had been cut off just as he had taken the Sons of Temperance pledge and planned to marry Elmira Shelton.[25] For such contemporary observers, these two achievements carried equivalent middle-class credibility, as both sobriety and matrimony guaranteed respectability and defined success. In such bourgeois discourse, the (usually male) tale of alcohol rehabilitation was elevated to the level of the (usually female) marriage plot as a myth of self-actualization. Such a pairing fantasized a counter-narrative to Poe's personal tragedy, imagining a satisfying dénouement. Yet, as Poe's fictions hinted, curing alcoholism was neither easy nor inevitable. Indeed, Poe's pet- and wife-killing tale – no less than his own complicated home life – exposed the false or naïve promises of nineteenth-century sentimentalism and domesticity as well as the idealized trajectories of reform and redemption. From his long wrangle with alcohol, Poe understood how difficult any rehabilitation could be.

One of Poe's most illuminating critiques of Washingtonian methods in "The Black Cat," however, points to the possibility of better therapeutic outcomes. In the throes of his horrors, Poe's narrator cries out, "For what *disease* is like Alcohol!" (emphasis added). Medicalized understandings of alcohol addiction and rehabilitation, according to Harry Gene Devine, had begun to emerge in the late eighteenth century, but temperance advocates only gradually came to believe that alcoholics weren't sinful or vicious but suffered from an alcohol-induced disease.[26] The Washingtonians, with their secular distrust of concepts of sin, helped foster this development, but still they tended not to understand alcohol addiction as an illness, a condition potentially beyond the reach of their moral suasion; as Katherine Chavigny has observed, "Only rarely did Washingtonians attribute this loss of control to a disease-like process."[27] And although disease concepts – especially in the nineteenth century – are never free from social stigma, such emerging conceptualizations eventually gave alcohol rehabilitation new ways of engaging Poe's "imp of the perverse" and introduced more effective, if imperfect, methods for countering the ravages of alcoholism.

NOTES

1. *Banner of Temperance*, August 31, 1849.
2. Ian Tyrrell, *Sobering Up: From Temperance to Prohibition in Antebellum America* (Westport, CT: Greenwood Press, 1979), 135–51.
3. David S. Reynolds, "Black Cats and Delirium Tremens: Temperance and the American Renaissance," in *The Serpent in the Cup: Temperance in American Literature*, ed. David S. Reynolds and Debra J. Rosenthal (Amherst, MA: University of Massachusetts Press, 1997), 32, 22.
4. For Griswold's anonymous 1849 memoir and 1850 biography of Poe, see Benjamin F. Fisher, ed., *Poe in His Own Time: A Biographical Chronicle of His Life, Drawn from Recollections, Interviews, and Memoirs by Family, Friends, and Associates* (Iowa City: University of Iowa Press, 2010), 73–80, 100–53.
5. Susan Archer Weiss, "The Sister of Edgar A. Poe," *Continent* 3 (June 27, 1883), 817.
6. Jack S. Blocker, Jr., *American Temperance Movements: Cycles of Reform* (Boston: Twayne, 1989), 3; W. J. Rorabaugh, *The Alcoholic Republic: An American Tradition* (New York: Oxford University Press, 1979), 14.
7. Rorabaugh, *Alcoholic Republic*, 40–1, 138; Blocker, *American Temperance Movements*, 3, 7–8, 119.
8. Robert DeUnger to E. R. Reynolds, October 29, 1899, quoted in Dwight Thomas and David K. Jackson, eds., *The Poe Log: A Documentary Life of Edgar Allan Poe, 1809–1849* (Boston: G. K. Hall, 1987), 628; Blocker, *American Temperance Movements*, 9.

9. Rorabaugh, *Alcoholic Republic*, 89; William Poe to Poe, June 15, 1843, *The Complete Works of Edgar Allan Poe*, 17 vols. (New York: Crowell, 1902), vol. xvii, 145–6.

10. Blocker, *American Temperance Movements*, 21.

11. Edgar Allan Poe to Joseph Evans Snodgrass, April 1, 1841, *The Collected Letters of Edgar Allan Poe*, ed. John Ward Ostrom, Burton R. Pollin, and Jeffrey A. Savoye, 2 vols. (New York: Gordian, 2008), vol. i, 262–4. For a discussion of dram drinking versus binge drinking, see Rorabaugh, *Alcoholic Republic*, 163–9; and Thomas R. Pegram, *Battling Demon Rum: The Struggle for a Dry America* (Chicago: Ivan Dee, 1998), 10.

12. Michael Warner, "Whitman Drunk," in *Breaking Bounds: Whitman and American Cultural Studies*, ed. Betsy Erkkila and Jay Grossman (New York: Oxford University Press, 1996), 32.

13. Rorabaugh, *Alcoholic Republic*, 233.

14. Steven Mintz, *Moralists and Modernizers: America's Pre-Civil War Reformers* (Baltimore: Johns Hopkins University Press, 1995), 10.

15. Mark Edward Lender and Karen R. Karnchanapee, "'Temperance Tales': Anti-Liquor Fiction and American Attitudes toward Alcoholics in the Late Nineteenth and Early Twentieth Centuries," *Journal of Studies on Alcohol* 38 (1977), 1351.

16. Quoted in Thomas and Jackson, *Poe Log*, 590.

17. Blocker, *American Temperance Movements*, xii.

18. Glenn Hendler, "Bloated Bodies and Sober Sentiments: Masculinity in 1840s Temperance Narratives," in *Sentimental Men: Masculinity and the Politics of Affect in American Culture*, ed. Mary Chapman and Glenn Hendler (Berkeley: University of California Press, 1999), 125; Pegram, *Demon Rum*, 29; Reynolds, "Black Cats," 27.

19. Timothy Shay Arthur, *Six Nights with the Washingtonians: A Series of Temperance Tales, 1842* (Philadelphia: Godey & McMichael, 1843), 2.

20. Abraham Lincoln, *An Address Delivered before the Springfield Washingtonian Temperance Society* (Springfield, IL: Springfield Reform Club, 1882), 3–4.

21. Edgar Allan Poe, *The Collected Works of Edgar Allan Poe*, ed. Thomas Ollive Mabbott, 3 vols. (Cambridge, MA: Belknap Press, 1969–78), vol. iii, 850, 856–7, 849. Subsequent references to this story come from this edition.

22. Walt Whitman, *Franklin Evans, or The Inebriate: A Tale of the Times*, ed. Christopher Castiglia and Glenn Hendler (Durham: Duke University Press, 2007), 112.

23. Poe, *Collected Works*, vol. iii, 1219, 1223.

24. Ibid., vol. ii, 478–9.

25. Joseph P. Kennedy and John R. Thompson quoted in Thomas and Jackson, *Poe Log*, 852, 854.

26. Harry Gene Devine, "The Discovery of Addiction: Changing Conceptions of Habitual Drunkenness in America," *Journal of Studies on Alcohol* 39 (1978), 143–74.

27. Katherine A. Chavigny, "Reforming Drunkards in Nineteenth-Century America: Religion, Medicine, Therapy," in *Altering American Consciousness: The History of Alcohol and Drug Use in the United States, 1800–2000*, ed. Sarah W. Tracy and Caroline Jean Acker (Amherst: University of Massachusetts Press, 2004), 111.

CHAPTER II

Fashion, Furnishings, and Style

Patricia A. Cunningham

In Edgar Allan Poe's lifetime Americans became increasingly less dependent on European products. During the early years of the nation, Americans moved toward independence from foreign goods, not through household industry as seen in homespun, but rather through concerted efforts in the production of all sorts of consumer products. The early nineteenth century saw great advances toward industrialization and mass production. Of particular note was the rapid rise of the men's clothing industry, as well as the mass production of carpets, coverlets, furniture, wallpaper, and textiles of all types with which to decorate the home.

THE PRODUCTION AND ACQUISITION OF MENSWEAR

By the mid-1840s, the making of men's clothing was one of the largest industries in America. In New York, for instance, it had grown from a few waterfront warehouses and shops selling loose-fitting slops and other work clothes in 1812 to streets bustling with clothier and tailor shops offering custom and ready-made suits in 1821. By 1835, New York was the nation's leading manufacturer of ready-made clothing, with wholesale houses shipping goods to all parts of the United States and to foreign countries.[1]

The production of menswear was carried out by tailors in their own shops, as well as by clothiers. The latter hired journeyman tailors and seamstresses to make clothing to sell in their stores. Wholesalers did the same and shipped clothing to all parts of the United States and abroad. The speed at which a suit could be made was greatly aided by the introduction of the measuring tape and the use of pattern drafting systems that relied on body proportions. An ever-increasing market of young men coming into cities looking for jobs likewise supported growth. These young men eagerly sought out the shops that gave them the best deal on looking good with suits made from low-priced European fabrics – high-quality broadcloth, velvets, cotton fabrics of different sorts, and wool and cotton blends. In addition to suits and coats, many clothing entrepreneurs offered cravats, handkerchiefs, shirts, hosiery, suspenders, collars, under vests, and under drawers.

Men might make their choices based on a salesman's advice, but that could be augmented with informative fashion news available in a number of popular magazines such as the *Mirror of Fashion* and *Graham's Magazine*. Newspaper advertisements and shop windows likewise provided views of the latest styles in men's clothing.

The rapid influx of young men into the cities removed from traditional restraints on their conduct was cause for some concern. There was fear that these young men would either be taken in by the new breed of fashionable "confidence men" or worse yet, become one. As Poe suggests in "The Man of the Crowd," they were alone in the city, disoriented, and essentially without family and social controls. The potential for fraud was real, as Poe reveals in "The Business Man," his humorous account of the sundry schemes of Peter Proffit, which include work as a tailor's walking advertisement. Poe apparently enjoyed exposing the behavior of overenthusiastic merchants ready to defraud unwary customers. With rapid changes occurring in America, not knowing what to wear for different occasions had potential to generate new anxieties. Fortunately, books directed toward young men, including William A. Alcott's *Young Man's Guide* and Daniel Eddy's *Young Man's Friend*,[2] helped relieve these anxieties.

MEN'S STYLES

The Suit

From the mid-1820s until the late 1840s, the clothing worn by Poe and most middle-class men consisted of a dark suit that included slim trousers (also called pantaloons), frock coats or tailcoats, and one or more waistcoats. With this combination they wore large, full shirts and usually black cravats. They also might wear an overcoat. Shoes, stockings, and various accessories completed the look. The daguerreotypes of Poe show him wearing these garments. They might have constituted his best set of clothes since it was not unusual for individuals to have their picture made while they wore their Sunday best. Although it is not possible to tell if Poe is wearing a tailcoat or a frock style, it is clear that he wore his jackets quite tight, following the fashion of this period. A looser sack jacket was available, but did not become a major fashion until the middle of the century. One of Poe's waistcoats (vests) survives. The waistcoat was one of the few items in a man's wardrobe that could be colorful. It allowed the wearer to express some individuality through the color and choice of fabric. It could be lavish or simple; in that respect waistcoats were similar to a tie worn today. The suit, of course, became the American civic uniform. Men's dress was meant to inspire modesty, self-respect, decency, and morality. It was utilitarian, yet seen by some as a link between the self and the soul. Ultimately, according to Michael Zakim, the suit brought social order to a potentially disorderly America and aided in the preservation of democracy.[3]

Suit Coats

The tailcoat could be single- or double-breasted; the latter featured larger lapels than the single-breasted style. Coat collars were cut high at the back of the neck and rolled to join the lapel with either a V- or M-shaped notch. Coat sleeves were cut full at the arm's eye allowing for fullness at the top of the shoulder. By the 1840s this fullness disappeared. The frock coat was less formal than the tailcoat. Instead of the bottom of the coat cutting away in the front, the frock coat was one length, ending at or slightly above the knee. During the 1830s, it became the fashion to wear the frock coat during the day and for casual wear, whereas the tailcoat was reserved for evening.

Waistcoats

Waistcoats were sleeveless garments with a small or standing collar worn under coats. Sometimes men wore two waistcoats, especially in cold weather. The white waistcoat was often reserved for evening and special occasions, such as a wedding. By the 1840s the waistcoat lengthened and was constructed with a point in the front. They also began to have large lapels sometimes worn over the edge of the coat lapel and collar.

Trousers

Pants were close fitting with an ankle strap. Closures were either a buttoned front fall or the newer fly front with buttons.

Shirts and Neckwear

Shirts were cut full with tucked inserts in front for daywear; for evening the shirt fronts were frilled. Sleeves had cuffs fastened with either buttons or studs. Collars were large, ample enough for the wearer to fold the edges over the cravat. The cravat, a black silk square cloth folded diagonally, was placed around the neck under the collar and tied in a knot or bow. Another option was a stick, a wide neck piece fastened at the back of the neck.

Overcoats

Overcoats, or greatcoats as they were often called, were single- or double-breasted. They could be short or long. Tailors fashioned the coat to fit close to the body during the 1830s and earlier, but the fit gained fullness in the 1840s. A new style was the Chesterfield, a slimmer coat with one back vent and a velvet collar.

Hairstyles and Hats

Men wore their hair fairly long, but not chin length. They also might have closely cropped whiskers. Grooming was critical to one's overall appearance. Poe critiqued poet and painter Charles Pearse Cranch, finding his "thick whiskers meeting under the chin…much out of keeping with the shirt-collar à *la Byron*."[4] Top hats were the prevailing style for both daytime and evening. There were several styles with subtle differences. Caps were worn for sports. Later the bowler (derby) style became popular as a replacement for the top hat.

Footwear

Footwear consisted of square-toed, laced-up shoes with four eyelets, boots for riding, and, by the 1840s, rubber overshoes and galoshes. The caoutchouc overshoes the narrator wears as he walks through the streets of London in "The Man of the Crowd" mark him as an American. Stockings were knit of wool, cotton, or silk. Before galoshes were available men wore ankle length protective cloth spats (gaiters) over their shoes; for sports these could be knee high.

Accessories

The number of necessary accessories for men included gloves made of leather, cotton, a wool–silk blend, or fine kid (for evening), as well as canes and umbrellas. Jewelry consisted of cravat pins, shirt buttons and studs, watches, and decorative watch chains.[5]

THE PRODUCTION AND ACQUISITION
OF WOMEN'S CLOTHING

Unlike men's clothing, the production of women's clothing, especially dresses, remained unchanged. The requirements of fit at the time were unsuitable to the methods of mass production adopted by the men's fashion industry. Women with sewing skills (and most women had sewing skills at this time) could make their own clothes; in many cases families helped each other or hired a seamstress to spend time in their home to help with sewing seasonable garments for all family members. They might engage such help several times during a year. Another option for women's clothing was to visit a professional dressmaker.

Fabrics, notions, and trimmings were available in dry goods stores in major cities and shops specializing in these items. Individuals might purchase their own fabrics to take to a skilled dressmaker. In some cases, dressmakers provided fabrics. Information about the latest styles was available in magazines such as *Godey's Lady's Book*, *Lady's World of Fashion*, or the less well-known *Ladies Cabinet*.

Some outerwear and accessories were ready-made. These included mantles and cloaks, gloves, stockings, shoes, and jewelry. Women also purchased their hats and bonnets from milliners, many of whom offered other clothing items. Under clothing was usually made at home. These included chemises, petticoats, drawers, and corsets. However, since corsets were difficult to make, women often purchased them from artisans specializing in them.

FASHION AND ETIQUETTE

The sentimental view of dress from the 1820s through the 1840s was that women who dressed with simplicity would improve the moral character of those who entered their sphere. A woman's honesty and transparency was a natural foil to the dreaded, deceitful "confidence man." Women who dressed fashionably risked being taken for a "painted woman," the female version of the confidence man and considered a person to be feared. The question was: Could such a person be trusted? Was she using fashion and genteel behavior as a means to deceive others? Advice books and fashion magazines provided the necessary information on appropriate dress for different times of day and occasions, such as rites of passage. Women could consult advice books to maintain a balance between dressing too simply and going overboard and thus into the realm of the painted women.[6]

Though this period brought a great deal of concern about deception through fashion on the part of many Americans, by the late 1840s people's attitudes about the function of fashionable display were beginning to alter. The reaction to Anna Mowatt's 1847 comedy, *Fashion: or, Life in New York*, reveals this new attitude. The play critiques the life of fashion from the perspective of sentimental middle-class hostility toward the

ridiculous pretensions and blunders of a newly rich fictional family. The
sentimental critique of fashionable dress, etiquette, and other rituals was
giving way to an acceptance of such display as appropriate expressions of
the middle class. The play allowed audience members to laugh at themselves. The characters in the play were portrayed as true confidence men
and painted women, deceiving each other in attempts to gain wealth and
status. As Zakim notes, Mowatt wrote her play as a good-natured satire on
the follies of citizens in a new country, yet she was really showing how far
Americans had come since the days of homespun. Reviewing the play, Poe
noted that Mowatt's achievement was not simply a satire on fashion, but
rather writing the first satire of a satire of fashion.[7]

WOMEN'S STYLES

Dresses. During the 1820s, women's fashionable dresses abandoned the
simple classical tubular silhouette that had prevailed during the postrevo-
lutionary period. By the late 1820s, the skirts became fuller, the waistline
lower, and the sleeves voluminous. Dresses were usually one piece with
openings either in the front or back secured with hooks, buttons, or laces.
However, there were some two-piece styles. When emphasis began to set-
tle on a small waist, it became necessary for women to wear tightly drawn
corsets and many petticoats to hold out their skirts.

Dresses were identified according to the time of day when they were
to be worn, and were styled as described previously. Morning dresses, or
house gowns, were informal, usually made of cotton, and not meant to
be worn in public. They were simply constructed. Daytime dresses, sometimes called walking dresses or carriage dresses, did not have trains. The
bodice neckline often was cut with a V shape or cut high to the throat. It
was not unusual for the bodice fronts and backs to have V-shaped revers
extending from the shoulder to the waist. Wide cape collars likewise
became popular. Fabrics for daytime were printed cottons, light batiste,
muslin, and wool challis. Evening dresses had a similar silhouette but were
made of soft gauzes, silk satin, or organdy, and often had extensive trim-
ming of lace, ribbon, or artificial flowers. Necklines were cut lower and
sleeves shorter. By the 1830s sleeves could be off the shoulder for evening.

Sleeves for dresses came in a variety of styles. They could have a puff
at the shoulder with a straight sleeve attached or feature a leg-of-mutton
shape, with fullness at the shoulder that decreased in size to the wrist. A
style called the "imbecile" had very full sleeves from shoulder to the wrist.
A full sleeve tied in at intervals was called a Marie sleeve. Sleeve fullness

diminished in the late 1830s, and by 1840 narrowness prevailed with some fullness set at various points on a relatively tight-fitting sleeve.

The waistline on dresses was cut straight until the early 1830s when a V shape at center front became the fashion. Skirts were full and long, ending at the top of the foot. From 1828 until 1836, however, the skirt became ankle length or slightly shorter. During the 1840s, skirt styles again lengthened when the general silhouette became narrower.

Hair Styles and Headdresses. Women often styled their hair with a center part and soft curls at the sides and back. Their head coverings included a small cap worn indoors. Describing novelist Catherine Maria Sedgwick in "The Literati of New York City," Poe compared her personal appearance with a recently published engraving: "The portrait in *Graham's Magazine* is by no means a likeness, and, although the hair is represented as curled, (Miss Sedgwick at present wears a cap – at least most usually,) gives her the air of being much older than she is."[8] All women wore hats outdoors, either a bonnet or a hat with a brim. Hats and bonnets were trimmed with a variety of ribbons, braid, or artificial flowers, and could be worn with a veil. Materials included cloth of various types depending on the season, with straw reserved for summer. Sunbonnets were a necessity. Many had a protective cloth draped at the back to protect the neck from the sun.

Outerwear. When women needed protection from the elements, especially the cold, they wore a pelisse, a long coat that followed the general lines of the prevailing dress style. Mantles, capes, and shawls of varying lengths were also choices for warmth.

Footwear. Women wore a slipper style, sometimes with a square toe. After 1840 a small heel was added to the shoe. Shoes were made of soft leather or cloth. Colder weather required sturdy leather shoes and boots with gaiters, or galoshes. In Poe's lifetime, shoes were ready-made, but shoemakers still did not distinguish between the left and the right foot.

Accessories. Gloves, of course, were a necessity for both daytime and evening. They were not strictly for warmth. Evening gloves were long until after the 1830s. Cotton, silk, and kid were the choices for glove materials. Mitts that left the fingers free also were popular. Women carried small purses called reticules, larger handbags and purses, as well as fans, muffs, and parasols. Jewelry popular during the period included gold chains with lockets, or crosses and Chatelaines, which were chains worn at the waistline from which the wearer suspended any number of small items – thimbles, scissors, or pen knives. Women also wore a variety of brooches and bracelets, drop earrings, and hair ornaments.[9]

FASHIONING THE HOME

As a student at the University of Virginia, Poe would have been immersed in Thomas Jefferson's classical Roman revival designs for the university. By the 1830s the Empire style was in full bloom with more authentic pieces seen in the market. The Empire style first developed in France during Napoleon's reign and includes Greek, Roman, and Egyptian designs, the latter owing to Napoleon's expeditions to the Nile in 1798 and 1801. The style was brought to the masses through fashion publications such as Thomas Hope's *Household Furniture and Interior Decoration* (1807), and especially Rudolph Ackerman's *Repository of Arts, Literature, Commerce, Manufacture, Fashions and Politics* (1809–28).[10]

American furniture was produced by artisans called cabinetmakers. Boston, Philadelphia, New York, and Baltimore were the leading centers. In 1835, for instance, Boston boasted 275 cabinetmakers. Growth in the industry occurred through recent inventions that speeded up production. These included the introduction of the circular veneer saw, water-powered lathes, and a new finish that used lacquer rather than varnish.

In cities such as Boston and Philadelphia, cabinetmakers formed organizations to exhibit and sell their goods. Their furniture was distributed to the South and West, and even to South America. Cabinetmakers for the most part produced "shop work" sold from their own shops while large firms took orders from exporters and retailers.

Of all of the furniture produced, chairs comprised the largest portion, especially for larger makers such as Duncan Phyfe and Lambert Hitchcock. The Greek klismos chair was very popular, as was the painted Hitchcock chair with stenciled decorations of cornucopias, honeysuckle blossoms, spread eagles, Greek lyres, and similar classical forms. The less expensive chairs had rush seats, turned legs and stiles, and stenciling in place of expensive upholstery. The cabinetmakers provided necessary furniture for every room of a house, not simply chairs.

FURNISHINGS FOR THE HOME

The Dining Room

A sideboard for the dining room was the most expensive and elaborate piece in a home. Sideboards dominated the dining room much as the sofa did the living room. Dining tables did not permanently stand in the center of the dining room. When not in use the table was placed against a wall.

The Bed Chamber

In the bed chamber one would find standard dressers, washstands, chests, and, of course, a bed, the most impressive and expensive piece of furniture in a bed chamber. Four-poster beds fit well in the high-ceilinged rooms found in many houses. The French sleigh bed also was popular in America after 1815. Other bed chamber furnishings included a French desk, bookcases, and wardrobes or armoires, sometimes with drawers and space for hanging clothes.

The Hallway

The pier table that sat in hallways and sometimes in dining rooms for serving food also was an impressive piece of furniture. These sometimes included a mirror.

The Parlor

In the years before the Civil War, etiquette and fashion were forces shaping the social life of Americans and the activities that took place in their parlors. In Philadelphia, Poe and his wife, Virginia, frequently gathered with a group of literati and friends at the home of the Grahams, owner of *Graham's Magazine*. Virginia Poe often played the pianoforte and sang on these occasions. Such genteel performances would have been repeated in the parlors of homes all across America. The home was the middle-class woman's universe, and the parlor its center. The parlor was a sanctuary, the heart of the home.

Elegant parlors needed at least one sofa to balance the fireplace. Specific styles varied by city in America. New York sofas, for instance, were lighter than those made in Philadelphia. There were three main sofa types: plain based on the Roman fulcra, a box type with vertical boxes at each end, and the Grecian style made with complex carved scrolls. Other couches were the French Récamier day bed and Ottoman-style benches.

A table placed in the center of the parlor was very popular in the Empire period, and served a function similar to the modern coffee table. The most popular type was a pedestal style supported by a massive Doric column, often with a marble top. In some illustrations the center table is depicted draped with a cloth on which was placed a whale oil lamp or "solar" lamp for reading or needlework. The table apparently was viewed as a symbol of cultivation. Smaller versions of the pedestal table could be basin stands, work tables, or card tables. A major addition to the parlor during the 1820s was the pianoforte. The instrument was sold in the hundreds to middle-class and upper-class Americans who enjoyed music. Since mirrors were hung in nearly every room, there would be at least one in the parlor. They could be elaborate with gilded frames, large or small.[11]

POE AND THE PARLOR

During the 1830s, mass production entered the realm of household furnishings. New inventions made it possible for everyone to purchase tasteful carpets, chairs, wallpaper, and curtains. Manufacturers tried to outdo themselves in fanciness and frippery. The old Windsor chairs were sent to the attic. New mass manufactured items were advertised widely, but little information was provided on how they should be used in decorating the home. *Godey's Lady's Book* and *Lady's World of Fashion* did not offer such advice. Consequently into these homes went a variety of heavy horsehair sofas, elaborate mirrors with gilt frames, portraits of bonneted ladies, carpets covered with flowers in bright colors, tinted walls, and later wallpaper. Indeed, the parlor has been described as holding a clutter of small tables and knickknacks, bronzes, busts, cameos, vases, and other similar objects scattered about. It seemed that women needed guidance in decorating their homes.[12]

Poe must have seen such rooms. Perhaps "The Philosophy of Furniture" was his response to this plethora of what seemed to be bad taste. In this essay, Poe criticizes Americans for confusing good taste with a display of wealth, wherein the cost of an object determines its merit. More specifically Poe refers to the absence of keeping. *Keeping* here refers to the need to apply aesthetic principles in arranging a room and designing furniture. Poe seems to draw on William Hogarth's "principles of beauty" regarding the need to choose undulating lines as opposed to straight lines, and the avoidance of uniformity and overabundance, as in the use of drapery that may overwhelm a room. Poe calls carpet the soul of a room, meaning that the homeowner chooses the colors and furniture for a room based on the carpet. He again draws on Hogarth in observing the importance of unity, proportion, and simplicity regarding design and color.[13]

Poe's ideal room would be oblong, thirty feet long and twenty-five feet wide. It should have one door and two large floor-length windows on another side. These windows, with massive rosewood frames, should open to a veranda. The window treatment should be silver and rich crimson silk held back with gold-colored rope ties. The gold and crimson should echo throughout the room, particularly in the carpet. The walls of Poe's ideal room would be papered in silver gray with small crimson arabesques designs. Large landscape paintings and three or four portraits of women with ethereal beauty, in the manner of Thomas Sully, should cover the walls. There should be only one mirror in the room, hung in a manner to avoid showing the reflection of anyone seated in the room. Poe's choice for furniture in the room would be two sofas of crimson silk decorated with a modest gold pattern and two matching "conversation" side chairs. Other furniture for the room would be a pianoforte of rosewood with the keys visible, and in the center of the room an octagonal marble table left uncovered. He suggested having 200 to 300 "magnificently" bound books on display.[14] Poe's ideal parlor fits the mode of the time, but is more subdued and less cluttered than the previously described overdecorated room. If gentility was what men and women sought, they could find it in Poe's ideal room.

NOTES

1. Egal Feldman, *Fit for Men: A Study of New York's Clothing Trade* (Washington, DC: Public Affairs Press, 1960), 4.
2. Ibid.; Karen Halttunen, *Confidence Men and Painted Women: A Study of Middle-Class Culture in America, 1830–1870* (New Haven: Yale University Press, 1982), 1–2; Michael Zakim, *Ready-Made Democracy: A History of Men's Dress in the American Republic, 1760–1860* (Chicago: University of Chicago Press, 2003), 70–1.
3. Zakim, *Ready-Made Democracy*, 114.
4. Edgar Allan Poe, *Essays and Reviews*, ed. G. R. Thompson (New York: Library of America, 1984), 1171.
5. For more details of 1840s menswear see Joan Severa, *Dressed for the Photographer: Ordinary Americans and Fashion, 1840–1900* (Kent, OH: Kent State University Press, 1995).
6. Halttunen, *Confidence Men*, 56–91.
7. Zakim, *Ready-Made Democracy*, 185–9.
8. Poe, *Essays*, 1204.
9. See Severa, *Dressed for the Photographer*.
10. For further discussion see Oscar P. Fitzgerald, *Four Centuries of American Furniture* (Radnor, PA: Wallace-Homestead, 1995), 109–32.
11. Ibid., 10–11.
12. Ibid., 109–15.
13. Edgar Allan Poe, *The Collected Works of Edgar Allan Poe*, ed. Thomas Ollive Mabbott, 3 vols. (Cambridge, MA: Belknap Press, 1969–78), vol. ii, 495–503.
14. A replica of this room can be seen at the Edgar Allan Poe National Historic Site in Philadelphia.

CHAPTER 12

The American Stage

Philip Edward Phillips

When Edgar Allan Poe left the Richmond household of John and Frances Allan on March 19, 1827 after quarreling with his foster father, he went to Boston, the city of his birth and a place where his parents had performed on stage. Except for the 1815–20 period when he lived in England, Poe grew up in Richmond, educated alongside other children of the Southern aristocratic elite. Though taken in by the Allans, he was never formally adopted, and his heritage as the son of actors – a class looked down upon by polite society – set him apart. In Richmond, his mother, Elizabeth Arnold Hopkins Poe, last appeared on stage before dying from tuberculosis on December 8, 1811.[1] Poe cherished his shadowy memories of his parents and reveled in the stories of those who had known them. Poe remained proud of his parents' occupation, and the influence of the American stage on him is unmistakable. Though establishing himself as an acerbic literary critic and author of weird tales, Poe wrote several theater reviews in the 1840s. His best writings reflect his interest in drama and stagecraft, a context that deepens our appreciation of his life and work.

THE EARLY AMERICAN STAGE

Colonial settlers brought prejudices against the theater with them to North America. The South supported the theater more than the northern colonies, but some people in New England and the middle colonies enjoyed theatrical entertainments despite the objections of Boston Puritans and Pennsylvania Quakers. Philadelphia remained America's leading theatrical center until the mid-1820s, when Boston and New York became preeminent. From the late eighteenth to the early nineteenth century, such great venues as Philadelphia's Chestnut Street Theatre, Boston's Federal Street Theatre, and New York's Park Theatre imported stars from England and continental Europe. By the mid-nineteenth century, the theater became more Americanized with the introduction of native-born talent like

Edwin Forrest, the first American actor to garner attention both at home and abroad, and Anna Cora Mowatt, best known for her highly successful comedy of manners, *Fashion* (1845).[2]

Laurence Senelick calls attention to the improvisatory nature of theater in early nineteenth-century America, noting that American theater regularly "reinvented its definitions of 'American' and 'theatre'" by resisting institutionalization and engaging in "an ongoing dialogue with its public." In the "absence of such constraints as official censorship, state patronage of the arts, or centralized professional training," Senelick continues, the early American stage enjoyed some liberties, but it struggled to overcome the past's "deep-seated anti-theatrical prejudice."[3] The importation of English actors and repertoire and the general attitude among the self-righteous public created a climate that scarcely distinguished between actors and prostitutes. This attitude posed a significant challenge to the development and acceptance of theater in early nineteenth-century America. As the son of actors and later as an aspiring writer and critic, Poe faced similar difficulties as he sought to challenge the heavy influence of British writers on the New England luminaries of his time and to assert the need for originality in American letters.

POE'S PARENTS

Edgar Allan Poe had theater in his blood. His grandmother, Elizabeth Arnold, had appeared on the stage at Covent Garden, London in such productions as *Blue Beard*, *The Castle Andalusia*, and *Orpheus and Eurydice*. Elizabeth Arnold and her daughter, Elizabeth or Eliza, as she was known, reached Boston on January 5, 1796. Three months later, nine-year-old Eliza made her first stage appearance singing "The Market Lass." Until her death at twenty-four, Eliza would spend her life on the American stage, performing over 300 parts in several different dramatic genres: Shakespearean comedies, tragedies, and histories; sentimental comedies; comic operas; farces; poetic tragedies; and gothic melodramas.[4] Like her mother, Eliza was a highly talented and versatile performer. Although Mrs. Arnold remarried a Mr. Tubbs in America, providing their family a level of stability, she soon passed away, leaving Eliza in the care of her stepfather. Eliza continued acting, married a Mr. Hopkins, and, after his death, married David Poe, Jr.

Unlike his wife, David Poe, Jr. had no theater in his blood. His father, "General" David Poe, Sr., wished him to pursue a career in law. Instead, he sought a career on the stage, but with less success than Eliza. He did

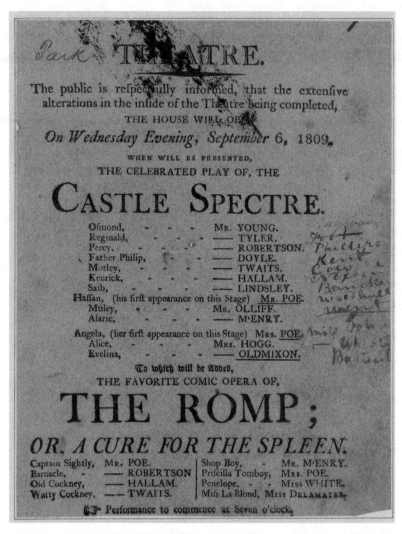

Figure 12.1 A playbill from the Park Theatre, New York, September 6, 1809, the first time David and Eliza Poe performed at the Park Theatre. Courtesy of the Harvard College Library.

perform several important roles, some Shakespearean, on the best stages in America. Regardless, David's relationship with his family deteriorated, and his performances were sometimes marred by "indisposition" – a euphemism for being drunk. The financial demands of his growing family further strained his personal situation, and he abandoned Eliza before she gave birth to their daughter, Rosalie. Some speculate that David died in Norfolk, but his ultimate fate is unknown.

Life on the stage was hard, both financially and physically. Eliza continued performing after David's departure, and her children traveled with her. Edgar was too young to remember the experience, but subsequent conversations with his older brother, William Henry Leonard Poe, helped him understand it. Their conversations may have supplied Poe with some characters (like Mr. and Mrs. Usher, for example, who had been fellow actors and intimate friends of their mother) and settings (derived from the gothic elements from such plays as *Castle Spectre*) for his works.

Eliza's death, which Poe witnessed, surely formed deep-seated associations between beauty, the theater, and death. These associations reemerge in his aesthetic theories involving the "death...of a beautiful woman," dramatic representations of "mournful and never-ending remembrance," and dark meditations upon our ultimate end, death.[5] Though John Allan took Poe in, he neither adopted him nor made him his heir. To his credit, Allan arranged for Eliza Poe's burial in the churchyard of St. John's Church in Richmond after meeting resistance because she had been an actress. As a schoolboy in Richmond, a young man preparing for university, an assistant editor of the *Southern Literary Messenger*, and later a visiting lecturer, Poe could have seen the unmarked grave and remembered one he had loved and lost.

POE'S EARLY THEATRICAL INTERESTS

Though the Allans were theatergoers, John Allan disapproved of acting, discouraged Poe's thespian activities, and frowned upon stage performers. But Poe demonstrated some dramatic talent, as attested by his involvement in minor theatrical productions during his schooldays in Richmond and recorded in an obituary notice for one of his former friends, Creed Thomas:

Dr. Thomas was a member with Poe, Beverly Anderson, and William F. Ritchie, of the Thespian Society, that had its headquarters in the old wooden building which stood on the northeast corner of Sixth and Marshall Streets. Poe was a member of this society, contrary to the wishes of Mr. Allan. He had undoubted talent in this direction. The audience usually numbered about forty or fifty. A small admission fee was charged, and this was divided between the actors, who used it as pin money.[6]

As Allan's ward, Poe received the education of a young gentleman. In Allan's mind, neither the stage nor the poetical arts were appropriate avocations. Poe's interests served only to drive a greater wedge between him and Allan, on whom his precarious position in Richmond society depended. When Poe quit Richmond for Boston, he left to seek a wider stage and proclaimed his connection to the city by signing his first published book of poems, *Tamerlane and Other Poems*, "by a Bostonian."[7] Arthur Hobson Quinn speculates that Poe sought places to perform on the stage in Boston. More likely, Poe sought venues associated with his origins, places such as the Boston or Federal Street Theatre, where his mother had performed to great acclaim from 1806 until his birth in 1809.

DRAMA AND DRAMATIC INFLUENCES

Poe's sole drama was *Politian, An Unfinished Tragedy* (1835), a revenge tragedy set in Rome but based on the "Kentucky Tragedy," that is, the murder of Colonel Solomon P. Sharp at the hands of Jereboam O. Beauchamp, who sought to avenge the honor of Ann Cook (or Cooke). Poe published five scenes from *Politian* during his lifetime; sections from other parts appeared posthumously. Not until the publication of Thomas Ollive Mabbott's 1923 edition did the work appear in its complete and final form.[8] In *Politian*, poetic sentiments and language take center stage, not the actors themselves.

Politian provides a touchstone for understanding Poe's view of Aristotelian tragedy, which reflects Aristotle's belief that tragic poets "keep their aim fixed on the effects they wish to produce." Poe was familiar, either directly or indirectly, with Aristotle's definition of tragedy as "an imitation of an action that is serious, complete, and possessing magnitude," whose constituent parts included "Plot, Character, Language, Thought, Spectacle, and Melody." Poe's critical and imaginative writings show he agreed with Aristotle that the plot's organization is the most important of a tragedy's constituent parts.[9] Aristotelian principles governed Poe's writing and critical thinking; the inconsistent application of them in *Politian* provided sufficient reason for Poe to keep it off the stage. N. Bryllion Fagin observes that Poe "advocated realism on the stage and excoriated American writers of drama for using the wrong models, yet his own play is definitely indebted to the Byron school of Romantic tragedy." As a closet drama, *Politian* deserves its author's own censure as an "anomaly" or a "paradox."[10] No evidence suggests that Poe intended his play to be performed.

When he came to work as an assistant editor under William E. Burton, Poe gained an additional source of information about the theater. Another

English actor who had established himself on the London stage, Burton came to the United States, where he earned a reputation as the greatest comedian on the Philadelphia stage. He used his theatrical fame to fulfill a lifelong ambition: to edit a magazine. For Poe, Burton proved to be a great source of anecdotes about the stage in both Great Britain and America. Burton also had the finest theatrical library in the nation. There's no telling how much Burton shared with Poe, but his library could have supplemented Poe's knowledge of both comedy and tragedy significantly. Burton owned copies of such revenge tragedies as *The Maid's Tragedy* by Francis Beaumont and John Fletcher; George Chapman's *The Tragedy of Bussy D'Ambois* and its sequel, *The Revenge of Bussy D'Ambois*; John Ford's '*Tis Pity She's a Whore*; Christopher Marlowe's *Jew of Malta*; John Marston's *The Malcontent*; and *The White Devil* and *The Duchess of Malfi*, both by John Webster.[11]

Two of Poe's later tales, "The Cask of Amontillado" and "Hop-Frog," belong to the revenge tragedy tradition and thus indicate his cognizance of this dramatic genre. The marginalized protagonists of these two works ultimately exact revenge upon their persecutors. Their actions may represent a revenge fantasy of an impecunious artist of early nineteenth-century America who, despite his genius and prodigious output, cannot gain recognition in an environment that favors the well-born gentleman or the Brahmin.

In other works, Poe combines the Aristotelian principles of imitation, plot, and dramatic unity with elements of the gothic, long popular on the American stage and ubiquitous in contemporary fiction, in order to heighten poetic effect and to universalize his subject matter. Two poems, "The Conqueror Worm" and "The Haunted Palace" function as *mises en scènes*, reflecting the dominant themes and central action of the tales in which they appear, "Ligeia" and "The Fall of the House of Usher," respectively. Mabbott reads "The Conqueror Worm" as a five-act tragedy presented by Ligeia to her husband on the ultimate end of humanity – death – in the play called life. "The Haunted Palace" functions as an *ekphrasis*, or a top-to-bottom description, of the house and, indeed, the mind, of Usher, in the process of collapse. Such multilayered mirroring dramatically suggests the deterioration of Roderick, the impending confrontation between sister and brother, the collapse of the house, and the cumulative effect on the narrator, who witnesses the final scene in the dank and lurid tarn (that closes like a curtain).

"The Raven," which can be read as a dramatic monologue, is an example of elegy without the comforts of consolation; the speaker's pleas to the ebony bird externalize his despair.[12] Poe explores the perennial theme of the death of the beautiful woman. He frequently recited or performed "The Raven" to rapt audiences in the salons of the poetesses of New York City until his fall from favor among that company. "The Masque of the Red Death," while drawing upon the literary tradition of Boccaccio's *Decameron*, also replicates in its details the genre of the court masque (Poe admired Milton's *Comus*), patronized by and written for the aristocratic elite, and its introduction of the red death, at the tale's conclusion, not only provides a check to the protagonist's hubris and the prerogatives of the cultural elite but also reiterates the connection between the theater and death (the death of Eliza Poe) that is characteristic of Poe's writings.

POE AS THEATER CRITIC

In his own time, Poe was best known as a literary critic, a "Tomahawk Man," whose vitriolic reviews sought to raise the bar for the standards of American letters, often at the expense of the writer being reviewed. Poe endeavored to combat plagiarism, cliques, and "namby-pambyism" in American literature and called for originality and beauty from his contemporaries, such as Henry Wadsworth Longfellow, who were, in his view, too often slavish followers of British models and tastes.

Poe's critical writings often reveal his fascination with stagecraft. Reading Friedrich von Raumer's *England in 1835*, Poe found intriguing Raumer's disappointment with the artificiality of a London production of *Macbeth*. More effective "ghostlike and supernatural" imagery, Raumer observed, could be created by using "some optical means."[13] In "Pinakidia," Poe remarks: "Speaking of the usual representation of the banquet-scene in *Macbeth*, Von Raumer, the German historian, mentions a shadowy figure thrown by optical means into the chair of Banquo, and producing intense effect upon the audience. Enslen, a German optician, conceived this idea, and accomplished it without difficulty."[14] Recirculating this tidbit of information, Poe revised his comments to include a cutting reference to the conservative and lackadaisical nature of contemporary stage production: "Von Raumer says that Enslen, a German optician, conceived the idea of throwing a shadowy figure, by optical means, into the chair of Banquo; and that the thing was readily done. Intense effect was produced; and I do not doubt that an American audience might be electrified by the feat. But our managers not only have no invention of their own, but no energy to avail themselves of that of others."[15] While Poe may have been helpless to coax contemporary stage managers into using modern technology to improve dramatic performance, he realized that he could do so to embellish his own imaginative writings. Poe's innovative visual imagery, including the use of both reflection and refraction, applies optical means to enhance his tales.

Poe wrote many theatrical reviews while living in New York in the mid-1840s. As the editor of the *Broadway Journal*, he received free passes to attend the theater, with the hope (or expectation) that he would review the productions favorably. His theater reviews often proved as savage as his book reviews. On one occasion, a theater manager revoked his passes. Nevertheless, Poe's reviews provide insight into his mindset as he reflected upon American drama and the acting profession. His reviews of a spectacularly successful production, *Fashion*, demonstrate his affinity for the stage and high regard and empathy for actors.

"Live theatre," according to John Lithgow, "is evanescent. It's like a flash of light whose after-image slowly fades. Its impact is most potent at the moment of contact between performer and audience. The moment lives on in memory for a while, and then it is gone."[16] This was true of early American theater as much as it remains true today. However, until the emergence of magazine culture in early nineteenth-century America, the primary records of the stage were playbills, few of which survive. The rise of magazines increased demand for artistic and cultural columns to fill their pages, and, as an editor, Poe sought to meet the demand. In his first review of *Fashion*, he criticizes the play for its lack of originality. Poe also uses the review to make general observations on the state of American drama while pointing out some of the merits of Mowatt's play, which coincided with his own Aristotelian standards in respect to character, plot, and dénouement.[17] A subsequent review indicates that Poe brought his meticulousness to the task of reviewing theatrical productions. He acknowledges that he returned again and again to the Park Theatre to watch *Fashion*, "making careful note of its merits and defects as they were more and more distinctly developed in the gradually perfected representation of the play."[18] As he ponders the future of American drama, he offers more glowing praise of Mowatt's performance.

Months later, Poe attended a performance of Mowatt's *Fashion* at Niblo's Garden. Once again, he appreciated Mowatt's play, her acting, and her physical features.[19] His close attention to detail and his repeated patronage of the play makes him a more appreciative theatergoer and sympathetic critic. After following her performances in *Fashion*, Poe praised Mowatt for her success on the stage and courage to embrace drama, despite the hypocritical prejudices of fashionable society: "We have no sympathies

Figure 12.2 H. Fossette, *Park Theatre – Park Row* (New York: Peabody and Co., 1832).
Courtesy of the Boston Athenaeum.

with the prejudices which would entirely have dissuaded Mrs. Mowatt
from the stage. There is no cant more contemptible than that which
habitually decries the theatrical profession – a profession which, in itself,
embraces all that can elevate and ennoble, and absolutely to degrade." Poe
understands and sympathizes with the pecuniary struggles inherent in the
actor's plight: "If some – if many – or if nearly all of its members are
dissolute, this is an evil not arising from the profession itself, but from
the unhappy circumstances which surround it." Following this defense of
actors, Poe identifies himself as "the son of an actress...who, although
well-born, hesitated not to consecrate to the drama her brief career of
genius and of beauty."[20] Indeed, Eliza Poe's example inspired her more
famous son throughout his literary career, even until the very end.

One of Poe's most famous tales, "The Gold-Bug," was adapted for
the stage during his lifetime. Poe won a much-needed cash prize of 100
dollars from the *Dollar Newspaper* for the June 1843 publication of "The
Gold-Bug." The treasure-hunting tale, written during a time of racial
tensions in Philadelphia and making use of cryptography, brought Poe
some measure of popularity as well. In fact, "The Gold-Bug" was so popular that by August, a dramatic adaptation was performed at the Walnut
Street Theatre, the oldest theater in America, founded in 1809. While Poe
derived no profits from the dramatic adaptation of his tale, he was able to
capitalize upon his newly earned fame by taking to the lecture circuit.

The lecture circuit provided Poe with a stage upon which to argue for originality in American poetry, to rail against the cliques and puffery that predominated the literary milieu of New England (as well as against the Transcendentalists), to promote his own literary standards by commenting upon the merits and demerits of the writers represented in the many editions of Rufus Griswold's anthologies – *The Poets and Poetry of America, The Female Poets of America* – and, finally, to recite his own works, often "The Raven," to the satisfaction of his audiences. Poe's peregrinations throughout his career would take him to all of the cities on whose stages his mother had performed. Just as his mother and his grandmother had aspired to reach their audiences on the stages of such cities as Boston, New York, Philadelphia, and Richmond, so too did Poe attempt to make America his stage as a writer of criticism, fiction, and poetry. It was indeed as a poet that Poe wished to be remembered, and it is in his poetry that his stagecraft can best be discerned and appreciated.

CONCLUSION

Throughout his life, Poe continued to cherish the memory of his mother, and he publicly defended his mother's profession and her artistic calling in the *Broadway Journal*. As a poet, a writer of fiction, a magazinist, and a critic, Poe attempted throughout his turbulent life to live up to his mother's legacy. Though Eliza Poe's example was one of hardship, it was, more importantly, one of dedication and perseverance. Understandably, Poe himself was attracted to and repulsed by the limelight that he sought; he wrote against the odds and against the cultural norms, and, as such, was destined to be consumed in the process, but he could do nothing other than take the literary stage for the sake of his idea of the beautiful, which was almost always dark, and almost always shrouded in death.

NOTES

1. Geddeth Smith, *The Brief Career of Eliza Poe* (Rutherford, NJ: Farleigh Dickinson University Press, 1988); Arthur Hobson Quinn, *Edgar Allan Poe: A Critical Biography* (New York: Appleton-Century, 1941), 1–50.
2. Don B. Wilmeth and Tice L. Miller, "Introduction: Survey from the Beginning to the Present," *Cambridge Guide to American Theatre* (New York: Cambridge University Press, 1993), 1–3.
3. Laurence Senelick, "Introduction," *The American Stage: Writing on Theatre from Irving to Tony Kushner*, ed. Laurence Senelick (New York: Library of America, 2010), xvii–xix.
4. Quinn, *Edgar Allan Poe*, 3, 1, 697–724.

5. Edgar Allan Poe, *Essays and Reviews*, ed. G. R. Thompson (New York: Library of America, 1984), 19, 25.

6. Dwight Thomas and David K. Jackson, *The Poe Log: A Documentary Life of Edgar Allan Poe, 1809–1849* (Boston: G. K. Hall, 1987), 57.

7. Philip Edward Phillips, "Poe's 1845 Boston Lyceum Appearance Reconsidered," *Deciphering Poe*, ed. Alexandra Urakova (Bethlehem, PA: Lehigh University Press, 2012).

8. Edgar Allan Poe, *Politian: An Unfinished Tragedy*, ed. Thomas Ollive Mabbott (Menasha, WI: George Banta, 1923).

9. Aristotle, *Poetics*, ed. and trans. James Hutton (New York: Norton, 1982), 64, 50–2.

10. N. Bryllion Fagin, *The Histrionic Mr. Poe* (Baltimore: Johns Hopkins University Press, 1949), 77.

11. Joseph Sabin, *Bibliotheca Dramatica: Catalogue of the Theatrical and Miscellaneous Library of the Late William E. Burton, the Distinguished Comedian* (New York: J. Sabin, 1860), lots 865, 941, 948, 1122, 1289, 1299, 1716, 1717.

12. See Philip Edward Phillips, "Teaching Poe's 'The Raven' and 'Annabel Lee' as Elegies," *Approaches to Teaching Poe's Prose and Poetry*, ed. Jeffrey Andrew Weinstock and Tony Magistrale (New York: MLA, 2008), 76–80.

13. Frederick von Raumer, *England in 1835: Being a Series of Letters Written to Friends in Germany During a Residence in London and Excursions into the Provinces*, trans. Sarah Austin and E. E. Lloyd (Philadelphia: Carey, Lea, and Blanchard, 1836), 144.

14. Edgar Allan Poe, *The Brevities: Pinakidia, Marginialia, Fifty Suggestions, and Other Works*, ed. Burton R. Pollin (New York: Gordian, 1985), 14.

15. Ibid., 165.

16. John Lithgow, "Foreword," *The American Stage: Writing on Theatre from Washington Irving to Tony Cushner*, ed. Laurence Senelick (New York: Library of America, 2010), xiii.

17. Edgar Allan Poe, *The Complete Works of Edgar Allan Poe*, ed. James A. Harrison, 17 vols. (New York: Crowell, 1902), vol. xii, 119–20.

18. Ibid., vol. xii, 124.

19. Ibid., vol. xii, 189.

20. Ibid., vol. xii, 185–6. The author would like to thank the Faculty Research and Creative Activity Committee, Middle Tennessee State University for a 2010–11 Academic-Year Grant to support his research at the Harvard Theatre Collection and Boston Athenaeum.

CHAPTER 13

Lions and Bluestockings

Anne Boyd Rioux

The cultural life of New York in the 1820s and 1830s – presided over by James Fenimore Cooper, Washington Irving, William Cullen Bryant, and others – was centered in all-male clubs like Cooper's Bread and Cheese Club, the Literary Club, and the Sketch Club. But the literary New York Poe conquered in the 1840s was defined as much, if not more, by mixed-gender literary salons and soirees, many of them hosted by women, in which men and women vied for attention and fame. The journals in which men and women's writings appeared side by side, sometimes in conversation with each other, mimicked the literary performances of the salons. This cross-gendered milieu allowed women writers greater access to the city's culture and greater agency as hostesses, but it also positioned them as objects of romantic attraction in social and literary contexts. Indeed, a good deal of the poetry and prose of this era, including Poe's, reflects the gendered and sometimes sexually charged nature of the interactions between the "lions" and "bluestockings" of New York, liaisons that teetered between rivalry and romance. At the heart of these relationships and their literary manifestations was the desire for the kind of lasting fame already achieved by Bryant, Cooper, and Irving. Ultimately Poe and his male and female contemporaries became entangled in what can only be described as a kind of internecine warfare that inspired a series of illuminating literary ephemera as well as works that contributed to Poe's lasting fame.

Poe's satirical sketch "Lionizing" (1835) suggests that he viewed literary celebrity as a fickle and vain affair. It was inspired in part by the rise to fame of Nathaniel Parker Willis, who since 1832 had been publishing wildly popular, gossipy letters about English high society for the *New York Evening Mirror*. In Poe's "Lionizing," the young narrator sets all "Fum-Fudge" aflame simply by possessing "a nose sufficiently conspicuous" and "following it" to a "Lionship." In Poe's estimation, the "lions" were nothing more than men who flattered themselves and each other for their large appendages and attracted the admiration of women like "little Miss Bas-Bleu" (a reference to bluestockings) and the "Duchess of Bless-my-Soul." The narrator's celebrity ends as abruptly as it began, however, when he shoots off the nose of a prominent society man in a duel.[1]

Willis's fame was more lasting. Despite the fact that he had abused the hospitality of Lady Blessington and other members of the London aristocracy by publishing unflattering portraits of them, upon his return to New York, he "parleyed his infamy and social blunders into the most commercially successful literary career of the era."[2] The key to his success, according to Poe, who a decade later became a friend and admirer of Willis, is that he sought not merely a literary reputation; rather, he had united "the éclat of the littérateur with that of the man of fashion or of society." In other words, he achieved his reputation as much in society as in the pages of magazines. "He 'pushed himself,' went much into the world,...sought the intimacy of noted women, and got into quarrels with notorious men." Although Poe had earlier satirized such a path to fame, he had witnessed Willis's rise to lionhood and fortune, and there is considerable evidence that Poe sought to follow in his footsteps precisely by adopting his method of attacking the lions and romancing the bluestockings.[3]

Poe's assaults on the lions had begun in the 1830s as he lashed out at what he viewed as the Boston and New York literary cliques from which he was excluded. He cultivated an irascible persona as a principled but contemptuous critic in reviews that charged Longfellow with plagiarism and outed Theodore S. Fay, an editor of the *New York Mirror*, for puffing his own novel. He also wasn't beneath fueling the flames of heated disputes with anonymous or pseudonymous attacks upon himself. As Sandra Tomc has argued, "cultivating sensationalism, scandal, and notoriety" were methods of survival in an "inhospitable system" of commodified public authorship.[4] But the publication of his poem "The Raven" in 1845 established his literary celebrity and brought him into the society that Willis had mastered and that Poe ultimately would be forced to leave in disgrace.

Poe had returned to New York in 1844, convinced that it was "the focus of American letters."[5] The commercial and literary influence of Boston and Philadelphia was waning, leaving New York at the head of a budding national culture. The city's population would nearly double in the 1840s from three hundred thousand to more than a half million. Although Poe struggled to find a position with one of the city's fifty magazines, he secured editorial work on Willis's *New York Mirror* and in early 1845 began to work for the *Broadway Journal*. His foray into New York literary society commenced in February at the home of Caroline Kirkland, an author famous for her sketches of Western life, *A New Home – Who'll Follow?* (1839). According to the editor of the *Broadway Journal*, Charles Briggs, Poe excited "great curiosity" among "the New York literati [present], not one of whom had ever before seen him" but who all wanted to meet the author of "The Raven," which had just been published. Shortly thereafter, at the home of a prominent physician and patron of the arts, Poe's arrival "betokened the visit of a celebrity," and he was introduced as "The Raven" in the midst of "an ominous silence."[6] Soon Poe was the man of the moment and the most sought-after guest in the city's literary salons.

The tradition of the salon had its origins in France and reached its height with the soirees hosted by Madame de Staël and Madame Recamier in the late eighteenth and early nineteenth centuries. As Amelia Gere Mason explains, in her comparison of the French salons to the women's clubs of the 1890s, "The salon, like the club, was founded and led by clever women in the interests of culture, both literary and social; but, unlike the club, it was devoted to bringing into relief the talents of men."[7] While the male literary lions may have been the guests of honor at the salons that proliferated in London and later New York, salons also afforded women the opportunity to gain positions of relative power as hostesses who brought together prominent men and, increasingly, women who had themselves achieved fame, most often as authors. The most prominent of the New York literary hostesses was Anne C. Lynch, an unmarried teacher and poet who lived with her mother at 116 Waverly Place, where, on Saturday evenings, the cream of the city's literary society gathered, including N. P. Willis, Caroline Kirkland, Horace Greeley, Margaret Fuller, Catharine Sedgwick, Rufus Griswold, Frances Osgood, Emma Embury, Sara Jane Clarke Lippincott (a.k.a. Grace Greenwood), and Elizabeth Oakes Smith. The primary attraction of the salon was celebrities, as Ida Tarbell explained in her 1894 essay on the French salon: "The first and most important preoccupation of a salon is the people who shall form it. Nothing is so interesting as a person. The wise woman knows this and makes it her first duty to secure habitués who will draw. Usually she seeks to have as constant visitors, one, two, or three 'stars,' men whom everybody wants to know."[8] In 1845, Poe was the "star" everyone, particularly the women, wanted to know.

At Anne Lynch's salon, the entertainment for the evening was simply, she wrote, "what they [guests] find in each other."[9] With only tea and cookies as lubricants, attendees entertained each other with readings and performances. Poe's were particularly memorable. In his recitation of "The Raven," he "presented himself as a mesmeric poet," wrote Eliza Richards, captivating his audience with his magnetic personality. Rufus Griswold remembered: "His conversation was at times almost supra-mortal in its eloquence. His voice was modulated with astonishing skill, and his large and variably expressive eyes looked repose or shot fiery tumult into theirs who listened."[10] Poet Elizabeth Oakes Smith recalled that Poe's mesmerizing style appealed primarily to women: "He did not affect the society of men, rather that of highly intellectual women with whom he liked to fall into a sort of eloquent monologue, half dream, half poetry. Men were intolerant of all this, but women fell under his fascination and listened in silence."[11]

The conventional view of the bluestockings who admired Poe has been that they were inferior "hangers-on," lesser lights who "happily sat at Poe's feet and luxuriated in the pride of knowing a famous writer on a first-name basis."[12] The term *bluestockings*, which continues to proliferate in Poe criticism in reference to these female writers, was often used in the nineteenth century as a derogatory epithet to describe a woman whose intellectual or literary pursuits made her mannish. Although women writers did refer at times neutrally or positively to "bluestockingdom" or "belle-blues" in their writings, others, including Catharine Sedgwick, tried to dismantle the negative associations of the term and reconstruct the image of literary women. By the 1840s, negative attitudes toward women writers as competitors and imitators of men had become wrapped up in the term "bluestocking."[13] More problematic, though, is the portrayal of the circle of women writers in which Poe moved as sycophantic admirers. Poe, for his part, could be just as mesmerized by the female poets he met in the literary salons, including Smith. Her poem "The Sinless Child" elicited extraordinary adulation from Poe, who, Smith wrote, "was an adroit and elegant flatterer for the time being, his imagination being struck by some fine woman." Poe himself wrote to Smith, "Such women as you, and Helena [Sarah Helen Whitman], and a few others, ought to be installed as queens, and artists of all kinds should be privileged to pay you court. They would grow wise and holy under such companionship." And, as Eliza Richards has demonstrated, it was just as likely that Poe desired to associate his name with those of the poetesses who had won fame long before his brief flirtation with celebrity.[14]

Chief among the women writers Poe admired was Fanny Osgood, one of the most famous female poets of the time. Thought of as a modern-day Corinne (the heroine of Madame de Staël's autobiographical novel), she was lauded by her contemporaries as an improvisatrice whose "beautiful songs," wrote Griswold, "were written with almost the fluency of conversation." Grace Greenwood, whose affection for Osgood bordered on worship, confirmed her particular appeal to literary men like Poe: "She charms lions to sleep, with her silver lute, and then throws around them the delicate network of her exquisite fancy, and lo! when they wake, they are well content in their silken prison."[15] The particular charm of Osgood's seductive performances was the sense that her poetry simply sprang organically and effortlessly from some hidden source. She embodied the ideal of the "poetess": "an artless songstress whose effusions gushed forth as naturally as bird song."[16] In that sense, then, she transcended the maligned bluestocking, whose learning was deemed affected and pretentious. Osgood's ultra-feminine literary persona thus made her alluring rather than threatening (as the bluestocking was). Her sexually charged lyrics found their way from soiree performances to the pages of the popular magazines and back again.

Although Osgood was married, she was likely separated from her husband when she met Poe in March 1845. Whether or not he was the one to seek an introduction, as she later claimed, it is clear that the admiration was mutual. In April, Osgood began sending poems, most of them pseudonymous, to the *Broadway Journal*, which Poe was editing with Charles Briggs. In the words of Mary de Jong, Osgood "secured [Poe's] editorial attention by portraying wistful and admiring females that Poe might, if he wished, take as representatives of herself, and by casting him as a loved one, intimate friend, genius, and guide." That he did read her poems as personally addressing him is clear, as he began to publish his own responses and often placed their works next to or on top of each other.[17]

In a representative exchange, Osgood published the poem "Echo-Song":

> I know a noble heart that beats
> For one it loves how "wildly well!"
> I only know for whom it beats;
> But I must never tell.

In response, Poe published "To F – – – ":

> Thou wouldst be loved? – then let thy heart
> From its present pathway part not!
> Being everything which now thou art,
> Be nothing which thou are not![18]

Thus their published poems performed the kind of Valentine exchange that had become popular at Lynch and other's soirees. Often the Valentines were read anonymously and guests were invited to guess for whom they were intended.[19] Sometimes the recipient's name was encoded in the poem, as in the acrostic Valentine Poe wrote to Osgood in 1846. The poem, which debuted at Lynch's Valentines' Day soiree, was subsequently published in the *Evening Mirror*. By that time, the *Broadway Journal* had folded and the flirtation between editor-poet and poetess had lost its platform. In addition, Osgood's husband had returned to New York, and she was pregnant with her third child. Poe and Osgood's affair, whether platonic or sexual, was rapidly coming to an end.

Poe also had worn out his welcome at Lynch's salon. As she explained nearly two years later, "There was a great war in bluestockingdom some time ago and Poe did not behave very honorably in it...I now scarcely ever see him."[20] The "great war" had begun in January 1846 at the hands of Elizabeth Ellet, a widely published writer who frequented Lynch's salon and whose poems had begun to appear prominently in the *Broadway Journal* (after Poe had become its sole editor), seemingly displacing Osgood as the editor's favorite. During a visit to the Poe household, Ellet claimed to have seen an indiscreet letter from Osgood and subsequently advised her to request the return of her letters. Fearful of further scandal – rumors of an affair between her and Poe had already begun to circulate – Osgood enlisted the aid of Lynch and Margaret Fuller. When they visited Poe, he testily suggested that Ellet should be concerned about her own letters. Poe claimed later to have soon thereafter returned Ellet's letters, leaving them at her door, but Ellet insisted she had never written him any compromising letters. Her brother soon confronted him, threatening violence. To protect himself, Poe asked his friend Thomas Dunn English for permission to borrow his gun. When English refused, suggesting the story was fabricated, Poe and English began a fistfight in which Poe received, in English's words, "a sound cuffing." Poe suffered thereafter what appears to have been a breakdown and wrote to Ellet that his accusation against her was the result of a bout of insanity.[21]

The public display of their romantic attraction in verses addressed to each other led both Poe and Osgood down a path of self and mutual destruction. Poe's reputation in society was forever shattered and his health began to deteriorate. (His wife was also dying.) Osgood's reputation did not suffer to such an extent; she continued to attend Lynch's salon, and she soon received the support and affection of Griswold, the era's chief anthologist and promoter of other writers, many of them women. Yet she also suffered from the imputations of compromising behavior and spent the remaining years of her life (she died of consumption in 1850) asserting her innocence and battling with Ellet, who began to feud with

Griswold as well.[22] Poe and Osgood's love poems were the outgrowth of a sentimental popular culture that valued a spontaneous outpouring of emotion in poetry, engaging them in a dangerous emotional game that threatened not only their reputations but also their health and sanity. The poem "In Memory of Mrs. Osgood" by her friend Emily Waters sentimentally interprets Osgood's poetry as the cause of her own demise:

> Yet, as thy pen interpreted the spirit,
> That rules the female heart, it was thy doom
> To show thine own, and in the world's gaze wear it,
> Until it sunk exhausted to the tomb.[23]

Poe also spent his final years (he died in 1849) defending himself, in his case by directly assailing his enemies. In May 1846, he began publishing his series "The Literati of New York," in which he wrote flattering assessments of Osgood, Fuller, and Lynch but declined to notice Ellet, reserving his venom for English and his former associate Charles Briggs. English, in particular, resented Poe's malice and published his rejoinder under the heading "War of the Literati" in the *Evening Mirror*, published by Hiram Fuller, under whom Poe had worked at the paper in 1844 and with whom he also had a rocky relationship. But it was English's charges in print that Poe was guilty of forgery and had not paid his debts, besides being generally "thoroughly unprincipled, base and depraved . . . an assassin in morals," that led Poe to file suit against Fuller and, indirectly, English.[24] English responded by publishing a novel, serialized in the *New York Mirror*, called "1844, or, the Power of the 'S. F.,'" that satirized Poe as the drunk and plagiarizing critic Marmaduke Hammerhead, who "deemed himself the object of persecution on the part of the combined literati of the country, and commenced writing criticisms upon their character." Poe would ultimately win the libel suit, and, perhaps more important, the battle for lasting fame with his literary contribution to the war of the literati, "The Cask of Amontillado." In the story, Montresor's (Poe's) desire for revenge with impunity is satisfied when he entombs Fortunato (English), although the story's European setting removes it from the context of the literary battles that inspired Poe to write this "meditation on the art and passion of revenge," making it a story whose psychological terror has captured readers' imaginations since it was published.[25]

One could argue that Poe's ongoing battles with Ellet and English ultimately contributed to his lasting fame, as "Cask" remains one of his most famous stories. And in another way his entanglements with the bluestockings did as well. Richards has argued, "Poe stood among the women writers as one who sought to harness their receptive powers and upstage their popular success." His mastery of "poetic conventions of romantic exchange," in poems such as "Annabel Lee" and "Lenore," arguably inspired by the work of female poets, has gained him many more readers over the years than the works of the poetesses who were not only the objects of that exchange but also participants in it.[26] Although his status as a literary lion was fleeting, just as he had predicted fame would be in "Lionizing," he has towered above his New York contemporaries, male and female, ever since. While Willis had seemed more successful at courting the bluestockings and attacking the lions, Poe managed to generate enduring literary capital out of his wars with the literati.

NOTES

1. Edgar Allan Poe, *Tales* (New York: Wiley and Putnam, 1845), 58, 59. Poe reprinted the story in the *Broadway Journal* under the title "Some Passages in the Life of a Lion," in May 1845, in the midst of his own rise to fame.

2. Sandra M. Tomc, "Poe and His Circle," in *The Cambridge Companion to Edgar Allan Poe*, ed. Kevin J. Hayes (New York: Cambridge University Press, 2002), 28.

3. Edgar Allan Poe, *Essays and Reviews*, ed. G. R. Thompson (New York: Library of America, 1984), 1124. Tomc, "Poe and His Circle," 28–9, argues that Poe patterned his professional and, in part, his social career on Willis.

4. Tomc, "Poe and His Circle," 27. For examples of Poe fanning the flames of controversy, see Kenneth Silverman, *Edgar A. Poe: Mournful and Never-Ending Remembrance* (New York: HarperCollins, 1991), 251–3.

5. Poe, *Essays*, 1120.

6. Charles F. Briggs, "The Personality of Poe," *Independent* 29 (December 13, 1877), 1–2.

7. Amelia Gere Mason, "Club and Salon," *Century Illustrated Magazine* 56 (1898), 123.

8. Ida M. Tarbell, "The Principles and Pastimes of the French Salon," *The Chautauquan* 18 (1894), 573.

9. Quoted in Dwight Thomas and David K. Jackson, *The Poe Log: A Documentary Life of Edgar Allan Poe, 1809–1849* (Boston: G. K. Hall, 1987), 620.

10. Eliza Richards, *Gender and the Poetics of Reception in Poe's Circle* (New York: Cambridge University Press, 2004), 32; Rufus W. Griswold, "Memoir of the Author," *The Works of Edgar Allan Poe*, ed. Rufus W. Griswold, 4 vols. (New York: W. J. Widdleton, n.d.), vol. i, liv.

11. Elizabeth Oakes Smith, *Selections from the Autobiography*, ed. Mary Alice Wyman (Lewiston, ME: Lewiston Journal, 1924), 88;

12. Smith, *Selections*, 88; James Hutchisson, *Poe* (Jackson: University Press of Mississippi, 2005), 179, 180.

13. *Oxford English Dictionary* contains an etymology of the term and its uses, which were often derogatory. Anne Lynch refers to "bluestockingdom" in a quote cited later in this chapter. Osgood referred to a "blue-belle" in "Life in New York: Sketch of Literary Soiree," *Graham's* 30 (March 1847), 177, and addresses "My brilliant Blue Belle" in "To a Slandered Poetess [1850]," *Wielding the Pen: Writings on Authorship by American Women of the Nineteenth Century*, ed. Anne E. Boyd (Baltimore: Johns Hopkins University Press, 2009), 84. See Catharine Sedgwick's rejoinder to the pejorative attitudes toward learned and literary women, "A Sketch of a Bluestocking [1832]," *Wielding the Pen*, 28–36.

14. Smith, *Selections*, 88, 124. Richards, *Gender and the Poetics*, 29.

15. Rufus Griswold, "Frances Sargent Osgood," *Laurel Leaves: A Chaplet Woven by the Friends of the Late Mrs. Osgood*, ed. Mary E. Hewitt (New York: Lamport, Blakeman and Law, 1854), 21, 18.

16. Mary G. De Jong, "Lines from a Partly Published Drama: The Romance of Frances Sargent Osgood and Edgar Allan Poe," *Patrons and Protégées: Gender, Friendship, and Writing in Nineteenth- Century America*, ed. Shirley Marchalonis (New Brunswick: Rutgers University Press, 1994), 34.

17. De Jong, "Lines," 35–6. See also Richards, *Gender and the Poetics*, chap. 2.

18. Quoted in De Jong, "Lines," 40.

19. Examples of the types of Valentine poems exchanged at soirees can be found in Frances Osgood's "Kate Carol to Mary S.," *Columbian Lady's and Gentleman's Magazine* 7 (1847), 203–6. Many Valentines were also subsequently published in Willis's *Home Journal*.

20. Quoted in Thomas and Jackson, *Poe Log*, 719.

21. De Jong, "Lines," 42–4, describes Ellet's displacement of Osgood in the *Broadway Journal*, the ensuing rivalry that played out in its pages, and the affair of the letters; Silverman, *Edgar A. Poe*, 290–2; Thomas and Jackson, *Poe Log*, 622–3; and James B. Reece, "A Reexamination of a Poe Date: Mrs. Ellet's Letters," *American Literature* 42 (1970), 157–64. English quoted in Francis B. Dedmond, "'The Cask of Amontillado' and the War of the Literati," *Modern Language Quarterly* 15 (1954), 141.

22. De Jong, "Lines," 45–8, describes Osgood's literary attempts to salvage her reputation and her responses to Ellet.

23. Emily Waters, "In Memory of Mrs. Osgood," *Laurel Leaves*, 151.

24. Quoted in Dedmond, "'The Cask,'" 141.

25. English's novel quoted in Silverman, *Edgar A. Poe*, 315–16, which assesses how Poe's feud with English inspired this tale. See also, Dedmond, "'The Cask.'"

26. Richards, *Gender and the Poetics*, 3.

CHAPTER 14

Slavery and Abolitionism

Paul Christian Jones

Alone among the major writers of the antebellum period, Edgar Allan Poe spent a substantial portion of his life in slaveholding sections of the United States. Poe's Southern upbringing has led scholars to pore over his writing for his views about the region's "peculiar institution" to discover whether he was slavery's defender, its critic, or somehow ambivalent about its horrors. Poe's well-known distaste for the didactic likely prevented him from making explicit arguments about slavery, either justification of the institution or criticism of its faults. Indeed, he even attacked writers for using literary works to advance their positions on this subject. For example, he denounced James Russell Lowell's *Fable for Critics* because "his prejudices on the topic of slavery break out every where in his present book," implying that such prejudices should be obscured from the readers' view.[1] However, even though unambiguous arguments about slavery are difficult to find in Poe's writing, a number of his works – including some of his most famous creations – reflect the prejudices of the proslavery South and its anxieties about the risks and consequences of slaveholding.

Brought up from the age of three in the household of John Allan, a prosperous Richmond, Virginia merchant, Poe spent his childhood and adolescence surrounded by slaves, likely in the care of a mammy and with slave children as playmates. During his year at the University of Virginia, he was attended by a black servant, probably a slave hired from a local slaveholder.[2] Despite his tenuous status in the Allan family (he was never legally adopted), young Poe likely held views common to members of the slave-owning class in the South, including pretensions to aristocracy, a conviction of the necessity (if not the justice) of the institution of slavery, and a belief in white racial superiority over the black underclass. A glimpse of this attitude is revealed in an 1827 letter from eighteen-year-old Poe detailing his outrage at his foster father, who has "suffered me to be subjected to the whims and caprice, not only of your white family, but the complete authority of the blacks – these grievances I could not submit to; and I am gone."³

In the years of his early adulthood, as Poe no longer relied upon the Allan family for support, he continued to inhabit a world where slavery was a part of everyday life. He spent over a year as a soldier at Fort Moultrie in Charleston, South Carolina, from late 1827 to late 1828. In Baltimore in 1829, he participated in the sale of a slave for his aunt, Maria Clemm.⁴ And, when he accepted his first literary job in 1835 as editorial assistant for the *Southern Literary Messenger* in Richmond, he worked in a setting wherein defending slavery from criticism was essentially editorial policy. The *Messenger* published a number of proslavery reviews and essays in Poe's time there. The most controversial has been the so-called Paulding-Drayton Review, an 1836 review praising James Kirke Paulding's *Slavery in the United States* and William Drayton's *The South Vindicated from the Treason and Fanaticism of the Northern Abolitionists*, which for decades was attributed to Poe and seen as explicit evidence of his support of slavery.⁵ While recent scholarship has convincingly attributed this review to Beverley Tucker instead, Poe did positively review for the *Messenger* books like Thomas Dew's *Address*, Joseph Holt Ingraham's *The South-West*, and Anne Grant's *Memoirs of an American Lady* that depicted slavery in a favorable light. For example, in his review of Ingraham's book, Poe applauds the author for avoiding "the general prejudices of a Yankee" and not casting "a jaundiced eye upon the South – to pervert its misfortunes into crimes – or distort its necessities into sins of volition." Asserting that Ingraham has "spoken of slavery as he found it," Poe notes that he "discovered...that while the physical condition of the slave is not what it has been represented, the slave himself is utterly incompetent to feel the *moral* galling of his chain."⁶ It is difficult to know whether the sentiments expressed in these reviews are Poe's own views or whether he tailored them to be in line with the *Messenger*'s largely proslavery readership. In either case, they illustrate Poe's willingness to advocate these views.

Poe's fiction has similarly been read as revealing a racist and proslavery ideology, even that written after he relocated to Philadelphia and New York, when he was no longer addressing a specifically Southern audience. Indeed, his slave characters are indistinguishable from the contentedly servile blacks abundant in antebellum plantation romance and the Sambo stereotypes of popular culture. For example, the slaves in "The Journal of Julius Rodman" (1840) and "The Gold-Bug" (1843) are consistent with the standard presentation of slaves in proslavery fiction as comic slaves loyally serving and amusing their masters. Toby in "Julius Rodman" is "a faithful negro," accompanying his master on his journey to the Rocky Mountains and entertaining Indians with his "jig dance."[7] Jupiter in "The Gold-Bug" is a manumitted slave, "who could be induced, neither by threats nor by promises, to abandon what he considered his right of attendance upon the foot-steps" of his master, William Legrand.[8] The black servants, both named Pompey, in "How to Write a Blackwood Article" (1838) and "The Man that Was Used Up" (1839) are similarly long-suffering, loyal attendants to their masters, Psyche Zenobia and General Smith. And Toby in "Julius Rodman" and Pompey in "Blackwood Article" are portrayed as racially offensive physical grotesques. Toby, for example, is "ugly...having all the peculiar features of his race; the swollen lips, large white protruding eyes, flat nose, long ears, double head, pot-belly, and bow legs."[9] While these stories do not offer explicit arguments, readers can infer a defense of slavery in these depictions of blacks as members of an inferior race, happy to serve white superiors.

Other readers might see in these tales a critique of slavery's effects, especially upon the whites influenced by what Frederick Douglass called "the fatal poison of irresponsible power." Poe's tales do present, as Douglass does, "the brutalizing effects of slavery" upon the slaveholder.[10] These masters all degrade their servants in a range of cruel behaviors, including General Smith's verbal insults of Pompey and Legrand's violent threats to Jupiter. The most extreme case is Psyche Zenobia's attack on Pompey; she seizes "him furiously by the wool with both hands" and tears "out a vast quantity of the black, and crisp, and curling material."[11] Beyond the abusive behavior of these figures, such depictions also suggest that slaveholding fosters an enfeebling dependency for the owners on their slaves. For example, General Smith depends on Pompey literally to assemble him each day, suggesting that he could not function without his servant's cooperation. And Psyche Zenobia's reliance on Pompey (whom she uses as a platform to stand on) enables her beheading by a large clock's hand. At the story's conclusion, she is left helpless (not only "headless," but also "niggerless").[12] Though cast as comic, Poe's presentation of these relationships resonates with the anxiety some readers must have felt about the potentially harmful effects of slave ownership.

In antebellum culture, these comic depictions of slaves coexisted along with and often obscured anxieties about the potential for violent slave uprising. Poe was living in Baltimore in August 1831 when Nat Turner led his slave revolt in Southampton County, Virginia, which claimed at least fifty-five white lives, mostly women and children, and Poe would have been well aware of the fearful responses of the white public, even outside of Virginia, to this event and the potential for recurrence. Much of his fiction can be read as exploiting these public concerns in the wake of Turner's Rebellion. In *The Narrative of Arthur Gordon Pym* (1838), a black cook leads a shipboard mutiny and, engaging in "most horrible butchery," executes twenty-two crew members with an axe and tosses their bodies into the sea. This mutinous black, a specter of Turner, is described by Pym as "a perfect demon." Later in the narrative, Pym and his companions, free of the mutineers, arrive on the island of Tsalal, where they encounter natives who are "jet black, with thick and long woolly hair." When it becomes apparent that the Tsalalians intend to kill the white men, they struggle to flee the "savages" – "the most barbarous, subtle, and bloodthirsty wretches that ever contaminated the face of the globe." Upon departing the island, Pym condemns these dark natives as "the most wicked, hypocritical, vindictive, bloodthirsty, and altogether fiendish race of men upon the face of the globe" and states, "we should have had no mercy had we fallen into their hands," echoing the anxiety that whites, both Southern and Northern, might have held about the imagined consequences of slave uprising.[13]

Though less explicit than *Pym*, a number of Poe's stories seem likewise grounded in fear of slave uprising. In these texts, Poe creates horrific figures who cannot be labeled actual representations of slaves but who are nevertheless marked with signs (including forced servitude or status as property) that encourage readers to consider them as figurative slaves; Poe thus achieves an effect of horror, exploiting white fears of slave rebellion, without writing tales that are proslavery polemic. In tales like "The Murders in the Rue Morgue" (1841) and "Hop-Frog" (1849), figurative slaves escape their enslavement to violent consequences. The orangutan in "Rue Morgue" is the "possession" of a sailor who brought it to Paris from Borneo to sell. Likely exploiting racist rhetoric linking Africans and primates, this orangutan represents a racial other who has become the "property" of a white owner.[14] The sailor's plans change when he finds the ape free from its closet, standing before a mirror with "razor in hand . . . attempting the operation of shaving." Terrified about "so dangerous a weapon in the possession of an animal so ferocious," the sailor attempts to whip it into submission, causing the animal to escape. The beast eventually attacks a mother and daughter in their apartment, first assaulting the mother with the razor and almost severing "her head from her body." Then "it flew upon the body of the girl, and imbedded its fearful talons in her throat, retaining its grasp until she expired."[15] Consistent with racist, proslavery rhetoric of the period, this story imagines the consequence of this rebellious property's attempt to escape its enslavement as gruesome violence upon the bodies of white women.

A similar narrative occurs in "Hop-Frog," wherein the title character, a jester enslaved to a tyrannical king, fights against degrading oppression. Hop-Frog comes "from some barbarous region...that no person ever heard of," where he and a female servant, Trippetta, "had been forcibly carried off from their respective homes...and sent as presents to the king." As a slave figure, Hop-Frog is initially presented sympathetically; not only is he a dwarf, crippled, and deformed, but he and Trippetta also endure frequent abuse from their master. Yet this sympathetic figure becomes a monstrous avenger with "fang-like teeth" who "foamed at the mouth...with an expression of maniacal rage." He enacts vengeance upon the king and his courtiers when he, helping to plan a masquerade, proposes the men portray "Eight Chained Ourang-Outangs"; the drunken courtiers and king allow the jester to cover them with tar and flax and to chain them together "after the fashion" of "those who capture Chimpanzees, or other larger apes, in Borneo." During the festivities, Hop-Frog chains the king and his courtiers to a chandelier, raises them into the air, and sets them on fire until "the whole eight ourang-outangs were blazing fiercely." While the crowd in attendance watches in terror, Hop-Frog and Trippetta escape, leaving the eight corpses "a fetid, blackened, hideous, and indistinguishable mass."[16] As in "Rue Morgue," grotesque white corpses in this tale represent the horrific consequence of a slave's resistance.

The narrative twist in "Hop-Frog" wherein this rebellious slave turns his masters into "ourang-outangs" reflects another anxiety about slave rebellion, the potential for racial hierarchies being overturned as the slaveholding class might become enslaved to those considered their inferiors. "The System of Doctor Tarr and Professor Fether" (1845) also registers this anxiety. In this story, the narrator visits a French insane asylum, takes a guided tour, and dines with what he believes to be the asylum's staff before learning that "the lunatics...had usurped the offices of the keepers" and thrown them "into the cells, where they were attended, as if they were the lunatics, by the lunatics themselves." While previously the asylum had practiced "the soothing system" where "all punishments were avoided" (suggesting a romanticized view of slavery as benign), after "the keepers and kept...exchange places," the newly empowered inmates implement a system of violent retribution, including tarring and feathering.[17]

As William Gilmore Simms demonstrates in an essay he contributed to *Southern Literary Messenger*, slavery's defenders argued that it played a valuable role in civilization but that not all races were capable of functioning as masters, claiming that civilization "conquers only to improve, while the savage only conquers to destroy." Accordingly, he asserts, civilization is "the only legitimate conquest, and every other is but tyranny."[18] These fears about the destructive and tyrannical nature of the "savage's" conquest are exploited in "Tarr and Fether." The inmates treat their keepers brutally; after being "suddenly overpowered," the asylum staff "were first well tarred, then carefully feathered, then shut up in underground cells," where an "abundance of water...was pumped on them daily." When the keepers finally escape their confinement and break into the dinner party, they appear to the frightened narrator as "a perfect army of...Chimpanzees, Ourang-Outangs, or big black baboons."[19] The reversal in roles has transformed the masters into beastlike creatures usually equated with slaves.

Poe's exploitation of anxieties about slave uprising is not confined to his fiction but appears in his verse as well. In "The Haunted Palace" (1839), for instance, the "evil things" that arose in a "hideous throng" and "assailed the monarch's high estate" might be grounded in fears of slave rebellion. One of Poe's most famous creations, the titular bird in "The Raven" (1845), also resonates with such concerns. The "ebony bird" tapping upon the speaker's window and tormenting him with its utterance is a black creature assumed to have escaped from "some unhappy master." This runaway possession, a less violent version of the "Rue Morgue" ape, outrages its auditor with its speaking of the single word "nevermore," a repeated and determined assertion of defiance. Similarly offensive to the speaker is the bird's refusal of "the least obeisance" to him and its assumption of the "mien of lord or lady." The raven's threatening perch upon the "bust of Pallas" – a figure of a white female – suggests its potential to defile white women. By the end of the poem, the narrator calls the bird "a thing of evil," a "fiend," and a "demon."[20] Yet again, the thought of a black possession refusing submission to a white "superior" figures as a horrifying act in Poe's work.

Though Poe's literary texts abound with these scenarios that dramatize cultural anxiety about resistant slaves, they seldom reveal his sentiments about abolitionists. However, his book reviews do articulate some of his objections to abolitionist positions and techniques. For example, his review of Henry Wadsworth Longfellow's *Poems on Slavery* (1842) criticizes the poet's antislavery verse as "a shameless medley of the grossest misrepresentation" and "incendiary doggerel," suggesting there is little truth in Longfellow's depictions of slavery.[21] His charges of propagandistic falsehood in abolitionist literary texts continue in his review of Lowell's *Fable for Critics* where he not only denounces Lowell as "the most rabid of the Abolition fanatics" but also raises concerns about how fanaticism of any sort can diminish a writer's work. Indeed, in the review, Poe criticizes what he considers fanatical views on both sides of the slavery question: Lowell's "fanaticism about slavery is a mere local outbreak of the same innate wrong-headedness which, if he owned slaves, would manifest itself in atrocious ill-treatment of them, with murder of any abolitionist who should endeavor to set them free." In Lowell's case, Poe asserts, his fanaticism creates an unfair bias against all Southerners. Poe suggests that "no Southerner who does not wish to be insulted, and at the same time revolted by a bigotry the most obstinately blind and deaf, should ever touch a volume by this author" because Lowell "has not the common honesty to speak well, even in a literary sense, of any man who is not a ranting abolitionist."[22] These reviews suggest Poe's belief that abolitionist rhetoric presented a dishonest depiction of the institution of slavery (and by implication the South as a region) that created a bias against Southerners like himself.

In his review of Robert Montgomery Bird's *Sheppard Lee* (1836), Poe reveals his perception of more dangerous consequences of abolitionist efforts. Poe praises the sequence in Bird's novel that offers "a spirited picture of a negro insurrection" and concludes "with the hanging of Nigger Tom," describing this sequence as "very excellent chapters upon abolition and the exciting effects of incendiary pamphlets and pictures, among our slaves in the South."[23] These chapters depict a group of slaves discovering an abolitionist pamphlet, "An Address to the Owners of Slaves," which causes them to revise their view of their bondage. They begin to "think of their master as a foe and usurper" and of themselves as "victims of avarice" and "the most injured people in the world." The effect of this abolitionist appeal upon them, clearly meant to evoke memories of Nat Turner, is that the slaves arm themselves and vow to "exterminate all the white men in Virginia, beginning with our master and his family."[24] Bird's narrative dramatizes starkly the black retributive violence that some Southerners believed would be stoked by abolitionists.

While Poe's favorable review of *Sheppard Lee* suggests that he agreed that abolitionist efforts could have such "exciting effects" upon the slave population, there is little reflection of this specific concern in the tales, like "Rue Morgue" and "Hop-Frog," that feature variations on slave rebellion. Only in "Tarr and Fether" does Poe present a link between an uprising – of the inmates against their keepers – and external instigation comparable to the influence of abolitionist literature. The asylum's superintendent, Maillard, laments to the narrator that, "more than once, some unhappy *contre-temps* has occurred in consequence of thoughtlessness on the part of our visitors," noting that the patients "were often aroused to a dangerous frenzy by injudicious persons who called to inspect the house."[25] The fear that slaves would be excited to "frenzy" by "injudicious" abolitionists seems validated here. "Hop-Frog" similarly offers readers a cautionary tale about the harmful potential of abolitionist rhetoric.[26] As it first follows the abolitionist approach of sympathetically depicting the travails of a slave before reversing course completely by unmasking its sympathetic slave as a terrifyingly vengeful "maniac" who leaves the "blackened, hideous" remains of "eight corpses" as testament to his rage and capacity for violence, "Hop-Frog" evokes fears about the "incendiary" possibilities of slave uprising.[27]

However, as suggested earlier, Poe appears attuned to anxieties on both sides of this debate and is quite willing to exploit all of these anxieties in his work regardless of the social implication. So, while horrifying images of rebellious slaves appear frequently in his work, so too appear images of brutish slave owners, like the king in "Hop-Frog" or Psyche Zenobia. Indeed, some of the most frightening figures in Poe's work might be these monstrous masters. "The Black Cat" (1843) provides the most striking example as its narrator, initially a loving and tender man, becomes increasingly abusive to his dependents, both human and animal. His favorite pet, Pluto, a large black cat that "loved me" and "attended me wherever I went" seems a composite of the devoted servants in "The Gold-Bug" and "The Man that Was Used Up" and the threatening animals in "Rue Morgue" and "The Raven." He becomes the special target of his drunken owner's abuse. In a gruesome sequence, the narrator "cut one of its eyes from the socket" and later "slipped a noose about its neck and hung it to a limb of a tree." He expresses "horror" at his own actions and his belief that he is committing a "deadly sin that would so jeopardize my immortal soul as to place it . . . beyond the reach of the infinite mercy of the Most Merciful and Most Terrible God."[28] This reference to God's disapproval of the narrator's actions – his abuse and murder of his black possession – echoes many antislavery arguments, including those in Thomas Jefferson's *Notes on the State of Virginia*, where he insists that "God is just" and "his justice cannot sleep for ever" as "The Almighty has no attribute which can take side with us" in debates over slavery.[29] While Poe's tale does not depict divine retribution, it does cast its narrator's brutal behavior as beyond redemption as he abuses yet another black cat, Pluto's double, and then turns on his own wife when she defends the poor creature: "goaded, by the interference, into a rage more than demoniacal, I withdrew my arm from her grasp and buried the axe in her brain."[30] This violent oppressor appears as monstrous as the rebellious slave in Poe's other work. Rather than making explicit or persuasive arguments about slavery, Poe seemed content to mine a variety of his time's anxieties about the institution of slavery – from the potential vengeance of an escaped slave to the brutalizing nature of slave owner- ship – and to construct haunting tales that pushed the necessary buttons to create the intended effect of horror.

NOTES

1. Edgar Allan Poe, *Essays and Reviews*, ed. G. R. Thompson (New York: Library of America, 1984), 819.
2. J. Gerald Kennedy provides an excellent account of Poe's early life in the milieu of slavery: "'Trust No Man': Poe, Douglass, and the Culture of Slavery," in *Romancing the Shadow: Poe and Race*, eds. J. Gerald Kennedy and Liliane Weissberg (New York: Oxford University Press, 2001), 233–6.
3. Poe to John Allan, March 19, 1827, *The Collected Letters of Edgar Allan Poe*, ed. John Ward Ostrom, Burton R. Pollin, and Jeffrey A. Savoye, 2 vols. (New York: Gordian, 2008), vol. i, 11.
4. John Miller, "Did Edgar Allan Poe Really Sell a Slave?" *Poe Studies* 9 (1976), 52–3.
5. Terence Whalen has convincingly argued against Poe's authorship of the "Paulding-Drayton Review" in *Edgar Allan Poe and the Masses: The Political Economy of Literature in Antebellum America* (Princeton: Princeton University Press, 1999), 181.
6. [Edgar Allan Poe], "The South-West," *Southern Literary Messenger* 2 (1836), 122.
7. Edgar Allan Poe, *Poetry and Tales*, ed. Patrick F. Quinn (New York: Library of America, 1984), 1200, 1243.
8. Edgar Allan Poe, *The Collected Works of Edgar Allan Poe*, ed. Thomas Ollive Mabbott, 3 vols. (Cambridge, MA: Belknap Press, 1969–78), vol. iii, 807.
9. Poe, *Poetry and Tales*, 1242.
10. Frederick Douglass, *The Oxford Frederick Douglass Reader*, ed. William Andrews (New York: Oxford University Press, 1996), 47–8, 54.
11. Poe, *Collected Works*, vol. ii, 351, 357.
12. Ibid., vol. ii, 351, 357.
13. Poe, *Poetry and Tales*, 1042–3, 1136, 1150, 1174.
14. Poe, *Collected Works*, vol. ii, 561–2. For a discussion of the racial codes evoked in this tale to encourage antebellum readers to equate the tale's orangutan with African Americans, see Elise Lemire, "'The Murders in the Rue Morgue': Amalgamation Discourses and the Race Riots of 1838 in Poe's Philadelphia," in *Romancing the Shadow*, 177–204.
15. Poe, *Collected Works*, vol. ii, 562–8.
16. Ibid., vol. iii, 1346–54.

17. Ibid., vol. iii, 1018–19.
18. William Gilmore Simms, "Miss Martineau on Slavery," *Southern Literary Messenger* 3 (1837), 654.
19. Poe, *Collected Works*, vol. iii, 1021.
20. Ibid., vol. i, 364–9.
21. Poe, *Essays*, 763–4, 762.
22. Ibid., 819.
23. Ibid., 399.
24. Robert Montgomery Bird, *Sheppard Lee*, 2 vols. (New York: Harper, 1836), vol. ii, 185, 187, 191, 196.
25. Poe, *Collected Works*, vol. iii, 1005.
26. Paul Christian Jones, "The Danger of Sympathy: Edgar Allan Poe's 'Hop-Frog' and the Abolitionist Rhetoric of Pathos," *Journal of American Studies* 35 (2001), 239–54.
27. Poe, *Collected Works*, vol. iii, 1354.
28. Ibid., vol. iii, 850–851.
29. Thomas Jefferson, *Writings*, ed. Merrill Peterson (New York: Library of America, 1984), 289.
30. Poe, *Collected Works*, vol. iii, 856.

CHAPTER 15

The Cult of Mourning

Therese M. Rizzo

Starting in the eighteenth century, Americans began to reformulate religious and social doctrines dictating a fundamental cultural practice: the way that society handled death. Rather than treating death as a function of biology or religious beliefs, the events surrounding death became ritualized, even commercialized, as people became consumers of cultural artifacts meant to memorialize death as an occasion greater than the natural cessation of life. Part of this shift in consciousness resulted from changing beliefs about the afterlife; James J. Farrell argues that Puritanical fears about a hellish afterlife were replaced with images of an inviting heaven. In an attempt to "destroy fears of death," much was written about the beauty, serenity, and peace that would follow after death.[1]

The 1799 death of George Washington, America's preeminent statesman and hero, is often cited as the cultural event that began a movement or, as one historian calls it, "an orgy of weeping and mourning," that became known as the cult of mourning.[2] The cult of mourning was a belief system that glorified the process of postdeath rituals, so much so that followers of this cultural movement "cherished" death "as the occasion for two of the deepest 'right feelings' in human experience: bereavement, or direct mourning for the dead, and sympathy, or mournful condolence for the bereaved."[3] In the years that followed Washington's death, changes in religious beliefs held by the flourishing American middle class caused a commercial and social revolution in the way that people were memorialized after death. Art, literature, architecture, music, and mass media were all affected by the cult of mourning as each field produced works meant to commemorate, direct, or promote correct methods of mourning.[4] If Washington's death was the event upon which this movement was modeled, then the nation's tribute to its lost leader through hundreds of public eulogies, countless hymns and poetic odes, and numerous personal testimonials printed in newspapers and pamphlets was only the beginning of a national fascination with communal grieving.[5]

That fascination extends to much of Edgar Allan Poe's work portraying the human psychology of dying and mourning. Although the poetry and stories most famously aligned with death, such as "The Raven" and "The Fall of the House of Usher," are often interpreted as macabre, gothic portrayals of the subject, Poe's work indicates an awareness of the growing importance placed on the rituals of death. At times, Poe's fiction and poetry seem to bring an added aura of beauty and mystery to the practices of mourning, thereby contributing in his distinct way to the cult of mourning. While certain pieces reify the cultural practices and human emotions following death, other works question the voyeuristic, consumer-based fascination with death practices inherent in the cult of mourning. Since Poe neither followed nor criticized these rituals, his relationship to the national fascination with communal rituals surrounding death remains as enigmatic as one of his most famous death omens, the raven.

Historians and critics suggest that the rise of Sentimentalism, a movement not often associated with Poe's work, greatly influenced the way in which private mourning was made public, but the cult of mourning was a widespread phenomenon that encompassed more than Sentimental artistic and material productions. Sentimental Americans "domesticated death" in an attempt to destroy the fear many felt about the unknown by enacting scenes of public mourning, such as wearing ostentatious mourning clothes and decorating their homes in black crepe and other indicators of loss.[6] Thus, death became a community event akin to a holiday. Elaborate burial plots, ideally located in rural locations reminiscent of Romantic landscapes, and ornate headstones or monuments became a necessary and expected part of the postdeath experience for mourners. Since all of these elaborate events cost money and involved the entire community, American mourning transformed what was once an event for a small group of people into a larger labor that "established itself as a civic virtue."[7] Despite low-cost memorials such as hair wreaths or death portraits, the cult of mourning was part of the economy of the nineteenth century, which enabled a kind of patriotic zeal for this community event.

Despite the codified rituals perpetuated by the growing middle class, the cult of mourning also extended to the working classes. Vincent DiGirolamo explores the media attention paid to pauper funerals, specifically funerals for newsboys. DiGirolamo presents a story of impoverished newsboys' attempts to gather enough money to buy a funeral wreath for an orphaned coworker with no one to pay for his funeral. The story suggests both the absurdity and poignancy of a group of uneducated children trying to convince a local florist to enshrine the name "Skinny" across the traditional mourning flower wreath.[8] Because the trappings of middle-class funerals cost so much, the rituals of mourning could be both exclusionary and ridiculous when mimicked by those who could not afford the luxury of mourning commodities.

The paradox of the ridiculous and the sincere in the ritualized nature of the cult of mourning is the theme most often repeated in Poe's works. "The Raven," first published in 1845, presents scenes familiar to the nineteenth-century mourner. The narrator says he looks to books for the "surcease of my sorrow" (line 10), an act not uncommon in ritualized mourning. Mary Louise Kete argues that the abundant production of stylized personal and public grief literature was done "as a means of transforming…grief into restorative mourning, skepticism into optimism."[9] The act of writing to share grief became a cathartic experience that would enable healing. The narrator of "The Raven," however, does not find solace in the books he consults because his "lost Lenore" has become "nameless here forever-more" (lines 10, 12). His words suggest that the discourse of mourning found in books is too impersonal and generalized. Lenore is not named in the books he consults; thus, the public discourse is not specific to his personal loss, so, for the narrator, his pain cannot be transformed by another author's depiction of grief.

The narrator of "The Raven" feels isolated in his grief with only the monosyllabic raven as his companion, yet he instinctively interprets the raven as a messenger sent from "these angels" or as a "Prophet…thing of evil!" The raven becomes more than a symbol of the narrator's grief; he is an agent of mourning who can "tell" the narrator "truly" if he will ever find peace and "balm" in the biblical "Gilead," or the place where all truth will be witnessed (lines 81, 85, 88–9). For those who took solace in the belief that mourning rituals were meant to honor the dead and transform grief into hope, the raven's ambiguous "Nevermore" either reaffirms the search for meaning in death or critiques the very premise upon which the cult of mourning promised solace to followers.

The ambiguity displayed in "The Raven" contrasts with Poe's 1838 short story "Ligeia," which clearly perverts and challenges the religious foundations for the cult of mourning. The post-Calvinist, Evangelical movement of the 1830s was the fundamental element in revisionist beliefs in a heavenly afterlife, rather than the perils of hell, as the just reward to all good Christians.[10] The Evangelical movement in both America and England called for a return to scriptural study, and even early practitioners clearly delineated between the outcomes for those who accepted and practiced correct Christian doctrines and those who did not. The Rev. Samuel

Davies asserted in a 1756 funeral sermon that misreading the Bible led to "tremendous gloom" in those who believed that life "was not worth while to come into being, if it must be resigned so soon." He rejects this spiritual pessimism by suggesting that after death Christians will have new, improved bodies impervious to death "so that they shall be as though death never had had any power over them; and thus death shall be abolished, annihilated, and all traces of the ruins it had made for ever disappear, as though they had never been."[11] The enemy here is clearly the sadness surrounding death, and belief in Christianity allows followers to partake in the abolition of death.

Almost eighty years later, William Sprague, another Presbyterian minister, echoes Davies's sentiment in *Letters on Practical Subjects to a Daughter* (1831) as he describes "the amazing scenes which must open upon the spirit the moment death has done its work, and on the riches of that grace which secures to the believer a complete victory in his conflict and triumphant entry into heaven."[12] Despite the physical pains of death, the acknowledgment of these amazing scenes should be part of the celebratory nature of death. Mourning for the triumphant dead turned, then, from a quiet and solemn affair into a celebration that reaffirmed the destruction of the very notion of death.

"Ligeia" consciously echoes the notion of this victory over death; however, the narrator's victory is not in finding consolation through the promise of a Christian afterlife, but in the destruction of death through the bodily resurrection of his beloved Ligeia. As the unnamed narrator of the story watches his enigmatic wife slowly die, he recites a poem she has written that predicts how "The curtain, a funeral pall, / Comes down with the rush of a storm" only to discover that "the play is the tragedy, 'Man,' / And its hero the Conqueror Worm."[13] In these lines, the funeral and its ritual are nothing more than an allegory for the performance of death, which cannot be conquered by a belief in Christ's supremacy. Despite the Evangelicals' assertions, Ligeia claims that only the worm feasting on the buried corpse stands as triumphant conqueror. Directly after the narrator recites Ligeia's poem, we hear her speak for the first time in the story as she calls out in her death throes: "O God! O Divine Father! – shall these things be undeviatingly so? – shall this Conqueror be not once conquered? Are we not part and parcel in Thee? Who – who knoweth the mysteries of the will with its vigor? Man doth not yield him to the angels, nor unto death utterly, save only through the weakness of his feeble will."[14] In her sole utterance, Ligeia poses a question not dissimilar to the emerging Evangelical revisionist philosophy on death. She deviates

from Christian doctrine, however, when she places human will on par
with divine agency and insinuates that man, rather than God, should con-
quer death. Although Ligeia dies, the narrator somehow mysteriously res-
urrects her by using his second wife, Lady Rowena, as a bodily vessel for
Ligeia's reemergence.

"Ligeia" ends with the resurrected body of its eponymous heroine, the
embodied conqueror of death. Poe subverts the emerging belief systems
that encouraged people to celebrate death as God's gift to humanity. In
the notion of asserted agency found in the story's epigraph attributed to
Joseph Glanvill, a seventeenth-century English philosopher and vicar in
the Church of England, Poe situates his reader in a philosophical counter-
narrative where humanity, not God, will determine how death is interpreted and enacted. In Poe's version of mourning the beloved dead, he
creates a husband who cannot, or will not, rejoice in the comforting
notion that he will be reunited with his wife. Instead, the narrator privately mourns Ligeia in a confused haze of grief and torment, only to
watch as his beloved reemerges into the world through decidedly un-
Christian means. In almost direct contrast to the doctrine that enabled
the cult of mourning to publicly share death, the narrator "after months
of weary and aimless wandering" settles in a deserted English abbey to privately mourn his loss, even after his remarriage. The narrator eschews religious consolation – the deserted abbey serves as a monument to his loss
of religious belief – and he erects no public monuments to the memory of
the woman whose "beauty," he says, "passed into my spirit, there dwelling as in a shrine."[15] The narrator memorializes Ligeia in life, not death,
through his worship of her and his complete abandonment to the transcendence of her spirit.

"Ligeia" questions the religious doctrines upon which the cult of mourning based its revisionist death rhetoric, while "The Cask of Amontillado"
(1846) makes a pointed criticism of the absurd practices of middle-class
mourning. The villainous narrator in "The Cask of Amontillado" uses a
highly stylized, ritualistic, and methodical technique to lure his adversary to an untimely death. The style and ritual involved in the murder,
rather than the burial, of the victim offers an inversion of the typical postdeath practices. "The Cask of Amontillado" was first published in *Godey's
Lady's Book*, a bastion of etiquette and advice for middle-class American
women. *Godey's* often published sensational and sentimental stories from
well-known authors, and the publication of Poe's perverse story suggests
that middle-class mourning mores were so ingrained in the culture that
the typical reader might find this story doubly horrifying. The expensive

and formulaic traditions of mourning "offered middle-class men and women an opportunity to demonstrate true gentility" that was a performative public expression of "bourgeois conduct."[16] Like any good reader of *Godey's*, the narrator of "The Cask of Amontillado" adheres to a genteel performance in the tone of his storytelling, yet the elaborate construction of his revenge tragedy shows the absurdity of those performances.

The first line of the story asserts without hesitancy that the narrator must kill his enemy, Fortunato, to maintain an appearance of honor after the "thousand injuries" Fortunato had inflicted. The narrator continues by addressing an unknown reader with familiarity, "You, who so well know the nature of my soul, will not suppose, however, that I gave utterance to a threat," thereby including the reader in his plan. This belief in the reader's a priori acceptance of the narrator's response to Fortunato's insults suggests that any person of similar circumstances would understand the narrator's reasons for his ritualistic yet nonsensical murder. The assumption of a shared set of beliefs about honor hints at the false gentility the narrator shares with the cult of mourning adherent. Leading his victim to a catacomb with "a range of low arches" that eventually comes to a "deep crypt" with "human remains piled to the vault overhead," now being used to store wine and other spirits for those who could afford to be laid to rest elsewhere, would have seemed less of an unusual setting for a wine tasting in the nineteenth century.[17] By mid-century, undertakers, rather than family members, prepared the body for death, and those laid to rest were housed in hardwood caskets and spacious cemeteries outside of the town's center rather than cramped churchyards or catacombs. After the Civil War, it was uncommon to have a funeral that did not contain such niceties as "a Lacquered hearse, ornate casket, floral wreaths, and rented banners, crape, cloves, and sashes."[18] The narrator's choice of burial location, no longer the preferable location for those who could afford better, reinforces his desire to respond to Fortunato's insults by violating acceptable death practices. Moreover, the narrator's elaborate entombing of his enemy also violates newly emerging burial methods. As one who identifies himself as bent on revenge for ill usage, the narrator's violation of, or disdain for, correct burial etiquette acts as a deliberate insult to Fortunato, whom the narrator deems undeserving of the respect afforded to any other genteel person.

The narrator's inability to identify his own psychosis and curb his psychopathic response to an acquaintance's rudeness underscores the notion that the rigid etiquette demanded by the cult of mourning remained similarly unquestioned. One of the newest trends was to find isolated, rural spots of great beauty to bury the dead – an added cost to an already expensive affair – so that mourners would always want to visit the burial place of their loved ones.[19] In Poe's interpretation of this troublesome trend, Fortunato's body is laid to rest in a cold, dark, and dank spot where no one can find him or memorialize his existence.

In "The Premature Burial" (1844), Poe similarly addresses an almost blasphemous idea to the cult of mourning, that of burying someone alive and enacting scenes of mourning where no death should have occurred. The narrator shudders at the idea of creating a fictionalized account of a premature burial, which of course happens in both "The Premature Burial" and "The Cask of Amontillado," but he says that "we thrill" at factual accounts of folks buried alive because "it is the history which excites."[20] The narrator recounts purportedly true stories about individuals buried alive for various reasons before coming to his own story of the phenomenon. The particularity of the individual stories is key, for the narrator argues that "the true wretchedness, indeed – the ultimate woe – is particular, not diffuse. That the ghastly extremes of agony are endured by man the unit, and never by man the mass – for this let us thank a merciful God!" Poe argues that the fear of an accidental burial is heightened when the individual is made to feel vulnerable. The narrator's sarcastic comment that it is a blessing that the individual, rather than the community, has to feel the actual, physical trauma of a premature burial seems to indicate that the proliferation of the culture of mourning as a vicarious pain-sharing event is a decided non-blessing. That might be so, but the almost universal acceptance of the societal constructs mandated by the cult of mourning would suggest that metaphorical pain was meant to be shared, even if physical trauma was meant only for the individual.

While pondering the depth of terror produced by the possibility of premature death, Poe notes that the line between life and death was increasingly permeable: "The boundaries which divide Life from Death are at best shadowy and vague. Who shall say where the one ends, and where the other begins?"[21] Although the narrator offers this line as part of the explanation for the abject terror created by stories of those buried alive, the sentiment is also made true because of the increasingly time-consuming and detailed mourning rituals that caused the celebration of death to bleed into life. The middle-class desire to use mourning etiquette as a means to mimic stereotypical notions of gentility impacted the culture so that "middle-class attention shifted from the sentiment to its forms of expression, and the ideal of private feeling yielded to bourgeois demands for its public performance."[22] Because of this performative aspect, a counterculture movement criticizing the superfluity of the cult of mourning developed. As an obvious part of that counterculture because he "stressed the horror of death in order to elicit fear, the strongest of human emotions,"[23] Poe's observation about the permeability of life and death seems more a warning than a threat. With the continual emphasis on the celebration of death as an extravagant event that for some encapsulated or represented the community's esteem for an individual, it became increasingly easy to focus on death, rather than the act of living.

In "The Philosophy of Composition" (1846), Poe famously said that "'of all melancholy topics, what, according to the universal understanding of mankind, is the most melancholy?' Death – was the obvious reply. 'And when,' I said, 'is this most melancholy of topics most poetical?' From what I have already explained at some length, the answer, here also, is obvious – 'When it most closely allies itself to Beauty: the death, then, of a beautiful woman is, unquestionably, the most poetical topic in the world – and equally is it beyond doubt that the lips best suited for such topic are those of a bereaved lover.'"[24] Although the idea that death, especially the death of a beautiful and vulnerable woman, is the height of sadness might seem contradictory to newly established mourning mores, Poe's assertion here is, like his work, ambiguous and possibly misleading. In his essay Poe attempts to explain how he creates poetry for public consumption or to affect universal appeal. While the cult of mourning transformed the culture's religious beliefs, as well as the social constraints placed upon the mourner, it did not negate all the sadness of the event. If anything, adherents to the cult of mourning attempted to share that melancholy to create a transformative effect in those left behind. Poe's ideal subject, a bereaved lover, is a melancholy figure indeed; however, by sharing his experience with the raven and the world, he becomes part of a communal phenomenon of shared and, sometimes, staged grief.

NOTES

1. James J. Farrell, *Inventing the American Way of Death: 1830–1920* (Philadelphia: Temple University Press, 1980), 6, 19.
2. Sterling E. Murray, "Weeping and Mourning: Funeral Dirges in Honor of General Washington," *Journal of the American Musicological Society* 31 (1978), 282.
3. Karen Halttunen, *Confidence Men and Painted Women: A Study of Middle-Class Culture in America, 1830–1870* (New Haven: Yale University Press, 1982), 124.
4. Anita Schorsch, "Mourning Art: A Neoclassical Reflection in America," *American Art Journal* 8 (1976), 5; Murray, "Weeping," 283; Halttunen, *Confidence Men*, 126.

5. Murray, "Weeping," 282–3.
6. Farrell, *Inventing*, 34.
7. Ibid.
8. Vincent DiGirolamo, "Newsboy Funerals: Tales of Sorrow and Solidarity in Urban America," *Journal of Social History* 36 (2002), 5–6.
9. Mary Louise Kete, *Sentimental Collaborations: Mourning and Middle-Class Identity in Nineteenth-Century America* (Durham: Duke University Press, 2000), 7.
10. According to Farrell, *Inventing*, 35, the Evangelical movement in America became quite influential by 1830 and was led by men like Charles Finney, whose revivals "emphasized the importance of scripture, a conversion experience, and a life (and death) of Christian Witness." This movement offered a dramatic break from seventeenth-century Puritanism, which held that believers should never feel safe in the knowledge of their salvation. The omnipresent knowledge that anyone could be damned created a much soberer atmosphere for mourning.
11. Samuel Davies, *Sermons*, 3 vols. (Philadelphia: Presbyterian Board of Publication, 1864), vol. ii, 35.
12. William B. Sprague, *Letters of Practical Subjects to a Daughter*, 2d ed. (New York: John P. Haven, 1831), 212.
13. Edgar Allan Poe, *The Collected Works of Edgar Allan Poe*, ed. Thomas Ollive Mabbott, 3 vols. (Cambridge, MA: Belknap Press, 1969–78), vol. II, 319.
14. Ibid., vol. ii, 319.
15. Ibid., vol. ii, 320, 314.
16. Halttunen *Confidence Men*, 124.
17. Poe, *Collected Works*, vol. iii, 1256, 1261.
18. DiGirolamo, "Newsboy Funerals," 11.
19. Halttunen, *Confidence Men*, 127.
20. Poe, *Collected Works*, vol. iii, 955.
21. Ibid., vol. iii, 955.
22. Halttunen, *Confidence Men*, 138.
23. Farrell, *Inventing*, 33.
24. Edgar Allan Poe, *Essays and Reviews*, ed. G. R. Thompson (New York: Library of America, 1984), 19.

PART THREE

The Contexts of Publishing

CHAPTER 16

The Literary Profession

John Evelev

Here are some of the paradoxical roles that Edgar Allan Poe was known by over the course of his literary career in the antebellum era: widely reprinted producer of popular genres of fiction and poetry and desperate entrant in magazine prize competitions, serial literary hoaxer and "art for art's sake" poetic aesthete, serious literary critic and scandalmongering literary libeler. Perhaps no other antebellum author embodied such seemingly contradictory stances: many of Poe's literary peers could only explain his career through accusations of madness or alcoholism. Even with his recuperation into the critical canon of nineteenth-century American literature in the twentieth century, Poe has been read as *sui generis*, the exception to our understanding of the antebellum literary profession. Rather than viewing Poe's literary career as eccentric or exceptional, however, we can read it as an illuminating window into the complex world of the antebellum literary profession in which a mass market-oriented professionalism competed with a more rarified vocational model privileging aesthetic autonomy and cultural authority. The contradictions of Poe's career are nothing less than the contradictions of the literary profession in the period in which he wrote.

When Poe decided upon a career as a writer in the mid-1830s, the literary profession was very much in flux. Not so long before, the profession was dominated by what Poe would himself call wealthy "gentlemen of elegant leisure," reflecting the standard expectation that writers were of an elite, moneyed class who didn't need income from their writing to survive.[1] The literary marketplace of the 1830s and 1840s, however, greatly expanded, with circulation of literary magazines and the sales of novels growing exponentially and offering the prospect of a literary living wage. There was not a national market for literature per se, but distinct regions associated with urban centers such as Richmond, Philadelphia, and New York City became publishing and circulation hubs.[2] It is a mark of Poe's deep commitment to the market opportunities of the literary profession that he tried working in all these cities, moving up and down the eastern seaboard in an attempt to fashion a stable literary career. His inability to secure that stable career in spite of his remarkable productivity reveals how difficult it was to be a self-sustaining literary professional in this period.

Despite his repeated failures, Poe's investment in a market-based model of literary professionalism can be seen in the kind of writing he produced over the span of his career, designed to reach the widest possible audience. His 1835 short story "Berenice" is characteristic: published in Richmond's *Southern Literary Messenger*, it tells the gruesome story of the narrator's obsession with the beloved title character's teeth and her death, whereupon the narrator in an unconscious state exhumes her corpse and removes her teeth, only to find that she was not dead after all. After publishing this story and receiving complaints from scandalized readers, Thomas W. White, the magazine's editor and proprietor, expressed his displeasure to Poe, who sought an editorial position there. Poe responded, demonstrating his thoughtful consideration of the mechanisms of the literary marketplace and mass audience preferences:

You may say all this is in bad taste. I have my doubts about it. The history of all magazines shows plainly that those which have attained celebrity were indebted for it to articles similar in nature to Berenice.... But whether the articles of which I speak are, or are not in bad taste is little to the purpose. To be appreciated you must be read, and these things are invariably sought after with avidity.... I propose to furnish you every month with a Tale of the nature which I have alluded to. The effect – if any – will be estimated better by the circulation of the Magazine than by any comments upon its contents.[3]

Under the regime of a mass market-oriented literary marketplace, the aesthetic question of "taste" is, as Poe avers, "little to the purpose." Given that such stories were read with "avidity," it behooves a literary magazine (and author) to traffic in them, paying attention to circulation numbers – rather than any complaints that might be registered – to gauge success. Poe's famous style, characterized by heightened tone, exaggerated plots, and grotesque subject matter and deployed in a range of popular fiction and poetic genres over the course of his career, was all part of a concerted effort to reach the broadest possible audience.

Poe's self-conscious orientation of his work toward a mass audience can also be seen in his embrace of what Meredith McGill calls "the culture of reprinting." Besides reprinting stories, articles, and novels from foreign journals and presses without recompensing the authors, editors showed little reluctance in pirating or reprinting domestic literary works. The regionalism of the publishing industry in the period meant that a single work could be reprinted many times, moving from one publishing center to another, often losing original attribution of publication source and author. Perhaps the most famous example of domestic reprinting is Poe's poem "The Raven," which was first published under a pseudonym in New York's *American Review* in 1845, but eventually appeared in a host of newspapers and magazines in New York, Philadelphia, Richmond, and London.[4] Traditional histories of American authorship present reprinting and piracy as banes of mid-nineteenth-century literary professionalism, but evidence suggests that many authors of the era, including Nathaniel Hawthorne and Poe, actively courted reprinting.[5] While Poe spoke out against reprinting foreign works, he embraced the practice of reprinting domestic literature. In the same 1835 letter to White, Poe noted that stories like "Berenice" "find their way into other periodicals, and into the papers, and in this manner, taking hold upon the public mind they augment the reputation of the source where they originated."[6] Though neither writer nor original publisher received remuneration for the reprinted work, the circulation of the text and publication source name accrued a kind of symbolic capital (Poe calls it "celebrity," but French sociologist Pierre Bourdieu could have termed it "cultural capital") that could be converted into more material capital (i.e., higher price per story or more favorable terms for book publication for the author, greater sales or more subscriptions for the source publication) at some future date.[7] Poe consistently tailored his stories and poems for reprinting, using what McGill has called "strategic generality." From his intentionally open-ended appropriation of the popular figure of direct address in poetry ("To – ," "To the River – ," and "To F – ") to his stories, which similarly made use of common fictional genres but typically eschewed contemporary time frames and local American settings for vaguely specified European settings and times, Poe wrote with reprinting in mind, making the text available or open for appropriation into as many publishing contexts as possible.[8] Writing with a self-consciously exaggerated style, using conventional generic forms and intentionally vague settings, Poe was trying to harness – rather than fight against – the mechanisms of the popular literary marketplace and, in doing so, reflected his investment in a market-based model of literary professionalism.

It has been a long-standing convention of Poe criticism to read his work as antagonistic to mass or popular readership, embodied most cogently in his famous use of the hoax, cryptography, and detective stories – all forms that seek to deceive, puzzle, or misdirect readers. However, Poe's interest in cryptography and his invention of the detective story can be seen as examples of what has been called "the operational aesthetic," a popular mode of the antebellum era that sought to attract a wide audience by encouraging its participation in questioning, explaining, validating, and debunking a range of cultural products from inventions to elaborate hoaxes. This mode of cultural production has been seen as distinctive for its demand of active, rather than passive, consumption.[9] Just as the detective story encourages readers to develop their own theories about the crime and makes the experience of reading akin to investigation, Poe also at one point invited his readers to send him text in code, claiming that he could decipher any cryptogram. Like other antebellum cultural producers who made use of the operational aesthetic, Poe's writings portray not a simplistic pandering to mass market demands or dismissive abuse of popular gullibility, but a thoughtful engagement with the financial and other exchanges at the heart of the popular cultural marketplace.[10]

For all his career-long investment in a mass-market directed literary professionalism, Poe constantly struggled and never truly succeeded in generating a self-sustaining income for himself from writing. Confident, impulsive, and always desperate for cash, he was repeatedly drawn into literary competitions, a common practice of antebellum magazines and newspapers seeking to draw attention to themselves and to find new authors by offering a lucrative cash prize for the winning story or poem. Unable to resist the temptation of a quick and lucrative prize, Poe entered many of these competitions, winning a few for some of his best-loved stories such as "Manuscript Found in a Bottle" and "The Gold-Bug," but losing others. Adding to the indignity of not winning the prize, losing entrants in these literary competitions lost all rights to the works submitted, which the magazines could then publish without recompense to the author.[11] In general, the market for literary production was irrevocably skewed in favor of publishers (on the relatively rare occasions that they made any profit themselves). No matter the circulation of the story or poems, authors seldom saw significant financial returns for their work. Recognizing this early on, Poe turned to editing magazines as an attempt to earn a steady wage as an employee, a very different model of work from the entrepreneurial market-oriented writer. Trading the ostensible autonomy of self-directed authorship for the reasonably consistent wage of editorship, Poe was trying to hedge his bets and cushion himself against the full demands of the literary marketplace. Magazine editing positions would carry him from Richmond (*Southern Literary Messenger* [1835–7]); to Philadelphia (*Burton's Gentlemen's Magazine* [1839–40], *Graham's Magazine* [1841–2]); to New York (*Broadway Journal* [1845–6]). Never wholly content serving other people's vision of the demands of the literary marketplace, Poe dreamed of not merely editing, but also publishing his own magazine, producing a number of prospectuses for what he first imagined would be called *The Penn Magazine* and later *The Stylus* in an effort to generate support and begin publishing. Throughout his struggles, Poe never abandoned the dream of magazine proprietorship and, with it, literary market success.

During this same period that the literary marketplace was expanding, many authors sought to articulate a vocational model of professional authorship, one that rejected both the earlier dilettante model and the market-oriented model that replaced it. This new literary professionalism reflected a broader cultural shift in the professions: in the mid-nineteenth century, the traditional professions – ministers, doctors, and lawyers – began to be associated with the middle class and redefined their authority through the codification of specialized knowledge with more formalized educational requirements and the establishment of self-governing legislative bodies, particularly the formation of professional organizations such as the American Medical Association (founded in 1847) or the American Legal Association (1849; ancestor to the American Bar Association).[12] Very much like the literary realm, the professions had been strongly associated with elite culture and social privilege early in the nineteenth century, but had been opened up to new constituencies and became more market directed under a range of populist measures in the 1820s. The new professionalism of the 1840s and 1850s sought to counter this trend by establishing objective standards for professional practice and linking professional authority to merit, rather than privileged social standing or the more populist standard of sales. Although Poe's use of popular genres, exaggerated style, and hyperbolic content reflected his investment in a market-directed model of literary professionalism, another side of his career reflected this alternative model of specialization, embodied particularly in his literary theory and criticism.

During his lifetime, Poe was widely recognized as one of the period's most important literary critics, actively rejecting the "cliques" (groups of affiliated or friendly writers who sought to forward each others' careers through publicity) and "puffing" (the common practice of positively reviewing works of friends and familiars) that typified the period and reflected the old model of literary work as the product of "gentlemen of elegant leisure." In 1845, James Russell Lowell called Poe "the most discriminating, philosophical, and fearless critic upon imaginative works who has written in America."[13] In his theory and criticism, Poe sought to establish himself as a literary professional whose legitimacy and hierarchical standing came from his specialized knowledge of the literary object and his objective and autonomous critical practice. Poe promised readers in each of his prospectuses to *The Penn Magazine* (1840) and *The Stylus* (1843) that his magazine would "demonstrate...the advantages, of an absolutely independent criticism – a criticism self-sustained; guiding itself only by the purest rules of Art...[and] holding itself aloof from all personal bias."[14] Poe's emphasis on critical independence and autonomy as the best resource to claims of authority reflects similar claims from newly professionalizing doctors and lawyers in the antebellum era. The repetition of the same promise about critical practices in both prospectuses reflects Poe's fervent belief that the new professionalized model of literary criticism was a path to success and cultural authority.

In addition to critiquing contemporary critical practices and offering an "independent" and "objective" alternative, Poe was deeply invested in producing a literary theory that codified rules or laws of aesthetic effect, reflecting the common professionalizing practice of defining a specialized practice or field of knowledge. In "The Philosophy of Composition," and subsequent works of aesthetic theory such as "The Rationale of Verse" and "The Poetic Principle," Poe sought to undercut the notion that writers "compose by a species of fine frenzy – an ecstatic intuition," presenting his own process of composition as a matter of "precision and [the] rigid consequence of a mathematical problem."[15] Writing a poem is a technical matter, one separate from the imagined audience: "Let us dismiss, as irrelevant to the poem per se, the circumstance – or say the necessity – which in the first place, gave rise to the intention of composing a poem that should suit at once the popular and the critical taste."[16] Although Poe's theory of poetic effect depends on generating a particular response within the reader, that response is wholly dependent on the design of the poet, who has specialized knowledge of the mechanism of the poem. Without denying the financial or status incentives of creating a poem that might appeal to both "popular and...critical taste," Poe's aesthetic theory claims a certain degree of autonomy for the act of creating a poem. His highly formalist theory of poetics was a notable precursor to the kind of literary analysis associated with the New Critics, the first wave of professionalized academic literary scholars of the twentieth century. In creating this semiautonomous vision of the poetic, Poe, like the new antebellum professional doctors and lawyers with whom he could be compared, sought to establish the autonomy of his practice outside of the marketplace. The rules of composition, which only the trained specialist knows, exist irrespective of audience demand. Poe's argument is not just an attack on romanticized "autorial vanity," but an assertion of literary authority based upon mastery over a field of cultural knowledge.[17] If this seems a direct contradiction to Poe's 1835 comments to his *Southern Literary Messenger* editor, this should be seen as reflective of the tensions within the literary profession of the period.

Poe has been stereotypically depicted as solitary figure, even an outcast, but more recent scholarship has demonstrated the extent of Poe's involvement – both professionally and socially – in the antebellum literary world.[18] His relations with other writers could be problematic: with his persistent attacks against Henry Wadsworth Longfellow, arguably the most popular poet of the era, and his successful libel suit against the *New York Evening Mirror*, Poe earned his reputation as a contentious and divisive figure in the literary circles of his day.[19] But Poe had many supporters within the community of writers and was himself invested in the notion of a literary community whose private opinion of authors was a matter of consensus, but differed dramatically from the public opinions offered to the reading public. In his 1840 prospectus of the *Penn Magazine*, Poe criticized "the involute and anonymous cant of the Quarterlies...which, hanging like nightmares upon American literature, manufacture, at the nod of our principal booksellers, a pseudo-public-opinion by wholesale."[20] In contrast to the manufactured "pseudo-public-opinions" of the literary press, produced only to sell literary goods, Poe posited a private community of opinion among editors and writers themselves in his 1846 literary profile series "The Literati of New York," published in the Philadelphia magazine *Godey's Lady's Book*. "[T]he very editors who hesitate at saying in print an ill word of an author personally known, are usually the most frank in speaking about him privately," Poe reported, and he promised in his series to give not only his "own unbiased opinion" but also that "of conversational society in literary circles." Far from imagining a deeply contentious literary society, Poe depicted one in which "on all literary topics there is in society a seemingly wonderful coincidence of opinion."[21] In constructing this vision of the literary community, Poe again reflected the early professionalizing impulse of the antebellum era, which saw the establishment of a community or collective of autonomous skilled practitioners as crucial to its legitimation.

In this self-legitimizing move, the professionalizing group distinguishes between itself, inferior practitioners (often labeled "amateurs" or "quacks"), and the general public. As introductory examples for his study of New York literati, Poe compared Hawthorne, who he asserted was "scarcely recognized by the press or by the public, and when noticed at all, is noticed merely to be damned by faint praise," to his *bête noir*, Longfellow, held to be "a poetical phenomenon, as entirely without fault as is the luxurious paper upon which his poems are invariably borne to the public eye." Within the private literary community, however, Hawthorne is described as "evinc[ing] extraordinary genius...and this opinion I have never heard gainsaid by any one literary person in the country." The consensus "one voice" judgment on Longfellow, by contrast, is that of a "skillful artist and a well-read man, but less remarkable in either capacity than as a determined imitator and dexterous adopter of the ideas of other people."[22] This accusation rehearses Poe's highly controversial claims that Longfellow was a plagiarist, but more notable even than how this assessment fits the modern critical consensus toward the two writers is Poe's investment in making his individual view stand in as a collective judgment. For all of his supposed status as an outsider, Poe actively sought to legitimize himself and the antebellum literary field by imagining writers as a community with shared values and opinions. Whether or not such a critical consensus existed amidst the American literary community of the antebellum era, Poe's argument about that imagined or real community at the beginning of "The Literati of New York" highlights the ways in which he was invested in claiming the legitimacy and autonomy of the new professionalizing middle-class vocational model.

Seen in this light, Poe's literary attitudes seem less strange, exotic, or eccentric and more familiar, more in line with some of our most cherished critical suppositions about the literary profession. Returning to Poe's comparison of Hawthorne and Longfellow – a comparison that now inspires thought about the rise and fall of literary reputations (at least Hawthorne's rise and Longfellow's fall) and the modern construction of an American literary canon – we see Poe articulating a very modern logic of literary merit. Using the common terms of antebellum professionalizers, Poe asserts that Hawthorne "is not an ubiquitous quack," while Longfellow "although little quacky per se, has...a whole legion of active quacks at his control."[23] Posing professionalized experts who direct their work to a select community of like-minded practitioners against quacks who speak to a wider, more commercially oriented market, Poe rehearses a logic of literary professionalism that has come to legitimize a range of mid-nineteenth-century American authors largely ignored during their lifetimes – including Hawthorne, Melville, Thoreau, and Whitman – yet have come to define the canon of American romantic literature as it was formalized in the twentieth century.

Poe himself has had a decidedly ambiguous place in that canon of American romantic literature. Was Poe a quack whose skill was in marketing himself to a mass audience eager for novelty and sensations? Or was he a genius or an expert skillfully addressing himself to the shared critical consensus of the meritorious few? Modern literary critics have struggled to place Poe, just as Poe's contemporaries struggled to understand him. Rather than labeling Poe "crazy" as did many of his antebellum enemies, we locate the craziness or schizophrenia within the antebellum field of cultural production itself, which offered competing models of literary professionalism, neither of which could fulfill its promise of offering financial security or hierarchical social status to writers of the period. Poe's dramatic literary career offers a vivid example of the contradictions within the literary profession of his era and his successes and failures, far from being unusual, are merely more extreme versions of the stories of all writers of the period. Edgar Allan Poe's literary career is the best, most representative embodiment of the tensions within the American literary profession in its transition from genteel eighteenth-century literary production to a modern, divided high–low cultural field, a field we still live in today.

NOTES

1. Kevin J. Hayes, *Poe and the Printed Word* (New York: Cambridge University Press, 2000), 38.
2. On sectionalism in book distribution, see Ronald J. Zboray, *A Fictive People: Antebellum Economic Development and the American Reading Public* (New York: Oxford University Press, 1993), 55–68.
3. Poe to Thomas W. White, April 30, 1835, *The Collected Letters of Edgar Allan Poe*, ed. John Ward Ostrom, Burton R. Pollin, and Jeffrey A. Savoye, 2 vols. (New York: Gordian, 2008), vol. i, 84–5.
4. For the reprintings of "The Raven," see Edgar Allan Poe, *The Collected Works of Edgar Allan Poe*, ed. Thomas Ollive Mabbott, 3 vols. (Cambridge, MA: Belknap Press, 1969–78), vol. i, 359–64.
5. For the central statement on the role of copyright on nineteenth-century American authorship, see William Charvat, *The Profession of Authorship in America, 1800–1870* (1968; reprinted, New York: Columbia University Press, 1992). For a history of the local debates around the topic in antebellum New York and Poe's role in them, see Perry Miller, *The Raven and the Whale: The War of Words and Wits in the Era of Poe and Melville* (New York: Harcourt, 1956). For a revisionist consideration of "the culture of reprinting," see Meredith McGill, *American Literature and the Culture of Reprinting, 1834–1853* (Philadelphia: University of Pennsylvania Press, 2003).
6. Poe to Thomas W. White, April 30, 1835, *Collected Letters*, vol. i, 85.

7. For applications of the work of Pierre Bourdieu in the context of the antebellum American literary marketplace, see Leon Jackson, *The Business of Letters: Authorial Economies in Antebellum America* (Stanford: Stanford University Press, 2008), 32–7. For Bourdieu's own analysis of the literary field of late nineteenth-century France, see his *The Rules of Art: Genesis and Structure of the Literary Field*, trans. Susan Emanuel (Stanford: Stanford University Press, 1996).

8. McGill, *American Literature*, 155–64.

9. On the operational aesthetic, see Neil Harris, *Humbug: The Art of P. T. Barnum* (Boston: Little, Brown, 1973).

10. Jonathan Elmer, *Reading at the Social Limit: Affect, Mass Culture, and Edgar Allan Poe* (Stanford, CA: Stanford University Press, 1995), 174–223.

11. Kevin J. Hayes, *Edgar Allan Poe* (London: Reaktion, 2009), 19.

12. On the antebellum rise of modern professionalism, see Magali S. Larson, *The Rise of Professionalism: A Sociological Analysis* (Berkeley: University of California Press, 1977) and Thomas Bender, *Intellect and Public Life: Essays on the Social History of Academic Intellectuals in the United States* (Baltimore: Johns Hopkins University Press, 1993).

13. James Russell Lowell, "Our Contributors: No. XVII: Edgar Allan Poe [1845]," in *The Shock of Recognition*, ed. Edmund Wilson (New York: Modern Library, 1955), 7. It is notable that Wilson uses this review essay as the first entry in his survey of the rise of an American literary criticism.

14. Edgar Allan Poe, *Essays and Reviews*, ed. G. R. Thompson (New York: Library of America, 1984), 1025, 1035.

15. Ibid., 14–15.

16. Ibid., 15.

17. Ibid., 14.

18. On Poe's complex relations with female poets of the period, see Eliza Richards, *Gender and the Poetics of Reception in Poe's Circle* (New York: Cambridge University Press, 2004).

19. Poe is the only antebellum author to have a book devoted entirely to his various conflicts with other writers: Sidney Moss's *Poe's Literary Battles* (Durham: Duke University Press, 1963).

20. Poe, *Essays*, 1025.

21. Ibid., 1119–20.

22. Ibid.

23. Ibid., 1120.

CHAPTER 17

Magazines

Jeffrey Andrew Weinstock

Among the most significant forces molding Poe's experience was the dramatic expansion of magazine publishing that coincided with his adult years and shaped what he considered the "ultimate purpose" of his life – what Terence Whalen characterizes as Poe's "desperate and consuming passion": his desire to found his own magazine.[1] This chapter will consider this unrealized dream within the context of the antebellum "golden age" of magazine journalism, offering an overview to the development of magazine publishing during the period, considering Poe's experience as a "magazinist" and his editorial connections to five different periodicals, and concluding with a brief look at how magazine publication surfaces as an important theme within his own writing.

MAGAZINES IN ANTEBELLUM AMERICA

Poe's adult life coincided with a remarkable expansion in magazine publication that led one commentator in 1831 in the *Illinois Monthly Magazine* to characterize the period as "the golden age of periodicals."[2] At the beginning of the nineteenth century, there were only about a dozen American magazines; by 1810, there were forty or so; and by 1825, nearly 100.[3] That number would increase sixfold in the next twenty-five years, with about 600 by 1850. Frank Luther Mott estimates that for every magazine operating in 1850 another seven or so had failed over the preceding two and a half decades – which means that some four or five thousand magazines in total were published during the period.[4] Taking note of this sudden profusion of periodicals, the *New York Mirror* commented, "These United States are fertile in most things, but in periodicals they are extremely luxuriant. They spring up as fast as mushrooms, in every corner." This newspaper added that although hundreds quickly fail, "hundreds more are found to supply their place."[5]

A variety of factors contributed to the proliferation of magazines in the United States between 1825 and 1850. Prior to this point, authorship had not been a profession in the modern sense. Primarily "the province of gentlemen and clergymen," authorship in the early republic generally consisted of finding a supporting patron to fund one's writing endeavors rather than pleasing a reading public, and most authors were likely to take their books to a local printer at their own expense.[6] In addition, American publishing had been hampered by a number of obstacles, including a lack of capital and a national currency, high production costs, an inefficient distribution system, and an absence of a predictable market.[7] As the nineteenth century progressed, a series of social and technological changes worked together to alter this conception of authorship, to facilitate print publication, and to expand the potential market for published works.

To begin with, radical changes in printing and papermaking technologies made possible the publication of low-priced periodicals and books at a greatly accelerated pace. Hand manufacture gave way to cylinder papermaking machines starting in the 1820s, which were followed by the introduction of Fourdrinier papermaking machines in the 1840s – the first to produce continuous sheets rather than single separate pages. Printing presses became increasingly efficient as the nineteenth century advanced. Printing from plates rather than type began in 1812; the use of steam power for running presses was pioneered around the same time, as was the replacement of the printing flatbed with the rotary cylinder – the latter of which was developed to print both sides of a sheet at once. By the 1840s, the combination of rolled paper and steam-powered printing allowed for thousands of copies of a page to be produced in a single day and helped mass production of printed works to thrive.[8]

The flourishing of periodical literature between 1825 and 1850 also benefited from a revolution of another sort. New and better roads, the Erie Canal – completed in 1825 – and an expanding railroad system (construction of the Baltimore and Ohio Railroad began in 1828), made it easier and cheaper to distribute printed materials to a growing country.[9] Also assisting in the distribution of periodical literature were reduced postal rates and an expanding market. In the years leading up to the American Civil War, different types of printed matter were handled by the Post Office in different ways. Newspapers, notes Peter Hutchinson, "had always been recognized for their value in promoting democratic discourse, and this implicit recognition of their social benefits led to preferential postal handling and subsidized postage rates." Magazines, however, were not regarded with the same esteem and therefore paid higher postage rates. According to Hutchinson, it cost more than ten times as much to mail a magazine over 100 miles in 1825 than it did a newspaper. Postage rate reform in 1845 lowered the cost of mailing magazines substantially – from 17.5 cents per piece to 7.5 cents per piece. Postage remained the biggest expense for most magazines, but the reduction in rates was beneficial.

As the century progressed, there were quite simply many more potential magazine consumers in the United States. When Poe was born in 1809, the population of the United States numbered seven million inhabitants; by the time he died in 1849, the population had more than tripled to twenty-two million. The period between 1820 and 1860 also witnessed the fastest rate of urban growth in American history, which created large, centralized consumer bases for periodical literature.[10]

Periodicals became easier and cheaper to produce and distribute, and as literacy rates – already extremely high among the white Northern population at the turn of the eighteenth century – continued to increase, a shift in attitude toward reading as entertainment occurred.[11] A growing and increasingly literate population grew hungrier for reading material. In order to cater to this multifaceted and expanding reading public, periodicals entered a period of diversification in the 1820s and 1830s. Specialization within periodicals was virtually unheard of in the eighteenth century.

The 1820s and afterward, however, saw the proliferation of periodicals devoted to particular topics and with specific readers in mind. Notable during this period (and connected to Poe) were the closely related categories of magazines of general literature, such as *Knickerbocker Magazine*, *Graham's Magazine*, and *Burton's Gentleman's Magazine*, and magazines for women including *Godey's Lady's Book*, *The Lady's Magazine*, and *Peterson's Ladies' National Magazine*. In addition, the period saw the development of religious periodicals of all denominational stripes; magazines devoted to particular topics such as agriculture, humor, medicine, and even phrenology; and of a peculiar category of magazine referred to as "knowledge magazines" that offered all kinds of factual information. These magazines were published weekly, monthly, or quarterly, and came in three "grades" with annual subscriptions costing one dollar, three dollars, or five dollars – this at a time when the average laborer made about one dollar a day working about 200 days a year. While annual subscriptions to *The Knickerbocker*, *Southern Literary Messenger*, and *Democratic Review* cost five dollars, three dollars tended to be the standard rate.[12]

The period from 1825 to 1850, while certainly a golden age for periodical publication, was not so golden for the vast majority of publishers, editors, and those who attempted to make a living as what Poe referred to as "magazinists." The literary profession was, as characterized by William Charvat, in its "adolescence" in the 1820s and 1830s, and both authorship and editing were transitioning from gentlemanly pursuits to professional endeavors. Mott notes that fair payment to authors for magazine contributions was rare prior to 1842.[13] The rate an author received depended on the size and financial condition of the magazine. Tebbel observes that the *North American Review*'s rate of a dollar a page for prose was something of a standard. Other magazines paid more or less depending on the reputation of the author. *The Knickerbocker*, for example, paid five dollars a page "for such contributions as we consider best," but might not pay lesser-known authors at all. Similarly, *Godey's Lady's Book* refused to pay unknown authors anything at all.[14] During the economic depression of 1837–43, Poe himself, as editor of *Burton's Gentleman's Magazine*, was forced to inform fellow writers that "the intense pressure has obliged Mr. B. with nearly, if not every, publisher in the country, to discontinue paying for contributions."[15] Things began to improve for magazinists when *Graham's* committed itself to compensating all authors and offered between four dollars and twelve dollars per page of prose and between ten dollars and fifty dollars for a poem. (Alas, Poe seems to have been at the low end of the scale, receiving only four or five dollars per page).[16] Whereas contributions had been anonymous in the earlier magazines, *Graham's* inaugurated the practice of advertising the names of famous writers on its front cover. The success of *Graham's Magazine* demonstrated that decent compensation produced excellent results, and a handful of other publications followed suit by adopting similar payment practices.

Poor compensation was not the only problem facing aspiring magazinists during Poe's lifetime; in addition, authors had few rights that editors felt obligated to respect. Once an author turned his manuscript over to an editor, not only could he find it rewritten (with or without his permission), but he might find it reprinted elsewhere without his knowledge or consent and with no additional payment. Ownership of magazine content was not well defined and the reprinting of magazine content in newspapers and other magazines was common. In fact, some magazines consisted almost entirely of reprinted material. Editors, it should be pointed out, did not have it substantially better. In many cases, editors received no salary at all or they were paid in proportion to the magazine's financial condition, and most of the monthly magazines limped along with subscription numbers of seven thousand or less. As a result, editing was in most cases part-time employment.[17]

Another problem for magazines in the nineteenth century (as today) was covering their costs. Advertising during Poe's lifetime was still relatively undeveloped and appeared primarily on the covers of the most expensive magazines or in a few pages at the back. While in many cases authors received little or no compensation, engravings on copper and steel were both common and costly. Mott observes, "A publisher sometimes paid more for one new plate than for all his literary contents."[18] The ladies' magazines had fashion plates, in some cases colored by hand, and often a few additional plates as well. *Graham's* stressed the use of illustration and included a mezzotint by artist John Sartain and a fashion plate in every issue, which helped to make pictorial illustration a "distinctive feature of American magazines."[19] While *Graham's* was one of the era's success stories, most magazines remained unprofitable and folded quickly.

EDGAR ALLAN POE AS MAGAZINIST

This background provides the context for understanding Poe's participation with some thirty different magazines during his lifetime, his editorial experience with five, and his personal dream of starting his own. His early fiction first appeared in periodicals in 1832 when the *Philadelphia Saturday Courier* published five tales he had submitted to a contest. Poe did not win, but the stories were published without his name attached, and it is unlikely he received any compensation. Poe subsequently won a contest sponsored by the *Baltimore Saturday Visiter* in 1833 with his short story "Manuscript Found in a Bottle." He received a fifty dollar award and the story appeared in the October 19, 1833 issue.

In addition to winning the *Baltimore Saturday Visiter* prize, his participation in the contest helped Poe in another way: it introduced him to one of the contest's judges, novelist John Pendleton Kennedy, who encouraged him to submit another story, "The Visionary," to *Godey's Lady's Book*. When it appeared there in January 1834, it became Poe's first publication in a widely circulated journal. Kennedy was also instrumental in advancing Poe's career in another way: he wrote a letter on Poe's behalf to T. W. White, publisher of the *Southern Literary Messenger*, a monthly magazine recently established in Richmond. Poe's "Berenice" appeared there in March 1835, and the magazine not only asked for more of his material, but offered him regular reviewing assignments. Later that year, Poe moved to Richmond, where he obtained full-time work on the magazine. His compensation was ten dollars a week, plus payment by the column for literary contributions. By December, he was a *Messenger* editor and his salary increased to $780 a year. In one year as an editor for the *Southern Literary Messenger*, Poe wrote more than 100 reviews and editorials and established his reputation as a fierce critic – indeed, the severity of his reviews led to him being nicknamed "Tomahawk Man" and "Bulldog the critick."

A variety of explanations have been proposed for Poe's split from the *Messenger* in 1837 – three of them from Poe himself, who referenced his own drinking, White's onerous control over him, and the "drudgery" and "contemptible" salary of his position.[20] In any event, Poe and his family relocated in February 1837 from Richmond to New York, where Poe attempted to make a living as a freelance writer, and they moved again in 1838 to Philadelphia, where William E. Burton offered Poe ten dollars a week for two hours of daily work on *Burton's Gentleman's Magazine* starting in May 1839. In his one year with Burton, Poe wrote over 125 reviews and a few articles and revised or reprinted earlier fiction.[21] "The Fall of the House of Usher" appeared in the magazine in September 1839, and the sonnet "Silence" followed in April 1840. In 1840, Poe also announced his plans for a new periodical called the *Penn Magazine*.

Poe and Burton parted company in mid-1840, but when Burton sold his magazine in 1840 to George R. Graham, who merged it with a magazine called *The Casket* to form *Graham's Magazine*, Poe signed on as literary editor in charge of book reviews in February 1841. His salary was $800 a year, plus payment for his literary contributions. Poe was with *Graham's* for fifteen months – a period that critics, including the author of Poe's slanderous biography, Rufus Griswold, acknowledge as "one of the most active and brilliant of his literary life."[22] Not only did he publish "The Murders in the Rue Morgue," "To Helen," and "The Masque of the Red Death" in *Graham's*, but he also published criticism, papers on cryptography, and his "Autography" series that purported to deduce the characters of established authors based on an analysis of their signatures. Although the circulation of *Graham's* continued to grow, Poe – in keeping with his pattern of self-destruction – left the magazine in 1842, declaring, "My reason for resigning was disgust at the namby-pamby character of the Magazine....I allude to the contemptible pictures, fashion-plates, music, and love-tales. The salary, moreover, did not pay me for the labor which I was forced to bestow. With Graham, who is really a very gentlemanly, although exceedingly weak man, I had no misunderstanding."[23] Despite this claim of being on good terms with Graham, Poe may in fact have been disgruntled with him for reneging on a promise to help him launch *Penn Magazine*.[24]

After Poe's break with Graham, he continued to publicize the ever-impending appearance of his own magazine, now called *The Stylus*, again relocated to New York, continued to try to make a living as a freelance author, and served a brief stint as a critic and subeditor for the *New York Evening Mirror*, a weekly newspaper, until he assumed another editorial position in February 1845 on the *Broadway Journal*. This periodical, launched on January 4, 1845, included Poe's writing in its first two editions. By July, Poe was sole editor and by the end of October, the sole owner as well. Poe finally had what he wanted – full control of the magazine – but the *Broadway Journal* was burdened with considerable debt and ceased publication in January 1846.

Poe was never to achieve what he referred to as the "grand purpose" of his life – the establishment of his own magazine.[25] After the demise of the *Broadway Journal*, he continued to attempt to earn a living through lecturing and freelance writing and published in a variety of journals, including *Godey's Lady's Book*, which ran six installments of his "The Literati of New York City" – a series of sketches of notable and not so notable authors and editors, some extremely vituperative in tone – as well as *Union Magazine, Columbian Lady's and Gentleman's Magazine, Graham's, Home Journal, Southern Literary Messenger, Sartain's Union Magazine,* and *Flag of Our Union*. In April 1849, Poe seemed on the verge of realizing his vision: an Illinois printer named Edward H. N. Patterson wanted to establish a national literary magazine with Poe as editor and half owner. Alas, Poe was to die in October of that year.

THE MAGAZINE PRISON HOUSE

In his sadly truncated magazine career, Poe performed the roles of author, proofreader, editor, reviewer, and – for a short time – proprietor of a journal. Staunch promoter of magazine journalism that he was, Poe altered the medium and helped make the magazine the main vehicle for literary fare during his time.[26] While as Meredith McGill notes, critical studies of Poe that insist on portraying Poe as a "figure of heroic resistance" standing "in staunch and principled opposition to the coteries that controlled the elite literary periodicals" turn a blind eye toward Poe's willingness to participate fully in that same system when it suited his needs and aspirations, it nevertheless is true that in various places Poe attacked many of the magazine practices of the day, including anonymous reviewing, "puffery" (false praise for promotional purposes), plagiarism, poor compensation for authors, unauthorized and uncompensated reprinting, and plain bad writing.[27] One article and two stories by Poe can illustrate his explicit critique of magazine practices of the day.

In "Some Secrets of the Magazine Prison-House," an article that ran in the January 15, 1845 issue of the *Broadway Journal*, Poe takes aim both at the absence of an international copyright law and at the illiberality of compensation for magazine contributions. He begins by explaining that the lack of an international copyright law creates an unfair playing ground for American authors by "rendering it nearly impossible to obtain anything from the booksellers in the way of remuneration for literary labor." Since American book and magazine publishers could simply pirate British and European titles without paying the authors, they had little incentive to pay for titles by American authors. This situation, notes Poe, "has had the effect of forcing many of our very best writers into the service of the Magazines and Reviews." Here as well, however, authors were frequently at the mercy of greedy publishers – a situation Poe illustrates with the tale of a generic "young author" who struggles "with Despair itself in the shape of a ghastly poverty." He composes an article for a magazine for which he is promised to be "handsomely paid"; however, the publisher keeps deferring payment with a series of excuses until the author dies of starvation and the "fat 'editor and proprietor' is fat henceforward and for ever to the amount of five and twenty dollars, very cleverly saved, to be spent generously in canvas-backs and champagne."[28]

In "The Literary Life of Thingum Bob, Esq.," first published in 1844 in the *Southern Literary Messenger*, Poe takes aim not just at greedy publishers who compensate authors poorly or not at all, but at plagiarism, puffery, and bad writing as well. In "Thingum Bob," the title character, who resides in the city of Smug, is inspired by a hackneyed ode to his barber father's hair oil to set his sights on becoming a poet and editor. His first attempts at publication, which consist of plagiarized passages from Dante, Homer, and other classical authors, are rebuffed not because they are lifted from other sources, but because the ignorant editors of the four principal magazines can't distinguish fine writing from trash. This point is then hammered home when Bob, writing under the pseudonym Snob, pens some doggerel:

> To pen an Ode upon the 'Oil-of-Bob'
> Is all sorts of a job.[29]

For this couplet, he is celebrated in increasingly inflated terms by the same four magazines. Despite the hyperbolic success of the magazines, any payment to Bob is endlessly deferred until, after serving for a time as the *Lollipop*'s "Thomas Hawk" reviewer, he himself becomes the proprietor of a magazine of his own.

Poe had previously taken aim at hackneyed writing in "How to Write a Blackwood Article," first published as "The Psyche Zenobia" in 1838 in the *American Museum*. This story, one of only two writings in which Poe adopts a female voice – the other is his poem "Bridal Ballad" – spoofs the formulaic horror stories typically published in the Scottish *Blackwood's Magazine* and similar periodicals. In this story, Signora Psyche Zenobia, a.k.a. Suky Snobbs, first seeks advice from Mr. Blackwood on the proper construction of a tale and is given such advice as to "pay minute attention to the sensations" and to give her writing an "air of erudition" by peppering it with obscure, "piquant" facts and expressions.[30] The embedded story, "A Predicament," then puts this advice into practice as Signora Psyche Zenobia offers up a story in which her head is improbably severed by the minute hand of a giant clock even as her narration continues unabated.

In articles and stories such as these, Poe proved himself an astute observer and critic of the magazine practices of the day. As Kevin J. Hayes notes, for Poe, the magazine "became the vehicle for serious, important literature, and he devoted much of the last decade of his life to imagining, planning, and trying to locate financial support for a magazine of his own and to writing short prose and verse which embodied his magazine aesthetic."[31] Although the magazine he hoped to found never materialized, Poe's contributions to and criticisms of the emergent medium influenced its development and the subsequent course of American literature.

NOTES

1. Terence Whalen, *Edgar Allan Poe and the Masses: The Political Economy of Literature in Antebellum America* (Princeton: Princeton University Press, 1999), 58.
2. Quoted in Frank Luther Mott, *A History of American Magazines* 5 vols. (Cambridge, MA: Belknap Press, 1938–68), vol. i, 341.
3. John Tebbel, *The American Magazine: A Compact History* (New York: Hawthorn Books, 1969), 169.
4. Mott, *History of American Magazines*, vol. i, 342.
5. Quoted in Mott, *History of American Magazines*, vol. i, 341.
6. Isabelle Lehuu, *Carnival on the Page: Popular Print Media in Antebellum America* (Chapel Hill: University of North Carolina Press, 2000), 17; Ann Douglas, *The Feminization of American Culture* (New York: Avon, 1977), 96.
7. Mary Kelley, *Private Woman, Public Stage: Literary Domesticity in Nineteenth-Century America* (New York: Oxford University Press, 1984), 7.
8. James D. Hart, *The Popular Book: A History of America's Literary Taste* (New York: Oxford University Press, 1950), 67.

9. Whalen, *Edgar Allan Poe and the Masses*, 32.
10. Peter Hutchinson, *A Publisher's History of American Magazine Publishing* (N.p.: Peter Hutchinson, 2008), 26–7; Kevin J. Hayes, *Edgar Allan Poe* (London: Reaktion, 2009), 135; Terence Whalen, "Poe and the American Publishing Industry," *A Historical Guide to Edgar Allan Poe*, ed. J. Gerald Kennedy (New York: Oxford University Press, 2001), 64–5; Karen Halttunen, *Confidence Men and Painted Women: A Study of Middle-Class Culture in America, 1830–1870* (New Haven: Yale University Press, 1982), 35.
11. Kelley, *Private Woman*, 10.
12. Kevin J. Hayes, *Poe and the Printed Word* (New York: Cambridge University Press, 2000), 93; Lehuu, *Carnival on the Page*, 75; Mott, *History of American Magazines*, vol. i, 513.
13. William Charvat, *Literary Publishing in American 1790–1850* (Philadelphia: University of Pennsylvania Press, 1959), 8; Hayes, *Poe and the Printed Word*, 38; Mott, *History of American Magazines*, vol. i, 504.
14. Tebbel, *American Magazine*, 71–2.
15. Quoted in Whalen, *Edgar Allan Poe and the Masses*, 24.
16. Kelley, *Private Woman*, 20; James Playsted Wood, *Magazines in the United States* (1949; reprinted, New York: Ronald Press, 1971), 62.
17. Mott, *History of American Magazines*, vol. i, 503; Meredith L. McGill, *American Literature and the Culture of Reprinting, 1834–1853* (Philadelphia: University of Pennsylvania Press, 2003), 2; John Tebbel and Mary Ellen Zuckerman, *The Magazine in America 1741–1990* (New York: Oxford University Press, 1991), 10; Tebbel, *American Magazine*, 73.
18. Mott, *History of American Magazines*, vol. i, 519.
19. Wood, *Magazines in the United States*, 45.
20. Poe to William Henry Poe, August 14, 1840, *The Collected Letters of Edgar Allan Poe*, ed. John Ward Ostrom, Burton R. Pollin, and Jeffrey A. Savoye, 2 vols. (New York: Gordian, 2008), vol. i, 235–8.
21. John Lent, "Edgar Allan Poe," *American Magazine Journalists, 1741–1850* (Detroit: Gale, 1988), 239.
22. Rufus Wilmot Griswold, "Memoir of the Author," *The Works of the Late Edgar Allan Poe* (New York: J. S. Redfield, 1850), xvii.
23. Poe to Frederick W. Thomas, May 25, 1842, *Collected Letters*, vol. i, 333–5.
24. Lent, "Edgar Allan Poe," 241.
25. Poe to George W. Eveleth, December 15, 1846, *Collected Letters*, vol. i, 600–5.
26. Lent, "Edgar Allan Poe," 246, 236.
27. McGill, *American Literature and the Culture of Reprinting*, 187; Whalen, "Poe and the American Publishing Industry," 82.
28. Edgar Allan Poe, "Some Secrets of the Magazine Prison-House," *Broadway Journal* 1 (February 15, 1845), 103–4.
29. Edgar Allan Poe, *Collected Works of Edgar Allan Poe*, ed. Thomas Ollive Mabbott, 3 vols. (Cambridge, MA: The Belknap Press of Harvard University Press, 1969–78), vol. iii, 1132.
30. Poe, *Collected Works*, vol. ii, 344.
31. Hayes, *Poe and the Printed Word*, 115.

CHAPTER 18

Gift Books

Kathryn K. Shinn

During the early nineteenth century, a gift book phenomenon swept across America, revolutionizing both literary creation and the art of publication. Gift books played a significant role in the development of American literature and in the careers of many highly celebrated American authors. In late 1825, the first American annual, *The Atlantic Souvenir*, was published in Philadelphia by Carey and Lea as a Christmas and New Year's book. Its preface explains: "Nothing would seem more naturally to suggest itself, as one of those marks of remembrance and affection, which old custom has associated with the gaiety of Christmas, than a little volume of lighter literature, adorned with beautiful specimens of art."[1] *The Atlantic Souvenir* was published annually until 1832, when it merged with *The Token*, Boston's most famous gift book. This new print genre would become an important aspect of Edgar Allan Poe's literary career. He never published in *The Atlantic Souvenir*, but this pioneering annual set the pattern for the gift books in which Poe would publish. By the time *The Atlantic Souvenir* merged with *The Token*, publishers throughout the United States had recognized the money-making potential of gift books and were publishing their own.

Some gift books contained much superficial writing, but other gift books contained superb poetry and fiction. The opportunities for publishing poetry, tales, and sketches they offered provided an outlet for many conventional authors, yet they also gave opportunities to groundbreaking writers as well. Poe's willingness to contribute to these annuals shows that not all gift book publications were for the faint of heart. Some intriguing genres of short fiction that remain popular today, including science fiction and detective stories, appeared in nineteenth-century gift books. Because they were so frequently purchased as gifts, they played a crucial role in cultivating American literary tastes. For a writer like Poe, gift books offered visibility. He could use them not only for financial gain, but also to advance his literary career. They paid better than the magazines, and their circulation expanded an author's readership, which could result in greater popularity, marketability, and publisher interest. Newspapers and magazines often reprinted works from the gift books. Though authors were not compensated for them, these reprints could sustain and expand literary reputations.

With a vision to shed cultural dependence on England, early nineteenth-century publishers, authors, and critics sought to produce great literature that was distinctly American. Many saw writing as a form of national development, and it eventually became a means of significant financial gain for those few who were commercially successful. As different print genres emerged, writers of all kinds could develop distinctly American themes for many different literary purposes.

More and more publishers emerged to meet the growing demand for literature in the nineteenth century. During a time when literary publication grew faster than the population, the circulation of newspapers and magazines increased significantly, but they could not meet the demands for pleasure reading fully. In the 1820s, the gift book emerged as one of the most popular kinds of books available. It provided a way for American publishers to increase their profits while simultaneously meeting the growing hunger for new American literature. Though they originated in Europe, nowhere were gift books as important or as popular as they became in the United States, particularly in New England.

When Poe met Isaac Lea, the junior partner in the firm that published *The Atlantic Souvenir*, in 1829, Lea suggested that Poe write something for the annual. Poe's follow-up letter to Lea makes it seem as if he would be open to publishing in *The Atlantic Souvenir*. He wrote: "I know nothing which could give me greater pleasure than to see any of my productions in so becoming a dress and in such good society as *The Souvenir* would ensure them."[2] Poe was being diplomatic. He remained wary of the gift book phenomenon. At the time, he much preferred to collect his individual works in separate volumes of his own.[3] When Poe and Lea first met, Poe was writing poetry almost exclusively. He would publish another volume of poetry before turning to short fiction in the early 1830s. Though he loved poetry and considered himself a poet throughout his life, Poe recognized that writing fiction was more lucrative, so he began writing short stories for the magazines, which offered an outlet for tales with different attitudes and subjects.

For the most part, American gift book literature was highly moral and very polite. Offering refinement, sentiment, and charm all in one package, they pleased audiences without risking offense. As their titles suggest, gift books were often exchanged between family members and friends. They also served as appropriate signs of affection during courtship. They were ideal for family sitting rooms, and their beauty made them desirable additions to any home library. They became fixtures in middle-class American households. Displayed prominently on parlor tables, they functioned as markers of taste and class.[4]

With their vibrantly colored bindings and handsome engravings, gift books were the most refined, aesthetically pleasing books many Americans had ever seen. Despite their sometimes high prices, they were a luxury people were willing to pay for. With women as the primary audience, each gift book volume was exceedingly sentimental. Walt Whitman, often critical of the gift book genre, referred to them as "those highly-refined imported and gilt-edged themes...causing tender spasms in the coteries, and warranted not to chafe the sensitive cuticle of the most exquisitely artificial gossamer delicacy."[5] Though the literary value of gift books has received a mixture of judgments, they became important vehicles for some of the nation's foremost authors. In addition to Poe, Nathaniel Hawthorne, Washington Irving, and Henry Wadsworth Longfellow all wrote for the gift book trade. Some of their most impressive works first appeared in this print genre. As gift books progressed, they helped nineteenth-century American readers experience the new literature that Poe and his contemporaries were creating.

The Gift contained some extraordinary literature. In the opinion of one contemporary, Carey and Hart were the "best-known and most popular publishers of belles-letters books in America."[6] This popularity was partly due to the reputation of *The Gift*, in which Poe is represented by five different works. With an emphasis on quality literature, as well as exceptional artwork, *The Gift*, according to one reviewer, could be regarded "as a dial by which to learn the progress of the arts in America."[7]

Poe's first gift book experience was the result of his submission of a manuscript volume of tales to a literary contest, which Poe won with "Manuscript Found in a Bottle." John Pendleton Kennedy, one of the contest's judges, found Poe's tales far superior to any of the other submissions and mentioned that the judges only struggled to decide which of the volume's tales should win the prize. Kennedy tried to help Poe publish a fuller collection, *Tales of the Folio Club*, with Carey and Lea, but Henry C. Carey hesitated to accept the work. A talented businessman, Carey understood how to maximize income for written works and decided that gift book publication would be a good choice for Poe. Publishers hesitated to pay authors up front for several stories in one volume, but the gift books paid well for individual tales. Carey sent Poe's manuscript volume of tales to Eliza Leslie, editor of *The Gift*. She, too, considered "Manuscript Found in a Bottle" as the strongest tale and included it in the inaugural issue of *The Gift* or, to use its full title, *The Gift: A Christmas and New Year's Present for 1836*. Conventionally, gift books appeared late in the year, that is, in time for gift givers to purchase them before Christmas, but they were intended to be enjoyed throughout the following year, the year mentioned in the title. A gift book for 1836 would be published in 1835. Leslie clearly recognized Poe's talent, and the two developed a strong working relationship that furthered Poe's literary career.

Poe's first gift book experience was also a lesson – that he was not chiefly in control of what publishers would include in their gift book volumes. In fact, the inclusion of "Manuscript Found in a Bottle" went against Poe's wishes. He complained to Kennedy: "*The Gift* is out. They have published 'The Ms. Found in a Bottle' although I not only told Mr. Carey himself that it had been published, but wrote him to that effect after my return from Baltimore, and sent him another tale in place of it. I cannot understand why they have published it – or why they have not published either 'Siope' or 'Epimanes.'"[8]

Despite the fact that "Manuscript Found in a Bottle" had actually been published a few years earlier, Leslie still believed it was the best choice for her annual. Since magazines and newspapers often reprinted tales from the gift books, Poe had no qualms about reprinting "Manuscript Found in a Bottle" himself after it had appeared in *The Gift*. Once he accepted an editorial position with the *Southern Literary Messenger*, he reprinted the story in the magazine as being from *The Gift* and thus personally reinforced the gift book's impact on the publishing scene.

As he grew savvier, Poe found he could exert more control over the publication of smaller, regional gift books like *The Baltimore Book*, to which he contributed "Siope – A Fable." Issued in late 1837 (though dated 1838), *The Baltimore Book* was patterned on such earlier regional books as *The Boston Book*, *The New York Book*, and *The Philadelphia Book*. Poe wrote to publishers Carpenter, Norris, and Brown that he would be glad to send something for their gift book, but that the theme should be left to his choice.[9] They agreed. *The Baltimore Book* was not particularly successful, but its publication of "Siope" earned it a lasting literary reputation.

Poe was not just a contributor to the gift books, he was also a consumer of them. When Washington Irving published "An Unwritten Drama of Lord Byron" in *The Gift for 1836*, Poe read the work and took inspiration from it. Irving's sketch became the basis for one of Poe's most accomplished short stories, "William Wilson." This great doppelganger tale took some years to gestate, but once Poe completed "William Wilson," he published it, appropriately enough, in *The Gift for 1840*.

The overall quality of *The Gift for 1840* is uneven. Besides "William Wilson," it includes the work of many local Philadelphia contributors. Gift books often gave inexperienced authors a venue to publish their works, regardless of talent. In some cases, the only requirement to publish was to know a publisher who would print a work. *The Gift for 1840* includes many names forgotten today. Beyond Poe, the only other notable name among the contributors is Harriet Beecher Stowe. One prominent female author who found success during the time period, Stowe, too, took advantage of the opportunities the gift books offered.

Gift books coincided with the female immersion into literary culture, and this print genre gave voice to many women with important things to say. The inclusion of so much work by women has earned the genre much criticism, despite notable female authors, including Lydia H. Sigourney and Frances S. Osgood, who both achieved considerable fame at the time. Unlike many of his contemporaries, Poe respected and valued female writers and readers and understood the importance of expanding his audience to include them. Volumes such as *The Gift* were helpful in sharing Poe's literary creativity and skill with the general reading public and in inspiring more women to take an active role in the literary production.

Even gift books that included high-quality fiction and verse earned their popularity largely from their physical appearance. Bindings were made from fancy embossed cloth or even more luxurious hand-tooled calf. Some special publications used fine materials such as velvet or silk. Though many American consumers judged these gift books by their covers, their beauty was not limited to their exteriors. Lovely art accompanied the literature inside the volumes. While the outside was beautiful, it was the art inside the books that people prized the most. Gift books typically contained about 300 pages of prose and poetry accompanied by many embellishments. In most cases, the literature was chosen to fit the illustration rather than vice versa. An American gift book's illustrations often reflected its publisher's personal taste. Though it might seem unimpressive by today's standards, at the time gift book art was new and exotic. American consumers were pleased that for the first time they could purchase work by American artists that exemplified refinement, good taste, and beauty.[10]

The combination of embellishments and original writing set certain gift books such as *The Token* and *The Gift* apart from the rest. The artwork in *The Gift* generated most of the praise this annual received. Despite its literary aspects, contemporary reviews focused largely on aesthetic appeal. As gift books were designed to please the eye, there was often more emphasis on aesthetic over literary value. Thus, the primary purpose of the gift book was ornamental. As peculiar as this seems, the function of the gift book reveals an important shift in American cultural development; for the first time, American publishers were creating fine artistic objects worthy of admiration.

Poe published "Eleonora," one of his most romantic tales, in *The Gift for 1842*. This installment of *The Gift* was also recognized for its handsome engravings. The publisher's advertisement at the beginning of the volume states: "All illustrations in the present volume are from pictures by our own artists and we flatter ourselves that they will be found to compare advantageously with any similar productions from abroad."[11] The advertisement mentions nothing of American literary production or the impressive fiction included. Whether the target audience knew it or not, the United States was continuing to develop a national literary identity, and annuals helped further this end. Publishers saw themselves playing an integral role in nation building, and the mass appeal of gift books, whether they were read or only enjoyed for their beauty, separated American artistic taste from European production.

Contemporary American publishers were often quite proud of the books they published, gift books included. They tried to contribute to the education of the American public and the intellectual growth of the nation. Matthew Carey – Henry's father and one of the previous generation's most prominent Philadelphia publishers – saw himself contributing to the national good and fostering the development of American arts and manufactures. He considered the books he published as works that educated, refined, and developed the nation. Following in his father's footsteps, Henry C. Carey became one of the most successful publishers of his time, perpetuating his father's optimistic philosophy and playing a vital role in the development of American print culture.[12]

Gift books well suited the beneficial ends of printing that nineteenth-century printers and publishers sought to fulfill. With their fine bindings, steel engravings, and handsomely printed pages, the annuals were products of good bookmanship. Though expensive to produce, they could be quite profitable for their publishers. Consequently, the gift book market was incredibly competitive. Gift books, with their high circulation, were among the first books to exploit new trends in literature, publishing, and marketing. The public grew increasingly interested in the new literature they could read in gift books. In Poe's case, readers were willing to set aside their desire for "light" literature and experience something revolutionary.

The Gift for 1843 includes "The Pit and the Pendulum," a tale of torture that doubles as a narrator's journey into the depths of his own self. Contrary to Whitman's comments on the delicate content of gift books, this tale was sure to "chafe the sensitive cuticle" or cause something more than "tender spasms" for readers. Poe continually pushed himself and wrote his way past existing literary boundaries. Never one to produce anything cliché, Poe managed to write complex, psychological, gothic fiction and poetry for a wider audience. Although his work was intellectually stimulating, readers did not have to be highly educated to enjoy it. Poe's last contribution to *The Gift* was his detective story, "The Purloined Letter," which explores methods of forensic science and implicitly questions artistic motivation. One reviewer called *The Gift for 1845* "an annual of which the publishers have reasons to be proud" and found "The Purloined Letter" an "exceedingly well-written tale."[13]

The year after *The Gift for 1845* appeared, George Graham enlisted James Russell Lowell to write an article about Poe for *Graham's Magazine*, which included a biography of Poe's life accompanied by a commentary on his works and influence on American literature. In this, one of the most sensitive portrayals of Poe to appear in his lifetime, Lowell observes: "In his tales, Mr. Poe has chosen to exhibit his power chiefly in that dim region which stretches from the very utmost limits of the probable into the weird confines of superstition and unreality."[14] Lowell's characterization shows how Poe's work contradicted the general trends of the gift book. Lowell continues: "In raising images of horror, also, he has a strange success, conveying to us sometimes by a dusky hint some terrible doubt which is the secret of all horror."[15] As Lowell's words suggest, Poe's tales added a darkness and sense of evil to the gift books that they otherwise often lacked.

Poe was detached from the usual content of gift books, but through the genre he found success and formed many important relationships. He is represented by five different contributions to *The Gift*, all of which impressed audiences and worked to carve a lasting place for Poe as one of the most important literary figures in American history. Even after his last publication in *The Gift*, Poe continued to find avenues to publish. The reading public became more and more attuned to the content of his work, and his contemporaries recognized his rare talent.

Poe's stories revolutionized American literature, and *The Gift* helped introduce the American public to Poe's new themes and forms that were not sentimental, moral, or idealistic. Both logical and creative, Poe's overall contribution to gift books is hard to categorize. He wrote nearly every form of prose and fiction, always inventing new narrative approaches. Poe could tell stories unlike any of his contemporaries. His gift book contributions seem to go against the very nature of the gift book, as his publications represent some of the most psychological, innovative, and important literature of the time.

He continued to find success with gift books outside of his important relationship with *The Gift*. Poe's career depended on the successful republication of his works in various gift books and illustrated magazines. He submitted prose and poetry to annuals including *The Opal*, which published his descriptive article, "Morning on the Wissachion." Sarah J. Hale, the editor of *The Opal*, also accepted Poe's story, "The Oblong Box," but Poe, frustrated by the rate of payment, sent her "A Chapter of Suggestions" instead. Always one to rebel against authority, he sent "The Oblong Box" to Louis Godey, knowing that Hale was also the editor of *Godey's Lady's Book*. Regardless, both stories were published and his positive relationship with Hale remained intact.[16] He republished "The Lake" in *The Missionary Memorial* and "The Imp of the Perverse" in *The Mayflower*. These smaller gift books played a much less significant role on the national stage, but aided in circulating his work. Most reprints circulated without payment or Poe's consent, but his reputation benefited by these indirect routes through which his works reached the public. Ultimately, reprints that circulated in the United States and abroad contributed to his literary career and his lasting legacy.

The gift book phenomenon outlived Poe, but his literary reach extends far beyond the beautifully bound volumes that included much of his finest work. By the start of the Civil War over a thousand different gift books had been published, but they lost public favor rather quickly. Though many gift books were published to promote certain causes, such as *The Liberty Bell*, written specifically to raise money for the antislavery cause, or *The Fountain*, which set out to warn people of the ill effects of strong alcoholic drinks, these politically motivated annuals were not enough to keep the public interested in gift books. As time progressed, public taste shifted from the ideal to the realistic, and there no longer existed the need to cater to publications printed at yearly intervals, especially those that might go unread. The fading interest in gift books coincides with the rise and spread of political and social inquiry, which publishers realized could be fostered without expensive ornamentation or elaborate leather bindings. For Poe, the gift book genre was as important as any other aspect of his literary career. It was through these books that he built important relationships, assembled his literary reputation as an outstanding author of the time period, and delivered revolutionary, visionary works to a new generation hungry for unique American literature.

NOTES

1. "Preface," *The Atlantic Souvenir: A Christmas and New Year's Offering, 1826* (Philadelphia: H. C. Carey and I. Lea, 1825), n.p.
2. Poe to Carey, Lea, and Carey, July 28, 1829, *The Collected Letters of Edgar Allan Poe*, ed. John Ward Ostrom, Burton R. Pollin, and Jeffrey A. Savoye, 2 vols. (New York: Gordian, 2008), vol. i, 40.
3. Kevin J. Hayes, *Poe and the Printed Word* (New York: Cambridge University Press, 2000), 18–20.
4. Isabelle Lehuu, *Carnival on the Page: Popular Print Media in Antebellum America* (Chapel Hill: University of North Carolina Press, 2000), 84.
5. Walt Whitman, *Complete Poetry and Collected Prose*, ed. Justin Kaplan (New York: Library of America, 1982), 980.
6. "Literary Souvenirs, &c." *Quarterly Review* 37 (1828), 99.
7. "Editor's Table," *Graham's Magazine* 21 (1842), 155.
8. Poe to John P. Kennedy, September 11, 1835, *Collected Letters*, vol. i, 108.
9. Poe to William Henry Carpenter, John Saurin Burns, and Janes Burns, February 28, 1837, *Collected Letters*, vol. i, 173.
10. Ralph Thompson, *American Literary Annuals and Gift Books, 1825–1865* (New York: H. W. Wilson, 1936), 39.
11. "Publishers' Advertisement," *The Gift: A Christmas and New Years Present for 1842* (Philadelphia: Carey and Hart, 1841), v.
12. Jeffrey D. Groves, "The Book Trade Transformed," in *Perspectives on American Book History*, eds. Scott E. Casper, Joanne D. Chaison, and Jeffrey D. Groves (Amherst: Massachusetts University Press, 2002), 109–32.
13. "Review of New Books," *Graham's Magazine* 26 (1844), 295.
14. James Russell Lowell, "Our Contributors: No. XVII," *Graham's Magazine* 27 (1845), 52.
15. Lowell, "Our Contributors," 52.
16. Kevin J. Hayes, *Edgar Allan Poe* (London: Reaktion, 2009), 128–9.

CHAPTER 19

Literary Piracy

Michael J. Everton

Like plagiarism, literary piracy is the unauthorized reproduction of another person's writing. Unlike plagiarism, however, piracy is not so much "intellectual fraud" as economic opportunism.[1] The pirate openly exploits the weakness of certain controls – technological controls like digital locks or legal controls like copyright – intended to enforce an author's property. But what if there are no controls in the first place? This was the situation in the antebellum United States, where a powerful publishing sector grew up in the absence of international copyright. Publishers, or "reprinters," could reproduce foreign texts and were under no legal obligation to pay writers for the right to do so, because according to American law these writers had no rights to begin with. That is exactly what reprinters did in increasingly large numbers, eventually establishing a vibrant market for foreign books. To many observers, it all seemed a bit mischievous, this commandeering of other people's property. To others it was downright immoral. What if all merchants, much less all Americans, acted this way? "For our own part," one literary monthly said, "we will never believe that the majority of our countrymen are so lacking in the first principles of morality, as to wish to thrive by plundering another people of their property."[2] Hence the epithet "pirate," which, though technically inaccurate, captured the sense of moral outrage critics felt at the perceived exploitation of foreign writers by a fraternity of blackguard businessmen. They understood that reprinting was not illegal, but they felt it ought to be. And they waged a long campaign to convince Americans they were right.

International copyright had more clamorous advocates in the 1830s and 1840s than Edgar Allan Poe, but none more competent. Poe possessed an exceptional understanding of copyright's theory and consequences. This may be the reason he argued both sides of the "copyright question," as the debate became known. Poe believed fundamentally that writers owned their creations regardless of geography. In the 1845 article "Anastatic Printing," for example, he celebrated a new printing process that would allow handwritten pages to be stereotyped, believing that "in depressing the value of the *physique* of a book, the invention will proportionately elevate the value of its *morale*, and since it is the latter value alone which the copy-right laws are needed to protect, the necessity of protection will be only the more urgent and more obvious."[3] By "*morale*," Poe meant the ideas of a text, though he was likely also alluding to the French legal concept of "moral rights" (*droit morale*): the notion that a text is an extension of its author, a physical gesture of metaphysical labor. At the same time, however, Poe recognized that reprinting, which often ignored these very rights, was not the evil some made it out to be. The rather anarchic literary culture created by the lack of international copyright was good for many readers and publishers and potentially even for writers, including Poe himself. This apparent inconsistency might frustrate students of Poe, but for students of piracy it is a symptom of the larger debate over literary property in antebellum America, a debate that could be as bewildering as the principle of copyright itself.[4]

United States copyright law dates to an act of the First Congress, which initially gave American writers and other copyright holders ownership of their literary property for up to twenty-eight years. The purview of the Copyright Act of 1790 was a product of the times. It protected authorship, obviously, but it also protected the domestic manufacturing of all manner of print, from books to newspapers to maps. Even more important was what it did not protect: foreign authors and publishers. This was not an oversight. In unusually deliberate language, Section 5 of the Act told printers and publishers that they were free to appropriate any and all foreign print. In the unsteady economic environment of the early republic, such protections made good sense. Thus, while the first federal copyright law is justly remembered for protecting writers, it was more concerned with stimulating American publishing, in part by encouraging piracy.

Few bothered with the inequities of the law until after the War of 1812, when domestic publishing stabilized and publishers, eager to serve a growing and literate population, began to exploit the so-called reprint clause more aggressively. Naturally, they looked to Europe, reprinting books frequently but not rampantly. As historian James N. Green puts it, the watershed came in 1820 in the form of "an avalanche of Scott."[5] Sir Walter Scott was already a steady seller in the early United States, but in 1820 his celebrity exploded. That year alone reprinters issued at least nine editions of his novels, the next year some thirty-one. The fact that these editions were issued by different reprinters indicates the catch in reprinting: if one house could reproduce a foreign title, so could others. Despite informal agreements among some publishers intended to reign in competition, the quest to be the first to market with a new foreign title was often a free-for-all in which capital, speed, and combativeness meant the difference between profit and loss. In this climate it did not take long for reprint-ers to earn a colorful reputation. The most damaging rumor involved the "Author of Waverley" himself. In 1832 Scott died insolvent, and it was widely reported that reprinters had grown fat and happy off profits from his books while the beloved author struggled to pay his bills. Though the Philadelphia firm Carey and Lea had long since worked out an arrange-ment with Scott's publisher – a deal that purportedly involved bribery – the story grew that American book pirates had consigned Scott to an early grave. It was apocryphal, but matters had grown so chaotic in the American trade that it was easy to see how such a story could be true. The "game," as the antic competition among reprinters became known, seemed more than a little ungentlemanly. Poe summed up the optics nicely, remarking that perhaps "robbing…literary Europe on the highway" was not good policy.[6] He believed the business of literature should be conducted in a gentlemanly way. Of course, gentlemanly conduct could be hard to come by, least of all in Poe. American print culture seldom lived up to its self-image, especially where reprinting was concerned.

Complain as they might, there was not much foreign publishers could do to curb reprinting. One London firm, Saunders and Otley, tried an end run around reprinters in 1836 by setting up a New York office. It was a bold but ultimately unsuccessful move: the firm quickly discov-ered that if anything were to change, American copyright law would have to change first. Backed by household names like Maria Edgeworth and William Wordsworth, it began to lobby Congress for a law recognizing the property rights of foreign authors. The next year a bill was proposed in Congress. Though the session ended before a vote, supporters were buoyed by the bill's favorable treatment and by a surprising lack of oppo-sition from reprinters. Briefly, international copyright seemed like a real possibility. Then, in the spring of 1837, an unprecedented banking and credit crisis sparked a vast economic downturn from which the country would not fully recover for five years. It hit publishing and allied trades hard, putting many firms in the red and some out of business altogether. By the time Congress reconvened late that year, the economic landscape had changed completely.

The new incarnation of the international copyright bill came under more and different kinds of scrutiny. The opposition had mobilized, anchored by reprinters. And by early 1838, when the bill went before the Senate Committee on Patents, opponents had a persuasive script, publisher Philip Nicklin's influential treatise, *Remarks on Literary Property*, which effectively summarized the case against extending copyright. In clear, dry prose Nicklin assured legislators that "the republication of foreign books...is merely an investment of capital, with a view to gain the common profit of trade."[7] And all those stories about Sir Walter Scott specifically and the trade generally? Nicklin brushed them aside. He suggested that if anyone were to blame for the unfortunate circumstances of "that illustrious and excellent man" it was his British creditors, not American publishers, who were models of commercial civility.[8] Nicklin spent the majority of his time, though, disabusing congressmen of any illusion that copyright did not matter. This was not just about protecting a few starry-eyed authors; the nation's commercial viability was at stake. In the end, international copyright did not survive the patent committee. Three more unsuccessful attempts followed between 1838 and 1842, after which the debate ebbed and flowed until 1891, when Congress adopted a law, complete with muscular protections for domestic manufacturing.

Half a century earlier, in Poe's time, reformers were undaunted by the trials and tribulations of congressional copyright reform. They took it for granted that they were right, and if anything they grew more idealistic, stimulated in part by the buzz of British Romanticism that lingered in the antebellum air. While advocates' belief that authors had natural rights that predated and ultimately superseded human law did not derive from Romanticism, it was more or less compatible with the Romantic belief in the social utility of original genius. In the words of Wordsworth's unambiguously titled poem, "A Plea for Authors, 1838," laws that failed to recognize authors' "natural rights" made a "mockery" of "social Justice."[9]

Wordsworth penned this poem in the wake of two high court decisions that seemed to do exactly that. In 1834, the Supreme Court ruled that under American copyright law authors forfeited whatever rights they had as creators when their works went into print. This interpretation of the Copyright Act of 1790 basically echoed Britain's House of Lords' 1774 interpretation of the law on which the American act was based, the Statute of Anne (1710). The courts essentially said that literary property was a function of the law, and the law did not recognize the literary property of foreign writers.

Neither of these cases was about international copyright, but both influenced the terms of the debate in the 1840s. In 1847, George Ticknor Curtis, co-counsel for Dred Scott in the 1857 Supreme Court case that would bear his name, published a treatise on copyright. In sometimes angry terms – his disappointment with juridical decisions on copyright is palpable – Curtis argued that the "author's exclusive title is not only theoretically perfect, but...practically acknowledged by mankind."[10] For Curtis, "public policy requires a recognition of the natural rights of authors, as the basis of legislation."[11] Poe agreed. "The right of property in a literary work is disputed merely for the sake of disputation, and no man should be at the trouble of arguing the point. Those who deny it, have made up their minds to deny every thing tending to further the law in contemplation."[12] Imagine, Poe said, "the demagogue-ridden public" allowing politicians to make "orations in our national halls...on the gross absurdity in especial of admitting so unprincipled a principle, that a man has any right and title either to his own brains or to the flimsy material that he chooses to spin out of them, like a confounded caterpillar as he is."[13]

Had times been better for publishers in the early 1840s more might have sympathized with such arguments. Even if a publisher did not accept the claim that an author's rights eclipsed all others – that is, that an author should have a perpetual monopoly over his works, a position at odds with the spirit of federal copyright law, though not without precedent in state law – he might at least agree that foreign authors deserved the same limited monopoly granted to their American counterparts, which was the gist of the 1837 bill. Publishers, however, had businesses to run. And by the early 1840s they had a new phenomenon to contend with: the trade revolution known as "cheap publishing."

The Panic of 1837 created opportunities for those who thought outside the box of traditional print formats. Enterprising literary tradesmen, among them Rufus Griswold, turned to the mass market periodical as a way to capitalize on the unprecedented factors created by the recession. Published as weekly newspapers, periodicals like the *New World, Brother Jonathan*, and the *Universal Yankee Nation* took advantage of new cylinder presses that could churn out some twenty thousand sheets an hour, sheets filled with pirated foreign texts. These newspapers could be sold over the counter, like conventional books, but they could also be hawked in the streets or mailed for next to nothing. Because of a loophole in government postal rates, a weekly newspaper measuring two feet by three feet could be sent from New York to New Orleans for far less than the cost of a single letter. So could special editions of these weeklies, some of which reached truly colossal proportions. One edition of the *Universal Yankee Nation*, the self-proclaimed "Mastodon of American Newspapers," measured more than four feet wide by ten feet long.[14] These editions could reproduce an entire novel in a single issue, much to the shock and chagrin of Charles Dickens, who came to America in 1842 and railed in person against the state of affairs that made such things possible. Though it lasted only as long as the recession, cheap publishing seemed to signal the triumph of piracy.

The conventional logic is that writers reacted to what Meredith L. McGill has aptly called the "culture of reprinting" with horror, followed by knee-jerk literary nationalism. Certainly many did. "Pirates have repeatedly seen the author die of starvation, or kill himself, or go mad, as a natural consequence of the ruin he brought on him by the act of piracy," British playwright Charles Reade charged; "in no single instance has one syllable of remorse escaped the murderer."[15] No, said New York writer and editor Cornelius Mathews: pirates were even worse than that. Riffing on the idea of moral rights, as Poe had in "Anastatic Printing," Mathews suggested – bizarrely – that reprinting "kills the image of god," because man and hence the author are made in "God's image."[16] Poe was not above a little exaggeration himself. In an 1842 letter he proposed that "Without an international copyright law, American authors may as well cut their throats."[17] In fact, while publishers did come to depend on the reprint trade, most did not discriminate against domestic authors, even during the Panic of 1837 and its aftermath.[18]

The hyperbole oversimplified the complex world not only of American print culture but of British print culture as well. While writers seldom spoke out publicly, some conceded being of two minds about reprinting, as Elizabeth Barrett Browning did in an 1850 letter about the piracy of Robert Browning's latest book of poetry:

Two hundred copies went off in the first fortnight, which is a good beginning in these days. – So I am to confess to a satisfaction in the American piracies. Well – I confess, then. Only it is a rather complex smile with which one hears ... "Sir or Madam, we are selling your book at half price, as well printed as in England." "Those apples we stole from your garden, we sell at a halfpenny, instead of a penny as you do; and they are much appreciated." It's worth while to rob us, that's plain – and there's something magnificent in supplying a distant market with apples out of one's garden. Still the smile is complex in its character, and the morality ... simple – that's all I meant to say.[19]

When not busy predicting the mass extinction of the American writer, Poe's sentiments corresponded with Elizabeth Barrett Browning's. He was explicit about his belief that reprinting was not to be feared in itself. "The immediate advantage arising to the pockets of our people is sufficiently plain. We get more reading for less money than if the international law existed."[20] He appreciated the greater dissemination of European works in the United States, fearing that without reprinting some of the best literature would become prohibitively expensive and scarce, and, despite his severe distaste for the cheap look of "cheap literature," he embraced the international literary culture it helped create. Suspicious of the brand of literary nationalism championed by contemporaries – "What is to be gained by it?" he asked – Poe welcomed the fact that, as Elizabeth Barrett Browning noted, a "distant market" was not so distant anymore.[21] (Poe should know: he was one of the relatively few American authors pirated by European publishers.[22]) The United States was too connected to Europe to follow a policy of cultural quarantine, however well intended. Literary globalization had begun, and there was no going back.

For Poe, the problem with the reprint trade was the way in which it was conducted and vindicated. Nations respected conventional commodities. Why not literature? Reprinters would respond that the law did not recognize literature as property the way it did, say, tobacco or cotton, and it was not their place to speculate on what should or should not be legal (though they worked behind the scenes to do just that). This legality made reprinting a matter of "expediency," by which reprinters meant economic pragmatism. In their writings, the term also took on a moral logic. It worked as a syllogism: reprinting is legal; whatever is legal is right; therefore, reprinting is right. Reprinters fell back on the government's definitions of right and wrong, definitions that were, in fact, neither moral nor immoral but amoral. Thus, when Elizabeth Barrett Browning called reprinters' morality "simple," she meant that it oversimplified the relationship between what was and what ought to be.

Poe was no moralist, but like other antebellum Americans his thinking on piracy relied on a moral grammar. On these grounds he too found the expediency defense problematic. The principle might be relevant in some cases, he admitted, but not this one. "Expediency is only to be discussed where no *rights* interfere," he wrote in *Godey's Lady's Book*. "It would no doubt be very expedient in any poor man to pick the pocket of his wealthy neighbour, (and as the poor are the majority the case is precisely parallel to the copyright case) but what would the rich think if expediency were permitted to overrule the right?"[23] Like Henry David Thoreau just a few years later, and like Mark Twain almost half a century later, Poe wondered what would happen if people decided what was right and wrong based on what was easiest or most profitable at the time.

He worried especially that reprinters' actions would come to characterize the United States, that they would be viewed as symptoms of a society incapable of recognizing right from "an open and continuous wrong."

Respect for literary property was, as Curtis said, a matter of "national character."[24] "There is scarcely any civilized people, who would not be shocked by a proposal to withdraw all protection from the interests of literary property."[25] To do so would be to invite the kinds of "retributive social ills" that were forever visited upon societies that abandoned the principles and "great maxims in which the essence of justice is enshrined."[26] Poe too spoke of the dangers to the "national character," mindful of what he called "the impolicy of our committing, in the national character, an open and continuous wrong on the frivolous pretext of its benefiting ourselves."[27] The copyright situation was not dangerous because it threatened the development of a national literary tradition. It was dangerous because it threatened the idea of the nation and the character of its people. The kinds of reprinting some powerful American publishers undertook during the 1830s and 1840s, in which they did not even attempt to remunerate the author and defended aggressively their right not to do so, was responsible for "that sense of insult and injury aroused in the whole intellect of the world, the bitter and fatal resentment excited in the universal heart of literature." It was, Poe said, "a resentment which will not and which cannot make nice distinctions between the temporary perpetrators of the wrong and that democracy in general which permits its perpetration."[28]

Notwithstanding the very real good it did for the nation's fledgling literary culture, reprinting was ultimately unsustainable because of the "remoter disadvantages" outlined earlier, according to Poe.[29] However "remote" or abstract, the moral, noneconomic costs of reprinting were simply too high. Still, as his language suggests, Poe was loathe to condemn reprinting wholesale. The lived experience of American print culture was not that simple. If anything, a surprising number of writers and publishers alike looked on literary piracy as Poe did, with something akin to Elizabeth Barrett Browning's "complex smile."

NOTES

1. Richard A. Posner, *The Little Book of Plagiarism* (New York: Pantheon, 2007), 106.
2. "International Copyright," *Putnam's Monthly Magazine* 1 (1853), 335.
3. Edgar Allan Poe, *The Complete Works of Edgar Allan Poe*, ed. James A. Harrison, 17 vols. (New York: Crowell, 1902), vol. xiv, 159.
4. On reprinting, see James J. Barnes, *Authors, Publishers and Politicians: The Quest for an Anglo-American Copyright Agreement, 1815–1854* (London: Routledge and Kegan Paul, 1974) and Meredith L. McGill, *American Literature and the Culture of Reprinting* (Philadelphia: University of Pennsylvania Press, 2003),

the ablest reconciliation of Poe's beliefs on piracy. On the history of piracy writ large, see Adrian Johns, *Piracy: The Intellectual Property Wars from Gutenberg to Gates* (Chicago: University of Chicago Press, 2009). On the moral aspects of antebellum print culture, see Michael J. Everton, *The Grand Chorus of Complaint: Authors and the Business Ethics of American Publishing* (New York: Oxford University Press, 2011). Volumes 2 and 3 of *The History of the Book in America* provide exemplary surveys of Poe's print culture: Robert A. Gross and Mary Kelley, eds., *An Extensive Republic: Print, Culture, and Society in the New Nation, 1790–1840* (Chapel Hill: University of North Carolina Press and the American Antiquarian Society, 2010); and Scott E. Casper, Jeffrey D. Groves, Stephen W. Nissenbaum, and Michael Winship, eds., *The Industrial Book, 1840–1880* (Chapel Hill: University of North Carolina Press and the American Antiquarian Society, 2007).

5. James N. Green, "The Rise of Book Publishing," in *An Extensive Republic*, 107.
6. Edgar Allan Poe, *Essays and Reviews*, ed. G. R. Thompson (New York: Library of America, 1984), 1037.
7. Philip Nicklin, *Remarks on Literary Property* (Philadelphia: P. H. Nicklin and T. Johnson, 1838), 20.
8. Ibid., 23.
9. William Wordsworth, *Last Poems, 1821–1850*, ed. Jared Curtis (Ithaca: Cornell University Press, 1999), 327.
10. George Ticknor Curtis, *A Treatise on the Law of Copyright* (Boston: Charles C. Little and James Brown, 1847), 13.
11. Ibid., 18.
12. Poe, *Essays*, 1374.
13. Ibid., 1037.
14. Quoted in Isabelle Lehuu, *Carnival on the Page: Popular Print Media in Antebellum America* (Chapel Hill: University of North Carolina Press, 2000), 68.
15. Charles Reade, *The Eighth Commandment* (Boston: Ticknor and Fields, 1860), 228.
16. [Cornelius Mathews], "The International Copyright Law, and Mr. Dickens," *Arcturus* 3 (1842), 244.
17. Poe to Frederick W. Thomas, August 27, 1842, *The Collected Letters of Edgar Allan Poe*, ed. John Ward Ostrom, Burton R. Pollin, and Jeffrey A. Savoye, 2 vols. (New York: Gordian, 2008), vol. i, 356.
18. Green, "The Rise of Book Publishing," 127.
19. Elizabeth Barrett Browning to Mary Russell Mitford, April 30, 1850, *Women of Letters: Selected Letters of Elizabeth Barrett Browning and Mary Russell Mitford*, ed. Meredith B. Raymond and Mary Rose Sullivan (Boston: Twayne, 1987), 226–7.
20. Poe, *Essays*, 1374.
21. Ibid., 1076.

22. Kevin J. Hayes, *Poe and the Printed Word* (New York: Cambridge University Press, 2000), 90–1.

23. Poe, *Essays*, 1374.

24. Curtis, *Treatise on the Law of Copyright*, 18.

25. Ibid., 19.

26. Ibid., 18–19.

27. Poe, *Essays*, 1375.

28. Ibid.

29. Ibid., 1374.

CHAPTER 20

The Art of Reviewing

Jonathan Hartmann

Poe first established a nationwide literary reputation during his time with the *Southern Literary Messenger*, not as a poet or an author of weird tales but as a critic. Before Poe came along, two basic impulses helped determine how books were reviewed. A gentlemanly tit for tat – "You say good things about my book, and I'll say good things about yours" – created a sense of camaraderie among authors and reviewers. Strongly influenced by their British counterparts, the authors of lengthier reviews used the publication of a book solely as a starting point to discuss whatever subject they wished, such as the proliferation of novel readers and novelists, the subject of an unsigned piece in the *American Monthly Magazine* for November 1835. Poe disagreed with both impulses, writing highly critical, tightly focused reviews under the firm belief that rigorous criticism could improve American literature.

In 1822, when Poe was writing his early poems, James Kirke Paulding declared in *A Sketch of Old England* that "personal, political, and religious antipathies or attachments" motivated ninety percent of Britain's literary reviews.[1] Paulding's observation largely held true for American critics. The typical anonymity of reviewers reinforced the process of critical puffing and critical damning. The majority of periodical reviews were voiced by an unknown figure, the editorial We, that appeared to speak for the journal itself. This was the standard of the British reviews upon which the *American*, *Democratic*, and *North American*, as well as the *Southern Literary Messenger* were founded. A common rationalization for this tendency was the need for the reviewer to seem objective. With their names affixed to their columns, editors might balk at pointing out the limitations of authors with whom they would inevitably come into personal and professional contact. In practice, however, anonymous reviewing facilitated critical aggression, such as the campaign of *Blackwood's Edinburgh Magazine* on the Cockney School, including Robert Southey, Leigh Hunt, and William Hazlitt. Anonymous reviewing also enabled authorial self-reviews of many thousands of books in England and the United States.[2]

Though Poe found common intellectual interest with most literary circles, he resented the advantages enjoyed by financially independent authors, particularly those based in the Northeast. These writers were especially well prepared to treat with publishers and magazine editors on either side of the Atlantic and hence to find a reading public. Poe singled out for special attention Transcendentalists such as William Ellery Channing, Ralph Waldo Emerson, and Margaret Fuller; the often Harvard-affiliated Brahmins such as Henry Wadsworth Longfellow and James Russell Lowell, whom he termed Frogpondians; and New York cliques including Washington Irving and Catherine Maria Sedgwick's Knickerbockers. Poe bristled at the remarks of reform-oriented critics such as Emerson and Lydia Maria Child, whom he perceived as self-styled exemplars of what Emerson in an 1844 speech termed the "Young American."

Even the staid and sober *North American Review* made certain its reviewers looked favorably upon the writers involved in its orbit. The *Review* gave Henry Wadsworth Longfellow, a college classmate of Hawthorne at Bowdoin College who had recently begun teaching at Harvard, the assignment of evaluating Hawthorne's *Twice-Told Tales*. Writing anonymously, Longfellow declared: "As to the pure mind all things are pure, so to the poetical mind all things are poetical. To such souls no age and no country can be utterly dull and prosaic. They make unto themselves their age and their country; dwelling in the universal mind of man, and in the universal forms of things. Of such is the author of this book."[3]

Longfellow was one of several important connections for Hawthorne. Emerson lent Hawthorne funds in 1836, and fellow Transcendentalist Elizabeth Peabody (Hawthorne's future sister-in-law) promoted his writing from her Salem bookstore by about 1840.[4] Five years later, Longfellow, again writing anonymously for the *North American Review*, noticed Hawthorne once more, speaking with added enthusiasm for his insight into the human condition: "It is the voice of a man who has seen and thought for himself, which addresses us; and the treasures which he offers to us are the harvests of much observation and deep reflection on man, and life, and the human heart."[5] This assessment is slightly more down to earth than its antecedent; Poe, however, would have been irritated by both. For Poe insisted on the practicality of literature, especially literary criticism, to speak the language of the heart and mind rather than the spirit.[6]

Although Hawthorne may not himself have aggressively promoted his fiction, Poe frequently observed that so-called self-made authors, often

sporting elite education and other important sources of professional
liaisons, were hard-nosed businessmen whose literary dealings contradicted
their professed goals as teachers, reformers, and/or Transcendentalists.[7] In
both "The Business Man" (1840; revised edition, 1843) and "The Literary
Life of Thingum Bob, Esq." (1844), Poe takes aim at Emerson's notion
of himself as a transparent eyeball, highlighting their protagonists' exceptional vision in designing schemes with which to fleece their neighbors.
Peter Proffit, Poe's businessman who presents himself as the soul of
practical reason, tallies up his earnings from practices such as cultivating
cats for the sake of vending their tails. Thingum Bob, whose name suggests
his function as a mere counter or unit of currency adrift in a vast matrix of
social forces, succeeds by devious means at elevating himself to the editor's
chair of a conglomerate of regional papers. Bob's achievement of success
by haphazardly cutting and pasting together the columns of other journals
calls attention to the newspaper exchange networks whereby such editors
as Thomas W. White of the *Messenger* obtained ready access to a wealth
of writing.[8]

The intricate networking of Northeastern writers is suggested by a
glance at the editorial matter for the opening issue of the *Knickerbocker
Magazine* (January 4, 1840). Here the *Knickerbocker* proclaims its achievements in a wide range of literature, trumpeting its stable of 100 illustrious
contributors guided by the frequent presence of James Fenimore Cooper,
Washington Irving, Henry Wadsworth Longfellow, and William Ware.
There follow "personal opinions" from Massachusetts' Governor Everett,
who finds the paper superior to many of the English journals. Charles
Dickens, listed as "The Author of *Pickwick, Oliver Twist*, etc." affirms his
pleasure in reading the *Knickerbocker*, and more important, his desire to
be published there. The final testimonial is offered by Edward Bulwer
Lytton, who, in offering his own contribution, calls the *Knickerbocker*
"the best periodical I have yet seen." The *Knickerbocker* completes its who's
who of collaborators with a baker's dozen of periodical endorsements
from the eastern United States and London. Much of the success of the
Knickerbocker may be attributed to its uniting members of early literary
circles such as The Calliopean Society and Bread and Cheese into collab-
orative harmony.

New York served as the leading center for literary clubs to pool their
resources and thus facilitate their members' advancement, for example,
by improving their access to publishers as well as government and private
patronage. Two well-connected club members proved themselves adept at
this game. Washington Irving was lavishly financed by John Jacob Astor

from 1834; James Kirke Paulding served as secretary of the navy from early 1838 to mid-1841. New York literary soirees brought together temperance advocates, women's rights activists, the Knickerbockers, and Young America with potential patrons and publishers as well as visitors such as Thomas Carlyle and Unitarian minister Frederic Henry Hedge.[9]

Poe, for his part, sought political and military appointment without tangible success. An early model for Poe was novelist John Neal, who had published a five-part series of off-the-cuff remarks on American literature for *Blackwood's Edinburgh Magazine* during 1824 and 1825. Beginning in the final weeks of 1834, John Pendleton Kennedy encouraged Poe's literary efforts for at least seventeen months, providing financial help and a recommendation to the *Southern Literary Messenger*. Poe's frequent impatience with America's system of patronage and puffing was hardly unique. Literary clubs often called for common efforts against the collusion of market forces and tightfisted publishers. Despite their stated aim of supporting needy brethren, literary associations may in fact have maintained the status quo ante of antebellum publishing.[10]

When Poe set up as an editorial assistant at Thomas W. White's *Southern Literary Messenger*, the epithet "Tomahawk Man," a term imported from the English magazines, was quickly applied to his criticism. Poe responded by celebrating this honorific in his fiction.[11] "The Man That Was Used Up" (1839) plays with the language of dismemberment. An ensemble of stock characters marvels at the handsome parts – each of which turns out to be man-made – of Brevet Brigadier General John A. B. C. Smith, decorated veteran of the Bugaboo and Kickapoo military campaigns. The general's laborious assembly by his colored servant calls attention to Poe's skill in verbally tearing apart writers who dared to test his critical mettle. One of Poe's earliest and most powerful demonstrations of this capacity decried the practice of advertising novels in putative reviews composed by the author and his associates.[12] The target of Poe's criticism was Harper and Brothers' anonymously published *Norman Leslie*:

Well! – here we have it! This is *the* book – *the* book *par excellence* – the book bepuffed, beplastered, and be-Mirrored: the book "attributed to" Mr. Blank, and "said to be from the pen" of Mr. Asterisk: the book which has been "about to appear" – "in press" – "in progress" – "in preparation" – and "forthcoming": the book "graphic" in anticipation – "talented" *a priori* – and God knows what *in prospectu*.[13]

Poe quickly identified Theodore S. Fay as the author, surmising that Fay had contributed both to the breathless publicity campaign of *Norman Leslie* and to the reviewing of his book in the *New York Mirror*, of which he was co-editor. Fay and his colleagues had put the techniques of anonymous publishing and reviewing to work toward a literary form of vertical integration.[14] The *Norman Leslie* review, published in the December 1835 *Messenger*, just as Poe was assuming official responsibilities, gained him editorial attention on a regional and national scale.

It must be noted that during the late 1830s, bold interrogation of one's subject was considered an essential part of the reviewer's task.[15] In fact, the tony *North American Review* performed evaluations of poets and novelists not unlike Poe's. However, its considerable social, cultural, and symbolic capital allowed it to impart a polite tone to its criticism without necessarily pulling any punches. Anonymously reviewing Frances Sargent Osgood's *Wreath of Wild Flowers* for the journal in 1840, Cornelius C. Felton found it too hastily assembled. After quoting four lines, Felton declares:

We do not insist that a critic is neither a pirate, nor a monster, nor a blighting frost, but a very harmless and Christian-like sort of person. It is the confusion of figures only, to which we object. These poems abound, also, too much in such splendid and dazzling things as jewels, pearls, golden locks, and flashing eyes. These do well in their places, but ought to be sparingly used.[16]

Felton's close attention to Osgood's mixture of metaphors as well as his reuse of them makes his review closely resemble Poe's own reviews. Poe's evaluation of Osgood for "The Literati of New York City" found her poetry the epitome of "*Grace*...a term applied, in despair, to that class of the impressions of beauty which admit neither of analysis nor of comprehension."[17] While Poe's sketch of Osgood has been often read as a positive endorsement, his negative definition of poetic grace may suggest otherwise.

When Poe began editing at the age of twenty-six for the *Southern Literary Messenger*, it was by no means clear what the purview of a reviewer should be. His first sixteen columns for the *Messenger*, spanning April 1835 to January 1836, treated prominent American and English work including Sedgwick's *The Linwoods*, the third volume of Washington Irving's *Crayon Miscellany*, John P. Kennedy's novel *Horse-Shoe Robinson*, William Gilmore Simms's *The Partisan*, and William Godwin's *Lives of the Necromancers*. Poe conveyed his keen assessment of the literary market in an April 30, 1835 letter to White informing him that in writing "Berenice," he had established a position at the very brink of obscenity. Poe also informed White that he found inspiration in authors such as Dickens and Thomas De Quincey. Examining the reception of these authors' work, Poe discovered that readers delighted in London's infestation of "Gin Shops" – passionately detailed in Dickens' *Sketches by Boz* (1836) – and narratives combining confession and sensation, such as De Quincey's *Confessions of an Opium Eater* (1821) and the true crime genre of Newgate novels.[18]

As poet-critic and advocate of art for art's sake, Poe maintained three basic principles: a work should aim for a single effect; the artist's technique should be completely devoted to this effect; and pleasure should be the primary goal of poetry and fiction.[19] Yet he frequently struggled to reconcile such an aesthetic with the need to please a broad public. Poe's point that to be appreciated, a writer must be entertaining enough to make himself read has recently been affirmed in the adjacent realm of Romantic poetry. While William Wordsworth has often received top billing in literary textbooks covering the period, close attention to publishing data acknowledging black market editions shows that the ballads of Lord Byron, often banned as indecent, outsold Wordsworth's collections by as much as fifty to one.[20] Though he does not provide hard numbers, Poe's reviews make the analogous point that Hawthorne is read by truly literary people; achieving only this goal, however, is not enough to earn a living.

Due largely to his willingness to take the subjects of his reviews to task for shortcomings of any and all kinds, Poe rarely displayed lasting allegiance to editors or publishers. Thus he managed, at one time or another, to offend nearly every literary coterie. Poe's two-year period of relatively placid criticism during the early 1840s was followed by "The Literati of New York City," published in *Godey's Lady's Book* from June to October 1846. The subtitle of this series – "Some Honest Opinions at Random Respecting Their Authorial Merits, with Occasional Words of Personality" – hints at the possibilities afforded Poe by the project.

A hypothesis that Poe deliberately reformed his critical headhunting of 1835–7 for his professional self-interest suggests two possible motives for such an action. The first, more reasonable claim is that Poe strove to stay politically neutral during the Depression of 1837–43. For example, he turned his focus from poetry to fiction during the 1830s, while adjusting his tales to offer a range of perspectives on the sobering state of literary affairs.[21] The second claim, that Poe kowtowed to the direction of the Young American literary clique from 1843–5, seems overblown due to Poe's thoroughly mixed treatment of the powerful men whose extensive horizontal and vertical literary connections allowed them to promote Poe's writing late in his career.

Poe waxed hot and cold when tabulating the merits of his chief supporters, Evert Duyckinck and James Russell Lowell. Poe's March 1844 review of Lowell's *Poems* found them exquisitely crafted yet preachy. Poe's "Editorial

Miscellanies" for the *Broadway Journal* (October 11, 1845) protested that John Wilson had recently insulted Lowell in the pages of *Blackwood's*. In reprinting Wilson's labels of "magpie," "ape," and "Yankee cockney," however, Poe likely did Lowell more harm than good. In a substantial review for the March 1849 *Messenger*, Poe characterized Lowell's *Fable for Critics* as stylistically execrable. One suspects, however, that Lowell's sending up Poe's criticism ("Three-fifths of him genius, and two-fifths sheer fudge") for its obsession with detail ("talks like a book of iambs and pentameters") had some influence on Poe's response.[22] Duyckinck won Poe's gift of faint praise, conveyed in a "Literati" sketch for July 1846. Poe was unhappy, however, with Duyckinck's selections for the Wiley and Putnam Library of American Books publication of *The Raven and Other Poems* (1845). Poe's preface suggests that the contents of this volume (and for that matter *Tales*, published earlier that year), were torn from Poe without any editorial input from their author.

The attention Poe gave to his review articles is suggested by his frequent comments on their style, presentation (binding, paper, and margins), and likely effect on their readers. He drove himself to describe the positive traits developed by novelists such as imagination, typically seen in the development of character, and skill, which he deemed necessary to constructing an effective plot. Poe's 1842 review of Dickens's *Barnaby Rudge* for *Graham's*, following his remarks on the same novel for the *Saturday Evening Post* (May 1, 1841), finds the novel a model of writing for both popular and critical tastes. Poe's treatment of his close contemporary Nathaniel Hawthorne displays admiration for Hawthorne's development of American settings. Indeed, Poe's reviews of Hawthorne's collections, for *Graham's* in April and May 1842 and for *Godey's* in November 1847, suggest that he saw an imperfect, Salem-addled version of himself in Hawthorne. Always ready to correct putative authorial presumption, Poe declared that many of Hawthorne's tales might be better termed essays. In the May 1842 article, however, Poe insisted that Hawthorne was the best teller of tales the United States had yet produced. Because the short story could command readers' undivided attention, Poe explained, it was the ideal form in which to achieve a literary effect. But for Hawthorne's insistence on intriguing critical tastes with moral allegory, he might have succeeded with the broader public.[23] Poe reemphasized this point in his self-review of *Tales* in the October 1845 *Aristidean*, and again in examining his hit poem "The Raven" in "The Philosophy of Composition" (1846).

Poe's 1840s rivals for most respected critic included Emerson and his Young American advocate Lowell. To twenty-first-century eyes, however, it was Margaret Fuller who offered a helpful social justice-minded counterweight to Poe's literary perspective. In her front-page review of Poe's *The Raven and Other Poems* for the *Daily Tribune* (November 26, 1845), Fuller admired Poe's attempt to maintain absolute critical objectivity but doubted the practicality of such a campaign. Fuller insisted that the practical value of criticism extended far beyond its possibilities for entertainment, as it had in the spectacular British quarrels over the Cockney School and its detractors. Her "Short Fable for Critics" held that the most valuable reviewers persist beyond mere egotism or identification with the artist to reach the status of "comprehensive critic": "The critic is beneath the maker, but is his needed friend... Next to invention is the power of interpreting invention; next to beauty the power of appreciating beauty."[24] Poe would have been pained by any implication that he had demoted himself by turning reviewer. Indeed, he held to the idea of a one-man poet-critic for two decades. In "The Philosophy of Composition," as in "Letter to B," Poe granted the truly successful poet the critical fortitude necessary to step back and competently evaluate his own work.[25]

Like Fuller, many of the professional respondents to the *Southern Literary Messenger*'s early criticism fretted that Poe was "using up" American authors who deserved more steady support. In response, Poe assembled an account of his reviewing evenhandedness, beginning with his assuming editorship of the journal during the final weeks of 1836. In the December 1835 *Messenger*, Lucian Minor had reported that some of the most popular reviews among general and critical audiences were the work of Poe, the only staffer he named. The assertion of Poe's letter to Richmond *Compiler* editors that seventy-nine of ninety-four reviews were "highly laudatory" may be accurate. However, a disparity in the apparent number of positive reviews and the figure reported by Poe may be due to the sharing of review duties with colleagues such as Minor. Nigel Barnes's tabulation of forty-seven reviews (excluding two brief book notices but including six reviews of periodicals) for Poe yields just over two-thirds laudatory, fifteen percent positive, just over ten percent negative, and six percent highly so.[26] Removing from Barnes's list the notices of other periodicals in operation, none of which Poe mentions in his letter to the *Compiler*, would greatly reduce the rate of highly positive reviews. Such an amended tabulation may approach an accurate report on Poe's own practice over the period in question.

Poe's canonization during 1845–6, the years in which his *The Raven and Other Poems* and *Tales* were published, has been credited to his ten years of determined work as a reviewer.[27] When Poe asked James Russell

Lowell, who with Margaret Fuller, ranked among the leading national critics, to assess his work for *Graham's Magazine*, Lowell complied. His essay was published in late January 1845, after which it was extensively reprinted in mid-Atlantic periodicals. This review, which met with warm assent from writers and editors including Fuller, Charles Briggs, Evert Duyckinck, and Nathaniel Parker Willis, provided Poe access to the New York scene. Here he wrote for and then edited the *Broadway Journal* while securing the attention-getting "Literati of New York City" series for *Godey's Lady's Book*. To this point, Poe's criticism had, like Fuller's, questioned the merits of writing motivated by a desire to raise the world standing of American letters. It is therefore unlikely that Poe ever fully embraced Young America's program of achieving literary independence from England.[28]

Poe's editorial treatment of women writers seems not unusual for his time. Writing anonymously for the *North American Review* in 1851, Anne W. Abbot cited the "custom to praise lady authors" with something akin to "the praise bestowed by a smiling school-committee man upon a smart school-girl's theme, after a whispered argument, that with some pruning and a little more thought, it would be really a surprising achievement *for a girl*."[29] Poe's reviews of female poetry and fiction often suggest that their authors would do better to leave the field to men. Margaret Fuller is the one woman whom Poe may have acknowledged as his intellectual equal. In his assessment of Fuller for "The Literati of New York City," Poe praised Fuller's sober *New York Tribune* appraisal of Longfellow's verse, but was less sanguine about the merits of her *Woman in the Nineteenth Century*, declaring, "She judges woman by the heart and intellect of Miss Fuller, but there are not more than one or two dozen Miss Fullers on the whole face of the earth."[30]

It is hardly surprising that as an editor paid for winnowing a vast field of submissions into literary notices for the *Messenger, Burton's Gentleman's Magazine, Graham's*, and the *Broadway Journal*, Poe strove to grasp the essence of his subjects as efficiently as possible. Poe compared such a feat to gazing at a star out of the corner of one's eye, a behavior that may produce more startling results than directly regarding the object. In critical practice, Poe's technique has been referred to as surface reading. The varieties of surface reading used by others have been used largely to slight Poe's reviewing. It is thus fortunate that we may recover Poe's critical insights using recent studies in periodical, reading, and publishing history. In the age of the Internet, Poe's dictum that one should be able to take in a successful work in one go is truer than ever.

NOTES

1. James Kirke Paulding, *A Sketch of Old England*, 2 vols. (New York: Charles Wiley, 1822), vol. ii, 88.
2. Lara Langer Cohen, "Democratic Representations: Puffery and the Antebellum Print Explosion," *American Literature* 79 (2007), 660.
3. [Henry Wadsworth Longfellow], "Hawthorne's *Twice-Told Tales*," *North American Review* 45 (1837), 60.
4. David Dowling, *The Business of Literary Circles in Nineteenth-Century America* (New York: Palgrave Macmillan, 2011), 96, 117.
5. [Henry Wadsworth Longfellow], "Hawthorne's *Twice-Told Tales*," *North American Review* 54 (1842), 499.
6. Edgar Allan Poe, *Essays and Reviews*, ed. G. R. Thompson (New York: Library of America, 1984), 1032.
7. Elizabeth Duquette, "Accounting for Value in 'The Business Man,'" *Studies in American Fiction* 35 (2007), 14.
8. Leon Jackson, *The Business of Letters: Authorial Economies in Antebellum America* (Stanford: Stanford University Press, 2008), 121–6.
9. Dowling, *Business of Literary Circles*, 59, 17.
10. Cohen, "Democratic Representations," 668.
11. Leon Jackson, "'Behold Our Literary Mohawk, Poe': Literary Nationalism and the 'Indianation' of Antebellum American Culture," *ESQ* (2002), 97–133.
12. See Nicholas Mason, "The Quack Has Become God," *Nineteenth-Century Literature* 60 (2005), 1–8, for a narrative of English advertisers deploying this technique as a way of reaching increasingly distracted readers.
13. Poe, *Essays*, 540.
14. Cohen, "Democratic Representations," 258.
15. Charles H. Brown, "Young Editor Whitman: An Individualist in Journalism," *Journalism Quarterly* 27 (1950), 141–8.
16. [Cornelius C. Felton], "Osgood's *Poems*," *North American Review* 50 (1840), 270.
17. Poe, *Essays*, 1102.
18. Poe to Thomas W. White, April 30, 1835, *The Collected Letters of Edgar Allan Poe*, ed. John Ward Ostrom, Burton R. Pollin, and Jeffrey A. Savoye, 2 vols. (New York: Gordian, 2008), vol. i, 84–5.
19. See R. E. Foust, "Aesthetician of Simultaneity: E. A. Poe and Modern Literary Theory," *South Atlantic Review* 46 (1981), 19.
20. William St. Clair, *The Reading Nation in the Romantic Period* (New York: Cambridge University Press, 2004), 192.
21. Terence Whalen, *Edgar Allan Poe and the Masses: The Political Economy of Literature in Antebellum America* (Princeton: Princeton University Press, 1999), 27.
22. Poe, *Essays*, 1077, 821, 820.
23. Ibid., 568, 579.
24. Margaret Fuller, "A Short Essay on Critics," *The Dial* 1 (1840), 8.

25. Poe, *Essays*, 6, 14.

26. Nigel Barnes, *A Dream within a Dream: The Life of Edgar Allan Poe* (London: Peter Owen, 2009), 304.

27. See Jackson, *Business of Letters*, 20, for in-depth discussion of the shift, by the 1840s, of literary exchange to blatantly financial considerations rather than the various forms of social exchange that had earlier prevailed.

28. See Meredith McGill, *American Literature and the Culture of Reprinting, 1834–1853* (Philadelphia: University of Pennsylvania Press, 2003), 188–9.

29. [Anne W. Abbot], "Female Authors," *North American Review* 72 (1851), 163.

30. Poe, *Essays*, 1173.

CHAPTER 21

The Politics of Publishing

Amy Branam

Pinpointing Poe's political affiliation has proven elusive. Scholars have pegged him as antidemocratic, anti-Jacksonian, a proslavery apologist, a Whig, and even apolitical. To complicate matters, only two of his tales, "The Gold-Bug" and "A Tale of the Ragged Mountains," are set in the South, and others seem to be set nowhere at all.[1] For proof of his Whig allegiance, the Law of Gradation has been posited as "one of Poe's most cherished principles."[2] The Whig platform favored the conservatism and education of the upper classes and bristled at the idea of giving too much freedom, and, by extension, power to an uneducated mob. Poe's negative view of the mob is detailed in many of his tales, including "The Man of the Crowd." In some stories, Poe lampoons Andrew Jackson and his administration, thus underscoring his alignment with the Whigs. But one issue on which the Whig party eventually failed Poe was the injustice that the magazinist faced in the publishing industry.

Probusiness laws were codified through American law early in the nation's history as American lawyers took hold of and reshaped English common law to benefit America's commercial interests. Whereas English law sought to thwart an individual's ability to amass too much wealth, American democracy wanted to stimulate the opposite through its capitalist economy.[3] Yet this system, like the system in England, favored those who already possessed wealth: they could afford the necessary starting costs to become successful entrepreneurs. For example, George Graham, a Whig, purchased two leading Whig newspapers by 1847 and combined them into the leading Philadelphia Whig periodical, the *North American and United States Gazette*.[4] Before aggressively acquiring many Philadelphia periodicals of his own, Graham worked briefly for the *Post* under Samuel Atkinson. He bought Atkinson's *Casket* in May 1839, which he combined with *Burton's* when he purchased that magazine in November. "The Man of the Crowd" benefited from the consolidation because Graham ran nearly identical issues for *Casket* and *Burton's* in

December 1840. In the same year, Graham moved from an employee to one of the proprietors of the *Post*.[5]

Though the Whig party did not coalesce into a major party until the Jacksonian era, the party's rise was characterized by support for, among other things, unfettered entrepreneurship as well as free and universal education. The future Whig party supporters came from a variety of movements and nascent parties that arose in reaction to the two-party system, including the soon to be supplanted Federalists, the Liberal Democrats, the Democrat Republicans, the National Republicans, and the Anti-Masonic party. Reinforcing Poe's Whig sympathies, a later tale, "The Cask of Amontillado," has been interpreted as an Anti-Masonic story.[6]

Poe's ability to navigate the publishing game may be partly attributed to his exposure to business while living in the Allan household. The experience taught him the language of commerce and helped him understand the economic value of information and the idea that literature was a commodity produced for sale in the capitalist marketplace.[7] In the sense of politicking as networking, many scholars have analyzed Poe's rise in the magazine world via contests, patronage, referrals by established magazine editors and contributors, securing editing positions, reprinting his works, and puffery. Less attention has been focused on the politics of the men who ran the magazines. Therefore, some of the magazines and key figures in Poe's literary life deserve consideration to understand just how challenging it was to publish in the antebellum print industry. In early nineteenth-century America, politicians increasingly exploited cheap print to impose their two-party perspective on public affairs by publicly subsidizing their private subsidies of partisan newspapers.[8] This entanglement of politics and print extended to Poe's magazine world.

Poe's first magazine publications are fraught with much complexity in that they appeared under his brother's initials, "W. H. P." William Henry Leonard Poe, who went by Henry Poe, lived in Baltimore with the descendants of David Poe, Sr., a Baltimore revolutionary hero, prominent member of the Whig Club, and local politician.[9] In 1827, after serving in the military and traveling the world, Henry Poe returned to Baltimore and became enmeshed in its literary scene. Around this same time, the Baltimore *Saturday Herald* was renamed the *North American* by its former publisher, Samuel Sands, who became its proprietor. Sands's earlier experience included working for the Whigs. In 1829, he bought a share of the *Marylander*, which became a Whig periodical, the *Commercial Chronicle and Daily Marylander*.[10]

A bit of a mystery exists as to how Poe's "The Happiest Day" found its way to Baltimore while Poe was in Boston. A month after "The Happiest Day" appeared with Henry's initials affixed to it, Poe's "Dreams" ran with the same byline. However, the inclusion of both poems in *Tamerlane* has led scholars to deem them Edgar Poe's work, though no manuscript version survives for "The Happiest Day" to make that case as concretely as the one for "Dreams."[11] Poe may have sent a copy of his recently published *Tamerlane and Other Poems* to his brother. Having literary connections and inclinations himself, Henry Poe could have submitted the poems under his own name. The political bent of the *North American* had less to do with party politics expressed in literary pieces than the party affiliations of the men connected through the magazines.

As entrepreneurs, magazine publishers and editors realized they could create sensation and increase sales and subscriptions by holding writing contests. Poe's career as a writer of tales began with these contests, which helped him form a literary network. The *Saturday Courier* and the *Saturday Visiter* proved instrumental. "Duc de L'Omelette," "Metzengerstein," "The Bargain Lost," "A Decided Loss," and "Tale of Jerusalem" all ran in Philadelphia's *Courier* during 1832. Poe's entries to the magazine contest were published, although he lost to a more famous writer. He did not receive a byline for each story; rather, each one began with the phrase "Written for the Saturday Courier." Of the six judges, Charles Alexander had numerous ties to future Poe associates. This prominent Philadelphia publisher was already acquainted with Samuel Atkinson, who would eventually run *Casket*. Together, they published the Philadelphia-based *Saturday Evening Post*. Alexander also conducted business with William Evans Burton and George R. Graham, with whom Poe eventually took an assistant editor and editor position, respectively.[12]

The second contest Poe entered was for the *Visiter*. His brother knew the current editor, John Hill Hewitt, who, in 1830, held an editorial position at the *Minerva*, a periodical that published some of Henry's poetry.[13] Poe's "Manuscript Found in a Bottle" won for best short story. In a notorious debacle, Poe lost the poetry contest to Hewitt, who used a nom de plume to enter a poem in his own contest.[14] Yet Poe benefited with the publication of some of his poems, including "Coliseum" and "Serenade," during 1833. The poems were printed with his name attached. Of the three judges for this contest, John Pendleton Kennedy remained in touch with Poe, becoming a good friend as well as a referral for Poe when Thomas W. White was in search of assistance with the *Southern Literary Messenger*. Like Sands, Kennedy was also a prominent Baltimore Whig. In

1841, running on the Whig ticket, Kennedy won a race for the House of Representatives.[15]

When Poe took the position with White, he wrote a couple of pieces for this so-called apolitical magazine that betrayed Whig sympathies.[16] "King Pest," published in September 1835, and "Epimanes" (later titled "Four Beasts in One"), published in March 1836, attacked Andrew Jackson, his cabinet, and the unenlightened democratic mob. The caricatures in "King Pest" closely resemble the political cartoons depicting Andrew Jackson.[17] A year earlier, Lucian Minor submitted to the *Messenger* "An Address on Education," in which he quotes Thomas Jefferson's definition of a Whig as follows: "The parties of Whig and Tory are those of nature. They exist in all countries, whether called by these names, or by those of Aristocrats and Democrats.... The sickly, weakly, timid man, fears the people, and is a tory by nature. The healthy, strong, and bold, cherishes them, and is a whig by nature."[18] Minor asserts that he is "a true Whig." His overriding point in this address fit the current Whig platform, which was to educate the public to make it informed enough to govern itself. Although White asked Poe to edit Minor's text to eliminate most of the potentially controversial, because overt, political content, this outspoken Whig was White's initial choice for editor over Poe.[19]

In 1837, Horace Greeley, a fervent Whig supporter, ran a notice in *The New-Yorker* that began: "Among all the magazines of our own country, after those of our own city, we have felt the most lively concern for the prosperity of the *Southern Literary Messenger*, as the first well-sustained attempt to establish a monthly periodical of distinguished character in the South."[20] On one hand, this endorsement may indicate a philanthropic impulse to see this Southern magazine remain afloat; however, since the *Messenger* relied upon Northern and Eastern subscribers, the promotion of a competing magazine for purely unselfish gain seems unlikely. Also, in its inaugural issue, in addition to writers such as Washington Irving and John P. Kennedy, John Quincy Adams – a former Whig president who lost to Jackson when running for his second term – is listed as one of the "eminent literary men" who endorsed the creation of the *Messenger*.[21]

The same year, Poe published "Von Jung, the Mystific" in the *American Monthly Magazine* for June 1837. The magazine's first editor, Henry William Herbert (also known as Frank Forester), resigned in 1835 when he quarreled with Charles Fenno Hoffman over what he perceived as too much political intrusion in its pages. Park Benjamin joined Hoffman, and, by 1837, the *American Monthly* became a Whig periodical. Once it took this partisan turn, Greeley bought it in 1838, and Park Benjamin continued to serve as an editor.[22]

Two more pro-Whig tales appeared in 1839: "The Devil in the Belfry" and "The Man that Was Used Up." In May, the former ran in Philadelphia's *Saturday Chronicle*. Benjamin Mathias, a founder of the *Chronicle*, became an elected Whig politician from 1848 to 1852, and later became speaker of the Pennsylvania legislature.[23] "The Devil in the Belfry" mocks Jackson's successor, Martin Van Buren, and his "Regency." *Burton's* published "The Man That Was Used Up" in August. In this tale, Poe bypassed the president and ridiculed Vice President Richard M. Johnson.[24]

Excepting the caricatures of Jacksonian figures, Poe's remaining works are more difficult to label politically; instead, he seems to rely more on his burgeoning literary reputation and old friends to secure publications. During 1838 and 1839, Nathan C. Brooks and Joseph E. Snodgrass, two of Poe's Baltimore friends, ran some of his poems and stories in their *American Museum*.[25] These works included "Ligeia," "The Psyche Zenobia," and "The Haunted Palace." As a result of an inquiry letter to William E. Burton, Poe obtained a position with *Burton's Gentleman's Magazine*. During his stint as a co-editor from July 1839 to June 1840, he published tales, poems, and criticism, including "The Fall of the House of Usher," "The Business Man," and "To the River – ." In November 1839, George R. Graham bought the magazine. He subsequently hired Poe as an assistant editor. For seven months, Poe again worked for a Whig supporter.

Faced with the reality of working hard for little financial gain, Poe's frustration with the Whig party became apparent by 1842. In the preceding year, he had attempted to secure a government position in John Tyler's administration. With high hopes of receiving a post, he wrote to Frederick Thomas in June 1841, professing his allegiance to the Whig party: "My political principles have always been as nearly as may be, with the existing administration, and I battled with right good will for Harrison, when opportunity offered."[26] Despite his optimism, Poe was humiliated by Thomas S. Smith, "the worst type of Whig," who refused to appoint him. Poe snipes in another letter to Thomas that "Mr. Smith has excited the thorough disgust of every Tyler man here. He is a Whig of the worst stamp and will appoint none but Whigs if he can possibly avoid it. People here laugh at the idea of his being a Tyler man. He is notoriously not such."[27] This event, his inability to care for his now ailing Virginia, and his dissatisfaction over the pay at *Graham's* may have all contributed to his decision to resign from *Graham's* in 1842.

Without the financial means of George Graham, prospective entrepreneurs in the magazine business often failed, as in the case of James Russell Lowell. He and Robert Carter founded *The Pioneer* in 1843. Aiming to publish "entirely original content and chiefly American," Lowell and Carter included Poe's "Tell-Tale Heart" among the items in *The Pioneer*'s first issue.[28] The magazine failed quickly, and Lowell could not afford to pay the contributors. What he lacked in economic prosperity he more than made up for with the currency of his literary reputation. Lowell made restitution to Poe by publishing a biographical sketch in February 1845 in *Graham's*, which was reprinted in the New York-based *Mirror*. This gesture placed Poe directly in the sights of the Young America leadership. Exactly why Poe aligned himself with this group is unclear. To some extent, Poe is co-opted for Young America's ends. One modern commentator observes, "Within this period, Poe repeatedly compromised his critical principles to curry favor with the Duyckinck circle, sacrificing his independent critical voice to promote the literary and political goals for the Young Americans."[29] Whether he firmly believed in the Young America platform or not, he created important literary associations, including those with Evert Duyckinck, John O'Sullivan, Nathaniel Parker Willis, and Charles Briggs. Duyckinck commissioned *The Raven and Other Poems* and *Tales* for his Library of American Books series, which he edited for Wiley and Putnam, a prominent New York publishing firm. Duyckinck also published "Ulalume" in his anti-Transcendentalist *Literary World*.[30] John O'Sullivan published "The Power of Words" in his *Democratic Review*. N. P. Willis, who had already met Poe when he took a job at the *Mirror* in 1843, continued to work with Poe, publishing three of his poems in his *Home Journal*. Lowell also introduced Poe to Charles Briggs, who worked with Poe on the *Broadway Journal*. This connection with Briggs proved one of his most strategic because it allowed Poe to revise and reprint most of his works.

Despite these connections and publications, Poe's financial struggle in the magazine industry continued. "The Literary Life of Thingum Bob, Esq." (December 1844) and "Some Secrets of the Magazine Prison-House" (February 1845) were published in the *Messenger* and the *Broadway Journal* respectively. Both served as exposés. "Some Secrets of the Magazine Prison-House," for example, illuminates the inequalities built into the publishing industry. Poe decries that "publishers, we say, who, under certain conditions of good conduct, occasional puffs, and decent subserviency at all times, make it a point of conscience to encourage the poor devil author with a dollar or two, more or less as he behaves himself properly and abstains from the indecent habit of turning up his nose."[31] Many of Poe's

contemporaries – authors, editors, and publishers – celebrated the proliferation of print as evidence of the flowering of American democracy.[32]
"Some Secrets of the Magazine Prison- House," alternatively, threatens to
expose the democracy of the printed word as an illusion: everyone did
not have an equal chance to achieve fame in the American literary marketplace. Though he may have loathed the system of puffery and critical
back scratching, Poe nonetheless participated in it. In 1844 he wrote a laudatory biographical sketch of Robert T. Conrad for *Graham's*.[33] The previous year Conrad had been on the panel of contest judges for the *Dollar
Newspaper* that awarded "The Gold-Bug" first place.[34] Poe's positive depiction of Conrad may reflect his gratitude. In addition, Poe puffed his own
"The Literary Life of Thingum Bob, Esq." by anonymously publishing it
in the *Southern Literary Messenger* and then favorably reviewing it in the
Broadway Journal.[35] In an especially deft case of self-puffery, a Poe review
of Hawthorne covertly suggested that Poe was the better tale writer.[36]

Though Poe seemed to have joined the Democratic Party, he retained an
entrepreneurial impulse. In an attempt to take total control of his literary
productions and critical voice, he took over the *Broadway Journal*. Unable
to purchase it on his own, he turned to two prominent Whigs in the New
York publishing arena: Horace Greeley and Rufus W. Griswold. Both
men floated him loans, but the magazine folded in early 1846. Poe did
not mind its failure too much: he kept the magazine afloat long enough
to suit his purpose, that is, to reprint in its pages enough of its own stories
that he could use bound volumes of the magazine as a showcase to attract
investors to the ideal magazine he was planning.[37]

In his remaining days, Poe published mostly in women's periodicals
and cheap magazines. His literary network with female writers, particularly in Philadelphia and New York, opened up even more publishing
opportunities for him. His content shifted to meet the demands of the
residual gothic tastes in *Godey's* and *Graham's*. Turning away from politics,
considered improper material for ladies to read, Poe had more freedom to
cultivate encomiums to women, his death poems, and the horror tales for
which he would become famous in later ages.

In a comment reminiscent of a Whig who distrusted the indiscriminate
proliferation of print material for the masses that faded into ephemera,
Poe equated publishing in the *Flag of Our Union* with sending his works
to a dead-end periodical. In his prospectus for the *Stylus*, Poe referred to
"the cheap literature of the day" with disdain.[38] Before he died, Poe had
also reached out to an old Philadelphia friend, John Sartain, whose *Union
Magazine* printed some of the last items during Poe's life and printed other

works, such as "The Bells," posthumously. Sartain had purchased the magazine with George Graham.[39]

To assert that Poe was not a Whig nationalist is accurate, but his career was clearly indebted to his Whig family, friends, and business associates.[40] Though he did not secure the Tyler post, over the years many Whigs repaid him for his avowed support. More important, Poe's political ambiguity has helped to ensure that his works have been read and studied for nearly 200 years.

NOTES

1. Terence Whalen, *Edgar Allan Poe and the Masses: The Political Economy of Literature in Antebellum America* (Princeton: Princeton University Press, 1999), 138.

2. Katrina E. Bachinger, "Peacock's Melincourt and the Politics of Poe's 'The Sphinx,'" *Nineteenth-Century Literature* 42 (1987), 217.

3. Charles Sellers, *The Market Revolution: Jacksonian America, 1815–1846* (New York: Oxford University Press, 1991), 48, 44.

4. J. Albert Robbins, "George R. Graham, Philadelphia Publisher," *Pennsylvania Magazine of History and Biography* 75 (1951), 287.

5. Frank Luther Mott, *A History of American Magazines* 5 vols. (Cambridge, MA: Belknap Press, 1938–68), vol. i, 546, 545; Robbins, "George R. Graham," 282.

6. Robert Con Davis-Undiano, "Poe and the American Affiliation with Freemasonry," *Symploke* 7 (1999), 119–38.

7. Terence Whalen, "Poe and the American Publishing Industry," in *A Historical Guide to Edgar Allan Poe*, ed. J. Gerald Kennedy (New York: Oxford University Press, 2001), 66.

8. Sellers, *Market Revolution*, 370.

9. John Thomas Scharf, *The Chronicles of Baltimore: Being a Complete History of "Baltimore Town" and Baltimore City from the Earliest Period to the Present Time* (Baltimore: Turnbull Brothers, 1874), 159, 187.

10. Scharf, *Chronicles of Baltimore*, 90–1; John Thomas Scharf, *History of Baltimore City and County* (Philadelphia: Louis H. Everts, 1881), 615.

11. Edgar Allan Poe, *The Collected Works of Edgar Allan Poe*, ed. Thomas Ollive Mabbott, 3 vols. (Cambridge, MA: Belknap Press, 1969–78), vol. i, 68.

12. Thomas Scharf and Thompson Westcott, *History of Philadelphia, 1609–1884*, 3 vols. (Philadelphia: L. H. Everts, 1884), vol. iii, 1988.

13. Scharf, *History of Baltimore City and County*, 646.

14. Kevin J. Hayes, *Edgar Allan Poe* (London: Reaktion, 2009), 15–17.

15. Dwight R. Thomas, "Poe in Philadelphia, 1838–1844: A Documentary Record," PhD diss., University of Pennsylvania, 1978, 241.

16. Whalen, *Edgar Allan Poe and the Masses*, 123.

17. William Whipple, "Poe's Political Satire," *University of Texas Studies in English* 35 (1956), 86.

18. Lucian Minor, "An Address on Education," *Southern Literary Messenger* 2 (1835), 17.
19. Whalen, *Edgar Allan Poe and the Masses*, 125.
20. "Southern Literary Messenger," *New-Yorker*, September 9, 1837, 397; Horace Greeley, *The Autobiography of Horace Greeley* (New York: E. B. Treat, 1872), 106–13, 215.
21. "Publisher"s Notice," *Southern Literary Messenger* 1 (1834), 1.
22. Mott, *History of American Magazines*, vol. i, 619, 345.
23. Scharf and Westcott, *History of Philadelphia*, vol. iii, 1988.
24. Whipple, "Poe"s Political Satire," 89, 91.
25. Hayes, *Edgar Allan Poe*, 72–3.
26. Dwight Thomas and David K. Jackson, *The Poe Log: A Documentary Life of Edgar Allan Poe, 1809–1849* (Boston: G. K. Hall, 1987), 332.
27. Arthur Hobson Quinn, *Edgar Allan Poe: A Critical Biography* (New York: Appleton-Century, 1941), 362.
28. Mott, *History of American Magazines*, vol. i, 735–6.
29. Meredith L. McGill, *American Literature and the Culture of Reprinting, 1834–1853* (Philadelphia: University of Pennsylvania Press, 2003), 188–9.
30. McGill, *American Literature*, 190; Mott, *History of American Magazines*, vol. i, 767.
31. Edgar Allan Poe, *Essays and Reviews*, ed. G. R. Thompson (New York: Library of America, 1984), 1036–7.
32. Lara Langer Cohen, "Democratic Representations: Puffery and the Antebellum Print Explosion," *American Literature* 79 (2007), 643.
33. Quinn, *Edgar Allan Poe*, 413–14.
34. Scharf and Westcott, *History of Philadelphia*, vol. iii, 2014.
35. Timothy Scherman, "The Authority Effect: Poe and the Politics of Reputation in the Pre-Industry of American Publishing," *Arizona Quarterly* 49 (1993), 14.
36. G. R. Thompson, "Literary Politics and the 'Legitimate Sphere': Poe, Hawthorne, and the 'Tale Proper,'" *Nineteenth-Century Literature* 49 (1994), 192–3.
37. Hayes, *Edgar Allan Poe*, 146.
38. Edgar Allan Poe, "Prospectus for the Stylus," *Saturday Museum*, March 4, 1843, 3.
39. John Sartain, *The Reminiscences of a Very Old Man* (New York: Appleton, 1899), 218.
40. David Long, "Poe's Political Identity: A Mummy Unswathed," *Poe Studies* 23 (1990), 8.

PART FOUR

Literary Contexts

CHAPTER 22

Ancient Classics

Gregory Hays

The Small Special Collections Library at the University of Virginia contains a text of the Latin satirist Persius with a facing English translation by William Drummond, Esq., M.P.[1] The translation, in rhymed couplets, is both free and verbose; as a contribution to Latin scholarship it is of little significance. The volume is pocket-sized and its binding unremarkable. The importance of this copy stems rather from an early owner's inscription on the title page: "Edgar A. Poe / 1826 Virginia College." Only a handful of Poe's books can now be identified, and one might hope that this one would provide insight into the young Poe's mental world.[2] In fact, the haul is disappointing. Poe added a few lines of Latin (his own?) to the flyleaf. At *Satires* 6.13 he annotated the phrase "*infelix pecori*" with a reference to a similar phrase in Virgil (*Eclogue* 3.3 "infelix...pecus"). But the later compiler of "Marginalia" has left no other traces.[3] In some ways, the volume raises more questions than it answers. Persius was not a standard school author, and there is no evidence that he was assigned at the university when Poe was there. In his later works, Poe mentioned scores of classical authors – but never Persius.[4] Could the book have been a gift? What, if anything, connects the seventeen-year-old reader of the Neronian satirist with the author of "Metzengerstein" and "The Tell-Tale Heart"?

A CLASSICAL EDUCATION

Poe studied Latin from the ages of nine to seventeen.[5] From 1818 to 1820, during the Allan family's stay in London, he boarded at the establishment of the Rev. John Bransby in Stoke Newington. It is here that he would have begun his study of the language. There is some evidence that Poe once owned a Latin version of Aesop's fables; if so, it may have been acquired at this period.[6] According to a later student, by the time he left Bransby's Poe would have been able to "construe any easy Latin author."[7] But this is probably an exaggeration. Following the Allans' return to

Richmond in 1820, Poe attended a preparatory school run by Joseph H. Clarke, succeeded in 1823 by William Burke. Clarke told a biographer in 1876 that Poe when first admitted "had studied the grammar as far as the regular verbs," and could decline nouns and adjectives.[8] That suggests a fairly elementary knowledge. Clarke continues: "Edgar Poe was five years in my school. During that time he read Ovid, Caesar, Virgil, Cicero, and Horace in Latin, and Xenophon and Homer in Greek. He showed a much stronger taste for classic poetry than he did for classic prose...although not conspicuously studious, he always acquitted himself well in his classes." Clarke's memories of a student taught fifty-five years previously may not be entirely reliable. He was wrong about the chronology (backdating Poe's arrival to 1818). But his report of Poe's Latin reading is probably accurate. A bill sent to John Allan for June–September 1822 includes a charge for books: "Horace" and "Cicero de Offi[ciis]."[9] Cicero's *De officiis* (*On Duties*) was a standard school text, a treatise on moral philosophy by one of the greatest of Roman statesmen. "Horace" will be the *Odes*, another staple of the nineteenth-century curriculum. A schoolmate at Clarke's recalled that Poe "was very fond of the Odes of Horace, and repeated them...often in my hearing."[10] The rest of Clarke's reading list was equally conventional: according to the same classmate, he undertook to teach his students "only the pure latinity of the Augustan age."[11] This restriction reflects the twin goals of American classical schooling at this period: to create an American educational system equal to (because patterned on) that of England, and to groom future leaders of a republic modeled on classical Rome. The boys who read Horace and Cicero with Poe went on to become "a conspicuous lawyer in Virginia," "an Episcopal clergyman in New York," and an instructor at the Virginia Military Institute.[12]

After studying with Clarke and Burke, Poe attended the newly founded University of Virginia, where he remained from February to December 1826.[13] Records show him attending the lectures of George Long, who held the chair of ancient languages from 1825 to 1828. An import from Trinity College, Cambridge, Long was then near the beginning of a distinguished and productive career. His surviving lecture notes for this period cover Roman history, Greek and Latin languages, rhetoric, "translations," Tacitus, Herodotus, and the history and geography of Greece.[14] Poe probably heard at least the Tacitus lectures; a surviving letter to Allan requests "a copy of the *Historiae* of Tacitus" (along with "more soap").[15] As at Clarke's, Poe seems to have "acquitted himself well." He appears on a surviving list of students who performed well in Latin, grouped just below Long's star pupil, Gessner Harrison, who would later teach at the university himself.

Both at school and university, Poe's training involved intensive study of a small number of works. Class time consisted mainly of rote recitation, reading aloud with attention to meter, and literal translation (both Latin to English and English to Latin).[16] Literary appreciation played no role. Preparation was often eased by crude interlinear translations ("trots" or "ponies") passed down illicitly from pupil to pupil. Few students emerged from this regime with real fluency. The adult Poe might have returned to his text of Horace from time to time, but it is doubtful that he could have read an unfamiliar Latin work with any ease. As for Greek, the "Xenophon and Homer" mentioned by Clarke probably amount to short excerpts from a textbook like Andrew Dalzell's *Collectanea Graeca Majora*.[17] There is no evidence that Poe took any Greek in Charlottesville. In his writings he makes heavy use of a few talismanic phrases, like *mellonta tauta* ("these things are still to come") from Sophocles' *Antigone*, or the description of poetry as *spoudiotaton* [sic] *kai philosophikotaton genos* ("the most weighty and philosophic genre"), a shaky paraphrase of Aristotle.[18] When he quotes Greek in translation (the *Odyssey* in "Politian"; Plato's *Republic* in "Monos and Una"), the translations are always secondhand.

But reading texts in the original language is not the only way to absorb classical culture. Poe had enough Latin to benefit from facing-page translations, like his copy of Drummond's *Persius*. And he would have known freestanding English versions of ancient writers, like those by Thomas Moore of the Greek lyric poet Anacreon. Poe also read books about antiquity in English and French. A University of Virginia library register records him borrowing various volumes of the *Histoire ancienne* and *Histoire romaine* of Charles Rollin (1661–1741). His later work bears witness that he had at least dipped into Gibbon's *Decline and Fall*.[19] As a professional journalist, Poe reviewed hundreds of books, including various classical titles. Among these were a memoir of Roman historian B. G. Niebuhr, editions of Ovid by N. C. Brooks and of Plato's *Laws* by Tayler Lewis, several Latin grammars, and a translation of Euripides for the Classical Family Library. We should not assume that he read them all attentively, but he must have browsed through some. His theater reviewing included a production of Sophocles' *Antigone*.[20] He also read historical fiction and verse on classical themes. He wrote an indulgent review of Lydia Child's *Philothea*, a "Grecian romance," and another of Thomas Moore's *Alciphron*. He also knew Macaulay's *Lays of Ancient Rome* and Bulwer-Lytton's *Last Days of Pompeii*.

As a reviewer Poe enjoyed skewering other authors for linguistic errors: treating "sarcophagi" as singular, for example, or making "candelabri" the plural of "candelabrum."[21] A classical education taught one to avoid such slips. In "Pinakidia" and "Marginalia," he cultivates a second persona: not just the cultured gentleman, but the erudite scholar, discoursing offhandedly on the pseudo-Homeric *Batrachomyomachia*, the philosopher Porphyry's views on the gods, and Diodorus Siculus's account of the Amazons. Like the bogus cogs and gears of Maelzel's chess player, these impressive references conceal a more prosaic reality. Almost all of them can be traced to a handful of secondary sources: Jacob Bryant's *New System, or an Analysis of Antient Mythology* (1807); Isaac D'Israeli's *Curiosities of Literature*; Charles Anthon's edition of Lemprière's *Classical Dictionary*; and H. N. Coleridge's *Introductions to the Study of the Greek Classic Poets* (1830).[22]

If Poe's classical knowledge was largely derivative (and partly a sham), that is not altogether surprising. The general level of American classical scholarship at this period was low; even its best representatives were weak by comparison with contemporary German scholars.[23] We can gain some sense of the field in Poe's day by looking at the career of Charles Anthon (1797–1867), professor of classical languages at Columbia College.[24] Anthon was an occasional correspondent of Poe, and once approached his own publishers, Harpers, on Poe's behalf.[25] Poe, for his part, went out of his way to review Anthon's books, including a Greek grammar; a handbook of Latin verse composition; editions of Homer, Sallust, and Cicero; and a revision of William Smith's *Dictionary of Greek and Roman Antiquities*. In "The Literati of New York City," Poe described Anthon as "generally considered the best classicist in America."[26] This may well be true, but it is also revealing. Anthon was an energetic teacher who knew Greek and Latin well – certainly better than Poe. Like George Long's, his approach to classical studies was progressive for its day, looking beyond verb paradigms and syntax to the totality of ancient culture. But his actual publications consisted primarily of school texts and of revisions or abridgements of reference works by Lemprière, Smith, and others. His heavy, and often unacknowledged, use of others' work is another link with Poe (whose defense of Anthon on this score was perhaps not wholly disinterested).

CREATIVE WORKS

Classical references are scattered through Poe's creative works, but not all serve the same function. Some merely reflect the idioms of educated discourse. Poe's readers could be expected to field references to "a *quondam* cobbler" ("Murders in the Rue Morgue"), "a philippic" ("X-ing a

Paragrab"), "Draconian laws" ("William Wilson"), "a petty Caligula" ("Metzengerstein"), or "the *Ultima Thule* of... punishments" ("The Pit and the Pendulum"). Overuse of such tags is parodied in "The Man That Was Used Up," where the pretentious narrator's references to "the *ne plus ultra* of legs" and "the tremendous events *quorum pars magna fuit*" are of a piece with his incessant use of other foreign phrases. Poe made fun of such pedantry elsewhere. In "How to Write a Blackwood Article," Psyche Zenobia is told that "nothing makes so fine a show as your Greek." The self-satisfied narrator of "Loss of Breath" invokes Anaxagoras, Demosthenes, the bull of Phalaris, Mark Anthony, Epimenides, and Brutus, even supplying his own source references ("See Diodorus"; "as Laertius relates"; "this remark is from Epictetus"). The narrator of "Thou Art the Man" lectures us on the correct meaning of the phrase *cui bono?*, while the speaker in "Never Bet the Devil Your Head" discourses pretentiously on items Poe reused from "Pinakidia." Other characters are less well informed. Thingum Bob, Esq., asks plaintively if anyone can translate the Latin *quocunque modo rem* ("money, at any cost") – a phrase from Horace whose irony escapes him. This is one of several jokes that assume a knowledge of familiar tags. In "Three Sundays in a Week," Horace's *poeta nascitur non fit* ("a poet is born, not made") becomes "a nasty poet for nothing fit." In "X-ing a Paragrab," Cicero's famous exclamation *O tempora! o mores!* ("oh the times! oh the behavior!") reappears as "Oh tempora, oh Moses."

Classical allusions can also be used to create a poetic atmosphere. Lalage in "Politian" owes her name to Horace, and Ligeia shares hers with one of Odysseus's Sirens. The repeated references in "The Raven" to "Night's Plutonian shore" echo Horace *Odes* 1.4.17: *Iam te premet nox...| et domus exilis Plutonia* ["Already night oppresses you, ... | and the meagre *Plutonian* halls."] A more puzzling case is the reference in "To Helen" to the "Nicéan barks" that carry home Poe's "way-worn wanderer."[27] Was Poe thinking of traders from Nice in southern France, with cargoes of oil and perfume? Of the god Dionysus, borne back to Greece from his wanderings in Nysa? Or did the youthful Poe invent the adjective from hazy memories of classical reading without having any very clear referent in mind?

In the major tales, allusions often function as a signaling device, marking the speaker as an aristocrat, or at least a person of culture. The narrator of "Ligeia" describes his beloved in terms drawn from Greek literature. Her radiance recalls "the phantasies which hovered...about...the daughters of Delos." Her hair reveals "the full force of the Homeric epithet 'hyacinthine.'" Her chin possesses "the contour which the god Apollo revealed but in a dream, to Cleomenes." Her eyes are "twin stars of Leda," "more profound than the well of Democritus." (But her attractions are not solely physical: "in the classical tongues was she deeply proficient.") The narrator in "The Man of the Crowd" is similarly well educated. He quotes a Homeric phrase in Greek, dismisses the "flimsy rhetoric of Gorgias" (the fifth-century BCE sophist), and distinguishes airily between "the Eupatrid and the commonplaces of society" (i.e., aristocrats and commoners). Women are described as "putting one in mind of the statue in Lucian, with the surface of Parian marble and the interior filled with filth." The gaslit city is "dark and splendid, as that ebony to which has been likened the style of Tertullian." (This last reference, like so many others in Poe, comes from D'Israeli's *Curiosities*.)

Tertullian is a suggestive choice – an early Latin church father, as notable for his baroque Latin as for his heretical leanings. Poe's own schooling had focused on the classical Latin authors of the "golden age": Cicero, Horace, Virgil, and their contemporaries. But his characters tend to prefer post-classical Latin, or Greek. Another Tertullian reader is Egaeus in "Berenice," who also refers offhandedly to "Ptolemy Hephestion" – an obscure author known only from excerpts in later Byzantine sources. Most educated readers could have fielded a reference to "halcyon days," but Egaeus provides a learned footnote quoting the Greek lyric poet Simonides.

Particularly revealing is Poe's use of the first-century CE geographer Pomponius Mela. Mela's short *Description of the World* is mostly a dry recitation of coastlines and city names. But Poe makes of him a much more exotic figure. The narrator of "The Fall of the House of Usher" recalls "passages in Pomponius Mela, about the old African satyrs and Oegipans, over which Usher would sit dreaming for hours." The geographer crops up again in a footnote to "The Island of the Fay": "Speaking of the tides, Pomponius Mela, in his treatise *De situ orbis*, says 'either the world is a great animal, or' etc."[28] Both these references allude to real passages, but the "Pomponius Mela" they conjure up is effectively Poe's own creation.

The Dupin stories employ their own system of allusions. In "The Murders in the Rue Morgue," Dupin's virtuoso reconstruction of the narrator's thoughts traverses both "the theories of Epicurus" and a line from Ovid's Fasti "about which we have often conversed." Dupin also quotes Virgil twice near the end of "The Purloined Letter." Virgil and Ovid are canonical poets of the Augustan golden age, and that is part of their significance. The detective's full name – C. Auguste Dupin – evokes that same Augustan period, and even mimics the nomenclature of Roman aristocrats (compare "C. Julius Caesar" or "M. Tullius Cicero"). Dupin's quotations, like his name, align him with the values of reason and order; he is the

Aristotelian mean between the subhuman ape and the hypercivilized but amoral minister "D." Yet one of the Virgilian quotations in "The Purloined Letter" describes the monstrous Cyclops, and the story closes with an allusion to the gory Greek myth of Atreus and Thyestes – a hint that civilization may be no more than a veneer. In this sense, the classical references here recall the bust of Pallas in "The Raven," an emblem of culture and enlightenment counterposed to "darkness" and "fantastic terror."[29]

A few of Poe's tales have ancient settings. "Shadow, A Parable," is narrated by a Greek named Oinos, and set in a vague Greco-Egyptian milieu. "A Tale of Jerusalem" is set during a Roman siege in the first century BCE, and spoofs a contemporary historical novel. In "Four Beasts in One," time travelers visit the Greek city of Antioch in the Hellenistic period. All three stories are early, and none is among Poe's major achievements. At first glance, indeed, Poe's greatest works seem to owe relatively little to classical models. Ironically, he had probably never read the ancient works that now strike us as most Poe-esque, such as the Roman novelists Petronius and Apuleius, with their tales of witchcraft and werewolves. Poe might have run across these authors in his classical dictionaries (an Apuleian phrase in "The Spectacles" comes from D'Israeli), but he would have had a hard time finding copies of them. If anything, it is Poe and his successors who created the taste by which such works could be appreciated. Poe might conceivably have run across the necromancy episode in Lucan's epic *Pharsalia*, but none of his references to Lucan suggest real knowledge.

But classical elements can underlie even stories not obviously classical in subject or setting. In "Thou Art the Man," the narrator undertakes to "play the Oedipus to the Rattleborough enigma" – to solve it, that is, as Oedipus solves the riddle of the Sphinx.[30] Oedipus is also the detective who remorselessly uncovers his own guilt, a man "hurrying onward," like the narrator of "Manuscript Found in a Bottle," toward "some exciting knowledge…whose attainment is destruction." As such, he lurks within many of Poe's heroes: William Wilson, pursuing an adversary who turns out to have his own name and face; Egaeus in "Berenice," informed by his servant of the horrors he himself has unknowingly perpetrated; the ratiocinative Dupin (whose very name echoes "OeDIPUs"), solving a puzzle that brings about the downfall of his other self, the poet-mathematician "D."; even the nearsighted Napoleon Bonaparte Simpson, aghast at discovering in "The Spectacles" that he has married his own great-great-grandmother. Poe's acquaintance with Sophocles seems superficial – he once misattributes *Oedipus at Colonus* to Aeschylus – and he will have read *Oedipus the King* only in translation, if at all.[31] But Oedipus is an archetypal figure, like Faust or Hamlet, familiar even to those who have never seen or read the play.

In 1842 a friend of Poe's tried unsuccessfully to raise the issue of his drinking. Poe, he reported, "turned the subject off by telling an amusing dialogue of Lucian, the Greek writer."[32] Lucian wrote in the second century CE; his "Menippean" satires are noted for their mixture of philosophical content with comedy and fantasy (voyages to the moon, the underworld, or Mt. Olympus). Lucian's *True History*, for example, is a spoof of Odyssey-type travel accounts. Like *The Narrative of Arthur Gordon Pym*, it is told in the first person, foregrounds its own fictional status, is much concerned with food, and breaks off abruptly.[33] It also includes a visit to the moon, foreshadowing Poe's other Menippean narrative, "The Unparalleled Adventure of One Hans Pfaall." Other Lucianic works, like *Dialogues of the Dead* and *An Interview with Hesiod*, might be seen as forerunners of the postmortem colloquies in "King Pest" and "Some Words with a Mummy." Lucian enjoyed huge popularity from the Renaissance into the nineteenth century, and Poe may have been influenced as much by later imitators as by Lucian himself.[34] But without some awareness of the Lucianic tradition we will miss an important side of Poe.

If Poe's classical learning is mostly paste and plaster, there is one area where the effects of his Latin lessons are still discernible. This is his prose style. Many of Poe's most effective phrases depend on the juxtaposition of a single Latin derivative with shorter Anglo-Saxon words, often linked to it by alliteration:

"my gloomy, gray, hereditary halls" ("Berenice")

"a faint, indefinite shadow" ("Ligeia")

"the swelling of the black, stupendous seas" ("MS Found in a Bottle")

"stern, deep and irredeemable gloom" ("The Fall of the House of Usher").

In other cases Latin muscles out English almost entirely, as in the following passage from "William Wilson":

Thus far I had succumbed supinely to this imperious domination. The sentiment of deep awe with which I habitually regarded the elevated character, the majestic wisdom, the apparent omnipresence and omnipotence of Wilson, added to a feeling of even terror, with which certain other traits in his nature and assumptions inspired me, had operated, hitherto, to impress me with an idea of my own utter weakness and helplessness, and to suggest an implicit, although bitterly reluctant submission to his arbitrary will.

This Latinate idiom has been dubbed the "ratiocinative style" by one critic.[35] It has a faintly comic feel, and Poe sometimes uses it for comic effect. But in "William Wilson" it has a more serious function. In the opening pages of the tale we may find the narrator pompous and verbose. But as we read further, we realize that the pomposity masks a desperate attempt to maintain control, to paper over the cracks, by "translating" a brutal and terrifying reality into a more distanced and comforting form. So the narrator "succumb[s] supinely" to Wilson's "imperious domination," when the truth is that Wilson has a hold on him, that he cannot flee Wilson, that he is in Wilson's thrall. Despite the efforts of the internal translator, a few Anglo-Saxon words slip past to betray the true dynamic: "my own utter weakness and helplessness" and that ominous final "will." Only the mature Poe could have written this paragraph. But its roots can be traced back, like the struggle of the two Wilsons themselves, to Dr. Bransby's schoolroom.

NOTES

1. Persius, *The Satires of Persius*, ed. and trans. William Drummond (London: W. Bulmer and Co. for James Wright, 1797).
2. For other surviving volumes see Thomas Mabbott, "A List of Books from Poe's Library," *Notes and Queries* 200 (1955), 222–3; and Kevin J. Hayes, "More Books from Poe's Library," *Notes and Queries* 55 (2008), 457–9.
3. Another reader using pencil has underlined a few words in the introduction and added brief notes on pages 13 and 20.
4. Classical citations and allusions are quantified by Killis Campbell, "Poe's Reading," *Texas Studies in English* 5 (1925), 191–2. Latin quotations are listed by E. K. Norman, "Poe's Knowledge of Latin," *American Literature* 6 (1934), 72–7.
5. For Poe's education see Kevin J. Hayes, *Poe and the Printed Word* (New York: Cambridge University Press, 2000), 1–16.
6. The book's present location is unknown.
7. W. E. Hunter, "Poe and his English Schoolmaster," *Athenaeum*, October 19, 1878, 497.
8. E. L. Didier, *Life of Edgar A. Poe* (New York: W. J. Widdleton, 1879), 29–30.
9. Arthur Hobson Quinn, *Edgar Allan Poe: A Critical Biography* (New York: Appleton-Century, 1941), 83.
10. J. T. L. Preston, "Some Reminiscences of Edgar A. Poe as a Schoolboy," *Edgar Allan Poe: A Memorial Volume*, ed. Sara Sigourney Rice (Baltimore: Turnbull, 1877), 40. See also J. P. Pritchard, "Horace and Edgar Allan Poe," *Classical Weekly* 26 (1933), 129–33.
11. Preston, "Some Reminiscences," 37.
12. Didier, *Life*, 32.
13. Floyd Stovall, "Edgar Poe and the University of Virginia," *Virginia Quarterly Review* 43 (1967), 297–317.

14. I draw this list from a description of a microfilm (now lost) in the library catalogue of the University of Virginia. The originals, which I have not been able to see, are in the Jubilee Library, Brighton. Norman, "Poe's Knowledge of Latin," 73, cites an 1829 course list as evidence for offerings in 1826, but Long had returned to England by then.

15. Poe to John Allan, May 25, 1826, *The Collected Letters of Edgar Allan Poe*, ed. John Ward Ostrom, Burton R. Pollin, and Jeffrey A. Savoye, 2 vols. (New York: Gordian, 2008), vol. i, 6.

16. On the actual content of early American classics teaching, see Caroline Winterer, *The Culture of Classicism. Ancient Greece and Rome in American Intellecual Life, 1780–1910* (Baltimore: Johns Hopkins University Press, 2002), 29–43.

17. For this work see Winterer, *Culture of Classicism*, 60.

18. *Poetics* 1451b6. See Edgar Allan Poe, *Writings in the Broadway Journal*, ed. Burton R. Pollin, 2 vols. (New York: Gordian Press, 1986), vol. ii, 7–8.

19. Poe, *Essays*, 1063–4.

20. Kenneth Silverman, *Edgar A. Poe: Mournful and Never-ending Remembrance* (New York: HarperCollins, 1991), 250.

21. Poe, *Essays*, 495.

22. Palmer C. Holt, "Poe and H. N. Coleridge's Greek Classic Poets: 'Pinakidia,' 'Politian' and 'Morella' Sources," *American Literature* 34 (1962), 8–30.

23. For the general level, see Meyer Reinhold, *Classica Americana* (Detroit: Wayne State University Press, 1984), 174–203; Winterer, *Culture of Classicism*, 77–98.

24. See Henry Drisler, *Charles Anthon, LL.D. A Commemorative Discourse* (New York: Van Nostrand, 1868); S. Newmyer, "Charles Anthon: Knickerbocker Scholar," *Classical Outlook* 59 (1981), 41–4.

25. Silverman, *Edgar A. Poe*, 250.

26. Poe, *Essays*, 1142.

27. E. A. Havelock, "Homer, Catullus and Poe," *Classical Weekly* 36 (1943), 248–9; E. D. Snyder, "Poe's Nicéan Barks," *Classical Journal* 48 (1953), 159–69.

28. The footnote, added by Poe in later printings, is omitted from some modern editions.

29. On this symbolic opposition see D. H. Unrue, "Edgar Allan Poe: The Romantic as Classicist," *International Journal of the Classical Tradition* 1 (1995), 112–19.

30. Variants of the phrase appear in "Eleonora" ("play unto its riddle the Oedipus") and other works.

31. For the misattribution (in a review of Elizabeth Barrett Browning), see Poe, *Essays*, 118.

32. F. W. Thomas, as reported in J. H. Whitty, *The Complete Poems of Edgar Allan Poe* (Boston: Highton Mifflin, 1911), xliii.

33. For Menippean elements in the novel, see Evelyn J. Hinz, "'Tekeli-li': *The Narrative of Arthur Gordon Pym* as Satire," *Genre* 3 (1970), 379–99, though her use of the term owes more to Northrop Frye than Lucian.

34. On Lucian's European reception see *Lucian of Samosata Vivus et Redivivus*, ed. Christopher Ligota and Letizia Panizza (London: Warburg Institute, 2007).

35. Donald Barlow Stauffer, "The Language and Style of the Prose," *A Companion to Poe Studies*, ed. Eric W. Carlson (Westport, CT: Greenwood, 1996), 448–67.

CHAPTER 23

Rabelais and Lesage

Lois Davis Vines

Among the French authors who influenced Edgar Allan Poe, few were more important than François Rabelais (1494–1553) and Alain-René Lesage (1668–1747). These two authors occupied a somewhat different place within the context of nineteenth-century American literary culture than they do now. Rabelais' stature in the history of world literature is huge; Poe and his American contemporaries recognized him as a major French author, yet few read Rabelais extensively. Lesage, alternatively, is seldom read today, but he was quite popular in Poe's time. *Gil Blas*, his masterwork, was readily available in English translation, and many boys, Poe included, read the work in their youth. Together the reputation of Rabelais and the writings of Lesage exerted a crucial, but so far largely neglected influence on the development of American literature in general and specifically on the writings of Edgar Allan Poe.

Poe mentions Rabelais in both his critical and imaginative writings. Reviewing Henry Wadsworth Longfellow's *Hyperion*, Poe found the work somewhat reminiscent of "a few of the heartier drolleries of Rabelais." In "The Literati of New York City," Poe appreciated John W. Francis's sense of humor, calling it "a compound of Swift, Rabelais, and the clown in the Pantomime."[1] In "The Facts in the Case of M. Valdemar," the narrator's friend M. Ernest Valdemar is credited with having translated *Gargantua* into Polish, and the narrator of "Hop-Frog" notes that the king "would have preferred Rabelais' *Gargantua* to the *Zadig* of Voltaire."[2] These references convey Poe's general appreciation of Rabelaisian humor but indicate little additional knowledge.

Other references in Poe's critical writings are more specific. In another book review, he mentioned "the appetite of a Grandgousier," referring to one of the giants in *Gargantua*.[3] Poe's fullest reference to Rabelais occurs in his review of Lambert Wilmer's *Quacks of Helicon*, a scathing verse satire of contemporary American poetry. Refuting Wilmer, Poe suggests: "Mr. Wilmer must read the chapter in Rabelais' *Gargantua*, 'de ce *qu'est signifié par les couleurs blanc et bleu'* – for there is *some* difference after all."[4]

Brett Zimmerman uses this passage as proof that Poe had read Rabelais in the original French.[5] More likely, Poe picked up the French chapter title secondhand as he did so many of his foreign quotations. William Harrison Ainsworth's novel *Crichton* – a work Poe knew well – is the surest possibility.[6] Glossing a reference to the sacrifice of a snow-white cock at the Jewish Feast of the Reconciliation, Ainsworth notes, "The reader of Rabelais will also call to mind what is said respecting *le cocq blanc* in the chapter of *Gargantua* treating *"de ce qu'est signifié par les couleurs blanc et bleu."*[7] Poe's reuse of this phrase does not necessarily mean that he had not read Rabelais in the original, but it is not the only evidence that he borrowed reference to Rabelais from Ainsworth. The second volume of *Crichton* contains a song titled "The Chronicle of Gargantua," which includes the following stanza:

No sooner was Gargantua born, than from his infant throttle,

Arose a most melodious cry to his nurse to bring the bottle!

Whereat Grandgousier much rejoiced – as it seemed, unto his thinking,

A certain sign of a humour fine for most immoderate drinking![8]

Combined with the French quote, Ainsworth's use of Grandgousier provides compelling evidence that Poe took his reference to Rabelais from *Crichton*, not *Gargantua*. A four-volume English edition of Rabelais appeared in 1844, that is, in time to exert a significant influence on Herman Melville. There is no indication that Poe read this translation, either. The only subsequent reference in his collected writings that mentions Rabelais occurs in "Fifty Suggestions," an 1849 article that merely repeats the same information from his review of Lambert's *Quacks of Helicon*.[9]

Though Poe's knowledge of *Gargantua* remains circumspect, he and Rabelais nevertheless share a certain satirical outlook. The two often based their parodies and satires on the "establishment," which in Rabelais' case was the church and the intellectual snobs at the Sorbonne. The Transcendentalists and the New York and Boston literati were Poe's chosen enemies. He used the derogatory term "Frogpondians" to refer to writers in New England, particularly in Boston, where the Frog Pond is located on Boston Common.

Frequent dictionary definitions of "Rabelaisian" are "lustily humorous" and "marked by gross humor and coarse jokes." Although true, these descriptions of Rabelais' literary output are reductive and are not elements found in Poe.[10] Mikhail Bakhtin's *Rabelais and His World*, first published in English in 1968, is a pivotal study in which the Russian intellectual brings to the fore the connection between popular culture and literary tradition. As he points out: "Rabelais is difficult. But his work, correctly understood, casts a retrospective light on this thousand-year-old development of the folk culture of humor, which has found in his works its greatest literary expression."[11] In Bakhtin's view, Rabelais' style is itself a revolt against commonly accepted standards for the learned works we call literature. The major contribution of Bakhtin's study is his analysis of the role of popular folk culture in Rabelais' depiction of society in the Middle Ages, many aspects of which still hold true today. In Bakhtin's words:

All the symbols of the carnival idiom are filled with the pathos of change and renewal, with the sense of the gay relativity of prevailing truths and authorities. We find here a characteristic logic, the peculiar logic of the "inside out," of a continual shifting from top to bottom, from front to rear, of numerous parodies and travesties, humiliations, profanations, comic crownings and uncrownings. A second life, a second world of folk culture is thus constructed; it is to a certain extent a parody of the extra-carnival life, a "world inside out."[12]

RABELAISIAN CARNIVAL REPRESENTATIONS IN POE'S SHORT STORIES

Poe's "Hop-Frog" is a tale of laughter and merrymaking reminiscent of Rabelais's carnival scenes, except that the American writer's story ends in horror. The action takes place at court, where the major preoccupation of the king and his ministers is to be constantly entertained. The court jester, Hop-Frog, a crippled dwarf who also happens to be very clever and creative, strives to provide distractions to keep everyone laughing. After the king throws wine into the face of the petite dancer Trippetta, Hop-Frog, inspired by revenge, comes up with an extravagant plan for a novel idea to entertain the court – a masquerade party with Hop-Frog in charge of the costumes for the king and his seven ministers. He convinces them that their disguise will be the most original and will garner the admiration of all the guests at the carnival. Hop-Frog has them dress in tight, tar-covered suits to which he attaches bunches of flax, making them look like orangutans. At midnight, when guests traditionally take off their masks, Hop-Frog attaches the eight beasts to a chain connected to a chandelier, hoists them high in the air and sets them on fire. Escaping the flames, the dwarf climbs upward through a hole in the ceiling, leaving behind a horrifying spectacle for the guests, who suddenly stop laughing. Describing the *folie* of a Rabelaisian banquet scene, Bakhtin remarks: "The fool or clown is the king of the upside-down world."[13] This phrase appropriately sums up Poe's carnival scene in which Hop-Frog, the crippled dwarf clown, literally comes out on top.

Poe's tale "Lionizing" is a satire of a literary banquet during which attendees are praised with a great deal of puffery for their accomplishments. As a young man the narrator, Robert Jones from Fum-Fudge, was asked by his father to explain what he intended to do with his life. The son replied that his goal was to be an expert in the study of Nosology, which he defines as the Science of Noses. The play on the term "nosology," which refers to the branch of medicine that deals with the classification of diseases, is the absurd element in the story. Young Robert reassures his father by saying that the nose "has been variously defined by a thousand different authors," then he begins to expound upon the subject before his father throws him out of the house and orders him to earn a living on his own. Following his nose, Robert writes a pamphlet on Nosology, which garners the admiration of the important people in Fum-Fudge, who flatter him with phrases such as "wonderful genius" and "superb physiologist." All of the individuals and publications praising him are thinly veiled references to those whom Poe held in little esteem in the literary and intellectual society of his time.[14] The Duchess of Bless-my-Soul, in swooning admiration of his nose, invites Robert to a grand ball, where unfortunately one of the guests insults him. The expert on Nosology challenges the impertinent Elector of Blunddennuf to a duel and shoots off his nose. The victim is praised and Robert is condemned by all his friends. His father is sympathetic, saying, "I grant you that in Fum-Fudge the greatness of a lion is in proportion to the size of his proboscis – but, good heavens! There is no competing with a lion who has no proboscis at all."[15] This final remark in the story is aimed at the intelligentsia and literati whom Poe considered conceited and highly overrated. In short, with their noses up in the air they are nonetheless undistinguished and lack talent. The use of the word "proboscis," a synonym for nose, can be interpreted as the "phallus" which has been shot off, suggesting the impotence of those who have a very high opinion of themselves.

The theme of the nose being the most admired feature of a person otherwise lacking in worth is found in *Gargantua*, chapter 40: "Why monks are shunned by everyone and why some people have bigger noses than others." Over half of the two-page chapter describes how monks are useless and annoying as they chatter prayers morning, noon, and evening. Then Gargantua asks, "Why does Frère Jean have such a fine nose?" The question brings attention to his one redeeming quality, the beauty of his proboscis. Panocrate responds, saying "Because he was one of the first at the nose-fair. He took one of the biggest and finest." The monk offers an explanation based on church doctrine: "According to true monastic philosophy, it's because my wet nurses had soft teats; in suckling her, my nose went in as into butter, and it rose and grew like dough in the kneading trough. Hard teats of wet nurses make children snubnosed. But merrily, merrily! *Ad forman nasi cognoscitur ad te levavi* [By the form of the nose is known, I raised unto Thee]."[16] He then orders a round of drinks. The monk is praised and admired for a quality of seemingly little importance that he acquired by chance.

These two examples from Poe and Rabelais are satiric representations of aspects of society they dislike the most. Poe makes fun of the literary and intellectual snobs through exaggeration and the use of comic names, such as the President of Fum-Fudge University, Delphinum Polyglott, Sir Positive Paradox, and Aestheticus Ethix, among others. Rabelais, having been a monk, uses his character Gargantua to mock the useless activities of God's servants. Through their use of negative laughter, Poe and Rabelais place themselves above the objects of their mockery.[17]

Perhaps none of Poe's tales highlights his affinity to and departure from Rabelais more than "The Cask of Amontillado." This short story makes considerable use of the carnivalesque. Not only is it set "during the supreme madness of the carnival season," but the character of Fortunato is drunk and dressed in motley: "He had on a tight-fitting parti-striped dress, and his head was surmounted by the conical cap and bells."[18] The carnival setting aligns "The Cask of Amontillado" with *Gargantua*, but, as Bakhtin observes, the ensuing events in Poe's tale establish a stark contrast between the celebratory carnival and the somber catacombs, a symbol and setting of death. Whereas the Rabelaisian carnivalesque integrates life and death in triumphant celebration, Poe's carnival creates an oppressive contrast to emphasize the omnipresence of death.[19]

THE DEVIL THEME IN LESAGE AND POE

Lesage (older spelling, Le Sage) was educated by the Jesuits in Brittany and later completed law studies in Paris, where he became fascinated by the theater. Early in his writing career he translated works by Spanish authors, which inspired him to create some of his own plays and novels in a Spanish setting. Lesage was so determined to pursue a literary career he abandoned the practice of law and struggled to support his wife and five children with his writing, which included comic plays and novels.

When the prestigious *Théâtre français* refused his submissions, he wrote over 100 plays for the *Théâtre de la Foire*, a popular venue that catered to a less demanding public that enjoyed burlesque comedies. His resentment toward the power of money and the high-brow literati motivated his biting satires. Having read Lesage's picaresque novel *Gil Blas* as a boy, Poe returned to it in college. His impressions of the book's robbers and their secret cave long endured in his memory.[20] In a review of Morris Mattson's *Paul Ulric*, Poe pointed out details he claimed had been plagiarized from *Gil Blas*, thus indicating that Poe knew Lesage's work well.[21]

Before the publication of *Gil Blas*, another novel by Lesage had gained popularity. *Le Diable boiteux*, meaning literally "the limping devil," came out in translation as *The Devil on Two Sticks*.[22] This work probably inspired Poe as he wrote several tales in which the devil plays a central role. For both Poe and Lesage the devil is a metaphor for the absurd, the elements in life that escape reason and logic.

In Lesage's novel, the devil Asmodeus, whose name is a variant of Asmoday, an evil spirit who can fly and predict the future, becomes the mentor of a young man by the name of Don Cleofas Leandro Perez Zambullo. In order to teach his student that people and situations are not what they seem in so-called reality, he peels away the roofs on the houses in Madrid to clearly expose all that is beneath them. He then takes Don Cleofas on a tour of these scenes to show him the truth behind appearances. In a comic mode, Asmodeus expresses his resentment at being blamed for situations for which he is not responsible, saying "when men are in a very uneasy, rickety coach, and cry out, 'This is a coach for the devil!' do you think they do us justice?"[23] While viewing civilization from above and revealing its pretentions, dissimulations, and lies, Lesage's demon uses comedy, parody, and satire to teach his student the absurd nature of elements that are incomprehensible to humans.

In one home, Asmodeus points out to Don Cleofas two people preparing to retire for the evening. One of them is a superannuated coquette going to bed after leaving her hair, eyebrows, and teeth on her toilet. The other is an amorous dotard of sixty, just come from making love. He has already laid down his eye, false whiskers, and peruke which hid his bald pate, and waits for his servant to take off his wooden arm and leg, to go to bed with the rest. As George Wetzel observes, the episode influenced the figure of General John A. B. C. Smith in "The Man That Was Used Up," a character similarly assembled from a set of manufactured parts.[24] Though Wetzel does not say so, the old woman from this episode anticipates Madame Eugénie Lalande in "The Spectacles." She, too, reveals her identity by removing her wig and various other body parts.

In "Never Bet the Devil Your Head," the absurd takes place at the end of the tale. Poe wrote this piece to make fun of critics who believed a good tale had to have a moral. He recounts the life of Toby Dammit who "indulged himself in some very equivocal behavior." Among other bad habits, Dammit, often repeated the phrase "I'll bet the devil my head." The narrator tries to correct Toby's misdeeds, but remarks in frustration, "I really could not make up my mind whether to kick or to pity him."[25] While taking a walk they come upon a bridge with a turnstile. Toby decides to leap over the obstacle, betting the devil his head that he will land safely on the other side. Unbeknownst to him, there is a flat iron bar above the stile supporting the structure. Toby lands flat on his back, decapitated. His friend sees in the darkness a "gentleman limping off at the top of his speed, having caught and wrapped up in his apron something that fell heavily into it from the arch just over the turnstile."[26] The image of the limping demon waiting at the turnstile is reminiscent of the *diable boiteux* in Lesage's novel.

Poe's "The Angel of the Odd" recounts the strange experience of the narrator who professes to "believe nothing henceforth that has anything of the 'singular' about it" after reading accounts in the newspaper that are so unusual they seem to have been made up.[27] While drinking his after dinner wine he is joined by a strange creature whose legs appear to be two kegs and his arms "long bottles with the necks outward for hands."[28] Speaking with a strange accent, the weird visitor represents the irrational spirit "whose business it was to bring about *odd accidents* which are continually astonishing to the skeptic."[29] A series of highly improbable events happen to the narrator, who wakes up, realizes he is still alive, and is forced to admit that there exists another world of inexplicable happenings and absurdities that oppose his skepticism. The "Angel of the Odd" is an ironic name for the devil, who confounds the human desire for reason and logic.

Another episode in *The Devil on Two Sticks* relates to a theme in "The System of Doctor Tarr and Professor Fether," a tale in which the narrator visits a mental health care facility in France to observe the innovative therapy called "system of soothing." In the course of his visit, hosted by the Superintendent Maillard, he discovers an unusual situation in which the staff appears deranged. The visit culminates with an outrageous banquet during which the guests laugh, shout, and "perpetrate a thousand absurdities." The climax comes when the narrator witnesses a gang of ten creatures bursting through the window appearing to be an "army of chimpanzees, orangutans, or big black baboons."[30] It turns out that they are the keepers who have been overpowered by the lunatics, then tarred, feathered, and kept captive. The system of Doctor Tarr and Professor Fether has changed the hierarchy. In Poe's story, it is evident that there is a thin line between the sane and insane. In Lesage's novel, the devil Asmodeus has his protegé observe the patients in an insane asylum as he points out the strange behavior of several individuals. After the visit, while looking down upon other households, Asmodeus and Don Cleofas observe a man who visited a former lover, "broke part of her furniture, threw the rest out of the window, and the next day married her." Don Cleofas remarks "Such a man certainly deserves the first vacancy in the asylum."[31]

Lesage's "devil on two sticks" bears witness to the ambiguity, the incomprehensibility, and the stupidity that are all part of the human experience. In a world where humans seek reason, continuity, and foreseen outcomes, the drama and trauma of the inexplicable never cease to confound even the most ardent skeptic. It's not hard to see why Poe found Lesage's satire so attractive.

CONCLUSION

Rabelais, Lesage, and Poe are what we call today "outliers," meaning in this case writers and thinkers who go against the grain, who are outside the norm. Rabelais, a monk and medical doctor, used his experience to create satiric, joyous, and outrageous literature that brings a critical perspective to religion and highly regarded professions. In Bakhtin's words, Rabelais became "the greatest writer to complete the cycle of the people's carnival laughter and bring it into world literature."[32] Lesage, trained as a lawyer in Paris, wrote novels and plays that make fun of his own class in society. Poe was an outlier in relation to the writers whom he saw as the New England clique, the Transcendentalists and the New York literati. His satiric and comic prose targets those who appear to have a very high opinion of themselves and, in his estimation, often lack talent and literary sensitivity.

NOTES

1. Edgar Allan Poe, *Essays and Reviews*, ed. G. R. Thompson (New York: Library of America, 1984), 670, 1136.
2. Edgar Allan Poe, *The Collected Works of Edgar Allan Poe*, ed. Thomas Ollive Mabbott, 3 vols. (Cambridge, MA: Belknap Press, 1969–78), vol. iii, 1234, 1345.
3. Poe, *Essays*, 823.

4. Ibid., 1013.
5. Brett Zimmerman, *Edgar Allan Poe: Rhetoric and Style* (Montreal: McGill-Queen's University Press, 2005), 68.
6. Poe, *Essays*, 101–3.
7. W. Harrison Ainsworth, *Crichton*, 2 vols. (New York: Harper and Brothers, 1837), vol. i, 247–8.
8. Ibid., vol. ii, 45.
9. Merton M. Sealts, Jr., *Melville's Reading*, rev. ed. (Columbia: University of South Carolina Press, 1988), 207; Poe, *Essays*, 1297.
10. Zimmerman, *Edgar Allan Poe*, 67.
11. Mikhail Bakhtin, *Rabelais and His World*, trans. Helene Iswolsky (Bloomington: Indiana University Press, 1984). 4.
12. Ibid., 11.
13. Ibid., 426.
14. Poe, *Collected Works*, vol. ii, 174.
15. Ibid., vol. ii, 183.
16. François Rabelais, *The Complete Works of François Rabelais*, trans. Donald M. Frame (Berkeley: University of California Press, 1991), 94.
17. Bakhtin, *Rabelais and His World*, 12.
18. Poe, *Collected Works*, vol. iii, 1257.
19. M. M. Bakhtin, *The Dialogic Imagination: Four Essays*, trans. Varyl Emerson and Michael Holquist (Austin: University of Texas Press, 1981), 199–200.
20. Kevin J. Hayes, *Poe and the Printed Word* (New York: Cambridge University Press, 2000), 14–15.
21. Poe, *Essays*, 851.
22. Alain-René Lesage, *The Devil on Two Sticks*, trans. William Strange (1841; reprinted, London: The Navarre Society, 1950).
23. Ibid., 14.
24. George Wetzel, "The Source of Poe's 'Man that Was Used Up,'" *Notes and Queries* 198 (1953), 38.
25. Poe, *Collected Works*, vol. ii, 625.
26. Ibid., vol. ii, 630.
27. Ibid., vol. iii, 1102.
28. Ibid.
29. Ibid., vol. iii, 1104.
30. Ibid., vol. iii, 1021.
31. Lesage, *Devil on Two Sticks*, 168.
32. Bakhtin, *Rabelais and His World*, 121.

CHAPTER 24

The Gothic Movement

Alan Brown

The birth of the gothic movement can be traced back to a single novel: British author Horace Walpole's *Castle of Otranto* (1764). The gothic novel in Britain continued to develop throughout the 1820s. According to G. R. Thompson, gothic fiction developed in two stages. In the first stage, extremely popular at the end of the eighteenth century, supernatural occurrences are explained away logically in the end of the tale. The most prominent purveyor of this type of fiction was Ann Radcliffe, who filtered the gloomy, obscure atmosphere of Gothic buildings through the sensitive minds of her innocent – but always threatened – heroines in works like *The Mysteries of Udolpho* (1794). Gothic works produced during the second stage were heavily influenced by the recent translations of German gothic tales. In these works, such as Matthew Lewis's *The Monk* (1794), Mary Shelley's *Frankenstein* (1818), Charles Maturin's *Melmoth the Wanderer* (1820), and Bram Stoker's *Dracula* (1897), the supernatural is real. Ghosts, the walking dead, witches, and demons are depicted as being actually supernatural. The emphasis on the actuality of the supernatural in these works can be interpreted as a reaction against the Enlightenment writers of the eighteenth century, who promoted the power of the rational mind and railed against the propagation of superstition.[1] Furthermore, the imagined dangers dreamed up by Mrs. Radcliffe's heroines are replaced in the second stage by genuine acts of violence. Murder and rape, commonplace in these works, point to the dark recesses of the human soul.

Gothic fiction became identified with a number of tropes that appear in many of the works produced at this time. *The Castle of Otranto* contains many pioneering gothic elements: an ancient prophecy, the castle setting, mystery, omens, overwrought emotion, supernatural occurrences, suspense, tyrannical men, and women in distress. Eve Kosofsky Sedgwick identifies the following tropes common to much gothic literature: "the priesthood and other monastic institutions; sleeplike and deathlike states, affinities between narrative and pictorial art; possibilities of incest, unnatural echoes and silences; unintelligible writings; the unspeakable, garrulous retainers, the poisonous effects of guilt and shame; nocturnal landscapes and dreams; apparitions from the past; Faust- and Wandering Jew-like figures; civil insurrections and fires; the charnal house and the madhouse."[2] Irving Malin's shorter list focuses on the tropes common to many American gothic works of the nineteenth and twentieth centuries: dreams, family conflicts, haunted houses, narcissism, the psyche, and silences.[3] Benjamin Fisher identifies the gothic elements in Poe's stories and poems as "decaying architecture or bleak landscapes and the stereotypical plot of vicious pursuit of innocence for purposes of lust, money or power, often related to family identity involving physically or emotionally debilitated characters, gender issues, sexuality, and perhaps, as some critics argue, even racial issues."[4]

The gothic movement first took root in America in the 1790s with the production of plays by one of America's first playwrights, William Dunlap. He wrote or adapted over sixty plays, many indebted to German writers. *The Fatal Deception or the Progress of Guilt* (1794), Dunlap's dramatic portrayal of murder and madness, borrows much from *Macbeth*. Another play, *Fountainville Abbey* (1795), is an adaptation of a novel by Ann Radcliffe. Dunlap's works were followed by the gothic novels of Charles Brockden Brown: *Wieland* (1798), *Ormond* (1799), *Edgar Huntly* (1799), and *Arthur Mervyn* (1799–1800). Leslie Fiedler argues that *Edgar Huntley* wrought changes in the gothic novel that paved the way for the development of what he calls "American Gothic."[5] Brown substitutes cliffs for castles and caves for dungeons. The medieval power structures commonly found in eighteenth-century English gothic novels were replaced in Brown's novel by the fury of nature. Villainous noblemen who preyed on the peasantry gave way in the American Gothic movement to savage Indians and bears and wolves.[6] Brown, generally credited with Americanizing the gothic, was an influential precursor to both Edgar Allan Poe and Nathaniel Hawthorne.

When Poe tried to make a living by writing popular fiction, he decided to write similar fiction to what appeared in *Blackwood's Edinburgh Magazine* and other British periodicals. Most of these stories can best be described as "terror tales," which descended from the gothic novels that flourished from the 1790s into the early nineteenth century.[7] In the early 1830s, when Poe began writing short stories in earnest, the mainstay of gothic tales were the "sensation tales," in which the protagonists found themselves in bizarre, life-threatening situations. As they tried to extricate themselves, the victims described their feelings in graphic detail.

Poe lampooned these tales and the often absurd tropes on which they depended in a number of stories, usually through subtle – and sometimes not so subtle – exaggeration.[8]

In "How to Write a Blackwood Article" (1838), for example, a budding young writer with the improbable name of Signora Psyche Zenobia visits the editor of *Blackwood's*. After telling her that "the writer of intensities must have very black ink, and a very big pen, with a very blunt nib" to produce as many words as possible, Mr. Blackwood says that "when manuscript can be read, it is never worth reading" because verbosity and unintelligibility are among the key features of the Blackwood story. He cites several examples of the typical stories that he selects for publication, such as "The Dead Alive," which provides "a gentleman's sensations when entombed before the breath was out of his body – full of taste, terror, sentiment, metaphysics, and erudition." Mr. Blackwood confesses that another highly successful story – "Confessions of an Opium Eater" – which he describes as "a nice bit of flummery" and that many readers mistook as one of Samuel Taylor Coleridge's compositions – was actually written by his pet baboon, Juniper, after he consumed a glass of Hollands and water.[9]

Another tale that records the sensations of its main character is "The Man in the Bell," which dramatizes the plight of a young man who falls asleep under the clapper of a church bell and is rudely awakened when it begins tolling during a funeral. Mr. Blackwood instructs Miss Zenobia to take a dose of Brandreth's pills and explain her sensations. To make her story even more impressive, he has her use big words, make allusions to Archytas, Gorgias, and Alcmaeon, and sprinkle a smattering of German phrases throughout to lend her tale more of a "German" air. Whenever she can, Mr. Blackwood advises, Miss Zenobia should "abuse a man named Locke."[10] English philosopher John Locke heavily influenced Enlightenment figures like Thomas Jefferson with his writing about government and about the power of the human mind. Because Blackwood stories in general emphasize emotion over rational thinking, John Locke would be the perfect nemesis for writers of gothic tales.

The end result of Miss Zenobia's interview with Mr. Blackwood is the often hilarious story, "A Predicament," in which Poe succeeds in making the conventions of the typical Blackwood story look ridiculous. Accompanied by the requisite grotesque, a three-foot tall African American dwarf named Pompey and her five-inch tall poodle Diana, Miss Zenobia visits Edinburgh. Overcome with an irresistible impulse to climb to the pinnacle of a Gothic cathedral, the trio walk up the nearly endless flight of stairs to the belfry. Searching for a window in the tower that will offer a panoramic view of the city, Miss Zenobia pokes her head through a hole in the wall and discovers, to her chagrin, that she is stuck. As she gazes up and down, she realizes, to her horror, that her head is poking through the face of a gigantic clock, the minute hand of which is lodged on her neck. The increasing pressure of the immense iron bar on her neck causes both of her eyes to pop out before decapitating her entirely. She then describes her most "singular" feelings, produced by the sight of her head rolling into the gutter: "My senses were here and there at one and the same moment." Unable to understand why Pompey is so shocked at her appearance, Miss Zenobia makes the following totally inappropriate allusion to Demosthenses as he runs away: "Andrew O'Phlegethon, you really make haste to fly."[11] In this burlesque of the typical German-inspired gothic story that often appeared alongside Poe's works in the 1830s, Poe parodies a number of gothic tropes including the damsel in distress, deformity, and gore.

In Poe's first gothic tale, "Metzengerstein" (1832), a bizarre, fable-like story, the dissolute teenage heir to the Metzengerstein estate in Hungary is implicated in the death of the patriarch of the Berlifitzing family, William von Berlifitzing, who died mysteriously in a fire in his stables. Afterward, young Metzengerstein is gazing at a tapestry depicting the death of a member of the Berlifitzing at the hands of one of the baron's ancestors when the dead man's horse suddenly assumes "an energetic and human expression."[12] Not long thereafter, an equerry informs him that a fiery-colored horse with the temperament of a demon has been found in his stables. The letters W. V. B. are branded on the forehead of the beast. The baron soon develops an unusual attachment to the animal, spending his time trying to break his new acquisition. One night, while the baron is riding the horse, his castle catches fire. The baron's mount gallops toward the castle and leaps into the flames. Hovering above the ruins of the castle is a cloud of smoke that resembles the figure of a gigantic horse.

Some critics read the story as a gothic spoof. Davidson points to the exaggerated elements of the tale, particularly the ending, as proof that "Metzengerstein" is a parody of the gothic genre as a whole. Thompson believes that through the use of turgid narration and awkward dialog, Poe is satirizing gothic elements found in a number of British gothic works, including *Castle of Otranto*, *The Monk*, and Sir Walter Scott's *The Antiquary* (1816).[13] For example, the ending of the tale is predicated by an ancient – and ominous sounding – prophecy: "A lofty name shall have a fearful fall when, as the rider over his horse, the mortality of Metzengerstein shall triumph over the immortality of Berlifitzing." Poe also interjects in the very end of the tale an "insignificant and misshapen little page...whose opinions were of the least possible importance." Gothic authors often introduce grotesque characters to instill revulsion in the reader. In Poe's tale, however, this "incidental" character makes some astute observations: that the young baron always shuddered when he climbed on the back of the beast and that when he returned from his daily ride, his face was distorted with "an expression of triumphant malignity."[14]

One of Poe's funniest gothic farces is "Loss of Breath" (1832), which chronicles the misadventures of a man who loses his ability to breathe the day after his wedding. In a typical gothic tale, physical disability, such as the loss of an eye or a hunchback, produces feelings of horror and repulsion in the reader. In "Loss of Breath," however, Poe uses his protagonist's handicap to comic effect. The self-absorbed narrator, whose relationship with his wife is typically dysfunctional, is in the process of calling her names such as "witch," "vixen," and "hag" when he suddenly finds himself unable to speak. After kissing her on one cheek and patting her on the other, the man retreats to his bedroom and contemplates suicide. His feelings of despair give way to anger when his pets diffuse the gloom: "Thus I shuddered at self-murder as the most decided of atrocities while the tabby cat purred strenuously upon the rug and the very water-dog wheezed assiduously under the table."[15]

His humorous efforts to communicate with his wife in deep, guttural tones lead her and others to believe that he should be confined to a straitjacket. To avoid commitment to an insane asylum, the narrator boards a stage, hoping to uncover the cause of his malady. Because he cannot breathe, his fellow passengers on board a mail stage mistake him for a corpse and throw him off. The slapstick elements are accentuated when they throw his trunk after him and it bounces off his head.

"Loss of Breath" pokes fun at gothic elements that, ironically, would make their way into several of Poe's serious gothic tales. For example, the narrator's pet cat and the bird after which a tavern is named – "The Crow" – appear years later in "The Black Cat" and "The Raven." The narrator's hanging – the consequence of his uncanny resemblance to a highwayman – brings to mind the fate suffered by the criminals in "The Black Cat" and "Imp of the Perverse." His execution, which conventionally instilled horror in the readers of gothic tales, is presented for comic effect: "For good reasons, however, I did my best to give the crowd the worth of their trouble. My convulsions were said to be extraordinary." The sensations he experiences at the end of the rope are decidedly understated and, therefore, not horrific at all: "But for the knot under my left ear...I dare say that I should have experienced very little inconvenience." Poe also peppers his story with quotations by and references to a number of ancient "philosophers, such as Anaxagoras, who made the quizzical observation that 'snow is black.'"[16] The narrator's interment in a public burial vault sustains the comic tone that permeates the tale. The man who stole his breath is, coincidentally, buried in the same vault, and the two men commence yelling until they are freed. The fear of being buried alive receives more treatment years later in the most gothic of Poe's tales, "The Fall of the House of Usher."

"The Premature Burial" (1844) appears to be a serious examination of several cases in which people were buried alive. The narrator, an avid fan of gothic tales of premature burial, devotes three-quarters of his story to a series of "factual" histories. In his description of the feelings of the people who find themselves in this predicament, he seems to be taking the advice of the editor in "How to Write a Blackwood Article." The subject of one of these histories, an officer of the artillery, is buried with "indecent haste" after being thrown from a horse and knocked senseless. Following his exhumation, he reports thinking that he was in a deep sleep until the ruckus made by the visitors to the cemetery makes him "fully aware of the awful horrors of his position." In another case history, Edward Stapleton is hastily pronounced dead from typhoid fever. Stapleton declared that "at no period was he altogether insensible – that, dully and confusedly he was aware of every thing which happened to him." When he realizes that he has been transferred to the dissecting room, he tries in vain to utter the words, "I am alive."[17]

When the narrator of "The Premature Burial" awakes to find himself in a very confined space, he leaps to the conclusion that he too has been buried alive. His account is riddled with the type of overwrought sensations commonly found in gothic tales at that time. For example, just before he is released, the narrator says, "I endeavored to shriek; and my lips and my parched tongue moved convulsively together in the attempt – but no voice issued from the cavernous lungs, which, oppressed as if by the weight of some incumbent mountain, gasped and palpitated, with the heart, at every elaborate and struggling inspiration." The horror of his situation is completely diffused in the end of the story when the narrator confesses that he was actually sleeping in the very narrow berth of a ship. His fears were groundless, and he had, in fact, gotten himself "worked up" over nothing at all. However, instead of laughing at his overreaction to his rather absurd predicament, the narrator somberly declares in the end of the tale that "from that memorable night, I dismissed forever my charnel apprehensions."[18]

Even though Poe achieved notoriety as a writer of "German" stories, he seems to have lamented his reliance on gothic fiction for his income. In a letter he wrote to Thomas White in April 1835, Poe said, "To be appreciated, you must be read, and these things [i.e., Gothic tales] are invariably sought after with avidity.[19] Indeed, one can construe his burlesques of gothic tales, which he wrote throughout his career, as proof that he resented having to compromise his art by writing in a format he considered beneath him but that paid the bills. However, in Poe's finest gothic tales, he clearly demonstrates his ability to improve on the standard gothic tale, which he believed depended primarily on cheap thrills generated by a number of rather absurd stock tropes. Fisher identifies Poe's use of psychological terror as his greatest contribution to the gothic.[20]

"Ligeia," which Poe considered his best story, is also one of his most gothic tales. Many of the trappings of the typical gothic tale are present in Poe's story: the tyrannical male (the narrator) who preys upon the helpless heroine (Rowena); the decaying "castle" (an abbey, this case); pursuit of money (the narrator marries wealthy women); and emotionally debilitated characters (the narrator himself). In the beginning of the tale, the narrator admits that one of Ligeia's most defining qualities was her "gigantic volition," which, in the end, enables her to overcome death itself. Because the narrator cannot remember when he first met his wife, Thompson suggests that Ligeia is a demon conjured up by his own fevered imagination.[21] In the end of the tale, when Ligeia is lying on her deathbed, he says he saw "three or four large drops of a brilliant and ruby colored fluid" fall into the glass of her wine.[22] Poe thus undercuts the ostensible supernaturalism and plants the seed in the reader's mind that the narrator – not the specter of his dead wife – may have poisoned Rowena as he was in the throes of an opium-induced mania.

While Poe was demonstrating the full potential of the gothic tale, he was also highlighting its deficiencies. Clark Griffith points out that the triumph of the dark, German Ligeia over the blonde, British Rowena implies the superiority of German gothic fiction (supernatural gothic) over British gothic fiction (explained gothic).[23] Poe also satirizes the excess of the overdone style of gothic writing in general in his description of Rowena's bed chamber: "And there was a couch, too – the bridal couch – of an Indian model, and low, and sculptured of solid ebony, with a pall-like canopy above. In each of the angles of the chamber stood on end a gigantic sarcophagus of black granite, from the tombs of the kings over against Luxor, with their aged lids full of immemorial sculpture...the phantasmagoric effect was vastly heightened by the artificial introduction of a strong continual current of wind behind the draperies – giving a hideous and uneasy animation to the whole." The overall effect of the narrator's questionable interior decorating skills was to transform the bridal chamber into a funeral chamber. Poe's description not only foreshadows the end of the tale, it also reveals the narrator's love of death.[24]

At first glance, "The Fall of the House of Usher" appears to be what Daniel Hoffman describes as "a thesaurus of Gothic clichés," which include the decaying castle, the lonely wanderer, the ghostly sister, the incestuous attachment between brother and sister, and premature burial.[25] However, in this, Poe's finest short story, the surface gothic details become realistically psychological. The most iconic of gothic tropes – the haunted castle – is immediately transformed into the haunted mind in the first paragraph of Poe's tale: "I looked upon the scene before me – upon the mere house, and the simple landscape features of the domain – upon the bleak walls – upon the vacant eye-like windows – upon a few rank sedges – and upon a few white trunks of decayed trees – with an utter depression of soul."[26] The bone-like whiteness of the trees and the skull-like appearance of the house instill an uneasy awareness of the presence of death in the reader. The fissure, which splits the façade of the skull-like mansion, reflects the fragmented landscape of the mind of Roderick Usher. Thompson likens the sinking of the House of Usher into the black tarn to the sinking of the rational mind into madness. The fear of death that propels the story is actually the fear of the death of sanity.

The gothic theme of madness introduced symbolically into Poe's tale is also present in the poem "The Haunted Palace." For the second time in the tale, a haunted mansion is a symbolic representation of the human head. In line five, Poe describes the haunted palace as "the monarch Thought's dominion," just as the human can be said to "reside" inside the human skull. The hideous throng who rush out of the haunted palace "and laugh – but smile not more" presage the impending insanity of Roderick Usher and his sister Madeleine. Daniel Hoffman asserts that dethroning of "the monarch Thought" in Roderick Usher's poem mirrors the toppling of Roderick Usher's tottering sanity.[27]

During his lifetime and after his death, critics deplored Poe's propensity for shrouding his terrifying tales in German gloom and doom, especially in those sensationalistic stories in which his primary intent seems to be to horrify the reader, like "Berenice."[28] The fact remains, though, that Poe learned to write gothic fiction better than any of his contemporaries. In

Poe's best gothic fiction, like "Ligeia" and "Fall of the House of Usher," the supernatural aspects of the tales are not totally destroyed by rational explanation, thereby enabling even the most skeptical reader to experience the thrill of the uncanny. In tales such as these, one can discern the genesis of psychological realism, which came to full flowering by the end of the nineteenth century in the works of Ambrose Bierce, William Dean Howells, and Henry James.

NOTES

1. Teresa A. Goddu, *Gothic America: Narrative, History and Nation* (New York: Columbia University Press, 1997), 3; G. R. Thompson, *Poe's Fiction: Romantic Irony in the Gothic Tales* (Madison: University of Wisconsin Press, 1973), 74–6.
2. Eve Kosofsky Sedgwick, *The Coherence of Gothic Convention* (New York: Methuen, 1986), 9–10.
3. Irving Malin, *New American Gothic* (Carbondale: Southern Illinois University Press, 1962), 5–12.
4. Benjamin F. Fisher, *The Cambridge Introduction to Edgar Allan Poe* (New York: Cambridge University Press, 2008), 56.
5. Leslie Fiedler, *Love and Death in the American Novel* (1966; reprinted, Normal, IL: Dalkey Archive Press, 1998), 145–53.
6. Renée L. Bergland, "Diseased States, Public Minds: Native American Ghosts in Early National Literature," *The Gothic Other: Racial and Social Constructions in the Literary Imagination*, ed. Ruth Bienstock Anolik and Douglas L. Howard (Jefferson, NC: McFarland, 2004), 94–5.
7. Fisher, *Cambridge Introduction*, 49.
8. Thompson, *Poe's Fiction*, 73.
9. Edgar Allan Poe, *The Collected Works of Edgar Allan Poe*, ed. Thomas Ollive Mabbott, 3 vols. (Cambridge, MA: Belknap Press, 1969–78), vol. ii, 339.
10. Ibid., vol. ii, 341.
11. Ibid., vol. ii, 355–6.
12. Ibid., vol. ii, 23.
13. Edward Davidson, *Poe: A Critical Study* (Cambridge, MA: Harvard University Press, 1957), 138; Thompson, *Poe's Fiction*, 54.
14. Poe, *Collected Works*, vol. ii, 19, 28.
15. Ibid., vol. ii, 63.
16. Ibid., vol. ii, 69.
17. Ibid., vol. ii, 961.
18. Ibid., vol. ii, 969.
19. Fisher, *Cambridge Introduction*, 110.
20. Ibid., 84.
21. Thompson, *Poe's Fiction*, 84.
22. Poe, *Collected Works*, vol. ii, 325.

23. Clark Griffith, "Poe's 'Ligeia' and the English Romantics," *University of Toronto Quarterly* 24 (1954), 8.
24. Poe, *Collected Works*, vol. ii, 321–2; Thompson, *Poe's Fiction*, 87.
25. Daniel Hoffman, *Poe Poe Poe Poe Poe Poe Poe* (Garden City, NY: Doubleday, 1972), 296.
26. Poe, *Collected Works*, vol. ii, 397.
27. Poe, *Collected Works*, vol. ii, 406–7; Hoffman, *Poe*, 306.
28. Fisher, *Cambridge Introduction*, 120; Thompson, *Poe's Fiction*, 77.

CHAPTER 25

Byron

Chris Beyers

When Thomas Holley Chivers asked Edgar Allan Poe to identify "the present Pantheon of English poets," Poe named Alfred, Lord Tennyson as the greatest living poet, disparaging the English Romantic poets Chivers revered and adding that most of the corpus of George Gordon, Lord Byron (among others) is not really poetic. This assertion may seem odd considering the obvious influence the British poet exerted on Poe's works. Poe openly admitted using Byronic materials for a few works, and many references in his letters and essays demonstrate a more than passing knowledge of Byron's works. Poe used lines from Byron to exemplify excellence in both "The Rationale of Verse" and "The Poetic Principle," and the standard edition of Poe's verse lists some sixty quotations, allusions, adaptations of, and parallels to Byron.[1] That Poe should know Byron's poems well is not surprising, since in Poe's life, Byron was the most read, richest (at least most people assumed so), and most famous poet alive. In Poe's time, by one estimate, Byron outsold all other authors five to one.[2] Poe's borrowings have often been taken to indicate a mental or moral defect. Time and again, critics assert that Poe wanted to be Byron.

Nineteenth-century Poe biographer George Woodberry, among others, censured poems "affected by the artificiality and turgidity, the false sentiment, the low motive, and the sensational accessories of the Byronic model." More sympathetically, Charles Baudelaire claimed Poe was "a Byron wandering in an evil world." Such claims are still common. Kenneth Silverman suggests, "Byron offered Edgar a perspective from which to evaluate his own life and legitimized his experiences as authentic for a young poet to have." And Burton Pollin claims Poe was obsessed with the British poet and felt at times that he was "an avatar of Byron."[3]

Some find Byronic influence only in Poe's early works because they take Poe at his word when he told John Allan in 1829, "I have long given up *Byron* as a model."[4] Yet Poe says this as he is begging for $100 from a guardian who shared Woodberry's low estimation of the British poet;

moreover, many of Poe's references to Byron come after 1829. Still, the claim that Poe was trying to turn himself into Byron Redux is based on evidence more often repeated than scrutinized. Some, for example, point to a supposed portrait of Poe by British artist Thomas Sully, in which Poe is posed in a Byronic way – overlooking the fact that 1) the portrait was probably never painted, and 2) the anecdote that mentions the painting also indicates the pose was Sully's idea, not Poe's. Likewise, Poe's great athletic feat, swimming six miles against the current in the James River, presumably emulated Byron's famous swim from Sestos to Abydos. But the connection was suggested by others, not Poe, who scoffed at the comparison, saying that Byron's swim was "nothing" compared to his feat.[5] It seems Poe's contemporaries were at least as active in trying to liken the two poets as Poe was to model himself on Byron. Indeed, the autobiographical note Poe wrote for Rufus Griswold, in which he falsely claimed that he had tried to join the Greek fight for independence (as Byron had earlier), is more likely an attempt to mock those who would make him into Byron than it is a case of self-fashioning. If Poe did envy Byron, perhaps it was for the latter's seemingly endless access to credit.

Instead of the unconscious result of identity formation, Poe's use of Byronic materials appears to be a very conscious and far-reaching intellectual reaction to Romantic ideas and motifs. For instance, Poe dismisses Byron in his conversation with Chivers because he saw British Romantic poetry as a record of overflowing emotion – rather than what Wordsworth claimed, an overflow recollected in tranquility (and with a philosophic mind). "You are mistaken in supposing that passion is the primum mobile of the true Poet," Poe tells Chivers, "for it is just the reverse. A pure Poem proper is one that is wholly destitute of a particle of passion." He goes on to say that a true poem "is a rhythmical creation of Beauty wholly destitute of every-thing, but that which constitutes purity, namely etheriality." Rather shocked, Chivers remarks that, if this were true, then two-thirds of Shakespeare's works would be "good for nothing." Poe rejoins, "Certainly it is good for nothing. Nothing is good for any thing except that which contains within itself the essence of its own vitality." He adds, "Otherwise it is mortal and ought to die."[6]

Poe here proposes the organic theory of poetry (and artistic production in general) most famously articulated by Samuel Taylor Coleridge, in which the work of art grows naturally out of itself and not according to a preconceived form. Some have taken this to mean that the true poem is the inevitable emanation of the poet's true self, yet Poe insists the poem is an integral aesthetic object growing as a seed grows in the ground: it is tended by the poet, perhaps, but it finds material and form entirely from within itself. For this reason, most of "Byron, Wordsworth, Coleridge, Montgomery, Southey" are not really poetry at all, and would benefit from severe pruning. Indeed, this attitude makes Poe impatient of all narrative poetry, since, he tells James Russell Lowell in a letter, it is too often interlarded with "connecting links of a narration."[7] For Poe, opera is all about arias.

Further, Poe's theory of organic unity insists that work should be short enough, as he says in "Philosophy of Composition," to be "read in one sitting." When a reader puts down the book, inevitably "the affairs of the world interfere, and every thing like totality is at once destroyed."[8] Poe's theory of unity is thus ultimately affective, focusing on the reader's experience. Poe assumes that the perception of unity is limited by the human mind, which cannot retain its integrity for very long, a phenomena evident in many of his tales.

Just as Poe's poetic theory partakes of and departs from Romantic theory, so do his works demonstrate a divided reaction to Byron's mystique. This is most evident in the tale "The Assignation," the source of which is Thomas Moore's *Letters and Journals of Lord Byron*. Some of Poe's descriptive passages clearly derive from Moore, and the central love triangle connecting a mysterious English poet, a beautiful young Italian woman named Aphrodite, and her cruel husband, Count Mentoni, are modeled on the triangle of Byron, Countess Guiccioli, and the count. Still, the tale's two outstanding events – the drowning baby and the lovers' deaths at the end – are not part of the story portrayed in Moore.[9] The two episodes, in fact, demonstrate Poe's recoil from aspects of Byronism.

Poe's story begins with the narrator hearing the "wild, hysterical, and long continued shriek" of a mother, whose baby has fallen into a Venetian canal. The narrator wants to believe the whole thing is a terrible accident, and he tries hard not to be troubled by many details. For example, he points out that the mother was not gazing "downwards upon that grave wherein her brightest hope lay buried" (that is, the canal), but at a building where the Byron character resides. The narrator assures the reader (and himself) that "at such a time as this, the eye, like a shattered mirror, multiplies the images of its sorrow, and sees in innumerable far off places the wo which is close at hand."[10] This rather far-fetched explanation is one of many such rationalizations in the tale, showing that the narrator is a precursor of Lambert Strether: he is the careful observer whose sense of decency keeps him from seeing what is obvious to everyone else. Similarly, after the Byron character bursts out of his residence to save the child, the marchesa starts trembling and blushing – "the entire woman thrills through the soul" is how the narrator characterizes it – and the narrator tries to explain this by suggesting the marchesa is embarrassed about being seen without her shoes and wrap. The narrator does not want to say that she is filled with erotic longing for her lover.

Poe's source for the near drowning incident is revealing. It probably was drawn from another part of Moore's documentary biography of Byron, the story of Margarita Cogni, a married woman who became infatuated with Byron, the kind of person we would call a stalker today. She simply showed up to live in his house, but Byron did not throw her out because of his own "indolence," as well as her "other powers of persuasion," which she exerted with "the usual tact and success of all she-things; high and low, they are all alike for that."[11] *Cosi Fan Tutte*, of course, might be said to be Byron's motto as far as most women go.

Eventually, she becomes very jealous and "ungovernable," and Byron tells her she must leave. She reacts by throwing herself in the canal. "That she intended to destroy herself, I do not believe," Byron remarks coolly; the incident only shows that "she had a devilish spirit of some sort within her." He suffers her further presence only enough for her to recover, then kicks her out for good. Byron's lack of real concern for the apparently drowning woman mirrors that of Count Mentoni's similar emotional distance when his child is submerged in the canal – he was "occasionally occupied in thrumming a guitar, and seemed *ennuyé* to the very death, as at intervals he gave directions for the recovery of his child."[12]

Reading "The Assignation" alongside the Cogni narrative, the tale takes a very dark turn typical of Poe's critique of Byron. When Margarita Cogni throws herself into the canal, she is trying to say, "I can't live without you." However, when the marchesa cares more about her lover than her child, she is saying, "I will give up everything for you." She is not moved by what the narrator assumes is the most basic impulse for all women – the maternal instinct.

One other anecdote in Moore's biography resonated with Poe. In an episode that apparently happened around that time, Byron asks Moore, "Have you any notion – but I suppose you have – of what they call the parental feeling? For myself, I have not the least."[13] Moore is quick to say that this was an example of Byron "falsifying his own character," pointing to his tender regard for his daughter, Ada, yet Poe likely read this as another attempt by Moore to whitewash the unpleasant aspects of Byron's character. "The Assignation" does indeed pay homage to the tale's romantic (small "r") aspects – the risks the lovers take for each other, the intensity of their ardor – but Poe explores aspects of such relationships that Byron and Moore seem to gloss over. Given his own feelings of being abandoned by his guardian, Poe cannot condone the neglect of a child. In the final paragraphs of "The Assignation," we find that the end of sexual freedom is death, not self-fulfillment.

Poe's other obvious borrowing from Byron's life shows a similar suspicion of physical relationships. "Byron and Miss Chaworth" describes Byron's early infatuation with Mary Chaworth, which Poe calls "boyish poet-love." It is the "human sentiment which most nearly realizes our dreams of the chastened voluptuousness of heaven," standing in the stark contrast to the unchastened (and unchaste) voluptuousness of "The Assignation."[14] Poe describes the relationship as "romantic, shadowy, and imaginative" and, implicitly, unconsummated – and more beautiful because of this. Byron's poems about the relationship are conspicuous for their "spiritual tenderness and purity" as opposed to the "gross earthliness" of Byron's other love poetry. Love is beautiful, apparently, so long as it is unconnected to flesh.

For this reason, Poe's general approach to beautiful female flesh is to idealize it beyond recognition, a technique he shares with his British precursor. The main figure in Byron's "She Walks in Beauty," to take just one example, is praised for her night-like walking, her "nameless grace," her raven tresses, and more generally her purity and innocence. She does not need to talk since her cheeks and brow are "eloquent" (lines 8–9). Apart from a general notion that she has dark hair and a light complexion, there is no description of her beauty. Poe's poems about female beauty likewise include very little physical description. Although in "The Philosophy of Composition," Poe tells us "The Raven" is about the death of a beautiful maiden, the only trace of her appearance in the poem is the speaker's assertion that Lenore was a "rare and radiant maiden" (line 11). Likewise, in "To Helen," the title character has "hyacinth hair," a "classic face," and somehow embodies Greek glory and Roman grandeur. The description is so idealized that it really cannot be called a visual image – it is really just the idea of beauty.

Manfred is a key text for understanding both Byron and Poe's approach to women. Thinking of Astarte, Manfred says, "She was like me in lineaments; her eyes / Her hair, her features, all to the very tone / Even of her voice" (II.105–7). Astarte is in fact just an improved female version of Manfred, with his same Faustian thirst for knowledge tempered by Christian virtues. Byron's friend Percy Shelley depicts a similar lover in *Alastor*. The poem's hero spurns the silent devotion of an "Arab maiden" in order to pursue the "veiled maid" of his imaginings, who is only described as having a voice "like the voice of his own soul" (line 129, 151–2). She is a female version of him. Tragically, Alastor can only join with the veiled maid in his dreams and eventually dies in futile pursuit. Similarly, after Manfred conjures up Astarte from the dead, he does not get a flesh and blood paramour, just a phantom who tells him he will die the next day, bidding farewell without giving him either forgiveness or the simple assurance that she loves him.

In these and other stories, it seems that Romantic poets stumbled upon a key feminist observation unaware that they had done any such thing. Men in these stories fall in love not with actual people but projections of their imagination. Like Narcissus, they adore reflections of themselves. Even in stories in which the beloved is not a female version of the male, there is a good deal of projection in lieu of observation. For example, in Keats' "La Belle Dame Sans Merci," the lonely and palely loitering knight meets a beautiful fairy and romps around with her all day, certain that she loves him as much as he loves her. Unfortunately, she speaks only a strange fairy language, so her apparent statement, "I love thee true" (line 337) is really just his uncertain interpretation. When she bursts out crying a stanza later, the speaker's reaction is to kiss her four times. With communication like this, is it any wonder he ends up sad and alone? He translates her ambiguous sounds into a straightforward declaration of love and ends up desolated when it turns out the words did not mean what he thought they meant.

While British poets tended to leave open the question of whether we love our illusions or our fellow humans, Poe offers a clearer answer. In "The Oval Portrait," for instance, an artist is married to a "maiden of the rarest beauty," yet he neglects her in order to depict her in paint. She dies the moment the painting is complete, only to have her husband remark of his own creation, "This is indeed *Life* itself!" Turning to his wife's corpse, he adds, "*She was dead.*"[15]

For Poe and the British Romantics, this problem of understanding women as embodiments of their own ideas is compounded by the fact that they have trouble coming to grips with themselves. Byron generally depicts the self in the Hegelian state of becoming. In *Childe Harold's Pilgrimmage*, the speaker asks, "What am I?" only to answer his own question with one word: "Nothing." Yet this stance is not nihilistic since it anticipates the existential idea that the self and meaning must be created through action. By creating – and by this the speaker seems to mean both artistic creation and the imaginative act of making something out of experience (that is, interpreting it meaningfully) – we can "live" and become a "being more intense" (3.6.1–5.)

Byron here posits a malleable self subject to potentially infinite expansion, yet this concept has a Janus face. The speaker tells us not that he has been created by experience so much as he has been created by his *reaction* to experiences. Put another way, he creates a self by rebelling against that which society and life seems dedicated to reducing him to. Finding himself close to being absorbed into the "agony and strife" of human existence only spurs the speaker to mount again on fresh wings to soar above it all, "spurning the clay-cold bonds" of earthly, material existence (3.73.3–9), imagining a day when his mind might be totally freed from "carnal life" (3.74.3). But such is a futile hope, because leaving carnality behind leaves him subject to his own mind. "I *have* thought / Too long and darkly," the speaker remarks, "till my mind became / In its own eddy, boiling and o'erwrought" (3.7.1–3). The spectacle of a speaker lost in confusing convolutions of his own thought processes is reminiscent of Coleridge and Thomas De Quincey, and anticipates contemporary conceptual frameworks for clinical depression.

Thus, when Byron's speakers reject physical existence, they find themselves caught in the downward tending mazes of their own minds. They live a dialectic in which every gesture toward transcendence hearkens to its opposite, dissolution. The famous description of Napoleon as a man whose "spirit" is "antithetically mixed" (3.36.2) is extended by the speaker of *Don Juan* to all humanity: "flesh is formed of fiery dust" (II.212), the speaker tells us ruefully. We are part divine spark, part clay – or perhaps, part burning, part already burnt out.

This antithetical mix is very much in evidence in *Manfred*. The fiery, spiritual side of his nature makes him scorn the sorts of things, such as earthly power, that might suffice a lesser man, yet his clay demands the sorts of things ethereal beings do not need – an actual embrace with his beloved, assurance of love, and forgiveness for earthly failings. Unfortunately, the world of Manfred operates on binaries, and the spirit world can offer only intellectual benefits, the material world only material ones, and Manfred needs a combination of both. He rejects the ethereal offers of the various spirits and the joys of the simple earthly life offered by the chamois hunter. Manfred's antithetical nature suits him neither for this world nor the next, keeping him on the Faustian task of endless questing, ironically scouring the empyrean to satisfy his very human need for forgiveness and love. A strong desire for affection from a dead loved one makes no rational sense, of course, but it makes a great deal of psychological sense, and many a person has gone into therapy to deal with these feelings.

Thus Byron portrays the individual mind as perpetually upsetting its own ease, and this drama appears time and again in Poe's works. Poe had good reason to connect this notion of the mind against itself to Byron. In "An Unwritten Drama of Lord Byron," the sketch that inspired "William Wilson," Washington Irving identifies the drama's doppelganger as "an allegorical being, the personification of conscience," which the second William Wilson represents in Poe's story.[16] Poe's narrator scorns the double that literalizes the speaker's moral conscience. As the speaker becomes dissolute, drinking too much and cheating at cards, his double more and more asserts himself, albeit speaking in a whisper. This secret voice that only the narrator can hear is an obvious symbol of conscience, yet the speaker conceptualizes it as something alien and destructive to the self. In the end, the narrator confronts his nemesis and runs him through with a sword. In his dying breath, the second William Wilson tells the first that he has killed himself.

This disassociation of the divisions within the self is evident in many of Poe's stories. While Byron's characters recognize the deep divisions within themselves, Poe's main characters see their other half as outside themselves, as a treacherous nemesis. Their confessions release the tensions building inside, but do not otherwise bring relief – the narrator of "The Imp of the Perverse," for instance, remarks that confessing has "consigned me to the hangman and to hell."[17] A more conventionally spiritual person might find confession a step toward heaven.

This unacknowledged division is evident even for one of Poe's most self-possessed narrators, Montressor of "The Cask of Amontillado." Like the speaker of "The Tell-Tale Heart," he assumes, unrealistically, that his reader will agree that his adversary's provocations are an adequate reason to kill. Without an interlocutor to object, he leads Fortunato to his death in the catacombs. Shortly before placing the last stone that will entomb his enemy, Montressor remarks, "My heart grew sick – on account of the dampness of the catacombs."[18] The pang of conscience is projected outside the self, and the speaker implicitly tells himself that as soon as he leaves the dank crypts, the heartsick feeling will dissipate. The fact that he feels compelled to tell a story now fifty years old suggests that it has not.

Thus Poe's narrators have divided consciousness at least as antithetically mixed as Byron's Napoleon. There is a part of the self that, if expressed, means death and dissolution to the other part, and the speaker's only antidote is to keep it bottled up. The inability to keep that other self from bubbling up leads to the dissolution of such characters as Roderick Usher and the narrator of "The Raven," who, at the poem's end, shrieks at the bird and contemplates his own soul that, he says, will never be lifted.

In all, Poe went much further than Byron, more seriously considering the psychological implications of Byronic solipsism. Simply put, Byron opened the door but only peeked in, while Poe went in to stay. Byron, finally, was trying to explore the possibilities of the infinite expansion of consciousness; Poe, on the other hand, says it is all about the consequences.

NOTES

1. T. H. Chivers, *Life of Poe*, ed. Richard Beale Davis (New York: Dutton, 1952), 29; Edgar Allan Poe, *The Collected Works of Edgar Allan Poe*, ed. Thomas Ollive Mabbott, 3 vols. (Cambridge, MA: Belknap Press, 1969–78), vol. i, passim; For additional Byron references, see Katarina Bachinger, *The Multi-Man Genre and Poe's Byrons* (Salzburg: Institut fur Anglistik und Amerikanistik, 1987).
2. Arthur Hobson Quinn, *Edgar Allan Poe: A Critical Biography* (New York: Appleton-Century, 1941), 104.
3. George E. Woodberry, *Edgar Allan Poe* (Boston: Houghton Mifflin, 1885), 33; Edgar Allan Poe, *Nouvelles Histoires Extraordinaires*, trans. Charles Baudelaire (Paris: Michel Lévy Frérés, 1857), viii; Kenneth Silverman, *Edgar A. Poe: A Mournful and Never-Ending Remembrance* (New York: Harper Collins, 1991), 41; Burton R. Pollin, *Discoveries in Poe* (Notre Dame: University of Notre Dame Press, 1970), 95.
4. Poe to John Allan, May 29, 1829, *The Collected Letters of Edgar Allan Poe*, ed. John Ward Ostrom, Burton R. Pollin, and Jeffrey A. Savoye, 2 vols. (New York: Gordian, 2008), vol. i, 30.
5. Poe to Thomas W. White, April 30, 1835, *Collected Letters*, vol. i, 84.
6. Chivers, *Life of Poe*, 48.
7. Poe to James Russell Lowell, October 19, 1843, *Collected Letters*, vol. i, 413.
8. Edgar Allan Poe, *Essays and Reviews*, ed. G. R. Thompson (New York: Library of America, 1984), 15.
9. Richard P. Benton, "Is Poe's 'The Assignation' a Hoax?" *Nineteenth-Century Literature* 18 (1963), 193–7.
10. Poe, *Collected Works*, vol. ii, 151–3.
11. Thomas Moore, *Letters and Journals of Lord Byron, with Notices of His Life*, 6 vols. (London: John Murray, 1854), vol. iv, 116.
12. Poe, *Collected Works*, vol. ii, 153.
13. Moore, *Letters*, vol. iv, 242.
14. Poe, *Collected Works*, vol. iii, 1122.
15. Ibid., vol. ii, 664–6.
16. Washington Irving, "An Unwritten Drama of Lord Byron," *The Gift: A Christmas and New Year's Present for 1836* (Philadelphia: E. L. Carey and A. Hart, 1835), 169.
17. Poe, *Collected Works*, vol. iii, 859.
18. Ibid., vol. iii, 1263.

CHAPTER 26

Folk Narrative

Katherine Kim

Though literary scholars have uncovered numerous literary sources of inspiration for Edgar Allan Poe's poetry and fiction, relatively little has been published regarding the extent to which folklore appears in his work. But Poe made significant use of folk materials in his writings. Folklore not only gave him a rich set of sources, it also helped him take advantage of his readers' familiarity with different forms of traditional narrative: legends, tall tales, folktales, fairy tales. In the process, Poe created original variations using traditional themes, plots, and motifs. His work contributes significantly to the rich corpus of appropriated folklore in American antebellum literature.

Put simply, legend is folk history. In other words, legends are traditional narratives considered true within the folk groups in which they are told.[1] Legends inspired many nineteenth-century American writers, including Nathaniel Hawthorne, Washington Irving, Herman Melville, and Edgar Allan Poe. Melville, for one, has received much critical attention regarding his use of folklore, especially legends related to sailing and sea life.[2] Though Poe did not write as extensively on nautical matters as Melville, he did appreciate one of the most prominent nautical legends of the day, the Flying Dutchman (motif E511). Reviewing Captain Frederick Marryat's *The Phantom Ship*, Poe observed that the story of the Flying Dutchman possesses "all the rich *materiel* which a vigorous imagination could desire."[3] According to one well-known version of the Flying Dutchman legend, the devil condemns the ship to sail forever around the Cape of Good Hope because its captain (named Vanderdecken in many accounts) "swore a blasphemous oath that he would round the Cape if it took him till Doomsday."[4] The Flying Dutchman, in turn, would doom any vessel that approached it.

Poe took inspiration from the Flying Dutchman legend, which he employed in both "Manuscript Found in a Bottle" (1833) and *The Narrative of Arthur Gordon Pym of Nantucket* (1838). In the earlier work, the nameless narrator sights an enormous and antiquated vessel just before his own ship sinks into turbulent and mysterious waters. The sudden appearance of the eerie vessel aligns it with the Flying Dutchman, which, according to legend, would appear prior to the sinking of a vessel that spotted it.[5] In Poe's tale, the narrator is hurled onto this strange craft, saving his life for the present. He soon discovers that an otherworldly crew operates the ship. The crew members glide "to and fro like the ghosts of buried centuries; their eyes have an eager and uneasy meaning." The narrator later sees the ship's Vanderdecken-like captain in a cabin "thickly strewn with strange, iron-clasped folios, and mouldering instruments of science, and obsolete long-forgotten charts." Like his spectral sailors, the captain does not notice the narrator, who moves freely about the ship. In contrast, the narrator examines the captain, who evokes a peculiar sense of timelessness and age: "His forehead, although little wrinkled, seems to bear upon it the stamp of a myriad of years." The outdated instruments and charts, along with the sense of the captain's extreme age, emphasize the antiquity of the beings and objects aboard. The narrator constructs a haunting vision of a captain futilely attempting to conclude his voyage: "His head was bowed down upon his hands, and he pored, with a fiery unquiet eye, over a paper which I took to be a commission, and which, at all events, bore the signature of a monarch. He muttered to himself... some low peevish syllables of a foreign tongue."[6] The foreign words mark the captain as not of English origin (though not necessarily from Holland) while his bowed head and "unquiet eye" reflect desperation and despondency due to his unending voyage.

Poe's tale further hints at the Flying Dutchman legend as the narrator recalls "an old weather-beaten Dutch navigator" and his apothegm: "As sure as there is a sea where the ship itself will grow in bulk like the living body of the seaman." Here, Poe not only inserts wordplay regarding a "Dutch man," but he also links the physicality of the ship to sailors' bodies. The narrator remembers the Dutch navigator and his apothegm when describing the "distended" look of the mysterious ship's planks, creating the sense that the ship paranormally expands with time. Attempting to identify the ship, the narrator seems haunted by ghostly memories: "There will occasionally flash across my mind a sensation of familiar things, and there is always mixed up with such indistinct shadows of recollection, an unaccountable memory of old foreign chronicles and ages long ago."[7] Why doesn't the narrator name the ship? Is he unable to solve its mystery, or does his fear of the possible truth – that the ship is indeed the legendary Flying Dutchman – somehow prevent him from verbalizing this frightful prospect? In either case, by describing a strange, antiquated ship manned by ghostly sailors and captained by an old man futilely attempting to reach port, Poe guides readers to connect his story with the Flying Dutchman while formulating a distinctive rendition of the cursed vessel's legend. In utilizing the Flying Dutchman to create "Manuscript Found in a Bottle," Poe disseminates the legend even as he expands its creative potential.

Poe also used the Flying Dutchman for inspiration in *The Narrative of Arthur Gordon Pym*. In chapter 10, Pym and three other shipwreck survivors attempt to hail an erratically sailing vessel "of a Dutch build."[8] They see from a distance three men "whom by their dress we took to be Hollanders." But instead of welcome aid or ghostly seamen sailing the ship as in "Manuscript Found in a Bottle," Pym and his companions eventually drift close enough to the vessel to witness perhaps "thirty human bodies...in the last and most loathsome state of putrefaction!"[9] In this imaginative application of the Flying Dutchman, according to Richard Kopley, Poe employs a lesser known version of the legend involving yellow fever.[10] Poe thus appears to have known multiple versions of the Flying Dutchman legend. In *Pym*, the dead seafaring Hollanders (one whom Pym even mistakes as interestedly staring at him and his companions) force the living to confront human mortality face to face. But instead of recoiling, the shipwreck survivors desperately shout to the dead, begging "that those silent and disgusting images...would receive us among their goodly company!"[11] Though it lacks the supernatural aspects of many Flying Dutchman tales, Poe's brief account of this vessel depicts a ship fated to sail for all eternity. Making the encounter even more horrifying, Poe then suggests that the living desire the company and aid of the dead and decaying seafarers.

In addition to the Flying Dutchman legend, Poe's seafaring novel employs lore regarding sea burial and haunting. Arthur Gordon Pym consciously takes advantage of the powerful folk beliefs among the superstitious sailors aboard the *Grampus* to survive a mutiny. Pym's friend, Augustus Barnard, and seaman Dirk Peters – himself a variation of an emerging type of American folk hero, the mountain man – dress Pym, so far an unnoticed stowaway, as the ghost of Hartman Rogers, a sailor who had died aboard the *Grampus*, possibly poisoned by the first mate, but who had not been properly interred. Upon seeing the corpse, the first mate, "being either touched with remorse for his crime or struck with terror at so horrible a sight, ordered the men to sew the body up in its hammock, and allow it the usual rites of sea-burial." Pym continues to explain that a violent storm prevents the crew from completing the rites, leaving the corpse "washed into the larboard scuppers...floundering about with the furious lurches of the brig."[12]

Poe's use of folk motifs and beliefs regarding improper burial and haunting is unsurprising; Poe employs such concepts in a number of works, such as "The Premature Burial" (1844), which not only references interment in its title, but also describes multiple tales and supposedly true accounts of live burial. In the case of sea burials, folk tradition and superstition dictate that a sailor who dies at sea receive a proper interment and burial ceremony to ensure that the vessel is not cursed with bad luck or the dead's returning ghost. Common tradition held that after wrapping and sewing a sailor's corpse into his hammock, the final stitch should be run through the corpse's nose to assure not only that the sailor's ghost did not return to haunt the ship, but also that the sailor was truly dead and the shroud would remain attached to the corpse once dropped into the water; proper interment of a sailor's corpse was imbued with both intense superstitions and practical purposes.[13] Having Pym successfully frighten the mutineers by pretending to be Hartman Rogers' ghost, Poe illustrates the potency of folkloric mandates and superstitious beliefs to his readers.

If legends are folk history, tales are folk fiction. The tall tale, one particular brand of folktale, assumes the guise of truth but contains incredible, unbelievable, and/or exaggerated elements. Within the folk groups in which they are told, the tall tale effectively determines group membership. Those who recognize the fantastic elements as fiction but winkingly go along with the tale rightfully belong to the group. Those who cannot discern truth from fiction do not. Tall tales permeate the mythos of the American frontier and the construction of the American identity through extraordinary characters like Davy Crockett, Johnny Appleseed, and Paul Bunyan.

While American folklore is rife with tall tales regarding nation-building figures, Poe fashioned a short story reminiscent of a tall tale – with a twist: the literal deconstruction of Brevet Brigadier-General John A. B. C. Smith in "The Man That Was Used Up" (1839). In this satiric work, the narrator attempts to ascertain more about the "remarkable" Smith, unsuccessfully asking a number of acquaintances about the brave, handsome, seemingly perfect man. Ironically, the narrator repeatedly calls Smith "remarkable" even though the narrator's trouble throughout the story is that he is not "able" to "remark" on what is remarkable about Smith. Acquaintances praise Smith's career and valor when the narrator asks about Smith, yet their remarks regarding the military hero who routinely risked his life fighting for his country are always cut short by interruptions such as loud theater music or a sudden change in conversation; their remarks are continuously interrupted whenever they are about to finish the phrase, "He's the man . . ."

The remarkable thing about Smith that the narrator cannot fully comprehend or articulate ("the odd air of *je ne sais quoi*") is finally clarified by the general himself once the narrator visits him. The narrator learns that Smith lost limbs, scalp, teeth, an eye, his tongue, and various other body parts throughout his military career. Poe was indebted to folk tradition for the details of his story.[14] He echoes a tall tale about a similarly debilitated Indian fighter. Confronted by hostile Indians, the man pulled out his false teeth, unstrapped his cork leg, and seemed about to unscrew his head. In doing so, he informed the Indians that he would dismember them similarly (motif K547.2).

In "The Man That Was Used Up," General Smith only appears physically "whole" once he is systematically assembled using artificial replacement parts. What further shocks the narrator about this revelation is that Smith recommends the specific makers of his artificial body parts to the narrator even though the narrator does not need or desire replacement parts. The violence of the country's nation building, according to Gerald Kennedy, is brutally displaced onto the patriotic military man's body.[15] Instead of a tall tale hero helping to construct and defend the nation, the nation's construction and defense lead to a hero's deconstruction.

Other folktales influenced Poe's fiction, as well. "The Murders in the Rue Morgue" (1841), the first modern detective story, is a redaction of a traditional narrative about an annoyingly imitative monkey.[16] In this folktale, which Charles Clay Doyle traces back to sixteenth-century France (though it could be older), the owner becomes frustrated at his monkey's constant imitations of him. So one day, the owner shaves himself and quickly draws the back of his razor across his throat in front of the watching monkey. Once the owner leaves, the monkey attempts to imitate its owner. However, the monkey does not turn the blade over before jerking it across its throat, consequently leading to unintentional suicide (motif J2413.4.3). Though Doyle does not locate versions of this folktale from Poe's day, it circulated in many different versions during the late eighteenth and nineteenth centuries. *The Cabinet of Momus*, a collection of English and Scottish stories, contains the very similar story, "The Monkey, Who Shaved Himself and His Friends."[17] Furthermore, Lawrence Levine relates an almost identical story known throughout the nineteenth-century American South entitled "Fatal Imitation."[18]

Such tales share striking similarities with the mystery Dupin correctly deduces in "The Murders in the Rue Morgue," in which an escaped "Ourang-Outang" at first imitates its owner's shaving on itself, and then leaps into Madame L'Espanaye's home and attempts to shave her, brandishing the razor "in imitation of the motions of a barber."[19] The frightened screaming of Madame L'Espanaye and her daughter enrages the primate, who then brutally kills both women in a mad frenzy. Poe transforms a folk narrative's monkey's suicide into an unintended and gory double homicide. Poe eliminates any callousness from the creature's owner; the orangutan's owner never means for harm to come to his wild pet or anyone else. Although Poe produces a gorier version of the imitative monkey story than the folk narrative, he relieves the pet owner of evil intent. Thus, the horrifying deeds in this tale are not due to issues that frequently occur in other Poe stories, such as vengeance, mania, or the supernatural. Instead, the gruesome murders are unfortunate, almost unbelievable accidents.

By placing the events of "The Murders in the Rue Morgue" in the urban setting of Paris, Poe can be interpreted as morphing a blade-wielding monkey tale into an early form of contemporary urban legend. This relatively modern form of legend exhibits the vitality of folklore in modern times, and Poe's story contains the horror, mystery, and strangeness of most urban legends. In addition, this short story reflects a possibility of truth also present in many urban legends since it possesses a complete and logical, though extraordinary, explanation of the murders.[20] Poe's tale further resembles urban legend through the choice of narrator. Similar to the common claim that the incidents of an urban legend happened to "a friend of a friend," "The Murders in the Rue Morgue" is narrated not by Dupin, but by an unnamed friend who conveniently resides temporarily with Dupin at the time of the murders. Consequently the reader, like the audience of an urban legend, is denied direct access to the main people in the story's events due to the anonymity of the narrator and the narrator relating a story of a friend. Perhaps, then, Poe can be considered not only the inventor of the modern detective story, but also an early literary raconteur of what is today widely known as the urban legend.

The fairy tale is yet another form of folklore Poe incorporates into a number of his works. Despite its name, a fairy tale need not contain fairies. This form of folk narrative often avoids mention of specifically delineated times (thus the common opening formula of the fairy tale: "Once upon a time"). It also avoids naming specific places and characters, instead utilizing generic terms: a castle, the woods, the king, the princess. In "Hop-Frog" (1849), Poe uses the conventions of the fairy tale, complete with an unnamed king in an unidentified land, a royal court, and a lavish masquerade. Furthermore, "Hop-Frog" uses the outer appearances of the characters to reflect inner attributes: another recurrent device in fairy tales.[21] Some commentators have identified the fairy tale qualities of "Hop-Frog," in which the deformed dwarf court jester exacts revenge against his cruel master, the king, by fooling and brutally murdering him and his seven sycophant ministers. Stuart Levine, for one, connects the gruesomeness in "Hop-Frog" to the violence characteristic of European fairy tales prior to the mid-nineteenth century, proposing that Poe may have employed features like those in the "thoroughly ghoulish" fairy tales published by Jakob and Wilhelm Grimm in "Hop-Frog."[22] Indeed, some of the Grimms' tales, such as their rendition of the Cinderella-like "Thousandfurs" in which a princess is lusted for by her own father, do seem quite grisly and horrible.[23]

Levine also likens the conclusion of "Hop-Frog" to the formulaic "they lived happily ever after" ending: "It is supposed that Trippetta, stationed on the roof of the saloon, had been the accomplice of her friend in his fiery revenge, and that, together, they effected their escape to their own country: for neither was seen again."[24] Although the premeditated homicidal ending of "Hop-Frog" may appear to add a gothic twist to a tale that uses fairy tale features, the ending is in fact very much like those of traditional European fairy tales. For example, the ending to one of the Grimms' versions of "Snow White" depicts the heroine's evil stepmother forced to dance in heated iron shoes at Snow White's wedding until she dies.[25] However, in using first person omniscient narration for "Hop-Frog," Poe breaks from the more traditional fairy tale use of a third person (many times omniscient) narrator, creating a mutated, hybrid form of fairy tale and first person narrated short story. Poe's application of fairy tale tropes and features in "Hop-Frog" relies upon his reader's familiarity with fairy tales; instead of directly drawing attention to the genre via references to fairies (as he does with "Fairy-Land" [1829] and "The Island of the Fay" [1841]), Poe evokes such comparisons from within the reader. Consequently the reader, drawing on prior knowledge of fairy tales, is impelled to notice not only the differences, but also the eerily close similarities between fairy tales and Poe's macabre story of an evil king and the deadly repercussions for his cruelty.

In *Form and Fable in American Fiction*, Daniel Hoffman describes the legend of Sam Patch, an early nineteenth-century Rhode Island textile worker who gained local fame through spectacular dives into rivers and waterfalls. Sam Patch's final, unsuccessful plunge down the Falls of Genesee became the stuff of legends; because his body did not surface for months after his leap, imaginative stories about him began to spread: "He had jumped through the bowels of the world and turned up alive in the South Seas. He was also knocking about the American West, as alleged by many travelers. While some might scoff, none could deny that he had been on the stage of many a theatre."[26] Stories regarding Sam Patch transformed the former textile worker and diver into a local legend. Edgar Allan Poe has himself become a legendary (albeit tragic) figure in American lore. In part thanks to his mysterious death and Rufus Griswold's obituary notice, which bolstered the perception of Poe as an unsociable, plagiarizing alcoholic, the Poe of popular culture sometimes transforms into larger than life versions of the haunted lover, the deranged addict, and the tortured artist. Poe appropriated folklore for his writings, and American lore has returned the favor by immortalizing Poe in the nation's popular and literary culture.

NOTES

1. For basic definitions of folklore terms, see *The Funk and Wagnalls Standard Dictionary of Folklore, Mythology, and Legend*, ed. Maria Leach (New York: Funk and Wagnalls, 1949). For more on the difficulty of defining folklore genres and terms, see *Folklore Genres*, ed. Dan Ben-Amos (Austin: University of Texas Press, 1976).

2. Kevin J. Hayes, *Melville's Folk Roots* (Kent, OH: Kent State University Press, 1999); Daniel Hoffman, *Form and Fable in American Fiction* (New York: Oxford University Press, 1961). A good starting point for approaching the use of folk motifs in literature is Stith Thompson, *Motif-Index of Folk-Literature: A Classification of Narrative Elements in Folktales, Ballads, Myths, Fables, Mediaeval Romances, Exempla, Fabliaux, Jest-Books, and Local Legends*, rev. ed., 6 vols. (Bloomington: Indiana University Press, 1955–8). Motif numbers are cited parenthetically within the text of this chapter.

3. [Edgar Allan Poe], review of Frederick Marryat, *The Phantom Ship*, *Burton's Gentleman's Magazine* 4 (1839), 358–9.

4. Willard Hallam Bonner, "The Flying Dutchman of the Western World," *Journal of American Folklore* 59 (1946), 283.

5. Edgar Allan Poe, *The Short Fiction of Edgar Allan Poe*, ed. Stuart Levine and Susan Levine (1976; reprinted, Urbana: University of Illinois Press, 1990), 631.

6. Edgar Allan Poe, *The Collected Works of Edgar Allan Poe*, ed. Thomas Ollive Mabbott, 3 vols. (Cambridge, MA: Belknap Press, 1969–78), vol. ii, 144.

7. Poe, *Collected Works*, vol. ii, 142.

8. Edgar Allan Poe, *Poetry and Tales*, ed. Patrick F. Quinn (New York: Library of America, 1984), 1084.

9. Poe, *Poetry and Tales*, 1086.

10. Richard Kopley, "Explanatory Notes," in *The Narrative of Arthur Gordon Pym of Nantucket* (New York: Penguin, 1999), 229.

11. Poe, *Poetry and Tales*, 1086.

12. Poe, *Poetry and Tales*, 1067.

13. Hayes, *Melville's Folk Roots*, 45–6.

14. Richard Dorson, *American Folklore* (Chicago: University of Chicago Press, 1959), 21; Elmer R. Pry, "A Folklore Source for 'The Man That Was Used Up,'" *Poe Studies* 8 (1975), 46.

15. J. Gerald Kennedy, "'A Mania for Composition': Poe's Annus Mirabilis and the Violence of Nation-Building," *American Literary History*, 17 (2005), 18.

16. Charles Clay Doyle, "The Imitating Monkey: A Folktale Motif in Poe," *North Carolina Folklore Journal* 23 (1975), 89–91.

17. Tim Broadgrin, pseud., *The Cabinet of Momus, and Caledonian Humorist; Being a Collection of the Most Entertaining English and Scotch Stories* (London: G. Auld, 1786).

18. Lawrence W. Levine, *Black Culture and Black Consciousness: Afro-American Folk Thought From Slavery To Freedom* (New York: Oxford University Press, 1977), 96–7.

19. Poe, *Collected Works*, vol. ii, 572.

20. For a review of debates regarding the naming and categorizing of stories as urban legends, see Timothy R. Tangherlini, "'It Happened Not Too Far from Here...': A Survey of Legend Theory and Characterization," *Western Folklore* 49 (1990), 381–3.

21. For a fairy tale containing all these attributes that was well known by the nineteenth century, see "Beauty and the Beast," such as the seminal eighteenth-century version by Jeanne-Marie Leprince de Beaumont in *The Classic Fairy Tales*, ed. Maria Tatar (New York: Norton, 1999).

22. Stuart Levine, *Edgar Poe: Seer and Craftsman* (DeLand, FL: Everett / Edwards, 1972), 74.

23. Jakob Ludwig Karl Grimm and Wilhelm Karl Grimm, *Grimms' Tales For Young and Old: The Complete Stories*, trans. Ralph Manheim (New York: Doubleday, 1977), 245–9.

24. Poe, *Collected Works*, vol. iii, 1354.

25. *Grimms' Tales*, 184–91.

26. Hoffman, *Form and Fable*, 55.

CHAPTER 27

Transcendentalism

Heidi Silcox

In 1844, Poe told his friend Thomas Holley Chivers: "You mistake me in supposing I dislike the transcendentalists – it is only the pretenders and sophists among them."[1] There is, however, good reason to believe that Poe disdained the New England Transcendentalists, especially in light of his public declarations about notable figures within the movement. For example, Poe announced that he had no patience with Ralph Waldo Emerson.[2] Furthermore, he openly mocks Coleridge, Kant, Carlyle, and Emerson in "Never Bet the Devil Your Head," and the Psyche Zenobia confesses confusion as to whether Kant is spelled with a "C" or a "K."[3] Poe's contrasting sentiments have sparked debate concerning the nature of the author's relationship to the most influential intellectual movement of his day. The research has chronicled Poe's vitriol, his motivations, and his influences in this notorious literary battle. Ottavio Casale ultimately finds Poe both repulsed and attracted to the movement.[4] Casale's thesis is compelling but not exhaustive. The specific areas of contention between Poe and the Transcendentalists within the larger philosophic debates have yet to be examined.

While Poe may have adopted a conciliatory attitude at times, he did not consider himself a Transcendentalist, nor was he sympathetic to the movement's major views. In the same letter to Chivers, Poe maintains, "My own faith is indeed my own." Here, Poe professes his independence from other contemporary philosophical movements. This desire to separate himself from other theorists may explain Poe's negative reaction to the major figures within Transcendentalism. It was Transcendentalism's most prolific spokesperson, Ralph Waldo Emerson, who articulated the movement's doctrines on epistemology, metaphysics, and aesthetics. Poe also delineated his distinct philosophical commitments on these topics. An analysis reveals that Poe and Emerson held several minor views in common. These two men also maintained distinctive positions on major tenets within these areas of philosophic inquiry.

Poe's writings reveal an interest in the nature of human knowledge, the object of concern in epistemology. His characters Morella and Ligeia are exceedingly intelligent and well read. Ligeia's "reading alone, rendered vividly luminous the many mysteries of the *transcendentalism* in which we were immersed."[5] Similarly, the narrator of "Morella" notes that his wife's "erudition was profound." She reads Fichte, the Pythagoreans, Schelling, and Locke.[6] The reading material with which Morella engages is not accidental.

The theories of Friedrich Wilhelm Joseph von Schelling and Johann Gottlieb Fichte supplied much of the philosophical groundwork for the New England Transcendentalists. One contemporary noticed that the ideas of these philosophers influenced Ralph Waldo Emerson greatly.[7] Idealists sought the basis of all human knowledge, which they thought logic could ultimately reveal. Accordingly, those who engage in dialectic reasoning eventually discover such a foundation of knowledge. The dialectical system involves the discord between a thesis and antithesis, which, in turn, produces a synthesis of ideas. The resulting synthesis serves as the thesis in a further dialectic scheme. Additionally, Schelling postulated that those who engage in dialectic reasoning will soon realize that the outside world and the individual thinking mind are both manifestations of one divine principle.[8]

Immanuel Kant supplied Emerson with the term *Transcendentalism*, which has an epistemological context. The label refers to a class of ideas that are known, not by experience, but by intuition. Emerson deduced that "whatever belongs to the class of intuitive thought, is popularly called at the present day, *Transcendental*."[9] In essence, Transcendentalism focuses on the primacy of *a priori*, as opposed to *a posteriori*, knowledge. Kant's theories were the product of debate within epistemology. He reacted negatively to John Locke's belief that the human mind is a *tabula rasa*, or blank slate. Essentially, Locke questioned the existence of innate ideas. He "insisted that there was nothing in the intellect which was not previously in the experience of the senses."[10]

In "Nature," Emerson advocates German Idealism to an American audience. He writes, "Idealism acquaints us with the total disparity between the evidence of our own being, and the evidence of the world's being. The one is perfect; the other, incapable of any assurance; the mind is a part of the nature of things; the world is a divine dream."[11] According to Emerson, human beings can have certain and "stable" knowledge of their own existence. Conversely, God imparts knowledge of the outside world to humans, and so nature is a remoter, and hence, inferior incarnation of the divine. Knowledge of the outside world is simply not as reliable as the products of one's intuition. People are often deceived by appearances. This happens because they only see the world in small fragments. Generally, humans are incapable of observing the world completely; only a minority is capable of taking in the world as a whole. There are other reasons why people do not perceive the world accurately. For example, our various moods taint our perceptions of things.

Skepticism does not prevail in Transcendentalist philosophy because, as Emerson explains, there are true laws of nature that humans can know. Emerson postulates, "The soul is the perceiver and revealer of truth. We know truth when we see it, let sceptic and scoffer say what they choose."[12] Here, Emerson admits that human beings are fallible, but he denies that truth is inaccessible. There are absolute truths, which people can know due to the special nature of the soul. In essence, when a person perceives a natural law, such as justice or the soul's immortality, a portion of the divine passes through humans, revealing the essential truth of the idea. Consequently, the intuitive faculty, which is divinely inspired, is a reliable means of knowledge.

Conversely, Edgar Allan Poe held a unique theory of knowledge that denies provable truths, yet advances a type of epistemological faith. Unlike his Transcendentalist contemporaries, Poe does not subscribe to a grand narrative that explains an epistemological teleology. The speaker of "A Dream within a Dream" questions the Transcendentalist notion that persons, things, actions, and events preexist the mind of God. The speaker of the poem asks:

> Is *all* that we see or seem
> But a dream within a dream?[13]

Clearly, the dictates of Idealism held little sway for Poe, who believed that everything had a material basis, even God.[14]

According to Poe, human beings, like God, are material, but human existence is made of baser components than that which constitutes divine essence. Because of their crude natures, people are fallible. Poe often depicts the unreliability of human perception in his works. For example, the narrator of "Ligeia" is affected by opium when he observes his dead wife comes back to life. Consequently, the reader cannot tell whether the narrator's account is reliable or if he experiences a drug-induced delusion. Furthermore, in *The Narrative of Arthur Gordon Pym*, the narrator notes the fallibility of the human memory when he says, "I feared I should not be able to write, from mere memory, a statement so minute and connected as to have the *appearance* of that truth it would really possess, barring only the natural and unavoidable exaggeration to which all of us are prone when detailing events which have had powerful influence in exciting the imaginative faculties."[15] Sometimes, events stimulate the imagination into action, thereby making a retelling problematic. Like his Transcendentalist contemporaries, Poe observed that knowledge is largely unreliable. Unlike Emerson, however, Poe found no comfort in the stability of natural laws. In *Eureka*, he avers that even natural phenomena can deceive us. Poe asserts that "*sensitive perception* of Gravity as we experience it on Earth, beguiles mankind into the fancy of *centralization* or *especiality* respecting it."[16] Furthermore, Poe brings our attention to the fact that there are moments when conclusions will seem obvious to some people and not to others, and that an idea will seem more or less conclusive to the same person at different times.

This is not to say that individuals are generally incapable of holding propositions. In *Eureka*, Poe argues that intuition comes to our aid when we are confronted with an issue. He defines intuition as the conviction a person experiences based upon the unconscious inductive and deductive processes at work in the mind. Here, Poe sounds much like Emerson; however, there are some striking differences between them. Clearly, Poe did not believe in absolute truths. Poe maintained that one does not prove anything but merely attempts to convince others by suggestion. Consequently, there is common ground among these positions in spite of their differences. Emerson acknowledged similarities between Idealism and Materialism, which may explain why some confuse the two positions. Emerson also noted the irreconcilable differences between the two schools of thought and upheld Idealism as the more enlightened approach when he said, "Every materialist will be an idealist; but an idealist can never go backward to be a materialist."[17]

The schism between Poe and Emerson, materialist and idealist, continued into discussions pertaining to metaphysics, an area of philosophic inquiry that Poe despised. In his "Letter to B—," Poe laments that Coleridge's "mind should be buried in metaphysics."[18] While Poe was averse to mysticism, he was also enthralled with realities beyond what science can definitively answer. This absorption is seen in many of Poe's tales. Relating his experience in "Manuscript Found in a Bottle," the narrator ends suspensefully as he and his shipmates are sucked into a great whirlpool, never to be heard from again. The narrator of "A Descent into the Maelström" narrowly escapes a similar fate by means of his ingenuity. As he descends into the irresistible vortex, however, he is so awed by what he sees that he believes he witnesses "a manifestation of God's power."[19] This passage suggests that Poe believed in God's existence and power. By extension, he thought deeply about what life after death must be like.

As with other philosophic debates, the major difference between Poe and Emerson lies in Emerson's commitment to Idealism and Poe's fastidious adherence to the essential dictates of Materialism. As his letter to Chivers suggests, Poe believed in God, an idiosyncratic being made of "a matter without particles – of no atomic composition." It is hard to know precisely what Poe means by a thing composed of matter without particles. He does his best to enlighten readers when he suggests that God is a kind of material unlike "rudimentary" human beings, who are individualized "by being incorporated in the ordinary or particled matter." There is, therefore, a difference between two types of matter: one made of particles, and the other devoid of particles. As a result of their particled state, humans remain distinct and separated from God. Yet God's true nature remains a mystery. Poe told Chivers that, at death, people take "a new form, of a novel matter, pass everywhere, and act all things, by mere volition, and are cognizant of all secrets but *the one* – the nature of the volition of God." It seems that in spite of Poe's efforts to define the human and the divine, God's nature remains partly obscure.

Poe noted, however, that a portion of the individual is not "particled," which ensures man's continued existence after death. Poe explored the idea that human beings slowly change form when they die. Poe details this process of metamorphosis in his dialogue, "Monos and Una," in which two deceased lovers discuss the state of humanity and life after death. Monos explains to Una that when he first died, he retained his familiar five senses for a time. Eventually, he acquired a sixth sense, which he calls, "a mental pendulous pulsation."[20] Furthermore, Monos says that he gradually lost his sense of material being and developed a keen and exclusive awareness of place and time. The dialogue ends as the lovers prophesy that man will also experience a rebirth in death.

Poe and Emerson were both committed to a belief in reunification with God at death. In "The Poet," Emerson, like Poe, insists that human beings undergo a profound change when they die. Emerson argues that at death, the soul ascends to higher forms.[21] Here, the Transcendentalist implies a union with God upon physical death, which is possible only because "the foundations of man are not in matter, but in spirit. But the element of spirit is *eternity*." Emerson's theory of man's nature is not complicated. Emerson also explains what he means by the term *eternity*. In "Nature," Emerson envisions an infinite loop of phenomena without beginning, middle, or end. He notes that Idealism "beholds the whole circle of persons and things, of actions and events, of country and religion, not as painfully accumulated, atom after atom, act after act, in an aged creeping Past, but as one vast picture, which God paints on the instant eternity, for the contemplation of the soul."²² Here, Emerson postulates that God, the phenomenon, exists simultaneously in infinite time and space.

In *Eureka*, Poe proclaims that he "*cannot* conceive Infinity." Instead, he explains that unity is achieved upon return to the One, which will occur once God withdraws from the universe and its forward momentum ceases. At that time, an inverse reaction will commence. Poe envisions a linear progression to the universe. He knows these realities of the universe by means of his intuition, and true to his materialism, he employs all of his senses to support his notions. Poe is convinced that his cosmology is correct because he also "feels it, sees it and perceives it."²³

Ideas such as these have a profound effect on Poe; he thinks that they can partake in beauty. In response to Laplace's Nebular Theory, which he discusses at length in *Eureka*, Poe says, "we shall find it *beautifully* true. It is by far too beautiful, indeed, *not* to possess Truth as its essentiality." While appealing to intuition, Poe, like his Transcendentalist counterpart, emphasizes the individual's innate sense of the aesthetic. He believed that a sense of the beautiful is deeply ingrained in each individual. Hence, a successful work of art should be universally accessible. Striving for this type of general appeal is a daunting task; however, Poe realized that he needed to tap into the audience's pleasure center in order to bring about his desired effect. There are some qualities that appeal to most people. Poe says, "Music, when combined with a pleasurable idea, is poetry."²⁴ Here, Poe acknowledges the equal status of abstract reason and material reality.

Poe further delineates the material conditions that make a work of art pleasurable. In "The Philosophy of Composition," he says that the work should be short enough to be read at one sitting. As a result, readers can sustain their attention on one idea without interruption. Furthermore, the right musical pitch will appeal to a wide audience. Poe prefers a melancholy sound, which is best achieved through monotone. Additionally, repetition and certain vowel sounds help create this lugubrious mood. Not only should a poem be short and sad, but it should also have the right amount of detail. An idea might be flawed because it is trite. Therefore, the author must strive for complexity and suggestiveness, which make a work of art particularly rich. The perfect harmony of elements is not attained easily. A work should always be an original composition. Consequently, the job of a poet is not easy; he should have to work very hard in order to produce a distinctive work of art that appeals to a large audience.

Poe's contempt for some Transcendentalist art, which he considered derivative, partly explains his animosity to its practitioners. In the letter to Chivers, Poe scoffed at the "pretenders and sophists" among their numbers. In public, he criticized the most heinous offenders. For instance, Poe castigated William Ellery Channing for being infected by the work of Tennyson and Carlyle.[25]

He also suggests that the Transcendentalist poet unjustly capitalizes on his father's name. Both of these objections center on Poe's observation that Channing imitates others and capitalizes on their labor.

Even though some Transcendentalists may have fallen short of Poe's ideals, originality was a central tenet of the movement. Emerson insisted that each person remain true to himself or herself. In "Self-Reliance," he says, "Insist on yourself; never imitate. Your own gift you can present every moment with the cumulative force of a whole life's cultivation; but of the adopted talent of another, you have only an extemporaneous, half possession."[26]

According to Emerson's larger philosophical system, individuals are the unique manifestation of the mind of God. People should, therefore, celebrate the special gifts with which they are imbued. Conversely, those who consistently adopt another's views deny the world their unique contributions. While many individuals cannot comprehend the whole, some can. In "Nature," Emerson says that the artist "throws a light upon the mystery of humanity."[27] Consequently, it is the poet who has insight into the totality. But this vision does not come by hard work. Instead, the true artist cannot help but see what he does.

The ordinary individual observes only small sections of the world, yet the artist sees all and renders the whole intelligible. In "Nature," Emerson argues, "A work of art is an abstract or epitome of the world. It is the result or expression of nature, in miniature." The whole passes through the individual mind of the poet, who in turn communicates his observations through his work. The artist sees all and renders it anew. This genius, therefore, is divinely inspired. According to Emerson, the poet "delights us by animating nature like a creator, with his own thoughts, he differs from the philosopher only herein, that the one proposes Beauty as his main end; the other Truth." Both the philosopher and the poet convey the beauty of ideas. Emerson believed that this is possible because "the true philosopher and the true poet are one, and a beauty, which is truth, and a truth, which is beauty, is the aim of both."[28] Theory and practice are linked under a larger category of the aesthetic. The artistic genius composes ideas, which he sometimes puts to music in such a way that appeals to the intuitions of others.

Because the whole is a divine manifestation, Emerson maintained that moral instruction is essential in works of art. Again, in "Nature," he argues that "all things with which we deal preach to us." Furthermore, the moral law works in concert with the natural law in all things, and the true poet, who has special insight into the whole of nature, renders experience faithfully. Conversely, Poe unequivocally denied the necessity of moral lessons in art. In "Letter to B— ," he denounces Wordsworth and the other Lake Poets, whose philosophy was that "the end of poetry is, or should be, instruction."[29] There were times, however, when he considered the pleasurable effect of morality in art, and the result is particularly funny. Poe puts his disdain for moral platitudes in art to comic effect in "Never Bet the Devil Your Head." In this tale, the narrator notes that his purpose is to show that "there is no just ground, therefore, for the charge brought against me by certain ignoramuses – that I have never written a moral tale, or, in more precise words, a tale with a moral." Furthermore, Poe's flippant narrator insists that, "Every fiction *should have* a moral; and, what is more to the purpose, the critics have discovered that every fiction *has*...When the proper time arrives, all that the gentleman intended, and all that he did not intend, will be brought to light, in the *Dial*."[30] This reference to *The Dial*, a Transcendentalist magazine, is immediately recognizable. Here, Poe clearly mocks Transcendentalist aesthetics.

It is no wonder that scholars have been troubled by the relationship between Poe and the New England Transcendentalists. There are some clear differences between Poe and his Transcendentalist contemporaries, yet one can also see echoes of Transcendentalist theory in Poe's writing. Both schools delineated the ways that human beings acquire knowledge. Emerson hypothesized that absolute truths exist. Poe, on the other hand, remains skeptical about certain knowledge. He believed, instead, that one only suggests to others what his intuition tells him is true. Though they disagreed on the subject of absolute knowledge, Emerson and Poe agreed on the supremacy of intuition, which guides one's thinking.

Intuition helps one understand certain realities that science cannot yet fully explain, including the existence of God and the nature of life after death. For both men, instinct reveals the existence of God. Poe's vision of the universe is dependent on a Supreme Being, who initiated universal events but, at some point in the future, will withdraw, thereby causing all things to return to the epicenter. Conversely, the Transcendentalist argues that God and the products of God's thoughts exist in infinite time and space. Here and elsewhere, the primary dispute between Poe and Emerson is grounded in the Materialist–Idealist binary. Poe maintains his allegiance to sensual existence, even when it comes to God's nature, which is a type of unparticled material that humans partake in to an extent. Conversely, the Transcendentalist is committed to the position that God is a phenomenon. Nothing exists outside of thought, and even human beings are manifestations of the mind of God. It makes sense, therefore, to conclude as Emerson does, that death activates another stage in our relationship with God. While Poe was uncomfortable with Transcendentalist Idealism, he agreed that human beings will reunite with God at death. This occurs because a part of human physiology is unparticled. At that time, a metamorphosis alters the existing human structure.

Finally, both Poe and the Transcendentalist concur that the artist is distinct among his kind. According to Emerson, the poet, who stays true to himself, easily renders the realities of nature anew. Poe also places the original artist in high esteem, but the poet struggles to bring about the beautiful for a pleasurable response from the audience. The two theorists, however, could not agree on the proper subject of art. Emerson saw morality in everything and thought that didacticism was an appropriate, indeed necessary, component in works of art. Conversely, Poe notes that moral lessons should never be the end of poetry; instead, pleasure should be the poet's ultimate goal. Yet Poe shows us that there can be a place for morality in art. Through farce, even didacticism can be, in the end, pleasurable.

Ottavio Casale's thesis concerning Poe's relationship to the New England Transcendentalists is well founded. Indeed, Edgar Allan Poe had a complex relationship to Transcendentalism and its proponents. Poe's work clearly echoes some tenets found in Transcendentalist epistemology, metaphysics, and aesthetics. Poe is, therefore, somewhat disingenuous when he says that his faith is his own. Here, he implies that creativity operates in a vacuum, but this cannot possibly be the case. Influences from other sources are evident in both Poe's works and in Transcendentalism. This suggests that Poe may have had too limited a view of genius. He does not create *sui generis*, but ingeniously expands and innovates on existing ideas. Emerson, too, was highly influenced by other thinkers, especially German philosophers. Exchanges of ideas are inevitable in an innovative and creative culture. Although the concept of genius is in need of refinement, Poe and Emerson demonstrate what its application will entail.

NOTES

1. Poe to Thomas H. Chivers, July 10, 1844, *The Collected Letters of Edgar Allan Poe*, ed. John Ward Ostrom, Burton R. Pollin, and Jeffrey A. Savoye, 2 vols. (New York: Gordian, 2008), vol. i, 453.
2. Edgar Allan Poe, "An Appendix of Autographs," *Graham's Lady's and Gentleman's Magazine* 20 (1842), 44–50, 49.
3. Edgar Allan Poe, *The Collected Works of Edgar Allan Poe*, ed. Thomas Ollive Mabbott, 3 vols. (Cambridge, MA: Belknap Press, 1969–78), vol. ii, 338.
4. Ottavio Casale, "Poe on Transcendentalism," *ESQ* 50 (1968), 85.
5. Poe, *Collected Works*, vol. ii, 316.
6. Ibid., vol. ii, 225.
7. Richard D. Geldard, *The Essential Transcendentalists* (New York: Penguin, 2005), 21.
8. "Biographia Literaria; or Biographical Sketches of my Literary Life and Opinions," *Christian Examiner* 14 (1833), 126.
9. Ralph Waldo Emerson, *The Collected Works of Ralph Waldo Emerson*, ed. Robert E. Spiller et al., 9 vols. to date (Cambridge, MA: Belknap Press, 1971–), vol. i, 207.
10. Ibid., vol. i, 207.
11. Ibid., vol. i, 37.
12. Ibid., vol. ii, 166.
13. Poe, *Collected Works*, vol. i, 452.
14. Poe to James Russell Lowell, July 2, 1844, *Collected Letters*, vol. I, 449.
15. Edgar Allan Poe, *Poetry and Tales*, ed. Patrick F. Quinn (New York: Library of America, 1984), 1007.
16. Ibid., 1285.
17. Emerson, *Collected Works*, vol. i, 202.
18. Edgar Allan Poe, *Essays and Reviews*, ed. G. R. Thompson (New York: Library of America, 1984), 11.
19. Poe, *Collected Works*, vol. ii, 588.
20. Ibid., vol. ii, 615.
21. Emerson, *Collected Works*, 3: vol. iii, 14.
22. Ibid., vol. i, 42, 36.
23. Poe, *Poetry and Tales*, 1274.
24. Poe, *Essays*, 11.
25. Edgar Allan Poe, "Our Amateur Poets," *Graham's Lady's and Gentleman's Magazine* 23 (1843), 113.
26. Emerson, *Collected Works*, vol. ii, 47.
27. Ibid., vol. i, 16.
28. Ibid., vol. i, 33.
29. Poe, *Essays*, 7.
30. Poe, *Collected Works*, vol. ii, 621–2.

CHAPTER 28

Charles Dickens

Tara Moore

Charles Dickens moved easily among popular Victorian genres; in fact, he set the standard in several of them. Using the pen name "Boz," Dickens made his earliest fame writing comic pieces for periodicals. His first articles appeared in such American periodicals as *The Albion* and *The New-Yorker* in 1834.[1] Greater fame came with his serialized, wildly popular *Pickwick Papers* (1836–7). This comic novel, like many of Dickens's subsequent works, was published in monthly installments. He went on to publish a total of twenty novels, some in monthly or weekly periodicals, others in paperbound parts. He also edited several periodicals and led the way not only in the Christmas book trade after the popular success of *A Christmas Carol* (1843), but also with the Christmas numbers of the periodicals he edited. Poe's junior by three years, Dickens dominated the literary spotlight on both sides of the Atlantic from 1836 until his death in 1870.

American readers may have been influenced by Poe's early criticism of Dickens. Poe read all of Dickens's early novels and reviewed several of them. He may have been the first American to review the work of Dickens.[2] Regarding *Nicholas Nickleby* (1838), Poe wrote, "We think it somewhat surprising that his serious pieces have elicited so little attention; but, possibly, they have been lost in the blaze of his comic reputation."[3] Even in his earliest reviews of Dickens, Poe emerges as, in Peter Bracher's words, "one of the most perceptive of Dickens's early American readers."[4] In these reviews, Poe notes the importance of the British author's art and looks forward to the lasting impression that the young author would make. Poe subsequently reviewed *Master Humphrey's Clock* – Dickens's short-lived weekly miscellany – and *The Old Curiosity Shop* while he was employed by *Graham's Magazine* in 1841.[5]

Reviewing an early installment of *Barnaby Rudge* (1841) for the *Saturday Evening Post*, Poe correctly guessed how the unsolved murder at the heart of the plot really happened. Dickens was serializing *Barnaby Rudge* in *Master Humphrey's Clock*, so each week readers could buy the periodical and read approximately three chapters of the novel in its pages. With just three weeks' worth (or eleven chapters) of installments before him, Poe correctly judged the novel's plot and mystery. In later editions of the novel, Dickens buried the clues that tipped off Poe.[6]

Not only did Poe review Dickens's work, he gleaned ideas from it. "Why the Little Frenchman Wears His Hand in a Sling" and "The Man of the Crowd" both echo *Sketches by Boz* (1836).[7] Dickens's "Confession Found in a Prison in the Times of Charles the Second," first published in 1840 in *Master Humphrey's Clock*, impressed Poe, and may have inspired "The Tell-Tale Heart" and "The Black Cat." In Dickens's short story, the murderer takes issue with the victim's intense gaze, and he gives himself away in a manner made memorable in Poe's more famous tales. Elements of Dickens's short Christmas novel *The Chimes* (1844) recur in Poe's poem "The Bells." In *The Chimes*, a poor, downcast working-class man dreams that the spirits of the cathedral bells speak to him and counsel him to empathize with the depravities to which starvation and poverty drive people. The last stanza of Poe's poem similarly brings the bells alive and tolls their message. More notably, in Dickens's *Barnaby Rudge*, a raven named Grip waits in jail with an innocent man, and the melancholy bird repeats hopeless barks not unlike Poe's own famous bird in "The Raven." Poe's second review of the novel suggests that it would have been better if the character of Rudge's raven had been prophetic, a fault Poe rectifies in "The Raven."[8]

Unlike Poe, Dickens enjoyed a wide following among American readers, but his popularity in the New World brought the author no direct profit. As a child of poverty and a businessman keenly aware of his assets, the absence of an international copyright irked Dickens to no end. Though the Federal Act of 1790 initiated American copyright, it protected only the copyright of American citizens and specifically allowed the piracy of foreign books. More books by a British author might be published in the United States than by his British publisher, but he received no profit from the American sales. For example, the book that Dickens wrote following his first American trip, *American Notes*, appeared in England as a two-volume, 600-page text costing one guinea. In contrast, American firms – Harper and Brothers, Lea and Blanchard, Wilson and Company – produced pirated copies that sold for ten to twenty-five cents each. Moreover, Dickens grieved over his loss of control of the physical quality of his books. American reprints appeared with tiny type and narrow margins. For an author who carefully planned the paper quality, illustrations, and covers of his books whenever possible, as with the Christmas books, such cheap, uncontrollable printing caused pain.

The lack of an Anglo-American copyright law seriously damaged the profits of authors on both sides of the Atlantic. American authors could try to survive on the profit from poems and stories published in magazines, but they rarely had a chance to profit from their books. If Dickens was disconcerted by his brief face-to-face encounter with the American reprinting industry during his 1842 trip to the United States, Poe was forced to become versed in it for the survival of his career. Authors often could not control the circulation of their writing, neither could they depend on other ways to promote themselves to the reading public. They had no choice but to accept these limitations. Indeed, the European settings of many of Poe's tales show his writing to be chameleon-like: American periodicals reprinted so many British novels and stories that American readers might well expect to find foreign settings when they opened the pages to read fiction.[9]

Poe clearly saw the benefit of a new law, and he joined the American Copyright Club in 1842. That same year he deplored the state of his national literature in a letter: "Literature is at a sad discount.... Without an international copyright law, American authors may as well cut their throats."[10] He spoke from hard experience. In 1839 Poe struggled to find a publisher for his collected tales. When he did secure a publisher, Lea and Blanchard offered Poe only twenty free copies as their royalty payment for *Tales of the Grotesque and Arabesque*. To add further insult, one of the anthologized stories, "Why the Little Frenchman Wears His Hand in a Sling," became the first of Poe's works printed in London only because it was pirated by *Bentley's Miscellany* – though Dickens had no hand in this piracy. By the time "Little Frenchman" appeared in *Bentley's*, William Harrison Ainsworth had taken over the editorship from Dickens.[11] The lack of international copyright lasted until long after the deaths of both Poe and Dickens; it was not established until Congress passed laws in 1891 and 1909. Ironically, the system that strangled both men's profits resulted in Dickens's wild popularity among his American audience since huge pirated print runs and low prices gave him "a mass audience he could not possibly have had otherwise."[12]

In 1841, the *Southern Literary Messenger* reported Dickens's financial success, calling him the "most successful author of modern times" and saying that he earned up to an astounding two thousand pounds a year with his writing. Such a claim ignores the greater profit Dickens might have made from the American market, and it also paints a picture of wealth that fails to capture the financial trials Dickens experienced. By July of that same year Dickens owed his publisher an embarrassing debt of £3,019.9.5, due in part to the fine London house he kept with its five live-in servants, the social demands of the society in which the Dickenses traveled, and the financial burdens his brothers and spendthrift father continued to be.[13] The profitability of a book about America written for the curious British audience of this period, just after passage of the democratizing Reform Bill, was one of the inducements that took Dickens across the ocean and into the arms of his most star-struck fans.

American readers felt no compunction about reading pirated versions of Dickens's works, and the author became a beloved celebrity. When word of Dickens's imminent arrival spread, American periodicals extended warm and celebratory welcomes to this distinguished guest heralded as "a public benefactor," "the most popular writer in the literary world, of the present day," and "one of the noblest and foremost Republican Penman of the nineteenth century!" *Brother Jonathan* named him "more a literary idol than any other man ever was in this country; and we hazard little in saying that 'Boz,' in the abstract of a literary acquaintance, is more beloved here than at home."[14]

The reception Dickens found in America differed significantly from the British audience's esteem that had grown with his success. He wrote to his brother to complain: "Imagine, when I landed from a steam boat in New York, in a dense crowd, some twenty or thirty people, screwing *small dabs* of fur out of the back of that costly great coat I bought in Regent Street!"[15] A banquet had been held for him in Edinburgh, and periodicals frequently praised him, but he was unused to the physical presence and press of fans eager to shake his hand and experience him in the flesh. He wrote to his brother that he feared to have his hair cut lest the barber trim it all off to turn a profit on the memento each curl would make.[16] This distasteful mobbing would be the defining and overwhelming character of his trip to America.

Arriving in January and leaving in June, Dickens and his wife traveled throughout the East, south to Richmond, and as far west as St. Louis. William Cullen Bryant wrote that the public greeted him "with a feeling that was formerly rendered only to emperors and kings."[17] On his trip, Dickens toured Hartford's Insane Asylum, Philadelphia's Eastern Penitentiary, both Houses of Congress, a tobacco factory worked by slaves in Richmond, and Niagara Falls. In each city he made himself available to the public and in the course of two hours might shake the hands of 300 people or more. Several banquets were held in his honor, including one chaired by Washington Irving, until he quickly decided to forgo this honor during the rest of his trip in the interest of traveling more quietly.

Nonetheless, he attended a reception with President Tyler and organized a public theatrical in Montreal.[18]

Amid all his social engagements, Dickens jeopardized his own popularity by embarking on his quest for an Anglo-American copyright law. The writer of sentiment was suddenly seen as a selfish miser, an impression that the angry press pushed on its readers. Dickens had conceived of and brought about a petition, signed by twelve British authors, that pressed his case for copyright.[19] These he had printed in American newspapers, and he hand delivered one to the U.S. Congress. Thus began one of his less popular personal crusades. The press that worked to defend its free piracy of Dickens's work could not squelch the American public's fascination with the English celebrity. Fans mobbed him at nearly every stop on his journey.

Poe joined the throng of Americans hoping to meet Dickens. Along with a request for an interview, Poe sent clippings of his reviews of Dickens's books as well as a copy of *Tales of the Grotesque and Arabesque*. While Poe was well versed in Dickens's work before their March 1842 meeting, there is no evidence that Dickens had read anything of Poe's. At the interview the two authors discussed American poetry, a conversation that would have a lasting impact on Dickens's view of American literature. A letter Poe wrote to James Russell Lowell suggests that Poe and Dickens had a second meeting, but the date and location of this meeting, if it really happened, remain a mystery. Since there is no other mention of it, it has been suggested that Poe merely fabricated this meeting and the length of his time with Dickens to puff his own importance.[20]

One of Poe's motivations for seeking an audience with Dickens had been the hope of gaining a friend in the London publishing world. During their interview, Poe asked Dickens to help him secure a London publisher for his *Tales of the Grotesque and Arabesque*. Back in London, Dickens eventually kept his word. In a letter dated November 17, 1842, he wrote publisher Edward Moxon with a feeble appeal on Poe's behalf: "Pray write me such a reply as I can send to the author of the volumes; and to get absolution for my conscience in this matter."[21]

After Dickens returned to England, negative portrayals of American culture began popping up in periodicals associated with the author and his own books. He had expected a utopia, and he had found bad manners, social injustice, and physical discomfort. He had been disgusted by the tobacco spitting in the West, wearied by the constant application for an introduction by strangers, and outraged by the slavery he had witnessed in Richmond. The prestigious *Foreign Quarterly Review*, edited by Dickens's good friend John Foster, suddenly began to run unsigned articles on America, including "American Poetry," printed in the January 1844 issue. It is believed that Dickens contributed this series, and it is possible that Poe gave Dickens much of the research he needed to write the article on American verse.[22] During the one proven meeting between Poe and Dickens, the American brought along Rufus W. Griswold's anthology *The Poets and Poetry of America*. This anthology placed three of Poe's poems side by side with those of Ralph Waldo Emerson and Henry Wadsworth Longfellow. When Dickens returned to England, it is supposed that he used the book and the conversation with Poe to produce an article about American poets. This attribution does not come from Dickens, but from a letter Poe wrote to James Russell Lowell after reading Dickens's article: "Nearly everything in the critique, I heard from him, or suggested to him, personally. The poem of Emerson [referred to in Dickens's article] I read to him."[23] Poe also wrote, "The article affords so strong internal evidence of his hand that I would as soon think of doubting my existence."[24] Poe would later write with certainty of Dickens's authorship in an 1845 article for the *Broadway Journal*.[25]

If Poe took pride in having educated the British celebrity in American poetry, he could only shudder at the critique Dickens wrote of American poets and Poe's own work. The article reviews five books of poetry, including the Griswold anthology. Of this wealth of poetry, the reviewer writes that American poetry "is little better than a far-off echo of the fatherland" and "with two or three exceptions, there is not a poet of mark in the whole Union." The article goes on to claim, "The whole state of American society, from first to last, presents insuperable obstacles to the cultivation of letters, the expansion of intellect, the formation of great and original minds." Emerson, Longfellow, and William Cullen Bryant receive notice and praise as poets, but after years of Poe's favorable reviews of Dickens's work, Boz did not return the favor. "American Poetry" identified Poe as an American imitator of British poets: "Poe is a capital artist after the manner of Tennyson; and approaches the spirit of his original more closely than any of them." The article gives a brief, romanticized version of Poe's biography and quotes lines as a proof of Poe's imitative verse before leaving a parting shot, likening Poe to a mockingbird because his so-called imitation has a bit of spirituality that stands out as slightly original.[26] Such charges of imitation "shook Poe's confidence badly, the more so because of his own reputation as an exposer of imitators and plagiarists."[27] Poe had specifically accused Longfellow of plagiarizing Tennyson, and now Poe's literary hero was accusing him of the same thing. Poe defensively wrote to James Russell Lowell that the passages in his poetry that the unnamed critic had chosen to call imitations of Tennyson had been "published by me long before Tennyson was heard of."[28]

Poe's reviews of Dickens's subsequent novels cooled a bit following this public chastening and Dickens's failure to locate a London publisher for him. Nonetheless, Poe continued a professional regard for Dickens. He even applied to Dickens in 1846, hoping to be named as an American correspondent for the *Daily News*, a paper for which Dickens wrote. The British author was not in a position to hire Poe in this way, but the communication suggested that no feud existed between the two men who reviewed each other's work.[29]

After Poe's death in 1849, Dickens continued to have a successful literary career for two more decades. His periodicals *Household Words* (1850–9) and *All the Year Round* (1859–70) kept him constantly in touch with the most creative literary minds of his day. He went on to write some of his most masterly novels, such as *Bleak House* (serialized March 1852 to September 1853) and *Our Mutual Friend* (serialized May 1864 to November 1865). Caricature, social reform, and sentimentality characterized his writing. The daring scope of his urban novels, with their huge cast of memorable characters, has resulted in the continued use of the word "Dickensian." When, in 1858, Dickens began selling tickets to his public readings, newspaper reports emerged detailing audience members' laughter, sobs, and tears as the author – a skilled actor – played upon their emotions with amazing dexterity. These same emotional responses had been going on since the start of Dickens's fictional career, either in the family reading circle or in solitary reading experiences. He eventually counted the potential profit, buried his past animosity, and returned to America for an 1867 reading tour.

It was on this tour that Dickens made a final overture to Poe, now long dead. Dickens, like many celebrities before him, sought out Maria Clemm, Poe's mother-in-law, in Baltimore. Dickens pressed the elderly woman to take a gift of $150 as an expression of his sympathy for the dead poet.[30] This financial memento was not the last transmission between Dickens and Poe. Dickens's pet raven Grip, which had inspired the *Barnaby Rudge* bird and, thereby, Poe's own prophetic bird in "The Raven," has had a surprising afterlife. Dickens sent his pet to a taxidermist upon its death. That stuffed raven was eventually purchased by a Poe collector, Richard Gimbel, and added to the Poe collection, now housed by the Philadelphia Free Library.

NOTES

1. William J. Carlton, "Dickens's Debut in America," *Dickensian* 55 (1959), 55–6.
2. Fernando Galvan, "Poe Versus Dickens," *A Descent into Edgar Allan Poe and His Works: The Bicentennial*, ed. Beatriz González Moreno and Margarita Rigal Aragón (New York: Peter Lang, 2010), 3; Peter Bracher, "Poe as a Critic of Dickens," *Dickens Studies Newsletter* 9 (1978), 109.
3. [Edgar Allan Poe], "Review of New Books," *Burton's Gentleman's Magazine* 5 (1839), 330.
4. Bracher, "Poe as a Critic," 109, 111.
5. Edgar Allan Poe, *Essays and Reviews*, ed. G. R. Thompson (New York: Library of America, 1984), 208–18.
6. Barry Westburg, "How Poe Solved the Mystery of Barnaby Rudge," *Dickens Studies Newsletter* 5 (1974), 39–40.
7. Edgar Allan Poe, *The Annotated Poe*, ed. Kevin J. Hayes (Cambridge, MA: Belknap Press, 2013).
8. Fernando Galvan, "Plagiarism in Poe: Revisiting the Poe-Dickens Relationship," *Edgar Allan Poe Review* 10 (2009), 14–20.
9. Meredith L. McGill, *American Literature and the Culture of Reprinting, 1834–1853* (Philadelphia: University of Pennsylvania Press, 2003), 119, 151, 155.
10. Mary A. Tobin, "Dickens, Poe and the International Copyright Battle," *Dickensian* 98 (2002), 123; Poe to Frederick W. Thomas, August 27, 1842, *The Collected Letters of Edgar Allan Poe*, ed. John Ward Ostrom, Burton R. Pollin, and Jeffrey A. Savoye, 3d ed., 2 vols. (New York: Gordian, 2008), vol. i, 356.
11. Dawn B. Sova, *Critical Companion to Edgar Allan Poe: A Literary Reference to His Life and Work* (New York: Facts on File, 2007), 189; Kevin J. Hayes, "Understanding 'Why the Little Frenchman Wears His Hand in a Sling,'" *Edgar Allan Poe: Beyond Gothicism* (Newark: University of Delaware Press, 2011), 119.
12. Igor Webb, "Charles Dickens in America: The Writer and the Reality," *Dickens Studies Annual* 39 (2008), 63, 65.
13. Michael Slater, *Charles Dickens* (New Haven: Yale University Press, 2009), 154–5.
14. "Visiters to America," *New-York Mirror* 19 (December 4, 1841), 391; "Arrival of the Britannia," *Christian Secretary* 4 (January 28, 1842), 3; "A Welcome to Charles Dickens," *Arcturus* 3 (1842), 161; "Our Weekly Gossip," *Brother Jonathan* 1 (January 29, 1842), 126.
15. Charles Dickens to Daniel Maclise, March 22, 1842, *The Letters of Charles Dickens*, ed. Madeline House, Graham Storey, Kathleen Tillotson, 12 vols. (Oxford: Clarendon Press, 1965–2002), vol. iii, 154.
16. Charles Dickens to Frederick Dickens, March 22, 1842, *Letters*, vol. iii, 149.
17. Sidney P. Moss, *Charles Dickens's Quarrel with America* (Troy, NY: Whitston, 1984), 2.
18. Slater, *Charles Dickens*, 182–4, 188.

19. Moss, *Charles Dickens's Quarrel*, 4, 7–8.

20. Galvan, "Poe Versus Dickens," 5, 11.

21. Ibid., 10.

22. Moss, *Charles Dickens's Quarrel*, 16–17.

23. Sidney P. Moss, "Poe's 'Two Long Interviews' with Dickens," *Poe Studies* 11 (1978), 11.

24. Kenneth Silverman, *Edgar A. Poe: Mournful and Never-Ending Remembrance* (New York: HarperCollins, 1991), 199–200.

25. Sidney P. Moss and Carolyn Moss, *American Episodes Involving Charles Dickens* (Troy, NY: Whitston, 1999), 76.

26. "American Poetry," *Foreign Quarterly Review* 64 (1844), 291, 293, 321, 322.

27. Moss, "Poe's 'Two Long Interviews' with Dickens," 11.

28. Fernando Galvan, "Plagiarism in Poe," 13; Galvan, "Poe Versus Dickens," 13.

29. Galvan, "Poe Versus Dickens," 19.

30. John H. Ingram, *Edgar Allan Poe: His Life, Letters, and Opinions* (New York: Ward, Lock, Bowden, 1891), 433.

CHAPTER 29

Nathaniel Hawthorne and the Art of the Tale

Meghan A. Freeman

Spanning nearly a decade, Edgar Allan Poe's critical examination of the fiction of Nathaniel Hawthorne began on an auspicious note. Poe's review of *Twice-Told Tales* in the May 1842 issue of *Graham's Magazine* detects "something which resembles a plagiarism – but which *may* be a very flattering coincidence of thought" between Hawthorne's "Howe's Masquerade" and his own "William Wilson." Hawthorne's story appearing in print before Poe's, the charge of plagiarism does not hold water, leaving one to consider Poe's motivations for putting before the reading public two fictions the narrative climax of which is a man's disturbing recognition of his doppelganger, whose presence allows him to see as through a mirror darkly the hidden parts of his own psyche. One explanation might be that by drawing attention to their stories about doppelgangers, Poe is encouraging the reader to see the two authors as doppelgangers, notwithstanding surface distinctions, styles, and interests. Moreover, the appearance of one's doppelganger traditionally coincides with an event at which something important is at stake, and for Poe, what might be said to be at stake is the future of the genre to which these stories belong and of which the two men would become legendary practitioners: the tale.

Supporting this hypothesis is the fact that Poe's review begins with a disquisition on what constitutes a tale, his point being that only some of Hawthorne's *Twice-Told Tales* deserve that denomination. Poe divides the volume into two categories – the tale and the essay – deeming the latter a merely fanciful affair while stating that the former "affords unquestionably the fairest field for the exercise of the loftiest talent, which can be afforded by the wide domains of mere prose."[1] Given the privileged position Poe accords the tale, his assertion that Hawthorne's successful experiments in the genre "belong to the highest region of Art – an Art subservient to genius of a very lofty order" is high praise indeed.[2] That said, Poe's celebration of Hawthorne also affirms the literary theories and critical dicta that govern his own grotesque and arabesque fictions. We might therefore look at this and subsequent reviews as part of a battle over the nature of the tale in the pugnacious environs of nineteenth-century American print culture. This chapter traces the evolution of Poe's opinions on Hawthorne while considering how these opinions, often dismissed as inconsistent or contradictory, respond to conflicting theories of the tale in contemporary periodicals and the writings of Hawthorne himself. By casting Poe in the role of a critical William Wilson confronting in Hawthorne his literary double, it is possible to chart the confluences and divergences in their textual relations, as they worked to define the genre on which both would indelibly leave their mark.

Poe's critical engagement with Hawthorne actually began one month prior to the May 1842 article, in a notice in *Graham's*. Also beginning with an encomium of "the *Tale*" and its "peculiar advantages," Poe places *Twice-Told Tales* at the apex of American efforts in the genre, with only Irving's *Tales of a Traveller* and a few other volumes for company. Among Hawthorne's virtues, Poe commends the purity of his style, the effectiveness of his tone, and "his *originality* both of incident and reflection."[3] Poe also voices certain concerns that will receive fuller treatment in future reviews. Most notably, Poe insists that many of the tales are not tales at all; and, further, this generic imprecision on Hawthorne's part demands both criticism and correction. For Poe, each "class of composition" – poem, tale, essay, or novel – has specific objectives, their fullest achievement depending on the adherence to certain formal criteria. These genres exist in a hierarchy, with the prose tale ranked below only a species of "rhymed poem, not to exceed in length what might be perused in an hour."[4] The ideal tale, as *occasionally* exemplified by Hawthorne, Poe defines as "a short prose narrative, requiring from a half-hour to one or two hours in its perusal." Although seemingly arbitrary, Poe's strictures on length extend from his belief that "unity of effect or impression is a point of greatest importance" in any literary composition. To generate in the audience "a sense of the fullest satisfaction," the author must walk the line between undertaxing readers' affective faculties and overtaxing their powers of endurance. Too short a composition and no very forceful or enduring impression can be evoked; too long and the workaday world intrudes, ruining the sense of totality.

Given that Poe's task was reviewing a work of prose fiction, his expansion into the loftier subject of the relation between and hallmarks of various literary forms seems off topic – unless one had read previous notices of the *Twice-Told Tales*. Reviews before Poe's were not numerous, but there were two in *North American Review*, both by Henry Wadsworth

Longfellow – Hawthorne's Bowdoin College classmate – that the May 1842 *Graham's* article appears intent to refute. Longfellow's first review in the July 1838 issue praises *Twice-Told Tales* as "a spiritual star," which ere long "star-gazers" like himself "will inform the world of its magnitude and its place in the heaven of poetry." He continues, "the book, though in prose, is written nevertheless by a poet...to [Hawthorne] external form is but the representation of internal being."⁵ That Poe had Longfellow's review in mind when writing his own is supported by the fact that the April 1842 edition of *Graham's* containing Poe's first review of Hawthorne also featured Poe's review of Longfellow's *Ballads and Other Poems*. Therein, he criticizes Longfellow for his erroneous "conception of the aims of poesy"; of the "original poems in the volume before us," Poe says, "there is none in which the aim of instruction, or *truth*, has not been too obviously substituted for the legitimate aim [of poetry], beauty."⁶

Poe makes the same distinction in the May 1842 review of Hawthorne, claiming that "truth is often, and in very great degree, the aim of the tale" and "that the author who aims at the purely beautiful in a prose tale is laboring at a great disadvantage."⁷ Thus, in celebrating Hawthorne's tales as tales, Poe places himself in opposition to Longfellow's theory of creative transubstantiation, a theory underwritten by the egotistical assumption that all literature aspires to the condition of poetry. The danger of such a theory is that it erodes categorical distinctions among genres by privileging some inchoate meaning and morality over formal realization. For Poe, truth in literature depends on a clear understanding of the genre, not its "internal being." Such "didacticism" amounts to a utilitarian harnessing of art to worldly concerns.

In his April 1842 review of the second volume of *Twice-Told Tales*, Longfellow further praises Hawthorne's ability to extract "the subtile essence of poetry...from prose," and he develops another point that Poe challenges a month later: that Hawthorne's tales are original in the sense of being uniquely American. For Longfellow, Hawthorne "gives us no poor copies of poor originals in English magazines and souvenirs. He has caught nothing of the intensity of the French, or the extravagance of the German schools of fiction.... His writings retain the racy flavor of the soil. They have the healthy vigor and free grace of indigenous plants."⁸

Originality is here figured as an absence of an unhealthy, corrupting foreign influence, Hawthorne's genius apparently having sprung fully formed from the forehead of Brother Jonathan. Poe's feelings on the subject are quite different, as befits the more cosmopolitan outlook that set him at odds with many of his literary contemporaries. The parade of national stereotypes in Longfellow's article exemplifies what Poe lambasts as "the usual animadversions against those tales of effect many fine examples of which were found in the earlier numbers of *Blackwood*," the British magazine that published many tales of the German Romantics.[9]

To dismiss the "tale of effect" is, Poe suggests, to misunderstand the function of the tale itself. Unlike the essay – the dominant characteristic of which is "repose," a painterly term that Poe employs to typify an affective experience of restfulness bordering on stagnation – the tale is meant to produce "impressions...wrought in a legitimate sphere of action." Thus, the other reviewer's ecstasies regarding the "quiet pathos," "tranquil beauty," and atmosphere of "soft and calm melancholy" in some of Hawthorne's stories reveal Longfellow's failure to understand the rules of the genre, rules that transcend petty national differences and that determine the status of an author's work within the corpus of Western literature.[10] So, when Poe says that "as Americans, we feel proud" of the *Twice-Told Tales*, he means not that he is proud of these tales' Americanness, but that he sees them as contributions to a literary genre in which few Americans yet had been worthy of distinction.

"The true critic," Poe pronounces, "will but demand that the design intended be accomplished, to the fullest extent, by the means most advantageously applicable." That Hawthorne produced tales that met the standards of Poe's true critic is evident from his May 1842 review, as he commends many for their "singular power," being both "exceedingly well imagined and executed with surpassing ability." Even in such moments of admiration, however, Poe's evaluations often serve a heuristic function, allowing him to make explicit, for example, why a particular story should be elevated to the rank of tale or demoted to that of essay. That he sees himself as correcting the faulty thinking of critics like Longfellow is clear from his comments on "The Minister's Black Veil," in which he qualifies his praise of this "masterly composition" by insinuating that the obvious moral espoused by the dying minister is merely a bone tossed to the rabble, obfuscating the more subtly profound meaning only intelligible to "those minds congenial with that of the author."[11]

Here and elsewhere, Poe reveals his desire to steer Hawthorne and his literary reputation away from the influence of the New England literati. He admits to being "agreeably mistaken" in his initial supposition that Hawthorne "had been thrust into his present position by one of the impudent *cliques* which beset our literature," but his myriad cautions throughout the article regarding problematic tendencies in Hawthorne's fiction imply that he considers the situation precarious. Poe depicts Hawthorne as a talented author who must be saved from falling into the Bostonian literary "Frog-pond," and Poe's actions subsequent to the May 1842 review suggest that he nominated himself for the task.

What follows next is a strange series of letters written throughout the spring of 1843, in which Poe and Hawthorne communicate using poet James Russell Lowell as their proxy. Poe begins the exchange the first week of February, praising Lowell's short-lived literary magazine, *The Pioneer*, and hoping to establish his own: "If I can but succeed in engaging, as permanent contributors, Mr Hawthorne, Mr Neal, and two others, with a certain young poet of Boston who shall be nameless, I will engage to produce the best journal in America."[12] Planting the seed of the idea with the deft flattering touch of Hawthorne's name at the top of the list, Poe follows up a month later with a more explicit plea to Lowell:

> I would be indebted to you if you could put me in the way of procuring a brief article...from Mr Hawthorne – whom I believe you know personally. Whatever you gave him, we should be happy to give. A part of my design is to illustrate, whatever is fairly susceptible to illustration, with finely executed wood-engravings – after the fashion of Gigoux's "Gil Blas" or "Grandville's Gulliver" – and I wish to get a tale from Mr. Hawthorne as early as possible.[13]

If the request is ostensibly addressed to Lowell, Poe's promises of good financial compensation and quality illustrations are clearly intended for Hawthorne's ears. Also directed at Hawthorne, one suspects, are the hints as to the kind of "article" that Poe would like from him. He chooses his examples of woodcut styles from contemporary reprints (1835 for *Gil Blas* and 1838 for *Gulliver's Travels*) of famous eighteenth-century picaresque travel narratives, both comprised of loosely linked stories full of incident and effect, conveying not a sense of repose but rather lively impressions "susceptible to illustration." In light of his earlier reviews, Poe's general solicitation might be narrowed down to a specific type of contribution: a tale, in his sense of the word.

That Hawthorne read this much into Poe's request cannot be assumed, but it does account for his curious reluctance to respond to Poe directly. Instead, he allows Lowell to communicate his willingness to "send an article in the course of a week or two" as well as his financial terms.[14] The allotted time goes by, and in May, Lowell again writes Poe to say that he is waiting on Hawthorne's article. Then, soon after, Lowell receives the following missive from Hawthorne himself:

> I am greatly troubled about the contribution for Mr. Poe. Hitherto, I have never been accustomed to write during the summer weather, and now I find that my

thoughts fly out of the open window.... I am compelled, indeed, to write a monthly article for the Democratic, but it is only with great pain and dolor.... If I am to send anything to Mr. Poe, I should wish it be worth his reception.... When you write to him, do make my apologies.... He shall hear from me after the first frost.[15]

If Hawthorne's excuse of the summer weather seems rather fanciful, it does have a fictional analogue in the exact article Hawthorne was writing for the *Democratic Review*: "Buds and Bird Voices." Therein, the speaker meditates on the effect of "Balmy Spring," who "peeps brightly into my study window, inviting me to throw it open," after doing which, "forth into infinite space fly the innumerable forms of thought or fancy that have kept me company in...wintry weather."[16]

It is hardly a crime for an author to recycle his own material, but having kept two men waiting for more than a month, his explanation and apology are stunningly inadequate. We might ask, then, what is behind Hawthorne's diffidence toward Poe's complimentary request? A potential answer might be sought in his stated reluctance to send anything to Poe unless it be "worth his reception." For "Buds and Bird Voices" – a possible companion piece to the story "Snowflakes" from *Twice-Told Tales* – matches all of Poe's criteria for an essay, being "quiet, thoughtful, subdued" with "a strong undercurrent of suggestion run[ning] continuously beneath the upper stream of the tranquil thesis."[17] That being the case, is Hawthorne perhaps insinuating here that he is withholding such works for venues where they will meet with a more appreciative audience, one that will not push him to adapt his writing to meet standards not his own?

Regardless, Hawthorne never did get in touch with Poe, and *The Stylus* (Poe's prospective journal) never making it to press, the whole exchange came to naught. Still, their mediated interchange does make visible a particular dynamic between the two men, in which Poe's expressions of fellowship and patronage were met by Hawthorne with politic aloofness, a refusal to commit himself to Poe's vision of American *belles-lettres* and the obligations that vision placed upon him, both socially and creatively. When Poe tentatively asks after Hawthorne in a letter to Lowell more than a year later, his usual compliment – that Hawthorne is a "man of rare genius" – lacks some of its former enthusiasm, and his next public evaluation of Hawthorne (significantly, in the December 1844 edition of the *Democratic Review*) makes some important revisions to his reviews from 1842. Whereas before Hawthorne was "original at *all* points," now his "handling" of a theme is "always thoroughly original" even if the theme itself is not. Hawthorne's style is still "purity itself," but now it is to be regretted that it has never been "vigorous." And if previously, Poe noted "the insufficient diversity of tone," he now laments that Hawthorne has "little or no variety of tone," insofar as "he handles all subjects in the same subdued, misty, dreamy, suggestive, innuendo way."[18]

Poe's stridency in this critique most likely has something to do with the failure of his overtures, but it also seems connected to an increasing sense that what he once considered inconsistent tendencies in Hawthorne's writing are well on their way to becoming entrenched characteristics. Supporting this idea is another qualified pronouncement that Poe makes in this 1844 article: "although I think [Hawthorne] the truest genius, upon the whole, which our literature possesses, I can't help regarding him as the most desperate mannerist of our day."[19] A term that, like repose, originated in the visual arts, *mannerism* signifies a kind of exaggerated, perverse, and idiosyncratic perspective in which the world is refracted through the oddly colored and distorted lens of the artist's consciousness. Poe again charges Hawthorne with mannerism in a largely positive mention in "The Literati of New York City," wherein he differentiates Hawthorne from Longfellow and others by virtue of the fact that he is "not a quack."

The source of Poe's growing dissatisfaction is not made fully explicit until his longest and most detailed article on Hawthorne published in the May 1847 issue of *Godey's*, titled "Tale-Writing – Nathaniel Hawthorne." Supposedly a review of Hawthorne's next collection of tales, *Mosses from an Old Manse*, Poe spends the majority of the article expanding on points made in 1842, his elaborations evidencing a now uncompromising stance on matters regarding the tale previously treated with much more latitude. Among the reasons for this obduracy we might include an 1846 letter – the only known letter – Poe received from Hawthorne, the purpose of which was to inquire after Poe's receipt of a reviewer's copy of *Mosses*. With typical formality, Hawthorne writes, "I have read your occasional notices of my productions with interest – not so much because your judgment was on the whole favorable, as because it seemed given in earnest. I care for nothing but the truth." The truth of that assertion, though, is belied by what follows: "I confess, however, that I admire you rather as a writer of tales than as a critic of them. I might often – and often do – dissent from your opinions in the latter capacity, but could never fail to recognize your force and originality in the former."[20] A provocative remark to direct toward a reviewer, Hawthorne's celebration of Poe's tales at the expense of his criticism denies those tales what for Poe was their legitimizing force: that they were but manifestations of the literary theory that gave meaning and structure to his understanding of creative production. Moreover, as before, Hawthorne refuses to accept Poe's governance on the subject of tale writing; he acknowledges him as a gifted writer, but not as an authority on the genre that Poe once saw them as jointly revolutionizing.

Poe's disapproval of the direction in which Hawthorne's fiction is headed manifests itself in the 1847 review in two major ways. First, he retracts his earlier assertions regarding Hawthorne's originality. His judgment now is that Hawthorne is not "original," but rather "peculiar." True originality, he argues, is the product of a receptive, ever-evolving genius, one that lends "its own character to everything it touches, and, especially [is] *self impelled to touch everything.*" Poe ascribes Hawthorne's lack of widespread popularity to a habitual strangeness that has the effect of novelty when initially encountered, but grows stale upon review, especially for the reader well versed in continental writers like Ludwig Tieck. Refusing to roast the old critical chestnut that "to be original is to be unpopular," he contrarily asserts that "the excitable, undisciplined and child-like popular mind" has rejected Hawthorne because his tales fail to engage with the fancies, concerns, and sentiments of a broader humanity, which create a "bond of sympathy between" author and reader, a bond that "irradiates" the truly original production.

At the heart of Poe's critique of Hawthorne is his supposition that the tendency in Hawthorne's tales toward "dreamy innuendo" has developed into an infectious "strain of allegory." Poe's opposition to allegory is ubiquitous in his literary criticism; even in its best instances, he deems it "an abomination – a remnant of antique barbarism – appealing only to our faculties of comparison."[21] Allegory, to Poe's mind, is a type of imaginative writing commissioned by – and thus beholden to – the Real; it yokes "the transparent upper current of meaning" to "an under or suggestive one," "what we vaguely term the *moral.*"[22] The story's "unity of effect," on which depends its "verisimilitude," is sacrificed in allegory to a propagandistic effort to instill a particular message or meaning. Poe sees this as a betrayal of the tale writer's grand purpose, and his decision to take issue with it in this review makes sense when one considers that other contemporaneous reviewers of Hawthorne are beginning to praise his fiction for precisely this attribute. For example, Charles Wilkins Webber, in the September 1846 *American Review*, describes "Young Goodman Brown" as "an Allegory of simple New England Village Life" and pronounces it "as a Tale of the Supernatural … more exquisitely managed than anything we have seen in American Literature, at least!" He suggests that other native authors would do well to follow Hawthorne's example, particularly a "modern Prometheus" "the glorious promise of whose prime has been wasted in the fierce guerrilla wars of egoism for notoriety" that have left him "*Raven*-ous."[23]

Webber's unsubtle allegorizing of Poe as a selfish demigod who swallowed the fires he stole from Olympus and now writhes and "blasphemies" "as the molten hell goes scorching through his veins" paints an unflattering picture of Poe's critical project and helps to explain why Poe's 1847 review returns to the subject of tale writing with such fervor and conviction.[24] In Hawthorne's *Mosses*, Poe sees the American tale as drifting ever farther away from the generic ideal, and like William Wilson's double, his warnings gain in strength as the creative vices in which he views Hawthorne as indulging become harder to overlook and correct. If Hawthorne will not acknowledge the error of his ways, Poe must expose them to the world at large, making Hawthorne an example of what happens when one sacrifices what Poe calls the "Indian-summer sunshine" of Hawthorne's best stories for the "phalanx and phalanstery atmosphere" of the Northeastern cultural elite.[25] Poe still believes Hawthorne to be the most skilled American craftsman of the tale, but he mourns Hawthorne's decision to become a citizen of a literary utopia whose foundational ideas can only be upheld through isolationism and shows of critical force against outsiders. Into this hothouse environment, where matters of national prestige all but obscure formal concerns, where a Lotos-land desire for repose weighs down the questing, restless energy of genius, and where moral conservatism hinders the artist's ability to transcend the small concerns of lesser minds, Poe will not follow Hawthorne. Yet, his final admonition – that Hawthorne "mend his pen, get a bottle of visible ink, come out from the Old Manse, cut Mr. Alcott, hang (if possible) the editor of *The Dial*, and throw out of the window to the pigs all his odd numbers of *The North American Review*" – is his prescription for Hawthorne's recovery, testifying to his belief that not all hope is lost.[26] Though consigned himself to the fate of Hop-Frog (setting the literary world on fire before escaping into the great unknown), Edgar Allan Poe's 1847 review offers an alternative ending to the narrative of the doppelganger which bound him to Nathaniel Hawthorne, as brothers in arms as well as worthy adversaries: instead of rushing at the mirror, daggers drawn, Poe asks Hawthorne to put his talents in the service of "honest, upright, sensible, prehensible, and comprehensible things,"[27] and, by conquering himself, to save the tale from being – like Wilson – "dead to the World, dead to Heaven, dead to Hope."

NOTES

1. Edgar Allan Poe, *Essays and Reviews*, ed. G. R. Thompson (New York: Library of America, 1984), 571.
2. Ibid., 574.
3. Ibid., 569.
4. Ibid., 571.
5. [Henry Wadsworth Longfellow], "Hawthorne's *Twice-Told Tales* [I]," *North American Review* 45 (1837), 59–60.
6. Poe, *Essays*, 691.
7. Ibid., 573.
8. [Henry Wadsworth Longfellow], "Hawthorne's *Twice-Told Tales* [II]," *North American Review* 54 (1842), 496–7.
9. Poe, *Essays*, 573.
10. Longfellow, "Hawthorne's *Twice-Told Tales* [II]," 498.
11. Poe, *Essays*, 574–5.
12. Poe to James Russell Lowell, February 4, 1843, *The Collected Letters of Edgar Allan Poe*, ed. John Ward Ostrom, Burton R. Pollin, and Jeffrey A. Savoye, 2 vols. (New York: Gordian, 2008), vol. i, 377.
13. Poe to James Russell Lowell, March 27, 1843, *Collected Letters*, vol. i, 394.
14. James Russell Lowell to Poe, April 17, 1843, *The Complete Works of Edgar Allan Poe*, 17 vols. (New York: Crowell, 1902), vol. xvii, 142.
15. Nathaniel Hawthorne to James Russell Lowell, circa May 1843, *The Letters, 1813–1843*, ed. Thomas Woodson et al. (Columbus: Ohio State University Press, 1984), 684.
16. Nathaniel Hawthorne, *Mosses from an Old Manse*, ed. William Charvat et al. (Columbus: Ohio State University Press, 1974), 148.
17. Poe, *Essays*, 570.
18. Ibid., 1119.
19. Ibid., 1343.
20. Nathaniel Hawthorne to Poe, June 17, 1846, *The Letters, 1843–1853*, ed. Thomas Woodson et al. (Columbus: Ohio State University Press, 1985), 168.
21. Poe, *Essays*, 159.
22. Ibid., 337.
23. Charles Wilkins Webber, "Hawthorne," *American Review* 4 (1846), 311.
24. Webber, "Hawthorne," 303.
25. Poe, *Essays*, 587.
26. Ibid., 587–8.
27. Ibid., 587. The last quotation comes from the final paragraph of "William Wilson."

PART FIVE

Scientific and Pseudoscientific Contexts

CHAPTER 30

Phrenology

Brett Zimmerman

Madeleine Stern has called phrenology a "nineteenth-century equivalent of psychoanalysis, occupational guidance, and computerized mating."[1] Edward Hungerford, the first critic to explore phrenology in Poe's oeuvre, provides a similar note: "Not unlike the psychology of today [Hungerford was writing in 1930], it hoped to provide accurate vocational guidance for the young, to revolutionize our systems of education, to revise the care of the insane, to bring wisdom into the treatment of criminals, and ... to provide dependable information upon the advisability of marriages."[2] Phrenology (once called cranioscopy or craniology) is a psychological theory founded by German anatomist and physician Franz Joseph Gall. In *The Anatomy and Physiology of the Nervous System in General, and of the Brain in Particular* (1809–19), Gall proposes that faculties of the mind and character traits are manifested through special organs in separate portions of the brain. For instance, the part of the brain responsible for parental love was thought to be located at the very back of the head, while another character trait, conscientiousness, was associated with a part of the grey matter near the top of the head above the ear. Some of these characteristics are the same ones that humans share with animals, such as combativeness, destructiveness, and philoprogenitiveness (parental love). The bumps and ridges of the skull – the shape of one's head – could allegedly tell a phrenologist much about one's character, as these bumps and ridges would reflect the shape of the brain's surface beneath: "The size of the organ within the brain determines the degree of intensity with which the individual possesses the quality."[3] A broad forehead, such as Poe possessed, would suggest that those character traits supposedly localized at the front of the brain were highly developed, the organs enlarged as a result of their supreme development, employment, and capacities.

The books and journals on phrenology typically provide cranial maps outlining the various faculties of the human mind and personality, and the placement of the organs beneath the skull that are the seats of these

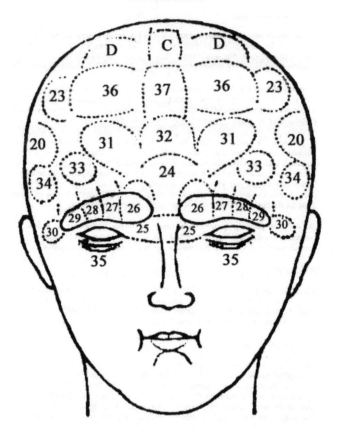

Figure 30.1 From O. S. Fowler, "Elementary Phrenology," *American Phrenological Journal* 2 (1839), 322. The letters and numbers have been digitally erased and resupplied for visual clarification.

faculties. We do not always find a consistency in the various diagrams used in terms of the number or even the names of the faculties. One suspects that the cranial maps evolved as the analysts "discovered" new cerebral organs.[4] The two-dimensional diagrams suggest that these various faculties were duplicated on the other side of the head; the left side of the brain is a mirror image of the right. A bump of sublimity, for example, would have a corresponding bump on the other side, as front-view phrenological maps demonstrate. The founders of this system devised several major groups: the Domestic Propensities, the Selfish Propensities, the Selfish Sentiments, the Moral and Religious Sentiments, the Intellectual Faculties, the Semi-Intellectual Sentiments, the Observing or Knowing (Literary)

Faculties, the Semi-Perceptive Faculties, and the Reflective or Reasoning (Intuitive) Faculties. These are the nine categories provided by O. S. Fowler in "Elementary Phrenology." His brother, Lorenzo Niles Fowler, on the other hand, became famous for his phrenology head. Lorenzo recognized only seven major groups. Clearly, phrenological "science" was a work in progress.

The uses and abuses of the many faculties of the human brain as "discovered" by Gall and as taught by his disciple, Johann Caspar Spurzheim, a great popularizer of phrenology in the United States and Great Britain, were legion; a few samples must suffice. As for the utility of cranial organs, Gall insisted that they demonstrated God's wisdom insofar as each was necessary for human survival and happiness. M. B. Sampson puts it this way:

[M]an is provided with special faculties to adapt him to each physical and moral law of the world in which he is placed, and that it is upon the harmonious and healthy action of such faculties that his happiness and safety are made entirely to depend. The phrenological system does not embrace a single organ, the deprivation of which would not prove in some way fatal to our physical or moral safety, or the functions of which could be supplied by the action of any other faculty.[5]

Spurzheim makes an additional significant claim: "the Creator could not bestow any faculty absolutely hurtful on man."[6] However, because we live in a postlapsarian world, these God-bestowed faculties are liable to become sickly if we are not careful. In his discussion of the Domestic Propensities (amativeness, philoprogenitiveness, adhesiveness, inhabitiveness), O. S. Fowler writes, "The proper, or improper, exercise of the domestic feelings have a most powerful influence on all the other faculties. When these organs are large, they cause an elongation and fulness in the middle and lower portion of the back part of the head; but when small, this part of the head presents a flattened and depressed appearance."[7] The largeness or smallness of the cerebral organs causes the bumps or depressions on a person's cranium. Fowler warns against what he calls the abuses of the various faculties. An abused organ would become hypertrophied through overuse or atrophied through underuse. While the faculty of cautiousness is necessary in a dangerous world, a hypertrophied organ of cautiousness would show not only in an enlargement of that part of the head but also in the sufferer's behavior: "procrastination; irresolution; timidity; cowardice; melancholy; want of promptness and enterprise."[8] Consider how Roderick displays these traits in "The Fall of the House of Usher." How many gothic heroines must have dangerously enlarged organs of ideality: "Abuses: ideal reveries; sickly sentimentalism; extravagant love of romance, poetry, the theatre, &c." – or Poe: "that sickly delicacy which is disgusted with the world as it is, and soars to dwell constantly in an ideal world."[9]

POE DISCOVERS PHRENOLOGY

Although phrenology was rejected by many scientists of the nineteenth century – not to mention the Catholic Church, which thought the theory blasphemous – it nevertheless spread rapidly throughout the Western world with numerous books and several journals devoted to explaining and publicizing the system. The New York firm of Fowler and Wells, which also had a branch in Philadelphia, was the most popular and successful one.[10] George Combe, who became a convert to phrenology through Spurzheim, founded the *Phrenological Journal* in Edinburgh (1832). Between 1838 and 1840 he made two visits to the United States, where he met many influential scientists, physicians, philosophers, and writers, including Poe's friend John Pendleton Kennedy. Combe gave a series of successful lectures on phrenology in numerous American cities. Poe may have attended some of these lectures, possibly the series that ended in Philadelphia on February 8, 1839.[11]

But Poe did not learn about the pseudoscience from Combe; he was already aware of it. How could he not have been, given his deep familiarity with the *Zeitgeist*? Certainly the magazine for which Poe would work from August 1835 to 1837, the *Southern Literary Messenger*, published articles on phrenology before Poe arrived at its offices – Daniel Patrick Thurs cites "Phrenological Examinations" in the January 1835 issue – and would continue publishing them long after he left.[12] In a March 1836 review of L. Miles's *Phrenology, and the Moral Influence of Phrenology* (1835) for the *Messenger*, Poe writes that phrenology "has assumed the majesty of a science; and as a science, ranks among the most important which can engage the attention of thinking beings."[13] Hungerford believes Miles's study first attracted Poe to the theory, after which references to phrenology are found fairly often in his prose. He adopted some of the terminology for his literary criticism as well. References to this "knowledge frame" occur in Poe's lesser known tales: Hungerford examines "The Business Man," "Diddling Considered as One of the Exact Sciences," and "Some Words with a Mummy." Further references appear many times in "The Literati of New York City." Perhaps Poe should have recognized it as sheer nonsense when he could not find a correspondence between an author's known character traits and the appearance of his cranium: "the forehead [of Charles Fenno Hoffman], to my surprise, although high, gives no indication, in the region of the temples, of that ideality (or love of the beautiful) which is the distinguishing trait of his moral nature."[14] In fact, by the early twentieth century, such instances of empirical refutation helped bring about the demise of phrenology as a pursuit for serious scientists.

PHRENOLOGY IN POE'S FICTION

Though the three tales mentioned earlier contain references to phrenology, Poe is not employing the "insights" of the system in any serious way. In some of his more famous tales, however, Poe depicts his main characters according to the findings of Gall and Spurzheim. One wonders if he had read the following passage in a Boston journal: "Writers who, in their delineation of character, have shown the deepest and most accurate knowledge of human nature, are throughout the most strictly phrenological;...characters drawn with a due attention to nature, may with ease, and in every case, admit of being translated, as it were, into phrenological language."[15] The original opening paragraph of "The Murders in the Rue Morgue" (1841), which Poe excised in later printings, clearly uses the terminology of the phrenologists.

This original paragraph is not the only time Poe sought to improve phrenological science; he does so as well in "The Black Cat" and "The Imp of the Perverse" in recommending a new organ or faculty of perverseness. After referring to the followers of Spurzheim ("Spurzheimites"), the narrator of "The Imp of the Perverse" finds fault not with phrenology but with its system of classification. The imp of the perverse is a fundamental human drive for which phrenologists have failed to assign a section of the brain. They have only accounted for those logical tendencies of humans such as the reasonable wish to nourish ourselves, to protect ourselves, and to continue the species. We remember Spurzheim's insistence that "the Creator could not bestow any faculty absolutely hurtful on man," but the imp of the perverse is an illogical motivating factor that compels us to want to bring harm or even destruction down upon ourselves.

In his way, Poe anticipates the twentieth-century existentialists in emphasizing the irrational aspects of human behavior. Perhaps he also anticipates modern psychological theories of masochism or the "death wish" or obsessive-compulsive neurosis, which involves persistent intrusions of unwanted thoughts or urges over which the person has no control.

Poe's interest in phrenology also explains why he provides such notable instances of *enargia* (vivid descriptions) in some of his tales, for the very appearance of characters such as Ligeia and Roderick Usher contributes to the themes of their respective stories. Ligeia's character certainly has a proper phrenological basis. An organ that the phrenologists speculated about but had trouble locating governs what they called a love of life. It might be identified with combativeness, a desire for self-preservation and well-being, but Spurzheim, for instance, refuses to conflate the two: "It is highly probable that there is a peculiar instinct to live, or love of life, and I look for its organ at the basis of the brain, between the posterior and middle lobes, inwardly of combativeness."[16] Combe – "than whom a more candid reasoner never, perhaps, wrote or spoke," as Poe wrote of him[17] – also considers that propensity:

Some individuals desire life so intensely, that they view death as the greatest calamity; they declare, that rather than part with existence, they would submit to live in endless misery; the bare idea of annihilation is unsupportable to their imaginations; – and they found an argument for immortality on the position that God cannot be guilty of the injustice of making them conscious of so great a boon as life, and subsequently depriving them of it; to have lived, according to them, gives an indefeasible title to continue to live.[18]

Ligeia's profound love of life, in this tale of metempsychosis, is central to her desire to be revived in another body. The narrator describes Ligeia's abhorrence of death: "It is this wild longing – it is this eager vehemence of desire for life – *but* for life – that I have no power to portray – no utterance capable of expressing."[19] So he procures the unsuspecting Rowena to function as the vessel for Ligeia's transmigrated spirit.

Unlike "Ligeia," where phrenology plays an important role in allowing us to understand the titular character, *The Narrative of Arthur Gordon Pym* (1838) only alludes to that pursuit, but this allusion would seem to have a deep significance, given Poe's ideas about the human races. Describing Dirk Peters, a half-breed Crow Indian, Pym says, "His head was equally deformed, being of immense size, with an indentation on the crown (*like that on the head of most negroes*)."[20] If this phrenological detail were in fact true, it would mean a deficiency in a number of key faculties located at the very top of the African cranium, most of them relating to moral and religious sentiments: benevolence (philanthropy, liberality, sympathy), veneration (worship), firmness (stability), spirituality (faith), and conscientiousness (justice, integrity). The supposed lack of these qualities can be seen to account for the unscrupulous behavior of the black islanders (the Tsalalians) in the novel as well as the mutinous black cook, Seymour, whom Pym describes as demonic. The contemporary phrenological literature supports the theory of moral depravity in blacks. In a discussion of veneration, a contributor to the *American Phrenological Journal* illustrates

VENERATION SMALL.

No. 46. NEGRO MURDERER.

Figure 30.2 From "Veneration: Its Definition, Location, Function, Adaptation, and Cultivation," *American Phrenological Journal* 9 (1847), 308.

the skull of a "Negro Murderer" indented in the area of the moral and religious sentiments.[21]

Not all of the literature suggests that blacks comprise a race of sociopathic killers, however; a few articles in fact discuss certain individuals more favorably – such as L. N. Fowler's report of Joseph Cinquez in the December 1839 issue of the *American Phrenological Journal* and the commendatory report on a former Santo Domingo slave named Eustache.[22] The phrenologists do acknowledge exceptional characters within races and nations but nevertheless cannot resist the urge to generalize: "in the Negro brain the moral and reflecting organs are of larger size, in proportion to the organs of the animal propensities now enumerated, than in that of the Indian. The Negro is, therefore, naturally more submissive, docile, intelligent, patient, trustworthy, and susceptible of kindly emotions, and less cruel, cunning, and vindictive, than the other race."[23] Clearly, phrenology supported the "romantic racialism" of such New England liberals as Harriet Beecher Stowe (*Uncle Tom's Cabin*) and Herman Melville's Captain Delano ("Benito Cereno"). But, as with religious texts, so with phrenological literature: people pick and choose what suits them. Poe, with a racist disposition typical of the times, would have seized upon "evidence" demonstrating that the "Negro brain" is deficient in the moral and religious sentiments. Unlike some of his coeval phrenologists, he had not forgotten the traumatizing lessons of Nat Turner's insurrection.

THE PROFESSIONAL PHRENOLOGISTS AND POE

Stern asserts that "phrenology was as deeply interested in Poe as Poe was in phrenology."[24] The Fowlers took a special interest in poets because of their allegedly large organs of ideality and language, and Stern suggests that Poe and the practitioners had opportunities to cross paths in New York or Philadelphia. Perhaps not surprising, then, Lorenzo Fowler did do an examination of Poe's head, either from life or from a likeness – perhaps a bust. "At all events," Stern writes, "upon several occasions after Poe's death the firm did publish their findings about the poet's phrenology."[25] She quotes Fowler in his *Illustrated Phrenological Almanac for 1851*: "[Poe's] phrenological developments, combined with the fiery intensity of his temperament, serve to explain many of the eccentricities of this remarkable man. [He inherited from his mother] strongly developed and highly excited faculties, an unusual degree of intellect, Ideality, Sublimity, Spirituality, and Language."[26] Upon examining the phrenological map or bust, we see that the regions of ideality and sublimity are located on the side of the skull above the ear just where the head begins to curve toward the top of the cranium. If we look at a picture of Poe, we see two large and unusual bumps just where the region of ideality is. His own contemporaries remarked on these bumps, which expanded Poe's already famously broad forehead even farther. In an 1862 lecture, Fowler informed his audience that Poe "was wanting in Firmness, Self-Esteem, Continuity, and in the basilar brain and vital power."[27] The regions of firmness and self-esteem are found at the top of the skull with firmness near the top, middle, and self-esteem in the middle sloping toward the back. Perhaps the phrenologists found Poe's head rather flattened in the alleged regions of these organs.

Still, we may begin to wonder to what extent a phrenological examination did indeed suggest those traits, or deficiencies therein, and to what extent Poe's own behavior, sometimes publicized and certainly legendary after his death, was actually behind the diagnosis. For instance, a subtrait of firmness is stability, and Poe's own *instability*, partly due to his drinking, was widely known in his time and after. It is easy to take that proven character trait and *guess* – without ever having examined Poe's skull – that he must have been deficient in the area of firmness. (In fact, a favorite pastime for phrenologists was to determine, *guess at*, the cranial appearance of absent characters, literary and historical, based on their known behavior and manifested talents.)

CONCLUSION: POE'S ATTRACTION TO PHRENOLOGY

Poe was attracted to phrenology for several reasons: it explained his own behavior, talents, and predispositions; it supported his way of looking at the world; and it informed his artistry both as a writer of fiction and as a literary critic. Consider the first: in 1841 he wrote to F. W. Thomas stating, "Speaking of heads – my own *has been examined* by several phrenologists – all of whom spoke of me in a species of extravaganza which I should be ashamed to repeat."[28] He seems to be hinting that the phrenologists raved about the extraordinary qualities that his cranium suggested. "Critics of phrenology," Thurs maintains, "almost universally stressed the pecuniary and commercial motivations of the traveling head readers, including the Fowlers and other 'itinerant self-seekers' who often catered to their clients' vanity with flattering assessments of character."[29] Now, at least, Poe could regard his unusually broad cranium, which some of his less friendly acquaintances considered an aesthetic defect – in his novel *1844*, Thomas Dunn English represents Poe as "Marmaduke *Hammerhead*" – as a physical trait of which he could be proud. Not all of Poe's supposed cranial traits were positive, though, as L. N. Fowler, Wells, and Sizer documented[30]; and we may wonder, given Poe's sometimes antisocial and self-destructive behavior, if his theory of perversity arose from his own unfortunate experiences and represents a covert or tangential explanation and apology for his social and vocational faux pas.

Phrenology also buttressed Poe's ideology and epistemology, his way of looking at and comprehending the world. As for his epistemology, he often used the concept of *analogy* as a way of understanding the natural and social arenas.[31] So did the phrenologists: "The use of analogy was a critical piece of most phrenologists' arguments for the notion of plural cerebral organs and the idea that larger organs indicated a stronger propensity for certain kinds of thought or behavior...natural examples of parallels between size and use abounded; the large muscles of the blacksmith's hammering arm showed this clearly."[32] Thus epistemology; as for ideology, phrenology assured Poe of the superiority of the Caucasian race. In Combe, Poe could have read this: "The brain of the different

EUROPEAN NATIONS... are decidedly larger than the Hindoo, American Indian, and Negro heads; and this indicates superior force of mental character."[33] With their craniometrical calipers, those clever "bumpologists" had been measuring the skulls of Caucasians, Mongolians, Malays, Native Americans, and Ethiopians, had been determining the volume of their specimens with sand or seeds, and had concluded that the Caucasian skull contains the largest brain capacity known to science. Even more, phrenology vindicated Poe's suspicions of blacks as a horde of Nat Turner types, murderous sociopaths deficient in morality and a proper sense of veneration. Phrenology "proved," in other words, that the South should be wary of its slaves, and Poe's use of that system validates our interpretation of *Pym* and "The Murders in the Rue Morgue" as allegorical warnings to slaveholders.

Finally, phrenology served Poe in his capacities as the notorious "Tomahawk Man" and as the painter of some of the most famous characters in American literature. It enabled him as a literary critic to evaluate the fictional characters of other authors in terms of phrenological verisimilitude. More significant, this system of mental philosophy afforded Poe a means by which he believed he could make his own characters true to life: Ligeia and Roderick Usher, especially, are the supreme examples in Poe's fiction of personages whose strengths, weaknesses, and behavior are firmly rooted in what many considered the cutting-edge psychological science of their day.[34] In the early twentieth century, as phrenology finally died, authors and critics, to depict and evaluate literary characters, turned to the psychological models of Freud and Jung – two other systems of mental philosophy that have not entirely withstood the test of time.

NOTES

1. Madeleine Stern, "Poe: 'The Mental Temperament' for Phrenologists," *American Literature* 40 (1968), 155.
2. Edward Hungerford, "Poe and Phrenology," *American Literature* 2 (1930), 210.
3. Ibid., 211.
4. John D. Davies, *Phrenology Fad and Science: A 19th-Century American Crusade* (New Haven: Yale University Press, 1955), 6.
5. M. B. Sampson, "On the Primary Function of the Organ Marked '?'," *American Phrenological Journal* 2 (1839), 205.
6. Johann Caspar Spurzheim, *Phrenology in Connexion with the Study of Physiognomy* (Boston: Marsh, Capen and Lyon, 1836), 30.

7. O. S. Fowler, "Elementary Phrenology," *American Phrenological Journal* 2 (1839), 322–3.
8. Fowler, "Elementary Phrenology," 324.
9. Fowler, "Elementary Phrenology," 327.
10. Stern, "Poe," 155.
11. Donald Barlow Stauffer, "Poe as Phrenologist: The Example of Monsieur Dupin," in *Papers on Poe: Essays in Honor of John Ward Ostrom*, ed. Richard P. Veler (Springfield, OH: Chantry Music Press, 1972), 114.
12. Daniel Patrick Thurs, *Science Talk: Changing Notions of Science in American Culture* (New Brunswick: Rutgers University Press, 2007), 194.
13. Edgar Allan Poe, *Essays and Reviews*, ed. G. R. Thompson (New York: Library of America, 1984), 329.
14. Ibid., 1211.
15. "Application of Phrenology to Criticism," *Annals of Phrenology* 2 (1834), 201–2.
16. Johann Caspar Spurzheim, *Phrenology, or the Doctrine of the Mental Phenomena*, 2 vols. (Boston: Marsh, Capen and Lyon, 1833), vol. i, 136.
17. Poe, *Essays*, 322.
18. George Combe, *A System of Phrenology*, 3rd ed. (London: Longman, 1830), 188.
19. Edgar Allan Poe, *Collected Works of Edgar Allan Poe*, ed. Thomas Ollive Mabbott, 3 vols. (Cambridge, MA: Belknap Press, 1969–78), vol. ii, 317.
20. Edgar Allan Poe, *Poetry and Tales*, ed. Patrick F. Quinn (New York: Library of America, 1984), 1043, emphasis added.
21. "Veneration: Its Definition, Location, Function, Adaptation, and Cultivation," *American Phrenological Journal* 9 (1847), 308.
22. L. N. Fowler, "Phrenological Developments of Joseph Cinquez, Alias Ginqua," *American Phrenological Journal* 2 (1839), 136–8; "Character of Eustache," *American Phrenological Journal* 2 (1840), 177–82.
23. George Combe, *A System of Phrenology*, 5th ed. (Edinburgh: Maclachlan, Stewart, 1843), 354–5.
24. Stern, "Poe," 155.
25. Ibid., 158.
26. Ibid. See also Madeleine Stern, *Heads and Headlines: The Phrenological Fowlers* (Norman: University of Oklahoma Press, 1971), 76.
27. Stern, "Poe," 159.
28. Poe to Frederick W. Thomas, October 27, 1841, *The Collected Letters of Edgar Allan Poe*, ed. John Ward Ostrom, Burton R. Pollin, and Jeffrey A. Savoye, 2 vols. (New York: Gordian, 2008), vol. i, 313.
29. Thurs, *Science Talk*, 37.
30. Stern, "Poe," 158–9. For documentation of what amateur phrenologists said about Poe, see Dwight Thomas and David K. Jackson, *The Poe Log: A Documentary Life of Edgar Allan Poe, 1809–1849* (Boston: G. K. Hall, 1987), 529, 643, 693, 844.

31. Brett Zimmerman, *Edgar Allan Poe: Rhetoric and Style* (Montreal: McGill-Queen's University Press, 2005), 123–7.
32. Thurs, *Science Talk*, 38–9.
33. Combe, *A System of Phrenology*, 618.
34. Brett Zimmerman, "Phrenological Allegory in Poe's 'The Fall of the House of Usher'," *Mosaic* 43 (2010), 57–72, and "Sensibility, Phrenology, and 'The Fall of the House of Usher'," *Edgar Allan Poe Review* 8 (2007), 47–56.

CHAPTER 31

Photography

Satwik Dasgupta

Louis Daguerre's invention of photography and Edgar Allan Poe's invention of the detective story, which occurred around roughly the same time, may not be as coincidental as they initially seem. Much as a photographic portrait captures the appearance of a person in a particular time and space, the deductive process involves examining the traces left behind as someone passes through a certain time and space. Recognizing the influence of photography on Poe can help illuminate his writings. Though the technology of reprinting photographs did not emerge until after Poe's death, the daguerreotype did give rise to a rich trade in engraved portraiture in books and magazines, which strongly reinforced the cultural significance of photography.

Daguerre was not the only one to introduce photography to the marketplace. In England, William Henry Fox Talbot unveiled his method of photogenic drawings. Though both Daguerre and Talbot were instrumental in revolutionizing the photographic process, the daguerreotype's success was more sensational in America and profoundly affected the popular imagination. Talbot's calotype process was not nearly as popular in the United States as the daguerreotype, partly because of a patent rights issue, but also because the paper print-based English invention lacked the minute details of the daguerreotype.[1] Conversely, the daguerreotype's lateral reversal of image – the mirror image familiar only to the sitter – made it less popular in Europe.[2] In addition, Talbot could not find a promoter in the United States, whereas Daguerre's agent, François Gouraud, visited New York in November 1839 and Boston soon thereafter to promote the daguerreotype.[3] Consequently, the calotypes (or talbotypes, as they would eventually be called) were relegated to the domain of licensed practitioners, amateur gentlemen, and scientists; clearly a class divide was also responsible for its inferior currency in the marketplace.

Poe was fascinated with these inventions. In "The Daguerreotype," an essay he contributed to *Alexander's Weekly Messenger* in January 1840 (the first of two appreciations of the daguerreotype he wrote for that magazine), Poe declared, "The instrument [the daguerreotype camera] itself must undoubtedly be regarded as the most important, and perhaps the most extraordinary triumph of modern science." He also claimed a photographic image to be truer than the original because "if we imagine the distinctness with which an object is reflected in a positively perfect mirror, we come as near the reality as by any other means." For Poe, "photogenic drawing discloses a more absolute truth, a more perfect identity of aspect with the thing represented."[4] Poe's enthusiastic essay in *Alexander's* both reflected and contributed to the burgeoning daguerreomania. By late 1840, the United States witnessed a flurry of activity involving the daguerreotype, particularly in New York and Philadelphia.

Romantic authors often emphasized the power of the written word to convey truth; photography provided a technological way to go the power of the word one better. *The Pencil of Nature* (1844), Henry Talbot's illustrated treatise describing his process of photogenic drawing, suggests a complex relationship between photography and writing.[5] One chapter, "A Scene in the Library," shows a photograph of two loaded bookshelves, as the accompanying text explains how photographs could be taken with "invisible rays" within a "darkened chamber." In other words, the photograph has the potential to convey hidden meaning beyond objective appearance. Without the accompanying text's explanation, however, the photograph cannot fulfill its role as a mediator of meaning. The invention of photography created a dialectic between word and image that significantly complicated the comprehension of texts.

Science and the popular imagination came together in the daguerreotype's evolution, and Poe became fascinated with the ways others used and interpreted this new form of imagery. His knowledge of photography clearly went beyond the daguerreotype. Poe's use of the terms *photogeny* and *photogenic drawings* points to his familiarity with Talbot's work. Furthermore, an anonymous contributor to *Burton's* during Poe's tenure as assistant editor of that magazine mentioned Talbot's efforts to record photographic images on paper: further evidence that Poe was aware of Talbot's process. In "The Spectacles," Poe includes a character named Talbot, who functions as a surrogate for the camera.[6]

For the most part, the daguerreotype's influence on Poe remains largely undocumented because he seldom mentioned it or evoked its working principles in his imaginative writings, but it is not totally absent. It does appear subtly in a few tales. In "The Black Cat," Poe describes a chemical process that creates an image of the dead cat, and his description recalls the chemical process involved in creating daguerreotypes. The image of the cat etched into a plaster wall by ammonia fumes from its decomposing body resembles the chemical processes of photography. Furthermore, serving as physical evidence of the narrator's wrongdoing, the cat's image offers a metaphor for the photograph. Another of Poe's tales emphasizes the agency of the sun in creating daguerreotypes. Among the modern wonders listed in "The Thousand-and-Second Tale of Scheherazade" is a person who can command the sun to paint his portrait.[7] Beyond these brief references, Poe's enthusiasm for photography can be discerned by exploring his works as manifestations of various photographic processes. Though they may not mention the daguerreotype, they nevertheless contribute to the discourse of photography.

Soon after Louis Daguerre made the invention of the daguerreotype process public in January 1839, news of it spread rapidly through Europe and across the Atlantic. In a matter of weeks, numerous articles announcing and extravagantly praising the new invention appeared in the American newspaper and periodical press. L. F. Tasistro reprinted an essay from the *London Court Journal* in the March issue of *The Expositor*, his miscellaneous New York weekly, which ended with the encomium: "Honor then to Mr. Daguerre! He is to the Fine Arts what Bacon was to Science. The Daguerreotype is the *novum organum* of art."[8] Daguerreotype exhibits went on display in major cities along the East Coast. Before the year was out, the first tentative efforts to produce daguerreotype portraits in the United States had begun. The enthusiastic press notices for the new invention continued through the following year.

Samuel Morse's letter from Paris to the New York *Observer* was especially influential.[9] Owing to Morse's friendship with Daguerre, the daguerreotype was not patented in America, and no restrictions were placed on its practice. Daguerreotypes were small in size (most popular sizes were 1/6 or 1/9 plates, about 3 by 2 1/2 inches), portable, cheap, and of unprecedented verisimilitude. Even though Americans were familiar with mechanical devices in portrait making and aware of the power of painting, daguerreotypes nevertheless yielded an unsurpassed, almost magical quality.

Upon seeing an early daguerreotype exhibit in New York, a contributor to the *Knickerbocker* called the photographic images displayed there "the most remarkable objects of curiosity and admiration, in the arts, that we have ever beheld." Like Poe, the *Knickerbocker* did not spare superlatives when it came to describing the daguerreotype. Unlike Poe, the *Knickerbocker* classified the newly invented photographic image as a "curiosity," that is, an object of popular scientific amusement rather than a serious scientific invention. Poe, however, intuitively recognized the invention's wide-ranging potential for contributing to the advancement of scientific knowledge. He was less certain about its potential as an artistic medium. In his first appreciation of photography for *Alexander's*, he observed, "The daguerreotype will never do for portrait painting. Its pictures are quite too natural to please any other than very beautiful sitters."[10] Poe suggests that the artistic process involved idealizing reality, not merely recording it.

Poe's appreciation of the daguerreotype in *Alexander's* has been subject to considerable interpretation. Sander Gilman, to name one modern commentator, sees little difference between the ideas Poe articulates and the comments of other contemporary journalists. Poe's acceptance of the photograph as a literal representation of reality, in Gilman's words, reflects the "naive realism of the first generation of writers" on photography.[11] Others have read much more into Poe's words. Richard Rudisill, for instance, finds Poe's idea about subjecting a photograph to a microscope analogous to Ralph Waldo Emerson's figurative sharpening of his sight in order to see beyond the surface of things. Emerson was conveying the mind's capacity for transcending the physicality of sight and seeing the unseen. Poe, alternatively, suggested how optical technology provided man with new ways of perceiving the physical world.[12]

Though some of Poe's comments are typical of the contemporary photographic discourse, his idea of subjecting the daguerreotype to a microscope is original. In a way, Poe's combination of two different optical technologies parallels his literary technique. He always sought originality in his writings, and he often achieved it by combining traditional literary forms and motifs in unique ways. The daguerreotype camera let a person capture a static image of reality. This image could then be subjected to intense scrutiny with the naked eye and could be scrutinized even further using another optical technology, the microscope.

Pondering Poe's juxtaposition of daguerreotype and microscope, Lisa Cartwright has suggested that the microscope reveals "the grain of the image, magnified and resolved so as to impute depth and volume to the smallest particle of the photographic surface." Poe, according to this view, saw photography as infinitely more accurate than painting, not because it provided a "more accurate rendering of pictorial space according to Renaissance perspective," but because it retained the "logic of perspective on a scale beyond the reach of the perception of the unaided eye." Cartwright compares the grain of the image surface of a daguerreotype to the stones that form the House of Usher: both "harbor a sentience identical with (and not merely reflective of) the life of the scene represented."[13] According to this view, the daguerreotype's reality stems from its materiality, evident only through the lens of the microscope.

Emphasizing the photograph's extraordinary mimetic powers, Poe elevated it above painting – but only in a technical sense. Mimetic veracity, needless to say, was not a part of Poe's visual aesthetic. Elaborating upon his visual aesthetic in a critical essay he wrote two years later, Poe specifically denied the need of art to reproduce reality. Refuting a commentator who asserted that the truth of a picture determined its merit, Poe observed: "That the chief merit of a picture is its *truth*, is an assertion deplorably erroneous. Even in Painting which is, more essentially than Poetry, a mimetic art, the proposition cannot be sustained. Truth is not even *the aim*. Indeed it is curious to observe how very slight a degree of truth is sufficient to satisfy the mind, which acquiesces in the absence of numerous essentials in the thing depicted."[14] Creating a work of art involved imaginatively selecting, arranging, and shaping its component parts, not replicating reality.

Poe did not totally rule out the possibility that photography could become a means of artistic expression.

In his second essay on the daguerreotype for *Alexander's*, he observes, "The invention will prove, upon the whole, highly beneficial to the interests of the fine arts."[15] He obviously hesitated to place any limits on this new medium. No one could possibly anticipate the wide-ranging future uses of photography, he asserted. In the last paragraph of his initial appreciation of the daguerreotype for *Alexander's*, he observes: "The results of the invention cannot, even remotely, be seen – but all experience, in matters of philosophical discovery, teaches us that, in such discovery, it is the unforeseen upon which we must calculate most largely. It is a theorem almost demonstrated, that the consequences of any new scientific invention will, at the present day exceed, by very much, the wildest expectations of the most imaginative."[16] Poe's careful prediction regarding the future of photography almost functions as a gloss on his visual aesthetic, for, he claimed, the unseen can often assume greater significance than the seen.

Like a detective, a daguerreotype could catch subjects in moments of private weakness and reveal the true person behind more careful public poses. Photography developed in tandem with physiognomy, that is, the analysis of facial features to interpret personality. In fact, daguerreotypes were often called "physiognomies." A time when social appearance and the question of identity were intertwined with perception of individuals, the nineteenth century also saw the emergence of the confidence man, someone who appears to be honest while actually hiding his true self. This dual impulse – to mask the self yet discern the hidden identity of others – forms a crucial aspect of nineteenth-century culture. The best photographers, then as now, capture surface reality while simultaneously unmasking the hidden truths beneath the surface. Poe's aim as a creative artist was not dissimilar: he sought to paint vivid word pictures, but ones that subtly revealed the psychological motivations lurking beneath the surface.

As the industry developed, daguerreotypes began to play a social role as an aid to personal memory. When family or friends were absent, portrait photographs began serving as physical reminders of them. Furthermore, once the subject of a daguerreotype portrait passed away, the photographic image often provided the sole visual indicator of their physical appearance. Read in terms of the discourse of photography, "The Oblong Box" addresses such issues as absence, death, and memory. This often neglected short story contains many elements pertinent to the profession of a daguerreotypist (detective work, study of physiognomies, art, mechanics of photography) and revolves around the core principle of photography (freezing time and space). The tale parallels the daguerreotype's powers by embracing the photographic principle of eternalizing past, present, and future through a conscious act of visually arresting a subject forever. Together memory, visualization, and representation combine to form a powerful tale.

In the story, Cornelius Wyatt, an old school chum of the narrator, books passage aboard a ship from Charleston, South Carolina to New York. The narrator is surprised when his old friend boards the ship with a veiled woman, presumably Mrs. Wyatt, and a mysterious oblong box. Both the box and Wyatt's extra stateroom puzzle the narrator. Soon, a storm breaks off Cape Hatteras and the passengers have to evacuate the ship for safety. Upon learning that the box must be left behind, however, Wyatt leaps from the lifeboat, returns to the ship, grabs hold of the box, ties himself to it, and plunges himself overboard, apparently determined to either save the box and its contents or go down with them. Once he and the oblong box disappear beneath the surface, Captain Hardy remarks, "They will soon rise again – *but not till the salt melts.*"[17] His words seem cryptic, but later, when the narrator meets the ship's captain on Broadway, the captain explains that the box had contained the body of Mrs. Wyatt, who had died shortly before the voyage. The extra stateroom was for the maid impersonating his wife. The deception was necessary, since none of the other passengers would have dared to travel with a dead body on board.

The narrator's role in the tale involves substantial, albeit unsuccessful detective work "to resolve the enigma," that is, to reach a suitable conclusion about Cornelius Wyatt and his mysterious box. The narrator passes through phases of speculation to arrive at an understanding of the goings-on through a close analysis of Wyatt. He even directly confronts his old friend to elicit some kind of response regarding the true nature of the box's contents but remains oblivious of the reality of the situation. The obtuse narrator conjectures that the box contained a painting. Not until Captain Hardy apprises him of the situation does he realize the box contained the body of Mrs. Wyatt. The captain's comment about the salt melting refers to the method in which the body had been packed for transportation, that is, in a large quantity of salt.

Yet salt had another meaning. During the initial enthusiasm surrounding the invention of the daguerreotype, people were curious about how the photographic process worked, and many descriptions of it appeared in the contemporary press. According to Daguerre's method, photographers could use common salt to fix the image onto the photographic plate. Daguerre instructed practitioners to fill a wide-mouthed bottle one-fourth with salt and three-fourths with pure water. Once the salt melted, the solution would be ready to use as a means of fixing the photographic impression.[18] In "The Oblong Box," Captain Hardy's curious words echo Daguerre's. The verbal parallel reinforces Wyatt's efforts to fix the impression of his wife, at least in his mind's eye, during the course of the story.

Poe's use of the discourse of photography in "The Oblong Box" reinforces the association between the daguerreotype and the dead. Before the invention of the daguerreotype, many people felt that once a person's coffin lid was closed, they had seen the last of a loved one.[19] With the invention of photography, people could look upon the faces of loved ones long after they had died. Indeed, the practice of daguerreotyping the deceased emerged as a new trade with the invention of photography. Wyatt's behavior aboard ship – lifting the lid of the oblong box to gaze at its contents – replicates the process of gazing at a photograph of a lost loved one. Though the narrator's conjecture that the box contained a painting is wrong, his description of Wyatt's behavior reveals much. He asserts that Wyatt "had opened his oblong box, in order to feast his eyes on the pictorial treasure within."[20] Wyatt's behavior, in other words, resembles the actions of someone gazing at a photograph of a loved one.

In Poe's day, daguerreotype images seldom circulated beyond a small group of family and friends, mainly because they could not be duplicated. The process of printing photographs for publication did not emerge until the late nineteenth century. Daguerreotypes did form the basis for steel-engraved portraits that appeared in the contemporary magazines. Poe recognized the utility of publishing the personal images of authors. When he planned his ideal magazine, *The Stylus*, he hoped to incorporate printed portraits of contemporary authors within its pages. Soliciting an article from Nathaniel Hawthorne, Poe specifically asked him to supply a daguerreotype with it.[21] Poe recognized the curiosity of contemporary readers to see images of the authors they were reading. Even before the technology of reproducing photographs, photographs, via the engraved portrait, were contributing to the nascent cult of celebrity.

Poe recognized that by sitting for a daguerreotype, people were doing more than merely creating an image for the times. They were also creating personal images that would last beyond their lives. Poe took no less care in shaping his personal image for the camera than in shaping his tales for publication.[22] After sitting for his first daguerreotype, he was disappointed with the resulting image. As a result, he became much more careful about how he posed for the camera. According to phrenologists, great poets had prominent foreheads. Poe himself had a remarkable forehead, though one can scarcely tell from that first daguerreotype. Subsequently, Poe made sure to comb his hair and position his head so that the camera would emphasize his poetic forehead. The careful poses that Poe made for his subsequent daguerreotype portraits succeeded, perhaps beyond his wildest imagination. Through the power of the daguerreotype, his face became the most widely recognized face in the history of American literature.

NOTES

1. Robert Taft, *Photography and the American Scene: A Social History, 1838–1889* (New York: Dover, 1964), 15–17.
2. Donald D. Keyes, "The Daguerreotype's Popularity in America," *Art Journal* 36 (1977), 121.
3. William Welling, *Photography in America: The Formative Years 1839–1900* (New York: Crowell, 1978), 8.
4. Edgar Allan Poe, *Contributions to Alexander's Weekly Messenger*, ed. Clarence S. Brigham (Worcester: American Antiquarian Society, 1943), 20–1.
5. Michael Sapir, "Cryptography in Artificial Light; Poe's stories and Nadar's Stills," *Weber Studies* 14 (1997), 19.
6. "Improvements in the Daguerreotype," *Burton's Gentleman's Magazine* 6 (1840), 193–4; Kevin J. Hayes, *Poe's "Spectacles" and the Camera Lens* (Baltimore: The Edgar Allan Poe Society of Baltimore, 2007), 7.
7. Edgar Allan Poe, *The Collected Works of Edgar Allan Poe*, ed. Thomas Ollive Mabbott, 3 vols. (Cambridge, MA: Belknap Press, 1969–78), vol. iii, 1168;

Benjamin McFarland and Thomas Peter Bennett, "The Image of Edgar Allan Poe: A Daguerreotype linked to the Academy of Natural Sciences of Philadelphia," *Proceedings of the Academy of Natural Sciences of Philadelphia* 147 (1997), 17.

8. "The Daguerreotype," *Expositor* 1 (March 30, 1839), 179.

9. Welling, *Photography in America*, 7.

10. "The 'Daguerreotype,'" *Knickerbocker* 14 (1839), 561.

11. Sander L. Gilman, *Inscribing the Other* (Lincoln: University of Nebraska Press, 1991), 90.

12. Richard Rudisill, *Mirror Image: The Influence of the Daguerreotype on American Society* (Albuquerque: University of New Mexico Press, 1971), 54–5.

13. Lisa Cartwright, "Science and the Film Avant-Garde," *Cinematograph* 4 (1991), 15.

14. Edgar Allan Poe, *Essays and Reviews*, ed. G. R. Thompson (New York: Library of America, 1984), 695.

15. Poe, *Contributions to Alexander's*, 82.

16. Ibid., 21–2.

17. Poe, *Collected Works*, vol. iii, 933.

18. Louis Daguerre, *A Full Description of the Daguerreotype Process*, trans. J. S. Memes (New York: J. R. Chilton, 1840), 7.

19. Susan Williams, "'The Inconstant Daguerreotype': The Narrative of Early Photography," *Narrative* 4 (1996), 164.

20. Poe, *Collected Works*, vol. iii, 929.

21. James Russell Lowell to Edgar Allan Poe, April 17, 1843, *The Complete Works of Edgar Allan Poe*, ed. James A. Harrison, 17 vols. (New York: Crowell, 1902), vol. xvii, 142.

22. Kevin J. Hayes, "Poe, The Daguerreotype, and the Autobiographical Art," *Biography* 25 (2002), 477–92.

CHAPTER 32

Mesmerism

Bruce Mills

Kenneth Silverman draws attention to an intriguing gap in Edgar Allan Poe's literary life often noted by biographers: "Poe's break with the [*Southern Literary*] *Messenger* seems to have brought him a long period of unemployment, poverty, and disenchantment with literary life," because "for about twenty-nine months after he left Richmond Poe virtually disappears from biographical view."[1] Describing this "blank period" from February 1837 until May 1839, Silverman notes that all that remains of Poe's private correspondence is one note, two letters by Poe, and another addressed to him. In 1928, Joseph Jackson filled in this gap with an intriguing assertion. In his preface to the republication of *The Philosophy of Animal Magnetism, by a Gentleman of Philadelphia* (1837), he attributes the anonymous book to Poe. While Jackson offers no convincing evidence of this assignment of authorship, it has the kind of appeal that feeds the popular myths of Poe's life. After all, what was he hiding behind his inscrutable smile? Thinking back upon his residence in Philadelphia during this lost period, is it not the stuff of Poe lore to imagine participation in mesmeric experiences and experiments?

If connecting Poe to the anonymous musings in *The Philosophy of Animal Magnetism* is a seductive conjecture, it is because the evidence of ensuing tales and criticism confirms that he had absorbed the era's fascination with mesmerism (also termed animal magnetism) from the "blank period" into the 1840s. In "A Tale of the Ragged Mountains," "Mesmeric Revelation," and "The Facts in the Case of M. Valdemar," for instance, Poe drew directly and quite knowledgeably from the science of animal magnetism. With this last narrative, in fact, many readers mistook fiction for a genuine description of a patient suspended between life and death through the induction of a mesmeric state. Even more important than providing plot materials for his short fiction, however, such works as Chauncy Hare Townshend's *Facts in Mesmerism, with Reasons for a Dispassionate Inquiry Into It* (1841) and Joseph Philippe François Deleuze's *Practical Instruction in Animal Magnetism* (1837) informed Poe's theorizing on the art of the short prose tale. The notion of the single effect articulated in his review of Nathaniel Hawthorne's *Twice-Told Tales* resonates meaningfully with Townshend's study of uniquely receptive states of consciousness. If Poe's work of the 1840s underscores one central pattern, it may be the effort to develop artistic choices consonant with psychological truths arising from an understanding of mesmerism.

By the latter decades of the eighteenth century, the science of mesmerism had evolved from a belief in an all-pervading fluid affecting animate and inanimate bodies to a conception of the suggestive power of words and gestures in evoking physical and psychological effects. The study of mesmerism arises from the work of Franz Anton Mesmer, an Austrian physician, who first published his theories on the nature of animal magnetism in 1766 and whose beliefs underwent formal scrutiny in the 1780s. According to Mesmer, "all bodies are mutually attractive or extend towards one another by means of a force which goes from individual particles of matter to all other individual particles."[2] In short, there exists an invisible fluid between bodies that can be acted upon to produce visible effects. Informed by findings regarding the gravitational influence of heavenly bodies and principles concerning magnetic and electric forces, Mesmer's ideas sought to explain the cures introduced through his medical practice. Having first used magnets, Mesmer discovered that the stones themselves could not explain the response of the nerves elicited by the passing of his hands over the bodies of his patients; he concluded that a force separate from the actual magnet (i.e., animal magnetism) explained physical responses. Given his observations, Mesmer refined strategies whereby he could manipulate this so-called animal fluid and thus produce a harmony conducive to physical and mental health.

Having moved to Paris in 1778 and gained prominence through the growing recognition of his practice, Mesmer came under greater examination, especially as his followers expanded his influence through the formation of the Society of Harmony, a group of individuals who paid a membership fee to study the theory of animal magnetism. While Mesmer insisted on the actual presence of an unseen but corporeal substance, many physicians and scientists came to doubt this theory, for the presence of an invisible fluid could not be empirically proven and seemed unnecessary to explain the behaviors of patients. As a result of the debate surrounding Mesmer's practice, King Louis XVI appointed a commission in 1784, headed by Benjamin Franklin, to study the legitimacy of animal magnetism. Ultimately, the commission concluded that, through their strategies to induce magnetic states, doctors elicited physical responses by appealing to patients' imaginations. In other words, the patient–doctor rapport was the cause of various effects.

With hindsight, of course, we can see this period as the beginning of the field of psychology and as an era that discovered the unconscious. Given the dramatic testimonies of remarkable cures and unique states of consciousness, a special interest naturally began to develop in the effects of magnetic sleep – what we now associate with hypnotic states. In these higher states, people appeared to demonstrate clairvoyant powers or special knowledge; in the terms of the time, they entered into and reported upon a transition state between material and spiritual worlds. Books and pamphlets on animal magnetism often devoted sections to somnambulism or clairvoyance. In addition, they consistently focused on the particular role of the physician-mesmerist in producing such conditions. According to these texts, the mesmerist could induce magnetic sleep through concentrated thought and attention. Imposing his will upon a receptive mind, that is, upon an individual trusting in the procedure and submitting willingly to the process, the magnetist could elicit striking effects.

In the United States, the science and spectacle of mesmerism gained prominence through print and the stage "performances" of Jane C. Rider, Loraina Brackett, and Miss Cynthia Ann Gleason. Published in book form as well as in the *Boston Medical and Surgical Journal* during the second half of 1834, the case of "somnambulist" Rider provided the public with astonishing depictions of her ability to perform complex domestic tasks in the dark, recall and recite long-forgotten poetry, and, seemingly, read without light. The report of Rider's case in the reputable venue of the *Boston Medical and Surgical Journal* marked the start of extensive public speculation concerning somnambulism and, of course, animal magnetism. Brackett entered national consciousness even more dramatically through a sustained public debate. In *Letter to Doctor A. Brigham, on Animal Magnetism: Being an Account of a Remarkable Interview between the Author and Miss Loraina Brackett While in a State of Somnambulism* (1837), William Stone brought the woman's case to the eyes of a broad readership. Addressing his "letter" to Dr. Amariah Brigham, one of the nation's most renowned physicians, Stone demonstrates how the discourse on animal magnetism engaged prominent cultural figures. (Among other books, Brigham shaped cultural notions of physical and mental health in *Remarks on the Influence of Mental Cultivation and Mental Excitement upon Health* [1833].) Stone's *Letter* initiated three notable replies – two challenging and one supporting reports of Brackett's abilities. Charles Durant's *Exposition, or a New Theory of Animal Magnetism with a Key to the Mysteries* (1837) and David Meredith Reese's *Humbugs of New York* (1838) argued that mesmerism could be explained through the self-delusion of participants. Between these works, Charles Poyen kept the debate alive through *A Letter to Col. Wm. L. Stone, of New York, on the Facts Related in His Letter to Dr. Brigham, and a Plain Refutation of Durant's Exposition on Animal Magnetism, &tc.* (1837). In the same year, he established his knowledge of mesmerism through *Progress of Animal Magnetism in New England,* a study drawing in part on his own public magnetizing of Cynthia Ann Gleason. Agreeing to assist Poyen after he had cured her of stomach ailments, Gleason served as a mesmeric subject in demonstrations to prominent Bostonians, including physicians at the Harvard Medical School.

In addition to this widespread (and often sensationalistic) documentation of animal magnetism, the 1830s and the beginning of the 1840s saw the publication of two central texts addressing the practice and philosophical underpinnings of the science: Deleuze's *Practical Instruction in Animal Magnetism* and Townshend's *Facts in Mesmerism*. In addition to Poe, some of the era's most well-known writers read Townshend's book, including Margaret Fuller, Lydia Maria Child, and Walt Whitman. Perhaps most evocative is Townshend's foregrounding of the key finding from the French commission headed by Franklin:

That which we have learned, or, at least, that which has been proved to us, in a clear and satisfactory manner, by our inquiry into the phenomena of mesmerism, is, that man can act upon man, at all times and almost at will, by striking the imagination; that signs and gestures the most simple may produce the most powerful effects; that the action of man upon the imagination may be reduced to an art, and concluded after a certain method, when exercised upon patients who have faith in the proceedings.[3]

Clearly, these conclusions suggest that mesmeric practice had far-reaching implications. After all, could we not see an author as engaged in an effort to "act upon man, at all times and almost at will, by striking the imagination"? Is not fiction writing an art that, if aiming to produce powerful outcomes, demands attention to method, to "signs and gestures" designed to call forth profound effects?

Given the cultural discourse on mesmerism, it is not surprising that Poe exploited the material in his fiction. After all, the history and practice of animal magnetism – its focus on interior consciousness, its depiction of the intermediary state between material and spiritual realms, its dramatis personae of mesmerists and mediums caught in a play of will and submission, its potential for gothic settings – provided the elements consistent with ongoing imaginary interests. Dramatic examples of this fictional use emerge in four pieces: "A Tale of the Ragged Mountains" (1844), "Mesmeric Revelation" (1844), "The Power of Words" (1845), and "The Facts in the Case of M. Valdemar" (1845).

Of these, the later story offers the most fascinating reception. In it, the first person narrator confesses his need to bring forth the "extraordinary case" of M. Valdemar, a patient who agreed to participate in mesmeric research by being magnetized at the point of his death. According to the narrator, the experiment provided the opportunity to explore a number of questions: "It remained to be seen, first, whether, in such condition, there existed in the patient any susceptibility to the magnetic influence; secondly, whether, if any existed, it was impaired or increased by the condition; thirdly, to what extent, or for how long a period, the encroachments of Death might be arrested by the process."[4] Evidence of the widespread speculation concerning the story and Poe's involvement in animal magnetism emerged in private as well as public correspondence. Writing Sarah Helen Whitman in January 1846, a friend (possibly Mary S. Hewitt) observed suggestively that "people seem to think there is something uncanny about him [Poe], and the strangest stories are told, what is more, *believed*, about his mesmeric experiences, at the mention of which he always smiles."[5]

That readers were inclined to believe that the dying Valdemar could be suspended near death for seven months and, upon being brought from the somnambulant state, immediately rot away to "a nearly liquid mass of loathsome – of detestible putridity" suggests Poe's knowledge of the medical history related to mesmerism.[6] Beginning in the late eighteenth century, doctors sometimes induced magnetic sleep as a form of anesthesia. For patients suffering from various conditions, then, the mesmeric literature – both medical journals and more popular texts – noted the remarkable ability for individuals to suspend the experience of surgical pain or the effects of disease. In Thomas Ollive Mabbott's preface to "The Facts in the Case of M. Valdemar," he quotes extensively from a letter describing such a procedure. Moreover, he also cites an experience to which Townshend alludes in *Facts in Mesmerism*: "I have watched the effects of mesmeric treatment upon a suffering friend, who was dying of that most fearful disorder – Lumbar Abscess. Unfortunately, through various hindrances, Mesmerism was not resorted to till late in the progress of the disease, so that, of course, that it should effect a cure was out of the question.... I have no hesitation in saying, that, under God, the life of my friend, R. T. was prolonged, at least, two months by the action of Mesmerism."[7]

In a letter to Poe printed in the *Broadway Journal*, Robert H. Collyer, a well-known supporter of animal magnetism who had started the *Mesmeric Magazine* in 1842 and published *Psychology, or The Embodiment of Thought; with Analysis of Phreno-magnetism, "Neurology," and Mental Hallucination, Including Rules to Govern and Produce the Magnetic State* (1843), noted the "great sensation" that the story elicited in Boston and his belief in the "possibility of such a phenomenon." He urged Poe to send on a reply in order to "put at rest the growing impression that your account is merely a *splendid creation* of your own brain, not having any truth in fact."[8]

Republishing "Valdemar" in the *Broadway Journal*, which he was currently editing, Poe initially did nothing to foreclose belief in the veracity of the tale's events. Acknowledging that the story had "given rise to some discussion – especially in regard to the truth or falsity of the statements made," he simply concludes: "We leave [the story] to speak for itself. We may observe, however, that there are a certain class of people who pride themselves upon Doubt, as a profession."[9] By the beginning of 1846, the story had made its way to British publications and, in one instance, was reprinted as a pamphlet entitled *Mesmerism, "In Articulo Mortis."* In the pamphlet's opening advertisement, the editor asserts that the narrative's "plain recital of facts" is given credence in America.

Perhaps the most significant evidence of Poe's embrace of the era's mesmeric science, however, arises in his short fiction theory integrating the psychological insights articulated by Townshend's philosophy and Deleuze's practice. Direct evidence that Poe was familiar with Townshend's text emerges in an article first published in the April 5, 1845 issue of the *Broadway Journal*. Reviewing William Newnham's *Human Magnetism; Its Claim to Dispassionate Inquiry* (1845), Poe compares the work unfavorably to Townshend's *Facts in Mesmerism*: "In some important points – his ideas of prevision, for example, and the curative effects of magnetism – we radically disagree – and most especially do we disagree with him in his (implied) disparagement of the work of Chauncey [*sic*] Hare Townshend, which we regard as one of the most truly profound and philosophical works of the day – a work to be valued properly only in a day to come."[10] In asserting that Newnham's book should still be read by those who "pretend to keep pace with modern philosophy," however, he appears to validate the role of such studies in illuminating the nature of magnetic states and thus the relationship between body and mind.[11] Moreover, it invites one to consider how, as a writer, he would have found discourse on the connection between material signs and interior processes relevant to artistic productions.

As underscored in his review of Newnham, Poe saw Townshend's work as an essential philosophical text, one that offered more than an authoritative study of animal magnetism. To see why Poe and other writers might have been drawn to this book, it is revealing to consider Townshend's chapter, "On the Mesmeric Consciousness." Attempting to show that such consciousness – that is, a higher perceptiveness that occurs in the elevated state of "sleep-waking" – actually harmonizes with normal states of awareness, Townshend delineates a third "law of our being":

Consciousness, whether it relate to sensation or to intellectual exertion, acts more forcibly the more it is brought to bear upon a single point.

Who has not felt that the senses, by their simultaneous action, are restrictions the one upon the other? How seldom can we be wholly absorbed in the pleasures of the eye! How seldom, when listening to sweet sounds, can we become "all ear!" There is almost always a something to be deducted from our feelings by the interference of some other sense than that we desire to exercise. Were all our capacities of sensation concentrated upon any one property of matter, we may judge how much stronger would be the force of our perceptions by observing that, where one sense is actually wanting (as in the blind or deaf, for instance), the vivacity of impressions received through the other organs is greatly increased.

Of particular importance here is the fact that Townshend finds in this new area of study even further evidence for seemingly self-evident or common sense "truths" of perception. He goes on to assert that, "as regards the exercise of our mental capacities, experience inculcates, as one of the precepts of wisdom, that if we wish to do a thing perfectly, we must do it singly."[12]

In this excerpt from *Facts in Mesmerism*, readers will hear a focus on the concentration of attention that resonates with Poe's review of Hawthorne's *Twice-Told Tales*. In his review, Poe asserts that the tale "affords unquestionably the fairest field for the exercise of the loftiest talent." Similar to a rhymed poem "not to exceed in length what might be perused in an hour," the potential of the tale arises in its concentration and compression. According to Poe, the "exaltation of the soul" elicited by a short prose tale emerges from its "continuity of effort" and a "certain duration or repetition of purpose." Speaking of the skillful tale writer, Poe later asserts: "If wise, he has not fashioned his thoughts to accommodate his incidents; but having conceived, with deliberate care, a certain unique or single effect to be wrought out, he then invents such incidents – he then combines such events as may best aid him in establishing this preconceived effect."[13] Given Poe's desire to develop a fictional practice that elicits powerful effects upon the soul, Townshend's speculation on "intellectual exertion" that is "brought to bear upon a single point" certainly provides psychological grounding for a fictional aesthetic.

Publications depicting the *practice* (or art) of inducing the mesmeric state further employ the language evoked in Townshend's description of this "law of our being." In *Practical Guide to Animal Magnetism*, Deleuze lays out principles and practices echoed in Townshend's views. For instance, he quantifies the optimal time for inducing a magnetic state during a mesmeric sitting: "The first sittings ought to be about an hour in duration, when there is no reason to prolong or abridge them."[14] Deleuze further underscores how the faculties of the somnambulist demonstrate a higher receptivity due to an exalted concentration: "Their surprising penetration may be regarded as the effect of a concentration upon one single class of sensations, upon one order of ideas; the more their attention is distracted by various objects, the less of it will they give to the essential object."[15] In a later section on how to develop and derive advantages from the magnetic faculties, the book also examines the critical relationship between patient and physician-mesmerist: "When a man magnetizes, he puts himself, by the exertion of his will, in a state different from his habitual one; he concentrates his attention upon a single object; he throws off and directs beyond himself the nervous or vital fluid; and this new manner of being renders him susceptible of new impressions."[16] Again, the mutually reinforcing acts of will, concentration, and sympathy between the mesmerist and the mesmerized provides rich possibilities to writers, especially those conceiving of their art as tied to inducing inward effects or, as Poe puts it, an "exaltation of the soul." Such views deepen an understanding of Poe's contention that the most vivid and enduring impressions derive from concentration and compression.

In a March 1846 "Marginalia" piece that in part addresses the power of words, Poe confesses that he has encountered a "class of fancies, of exquisite delicacy, which are not thoughts, and to which, *as yet*, [he has] found it absolutely impossible to adapt language." Such fancies are to be understood as "rather psychal than intellectual" and "arise in the soul... only at its epochs of most intense tranquility – when the bodily and mental health are in perfection – and at those mere points of time where the confines of the waking world blend with those of the world of dreams."[17] As Poe begins to discern the nature of this world between wakefulness and sleep, a state of awareness that seems to draw from both the conscious and unconscious mind and that can result in what he terms pleasurable ecstasies, he employs a language that resonates with descriptions of somnambulant or magnetic sleep and the truths that arise from such a condition:

I regard the visions, even as they arise, with an awe which, in some measure, moderates or tranquilizes the ecstasy – I so regard them, through a conviction (which seems a portion of the ecstasy itself) that this ecstasy, in itself, is of a character supernal to the Human Nature – is a glimpse of the spirit's outer world; and I arrive at this conclusion – if this term is at all applicable to instantaneous intuition – by a perception that the delight experienced has, as its element, but *the absoluteness of novelty.*[18]

Significantly, such thoughts suggest that creating works that reflect a degree of novelty indicative of a higher imagination engages writers in what might be termed mesmeric principles.

To see animal magnetism or mesmerism as a pseudoscience or as an antebellum spectacle overlooks its place in the evolution of our understanding of human psychology. As a writer, Poe partook fictionally in the sensationalistic elements of animal magnetism. From "Mesmeric Revelation" to the "The Facts in the Case of M. Valdemar," from criticism on the short prose tale to an ultimate effort to articulate an aesthetic cosmology in *Eureka*, however, Poe should not be seen as succumbing to his era's questionable science as much as productively engaging with early speculation on the nature of human thought. Not unlike current writers whose aesthetic takes into account neuroscientific findings related to human perception, he embraced a strain of thought that, in different forms, continues to illuminate the inward turn in Western notions of identity and the faculty of the imagination.

NOTES

1. Kenneth Silverman, *Edgar A. Poe: Mournful and Never-ending Remembrance* (New York: HarperCollins, 1991), 129.
2. Franz Anton Mesmer, *Mesmerism: A Translation of the Original Scientific and Medical Writings of F. A. Mesmer*, trans. and ed. George Bloch (Los Altos, CA: William Kaufman, 1980), 22.
3. Quoted in Chauncy Hare Townshend, *Facts in Mesmerism, with Reasons for a Dispassionate Inquiry into It* (1841; reprinted, New York: Da Capo, 1982), 18.
4. Edgar Allan Poe, *The Collected Works of Edgar Allan Poe*, ed. Thomas Ollive Mabbott, 3 vols. (Cambridge, MA: Belknap Press, 1969–78), vol. iii, 1233.
5. Quoted in Sarah Helen Whitman, "Introductory Letter," in *The Life and Poems of Edgar Allan Poe*, ed. Eugene L. Didier (New York: W. J. Widdleton, 1879), 13.
6. Poe, *Collected Works*, vol. iii, 1243.
7. Ibid., vol. iii, 1229.
8. Robert H. Collyer to Poe, December 16, 1845, *The Complete Works of Edgar Allan Poe*, 17 vols. (New York: Crowell, 1902), vol. xvii, 225.
9. Poe, *Collected Works*, vol. iii, 1230.

10. Poe, *Complete Works*, vol. xii, 123.
11. Ibid., vol. xii, 123.
12. Townshend, *Facts in Mesmerism*, 211–12.
13. Edgar Allan Poe, *Essays and Reviews*, ed. G. R. Thompson (New York: Library of America, 1984), 571–2.
14. J. P. F. Deleuze, *Practical Instruction in Animal Magnetism*, trans. Thomas C. Hartshorn (1843; reprinted, New York: Da Capo, 1982), 36.
15. Ibid., 75.
16. Ibid., 193.
17. Poe, *Essays*, 1383.
18. Ibid.

CHAPTER 33

Architecture

Alvin Holm

Edgar Allan Poe fit neatly into the architectural styles of his times in three significant ways. In terms of personal attitude, literary outlook, and dwelling place, Poe exemplified the Romantic era. Before continuing, a personal note: I write as a life-long devotee of Poe's work, an architect practicing in the classical tradition, and a restorationist with intimate knowledge of one of Poe's homes in Philadelphia. In 1982, I completed the Historic Structures Report commissioned by the National Park Service on the house Poe occupied for two years in the Spring Garden Section of Philadelphia. My job was to discover as accurately as possible how the house looked during the time Poe resided there with his wife and mother-in-law. Soon after their departure for New York, the house was greatly altered. What could have been considered a cottage became the rear portion of a large, four-story row house erected on the front of the lot.

During Poe's most prolific and turbulent period, the nation had just entered the Romantic era, exemplified in architecture by the cottage style of A. J. Downing and others. An equally Romantic ideal of landscape design accompanied this vision of an ideal domestic existence. The appropriate setting for the simple cottage was a naturalistic landscape, lightly cultivated, bounteous, and beautiful. This theme, begun a century earlier in England, was renewed by American painters like Thomas Cole and Frederick Church. Poe embraced this landscape aesthetic in his stories and poems, explicitly propounding it in "The Domain of Arnheim," "The Island of the Fay," "Morning on the Wissahiccon," and "Landor's Cottage." The architecture and landscape design ideas were inseparable, and Poe's literary art was perfectly in tune.

The cottage enthusiasm in America in the 1840s followed the popular Greek Revival that had emerged a decade earlier. That style trumped the Federal Style, which had in turn taken over from the Georgian. As a practicing architect, a designer myself, I am skeptical of all art historical terminology: throughout history, architects have seldom known what their work would be called by future generations. Having worked extensively as a historical restoration architect, I know how maddening it is to decide whether a building from 1800 should be described as Georgian or Federal when almost every building, to one degree or another, is actually transitional. Nonetheless, I am confident that Edgar Allan Poe knew the cottage style, and he did a great deal to promote and enjoy it.

The term "Romantic," which has different connotations for literature, music, painting, and architecture, may need a little clarification. I use the term in two distinct senses – Naturalizing Romanticism and Classicizing Romanticism. Poe embodied both. In his obvious adoration in "To Helen" of the "glory that was Greece and the grandeur that was Rome," and in countless other references he is a devout classicist. In his yearning for "Eldorado" or "Israfel," or any number of faraway Edens or pastoral destinations Poe is a Naturalist. These then, are the two faces of Poe the Romantic, at once Classicizing and Naturalizing. Small wonder that in the ongoing era of Greek Revival (classical) he was as well caught up in the cottage style and thence in the other Romantic revivals – the Gothic, the Egyptian, the Moorish – all aspects of the Picturesque movement. Common to these artistic modes was the drive, the Eros, the inner impulse to be beyond the "here and now" to a distant land before or yet to come. Poe's overarching goal was to achieve beauty, which he equated with truth and believed was inevitably tinged with sorrow.

In the summer of 1981, I was elated to receive word that I had been selected by the National Park Service to work on the Edgar Allan Poe House. Poe had been a kind of intellectual guru for me since childhood, and I confess that this intrigue had never really lost hold. Working on his house as a historical architect was an exciting prospect to contemplate. At the end of this research, I was pleased to report that the experience was even more exhilarating than I had anticipated. Part of this enjoyment was getting to know Poe better. Part of it was simply the discovery that such a plain little house could yield so much mystery.

The Poe House deceived us all. So many aspects of it that seemed so clear and simple at the outset of this study became quite complicated upon detailed examination. Some early conclusions have become problematic, and, though much has been revealed, more questions arise. All old houses have their mysteries, but appropriately the residence of Edgar Allan Poe has more than its share of enigma. The plainest surface here, when scratched, will continue to baffle the conscientious investigator for years to come.

If this introduction has begun to sound like a tale in itself, the experience of working on the Poe House during the course of that year resembled an unfolding narrative more suitable for the pen of Edgar Poe than that of a restoration architect. I confess to having been carried away again and again by a personal fascination with the details of Poe's life and work that have no proper place in a Historic Structures Report. Poe's "Imp of the Perverse" led me astray too often for a totally systematic investigation. Yet without that infatuation – that frequent foolishness that leaves one banging on blank walls too long – I think I might have missed many exciting facts. The Poe House might have remained blank walls, however meticulously documented.

Chief among the problems of conceptualizing Poe's life in his Spring Garden house on Seventh Street is squaring what we see today with the tradition of the rose-covered cottage. The image was promoted by Anthony Frayne in his small book of that name, but it has been persistent from the earliest writings about Poe. Even imagining the house without the front building, as it was when Poe lived there, the picture is a rather dry one, far removed from the cheerful descriptions of Virginia and Mrs. Clemm amidst the flowers. Was the connotation of the word "cottage" different in those days, that we have such trouble recognizing one when we see it? Surely not! For it was the mid-nineteenth century that formulated our current ideas of the domestic cottage and its romantic associations. A. J. Downing's influential *Cottage Residences* appeared in 1842, about the time Poe moved to Spring Garden. Downing, along with scores of other gardeners and carpenters, cultivated the very images we still share of what cottage life was like.

So long as we view the Poe House as an appendage, as it is today, or even as an appendage to be, as it was then, the cottage image is elusive. The key may be found in reconstructing the appearance of the one façade that has been completely obscured. Rather than thinking of the east elevation as a temporary stub end waiting for the grand house to appear we must consider the building as fully formed and an end in itself. Suddenly the little house is flooded with light and open to the breezes. When we can see it in a garden setting, the entire picture is changed.

These thoughts gave rise to a scrupulous study of the east wall, mostly by rapping and thumping but also through close visual examination and some demolition. Two stages of development prior to the present condition soon emerged. The most obvious from a logical standpoint consisted of the modifications that had been made on the east wall to facilitate access from the piazza[1] and stairway of the front building. For this phase there were plenty of clues in old interior photographs and in notes on the drawings for the 1978 renovation. It might have occurred to us that living memories also would have been very useful here because much of the work that concealed that phase is quite recent. The earliest phase of course is beyond recall, obliterated by the 1848 front addition.

The more recent, and less interesting, hidden construction consisted of three doors in the east wall, each giving access from a floor of the rear building to a start landing in the piazza. The first floor of the Poe House is eight inches lower than the piazza elevation so the step we see today at the doorway to the parlor was undoubtedly in place since the 1848 addition.

Contemporary descriptions of the Poe House as a cottage gain credibility with the realization that the east wall, now buried behind the front building, was the principal elevation, fully developed and well finished. A window was centered on each upper floor to match those on the southern elevation, and a doorway into the parlor was the principal entry from Seventh Street. But where was the picturesque porch so frequently mentioned?

Biographer Mary Phillips recounts the story of the Poes' arrival at their Spring Garden house, portraying Maria Clemm finding "in the neglected garden a struggling climbing rosebush, which she cheered into generous growing with attractive effects over their front porch.... This pretty aspect, with other plentiful flowers and vines about the place, named it 'the poet's rose-covered cottage.'" And again, "The neighbors noted Virginia as laughing among her flowers and sewing on their porch."[2] Where did this well-recollected porch go?

It has not been seen for 140 years. Speculation has ranged on the veracity of this tradition, and Anthony Frayne was apparently forced to assume the references must mistakenly have transformed the "rear shed" that existed when Richard Gimbel purchased the place in 1933 into the "front porch."[3] Others have also accepted the pretty description as a romantic embellishment of the reality. The discovery of the front door on the east, however, casts a whole new light on the question of the front porch. Where better to seek it than at the front door?

Phillips discusses the setting of the house with precision: "The absence of the present front building, in Poe's day left his home some ways from the corner of North 7th Street and Brandywine, a little lane north of Spring Garden, and inside a pale [picket] fence closed by two gates. A long narrow walk through his garden led to their door; and around the corner to a side entrance and small rear yard with its pear tree shade under which Poe legends seem sure he wrote part of all of 'Gold-Bug.'"[4] This passage puts everything in its proper place, and the entrance on Brandywine Street, for so long thought to be the front door, can now resume its former position at the side of the house. One of the gates is in front of the side entrance, and the other one would have been on Seventh Street at the end of the long walk through the garden from the front door.

Having found so plausible a location for the legendary front porch, it was only necessary to uncover the physical evidence. The eastern face of the Poe House wall, which had become the western wall of the piazza, proved to be a mine of good information once stripped of plaster to expose the original façade at the first floor level. In the first place the brick and pointing was found to be a finished exterior wall, and the location of the front door was established. In the second place enough small traces of white paint remained to show the shape, extent, and color of wood trim and cornice above the door. Similar paint traces identified a ledger beam across the face of the building at just the height of a shed porch roof. Wooden wedges were also found at intervals in the vertical brick joints with square nail holes indicating their use as nailers for the ledger. Searching the exterior portion of this wall outside the piazza, another vertical joint was found in the same course that appeared to have also housed a nailer plug, showing the porch extended the full width of the façade. At the party wall to the north, the trace of a raised block appears, presumably a flashing curb along the junction of the sloping roof and party wall.

Little plaster was removed from the north wall of the piazza because the party wall brick was not in itself worth exposing, but some exploratory holes were made to determine the depth of the porch. A tiny bit of white paint presumably marks the porch corner post, and, at a slightly higher level, a small cement-filled cavity in the brick could have been a point where the post was made secure to the wall. The porch then is seen to extend about eight feet out from the front wall and is as wide as the house itself.

Because of extensive renovations to this east wall at both the first floor and cellar levels, little of the original brick or stone remains below the first floor line. Nevertheless, one joist pocket in the brick was found as a vestige of the original porch framing, which establishes the porch deck at about fifteen inches above grade, or two steps up. The joist was tenoned into the brick in exactly the same way headers are let into joists in the cellar of the Poe House. In each case the mortise is a square two and one-quarter inches on a side. It is not likely that further traces of the porch framing will show up. The only additional material that may be found would be beneath the plaster on the party wall, and that may help to ascertain the pitch of the roof and perhaps some eave, gutter, or downspout information.

The poetic image of Virginia sitting amidst flowers on the vine-covered porch of the Poe cottage should no longer be considered to be stretching a point about life in Spring Garden. Ample physical evidence for the existence of this porch, as described in the romantic legends, has been uncovered. It was as wide as the house, two steps off the ground, framed with three-by-eight joists mortised into the front wall, and eight feet deep. The roof was probably covered with six-inch by twenty-seven-inch cedar shingles like the other roofs of the house, and it sloped from a ledger eight feet and four inches high about first floor wall down to the eave and a downspout. And there was undoubtedly a profusion of greenery. So much for the sunshine and cheer. Now for the scary, dark cellar.

The fascination of the Poe House cellar is obvious to any reader of "The Black Cat" or "The Cask of Amantillado." The damp darkness and the red-stained cellar walls suggest terrible secrets that visitors find nowhere else in the house. For many, it is the high point of their pilgrimage to the house of the master of horror. For the literary scholar it is especially interesting to see the brick piers supporting a chimney above which may well have given Poe the idea for walling up his fictional victims. "For a purpose such as this," Poe writes, "the cellar was well adapted. Its walls were loosely constructed and had lately been plastered throughout with rough plaster, which the dampness of the atmosphere had prevented from hardening." Such is the case today. He goes on, "Moreover, in one of the walls was a projection, caused by a false chimney, or fireplace, that had been filled up and made to resemble the rest of the cellar."[5] The description from "The Black Cat" is close, even to the filling in between the piers which today is only partially complete, apparently in order to provide a shelving niche.

From the gloom of the famous cellar, we turn to the bedroom. Tradition holds that the east room on the second floor was the bedroom of Edgar Allan Poe, and there is no reason to doubt it. A close reading of "The Black Cat," presumably written in this house, suggests that the first person protagonist occupied a similar bedroom in a similar house. It may be recalled that "On the night of the day on which [the] cruel deed was done" – that he murdered his cat – his house collapsed in flames. "The walls, with one exception, had fallen in. This exception was found in a compartment wall, not very thick, which stood about the middle of the house, and against which had rested the head of my bed. The plastering had here, in great measure, resisted the action of the fire."[6] There is only one wall in the eastern second floor room against which the headboard could be placed, considering the windows on the south and east walls and the closets and mantel on the north, and that wall is the plaster partition wall, not very thick, about in the middle of the house, just as described in Poe's passage.

Despite this slender reasoning, it is nevertheless tempting to deduce from "The Black Cat" context that a tree stood in the front yard to the east from which Poe imagined that his troubled hero might hang the murdered cat: "The cat, I remembered, had been hung in a garden adjacent to the house. Upon the alarm of fire, this garden had been immediately filled by the crowd – by some one of whom the animal must have been cut down from the tree and thrown, through an open window, into my chamber...with the view of arousing me from sleep."[7] The only adjacent area of this house where there could have stood a tree, and from which the cat could have been thrown through a window, is on the east, or in front, toward Seventh Street. Further, if we can envision the trajectory of the flung cat in the story that struck the wall above our hero's bed we can see that it must have been the second floor bedroom in question and not the third, which is the only other possible alternative.

This line of literary reasoning cannot be admitted as equivalent to any kind of proof that Poe occupied the second floor east bedroom. It is probably as good an indication as any, however, if we accept the obvious (and often demonstrated) fact that much of what Poe wrote about was drawn from his own experience. That other details in "The Black Cat" were also suggested by this particular house, such as the cellar wall where the murdered wife was buried, cannot be easily dismissed.

During the course of my study the image of the Poe House in Spring Garden slowly transformed from a bleak little brick shed in the rear of the more stately homes of Seventh Street. The picture that emerged is much closer to the more cheerful descriptions of the house found in the Poe biographies, many of which have been thought until now to be wishful romantic embellishments of a reality far more grim. The drawing that I prepared sought to render the house as it probably was in 1842, based on my research, with a view showing how it could fairly be described as "the rose-covered cottage of the poet."

First the setting must be understood to have been far different than today, with the front building not yet built and the little house sitting within a garden two or three times as large as its own area, surrounded by a white picket fence running across the frontage on Seventh Street and all the way down Wistar, a distance of eighty feet. To the rear stood a vacant lot with planting, and across Wistar Street the land was clear all the way to the farmers' market on Spring Garden Street, a full block away. Anthony Frayne's description – "delightful vista of well-kept lawns and neat gardens dotted with stately old shade trees" – somewhat exaggerates the suburban quality of the neighborhood, yet it was a well-settled area at this time when the larger land holdings, presumably small farms, were being parceled off as urban lots for development.[8] The "towering pear tree" beneath which Poe supposedly wrote "The Gold-Bug" suggests the site was cultivated long before William Alburger bought it to build his "three-story brick structure" in 1840. Frayne thought the tree was in the rear, which would have placed it in the neighboring lot beyond the property line and hence outside of Poe's yard. He claims the tree was still standing until 1920 when it was razed by lightning. More likely it stood in front of the house toward Seventh Street where it would have been within the garden and within the picket fence. In "Landor's Cottage," Poe describes just such a situation: "Not more than six steps from the main door of the cottage stood the dead trunk of a fantastic pear-tree, so clothed from head to foot in gorgeous bignonia blossoms that one required no little scrutiny to determine what manner of sweet thing it could be."[9] Any trace of this tree, so prominent in the literature of and about Poe, would have been effaced with the construction of the front building. It is possible that another tree to the rear, on property acquired in 1854, took on the role of the lost legendary tree when the rear shed became confused with the front porch, which had also been lost in the building of the front house.

From the many accounts of the abundant flowers and vines that envelop the house we may assume that the garden was well established before the Poes arrived. Thomas C. Clarke, for example, observes, "Their little garden in summer, and the house in winter, were overflowing with luxurious grape and other vines and ornamented with choice flowers of the poet's selection."[10] Because the Poes were there for little more, and perhaps less than, one cycle of seasons, it is hard to imagine that such a lavish garden could be solely their creation. According to the deed records, the house itself was barely two years old, so there could have been no more than one or at most two tenants before the Poes, who must have applied themselves with zeal to the business of gardening.

Certain details of the yard layout seem so explicit in the accounts – and reasonable – that we have assumed they are accurate. For instance, in Phillips we read about the "pale fence closed by two gates" and we may guess that one gate was on Wistar Street in front of the side entrance and the other was on Seventh Street in front of the lot. Her narrow walk through the garden fits perfectly the situation as it now appears. Writing in 1896, Thomas Dunn English observes, "the ground where the front

THE EDGAR ALLAN POE HOUSE

BY ALVIN HOLM A.I.A
1982

Figure 33.1 Alvin Holm, *The Edgar Allan Poe House* (1982). Courtesy of the artist.

[house] was to stand in the future had been turned into a grassplot, with a flower border against the adjoining brick wall." There were flowers also along the south wall of the house. Mayne Reid quotes a Spring Garden neighbor, who recalled: "I had to pass their house, and in the summer

time I often saw them. In the mornings Mrs. Clemm and her daughter would be generally watering the flowers, which they had in a bed under the windows."[11]

Throughout my studies and, indeed, throughout Poe biography, the abundant vines and flowers that surrounded the house seem characteristic of the Spring Garden tenure. They are important to Poe in his writings, and they are therefore important to the interpretation of this historic property. Some sort of garden including roses should be cultivated in any future restoration simply for the general effect, and substantial research should also be undertaken for an appropriately romantic 1840s flower garden. A further step should be considered in the recreation of a portion of Brandywine Street with whatever street furniture it might have had such as lamps or posts. Effective landscaping will greatly enhance the attraction of the site, as well as more clearly convey the sense of how it was when Poe lived there.

The issue of a possibly overromanticized view of Poe's Spring Garden house is an important one that could not be adequately argued in the context of my Historic Structures report. It should be noted however, that in my research I have tended to trust first, rather than doubt, the traditions and literary references, however florid or fantastic. And it must also be stated that this policy has proved exceptionally fruitful in the course of this work. The persistence of the cottage image, for instance, has been of critical importance to the discoveries made in this investigation. Accounts of the flower garden are integral to this picture and should not be discounted by reference to the inconsistency of any given witness. Hard evidence on the landscape issue is difficult to come by a century later, but the weight of the literary testimony is considerable – and consistent with the house as we have rediscovered it.

My continuing hope today, as I wistfully wrote in 1982 as "A Dream" is that one day visitors to the Edgar Allan Poe Historical Site may walk down Seventh Street to a gate in a white picket fence, enter a garden overflowing with flowers, and move down a long narrow path past a towering pear tree to arrive at the front porch of the little house where, as Poe wrote in "Landor's Cottage," his last published story:

The pillars of the piazza were enwreathed in jasmine and sweet honeysuckle; while from the angle formed by the main structure and its west wing, in front, sprang a grape-vine of unexampled luxuriance, scorning all restraint, it had clambered the latter, it continued to writhe on, throwing out tendrils to the right and left, until at length it fairly attained the east gable, and fell trailing over the stairs.

NOTES

1. The term *piazza* refers to the narrow link between the front and rear portions of these nineteenth-century row houses.
2. Mary E. Phillips, *Edgar Allan Poe: The Man*, 2 vols. (Chicago: John C. Winston, 1926), vol. i, 843.
3. Anthony J. Frayne, *The Rose-Covered Cottage of Edgar Allan Poe in Philadelphia* (Philadelphia: A. J. Frayne, 1934), 5.
4. Phillips, *Edgar Allan Poe*, vol. i, 821.
5. Edgar Allan Poe, *The Collected Works of Edgar Allan Poe*, ed. Thomas Ollive Mabbott, 3 vols. (Cambridge, MA: Belknap Press, 1969–78), vol. iii, 857.
6. Ibid., vol. iii, 853.
7. Ibid., vol. iii, 854.
8. Frayne, *Rose-Covered Cottage*, 7.
9. Poe, *Collected Works*, vol. iii, 1337.
10. Quoted in Phillips, *Edgar Allan Poe*, vol. i, 821.
11. Phillips, *Edgar Allan Poe*, vol. i, 821; Thomas Dunn English, "Reminiscences of Poe," *Independent*, October 22, 1896, 3; Mayne Reid, "A Dead Man Defended," *Onward* 1 (1869), 305–8.

CHAPTER 34

The Heritage of Fiction Science

Peter Swirski

Literary historians agree by and large that science fiction is a modern genre. When it comes to specifying what "modern" means, however, opinions vary rapidly. Some place the roots of modern science fiction in the early nineteenth century, more or less coeval with Mary Shelley's *Frankenstein; or The Modern Prometheus*. Others point to Poe and his notorious hoaxes and scientific satires or to Jules Verne and his romances of technological wonder. Others reserve the distinction for late nineteenth-century utopians like Edward Bellamy in America and William Morris in England.

Arguments over these literary lineages are as sterile as those of hydrologists quarreling over the exact point at which a brook becomes a stream. Historically speaking, the only assertion one can make without expecting to be contradicted is that at the beginning of the nineteenth century we are still talking about a science-fiction brook, whereas at the outset of the twentieth we are already facing a flowing stream. What lies in between is, in the absence of universal criteria about what might count as incontestable proof, a pursuit as aimless as the marble-playing game in Poe's "The Purloined Letter."

When it comes to science fiction, H. G. Wells's place as the father of the modern genre is unassailable, no matter how much he himself may have disparaged of his scientific romances in his unrequited campaign to be recognized for his "serious" novels. This is not to say that Wells was invariably the first to mine the themes associated with science fiction today. To take but one example, his landmark *The Time Machine*, published in book form in 1895 but serialized a year earlier as "The Time Traveller's Story," was far from the first modern tale of chronomotion. Barring the recent claims on behalf of Enrique Gaspar's *El Anacronopete* (1887), that distinction belongs to Edward Page Mitchell, editor of the *New York Sun*, who published his singularly undistinguished "The Clock That Went Backwards" as early as 1881.

What H. G. (as he would become known around the world) did, however, was to gather the diverse narrative and philosophical strands that stretch as far back as antiquity and refurbish them into a new literary form that boasted a thoroughly contemporary scientific sensibility. One of these literary strands was the gothic novel that peaked in popularity at the turn of the eighteenth century, only to become cannibalized by the likes of Mary Shelley, E. T. A. Hoffman, Hawthorne, and Poe in the ensuing decades. Their tales of scientific aspirations to change the course of nature were as much about usurpations of divine prerogatives – and suffering the inevitable retribution.

If Poe's name crops up again and again in these accounts, it is because he was in many ways the most modern writer of his era. It is not only that he felt perfectly at home in every one of the emerging genres that he did as much as anybody else to establish: the horror story, the detective story, the adventure story, the satirical hoax, literary criticism, metacritical poetics. Equally to the point, in synchrony with the sensibilities of his new-fangled magazine-reading public, he championed a thoroughly modern kind of art – the light "art"-illery of the mind designed to titillate his novelty-seeking audiences.

With hindsight, his literary goals – to entrance and entertain, and do so it forms compact enough to be consumed in one sitting – were a cultural watershed. Turning his "nobrow" brand of art into a popular gold mine, they turned his narrative descents into the human maelstrom into classics lionized far outside the United States. In France, for example, in a testimony to his crosscultural appeal, Poe was championed not only by Charles Baudelaire and his poetic peers but also by Jules Verne – who did not, however, think much of the American's (and the Americans') penchant for hoaxes and similar sensationalistic humbug. All that did not stop him, however, from paying Poe the highest tribute by penning a sequel to the latter's only novel, *The Narrative of Arthur Gordon Pym of Nantucket*, entitled *An Antarctic Mystery* (or *The Sphinx of the Ice Fields*).

Verne was, it must be said, a different species of a writer of tales of futurity and science. Keener than Poe on the verisimilitude of his fictional geographical discoveries or technological inventions – be it an electrically powered submarine or the mother of all Columbiads constructed to blast a manned missile to the moon – he purposefully tried to lay the foundations of what he envisioned as a new type of *belles lettres*. Full of popular science detail as well as optimistic (at least until his later period) extrapolation, they were crucial for establishing the narrative baseline for his and other writers' scientific romances. The ideals of what constituted good science fiction were so clear in his mind that he protested of Wells, with whom his works were increasingly compared, "*Mais, il invente!*"

The technological ferment of the nineteenth century that permeates the writings of Poe and other writers commonly touted as the precursors of science fiction is undoubtedly the greatest direct contributor to the development of the genre. But the century itself did not spring like Athena, fully formed and complete, from any one writer's head. The antecedents of science fiction boast a history that spans thousands of years, going back to some of the earliest literary efforts to take a measure of the ambient world. When Poe sat down to write *Eureka*, "Mellonta Tauta," "The Colloquy of Eiros and Charmion," or his "factional" mesmeric tales, he was tapping into a long tradition of literature in the speculative – as opposed to the romantically expressive – mode.

All this is to say that, even if science fiction is an exemplary modern genre, its history is quite ancient, going back in some cases to some of the greatest thinkers and writers of antiquity who speculated on new forms of social organization or instrumental power and their inevitable perils. Their literary endeavors to bring the wonders of their scientific, technological, or natural worlds to justice form as much of a context for Poe and his contemporaries as do *The Castle of Otranto* or Robert Fulton's *Nautilus*, the first practical submarine in history (commissioned by none other than Napoleon Bonaparte).

While it would be impossible to trace all of Poe's literary and historical predecessors within this short chapter, they can be synthesized into several dominant literary strands that converge on the nineteenth century to meld into modern science fiction. Here then are the historical antecedents of Poe and other genre pioneers.

THE IMAGINARY VOYAGE

The ur-narrative is *The Odyssey*, traditionally attributed to Homer, a historical enigma said to have lived in the twelfth century BCE, but whose verses were not written down until half a millennium later through an intercession of the Athenian despot Peisistratus. The story itself – memorable among others for its ichtyogynetic Sirens (whose haunting songs have been traced to humpback whales' songs resonating throughout the ancient mariners' wooden hulls), the monocular Cyclops, and the sorceress Circe who transformed Odysseus's crew into swine – became a template for countless imaginary voyages over the centuries before Poe's "The Thousand-and-Second Tale of Scheherazade" (1845).

As Poe's mock apocryphal title suggests, there were also the popular tales of the Orient and the South Seas, replete with imaginary beasts styled on the mythical Gorgons – women with serpents for hair, serpent's fangs and scales, and boar's tusks and claws – and later on the medieval Manticore, a hybrid of a lion, snake, and eagle. The tradition of imaginary travelogues, full of out of this world adventures and unearthly creatures, only intensified after Columbus's four voyages, with Old World writers populating their fictional worlds with anything from human beings with their heads in their bellies to, as in Gabriel Foigny's *A New Discovery of Terra Incognita Australis* (1676), a race of hermaphrodites who transform the entire Australian continent.

Poe's *Narrative of Arthur Gordon Pym* (1838) is a minor masterpiece of the genre that influenced Verne's famous *20,000 Leagues Under the Sea*, itself a precursor to one of the latter's modern classics, *Around the World in Eighty Days*. Beset like Coleridge's Ancient Mariner in equal proportions by an unquenchable yen for adventure and ill luck, Poe's young protagonist experiences a shipwreck, mutiny, and cannibalism before he is rescued by a vessel that will eventually take him deep south to a land of all-black natives (even their teeth are black) unnerved by everything white, on the way to the South Pole.

THE LUNAR VOYAGE

Cosmology, like astronomy, had been dormant for centuries in the light of the Roman Catholic Church's condemnation of natural philosophy as inimical to divine will, all couched in terms of neo-Aristotelian scholasticism. Galvanized, however, by Galileo's perfection of the telescope in 1609, literary voyages to the Earth's satellite began to appear with the regularity of the phases of the moon. Johannes Kepler's posthumous *Somnium* (1634), which cashed in on the notoriety kindled by the publication of his laws of planetary motion, advanced speculation about life forms adapted to the lunar conditions – tiny and short-lived, but with new generations born daily – decades before Thomas Hooke's breakthrough study of microscopic life, *Micrographia*.

Written to satisfy the enormous curiosity about speculation about life on other worlds, Bishop Francis Godwin's *The Man in the Moone* (1638) – Anglican clergy were beyond the pale of Rome's bulls – became a best seller not only in its own day but over the next two centuries. In marked contrast to Kepler, Domingo Gonzales, who trains a posse of swans to carry him to the moon, discovers there a utopia inhabited by long-lived giants who get rid of their social misfits by shipping them to Earth's North America (much like the real-life English did with felons in the seventeenth and eighteenth centuries, first in America and then in Australia and Tasmania).

Perhaps the most fanciful of these early lunar stories was Cyrano de Bergerac's *Voyage dans la lune* (1657), in which the voyager, in the manner of the next century's Baron Münchhausen, equips himself with an array of small bottles filled with dew which, as it evaporates in the heat of the sun, gives him the requisite lift. Bergerac's fantastic and satirical tone is revived in Poe's own "The Unparalleled Adventure of one Hans Pfaall" (1835), intended to be a hoax but beat to the punch by a rival publication. The story has the singularly named Dutch murderer plea for pardon to the assorted citizenry of Rotterdam in exchange for a manuscript of his balloon trip to the moon, enabled by a revolutionary apparatus that compresses molecules dispersed in a vacuum into breathable air.

THE STORY OF FORBIDDEN KNOWLEDGE

While the prototype is the parable of the tree of knowledge from the Hebrew Testament, its classic embodiment is the legend of Daedalus and Icarus. As soon as Daedalus builds the labyrinth in Crete to house the Minotaur, the genetically crossbred monster (half man, half bull), his proto-maze is deemed to be such a dangerous invention by King Minos that he imprisons the constructor in a tower. It is from there that Daedalus and his son escape with the aid of artificial wings in a proto-myth of perils of technology that has Icarus soar too close to the sun, which melts the wax in the wings and sends him plunging into the Aegean.

This cautionary, not to say homiletic, element will surge to the forefront in centuries of medieval *exempla* and in the modern classic of the genre, Christopher Marlowe's drama, *Doctor Faustus* (1604). Combining the Odyssean figure of a devil-may-care seeker of knowledge with the didacticism of a morality play, it fashions one of the modern age's enduring myths. Later on, weaving strands of Jewish mysticism in the figure of the artificial nonhuman Golem, E. T. A. Hoffman's "The Automaton" (1814) and Mary Shelley's *Frankenstein* (1818) pave the way for Poe's more lighthearted treatment of scientific genius in "Von Kempelen And His Discovery" (1849). "The Facts in the Case of M. Valdemar" (1845) is, on the other hand, decidedly more ghastly, purporting to be factographic record of a seven-month-long experiment in which a corpse is maintained in suspended animation with the aid of mesmerism, only to dissolve instantly into putrescence upon the termination of the séance.

THE CATASTROPHE STORY

Familiar from the biblical accounts of the Flood, stories of a catastrophic deluge come to us from most of the oldest Mediterranean civilizations, including the Sumerians, the Akkadians, the Egyptians – and, in the fifth century BCE, the Athenians. Plato's enduring legend of a great civilization on the island of Atlantis situated beyond the pillars of Hercules has now been traced to an earthquake and tsunami-destroyed Minoan culture on the island of Thera (modern Santorini).

Picked up by didactically minded medieval clerics who typically set the destructive events in the past in order to reform sinners in the present, catastrophe stories burgeoned again in the nineteenth century, this time fashioned as prophetic warnings of the future. Typical is Mary Shelley's virtually unknown three-volume epic *The Last Man* (1826), in which warfare and plague finish off humankind in the year 2100. In America, literary comets fell fast and hard in tales by Hawthorne and Poe, whose "The Colloquy of Eiros and Charmion" (1839) brims with apocalyptic imagery. Capitalizing on Adventist preacher William Miller's sensationalist predictions of the end of the world, Poe depicts the ravages of a comet whose approach thins out the nitrogen in the air, leaving people dizzy and delirious even before the nucleus strikes and catastrophically ignites the pure oxygen atmosphere.

THE PHILOSOPHICAL TALE (*CONTE PHILOSOPHIQUE*)

When Enlightenment philosophy finally separated itself from the yoke of theology, it became a powerful instrument of social criticism dressed up in counterfactual speculation. Montesquieu in France, Locke in England, and Franklin in America became the pillars of science-informed humanitarian philosophy, but it was Voltaire's *Micromegas* (1750) that provided the quintessential embodiment of the literary genre. The story describes two gigantic visitors from the stellar system of Sirius who pluck a seagoing vessel right out of the Baltic in order to interrogate the Lilliputian humans about their customs in a de-anthropomorphizing satire of Voltaire's times.

Few literary efforts, however, can rival the scope of Poe's prose poem cum philosophical treatise, *Eureka* (1848). An intellectual offspring of a professional man of letters and amateur philosopher, in 100 pages of alternatively rapturous and analytical prose the book attempts to forge a *modus vivendi* between Romantic sensibility and nineteenth-century science. Based on Poe's speculation on the fate of the material and spiritual universe, the first part of the treatise elaborates a novel epistemology grounded in poetic intuition, while the second outlines a sketch of an empirically grounded cosmogonic theory.

A good way to balance the ambition of Poe's philosophical essay may be to put it next to the countless cosmologies advanced since the beginning of written records. From the Sumerian epics through the pre-Socratic philosophers, the classical Hellenes, the Roman verse historians, the Scholastics, and the Renaissance and Enlightenment natural philosophers (including Kepler and Newton), all have labored to devise a cogent vision of humankind's place in the universe. Even though their theories have invariably turned out to be flawed either on logical or empirical grounds – or, as in Poe's case, both – grand designs of this nature are endemic to human thought, a record of our tireless efforts to understand the ways of the world.

CLASSICAL UTOPIA

Going back to the legend of Atlantis in Plato's *Kritias* and *Timaeus*, literary visions of a just and fair society are equally indebted to his *Republic* and *The Laws*, all of which set the agenda for the next two millennia. Be that as it may, there was something radically different about the blueprint masterminded by Thomas More in *Utopia* (1516). In a break from the preceding centuries of visions of the Christian City of God or folk legends of Cockaigne, it was thoroughly secular and reformist, far less interested in metaphysical speculation than in the hardcore problem of engineering a society less riven by the inequality between the rich and the poor.

The Renaissance and the Enlightenment followed in his footsteps, multiplying tales of futurity and enlightenment devoted to rationalizing the excesses of feudal monarchies. Andreae's *Christianopolis*, Bacon's *The New Atlantis*, Campanella's *The City of the Sun* (which Roderick Usher has in his personal library in "The Fall of the House of Usher"), and Harrington's *Oceana* were only some of the literary milestones on the road to a better social order – or at least a philosophical outline for it. The reformist spirit was perhaps best expressed by Louis-Sebastien Mercier in *Memoirs of the Year Two Thousand Five Hundred* (1772) and its elaborate projections of French society and culture. Mercier's utopia, which Poe mentions in a footnote to "Metzengerstein," is one of the first future-oriented rather than remote island utopias, and one of the first to depict and embrace a vision of a giant modern city, as memorable for its equitable social system as for the foresight of machines that lighten human toil.

For all their forward thinking, utopian visionaries have always borrowed from the past. No matter how different from one another, all share a number of elements with Plato: elite government, checks and balances, eugenics, education, meritocracy, redistribution of wealth. Once again, Poe puts a satirical spin on the shape of things to come in "Mellonta Tauta" (1849) – Greek for "Things of the Future." Letters from a transatlantic balloon voyage offer snippets of America in the year 2048 (the first dirigible was constructed in France only three years after Poe's story). Universal suffrage, a transatlantic telegraph, immense balloons racing at 150 miles an hour, trains running more than twice as fast, memories of an earthquake-flattened island called Paradise with its twenty-story building inhabited by Knickerbockers who worshipped the gods of wealth and fashion – all mingle with news of civil wars in Africa, pestilence decimating Europe and Asia, and a chilling rejoicing in the death of myriads.

IMAGINARY WAR STORY

This tabloid subgenre peaked in popularity mainly in Europe in the second half of the nineteenth century, too late to have influenced Poe, who passed away in 1849. Anticipating contemporary military techno-thrillers, fictive invasions, and conquests of the British isles – usually by the old enemy France or by the newly united Germany – were quite the rage in the days of the "Iron Chancellor" Otto von Bismarck, under whose leadership Germany began to dominate continental affairs after mid-century by modernizing and arming itself and by heavily investing in technical and (especially in Prussia) military education.

Massive engagements, dramatic use of advanced weapons technology, realistic depiction of panic, chaos, and massacres of civilian populations became familiar themes of these fictional military campaigns. H. G. Wells's classic *War of the Worlds* borrows all these elements from George Chesney's 1871 best seller *Battle of Dorking*, which has the dubious distinction of having been translated and published by the Nazis in 1940, just as they were gearing up for what was to be (or rather not to be) Operation Sea Lion. Little wonder: in the guise of fictitious journalism, Chesney's novel depicts a successful invasion of the British Isles by newly consolidated Germany.

Driven by the Industrial Revolution, the nineteenth century moved at a pace that made the transformation of the entire world by machines and technology seem only a matter of time. The instrumental extensions of modern society bestowed on it unprecedented powers to remake the natural world in the image of the future envisioned by thinkers of the past. In the United States, this Industrial Revelation was put to action in the first decades of the century with the dredging of the Erie Canal. It culminated with the 1898 Cuban war which turned the erstwhile republic into a global colonial superpower, even as the American economy became the world's largest.

The reaction among writers to the explosive development of new technologies in a new capital-driven society was polarized. In England, William Blake deplored the horror and the misery of the dark satanic mills of industrial mass production. Mercier, Verne, and in general the French *ecrivants* were altogether more optimistic, amazed at the new world of possibilities and embracing it with a sense of destiny. In America, straddling the two traditions, Poe reflected both the dark, foreboding, skeptical attitude to visions of paradise on earth that even in his time looked more like Hieronymus Bosch's grotesque *Garden of Earthy Delights*, as well as the can-do spirit of the era that hailed science as a universal panacea to all that ailed society.

After all, even in the notorious "Sonnet – To Science" (1829), Poe speaks out not against science, but against the triumph of mechanical reason. This interpretation squares aptly with his documented admiration for science, evident in breathless enumerations of the wonders of nature and technology in "The Thousand-and-Second Tale of Scheherazade," or in articles such as his little-known "A Chapter on Science and Art," in which Poe, the alleged Romantic reactionary, reviews many contemporary scientific inventions with a favorable eye and even recommends establishing a scientific foundation in Washington. Any lingering doubts about his views are dispelled in "Marginalia" where, in no ambiguous terms, he declares a poem about Saturn a paltry thing next to the breathtaking scientific facts about the planet!

CONCLUSION

If Poe continues to be read, written about, and celebrated the world over, it is at least in part because his fiction provides an apt context for judging the role that science and philosophy played in nineteenth-century society. Unlike the almost autonomous systems of thought like logic or mathematics, science is not cumulative in any straightforward way. Today's theories may be supplanted tomorrow by better and more comprehensive ones, consigning the old models to their rightful place in the history of a civilization: its galleries, museums, and libraries. Yet, although human inquiry is a fallible and daily outdated enterprise, science and its methods are the best means of learning about the world. And as such, as Poe was keenly aware, they demand our critical attention.

CHAPTER 35

Cosmology and Cosmogony

Jonathan Taylor

Given Edgar Allan Poe's avowed "identification of ... matter with God," it should come as no surprise that, in his science fiction, the scientific and cosmological context is bound up with a complex theological and philosophical inheritance.[1] In his story "The Power of Words" (1845), for example, Poe's view of the universe draws on an Enlightenment and Deistic inheritance, particularly in the conception of God as First Cause: "The Deity does not create.... In the beginning *only*, he created. The seeming creatures which are now, throughout the universe ... springing into being, can only be considered as the mediate or indirect, not as the direct or immediate results of the Divine creative power."[2]

"Among men," claims one of the characters in the story, "this idea would be considered heretical in the extreme." In many ways, though, Deistic ideas like that of God as First Cause had actually become commonplace – almost a new orthodoxy – among Enlightenment and post-Enlightenment thinkers. "In an atmosphere saturated with Newtonian science," argues Peter Gay, "Deism was a perfectly sensible religion to adopt," and if the reputation of the original English Deists had faded by the late eighteenth century, this was precisely "because their teachings and their criticisms had become commonplace [and] ... widely accepted." Isaac Kramnick notes of this Deistic inheritance that "central to the Enlightenment agenda was the assault on religious superstition and its replacement by a rational religion in which God became ... [a] supreme intelligence or craftsman who had set the machine that was the world to run according to its own natural and scientifically predictable laws."[3]

Herein lies an important point: as Kramnick suggests, the world runs according to its *own* laws, laws many scientists seemed to believe had precedence over God, and to which God was himself subject. The idea of God as First Cause is shot through with contradictions: for a start, a First Cause might be said to be *both* outside *and* inside creation. A First Cause is outside creation insofar as it originates that creation, but, according to the strictures of Newtonian physics, it must also be part of the mechanism as a sufficient cause for the machine to be set running. Since, as Poe and most other Newtonians would assume, "an effect is the measure of its cause," a cause must necessarily be connected with its effect, very much part of the same system, and implicated in the same laws.[4] Isaac Newton (1642–1727) himself often betrays this confusion; in a letter to Richard Bentley, he appears to argue straightforwardly for God as a First Cause preexisting creation when he writes:

Matter should divide itself into two sorts, and that Part of it, which is fit to compose a shining Body, should fall down into one Mass and make a Sun, and the rest, which is fit to compose an opaque Body, should coalesce...into many little ones.... I do not think explicable by mere natural Causes, but am forced to ascribe it to the Counsel and Contrivance of a voluntary Agent.... Why there is one Body in our System qualified to give Light and Heat to the rest, I know no Reason, but because the Author of the System thought it convenient...the Motions which the Planets now have could not spring from any natural Cause alone, but were impressed by an intelligent Agent.[5]

In this passage, it seems at first that Newton's God is in control, is the preexisting "Author of the System" and its physical laws. On closer inspection, however, Newton's language is peculiarly ambivalent: the word "Agent" can mean both someone who produces an effect or someone in a secondary position, standing in for someone or something else. Furthermore, Newton hovers on the verge of ascribing human traits to his Agent, and human beings are obviously a secondary phenomenon, subject to the already created universe. Rather than appearing faultless and omnipotent, Newton's First Cause is merely "intelligent" and "voluntary"; Newton makes his Agent sound almost capricious when he declares that he knows "no Reason" why only the sun gives off light and heat, except that "the Author of the System thought it convenient."

Even God's "convenience," though, is not as "voluntary" as it might seem in a Newtonian universe, as can be seen when Newton goes on to qualify the nature of his First Cause. "To make this System...with all its Motions," asserts Newton, "required a Cause which understood, and compared together, the Quantities of Matter in the several Bodies of the Sun and Planets, and the gravitating Powers resulting from thence," and all of this necessarily "argues that Cause to be not blind and fortuitous, but very well skilled in Mechanicks and Geometry."[6] Newton's First Cause is rather like Newton himself, with all his power to observe laws, but no power to change them. Here is a God who understands and compares the "Quantities of Matter," knows all about gravity, and is adept at the relevant branches of mathematics. Instead of being truly capricious or "fortuitous," Newton's First Cause, like Newton himself, sees and understands physical laws and obeys them when arranging the universe. God is logical in terms of Newtonian physics – God is subject to the same laws of mechanics, geometry, and even gravity as other scientists. As First Cause, God is at once outside creation and locked within it, subject to its natural (and Newtonian) laws.

There are insoluble paradoxes here: questions arise as to how a First Cause can still be a First Cause if subject to laws which seem to preexist it or him, and, conversely, how any laws can possibly be said to preexist a First Cause. In fact, questions like these, reformulated in the language of modern physics, still exercise cosmologists today; as John Barrow notes, "If the universe did begin at a singularity from which matter appeared ... then we are confronted with a number of problems. . . . If space and time do not exist before that singular beginning, how do we account for the laws of gravitation, or of ... mathematics? Did they exist 'before' the singularity? If so ... we must admit to a rationality larger than the material universe."[7]

Standing between Newton and modern cosmology, historically speaking, Poe seeks to tackle just such questions in his science fiction, often taking Newton's implications to their logical conclusion and preempting some of the concerns of twentieth-century cosmology. Just as, in "The Power of Words," Poe argues that "in the beginning only, [the Deity] ... created," in *Eureka* (1848), he writes that "'in the beginning' we can admit, indeed we can comprehend, but one first cause, the truly ultimate principle – the volition of God ... The thought of God is to be understood as originating the diffusion [of particles in the universe] ... and ... as being withdrawn from it upon its completion."[8]

Throughout *Eureka*, Poe continually underlines the idea that "the volition of God" is withdrawn from creation after its completion; in true Newtonian and Deistic style, he posits a mechanical, clockwork universe that, once set running, maintains itself without divine intervention. As one contemporary reviewer recognized, Poe speaks as a "Deist might speak."[9]

Indeed, he goes much further in this respect than some earlier Deists or Newton himself dared. Whereas the latter believed that "the Motions which the Planets now have could not spring from any natural Cause alone, but were impressed by an intelligent Agent," Poe claims that "the act of creation has long ago ceased." Poe resists *any* notion of divine interference or secondary creation after the origin of the universe in a single "primordial particle."[10] As Gay writes, "While there was room in [Newton's] ... system for divine intervention – God, Newton thought, set the universe right once in a while when it threatened to run down – the Newtonians could safely disregard this kind of theology."[11]

If one such Newtonian was Poe, another was French astronomer and mathematician Pierre-Simon Laplace (1749–1827), on whose cosmological findings some of Poe's theories depend. As John Gribbin points out, Newton had "suggested that after a long enough time...divine intervention would be required to put the planets back in their proper orbits and prevent the Solar System falling apart," owing to the fact that, over extended periods, the orbits of Saturn and Jupiter appear to drift; Laplace, however, "showed conclusively that these secular variations...can be explained within the framework of Newtonian theory and are caused by the disturbing influences of the two planets on one another."[12] Laplace's demonstration makes conceivable what Poe assumes – namely, the absence of divine intervention from the universe's day-to-day workings. Laplace's work makes possible Poe's rebuttal of any kind of divine intervention after the First Cause. "The willing into being [of] the primordial particle," asserts Poe, "*has completed* the act, or more properly the conception, of creation," and there is to be no secondary creation or interference.[13]

The single particle at creation is "of one kind...a particle, therefore, 'without form and void'...absolutely unique, individual, undivided," and yet somehow contained within it is the potential universe and its whole future history. "Oneness," writes Poe, "is all that I predicate of the originally created matter; but...this oneness is a principle abundantly sufficient to account for the constitution, the existing phenomena, and the plainly inevitable annihilation, of...the...universe." The original "oneness" is a sufficient cause for everything that is to follow: "all...laws...are but consequences of one primary exercise of the divine volition."[14]

Poe argues that "a perfect consistency can be nothing but an absolute truth," and he attacks many of his forebears for not adhering with perfect consistency to the doctrine of an all-sufficient First Cause. Writing about the orbital patterns of satellites, Poe seems almost to attack Newton himself – and his assumption that "the Motions" of planets are "impressed by an intelligent Agent" – when he derides "astronomical treatises" for their tendency

to seek beyond the limits of mere Nature... [for] a solution of the phenomenon of tangential velocity. This...they attribute directly to a first cause – to God. The force which carries a stellar body around its primary they assert to have originated in an impulse given immediately by the finger...of deity itself.... The planets...are conceived to have been hurled from the divine hand to a position in the vicinity of the suns with an impetus mathematically adapted to the masses, or attractive capacities, of the suns themselves.[15]

Here, Poe sneers at the Newtonian argument for a God who himself impresses the motions of planets – a God who, being "very well skilled in Mechanicks and Geometry," understands "the Quantities of Matter in the...Sun and Planets, and [their]...gravitating Powers." Newton's letter to Bentley and other astronomical treatises set up a distinction between God and physical laws such as "quantity" and "gravity," or, in Poe's terms, "mass" and "attractive capacities" – physical laws to which God, by intervening in creation, is himself subject. Poe, by contrast, refuses to acknowledge such a distinction. Rather, he absolutely identifies physical laws with God and vice versa: "that Nature and the God of Nature are distinct," he remarks, "no thinking being can long doubt. By the former we imply merely the laws of the latter." Since Poe's God in no way interferes in the workings of the universe after creation, he is not subject to its laws, but rather initiates those laws himself and, indeed, *is* those laws. Poe's First Cause is sufficient to account for all physical laws; the initial conditions of his universe are a sufficient cause for all that is to follow. As he remarks, "Each law of Nature is dependent at all points upon all other laws," and "all are but consequences of one primary exercise of the divine volition."[16]

Poe's conception of an all-sufficient First Cause, or "primary exercise of the divine volition," does not just look back to Laplace, Newton, and the Deists; strangely enough, it also anticipates twentieth-century cosmology. Poe self-consciously positions himself as a prophet in his science fiction, and many of the more recent theories concerning the universe's origins have come to support Poe's intuitions – particularly his idea that creation commenced with a "primordial particle," which split to form the universe. Stephen Hawking is one twentieth-century cosmologist who almost sounds like Poe when he describes the now-famous big bang theory: "At some time in the past...the distance between neighboring galaxies must have been zero. At that time, which we call the big bang, the density of the universe and the curvature of space-time would have been infinite.... Such a point is an example of what mathematicians call a *singularity*.... Any...expanding universe must have begun with a singularity." As Peter Coveney and Roger Highfield gloss the big bang theory, at "the birth of the universe...a pinpoint of featureless matter budded from nothing at all. From this putatively emphatic and utterly simple big bang, the universe ballooned."[17]

If contemporary cosmology supports Poe's idea of an original "singularity," it also assumes what Poe states when he claims that this singularity was the determinant for the whole future of the universe – that it was "a principle abundantly sufficient to account for the constitution, the existing

phenomena, and the plainly inevitable annihilation, of...the...universe."
As Barrow indicates, the whole science of cosmogony depends on the
assumption that it is possible to extrapolate the past from what is observed
of the "present" state of the universe – and that the present state of the
universe is determined by that past and, ultimately, by its origin: "If...the
present state of the universe emerges regardless of the starting conditions,
then our observations...will not be able to tell us anything about those
starting conditions.... But if the present structure of the universe...[is a]
reflection...of the way the universe began, then it might be possible to
determine something about the initial state of the universe by observing
it today."[18] In *Eureka*, Poe assumes something similar: that it is possible to
trace the present state of the universe back to its ultimate origin because
that origin was a sufficient cause to determine everything that followed.

Certainly, many scientists in the nineteenth century were well aware
that the observation of the present state of the universe might lead to an
understanding of the distant past – that, as Poe puts it, "the processes at
present observed" also encode "the phantoms of processes completed long
in the past." It is in this historical context that some of Poe's uncannily
prescient hypotheses might be placed and understood. In 1845, William
Parsons, third Earl of Rosse, built a huge telescope in his castle in Ireland.
Poe points out that looking through this telescope is really the same as
looking into the distant past: "So far removed from us are some of the
'nebulae' that even light...could not and does not reach us from those
mysterious regions in less than three million years...There are 'nebulae'...which, through the magical tube of Lord Rosse, are this instant
whispering in our ears the secrets of a million ages gone by."[19]

In 1929, Edwin Hubble discovered that these remarkable distances are
increasing – that the universe is expanding – just as Poe (in part) suggests
in *Eureka* when he talks about the "radiation" of matter from the original
particle: "from the one particle...[was] radiated spherically, in all directions, to immeasurable...distances...[an] inexpressibly great...number
of...atoms."[20] If Poe again seems remarkably prescient here, it is worth
remembering that he was aware of some of the major scientific and theo-
retical advances that made Hubble's discovery possible.

For a start, Poe avowedly takes his ideas on radiation, diffusion and,
indeed, condensation of particles from what he calls "the most magnificent of theories...the nebular cosmogony of Laplace."[21] As expounded
in the latter's *Exposition du système du monde* (1796), Laplace's "nebular hypothesis" proposed that the solar system and its planets had con-
densed from what was originally diffused, nebulous matter. Indeed, the

nebular hypothesis Poe assimilates can be traced back much further. In his early work, *Allgemeine Naturgeschichte und Theorie des Himmels* (1755), Immanuel Kant had preempted Laplace. Kant writes: "I assume that all the material of our solar system...was, at the beginning of all things, decomposed into its primary elements, and filled the whole space...in which the bodies formed out of it now revolve."[22] In turn, both Kant and Laplace's views of the solar system's origins can be traced all the way back to the philosopher Lucretius. In *On the Nature of the Universe*, Lucretius describes *"the stages by which the initial concentration of matter laid the foundation of earth and sky*, of the ocean depths and the orbits of sun and moon.... Multitudinous atoms, swept along in multitudinous courses, through infinite time by mutual clashes and their own weight, have come together in every possible way and tested everything that could be formed by their combinations."[23] In this vision of "multitudinous atoms" forming "everything that could be formed," Lucretius established a powerful philosophical tradition which, almost two thousand years later, developed into the nebular hypothesis of modern cosmogony.

By Poe's time, advances in telescopes meant that the nebular hypothesis was increasingly subject to empirical observation, which served both to confirm and modify it. The construction of Lord Rosse's telescope in 1845 facilitated a more detailed understanding of *distant* "nebulae." This new understanding led Poe to predict that "we have no reason to suppose the Milky Way really more extensive than the least of these 'nebulae.'"[24] Indeed, Hubble did eventually recognize the nebulae as separate galaxies in themselves. Hence Poe's prescience in *Eureka* can be understood as part of an historical continuum, in which he seems to gesture toward future cosmology by extrapolating hypotheses from past and contemporary cosmological observations, theories, and traditions. For example, Poe's hypothesis of an initial "radiation" and "diffusion" of matter, which looks forward to Hubble's expanding universe, is conceived only six years after the identification of what became known as the "Doppler effect" – the very effect that made possible Hubble's discovery that other galaxies are accelerating away from our own and from one another.[25]

In these ways, Poe's hypotheses look backward as well as forward, historically speaking; past and future are both important contexts for Poe's work. As well as anticipating Hubble, his conception of a universe that radiates from singularity also draws on traditional religious imagery. Robert Lawlor suggests that "the primal act" of creation has been envisaged by various religions in terms of "the division of unity." He writes: "Those who use geometric figures to describe the beginning of Creation must attempt to show how an absolute Unity can become multiplicity and diversity. Geometry attempts to recapture the orderly movement from an infinite formlessness to an endless interconnected array of forms, and in recreating this mysterious passage from One to Two, it renders it symbolically visible."[26]

In attempting to envisage the universe's origin, Poe seems to gesture toward geometry and its ability to recapture the "mysterious passage" from singularity to multiplicity. He uses a geometrical diagram to depict the radiation of particles, and suggests that it is possible for a scientist to "establish the universe on a purely geometrical basis" since it is founded on "'ultimate principles'...[of] a geometrical turn." These "'ultimate principles'" of geometry and science have spiritual overtones. After all, Poe names "the truly ultimate principle" as "the spiritual capacity of God," and declares one of his aims to be the discovery of the "principle...existing behind the law of gravity," a principle from which even "the great mind of Newton...shrank, and which "Laplace had not the courage to attack."[27]

Unlike Newton and Laplace – or, at least, apparently unlike them – Poe draws on an older tradition of mystical astronomy that attempted to discover ultimate principles, synthesizing the sciences, arts, and religion. Most significant, he looks back – and, oddly enough, forward as well – to seventeenth-century astronomer Johannes Kepler, whom Daniel Hoffman calls "the real hero of the piece."[28] Toward the start of *Eureka*, Poe looks forward to the year 2848, when he predicts that new "Keplers...[will] speculate [and] theorise" their way toward truth; and Poe clearly sees himself as both the precursor for these future Keplers and the standard-bearer for past Keplerian science, particularly in its intermixture of the physical and the metaphysical. Of Kepler's *Harmony of the World* (1618), Arthur Koestler suggests that "Kepler attempted...to bare the ultimate secret of the universe in an all-embracing synthesis of geometry, music, astrology, astronomy and epistemology," discovering "certain geometrical proportions...everywhere, [which are] the archetypes of universal order." Koestler asserts that Kepler's synthesis "was the first attempt of this kind since Plato, and it is the last to our day."[29] Other attempts might be cited as well, not the least of which is Poe's *Eureka*, which seeks to "bare the ultimate secret of the universe" in an all-embracing synthesis of science, mysticism, Euclidian and post-Euclidian geometry, Lucretian philosophy, Deistic theology, Newtonian and Laplacian cosmology, Enlightenment rationalism and Romantic Pantheism, prophecy and tradition, past and future, material and spiritual. In *Eureka*, Poe stands with Kepler, who once declared that "I do think the thoughts of God."[30]

NOTES

1. Edgar Allan Poe, *The Collected Works of Edgar Allan Poe*, ed. Thomas Ollive Mabbott, 3 vols. (Cambridge, MA: Belknap Press, 1969–78), vol. iii, 1024–42. For an extended discussion of Poe's religious, philosophical, and scientific contexts, see Jonathan Taylor, *Science and Omniscience in Nineteenth-Century Literature* (Brighton: Sussex Academic Press, 2007).

2. Poe, *Collected Works*, vol. iii, 1213.

3. Peter Gay, *The Enlightenment, An Interpretation: The Rise of Modern Paganism* (New York: Norton, 1966), 375; Isaac Kramnick, "Introduction," in *The Portable Enlightenment Reader*, ed. Isaac Kramnick (New York: Penguin, 1995), xii.

4. Edgar Allan Poe, *Eureka: A Prose Poem*, in *Poetry and Tales*, ed. Patrick F. Quinn (New York: Library of America, 1984), 1299. In the *Philosophiae Naturalis Principia Mathematica* (1687), Isaac Newton demands that "we are to admit no more causes of natural things than such as are both true *and sufficient* to explain their appearances" (*Philosophical Writings*, ed. Andrew Janiak [New York: Cambridge University Press, 2004], 87, emphasis added).

5. Newton, "Correspondence with Richard Bentley," *Philosophical Writings*, 94–5.

6. Newton, "Correspondence," 96.

7. John D. Barrow, *The Origin of the Universe* (London: Weidenfeld and Nicolson, 1994), 45.

8. Poe, *Eureka*, 1300.

9. [John Henry Hopkins], review in the *Literary World*, July 29, 1848, in *Edgar Allan Poe: The Critical Heritage*, ed. I. M. Walker (New York: Routledge and Kegan Paul, 1986), 284.

10. Poe, *Eureka*, 1320, 1277.

11. Peter Gay, "Part I: Deism," in *Deism: An Anthology*, ed. Peter Gay (Princeton: Van Nostrand, 1968), 24.

12. John Gribbin, *Science: A History, 1543–2001* (London: BCA, 2002), 296.

13. Poe, *Eureka*, 1277, emphasis added.

14. Ibid., 1277, 1314.

15. Ibid., 1269, 1313.

16. Ibid., 1313.

17. Stephen Hawking, *A Brief History of Time: From the Big Bang to Black Holes* (London: Bantam, 1998), 52, 56, emphasis added; Peter Coveney and Roger Highfield, *Frontiers of Complexity: The Search for Order in a Chaotic World* (London: Faber and Faber, 1995), 10.

18. Barrow, *Origin of the Universe*, 18.

19. Poe, *Eureka*, 1321, 1340.

20. Ibid., 1278.

21. Ibid., 1306.

22. Immanuel Kant, *Universal Natural History and Theory of the Heavens*, trans. W. Hastie (Ann Arbor: University of Michigan Press, 1969), 74.

23. Lucretius, *On the Nature of the Universe*, ed. John Godwin, trans. R. E. Latham (New York: Penguin, 1994), 139.

24. Poe, *Eureka*, 1325.

25. See David Hughes, "Doppler Effect," in *The Science Book*, ed. Peter Tallack (London: Weidenfeld and Nicolson, 2001), 156.

26. Robert Lawlor, *Sacred Geometry: Philosophy and Practice* (London: Thames and Hudson, 1982), 23.

27. Poe, *Eureka*, 1279, 1289, 1290.

28. Daniel Hoffman, *Poe Poe Poe Poe Poe Poe Poe* (Garden City, NY: Doubleday, 1972), 280

29. Arthur Koestler, *The Sleepwalkers: A History of Man's Changing Vision of the Universe* (New York: Penguin, 1968), 394.

30. Quoted in A. D. White, *A History of the Warfare of Science with Theology in Christendom*. 2 vols. (1896; reprinted, New York: Dover, 1960), vol. i, 168.

CHAPTER 36

Forensic Science

Benjamin F. Fisher

Though many of Poe's tales might well be classed as crime stories, "The Murders in the Rue Morgue" (1841) is the first detective story in the English language to "attain worldwide popularity" – so said the doyen of Poe studies, the late Thomas Ollive Mabbott, in his introduction to the tale.[1] Rightly placed by Mabbott, the piece contains essentials that have become commonplaces in detective fiction. To alert readers that here was some new species of writing, or at least not of the customary venue in fiction, the narrator moves from describing the analytic abilities and the noticeable physical features of sleuth, C. Auguste Dupin, when he engages analysis, to a disclaimer about the nature of his (the narrator's) narrative itself: "Let it not be supposed, from what I have just said, that I am detailing any mystery, or penning any romance. What I have described in the Frenchman was merely the result of an excited, or perhaps of a diseased intelligence."[2] What transpires in this and the two subsequent Dupin tales, "The Mystery of Marie Rogêt" (1842–3) and "The Purloined Letter" (1845), reinforces a likelihood that his intelligence is indeed excited when he mulls the nature of a crime and the criminal, rather than Dupin's, intelligence is diseased. Dupin employs analytic methods when he's working out the solution to a mystery, but he likewise depends on intuition to obtain results. Additional tales by Poe that qualify as detective fiction are "The Gold-Bug" (1843) and "Thou Art the Man" (1844). Earlier works by other authors have been categorized as detective fiction – Charles Brockden Brown's *Wieland; or, The Transformation* (1798), Nathaniel Hawthorne's "Mr. Higginbotham's Catastrophe" (1834) – though these fictions present neither the intellectual richness nor the methods of forensic science that inform Poe's detective tales.

Poe's heritage in gothic tradition also bears upon his detective tales, as does his interest in puzzles. Poe's modifications of gothicism are well known, and his techniques and themes in the detective tales illuminate yet another of those modifications. In many of its features, "The Murders in the Rue Morgue" betrays its gothic lineage. The eerie atmosphere established at the outset as the narrator notes Dupin and his unusual living arrangements, both in choice of residence (a descendant from many Gothic haunted castles) and habits (preferring to be most active at night). Add the horrifying and equally mystifying (initially) deaths of the mother and daughter, and we have gothic heaped upon gothic.

Poe's contemporaries would not have read far in "The Murders in the Rue Morgue" without anticipating that a gothic thriller would ensue. Subsequently, as Dupin notices the hair obviously shed by the murderer, the narrator's reaction might well recall those shocks typical of protagonists in innumerable gothic tales when they suddenly confront the unknown – and immediately assume that it is a supernatural manifestation. Dupin's explanations of various phenomena connected with the atrocious murders disturbs his companion almost to an emotional breaking point: "'Dupin!' I said, completely unnerved; 'this hair is most unusual – this is no *human* hair.'"[3] Given that Dupin has already alluded to the voice of the murderer, as described by witnesses within hearing distance of the murders, as nothing mundanely human, combined with the apparently difficult feat of gaining entrance into a supposedly locked second floor room and with the extraordinary strength and savagery involved in the deaths of the two women, the implication for most contemporaneous readers would be that a supernatural agency has committed these atrocities.

Even as Poe manipulates the gothic conventions, he anticipates the fundamental principles of forensic science. Dupin and the narrator visit the crime scene as a way of helping to solve the murder mystery. The unusual strands of hair Dupin discovered within the room where the murders occurred provide examples of evidence manifesting what would be called the Locard Exchange Principle. Edmond Locard, who founded the Lyons Police Technical Laboratory in 1910, devised the theory that "every contact leaves a trace," meaning that criminals cannot commit crimes without leaving evidence of their passage.[4] Dupin uses such trace evidence – to apply another term Locard coined – in order to solve the murders. Not content to limit his investigation to the room, Dupin also looks around the outside of the apartment, where he locates another crucial piece of trace evidence that manifests the Locard Exchange Principle: a small piece of ribbon suggesting a sailor's presence outside the apartment window.

The similarities between Dupin's method and the procedures of criminal investigation Locard describes in his detailed textbook, *L'Enquête criminelle et les méthodes scientifiques* (1920), are not coincidental. Eight years before Locard published his groundbreaking textbook of forensic science, in fact, he had published a sixteen-page appreciation of the investigative methods Poe developed in his short fiction: *Edgar Poe détective: Étude de technique policière* (1912). Even after his textbook appeared, Locard continued to think about Poe and the applicability of his fiction to the process of criminal investigation, subsequently publishing an article in a Paris weekly outlining Poe's qualifications as a crime scene investigator.[5]

Once Dupin realizes the hair had come from an orangutan, he devises a way to attract the attention of the animal's owner. The way he does so represents another first in the nascent field of forensic science. FBI criminal profiler John Douglas has called Dupin "history's first behavioral profiler."[6] Based on the trace evidence, both the hair and the ribbon, Dupin discerns not only that the orangutan is the killer but also that his keeper was a sailor who witnessed the killings. To coax the sailor out of hiding, Dupin places an advertisement in the newspaper, containing what facts he has discerned. His method, Douglas continues, represents "the first use of a proactive technique by the profiler to flush out an unknown subject and vindicate an innocent man imprisoned for the killings."[7]

In terms of his depiction of the detective process, Poe had some literary antecedents. Sir Walter Scott's *Count Robert of Paris* (1831) provided one model. Poe may also have learned from Voltaire's *Zadig* (1741) the importance of pursuing what seem to be minor, even irrelevant, clues, but that prove to be significant. Although this last work is not entirely devoted to forensic science, it offers more of that type of perspective than other sources published before "The Murders in the Rue Morgue." We might remember, in context, that Dickens's novels published up to this time – *Oliver Twist* (1839), *The Old Curiosity Shop* (1841), *Barnaby Rudge* (1841) – all include elements of detection, if no detective proper. Poe was attentive to Dickens's fiction, and his "solution" to *Barnaby Rudge* (1841), which must have been written while Poe was also at work on "Murders," if not wholly accurate in its findings, likewise shows that elements of detection were germinating in Poe's mind.

Poe's own writings may also figure into the backgrounds of "Murders." The circumstances in the tale undeniably present a puzzle, and Poe's fondness for puzzles, as Howard Haycraft has emphasized, and for cryptography would provide a natural impetus for his creating a story that is indeed a puzzle, which Dupin deftly assembles, and does so by pondering the unnoticed clues ignored by the police.[8] Poe's readers were fond of puzzles of all sorts, as is evident in the popularity of gothic and sentimental works, with another variety of puzzle or puzzlement having considerable appeal to those same readers. Several of Poe's tales were termed "quizzes" by his early readers; for example, his "Loss of Breath" and "The Duc De L'Omelette" were commended as respectively targeting the stereotypical *Blackwood's Edinburgh Magazine* terror tale and the habits and conduct of N. P. Willis, an American author much admired in the 1830s. Later, in an editorial headnote to the poem "For Annie," N. P. Willis perpetrated a quiz on what he presented as Poe's haste to publish. Although there were no quizzings involved, the later debate over the author's identity for "Ulalume" also created puzzlement.

Forensic science, or the science of detection, as should be evident by now, was by no means fully developed, indeed it was not much employed at all in detection as that activity came to be known by Poe's time. Detection, as we comprehend it today, as an organized or quasi-organized occupation, began only in the eighteenth century, and ideas about how to detect and practices emanating from such thinking were still new. Although Poe's Dupin is an amateur sleuth, not a police force employee, as detectives customarily had been preceding Poe's creation of his sleuth, Dupin's practices that verged on the scientific came to be emulated by many subsequent writers of detective fiction. As is indicated in the quotation cited earlier from "The Murders in the Rue Morgue," the narrator's viewpoint is that detection is a serious occupation, not a delicate frill to decorate (probably ephemerally) a bit of fiction. Dupin seems to possess a more latitudinarian conception of detection, hence of forensic science, because, as may be made clearer later in the chapter, his work, whatever seriousness is involved, carries a dimension of humor, more so in "Murders" and "The Purloined Letter" than in "The Mystery of Marie Rogêt."

Readers should not forget, however, that the corpus of Poe's fiction is rife with elements of hoax, so they should be cautious about interpreting the tales, *The Narrative of Arthur Gordon Pym*, or *Eureka: A Prose Poem*, as entirely straightforward writing. Many readers focus on the episodes of horrifics in Poe's fiction, seemingly unaware of coded dissimulation in any of them; such readings produce an off-center approach. That is, Poe continually published creative works that admit, with equal validity, a serious or comic intent – and it might be more precise to make the *or* an *or / and*. Though Poe was the first to employ any of the methods of forensic science in detective fiction, his handling of that discipline may not incline to undeviating sobriety. Not long after "The Murders in the Rue Morgue" was published, E. D. Forgues, reviewing Poe's *Tales* (1845), spoke of Poe's particular method in the tale, and in 1856 the Goncourt Brothers stated that Poe's Dupin tales anticipate the "literature of the twentieth century," in that the emphasis on the cerebral is significant.[9]

Especially in "The Murders in the Rue Morgue" and "The Purloined Letter," Dupin's perceiving and following less blatant possibilities permit his arriving at successful conclusions. "The Mystery of Marie Rogêt" may (but this is a tentative "may") in this respect fall short of the artistic achievements of the other Dupin tales, probably because it was based on an actual murder case, that of Mary Rogers, well known in New York City as the beautiful cigar girl.[10] Poe couldn't have known the details leading up to Mary's death because they were not known to anyone else for some time after he had begun serializing "The Mystery of Marie Rogêt." Furthermore, some readers find the very cerebral element too extended to maintain reader interest. To be sure, champions for this tale have defended Poe's techniques. Dorothy L. Sayers commended the intellectual makeup of the tale, which subsumes any of the melodramatic aspects in Poe's other detective stories, as well as melodrama far more poorly handled by other early writers of detective stories. Subsequently, Richard P. Benton and John T. Irwin persuasively argued that the tale has affinities with the calculus of probabilities.[11]

The technique in this tale is that of Dupin never leaving his chambers. Instead he considers the existing evidence concerning the murder of Marie Rogêt, which he finds in newspaper articles, draws his own conclusions from these documents, and closes with a fairly inconclusive conclusion. Poe's technique had been leading toward an outcome in which Marie Rogêt's lover murdered her, but revelation that Mary Rogers actually died from a bungled abortion necessitated Poe's changing the conclusion to "Marie Rogêt." Dupin resorts to duplicity, or if not to actual duplicity, to useful indirection, in his closing remarks. There he shifts to speaking about coincidence and mathematical theory, as applicable to his narrative. Although Poe's method here maintains high intellectuality, such technique would not elicit positive response from readers not attuned to forensic procedures, handled, of course, through the alembic of Poe's creative imagination. Here again we confront a tale that seems to offer decided elements of gothic gruesomeness – murder of an innocent by a crass, false lover – which Poe deftly channels into more intellectual planes by muting such physical details as might be revolting, just as the idea of abortion itself was a clandestine procedure, which in the very secrecy with it was accompanied presented terrors of the unknown. Ironically, because of its very foregrounded intellectual content, "The Mystery of Marie Rogêt" often loses appeal for many readers.

The third and most brief Dupin tale, "The Purloined Letter" (1845), like its predecessors, offers possibilities of gothic sensationalism. That sensationalism is, however, indirectly presented via Dupin's recounting of his regaining the letter, and although he takes great risks in securing the document, his own intelligence comes to his rescue. The sensationalism is located instead in the emotional damage possible to the lady from whom the letter was stolen should the letter's contents be publicized. Understandably, fear besets the lady in question, who is consequently a persecuted female recreated from earlier gothics, but because her plight is not depicted with any of the gory horrors given in the account of the corpses in "Murders" or the kindred but less grimly elaborated scenario of attention to Marie Rogêt's remains, she represents Poe's refinement of what well before his time had become a cliché gothic character.

"The Purloined Letter" is none the less exciting in that Dupin's report is so skillfully fashioned as to capture and sustain reader interest. Using forensic methods, he considers the less obvious clues, which, as in "Murders," have been overlooked by police investigators, whose painstaking searches of the Minister D – 's premises invite little sympathy (within the tale itself, as well as from those reading the tale. In all the Dupin tales, we encounter Poe's subtle uses of frame narrative methods, a technique he employed in his early projected book, *Tales of the Folio Club*. There, within the framework of a literary club's meetings, short stories and critiques of them, by increasingly intoxicated and gluttonous caricatures of best-selling authors, would have served as individual segments of the frame scheme. Poe's own fondness for this tale may reflect a sense that his art had reached a fine achievement, the success of which directly related to the compactness of the tale. The intellectual qualities in "The Purloined Letter" operate at a more rapid pace than we see in the other Dupin tales, so reader interest is unlikely to flag.

In "Murders" and "The Purloined Letter" Dupin seems able to penetrate to what lesser writers could not effect. Though he has no real antagonist in "Murders," he does face off the Minister D – in "The Purloined Letter," who, as we learn only in the conclusion, had once offended him. Dupin actually functions as something of a mind reader here, thus linking him with the supernatural characters who frequently appear in gothic fiction. Although "The Purloined Letter" is far more intellectual than many another gothic tale, Poe draws in a motif that was not confined to gothics, but that coursed through Romantic culture, that of identical twins and their uncannily similar mindsets. Though the nature of twinning is not presented with entire scientific accuracy in Romantic literature, the lore that identical twins are linked by special physical and emotional bonds was fascinating to the Romantic outlook. Poe repeatedly introduced motifs of such twinning into his tales, so that he should turn to such a trope in the interactions of Dupin and the Minister D –, who may be his identical twin, is not surprising.

In outwitting the Minister D –, Dupin's method is part forensic, part imaginative. He surveys the obvious clues, finds them useless, then turns his attention to what less overt clues may suggest. Poe's works are rife with motifs of sight, and in "The Purloined Letter" the sleuth's analytic mind rapidly divines that what is in plain sight is often ignored because it appears to be so innocuous, therefore not worth investigation. The minister much resembles Dupin in placing the letter where anybody might see it – and thus pay it no heed, but Dupin's wits are a match for his opponent's, so he speedily realizes where the letter is located, purloins it himself while he has the other's attention diverted, and thus finishes his quest in triumph.

"The Gold-Bug" includes no person whose profession or occupation is that of a sleuth, but William Legrand, the narrator's friend, fills that role as he comes to grips with the long secret location of buried treasure. Legrand, a descendant from a formerly wealthy, prestigious old family, sustains a livelihood of Spartan sorts because his fortune vanished. He is "educated, with unusual powers of mind," and those powers are put to use in mystifying his friend, the narrator, who participates in a treasure hunt. Legrand is also given to mood swings, so he enjoys playing on the superstitious nature of Jupiter, his old African American servant. Legrand is also descended from generations of moody, misanthropic characters, usually the villains, from gothic tradition, but he perpetrates no horrendous tortures or revenge, except of the mildest type, and that mingled with a comic impulse, when he uses the gold bug, an actual insect species, to foster superstitions and awe in others. The narrator had had doubts regarding Legrand's sanity; Legrand realized this distrust, and he enjoyed playing to his audience, so to speak. Though Poe never composed a successful drama, his keen sense of the dramatic was infused throughout his tales and poems.

To locate the treasure, Legrand's powers of the mind indeed come into play, and, rather like those of Dupin in "The Purloined Letter," he uses them for ironic means to achieve the end he desires. Like Dupin's disquisition on the nature of the mathematician and the poet, that is, between the rational and imaginative-creative aspects of mind, Legrand's staged progress toward the site of the treasure involved both characteristics of mind. What Poe creates in "The Gold-Bug" is an exciting intellectual tale, the nature of intellect thrown into greater illumination because of minds that are more dim-witted than Legrand's. Yet again we observe Poe subtly blending comedy with what may initially seem to be more unsettling circumstances. Jupiter's ascent of the great tree is fraught with potential hazards such as a limb being too weak to support him or the possibility of encountering a savage animal while he is high up in the tree. Poe neatly balances the humorous and the horrific.

Another exquisite blending of the horrifying and the humorous enlivens "Thou Art the Man" (1844), another tale of detection, but one in which Poe parodies the very type of detective story he himself created. Rather like Dupin's reaction to offense from the Minister D –, the narrator in "Thou Art the Man" witnesses a contretemps between Mr. Pennifeather, nephew to Mr. Shuttleworthy, the murdered man, and Old Charley Goodfellow, who had insinuated himself into the good graces of Mr. Shuttleworthy. Goodfellow murders Shuttleworthy, attempts to fasten the crime upon Pennifeather, and nearly succeeds. The narrator, who, like most of Poe's first person narrators, remains nameless, suspects Goodfellow's motives, analyses the evidence, giving close scrutiny to details overlooked as insignificant, and eventually frightens Goodfellow into confessing.

A case of what purports to be Goodfellow's favorite wine is delivered to him with a card that reads as if Mr. Shuttleworthy had ordered this gift for his great friend. At a gathering, Goodfellow opens the box, out of which springs the corpse of Shuttleworthy, who utters "Thou art the man!" causing Goodfellow to deteriorate emotionally, confess his crime, then drop dead from fright. The bullet with which Goodfellow killed Shuttleworthy's horse had been discovered, providing irrefutable evidence against Old Charley. This, the first example of ballistics being used to reveal the identity of a criminal, is an early use of such in crime fiction, just as the villain's being the least likely person (as murderer) stands as progenitor to many subsequent villains in detective fiction. "Thou Art the Man" represents another instance of Poe's adroit mingling of irony and sensational physical detail, making the tale indeed an outstanding example of grotesquerie.

In conclusion, one may readily see, from evidence provided in the foregoing assessments of Poe's detective tales, that he pioneered in drawing on forensic science for enriching his detective fiction. His sleuths depend on their analytic abilities, albeit those abilities betray no plodding dullness; any dullards are the narrators, except in "Thou Art the Man," where the narrator is an antagonistic protagonist, not antagonistic in any physical display, but, far more interesting, in psychological acumen. One may therefore wonder at Poe's dismissal of the Dupin stories as being not at all stimulating artistic accomplishments and lamenting their presence in a selection of his tales as taking up space that might be devoted to better choices. The five tales examined here stand as unquestionably fine detective fiction, and they simultaneously testify to Poe's working in contexts of his own literary awareness and experience. His mind and the tangible achievements that emanated from it paved the way for much that would later occur in literary endeavors, detective or other. Poe's pioneering was not crude after all, as may in part be attested if we compare the characterization of Dupin and the psychological depths that enable him to succeed where others might fail. That same psychological depth exists in the makeup of William Legrand and in the narrator of "Thou Art the Man."

NOTES

1. Edgar Allan Poe, *The Collected Works of Edgar Allan Poe*, ed. Thomas Ollive Mabbott, 3 vols. (Cambridge, MA: Belknap Press, 1969–78), vol. ii, 521.
2. Ibid., vol. ii, 533.
3. Ibid., vol. ii, 558.
4. John Horswell, and Craig Fowler, "Associative Evidence: The Locard Exchange Principle," in *The Practice of Crime Scene Investigation*, ed. John Horswell (Boca Raton, FL: CRC Press, 2004), 46.
5. Edmond Locard, "Edgar Poe détective," *La Revue hebdomadaire*, 30 juillet 1921, 527–44.
6. John Douglas and Mark Olshaker, *Mindhunter: Inside the FBI's Elite Serial Crime Unit* (New York: Scribner, 1995), 32.
7. Ibid.
8. Howard Haycraft, *Murder for Pleasure: The Life and Times of the Detective Story* (New York: D. Appleton-Century, 1941), 11.
9. Poe, *Collected Works*, vol. ii, 521.
10. John Evangelist Walsh, *Poe the Detective: The Curious Circumstances Behind "The Mystery of Marie Rogêt"* (New Brunswick: Rutgers University Press, 1967); Daniel Stashower, *The Beautiful Cigar Girl: Mary Rogers, Edgar Allan Poe, and the Invention of Murder* (New York: Dutton, 2006).
11. Dorothy L. Sayers, "Introduction," *The Omnibus of Crime*, ed. Dorothy L. Sayers (Garden City, NY: Garden City Publishing, 1929), 16–19; Richard P. Benton, "The Mystery of Marie Rogêt – A Defense," *Studies in Short Fiction* 6 (1969), 144–51; John T. Irwin, *The Mystery to a Solution: Poe, Borges, and the Analytic Detective Story* (Baltimore: Johns Hopkins University Press, 1994).

CHAPTER 37

Technology

John Tresch

The brief span of Poe's life coincided with America's first confident steps toward industrialization. In the 1830s and 1840s, railroads, telegraphs, electricity, and new printing technology were changing the way people worked, communicated, and understood themselves. Though Poe's work often took the character of otherworldly Romanticism, his writings show the unmistakable imprint of the machine. Technology in fact draws together a number of the contexts covered in this book's previous chapters: locomotives and improvements in navigation shifted the limits of the known world; in the city, gas lighting created both new light and new shadows; steam presses and cheaper paper created new readers and new opportunities for piracy; photography and other methods of observation and recording mechanically fixed both the human face and the surfaces of nature.[1]

Technology is a key not only to those works of Poe that feature new or imaginary inventions, but to those that express his views of writing and his philosophy of nature. As is well known, Poe frequently pointed out the limits of mechanism and ridiculed his contemporaries' faith in endless material progress. Yet he also espoused faith in an underlying pattern to the cosmos, and he portrayed the arts – poetry and music, as well as the mechanical arts – as a means of adapting to and harmonizing with it. Where science and technology were concerned, Poe was both skeptic and enthusiast. The tensions and paradoxes we find throughout his writings reflect his age's ambivalence toward an increasingly mechanized world.

THE GARDEN AND THE RAILROAD

Colonial America was guided by the mythology of the nation as an Edenic paradise. Yet by the early nineteenth century, this pastoral ideal was challenged by a view of the United States as a commercial and industrial power.[2] Did the destiny of the nation lie in the peaceful agricultural landscape or in cities and factories? Like his contemporaries, Poe wrestled with this tension. His Southern upbringing brought him into contact with the pastoral values of Jefferson's natural aristocracy; yet this way of life depended on slavery and the trade of merchants like John Allan, and was revitalized by Eli Whitney's cotton gin. Though he rhapsodized about solitary rambles through the sublime landscapes of the Hudson, the Wissahickon, and the Ragged Mountains, Poe spent much of his adult life in the cities where science and industry were taking root: in Philadelphia, "The Athens of America," he hobnobbed with scientists, artists, and inventors; in New York he was at the center of print and commerce. Even his education reflected this tension: at the University of Virginia he followed a humanistic curriculum, while as a cadet at West Point – the finest engineering school in the nation – he was drilled in mathematics, and his classmates went on to build the infrastructure of the nation, working in the railroad, the U.S. Coastal Survey, and the scientific reconnaissance of the Western territories.

Poe thus lived in a time when utilitarianism and mechanism encroached on all aspects of life. His tales "The Man That Was Used Up" and "The Business Man" depicted men transformed, by military and accounting techniques, into machines.[3] In a call for an American literature, he lamented: "Our necessities have been mistaken for our propensities. Having been forced to make railroads, it has been deemed impossible that we should make verse. Because it suited us to construct an engine in the first instance, it has been denied that we could complete an epic in the second. Because we were not all Homers in the beginning, it has been somewhat too harshly been taken for granted that we shall be all Jeremy Benthams to the end."[4]

Poe had further cause to be anxious about the effect of mechanism on literature: he was living through a media revolution. In the 1830s and 1840s, steam presses and new paper-making techniques increased the quantity and speed of publication, while canals, railroads, and the telegraph hastened the spread of information.[5] The growing mechanization of the press was particularly significant for Poe, who worked in every aspect of printing – as a writer, editor, and compositor. His frequent play with anagrams, reversed and scrambled letters, cryptography, and hieroglyphics shows close attention to the material composition of words; his tale X-ing a Paragrab" turned on the systematic errors that "the printer's devil" introduces to communication.

In the new popular journals, poems and tales of fiction were often published side by side with gossip, political reporting, and scientific reports.

In this crowded marketplace, Poe struggled to establish himself as an authority on literary matters.[6] His reviews and critical essays frequently employed analytical and scientific rhetoric. These efforts to make himself the spokesman for the "Rationale of Verse" exactly paralleled the attempts of scientists to create audiences and institutions to secure control over natural knowledge. Even though notions of rationality and natural law had been crucial for the founders of "the American experiment," promoters of science in the 1830s and 1840s in the United States complained that authoritative institutions, state funding, and appreciative audiences were painfully absent. The term "scientist" had only been coined in the 1830s; in the press and in popular lectures and spectacles, the boundaries between experts and charlatans, facts and hoaxes, established truth and mere speculation were in flux.[7]

Poe was in fact one of the nation's first popular science writers. His series of "Notes on Art and Science" evaluated discoveries and inventions; he also wrote articles on cryptography, phrenology, and handwriting analysis. The book of his that sold the most copies in his lifetime was *The Conchologist's First Book*, based on the classification for snails and shells laid out by Cuvier. His stories were also a repository of contemporary science. The plot of the "The Gold-Bug" turned on cryptography, cartography, and entomology; "Manuscript Found in a Bottle," *The Narrative of Arthur Gordon Pym*, and "A Tale of the Ragged Mountains" all detailed the combination of exploration, navigation, and cultural contact that marked many sciences of the time.[8] C. Auguste Dupin was not only the inspiration for Sherlock Holmes but an important source for later representations of scientific genius. Implicit and explicit allusions to technical and scientific debates, from the best means of paving streets ("Murders in the Rue Morgue") and the classification of mental faculties ("The Black Cat") to the possibility of human evolution and the formation of new stars ("Mesmeric Revelation," "The Power of Words"), wove through his tales.

Yet Poe's view of scientific and technical progress was insistently self-contradictory. Emphasizing the astounding, unbelievable aspects of new technology, "The Thousand and Second Tale of Scheherazade" purported to be the last chapter of the famous framework tale, presenting a fantastic account of "a nation of the most powerful magicians," whose feats included the domestication of "a huge horse whose bones were iron and whose blood was boiling water...so strong and swift that he would drag a load more weighty than the grandest temple."[9] Although the king interjected "Ridiculous!" "Absurd!" and "Twattle!" Poe's footnotes identified this wonder as the railroad, along with the similarly transformed daguerreotype, electrotelegraph, Maelzel's chess player, Babbage's calculating engine, and the steam press ("a thing of such prodigious strength, so that it erected or overthrew the mightiest empires at a breath."[10]) The tale suggested that modern inventions and discoveries were the realization of fairy tales and myths.

In "Some Words with a Mummy," Poe used an inventory of modern invention not to flatter but to tweak the pride of his contemporaries. A group of modern men (including Gliddon, a real-life Egyptologist with strong ties to Philadelphia's scientific community[11]) electrically reanimated the mummy of a pharaoh via "an experiment or two with the Voltaic pile." The Americans explained to the revivified king "the marked inferiority of the old Egyptians in all particulars of sciences, when compared with the moderns, and more especially with the Yankees."[12] Yet the pharaoh, "Allamistakeo," replied to each example of modern scientific achievement with proof of Egyptian superiority, citing his people's knowledge of chemistry, astronomy, artesian wells, mechanical conveyances, steam power, and architecture. The only discoveries lacked by the Egyptians, it appears, were democracy and quack medicine – innovations the pharaoh (and the author) seem to place on a par.

Even in these lighthearted tales, Poe oscillated between enthusiastic embrace of technical novelty and dismissive skepticism: if Scheherezade's tale highlighted all that was astounding in modern technology, Allamistakeo's conversation, on the contrary, deflated the contemporary faith in progress. The latter theme was dear to Poe: in "The Colloquy of Monos and Una," he wrote back from a distant future that "one or two of the wise among our forefathers – wise in fact, although not in the world's esteem – had ventured to doubt the propriety of the term 'improvement,' as applied to the progress of our civilization."[13] Similarly, in hoaxes, Poe mocked the knee-jerk credulity shown to reports of new discoveries by exploiting the scientific uncertainty created by the mass press. The tale now known as "The Balloon Hoax" was presented in an extra to the *New York Sun* as a true report of a voyage by balloon from England to the United States (one which, it was subsequently revealed, never took place). It used all the conventions of scientific reporting, along with a detailed, exact journal of one of the voyagers. This tale about a machine, assembled with machine-like literary conventions, and printed on new steam presses, produced a mechanical response in its readers. Such a state of affairs was both remarkable and unsettling.

THE POETIC AUTOMATON

The idea that machines might take the place of humans runs through Poe's writing. Often this took a comical slant. In the *Broadway Journal* he penned a hilarious review of a troupe of Swiss bell ringers – performing melodies with each performer chiming one note in synchronization with the others. Poe facetiously revealed that "they are ingenious pieces of mechanism, contrived on the principle of Maelzel's Automaton Trumpeter and Piano-forte player (exhibited here some years ago), but made so much more perfect and effective by the application to them of the same power which operates in the Electro-Magnetic Telegraph, but which should here be called Electro-tintinnabulic. A powerful electric battery under the stage communicates by a hidden wire with each of them, and its shocks are regulated and directed by the skilful musician and mechanician who secretly manages the whole affair."[14] Evert Duyckinck may have had this passage in mind when he wrote of a posthumous collection of Poe's: "His instrument is neither an organ nor a harp; he is neither a King David nor a Beethoven, but rather a Campanologian, a Swiss bell-ringer, who from little contrivances of his own, strikes a sharp melody which has all that is delightful and affecting, that is attainable without a soul. We feel greatly obliged to Messrs. Willis, Lowell, and Griswold, for helping to wheel into public view this excellent machine."[15]

In comparing Poe's literary output to that of a machine, the critic recalled an essay in which Poe argued against the possibility of mechanizing thought. "Maelzel's Chess-Player" of 1836 sought to convince the reader that the chess-playing automaton displayed by Maelzel (inventor of the metronome and the mechanical musicians mentioned in the bell ringers' review) had to be a fake: "The operations of the Automaton are regulated by *mind*, and by nothing else."[16] Through a rigorous chain of inferences, Poe demonstrated that beneath the screen of mechanism – created by false fronts and mirrors and the feints of the showman – must lurk a living, irreducible human, a chess-playing dwarf.

In this essay Poe positioned himself as the romantic defender of the soul against the encroachment of mechanization, unveiling the lie at the heart of the project of mechanical reduction. Yet Poe often presented the genres of the popular press as modes of mass production: "How to Write a Blackwood's Article" detailed the steps needed to write a popular "tale of sensation": quoting classical references, giving a first person account of a situation of extreme danger, with frequent breathless exclamations. Further, his argument in "Maelzel" was largely plagiarized from David Brewster's

Letters on Natural Magic, and his reasoning unfolded according to the formulaic conventions of a mechanical proof. The obsessive repetition of themes in his stories, his skillful deployment of the clichés he decried in his criticism, and the barrage of techniques through which he carefully constructed his own public persona – including, notably, the new technology of daguerreotypes – raise the specter that the human we assume to be hiding inside the literary automaton might himself be a machine.

Poe gave further strength to this identification in 1846 with "The Philosophy of Composition." After the success of "The Raven," Poe went on tour, following the poem with the explanation of the principles of its construction. Like the "making of" feature of today's DVDs, the essay offered a "peep behind the scenes" into the workshop of the poet, a view of "the wheels and pinions" of the poetic machinery. Poe presented himself as a kind of poetry automaton: "the work proceeded step by step, to its completion with the precision and rigid consequence of a mathematical problem."[17] The title winked at the American taste for handy manuals (as satirized in Dickens' *Martin Chuzzlewit*, which mentions edifying lectures on "The Philosophy of Matter," "The Philosophy of Crime," and "The Philosophy of Vegetables.")[18] It also recalled Andrew Ure's *Philosophy of Manufactures*, a manifesto for rationalizing industrial production. Further, composition meant not only the assembly of ideas but the craft of typesetting. Directly contradicting the organic conception of poetry, and Wordsworth's definition of poetry in *Lyrical Ballads* as "the spontaneous overflow of powerful emotion," "The Philosophy of Composition" can be read as an engineering manual, written by a cadet of West Point, analyzing the mode of construction best adapted to a sublime work of art. The poem is created by mechanical procedures and is itself a device built to produce an ideal effect.

Poe constantly oscillated between ridiculing or warning against mechanism and identifying with the machine. His skepticism, irony, and frequent self-contradictions have a consistency that can perhaps only be grasped by superhuman intelligences: "That a tree can be both a tree and not a tree, is an idea which the angels, or the devils, may entertain."[19] What appears contradictory to us might actually simply be the effect of the level at which we approach the work. Poe's writings, like his philosophy, frequently enacted the logic of stage sets, of screens and curtains that lift to reveal hidden depths. Just as Maelzel suggested that mechanism might lie behind seemingly human chess playing or musical performance, and Poe revealed a human behind the mechanical surface, another level down from the world immediately sensed another world was lurking.

THE TECHNOLOGICAL ARABESQUE

Along these lines, the structure of many of Poe's works has been linked to the literary and artistic style of the arabesque. Echoing the frames within frames of Islamic visual art, in arabesque writing, intricate visible details draw the attention of both protagonist and reader into a hidden reality, another world within this one – as Poe put it, a "dream within a dream," or "eternally beginning behind beginning."[20] In Poe's writing on early photography, for instance, this logic of metaphysical Russian dolls was given a technological spin. A daguerreotyped plate, he wrote, "is infinitely more accurate in its representation than any painting by human hands. If we examine a work of ordinary art, by means of a powerful microscope, all traces of resemblance to nature will disappear – but the closest scrutiny of the photogenic drawing discloses only a more absolute truth."[21] The visible surface of things may on closer look – with technically enhanced perceptions – reveal a hidden order of reality.

Poe's works were filled with revelations and apocalypses. He was one of the first to see industry as a cause of ecological catastrophe: "The Colloquy of Monos and Una" describes the death of the earth after "huge smoking cities arose, innumerable. Green leaves shrank before the hot breath of furnaces. The fair face of Nature was deformed as with the ravages of some loathsome disease."[22] Yet this destruction gave way to rebirth. Before their deaths, the spirits in the tale "discoursed of the days to come, when the Art-scarred surface of the Earth, having undergone that purification which alone could efface its rectangular obscenities, should clothe itself anew in the verdure and the mountain-slopes and the smiling waters of Paradise, and be rendered at length a fit dwelling-place for man... for the redeemed, regenerated, blissful, and now immortal, but still for the *material*."[23] After the earth was ravaged by technology ("Art-scarred") and disfigured by "rectangular obscenities," only an apocalyptic fire would allow nature to recreate itself in more perfect forms and prepare for a perfected humanity. The tale then focused in on the first person description of the death of Monos. During the last days of a terminal illness, as his senses faded away one by one, he was left only with "the sense of time, a pulsation" whose perfect, constant meter highlighted the grating imperfections of human clocks. This pulsating rhythm, Monos suggested, is what all poetry and music, strain to hear.

This sound might also be the source of the dull, regular beating that forced the guilty narrator of "The Tell-Tale Heart" to reveal his crime. In it we also hear the "throb of the heart Divine" whose rise and fall Poe sketched out in *Eureka*. Poe asked in one of his early sonnets how a poet "should love" science.[24] His cosmological prose-poem, *Eureka*, answered by identifying the aims of art and science: "Symmetry and consistency are convertible terms: – thus Poetry and Truth are one." *Eureka* took the fixed universe of Kepler, Newton, and Laplace and set it into motion, revealing the cosmos as a process. The universe unfolded from a first unity into a maximum of complexity and relation, followed by an apocalyptic collapse, returning the universe to the primary unity.[25] The cosmos is presented as a machine, terms, a living, breathing being, and a "beautifully true" work of art.

Eureka concludes by affirming that we humans are part of the divine being that is the universe – that despite our imperfections, we are part of God. Aesthetics becomes theology. The pleasure we get from a work of art depends on how closely it approximates the perfection of God's handiwork. "In the construction of *plot*, for example, in fictitious literature, we should aim at so arranging the incidents that we shall not be able to determine, of any one of them, whether it depends from any one other or upholds it. In this sense, of course, *perfection* of plot is really, or practically, unattainable – but only because it is a finite intelligence that constructs. The plots of God are perfect. The Universe is a plot of God."[26] Poe's search for perfectly crafted plots and poetic forms thus had a higher purpose: to approximate the unity and adaptation of the divine construction of the universe.

ANGELIC ENGINEERING

This sense of the divine potential of art and its metaphysical underpinnings was richly illustrated in Poe's late tale, "The Domain of Arnheim," which defined the ultimate medium of artwork as a landscape garden. The order imposed by God on nature appears as chaos to us; but our attempts at making order are obviously limited. The narrator speculates that what our eyes perceive as "unpicturesque" may well be perfectly adapted, by the art of the creator, to other eyes, to which "our disorder may seem order." What if, rather than either a perfect imitation of what appears the disorderly order given by God, or the too orderly order created by human artists, we instead aimed at creating an art with "the air of an intermediate or secondary nature – a nature which is not God, nor an emanation from God, but which still is nature in the sense of the handiwork of the angels that hover between man and God."[27] The Domain of Arnheim was the landscape garden that the unimaginably wealthy artist, Ellison, designed in service of that ideal.

The experience had by its visitors resembled both a voyage to the afterworld and the sublime closing sections of *Pym*. An empty boat awaited the visitor, who on entering it was immediately drawn by a gentle current through mazy, crystalline canyons and beds of flower blossoms that at one point resembled "a panoramic cataract of rubies, sapphires, opals and golden onyxes, rolling silently out of the sky."[28] The journey immersed the viewer in an arabesque landscape hallucinated into three dimensions. The artificial paradise of "The Domain of Arnheim" was a new nature designed for the eyes of angels but experienced by the eyes of humans as a combination of "beauty, magnificence, and strangeness," which appeared cared for and cultivated by invisible groundskeepers, "with an extent and novelty of beauty, so as to convey the sentiment of spiritual interference."[29] This was a world re-engineered to allow earth dwellers to experience, while still embodied, a taste of the visions beheld by beings "refined" by death. Such a view elevates and prepares the senses for their "purified" state, when bodily organs are left behind.

Eureka and "The Domain of Arnheim" expressed Poe's highest vision of the fine arts – as well as the mechanical arts. *Eureka* depicted the aim of the artist as that of approaching the perfection of God's construction through our own plots. More than music, poetry, short stories, "The Domain of Arnheim" framed art as a remaking of nature in line with angelic perfection. By lifting up the base materials of the world according to a visionary ideal, the sensitive soul would be elevated to a perspective like that of more perfect beings. Such art would transform the world of humans and the face of the earth.

Shaped by the technical obsessions of "the American experiment," Poe's works – his poems, his hoaxes, his landscapes – were often "social experiments," attempts to push the limits of reality, to test the limits of what is true and believed. They aimed at moving readers into new worlds, worlds more like his dreams. Poe disparaged science and technology when these acted as forces of reduction and limitation, when they arrogantly declared themselves to possess the last word of knowledge and nature; deeper experience, greater complexity, and higher "ideality" were always possible. Yet despite his suspicion toward mere reason and toward progress, Poe embraced science and technology (including poetry, music, and landscape gardening) when they were used to bring us nearer to perfection, when they helped continue processes of mental and material development that injected greater unity to the living, divine machine of nature.

Despite his emphasis on "strangeness" and his own miserable life, Poe's view of art was aligned with his age's widespread optimism toward the possibility of a nature harmonized with technology.[30] At the same time, his works – with their doubts, sarcasm, and tragic collapses – showed the blind spots in his contemporaries' narrow view of progress, warning of the twists that turn dreams of mechanical conquest into nightmares.

NOTES

1. Ruth Schwartz Cowan, *A Social History of American Technology* (New York: Oxford University Press, 1997).
2. Leo Marx, *The Machine in the Garden: Technology and the Pastoral Ideal in America* (New York: Oxford University Press, 1964).
3. Ken Egan, Jr., "Edgar Allan Poe and the Horror of Technology," *ESQ* 48 (2002), 187–208.
4. Edgar Allan Poe, *Essays and Reviews*, ed. G. R. Thompson (New York: Library of America, 1984), 549.
5. James Secord, *Victorian Sensation: The Extraordinary Publication, Reception, and Secret Authorship of Vestiges of the Natural History of Creation* (Chicago: University of Chicago Press, 2000).
6. Terence Whalen, *Edgar Allan Poe and the Masses: The Political Economy of Literature in Antebellum America* (Princeton: Princeton University Press, 1999).
7. David Schmit, "Re-visioning Antebellum American Psychology: The Dissemination of Mesmerism, 1836–1854," *History of Psychology* 8 (2005), 403–34.
8. Robert Bruce, *The Launching of Modern American Science, 1846–1876* (New York: Knopf, 1987).
9. Edgar Allan Poe, *The Collected Works of Edgar Allan Poe*, ed. Thomas Ollive Mabbott, 3 vols. (Cambridge, MA: Belknap Press, 1969–78), vol. iii, 1166.
10. Ibid., vol. iii, 1167.
11. Ann Fabian, *The Skull Collectors* (Chicago: University of Chicago Press, 2010), 103–12.
12. Poe, *Collected Works*, vol. iii, 1191.
13. Ibid., vol. ii, 609.
14. Ibid., vol. iii, 1119.
15. [Evert Duyckinck], "Poe's Works," *Literary World*, January 26, 1850, 81.
16. Poe, *Essays*, 1257.
17. Ibid., 15.
18. Kevin J. Hayes, "The Flaneur in the Parlor: Poe's 'Philosophy of Furniture,'" *Prospects* 27 (2002), 103–19.
19. Edgar Allan Poe, *Poetry and Tales*, ed. Patrick F. Quinn (New York: Library of America, 1984), 877.
20. David Ketterer, *New Worlds for Old: The Apocalyptic Imagination, Science Fiction, and American Literature* (Garden City: Anchor Press, 1974); G. R. Thompson, "The Arabesque Design of Arthur Gordon Pym," in *Poe's Pym:*

Critical Explorations, ed. Richard Kopley (Durham: Duke University Press, 1992), 118–213.

21. Edgar Allan Poe, *Contributions to Alexander's Weekly Messenger*, ed. Clarence S. Brigham (Worcester: American Antiquarian Society, 1943), 20–1.

22. Poe, *Collected Works*, vol. ii, 610.

23. Ibid., vol. ii, 612.

24. Ibid., vol. i, 91.

25. Scott Peeples, "Poe's 'Constructiveness' and 'The Fall of the House of Usher,'" *The Cambridge Companion to Edgar Allan Poe*, ed. Kevin J. Hayes (New York: Cambridge University Press, 2002), 187–8.

26. Poe, *Poetry and Tales*, 1342.

27. Poe, *Collected Works*, vol. iii, 1277.

28. Ibid., vol. iii, 1280.

29. This three-dimensional dream world and its invisible helpers recall Disneyworld, a twentieth-century artificial paradise. See Miles Orvell, "Virtual Culture and the Logic of American Technology," *Revue Française d'Etudes Americaines* 76 (1998), 12–27.

30. David Nye, *America as Second Creation: Technology and Narratives of New Beginnings* (Cambridge, MA: MIT Press, 2004).

Further Reading

What follows is a highly selective list of suggestions for further reading about Edgar Allan Poe and about the contexts examined in this collection. After the first section, which is devoted to biographies and biographical resources, each of the remaining thirty-seven sections pertains to a different chapter in this book. Many of the books and articles have been suggested for inclusion by multiple contributors; they have been placed in the section that seems most relevant. These suggestions for further reading are meant to supplement the notes at the end of each chapter.

BIOGRAPHY

Hayes, Kevin J., *Edgar Allan Poe*. London: Reaktion, 2009.

Hutchisson, James M., *Poe*. Jackson: University Press of Mississippi, 2005.

Miller, John Carl, ed. *Building Poe Biography*. Baton Rouge: Louisiana State University Press, 1977.

Phillips, Mary Elizabeth, *Edgar Allan Poe: The Man*, 2 vols. Chicago: John C. Winston, 1926.

Poe, Edgar Allan. *The Collected Letters of Edgar Allan Poe*, ed. John Ward Ostrom, Burton R. Pollin, and Jeffrey A. Savoye, 2 vols. New York: Gordian, 2008.

Quinn, Arthur Hobson, *Edgar Allan Poe: A Critical Biography*. New York: Appleton-Century, 1941.

Silverman, Kenneth, *Edgar A. Poe: Mournful and Never-Ending Remembrance*. New York: HarperCollins, 1991.

Thomas, Dwight, and David K. Jackson, *The Poe Log: A Documentary Life of Edgar Allan Poe, 1809–1849*. Boston: G. K. Hall, 1987.

Walsh, John Evangelist, *Midnight Dreary: The Mysterious Death of Edgar Allan Poe*. New Brunswick: Rutgers University Press, 1998.

Whitman, Sarah Helen. *Poe's Helen Remembers*, ed. John Carl Miller. Charlottesville: University Press of Virginia, 1979.

GREAT BRITAIN

Allen, Michael L. *Poe and the British Magazine Tradition*. New York: Oxford University Press, 1969.

Fisher, Benjamin F. "Poe in Great Britain," in *Poe Abroad: Influence, Reputation, Affinities*, ed. Lois Davis Vines. Iowa City: University of Iowa Press, 1999. 52–61.

Giles, Paul. *Transatlantic Insurrections: British Culture and the Formation of American Literature, 1730–1860*. Philadelphia: University of Pennsylvania Press, 2001.

Lease, Benjamin. *Anglo-American Encounters: England and the Rise of American Literature*. New York: Cambridge University Press, 1981.

THE SOUTH

Bondurant, Agnes Meredith. *Poe's Richmond*. Richmond: Garrett and Massie, 1942.

Branham, Amy. "Gothic Displacements: Poe's South in *Politian*," in *Edgar Allan Poe: Beyond Gothicism*, ed. James M. Hutchisson. Newark: University of Delaware Press, 2011. 69–87.

Gray, Richard J. *Southern Aberrations: Writers of the American South and the Problem of Regionalism*. Baton Rouge: Louisiana State University Press, 2000.

Hubbell, Jay B. *The South in American Literature, 1607–1900*. Durham: Duke University Press, 1954.

Jones, Paul C. *Unwelcome Voices: Subversive Fiction in the Antebellum South*. Knoxville: University of Tennessee Press, 2005.

Rubin, Louis D. *The Edge of the Swamp: A Study in the Literature and Society of the Old South*. Baton Rouge: Louisiana State University Press, 1989.

THE WEST

Fussell, Edwin S. *Frontier: American Literature and the American West*. Princeton: Princeton University Press, 1965.

Greenfield, Bruce R. *Narrating Discovery: The Romantic Explorer in American Literature, 1790–1855*. New York: Columbia University Press, 1992.

LeMenager, Stephanie. *Manifest and Other Destinies: Territorial Fictions of the Nineteenth-Century United States*. Lincoln: Nebraska University Press, 2004.

Lewis, Nathaniel. *Unsettling the Literary West: Authenticity and Authorship*. Lincoln: University of Nebraska Press, 2003.

Rusk, Ralph Leslie. *The Literature of the Midwestern Frontier*, 2 vols. New York: Columbia University Press, 1925.

THE SEA

Harvey, Ronald C. *The Critical History of Edgar Allan Poe's The Narrative of Arthur Gordon Pym: "A Dialogue with Unreason."* New York: Garland, 1998.

Kopley, Richard, ed. *Poe's Pym: Critical Explorations*. Durham: Duke University Press, 1992.

Lyons, Paul. *American Pacificism: Oceana in the U.S. Imagination*. New York: Routlege, 2006.

Sanborn, Geoffrey. "A Confused Beginning: *The Narrative of Arthur Gordon Pym, of Nantucket*," in *The Cambridge Companion to Edgar Allan Poe*, ed. Kevin J. Hayes. New York: Cambridge University Press, 2002. 163–77.

FRANCE

Baudelaire, Charles. *Baudelaire on Poe: Critical Papers*, ed. and trans. Lois Hyslop and Francis E. Hyslop, Jr. State College, PA: Bald Eagle Press, 1952.

Hayes, Kevin J. "One-Man Modernist," in *The Cambridge Companion to Edgar Allan Poe*, ed. Kevin J. Hayes. New York: Cambridge University Press, 2002. 225–40.

Quinn, Patrick F. *The French Face of Edgar Poe*. Carbondale: Southern Illinois University Press, 1957.

Vines, Lois Davis. "Charles Baudelaire," in *Poe Abroad: Influence, Reputation, Affinities*, ed. Lois Davis Vines. Iowa City: University of Iowa Press, 1999. 165–70.

"Poe in France," in *Poe Abroad: Influence, Reputation, Affinities*, ed. Lois Davis Vines. Iowa City: University of Iowa Press, 1999. 9–18.

"Stéphane Mallarmé and Paul Valéry," in *Poe Abroad: Influence, Reputation, Affinities*, ed. Lois Davis Vines. Iowa City: University of Iowa Press, 1999. 171–6.

THE NEAR EAST

Allison, Robert J. *The Crescent Obscured: the United States and the Muslim World, 1776–1815*. Chicago: University of Chicago Press, 2000.

Irwin, John T. *American Hieroglyphics: The Symbol of the Egyptian Hieroglyphics in the American Renaissance*. New Haven: Yale University Press, 1980.

Montgomery, Travis. "Poe's Oriental Gothic: 'Metzengerstein' (1832), 'The Visionary' (1834), 'Berenice' (1835), the Imagination, and Authorship's Perils." *Gothic Studies* 12 (2010): 4–28.

Turning East: Edgar Allan Poe's Poems (1831), the Orient, and the Renewal of American Verse. Baltimore: Edgar Allan Poe Society, 2011.

Trafton, Scott. *Egypt Land: Race and Nineteenth-Century American Egyptomania*. Durham: Duke University Press, 2004.

Yothers, Brian. 'Desert of the Blest': Poe's Anti-Representational Invocations of the Near East." *Gothic Studies* 12 (2010): 53–60.

THE POLAR REGIONS

Jones, Darryl. "Ultima Thule: *Arthur Gordon Pym*, the Polar Imaginary, and the Hollow Earth." *Edgar Allan Poe Review* 11 (2010): 51–69.

Nelson, Victoria. "Symmes Hole: or, The South Polar Romance." *Raritan* 17 (1997): 136–66.

Standish, David. *Hollow Earth: The Long and Curious History of Imagining Strange Lands, Fantastical Creatures, Advanced Civilizations, and Marvelous Machines Below the Earth's Surface*. Cambridge, MA: Da Capo, 2006.

Stanton, William. *The Great United States Exploring Expedition of 1838–1842*. Berkeley: University of California Press, 1975.

THE URBAN ENVIRONMENT

Brand, Dana. *The Spectator and the City: Fantasies of Urban Legibility in Nineteenth-Century England and America*. New York: Cambridge University Press, 1991.

Hayes, Kevin J. "Understanding 'Why the Little Frenchman Wears His Hand in a Sling,'" in *Edgar Allan Poe: Beyond Gothicism*, ed. James M. Hutchisson. Newark: University of Delaware Press, 2011. 119–28.

"Visual Culture and the Word in Edgar Allan Poe's 'Man of the Crowd.'" *Nineteenth-Century Literature* 56 (2002): 445–65.

Merivale, Patricia. "Gumshoe Gothics: Poe's 'The Man of the Crowd' and his Followers," in *Detecting Texts: The Metaphysical Detective Story from Poe to Postmodernism*, ed. Patricia Merivale and Susan Elizabeth Sweeney. Philadelphia: University of Pennsylvania Press, 1999. 101–16.

Werner, James V. *American Flaneur: The Cosmic Physiognomy of Edgar Allan Poe*. New York: Routledge, 2004.

CURIOSITY

Barnum, P. T. *The Colossal P. T. Barnum Reader: Nothing Else Like It in the Universe*, ed. James W. Cook. Urbana: University of Illinois Press, 2005.

Bogdan, Robert. *Freak Show: Presenting Human Oddities for Amusement and Profit*. Chicago: University of Chicago Press, 1988.

Harris, Neil. *Humbug: The Art of P. T. Barnum*. Chicago: University of Chicago Press, 1973.

Reiss, Benjamin. *The Showman and the Slave: Race, Death, and Memory in Barnum's America*. Cambridge, MA: Harvard University Press, 2001.

ALCOHOL, ADDICTION, AND REHABILITATION

Chavigny, Katherine A. "Reforming Drunkards in Nineteenth-Century America: Religion, Medicine, Therapy," in *Altering American Consciousness: The History of Alcohol and Drug Use in the United States, 1800–2000*, ed. Sarah W. Tracy and Caroline Jean Acker. Amherst: University of Massachusetts Press, 2004. 108–23.

Hendler, Glenn. "Bloated Bodies and Sober Sentiments: Masculinity in 1840s Temperance Narratives," in *Sentimental Men: Masculinity and the Politics of Affect in American Culture*, ed. Mary Chapman and Glenn Hendler. Berkeley: University of California Press, 1999. 125–48.

Mintz, Steven. *Moralists and Modernizers: America's Pre-Civil War Reformers.* Baltimore: Johns Hopkins University Press, 1995.

Reynolds, David S. "Black Cats and Delirium Tremens: Temperance and the American Renaissance," in *The Serpent in the Cup: Temperance in American Literature*, ed. David S. Reynolds and Debra J. Rosenthal. Amherst, MA: University of Massachusetts Press, 1997. 22–59.

Rorabaugh, W. J. *The Alcoholic Republic: An American Tradition.* New York: Oxford University Press, 1979.

Tyrrell, Ian. *Sobering Up: From Temperance to Prohibition in Antebellum America.* Westport, CT: Greenwood Press, 1979.

FASHION, FURNISHINGS, AND STYLE

Halttunen, Karen. *Confidence Men and Painted Women: A Study of Middle-Class Culture in America, 1830–1870.* New Haven: Yale University Press, 1982.

Hayes, Kevin J. "The Flaneur in the Parlor: Poe's 'Philosophy of Furniture.'" *Prospects* 27 (2002): 103–19.

Severa, Joan. *Dressed for the Photographer: Ordinary Americans and Fashion, 1840–1900.* Kent, OH: Kent State University Press, 1995.

Zakim, Michael. *Ready-Made Democracy: A History of Men's Dress in the American Republic, 1760–1860.* Chicago: University of Chicago Press, 2003.

THE AMERICAN STAGE

Fagin, Nathan Bryllion. *The Histrionic Mr. Poe.* Baltimore: Johns Hopkins Press, 1949.

Nathans, Heather S. *Early American Theatre from the Revolution to Thomas Jefferson: Into the Hands of the People.* New York: Cambridge University Press, 2003.

Shaffer, Jason. *Performing Patriotism: National Identity in the Colonial and Revolutionary American Theater.* Philadelphia: University of Pennsylvania Press, 2007.

Smith, Geddeth. *The Brief Career of Eliza Poe.* Rutherford, NJ: Farleigh Dickinson University Press, 1988.

Wilmeth, Don B., and C. W. E. Bigsby, eds. *The Cambridge History of American Theatre*, 3 vols. New York: Cambridge University Press, 1998–2000.

SLAVERY AND ABOLITIONISM

Goddu, Teresa A. "Poe, Sensationalism, and Slavery," in *The Cambridge Companion to Edgar Allan Poe*, ed. Kevin J. Hayes. New York: Cambridge University Press, 2002. 92–112.

Jones, Paul Christian. "The Danger of Sympathy: Edgar Allan Poe's 'Hop-Frog' and the Abolitionist Rhetoric of Pathos." *Journal of American Studies* 35 (2001): 239–54.

Kennedy, J. Gerald, and Liliane Weissberg, eds. *Romancing the Shadow: Poe and Race*. New York: Oxford University Press, 2001.

Otter, Samuel. *Philadelphia Stories: America's Literature of Race and Freedom*. New York: Oxford University Press, 2010.

Whalen, Terence. *Edgar Allan Poe and the Masses: The Political Economy of Literature in Antebellum America*. Princeton: Princeton University Press, 1999.

THE CULT OF MOURNING

Farrell, James J. *Inventing the American Way of Death: 1830–1920*. Philadelphia: Temple University Press, 1980.

Isenberg, Nancy, and Burstein, Andrew. *Mortal Remains: Death in Early America*. Philadelphia: University of Pennsylvania Press, 2003.

Kete, Mary Louise. *Sentimental Collaborations: Mourning and Middle-Class Identity in Nineteenth-Century America*. Durham: Duke University Press, 2000.

Schor, Esther H. *Bearing the Dead: The British Culture of Mourning from the Enlightenment to Victoria*. Princeton: Princeton University Press, 1994.

LIONS AND BLUESTOCKINGS

Boyd, Anne E., ed. *Wielding the Pen: Writings on Authorship by American Women of the Nineteenth Century*. Baltimore: Johns Hopkins University Press, 2009.

Marchalonis, Shirley, ed. *Patrons and Protégées: Gender, Friendship, and Writing in Nineteenth-Century America*. New Brunswick: Rutgers University Press, 1994.

Richards, Eliza *Gender and the Poetics of Reception in Poe's Circle*. New York: Cambridge University Press, 2004.

Tomc, Sandra M. "Poe and His Circle," in *The Cambridge Companion to Edgar Allan Poe*, ed. Kevin J. Hayes. New York: Cambridge University Press, 2002. 21–41.

THE LITERARY PROFESSION

Bender, Thomas. *Intellect and Public Life: Essays on the Social History of Academic Intellectuals in the United States*. Baltimore: Johns Hopkins University Press, 1993.

Charvat, William. *The Profession of Authorship in America, 1800–1870*. Columbus: Ohio State University Press, 1968.

Evelev, John. *Tolerable Entertainment: Herman Melville and Professionalism in Antebellum New York*. Amherst: University of Massachusetts Press, 2006.

Hayes, Kevin J. *Poe and the Printed Word*. New York: Cambridge University Press, 2000.

MAGAZINES

Jackson, David Kelly. *Poe and the Southern Literary Messenger*. Richmond: Dietz, 1934.

Jacobs, Robert D. *Poe, Journalist and Critic*. Baton Rouge: Louisiana State University Press, 1969.

Mott, Frank Luther. *A History of American Magazines*. 5 vols. Cambridge, MA: Belknap Press, 1938–68.

Tebbel, John, and Mary Ellen Zuckerman. *The Magazine in America 1741–1990*. New York: Oxford University Press, 1991.

GIFT BOOKS

Elliott, Jock. *Inventing Christmas: How Our Holiday Came to Be*. New York: H. N. Abrams, 2002.

Lehuu, Isabelle. *Carnival on the Page: Popular Print Media in Antebellum America*. Chapel Hill: University of North Carolina Press, 2000.

Piper, Andrew. *Dreaming in Books: The Making of the Bibliographic Imagination in the Romantic Age*. Chicago: University of Chicago Press, 2009.

Thompson, Ralph. *American Literary Annuals and Gift Books, 1825–1865*. New York: H. W. Wilson, 1936.

LITERARY PIRACY

Barnes, James J. *Authors, Publishers and Politicians: The Quest for an Anglo-American Copyright Agreement, 1815–1854*. London: Routledge and Keegan Paul, 1974.

Everton, Michael J. *The Grand Chorus of Complaint: Authors and the Business Ethics of American Publishing*. New York: Oxford University Press, 2011.

Johns, Adrian. *Piracy: The Intellectual Property Wars from Gutenberg to Gates*. Chicago: University of Chicago Press, 2009.

McGill, Meredith L. *American Literature and the Culture of Reprinting*. Philadelphia: University of Pennsylvania Press, 2003.

THE ART OF REVIEWING

Dameron, J. Lasley. "Poe and *Blackwood's* on the Art of Reviewing." *ESQ* 31 (1963): 29–30.

Ljungquist, Kent. "The Poet as Critic," in *The Cambridge Companion to Edgar Allan Poe*, ed. Kevin J. Hayes. New York: Cambridge University Press, 2002. 7–20.

Parks, Edd Winfield, *Edgar Allan Poe as Literary Critic*. Athens: University of Georgia Press, 1964.

Rowland, William G. *Literature and the Marketplace: Romantic Writers and Their Audiences in Great Britain and the United States*. Lincoln: University of Nebraska Press, 1996.

St. Clair, William. *The Reading Nation in the Romantic Period*. New York: Cambridge University Press, 2004.

THE POLITICS OF PUBLISHING

Dowling, David O. *The Business of Literary Circles in Nineteenth-Century America*. New York: Palgrave Macmillan, 2011.
    Capital Letters: Authorship in the Antebellum Literary Market. Iowa City: University of Iowa Press, 2009.
Hartmann, Jonathan H., *The Marketing of Edgar Allan Poe*. New York: Routledge, 2008.
Moss, Sidney P. Poe's *Literary Battles: The Critic in the Context of His Literary Milieu*. Durham: Duke University Press, 1963.
Scherman, Timothy. "The Authority Effect: Poe and the Politics of Reputation in the Pre-Industry of American Publishing." *Arizona Quarterly* 49 (1993): 1–19.
Thompson, G. R. "Literary Politics and the 'Legitimate Sphere': Poe, Hawthorne, and the 'Tale Proper.'" *Nineteenth-Century Literature* 49 (1994): 167–95.

ANCIENT CLASSICS

Campbell, Killis. "Poe's Reading." *Texas Studies in English* 5 (1925): 166–96.
Holt, Palmer C. "Poe and H. N. Coleridge's Greek Classic Poets: 'Pinakidia,' 'Politian' and 'Morella' Sources." *American Literature* 34 (1962): 8–30.
Norman, E. K. "Poe's Knowledge of Latin." *American Literature* 6 (1934): 72–7.
Preston, J. T. L. "Some Reminiscences of Edgar A. Poe as a Schoolboy," in *Edgar Allan Poe: A Memorial Volume*, ed. Sara Sigourney Rice. Baltimore: Turnbull, 1877. 37–42.
Reynhold, Meyer. *Classica Americana*. Detroit: Wayne State University Press, 1984.
Unrue, D. H. "Edgar Allan Poe: The Romantic as Classicist." *International Journal of the Classical Tradition* 1 (1995): 112–19.
Winterer, Caroline. *The Culture of Classicism. Ancient Greece and Rome in American Intellecual Life, 1780–1910*. Baltimore: Johns Hopkins University Press, 2002. 29–43.

RABELAIS AND LESAGE

Bakhtin, M. M. *The Dialogic Imagination: Four Essays*, trans. Varyl Emerson and Michael Holquist. Austin: University of Texas Press, 1981.
    Rabelais and His World, trans. Helene Iswolsky. Bloomington: Indiana University Press, 1984.
Royot, Daniel. "Poe's Humor," in *The Cambridge Companion to Edgar Allan Poe*, ed. Kevin J. Hayes. New York: Cambridge University Press, 2002. 57–71.
Wetzel, George. "The Source of Poe's 'Man that Was Used Up.'" *Notes and Queries* 198 (1953): 38.
Zimmerman, Brett. *Edgar Allan Poe: Rhetoric and Style*. Montreal: McGill-Queen's University Press, 2005.

THE GOTHIC MOVEMENT

Bailey, Dale. *American Nightmares: The Haunted House Formula in American Popular Fiction*. Bowling Green: Bowling Green State University Popular Press, 1999.

Crow, Charles L. *American Gothic*. Cardiff: University of Wales Press, 2009.

Fisher, Benjamin Franklin. "Poe and the Gothic Tradition," in *The Cambridge Companion to Edgar Allan Poe*, ed. Kevin J. Hayes. New York: Cambridge University Press, 2002. 72–91.

Goddu, Teresa A. *Gothic America: Narrative, History, and Nation*. New York: Columbia University Press, 1997.

Hayes, Kevin J. "Retzsch's Outlines and Poe's 'The Man of the Crowd.'" *Gothic Studies* 12 (2010): 29–41.

Ringe, Donald A. *American Gothic: Imagination and Reason in Nineteenth-Century Fiction*. Lexington: University Press of Kentucky, 1982.

Smith, Andrew. *Gothic Literature*. Edinburgh: Edinburgh University Press, 2007.

BYRON

Bachinger, Katarina. *The Multi-Man Genre and Poe's Byrons*. Salzburg: Institut fur Anglistik und Amerikanistik, 1987.

Campbell, Killis. "Poe's Indebtedness to Byron." *Nation*, 11 March 1909, 248–9.

Chivers, T. H. *Life of Poe*, ed. Richard Beale Davis. New York: Dutton, 1952.

Soule, George H., Jr. "Byronism in Poe's 'Metzengerstein" and "William Wilson." *ESQ* 24 (1978): 152–62.

FOLK NARRATIVE

Brown, Carolyn S. *The Tall Tale in American Folklore and Literature*. Knoxville: University of Tennessee Press, 1987.

Hayes, Kevin J. *Folklore and Book Culture*. Knoxville: University of Tennessee Press, 1997.

Melville's Folk Roots. Kent, OH: Kent State University Press, 1999.

Hoffman, Daniel. *Form and Fable in American Fiction*. New York: Oxford University Press, 1961.

Jones, Steven Swann. *Folklore and Literature in the United States: An Annotated Bibliography of Studies of Folklore in American Literature*. New York: Garland, 1984.

TRANSCENDENTALISM

Casale, Ottavio. "Poe on Transcendentalism." *ESQ* 50 (1968): 85–97.

Gardner, Stanton. "Emerson, Thoreau, and Poe's 'Double Dupin,'" in *Poe and His Times: The Artist and His Milieu*, ed. Benjamin F. Fisher (Baltimore: Edgar Allan Poe Society, 2. 130–45.

Griffith, Clark. "'Emersonianism' and 'Poeism': Some Versions of the Romantic Sensibility." *Modern Language Quarterly* 22 (1961): 125–34.

Myerson, Joel, ed. *The Transcendentalists: A Review of Research and Criticism.* New York: Modern Language Association of America, 1984.

CHARLES DICKENS

Bracher, Peter, "Poe as a Critic of Dickens," *Dickens Studies Newsletter* 9 (1978): 109–11.

Caserio, Robert L., *Plot, Story, and the Novel: From Dickens and Poe to the Modern Period.* Princeton: Princeton University Press, 1979.

Galvan, Fernando Galvan. "Plagiarism in Poe: Revisiting the Poe-Dickens Relationship." *Edgar Allan Poe Review*, 10 (2009): 14–20.

"Poe Versus Dickens," in *A Descent into Edgar Allan Poe and His Works: The Bicentennial*, ed. Beatriz González Moreno and Margarita Rigal Aragón (New York: Peter Lang, 2010). 3–24.

Moss, Sidney P. *Charles Dickens' Quarrel with America.* Troy, NY: Whitston, 1984.

Moss, Sidney P. and Carolyn Moss. *American Episodes Involving Charles Dickens.* Troy, NY: Whitston, 1999.

Slater, Michael. *Charles Dickens.* New Haven: Yale University Press, 2009.

NATHANIEL HAWTHORNE

Idol, John L., and Buford Jones. *Nathaniel Hawthorne: The Contemporary Reviews.* New York: Cambridge University Press, 1994.

Levin, Harry. *The Power of Blackness: Hawthorne, Poe, Melville.* New York: Knopf, 1958.

Miller, Edwin Haviland. *Salem is My Dwelling Place: A Life of Nathaniel Hawthorne.* Iowa City: University of Iowa Press, 1991.

Person, Leland S. *The Cambridge Introduction to Nathaniel Hawthorne.* New York: Cambridge University Press, 2007.

Sutherland, Judith L. *The Problematic Fictions of Poe, James, and Hawthorne.* Columbia: University of Missouri Press, 1984.

PHRENOLOGY

Colbert, Charles. *A Measure of Perfection: Phrenology and the Fine Arts in America.* Chapel Hill: University of North Carolina Press, 1997.

Cooter, Roger. *The Cultural Meaning of Popular Science: Phrenology and the Organization of Consent in Nineteenth-Century Britain.* New York: Cambridge University Press, 1984.

Stern, Madeleine B. *Heads and Headlines: The Phrenological Fowlers.* Norman: University of Oklahoma Press, 1971.

Tomlinson, Stephen. *Head Masters: Phrenology, Secular Education, and Nineteenth-Century Social Thought.* Tuscaloosa: University of Alabama Press, 2005.

PHOTOGRAPHY

Deas, Michael. *The Portraits and Daguerreotypes of Edgar Allan Poe.* Charlottesville: University Press of Virginia, 1989.

Hayes, Kevin J. "Poe, the Daguerreotype, and the Autobiographical Act." *Biography*, 25 (2002): 477–92.

Poe's "Spectacles" and the Camera Lens. Baltimore: The Edgar Allan Poe Society of Baltimore, 2007.

Rudisilll, Richard. *Mirror Image: The Influence of the Daguerreotype on American Society.* Albuquerque: University of New Mexico Press, 1971.

Tresch, John. "Estrangement of Vision: Edgar Allan Poe's Optics," in *Observing Nature / Representing Experience: The Osmotic Dynamics of Romanticism, 1800–1850,* ed. Erna Fiorenti. Berlin: Reimer Verlag, 2007. 126–57.

Williams, Susan S. *Confounding Images: Photography and Portraiture in Antebellum American Fiction.* Philadelphia: University of Pennsylvania Press, 1997.

MESMERISM

Coale, Samuel. *Mesmerism and Hawthorne: Mediums of American Romance.* Tuscaloosa: University of Alabama Press, 1998.

Mesmer, Franz Anton. *Mesmerism: A Translation of the Original Scientific and Medical Writings of F. A. Mesmer,* trans. and ed. George Bloch. Los Altos, CA: William Kaufman, 1980.

Mills, Bruce. *Poe, Fuller, and the Mesmeric Arts: Transition States in the American Renaissance.* Columbia: University of Missouri Press, 2006.

Schmit, David. "Re-visioning Antebellum American Psychology: The Dissemination of Mesmerism, 1836–1854." *History of Psychology* 8 (2005): 403–34.

Willis, Martin. *Mesmerists, Monsters, and Machines: Science Fiction and the Cultures of Science in the Nineteenth Century.* Kent, OH: Kent State University Press, 2006.

ARCHITECTURE

Clark, Clifford Edward. *The American Family Home, 1800–1960.* Chapel Hill: University of North Carolina Press, 1986.

Downing, A. J. *A. J. Downing's Cottage Residences, Rural Architecture and Landscape Gardening,* ed. Michael Hugo-Brunt. Watkins Glen, NY: Library of Victorian Culture, 1967.

Frayne, Anthony J. *The Rose-Covered Cottage of Edgar Allan Poe in Philadelphia.* Philadelphia: A. J. Frayne, 1934.

Hussey, E. C. *Cottage Architecture of Victorian America.* New York: Dover, 1994.

Maynard, W. Barksdale. *Architecture in the United States, 1800–1850.* New Haven: Yale University Press, 2002.

SCIENCE FICTION

Disch, Thomas M. *On SF*. Ann Arbor: University of Michigan Press, 2005.

Franklin, H. Bruce. *Future Perfect: American Science Fiction of the Nineteenth Century*. New York: Oxford University Press, 1966.

Goulet, Andrea. *Optiques: The Science of the Eye and the Birth of Modern French Fiction*. Philadelphia: University of Pennsylvania Press, 2006.

Limon, John. *The Place of Fiction in the Time of Science: A Disciplinary History of American Writing*. New York: Cambridge University Press, 1990.

Scholnick, Robert J. *American Literature and Science*. Lexington: University Press of Kentucky, 1992.

Tresch, John. "Extra! Extra! Poe Invents Science Fiction!" in *The Cambridge Companion to Edgar Allan Poe*, ed. Kevin J. Hayes. New York: Cambridge University Press, 2002. 113–32.

COSMOLOGY AND COSMOGONY

Coveney, Peter, and Roger Highfield. *Frontiers of Complexity: The Search for Order in a Chaotic World*. London: Faber and Faber, 1995.

Secord, James. *Victorian Sensation: The Extraordinary Publication, Reception, and Secret Authorship of Vestiges of the Natural History of Creation*. Chicago: University of Chicago Press, 2000.

Swirski, Peter. *Between Literature and Science: Poe, Lem, and Explorations in Aesthetics, Cognitive Science, and Literary Knowledge*. Montreal: McGill-Queen's University Press, 2000.

Taylor, Jonathan. *Science and Omniscience in Nineteenth Century Literature*. Brighton: Sussex Academic Press, 2007.

FORENSIC SCIENCE

Stashower, Daniel. *The Beautiful Cigar Girl: Mary Rogers, Edgar Allan Poe, and the Invention of Murder*. New York: Dutton, 2006.

Thomas, Ronald R. *Detective Fiction and the Rise of Forensic Science*. New York: Cambridge University Press, 1999.

Thoms, Peter. *Detection and Its Designs: Narrative and Power in 19th-Century Detective Fiction*. Athens: Ohio University Press, 1998.

Walsh, John Evangelist. *Poe the Detective: The Curious Circumstances behind "The Mystery of Marie Rogêt."* New Brunswick: Rutgers University Press, 1967.

TECHNOLOGY

Benesch, Klaus. *Romantic Cyborgs: Authorship and Technology in the American Renaissance*. Amherst: University of Massachusetts Press, 2002.

Cowan, Ruth Schwartz. *A Social History of American Technology*. New York: Oxford University Press, 1997.

Egan, Ken, Jr. "Edgar Allan Poe and the Horror of Technology." *ESQ* 48 (2002): 187–208.

Marx, Leo. *The Machine in the Garden: Technology and the Pastoral Ideal in America.* New York: Oxford University Press, 1964.

Nye, David. *America as Second Creation: Technology and Narratives of New Beginnings.* Cambridge, MA: MIT Press, 2004.

Orvell, Miles. "Virtual Culture and the Logic of American Technology." *Revue Française d'Etudes Americaines* 76 (1998): 12–27.

Tresch, John. "The Potent Magic of Verisimilitude: Edgar Allan Poe within the Mechanical Age." *British Journal for the History of Science* 30 (1997): 275–90.

Index

A Edgar Poe (Redon), 47
A Rebours (Huysmans), 47
Abbott, Anne W., 206
Ackerman, Rudolph
    Repository of Arts, 114
Adams, John Quincy, 212
Address (Dew), 139
Address (Reynolds), 32, 67
Address Delivered before the Springfield
    Washingtonian Temperance Society
    (Lincoln), 100
Aeschylus, 227
Aesop
    Fables, 221
Affaire Lerouge (Gaboriau), 48
Ainsworth, William Harrison, 281
    Crichton, 233
    Guy Fawkes, 54
Alastor (Shelley), 255–6
Albion, 279
Alciphron (Moore), 56, 223
Alcmaeon, 243
Alcott, Bronson, 296
Alcott, William A.
    Young Man's Guide, 108
Alexander, Charles, 211
Alexander's Weekly Messenger, 313–14,
    316–17
Algerine Captive (Tyler), 59
Allan, Frances, 5, 13, 118
Allan, John, 5, 13, 118, 121, 138, 210, 221–2,
    251, 373
Allan, Mary, 5
Allgemeine Naturgeschichte (Kant), 359
American Monthly Magazine, 198, 212
American Museum, 177, 213
American Notes (Dickens), 3, 24, 280
American Phrenological Journal, 307
American Phrenological Review, 306
"American Poetry," 284
American Review, 161, 198, 295

Ames, Nathaniel
    Mariner's Sketches, 64
Anacreon, 223
Anacronopete (Gaspar), 343
Anatomy and Physiology of the Nervous System
    (Gall), 301
Anaxagoras, 225, 246
Anderson, Beverly, 121
Andreae, Johann Valentin
    Christianopolis, 349
Antarctic Mystery (Verne), 344
Anthology of Black Humor (Breton), 49
Anthon, Charles, 224
Antigone (Sophocles), 223
Antiquary (Scott), 244
Antony, Mark, 225
Apuleius Madaurensis, 227
Arabian Nights, 54
Arcades Project (Benjamin), 76
Archytas, 243
Aristidean, 17, 204
Aristotle, 122, 223, 227
Arnold, Elizabeth, 119
Around the World in Eighty Days (Verne), 346
Arthur, Timothy Shay
    Six Nights with the Washingtonians, 100
    Ten Nights in a Bar-Room, 102
Arthur Mervyn (Brown), 242
Assassins (Campos), 50
Astor, John Jacob, 200–1
Atkinson, Samuel, 209
Atlantic Souvenir, 179–80

Babbage, Charles, 375
Bacon, Francis, 91, 315
    New Atlantis, 349
Bailey, J. O., 67
Bakhtin, Mikhail, 239
    Rabelais and His World, 233–4
Ballads and Other Poems (Longfellow), 17, 290
Baltimore Book, 182

Baltimore Saturday Visiter, 173, 211
Bande à part (Godard), 50
Banner of Temperance, 96
Barbey-d'Aurevilly, Jules-Amédée, 44–5
Barnaby Rudge (Dickens), 4, 204, 279–80, 285, 365
Barnes, Nigel, 205
Barnum, P. T., 86–7, 89, 91, 93
Batrachomyomachia, 224
Battle of Dorking (Chesney), 350
Baudelaire (Tarek), 50
Baudelaire, Charles, 41–4, 47, 75, 77, 251, 344
  "Bérénice," 42
  "Edgar Poe, sa vie et ses ouevres," 42
  Fleurs du mal, 42–3
  Histoires extraordinaires, 42
  Histoires grotesques et sérieuses, 42
  Nouvelles histoires extraordinaires, 42
  "Spleen," 43
  "Voyage à Cythère," 43
Beauchamp, Jereboam O., 122
Beaumont, Francis
  Maid's Tragedy, 123
Beckford, William
  Vathek, 55
Beecher, Lyman, 26
Beethoven, Ludwig van, 376
Bellamy, Edward, 343
Benjamin, Park, 212–13
Benjamin, Walter, 11, 77–9
  Arcades Project, 76
Bentham, Jeremy, 373
Bentley's Miscellany, 281
Benton, Richard P., 367
Bierce, Ambrose, 249
Billy Budd (Melville), 38
Bird, Robert Montgomery
  Sheppard Lee, 144
Bismarck, Otto von, 350
Blackwood's Edinburgh Magazine, 177, 198, 201, 204, 242, 291, 366
Blake, William, 351
Bleak House (Dickens), 4, 285
Blessington, Marguerite, *countess of*, 130
Blocker, Jack S., Jr., 98
Blue Beard, 119
Bogdan, Robert, 93
Bonaparte, Napoleon, 56, 114, 345
Bosch, Hieronymus
  Garden of Earthly Delights, 351
Boston Book, 182
Boston Medical and Surgical Journal, 324
Bourdieu, Pierre, 161
Brackett, Loraina, 324
Brand, Dana, 78–9

Bransby, John, 5, 7, 221, 229
Breton, André
  Anthology of Black Humor, 49
  Manifesto of Surrealism, 49
Brewster, David
  Letters on Natural Magic, 376–7
Bride of Abydos (Byron), 56
Briggs, Charles, 131, 135, 206, 214
Brigham, Amariah, 324
  Remarks on the Influence of Mental Cultivation, 324
Brix, Michel, 43
Broadway Journal, 7, 27, 125, 127, 130–1, 133–4, 162, 174, 176, 204, 206, 214–15, 284, 327, 376
Broche, Gaston, 69
Brooks, Nathan C., 213, 223
Brother Jonathan, 192, 282
Brown, Charles Brockden
  Arthur Mervyn, 242
  Edgar Huntly, 242
  Ormond, 242
  Wieland, 242, 363
Brown, William Wells,
  Narrative, 25
Browning, Elizabeth Barrett, 193–5
Browning, Robert, 193
Bruce, James
  Travels to Discover the Source of the Nile, 57
Brutus, Marcus Junius, 225
Bryant, Jacob
  New System: or, An Analysis of Antient Mythology, 224
Bryant, William Cullen, 18, 33, 129, 282, 284
  "Prairies," 27
Bulwer-Lytton, Edward, 200
  Last Days of Pompeii, 223
Burke, William, 222
Burton, William E., 32, 122–3, 174, 211
Burton's Gentleman's Magazine, 29, 56, 162, 171–2, 206, 209, 213, 314
Byer, Robert H., 78
Byron, George Gordon, *baron*, 55–6, 110, 122, 203, 251–9
  Bride of Abydos, 56
  Childe Harold's Pilgrimage, 256
  Corsair, 56
  Don Juan, 257
  Giaour, 56
  Lara, 56
  Manfred, 255–7
  "She Walks in Beauty," 255

Cabinet of Momus, 264
Caesar, Caius Julius, 222, 226

Calhoun, John C., 14
Campanella, Tommaso
 City of the Sun, 349
Campos, Claudia
 Assassins, 50
Captain Singleton (Defoe), 39
Captains Courageous (Kipling), 39
Carey, Henry C. 179–80, 184, 190
Carey, Matthew, 184
Carlyle, Thomas, 201, 269, 275
Carter, Robert, 214
Cartwright, Lisa, 316
Casale, Ottavio, 269, 277
Cash, W. J.
 Mind of the South, 14
Casket, 174, 209, 211
Castle Andalusia, 119
Castle of Otranto (Walpole), 241, 244, 345
Castle Spectre, 121
Chabrol, Claude, 49
Channing, William Ellery, 17, 199, 275
Chapman, George
 Revenge of Bussy D'Ambois, 123
 Tragedy of Bussy d'Ambois, 123
Charvat, William, 171
Chase, Owen
 Narrative of the … Shipwreck, 37–8
Chase, William Henry, 38
Chateaubriand, François-René, *vicomte de*
 Itinéraire de Paris, 58
Chavigny, Katherine, 104
Chesney, George
 Battle of Dorking, 350
Child, Lydia Maria, 199, 325
 Philothea, 223
Childe Harold's Pilgrimage (Byron), 256
Chimes (Dickens), 280
Chivers, Thomas Holley, 251–2, 269, 273, 275
Christian Philosopher (Mather), 64
Christianapolis (Andreae), 349
Christmas Carol (Dickens), 279
Church, Frederick, 332
Cicero, Marcus Tullius, 222, 224–6
 De officiis, 222
"Cinderella," 266
Cinq semaines en ballon (Verne), 48
Cinquez, Joseph, 307
City of the Sun (Campanella), 349
Civilization and Its Discontents (Freud), 82–3
Claretie, Jules, 45–6
Clark, William, 30, 63
Clarke, Joseph H., 222
Clarke, Thomas C., Jr., 339
Classical Dictionary (Lemprière), 224
Clemens, Samuel, 25, 194

Clemm, Maria, 139, 285, 334–5, 341
Cobb, William, 46
Cogni, Margarita, 254
Cole, Thomas, 332
Coleridge, H. N.
 Introductions to the Study of the Greek Classic Poets, 224
Coleridge, Samuel Taylor, 57, 243, 252–3, 257, 269, 272
 "Rime of the Ancient Mariner," 35–6, 346
Collectanea Graeca Majora (Dalzell), 223
Collyer, Robert H., 327
 Psychology: or, The Embodiment of Thought, 327
Columbian Lady's and Gentleman's Magazine, 175
Combe, George, 304, 306
Commercial Chronicle and Daily Marylander, 210
Comus (Milton), 124
Conchologist's First Book (Poe), 374
Confessions of an Opium Eater (De Quincey), 203, 243
Conrad, Joseph
 Heart of Darkness, 39
 "Secret Sharer," 39
Conrad, Peter
 Imagining America, 10
Conrad, Robert T., 215
Contes cruels (Villiers de l'Isle-Adam), 46
Contes macabres (Lacombe), 50
Cook, Ann, 122
Cook, James, *captain*, 36, 39, 63
Cooke, Philip Pendleton, 17–18
 "Rosalie Lee," 17
Cooper, James Fenimore, 14, 18, 23, 28, 129, 200
 Last of the Mohicans, 27
Corbeau (Mallarmé), 44
Corinne (Staël), 132
Corneille, Pierre, 41
Corsair (Byron), 56
Cottage Residences (Downing), 331
Count Robert of Paris (Scott), 365
Coveney, Peter, 357
Cranch, Charles Pearse, 110
Crane, Stephen
 "Open Boat," 39
Crayon Miscellany (Irving), 202
Crébillon, Prosper Jolyot de, 41
Crichton (Ainsworth), 233
Crockett, Davy, 263
Curiosities of Literature (D'Israeli), 224–5, 227
Curtis, George Ticknor, 191–2, 195
Cuvier, Georges, 374

Cyclopaedia (Rees), 57
Cyrano de Bergerac
  Voyage dans la lune, 347

Daguerre, Louis, 313, 315, 319
Daily News, 285
Dalzell, Andrew
  Collectanea Graeca Majora, 223
Dana, Richard Henry, 63
  Two Years before the Mast, 32, 39
Daniel John W., 42
Dante Alighieri, 176
David Copperfield (Dickens), 4
Davies, Samuel, 150–1
De la terre à la lune (Verne), 48
De officiis (Cicero), 222
De situ orbis (Mela), 226
"Dead Alive," 243
Defoe, Daniel
  Captain Singleton, 39
  Robinson Crusoe, 5, 32
Deleuze, Joseph Philippe François
  Practical Instruction in Animal Magnetism,
    322–3, 325, 329
Democratic Review, 55, 171, 198, 214, 293
Democritus, 226
Demosthenes, 225
De Quincey, Thomas, 202, 257
  Confessions of an Opium Eater, 203, 243
DeUnger, Robert, 98
Devil on Two Sticks (Lesage), 237–9
Devine, Harry Gene, 104
Dew, Thomas
  Address, 139
Dial, 276, 296
Dialogues of the Dead (Lucian), 228
Diary in America (Marryat), 85
Dickens, Charles, 3–4, 7, 9–11, 75, 78, 193, 200,
    202, 279–85
  American Notes, 3, 24, 280
  Barnaby Rudge, 4, 204, 279–80,
    285, 365
  Bleak House, 4, 285
  Chimes, 280
  Christmas Carol, 279
  "Confession Found in a Prison," 280
  David Copperfield, 4
  "Drunkard's Death," 10
  Household Words, 285
  Martin Chuzzlewit, 3–4, 10, 377
  Master Humphrey's Clock, 279–80
  Nicholas Nickleby, 279
  Old Curiosity Shop, 279, 365
  Oliver Twist, 365
  Our Mutual Friend, 285

Pickwick Papers, 4, 279
Sketches by Boz, 4, 10, 203, 280
Dictionary of Greek and Roman Antiquities
    (Smith), 224
Dickinson, Emily, 70
DiGirolamo, Vincent, 149
Diodorus Siculus, 224–5
D'Israeli, Isaac
  Curiosities of Literature, 224–5, 227
Doctor Faustus (Marlowe), 347
Dolin, Eric, 38
Dollar Newspaper, 126, 215
Domain of Arnheim (Magritte), 49
Domestic Manners of the Americans
    (Trollope), 26
Don Juan (Byron), 257
Douglas, John, 365
Douglass, Frederick, 140
Downing, A. J., 332
  Cottage Residences, 334
Doyle, Arthur Conan
  Study in Scarlet, 48
Doyle, Charles Clay, 264
Dracula (Stoker), 241
Drake, Daniel, 26–7
Drayton, William
  South Vindicated, 139
Drummond, William
  Satires of Persius, 221, 223
Dubourg, Misses, 5
Dumas, Alexandre, 41
Dunlap, William
  Fatal Deception, 242
  Fountainville Abbey, 242
Durant, Charles
  *Exposition: or, A New Theory of Animal
    Magnetism*, 324–5
Dutchess of Malfi (Webster), 123
Duyckinck, Evert A., 14, 203–4, 206, 214, 376

Eclogue (Villiers de l'Isle-Adam), 221
Eddy, Daniel
  Young Man's Friend, 108
Edgar Huntly (Brown), 242
Edgar Poe détective (Locard), 365
Edgeworth, Maria, 190
Ellet, Elizabeth, 134–5
Embury, Emma, 131
Emerson, Ralph Waldo, 3, 6, 18, 199–200, 204,
    269–77, 284, 316
  "American Scholar," 5, 14
  "Nature," 8, 270–1, 273–5
  "Poet," 273
  "Self-Reliance," 275
Engels, Friedrich, 75

England in 1835 (Raumer), 124–5
English, Thomas Dunn, 99, 134–5, 309, 339
   "1844: or, The Power of the S.F.," 135
Enquête criminelle et les méthodes scientifiques
   (Locard), 364
Epicurus, 226
Epimenides, 225
Epstein, Jean, 49
Ernst, Max, 49
Eureka (Poe), 42, 45, 272, 274, 330, 345, 348, 355,
   358, 360, 366, 379
Eve future (Villiers de l'Isle-Adam), 46
Exposition (Durant), 324–5
Exposition du système du monde (Laplace), 358
Expositor, 315
Eymery, Marguerite
   Jongleuse, 47
   Monsieur Vénus, 47

Fable for Critics (Lowell), 138, 143–4, 204
Fables (Aesop), 221
Facts in Mesmerism (Townshend), 322, 325–9
Fagin, N. Bryllion, 122
Farrell, James J., 148
Fashion (Mowatt), 111–12, 119, 125–6
Fasti (Ovid), 226
Fatal Deception (Dunlap), 242
"Fatal Imitation," 264
Faust (Goethe), 228, 242
Fay, Theodore, 130
   Norman Leslie, 201–2
Felton, Cornelius C., 202
Female Poets of America (Griswold), 127
Fichte, Johann Gottlieb, 270
Fiedler, Leslie, 242
Fielding, Henry
   History of Tom Jones, 39
Fisher, Benjamin F., 242
Flag of Our Union, 175, 215
Fletcher, John
   Maid's Tragedy, 123
Fleurs du mal (Baudelaire), 42–3
Flint, Timothy, 23, 26
Flying Dutchman (Wagner), 37
Foigny, Gabriel
   New Discovery of Terra Incognita Australis,
   346
Ford, John
   'Tis Pity She's a Whore, 123
Foreign Quarterly Review, 283–4
Forester, Frank, 212
Forgues, E. D., 366
Form and Fable in American Fiction (Hoffman),
   266
Forrest, Edwin, 119

Foster, John, 284
Foucault, Michel, 80
Fountain, 186
Fountainville Abbey (Dunlap), 242
Fowler, Lorenzo Niles, 303, 307–9
Fowler, O. S., 303, 308
Francis, John W., 232
Frankenstein (Shelley), 241, 343, 347
Franklin, Benjamin, 323, 325, 348
Franklin Evans (Whitman), 101
Frayne, Anthony, 335
Freud, Sigmund, 310
   Civilization and Its Discontents, 82–3
Fuller, Hiram, 135
Fuller, Margaret, 23, 131, 134–5, 199, 205–6, 325
   "Short Fable for Critics," 205
   Summer on the Lakes, 23
   Woman in the Nineteenth Century, 206
Fulton, Robert, 345
Fussell, Edwin, 23, 27

Gaboriau, Emile, 48
   Affaire Lerouge, 48
Gall, Franz Joseph, 303, 305
   *Anatomy and Physiology of the Nervous
   System*, 301
Galland, Antoine
   Mille et une Nuit, 54
Garden of Earthly Delights (Bosch), 351
Gardner, Eric, 25
Gargantua (Rabelais), 232–4
Gaspar, Enrique
   Anacronopete, 343
Gay, Peter, 353, 355
Gazette des Tribunaux, 48
Georgia Scenes (Longstreet), 18–19
Giaour (Byron) 56
Gibbon, Edward
   *History of the Decline and Fall of the Roman
   Empire*, 223
Gift, 181–6
Gigoux, Jean, 292
Gil Blas (Lesage), 232, 237, 292
Giles, Paul, 6–7
Gilman, Sander, 316
Gimbel, Richard, 285, 335
Gitelman, Lisa, 68
Glanvill, Joseph, 152
Glasgow, Ellen, 14
Gleason, Cynthia Ann, 324–5
Gliddon, George R., 375
Godard, Jean-Luc
   Bande à part, 50
   Pierrot le fou, 50
   Vivre sa vie, 50

Godey, Louis, 186
Godey's Lady's Book, 111, 116, 152, 165, 171–3, 175, 186, 194, 203–4, 206, 215, 294
Godwin, Francis
  Man in the Moone, 346
Godwin, William
  Lives of the Necromancers, 202
Goethe, Johann Wolfgang von
  Faust, 228, 242
Goncourt, Edmond, 45
Gorgias, 226, 243
Gough, John Bartholomew, 100
Gouraud, François, 313
Gourmont, Remy de, 50
Graham, George R., 185, 209–11, 213–14, 216
Graham's Magazine, 108, 113, 115, 162, 171–5, 185, 204, 206, 213, 215, 279, 288–90
Grandville, J. J., 292
Grant, Anne
  Memoirs of an American Lady, 139
Greeley, Horace, 131, 212–13, 215
Green, James N., 189
Greenwood, Grace, 131, 133
Gribbin, John, 356
Griffith, Clark, 247
Grimm, Jakob and Wilhelm
  "Thousandfurs," 266
Griswold, Rufus, 75, 97, 131–2, 174, 192, 215, 252, 267, 376
  Female Poets of America, 127
  Poets and Poetry of America, 127, 284
Guiccioli, Teresa, *contessa di*, 253
Gulliver's Travels (Swift), 32, 292
Gunning, Tom, 78
Guy Fawkes (Ainsworth), 54

Hale, Sarah J., 186
Hall, James, 23, 26
Halley, Edmond, 64
Hamlet (Shakespeare), 64, 228
Hannibal Courier, 25
Harmony of the World (Kepler), 360
Harrington, James
  Oceana, 349
Harris, Neil, 85–6
Harrison, Gessner, 222
Harrison, William Henry, 213
Hastings, Warren, 5
Hawking, Stephen, 357
Hawthorne, Nathaniel, 8–9, 11, 161, 165–6, 181, 204, 242, 260, 288–97, 320, 344, 348
  "Buds and Bird Voices," 293
  House of the Seven Gables, 9
  "Howe's Masquerade," 288
  "Minister's Black Veil," 291

"Mr. Higginbotham's Catastrophe," 363
Mosses from an Old Manse, 294, 296
Twice-Told Tales, 8, 199, 288–91, 293, 323, 328
"Young Goodman Brown," 295
Haycraft, Howard, 365
Hayes, Kevin J., 75, 177
Hazlitt, William, 198
Heart of Darkness (Conrad), 39
Hedge, Frederic Henry, 201
Hegel, Georg Wilhelm Friedrich, 256
Heine, Heinrich, 75
Herald of Truth, 92
Herbert, Henry William, 212
Herodotus, 222
Heth, Joice, 86–9
Hewitt, John Hill, 211
Hewitt, Mary S., 326
Highfield, Roger, 357
Histoire ancienne (Rollin), 53, 223
Histoire de masques (Lorrain), 47
Histoire romaine (Rollin), 223
Histoires extraordinaires (Baudelaire), 42
Histoires extraordinaires d'Edgar Poe (Roehmer), 50
Histoires extraordinaires d'Edgar Poe (Thourds), 50
Histoires grotesques et sérieuses (Baudelaire), 42
Histoires incroyables (Lermina), 46
Historiae (Tacitus), 222
History of Nourjahad (Sheridan), 55
History of the Decline and Fall of the Roman Empire (Gibbon), 223
History of Tom Jones (Fielding), 39
Hitchcock, Alfred, 49
Hitchcock, Lambert, 114
Hoffman, Charles Fenno, 23, 26, 212, 304
  Winter in the West, 27
Hoffman, Daniel, 248, 360
  Form and Fable in American Fiction, 266
Hoffmann, E. T. A., 45–6, 344
  "Automaton," 347
Hogarth, William, 116
Holmes, Oliver Wendell, 14
Home Journal, 175, 214
Homer, 176, 222–5, 373
  Odyssey, 223, 225, 228, 345, 347
Hooke, Thomas
  Micrographia, 346
Hope, Thomas
  Household Furniture, 114
Hopkins, Mr., 119
Horatius Flaccus, Quintus, 222, 225–6
  Odes, 222, 225
Horse-Shoe Robinson (Kennedy), 202
Hortulus Animae, 77

House of the Seven Gables (Hawthorne), 9
Household Furniture (Hope), 114
Household Words (Dickens), 285
Hovey, Kenneth Alan, 18
Howells, William Dean, 249
Hubble, Edwin, 358–9
Huckel, Oliver, 14
Human Magnetism (Newnham), 327–8
Hungerford, Edward, 301
Hunt, Leigh, 198
Hutchinson, Peter, 170
Huysmans, Joris Karl
    A Rebours, 47
Hyperion (Longfellow), 232

Illinois Monthly Magazine, 169
Illustrated Phrenological Almanac, 308
Imagining America (Conrad), 10
Imp of the Perverse (Margritte), 49
Incidents of Travel in Egypt (Stephens), 58
Ingraham, Joseph Holt
    South-West, 139
Inquiry into the Effects of Ardent Spirits (Rush), 97–8
Interview with Hesiod (Lucian), 228
Introductions to the Study of the Greek Classic Poets (Coleridge), 224
Irving, Washington, 14, 18, 23, 129, 181, 199–200, 212, 260, 282
    Crayon Miscellany, 202
    Tales of a Traveller, 289
    Tales of the Alhambra, 58
    Tour on the Prairies, 27
    "Unwritten Drama of Lord Byron," 182, 258
Irwin, John T., 57, 367
Itinéraire de Paris (Chateaubriand), 58

Jackson, Andrew, 34, 85, 87, 209, 212–13
Jackson, Joseph
    Philosophy of Animal Magnetism, 322
James, Henry, 3, 249
Jefferson, Thomas, 17, 114, 212, 243, 373
    Notes on the State of Virginia, 145
Jew of Malta (Marlowe), 123
Johnson, Richard M., 213
Johnson, Samuel
    Rasselas, 55
Jones, Darryl, 68–9
Jong, Mary de, 133
Jongleuse (Eymery), 47
Jung, C. G., 310

Kahn, Gustave, 44
Kant, Immanuel, 269–70
    Allgemeine Naturgeschichte, 359

Keats, John
    "Belle Dame Sans Merci," 256
Kennedy, John Pendleton, 18, 173, 181, 201, 211–12, 304
    Horse-Shoe Robinson, 202
Kepler, Johannes, 349, 360, 379
    Harmony of the World, 360
    Somnium, 346
Kete, Mary Louise, 150
Kipling, Rudyard
    Captains Courageous, 39
Kircher, Athanasius, 67
    Mundus subterraneus, 64
Kirkland, Caroline, 23, 27–9, 130–1
    New Home, 27, 131
    Western Clearings, 27
Knickerbocker Magazine, 24, 171–2, 200, 315
Koestler, Arthur, 360
Kopley, Richard, 67
Kramnick, Isaac, 353
Kritias (Plato), 349

La Bruyère, Jean de, 41
Lacombe, Benjamin
    Contes macabres, 50
Ladies Cabinet, 111
Lady's Magazine, 171
Lady's World of Fashion, 111, 116
Lalla Rookh (Moore), 54, 56
Landor, Edward Wilson
    "Maelstrom: A Fragment," 35
Laplace, Pierre-Simon, 274, 356, 358–60, 379
    Exposition du système du monde, 358
Lara (Byron), 56
Last Days of Pompeii (Bulwer-Lytton), 223
Last Man (Shelley), 348
Last of the Mohicans (Cooper), 27
Lawlor, Robert, 359
Laws (Plato), 223, 349
Lays of Ancient Rome (Macaulay), 223
Lea, Isaac, 179–81, 190
Lemprière, John
    Classical Dictionary, 224
Lermina, Jules, 45
    "Fous," 46
    Histoires incroyables, 46
Lesage, Alain-René, 232, 236–9
    Devil on Two Sticks, 237–9
    Gil Blas, 232, 237, 292
Leslie, Eliza, 182
Leslie, John, 64
Letter to Col. Wm. L. Stone (Poyen), 325
Letter to Doctor A. Brigham (Stone), 324

Letters and Journals of Lord Byron (Moore), 253
Letters on Natural Magic (Brewster), 376–7
Letters on Practical Subjects (Sprague), 151
Levine, Lawrence, 264
Lewis, Matthew
  Monk, 241, 244
Lewis, Meriwether, 29–30, 63
Lewis, Taylor, 223
Liberté de penser, 42
Liberty Bell, 186
Lincoln, Abraham
  Address Delivered before the Springfield
    Washingtonian Temperance Society, 100
Linwoods (Sedgwick), 202
Lippincott, Sara Jane Clarke,
  131, 133
Literary World, 214
Lithgow, John, 125, 243
Lives of the Necromancers (Godwin), 202
Locard, Edmond, 364–5
  Edgar Poe détective, 365
  Enquête criminelle et les méthodes
    scientifiques, 364
Locke, John, 270, 348
Locke, Richard, 88
London Court Journal, 315
Long, George, 222, 224
Longfellow, Henry Wadsworth, 17–18, 27, 124,
  165–6, 181, 199–200, 206, 289–91
  Ballads and Other Poems, 17, 290
  Hyperion, 232
  Poems on Slavery, 17, 143
  "Slave's Dream," 17–18
Longstreet, Augustus Baldwin
  Georgia Scenes, 18–19
Lorrain, Jean, 45
  Histoire de masques, 47
  "Homme au complet mauve," 47
  "Impossible alibi," 47
  Monsieur de Phocas, 47
Louis XVI, king of France, 323
Lowell, James Russell, 163, 185, 199, 203–6, 214,
  253, 283–5, 292, 376
  Fable for Critics, 138, 143–4, 204
  Poems, 203
Lucanus, Marcus Anneus
  Pharsalia, 227
Lucianus
  Dialogues of the Dead, 228
  Interview with Hesiod, 228
  True History, 228
Lucretius Carus, Titus
  On the Nature of the Universe, 359
Lynch, Anne C., 131, 133–5
Lyrical Ballads (Wordsworth), 377

Mabbott, Thomas Ollive, 122–3, 326, 363
Macaulay, Thomas Babington
  Lays of Ancient Rome, 223
Macbeth 124, 242
McBride, James, 64
McGill, Meredith, 160–1, 175, 193
Madison, James, 17
Maelzel, Johann, 86, 88, 224, 375–6
Magritte, René
  Domain of Arnheim, 49
  Imp of the Perverse, 49
  Reproduction interdite, 49
Maid's Tragedy (Beaumont and Fletcher), 123
Malcontent (Marston), 123
Malin, Irving, 242
Mallarmé, Stéphane, 42, 44
  Corbeau, 44
  "Tombeau d'Edgar Poe," 44
"Man in the Bell," 243
Man in the Moone (Godwin), 346
Manet, Edouard, 44
Manfred (Byron), 255–7
Manifesto of Surrealism (Breton), 49
Mariner's Sketches (Ames), 64
"Market Lass," 119
Marlowe, Christopher
  Doctor Faustus, 347
  Jew of Malta, 123
Marryat, Frederick
  Diary in America, 85
  Phantom Ship, 37, 260
Marston, John
  Malcontent, 123
Martin Chuzzlewit (Dickens), 3–4, 10, 377
Martineau, Harriet
  Retrospect of Western Travel, 26
Marylander, 210
Master Humphrey's Clock (Dickens), 279–80
Mather, Cotton
  Christian Philosopher, 64
Mathews, Cornelius, 193
Mathias, Benjamin, 213
Matthews, Thomas Johnston, 64
Matthiessen. F. O., 14
Mattson, Morris
  Paul Ulric, 237
Maturin, Charles
  Melmoth the Wanderer, 241
Maupassant, Guy de, 45
  "Apparition," 45
  "Fou?" 45
  "Horla," 45
  "Magnétisme," 45
Maurice, Sylvain, 50
Mayflower, 186

Mela, Pomponius
   De situ orbis, 226
Melmoth the Wanderer (Maturin), 241
Melville, Herman, 14, 32, 63, 166,
   233, 260
   "Benito Cereno," 307
   Billy Budd, 38
   Moby-Dick, 33, 37–9
Memoirs (Mercier), 349
Memoirs of an American Lady (Grant), 139
Mercier, Louis-Sebastien, 351
   Memoirs, 349
Merivale, Patricia, 78
Mesmer, Franz Anton, 323
Mesmeric Magazine, 327
Mesmerism, "in Articulo Mortis"
   (Poe), 327
Meunier, Isabelle, 42
Micrographia (Hooke), 346
Micromegas (Voltaire), 348
Miles, Mrs. L.
   Phrenology, 304
Mille et une Nuit (Galland), 54
Miller, William, 348
Milton, John
   Comus, 124
Mind of the South (Cash), 14
Minerva, 211
Minor, Lucian, 205
   "Address on Education," 212
Mintz, Steven, 99
Mirror of Fashion, 108
Missionary Memorial, 186
Missouri Courier, 25
Mitchell, Edward Page, 343
   "Clock That Went Backwards," 343
Moby-Dick (Melville), 33, 37–9
Monk (Lewis), 241, 244
"Monkey Who Shaved Himself," 264
Monroe, James, 17
Monsieur de Phocas (Lorrain), 47
Monsieur Vénus (Eymery), 47
Montesquieu, Charles de Secondat, *baron de*,
   348
Montgomery, James, 55, 253
Moore, Thomas, 223, 253–5
   Alciphron, 56, 223
   Lalla Rookh, 54, 56
   Letters and Journals of Lord Byron, 253
More, Thomas
   Utopia, 349
Moréas, Jean, 44
Morinière, Aurélien
   Baudelaire ou le roman rêvé d'Edgar Allan
   Poe, 50

Morrell, Benjamin
   Narrative of Four Voyages, 32, 34
Morris, William, 343
Morse, Samuel, 315
Mosses from an Old Manse (Hawthorne), 294,
   296
Mott, Frank Luther, 169
Mowatt, Anna
   Fashion, 111–12, 119, 125–6
Moxon, Edward, 283
Mundus subterraneus (Kircher), 64
Mysteries of Udolpho (Radcliffe), 241

Narrative (Brown), 25
Narrative (Riley), 59
Narrative of Arthur Gordon Pym (Poe), 15, 23,
   26, 32, 33, 35–7, 39, 42–3, 48–9, 57, 59, 63,
   65–8, 70, 141, 228, 260–3, 271, 306, 310,
   366, 374
Narrative of Four Voyages (Morrell), 32, 34
Narrative of the … Shipwreck (Chase), 37–8
Neal, John, 201, 292
New Atlantis (Bacon), 349
New Discovery of Terra Incognita Australis
   (Foigny), 346
New Home (Kirkland), 27, 131
New System (Bryant), 224
New York Book, 182
New York Daily Tribune, 205–6
New York Evening Mirror, 129–30, 134–5, 165,
   169, 175, 201, 214
New York Morning News, 14
New York Observer, 315
New York Sun, 88, 343, 375
New-Yorker, 212, 279
New World, 192
Newnham, William
   Human Magnetism, 327–8
Newton, Isaac, 349, 354–7, 360, 379
Nicholas Nickleby (Dickens), 279
Nicklin, Philip
   Remarks on Literary Property, 191
Niebuhr, B. G., 223
Niebuhr, Carsten, 58
Norman Leslie (Fay), 201–2
North American (Baltimore), 210–11
North American and United States Gazette, 209
North American Review, 172, 198–9, 202, 206,
   289, 296
Notes on the State of Virginia (Jefferson), 145
Nouvelles histoires extraordinaires (Baudelaire),
   42

Oceana (Harrington), 349
Odes (Horace), 222, 225

Odyssey (Homer), 223, 225, 228, 345, 347
Oedipus at Colonus (Sophocles), 227
Oedipus the King (Sophocles), 227
Old Curiosity Shop (Dickens), 279, 365
Oliver Twist (Dickens), 365
On the Nature of the Universe (Lucretius), 359
Opal, 186
Oquawka Spectator, 22
Oregon Trail (Paulding), 24
Orpheus and Eurydice, 119
Ormond (Brown), 242
Osgood, Frances, 131–5, 183, 202
    "Echo-Song," 133
    Wreath of Wild Flowers, 202
O'Sullivan, John, 214
Our Mutual Friend (Dickens), 285
Ovidius Naso, Publius, 222–3
    Fasti, 226

Parkman, Francis
    Oregon Trail, 24
Parsons, William, 358
Partisan (Simms), 202
Patch, Sam, 266–7
Patterson, E.H.N., 22–4, 175
Paul Ulric (Mattson), 237
Paulding, James Kirke, 201
    "Selim," 55
    Sketch of Old England, 198
    Slavery in the United States, 139
Pays, 48
Peabody, Elizabeth, 199
Peisistratus, 345
Pencil of Nature (Talbot), 314
Penn Magazine, 163–5
Persius
    Satires, 221, 223
Peterson's Ladies' National Magazine, 171
Petronius Arbiter, Titus, 227
Phalaris, 225
Phantom Ship (Marryat), 37, 260
Pharsalia (Lucan), 227
Philadelphia Book, 182
Philadelphia Saturday Chronicle, 213
Philadelphia Saturday Courier, 173, 211
Phillips, Mary, 335
Philosophical Transactions, 64
Philosophy of Animal Magnetism (Jackson), 322
Philosophy of Manufactures (Ure), 377
"Phrenological Examinations," 304
Phrenology (Miles), 304
Phyfe, Duncan, 114
Pickwick Papers (Dickens), 4, 279
Pierrot le fou (Godard), 50
Pinckney, Edward C. 19

Pioneer, 214, 292
Plato, 348
    Kritias, 349
    Laws, 223, 349
    Republic, 223, 349
    Timaeus, 349
Poe, David, Sr. (grandfather), 119, 210
Poe, David, Jr. (father), 119, 121
Poe, Edgar Allan
    "Al Aaraaf," 54, 56
    "Anastatic Printing," 188–9
    "Angel of the Odd," 238
    "Annabel Lee," 136
    "Assignation," 253–5
    "Balloon Hoax," 33, 48, 88, 375
    "Bargain Lost," 211
    "Bells," 216
    "Berenice," 42, 47, 49, 160–1, 173, 202,
        226–8, 248
    "Black Cat," 42, 50, 82, 96, 101–4, 145–6,
        245, 280, 305, 314, 337–8, 374
    "Bridal Ballad," 177
    "Business Man," 108, 200, 213, 304, 373
    "Byron and Miss Chaworth," 255
    "Cask of Amontillado," 101, 123, 135, 152–4,
        210, 236, 258, 337
    "Chapter of Suggestions," 186
    "Chapter on Science and Art," 351
    "City in the Sea," 37, 56–7
    "Coliseum," 211
    "Colloquy of Monos and Una," 19, 223, 345,
        348, 375, 378
    Conchologist's First Book, 374
    "Conqueror Worm," 123
    "Daguerreotype," 313
    "Decided Loss," 211
    "Descent into the Maelström," 32, 35, 65, 67,
        70, 272
    "Devil in the Belfry," 213
    "Diddling Considered as One of the Exact
        Sciences," 304
    "Domain of Arnheim," 49, 68, 332, 379–80
    "Doomed City," 57
    "Dream within a Dream," 271
    "Dream-Land," 69
    "Dreams," 211
    "Duc de L'Omelette," 211, 366
    "Editorial Miscellanies," 203–4
    "Eldorado," 23, 333
    "Eleonora," 184
    "Epimanes," 182
    Eureka, 42, 45, 272, 274, 330, 345, 348, 355,
        358, 360, 366, 379
    "Facts in the Case of M. Valdemar," 45, 232,
        322, 326–7, 330, 347

"Fairyland," 266
"Fall of the House of Usher," 15, 45, 47, 49–50, 68, 81, 123, 149, 213, 226, 228, 246, 248–9, 303, 305, 310, 316, 349
"Fifty Suggestions," 233
"For Annie," 366
"Four Beasts in One," 212, 227
"Gold-Bug," 13, 15, 126, 139–40, 144, 162, 209, 215, 339, 363, 369, 374
"Hans Pfaal," 43, 46, 48, 63, 67, 78, 228, 347
"Happiest Day," 211
"Haunted Palace," 68, 123, 143, 213, 248
"Hop-Frog," 46, 90–4, 123, 141–2, 144–5, 232, 234–5, 265–6, 296
"How to Write a Blackwood Article," 6, 140, 145, 177, 225, 242, 246, 376
"Imp of the Perverse," 47, 49, 102–3, 186, 245, 258, 305, 334
"Instinct versus Reason," 103
"International Copyright," 8
"Island of the Fay," 226, 266, 332
"Israfel," 54, 56, 333
"Journal of Julius Rodman," 23, 29, 139–40
"King Pest," 6, 212, 228
"Lake," 186
"Landor's Cottage," 332, 339, 341
"Lenore," 136
"Letter to B," 205, 272, 276
"Ligeia," 6, 46, 55–6, 123, 150–2, 213, 225, 228, 247, 249, 270, 305–6, 310
"Lionizing," 129, 136, 235
"Literary Life of Thingum Bob," 176, 200, 214–15, 225
"Literati of New York City," 55, 113, 165–6, 175, 203–4, 206, 224, 232, 294, 304
"Loss of Breath," 225, 245–6, 366
"Maelzel's Chess-Player," 87–8, 376
"Man of the Crowd," 10–11, 43, 46–7, 75–6, 79–81, 108, 110, 209, 225, 280
"Man That Was Used Up," 19, 86, 88–90, 94, 140, 144, 201, 213, 225, 237, 263–4, 373
"Manuscript Found in a Bottle," 32, 35–6, 63, 67, 70, 162, 173, 181–2, 211, 227–8, 262, 272, 374
"Marginalia," 221, 224, 329, 351
"Masque of the Red Death," 46, 124, 174
"Mellonta Tauta," 345, 350
"Mesmeric Revelation," 41, 322, 326, 374
Mesmerism, "in Articulo Mortis", 327
"Metzengerstein," 81, 211, 221, 225, 244–5, 349
"Morella," 46, 270
"Morning on the Wissahiccon," 5, 186, 332

"Murders in the Rue Morgue," 41, 46, 48–9, 79–80, 141–5, 174, 224, 226, 264–5, 305, 310, 363–4, 366–8, 374
"Mystery of Marie Rôget," 79–80, 363, 366–8
Narrative of Arthur Gordon Pym, 15, 23, 26, 32, 33, 35–7, 39, 42–3, 48–9, 57, 59, 63, 65–8, 70, 141, 228, 260–3, 271, 306, 310, 366, 374
"Nathaniel Hawthorne," 8
"Never Bet the Devil Your Head," 225, 238, 269, 276
"Notes on Art and Science," 374
"Oblong Box," 186, 318–19
"Oval Portrait," 256
"Palestine," 57–8
Penn Magazine, 163–5
"Philosophy of Composition," 3–4, 8, 16, 42–3, 155, 164, 205, 253, 255, 274, 377
"Philosophy of Furniture," 5–6, 9, 116
"Pinakidia," 124, 224–5
"Pit and the Pendulum," 69, 185, 225
"Poetic Principle," 17, 42, 164, 251
"Politian," 122, 223, 225
"Power of Words," 214, 326, 353, 355, 374
"Predicament," 15, 80, 177, 243
"Premature Burial," 154, 246, 263
"Psyche Zenobia," 177, 213
"Purloined Letter," 78–9, 185, 226–7, 343, 363, 366–9
"Rationale of Verse," 164, 251, 374
"Raven," 44, 49, 123–4, 127, 130–1, 143, 145, 149–50, 161, 225, 227, 245, 255, 258, 280, 285, 296, 377
Raven and Other Poems, 28, 204–5, 214
"Serenade," 211
"Shadow," 227
"Silence," 5
"Siope," 182
"Some Secrets of the Magazine Prison-House," 176, 214–15
"Some Words with a Mummy," 56, 228, 304, 375
"Sonnet: To Science," 19, 351
"Spectacles," 88–9, 94, 227, 238, 314
Stylus, 22, 164, 174, 215, 293, 320
"System of Doctor Tarr and Professor Fether," 46, 49, 142–3–, 144, 238–9
"Tale of Jerusalem," 58, 211, 227
"Tale of the Ragged Mountains," 5, 209, 322, 326, 374
"Tale Writing: Nathaniel Hawthorne," 294
Tales, 14, 28, 204, 214, 366
Tales of the Folio Club, 181, 368

Poe, Edgar Allan (*cont.*)
  Tales of the Grotesque and Arabesque, 53, 281, 283
  "Tamerlane," 55–6
  Tamerlane, Al Aaraaf, and Other Poems, 54
  Tamerlane and Other Poems, 122, 211
  "Tell-Tale Heart," 47, 50, 56, 82, 214, 221, 258, 280, 378
  "Thou Art the Man," 225, 227, 363, 370–1
  "Thousand and Second Tale of Scheherezade," 19, 54, 315, 345, 351, 374–5
  "Three Sundays in a Week," 48, 225
  "To – – –," 161
  "To F – – –," 133, 161
  "To Helen," 56, 174, 225, 333
  "To the River – – –," 161, 213
  "Ulalume," 214, 366
  "Valley of Unrest," 5
  "Visionary," 58, 173
  "Von Kempelen and His Discovery," 347
  "Von Jung, the Mystific," 212
  "Why the Little Frenchman Wears His Hand in a Sling," 6, 81, 280–1
  "William Wilson," 6, 68, 81, 183, 225, 227–9, 258, 288–9
  "X-ing a Paragrab," 224–5, 373
Poe, Eliza (mother), 13, 97, 118–21, 124, 126
Poe, Henry (brother), 121, 210
Poe, Rosalie (sister), 121
Poe, Virginia (wife), 115, 334
Poe, William (cousin), 16
Poe, William (uncle), 98
Poems (Lowell), 203
Poems on Slavery (Longfellow), 17, 143
Poets and Poetry of America (Griswold), 127, 284
Pollin, Burton, 251
Porphyry, 224
Poyen, Charles
  Letter to Col. Wm. L. Stone, 325
  Progress of Animal Magnetism, 325
Practical Instruction in Animal Magnetism (Deleuze), 322–3, 325, 329
Progress of Animal Magnetism (Poyen), 325
Psychology (Collyer), 327
Ptolemy Hephestion, 226
Putnam, George P., 24

Quacks of Helicon (Wilmer), 232–3
Quinn, Arthur Hobson, 66, 122
Qu'ran, 54

Rabelais, François, 232–5, 239
  Gargantua, 232–4
Rabelais and His World (Bakhtin), 233–4
Rachman, Stephen, 10–11

Radcliffe, Ann, 242
  Mysteries of Udolpho, 241
Rasselas (Johnson), 55
Raumer, Friedrich von,
  England in 1835, 124–5
Raven and Other Poems (Poe), 28, 204–5, 214
Reade, Charles, 193
Recamier, Madame, 131
Redon, Odilon
  A Edgar Poe, 47
  "Teeth," 47
  "Tell-Tale Heart," 47
Rees, Abraham
  Cyclopaedia, 57
Reid, Mayne, 340–1
Remarks on Literary Property (Nicklin), 191
Remarks on the Influence of Mental Cultivation (Brigham), 324
Repository of Arts (Ackerman), 114
Reproduction interdite (Magritte), 49
Republic (Plato), 223, 349
Retrospect of Western Travel (Martineau), 26
Revenge of Bussy D'Ambois (Chapman), 123
Reynolds, David, 96, 101
Reynolds, Jeremiah N., 36, 65–7, 69
  Address, 32, 67
  "Leaves from an Unpublished Journal," 67
Richards, Eliza, 131, 135
Richmond Compiler, 205
Rider, Jane C., 324
Riley, James
  Narrative, 59
Rimbaud, Arthur, 44
Ritchie, William F., 121
Rivière, Henri, 45
Robinson Crusoe (Defoe), 5, 32
Roderick Random (Smollett), 39
Roehmer, Eric
  Histoires extraordinaires d'Edgar Poe, 50
Rogers, Mary Cecilia, 79, 367
Rollin, Charles
  Histoire ancienne, 53, 223
  Histoire romaine, 223
Rorabaugh, W. J., 98
Ross, James Clark, 66
Rosse, Lord, 359
Rousseau, Jean-Jacques, 41
Rudisill, Richard, 316
Ruines (Volney), 57
Rush, Benjamin
  Inquiry into the Effects of Ardent Spirits, 97–8

Said, Edward W., 53
Sainte-Beuve, Charles-Augustin, 43
Sale, George, 54

Sallustius, Crispus Caius, 224
Sampson, M. B., 303
Sanders, J. Milton
  "Miami Valley," 29
Sands, Samuel, 210–11
Sartain, John, 173, 215
Sartrain's Union Magazine, 175, 215
Satires of Persius (Drummond), 221, 223
Saturday Evening Post, 101, 204, 209, 211, 279
Saturday Herald, 210
Sayers, Dorothy L., 367
Schelling, Friedrich Wilhelm Joseph von, 270
Scott, Dred, 191
Scott, Walter, 189–91
  Antiquary, 244
  Count Robert of Paris, 365
Seaborn, Adam, 64
Sedgwick, Catherine Maria, 113, 131–2, 199
  Linwoods, 202
Sedgwick, Eve Kosofsky, 241
Senelick, Laurence, 119
Shakespeare, William, 70, 119–20, 252
  Hamlet, 64, 228
  Macbeth, 124, 242
Sharp, Solomon P., 122
Shelley, Mary, 343–4
  Frankenstein, 241, 343, 347
  Last Man, 348
Shelley, Percy Bysshe, 57
  Alastor, 255–6
Shelton, Elmira, 103
Sheppard Lee (Bird), 144
Sheridan, Frances
  History of Nourjahad, 55
Sigourney, Lydia, 16, 183
Silverman, Kenneth, 7, 68, 251, 322
Simms, William Gilmore, 18, 142
  Partisan, 202
Six Nights with the Washingtonians (Arthur), 100
Sizer, Nelson, 309
Sketch of Old England (Paulding), 198
Sketches by Boz (Dickens), 4, 10, 203, 280
Slavery in the United States (Paulding), 139
Smith, Elizabeth Oakes, 131–2
  "Sinless Child," 132
Smith, Thomas S., 213
Smith, William
  Dictionary of Greek and Roman Antiquities, 224
Smollett, Tobias
  Roderick Random, 39
Snodgrass, Joseph, 16, 98, 213
"Snow White," 266
Somnium (Kepler), 346

Sophocles
  Antigone, 223
  Oedipus at Colonus, 227
  Oedipus the King, 227
South-West (Ingraham), 139
South Vindicated (Drayton), 139
Southern Literary Messenger, 13, 15–17, 19, 32–3, 66, 121, 139, 142, 160, 162, 165, 171, 173, 175–6, 182, 198, 200–2, 204–6, 211–12, 214–15, 281, 304, 322
Southey, Robert, 198, 253
Sphinx des glaces (Verne), 48, 344
Sprague, William
  Letters on Practical Subjects, 151
Spurzheim, Johann Caspar, 303–6
Stapleton, Edward, 246
Staël de Holstein, Anne Louise Necker Germaine, *baronne de*, 131
  Corinne, 132
Stephens, John L., 66
  Incidents of Travel in Egypt, 58
Stern, Madeleine, 301
Stoker, Bram
  Dracula, 241
Stone, William
  Letter to Doctor A. Brigham, 324
Stowe, Harriet Beecher, 183
  "Drunkard Reclaimed," 102
  Uncle Tom's Cabin, 307
Study in Scarlet (Doyle), 48
Stylus, 22, 164, 174, 215, 293, 320
Sully, Thomas, 117, 252
Summer on the Lakes (Fuller), 23
Swift, Jonathan
  Gulliver's Travels, 32, 292
Symmes, John Cleve, Jr., 35–6, 63–5, 67
Symmes's Theory of Concentric Spheres, 64
Symzonia, 64

Tacitus, Cornelius
  Historiae, 222
Talbot, William Henry Fox, 313
  Pencil of Nature, 314
Tales (Poe) 14, 28, 204, 214, 366
Tales of a Traveller (Irving), 289
Tales of the Alhambra (Irving), 58
Tales of the Folio Club (Poe), 181, 368
Tales of the Grotesque and Arabesque (Poe), 53, 281, 283
Tamerlane, Al Aaraaf, and Other Poems (Poe), 54
Tamerlane and Other Poems (Poe), 122, 211
Tarek
  Baudelaire ou le roman rêvé d'Edgar Allan Poe, 50

Tasistro, L. F., 315
Tate, Allen, 14
Tebbel, John, 172
Ten Nights in a Bar-Room (Arthur), 102
Tennyson, Alfred Tennyson, *baron*, 7, 251, 275, 285
Teorey, Matthew, 68
Tertullianus, Quintus Septimius Florens, 226
Thomas, Creed, 121
Thomas, Frederick W., 213, 309
Thompson, G. R., 241, 248
Thoreau, Henry David, 28, 166, 194
    "Resistance to Civil Government," 6
Thourds, Jean-Louis
    Histoires extraordinaires d'Edgar Poe, 50
    "Mort rouge," 50
    "Scarabée d'Or," 50
    "Usher," 50
Thurs, Daniel Patrick, 304, 309
Timaeus (Plato), 349
Time Machine (Wells), 343
'Tis Pity She's a Whore (Ford), 123
Token, 179, 183
Tomc, Sandra, 130
Tomlin, John, 16
Tour du monde en 80 jours (Verne), 48
Tour on the Prairies (Irving), 27
Townshend, Chauncy Hare
    Facts in Mesmerism, 322, 325–9
Trafton, Scott, 56–7
Tragedy of Bussy d'Ambois (Chapman), 123
Travels to Discover the Source of the Nile (Bruce), 57
Trollope, Frances
    Domestic Manners of the Americans, 26
True History (Lucian), 228
Tubbs, Mr., 119
Tucker, Beverley, 139
Turner, Nat, 140, 308, 310
Twain, Mark, 25, 194
20,000 Leagues Under the Sea (Verne), 346
Twice-Told Tales (Hawthorne), 8, 199, 288–91, 293, 323, 328
Two Years before the Mast (Dana), 32, 39
Tyler, John, 213, 283
Tyler, Royall
    Algerine Captive, 59

Uncle Tom's Cabin (Stowe), 307
Union Magazine, 175
Universal Yankee Nation, 192
Ure, Andrew
    Philosophy of Manufactures, 377

Usher, Harriet L'Estrange, 97
Utopia (More), 349

Valéry, Paul, 42, 44–5
Van Buren, Martin, 213
Vanderdecken, Captain, 260–1
Vathek (Beckford), 55
Vergilius Maro, Publius, 222, 226–7
Verne, Jules, 47–8, 343–4, 351
    Antarctic Mystery, 344
    Around the World in Eighty Days, 346
    Cinq semaines en ballon, 48
    De la terre à la lune, 48
    Sphinx des glaces, 48, 344
    Tour du monde en 80 jours, 48
    20,000 Leagues Under the Sea, 346
    Voyages extraordinaires, 48
Vidocq, François, 48
Vielé-Griffin, Francis, 44
Villiers de l'Isle-Adam, 45
    "Claire Lenoir," 46
    Contes cruels, 46
    Eclogue, 221
    Eve future, 46
    "Véra," 46
Vivre sa vie (Godard), 50
Volney, Constantin François de Chasseboeuf, *comte de*
    Ruines, 57
Voltaire, 41
    Micromegas, 348
    Zadig, 232, 365
Voyage dans la lune (Cyrano de Bergerac), 347
Voyages extraordinaires (Verne), 48

Wagner, Richard
    Flying Dutchman, 37
Walpole, Horace
    Castle of Otranto, 241, 244, 345
War of the Worlds (Wells), 350
Ware, William, 200
Warner, Michael, 99
Washington, George, 17, 86, 88, 148
Waters, Emily
    "In Memory of Mrs. Osgood," 135
Wauchope, George, 14
Webber, Charles Wilkins, 295
Webster, John
    Dutchess of Malfi, 123
    White Devil, 123
Wells, H. G., 343–5
    Time Machine, 343
    "Time Traveller's Story," 343
    War of the Worlds, 350
Wells, Samuel R., 309

Western Clearings (Kirkland), 27
Whalen, Terence, 169
White, Thomas W., 33, 160–1, 173, 200–1, 211, 247
White Devil (Webster), 123
Whitman, Sarah Helen, 132, 326
Whitman, Walt, 33, 166, 181, 325
  Franklin Evans, 101
Whitney, Eli, 373
Wieland (Brown), 242, 363
Wilkes, Charles, 32, 35, 65
Willis, Nathaniel Parker, 76, 129–31, 136, 206, 214, 366, 376
Wilmer, Lambert
  Quacks of Helicon, 232–3
Wilson, John, 204
Winter in the West (Hoffman), 27
Woman in the Nineteenth Century (Fuller), 206

Woodberry, George, 251
Wordsworth, William, 190, 203, 253
  Lyrical Ballads, 377
  "Plea for Authors," 191
Wreath of Wild Flowers (Osgood), 202
Wyatt-Brown, Bertram, 17

Xenophon, 222–3

Yakhlef, Ben
  Baudelaire ou le roman rêvé d'Edgar Allan Poe, 50
Young Man's Friend (Eddy), 108
Young Man's Guide (Alcott), 108

Zadig (Voltaire), 232, 365
Zakim, Michael, 109, 112
Zimmerman, Brett, 233